Communication Works

EIGHTH EDITION

Teri Kwal Gamble
College of New Rochelle

Michael Gamble
New York Institute of Technology

McGraw Hill

Boston   Burr Ridge, IL   Dubuque, IA   Madison, WI   New York   San Francisco   St. Louis
Bangkok   Bogotá   Caracas   Kuala Lumpur   Lisbon   London   Madrid   Mexico City
Milan   Montreal   New Delhi   Santiago   Seoul   Singapore   Sydney   Taipei   Toronto

The McGraw·Hill Companies

COMMUNICATION WORKS

Published by McGraw-Hill, a business unit of The McGraw-Hill Companies, Inc., 1221 Avenue of the Americas, New York, NY, 10020. Copyright © 2005, 2002, 1999, 1996, 1993, 1990, 1987, 1984, by The McGraw-Hill Companies, Inc. All rights reserved. No part of this publication may be reproduced or distributed in any form or by any means, or stored in a database or retrieval system, without the prior written consent of The McGraw-Hill Companies, Inc., including, but not limited to, in any network or other electronic storage or transmission, or broadcast for distance learning.

Some ancillaries, including electronic and print components, may not be available to customers outside the United States.

♻ This book is printed on recycled, acid-free paper.

2 3 4 5 6 7 8 9 0 QPD/QPD 0 9 8 7 6 5 4

ISBN 0–07–286282–3

Publisher: *Phillip A. Butcher*
Senior Sponsoring editor: *Nanette Giles*
Developmental editor: *Jennie Katsaros*
Senior marketing manager: *Leslie Oberhuber*
Producer, Media technology: *Jessica Bodie*
Project manager: *Rick Hecker*
Production supervisor: *Enboge Chong*
Senior designer: *Kim Menning*
Associate supplement producer: *Meghan Durko*
Associate photo research coordinator: *Natalia C. Peschiera*
Art editor: *Cristin Yancey*
Photo researcher: *David A. Tietz*
Permissions editor: *Marty Granahan*
Cover design: *Yvo Riezebos*
Interior design: *Glenda King*
Typeface: *10/12 Galliard*
Compositor: *GTS—York, PA Campus*
Printer: *Quebecor World Dubuque Inc.*

Library of Congress Cataloging-in-Publication Data

Gamble, Teri Kwal.
    Communication works / Teri Kwal Gamble, Michael Gamble.—8th ed.
        p.   cm.
    Includes bibliographical references and index.
    ISBN 0-07-286282-3 (alk. paper)
    1. Communication. I. Gamble, Michael, 1943- II. Title.
P90.G299 2005
302.2—dc22   2003066002

For Matthew Jon and Lindsay Michele—our children—who grew up with this book and who with the publishing of this new edition are on track to graduate from a Ph.D. program and college, respectively. They have proven themselves to be wonderful students of life and have taught us so much about how and why communication works.

For Martha and Marcel Kwal and Nan and Wesley Gamble, who helped us understand and address "the circle of life."

BRIEF CONTENTS

iv

CONTENTS

PART ONE

The Essentials of Communication

CHAPTER 3

Communication and the Self-Concept: Who Are You?   51

CHAPTER 4

Communication and Perception: I Am More Than a Camera   81

CHAPTER 5

Language and Meaning: Helping Minds Meet   113

CHAPTER 6

Nonverbal Communication: Silent Language Speaks   147

CHAPTER 9

Person to Person: Relationships in Context 263

CHAPTER 10

Interviewing: From Both Sides of the Desk 301

PART THREE

Communicating in the Small Group

CHAPTER 11

The Roles of the Group and Team in Decision Making and Problem Solving 335

PART FOUR

Communicating to the Public

CHAPTER 16

Designing Your
Speech: Organizing
Your Ideas   481

CHAPTER 17

Delivering Your Speech:
Presenting Your
Ideas   509

CHAPTER 18

Informative Speaking 529

CHAPTER 19

Persuasive Speaking 549

APPENDIX

Mass Communication and Media Literacy   A-1

Teri Kwal Gamble and Michael W. Gamble both have Ph.D.s in communication from New York University. They are professors of communication and award-winning teachers, with Teri at the College of New Rochelle, and Michael at the New York Institute of Technology in Manhattan. As cofounders of Interact Training Systems, a communication consulting firm, they have conducted seminars, workshops, and short courses for numerous business and professional organizations across the United States.

The Gambles are coauthors of several textbooks and training systems, including *Literature Alive!*, *Public Speaking in the Age of Diversity*, and *Contacts: Communicating Interpersonally*. Their trade books include *Sales Scripts That Sell*, *The Answer Book*, and *Phone Power*.

Teri and Michael live in New Jersey and spend much of their time interacting with and following the academic, athletic, and professional careers of their favorite communicators, their son, Matthew Jon, age 27, a Ph.D. candidate in cell and molecular biology, and their daughter, Lindsay Michele, 21, a scholar-athlete.

Teri and Michael Gamble with daughter Lindsay and son Matthew.

PREFACE

With the eighth edition of *Communication Works,* we find ourselves considering a world that is very different from the one we faced while writing any of the prior editions of the text. And our new reality is one that we would never have imagined. Indeed, our world has changed; however, the need for effective communication has not. If anything, this need has intensified. More than ever, we realize the costs of failed communication. We understand—from a personal, professional, and global perspective—how critical it is to do our part to make communication work.

With this in mind, we revised this text to ensure that its contents have immediate relevance. We took pains to contemporize the contents and offer comprehensive coverage of the most important communication topics. We made an even greater effort to write in an interactive style and to complement this with an interactive visual program, so that students will feel engaged by the text and its media resources. Furthermore, in recognition of the challenges that our world presents for students in the 21st century, we enhanced our coverage of ethical, cultural, and technological issues, all while maintaining the skill-building focus of the text.

EIGHTH EDITION HIGHLIGHTS: WHAT'S NEW AND REVISED

1. We have integrated **"speaking experiences"** throughout the text, thus providing opportunities for students to communicate publicly across the semester. We also have addressed communication anxiety issues relevant to each of the communication contexts we cover in the main parts of the text.
2. We have integrated **service-learning** suggestions into marginal notations and queries.
3. We have updated the songs, films, and reading suggestions contained in the *Listen to Me, View Me, Read Me,* and **new** *Tell Me* **features,** which are located in the *Wrap Up* section at the end of each chapter.
4. We have introduced **work-related issues** into text boxes.
5. We have improved our coverage of **culture and globalization issues,** including skill-building related to "seeing through the eyes of persons from other cultures," an essential communication behavior for meeting the challenges posed by living in an increasingly socially diverse society.

We revised this text to ensure that its contents have immediate relevance to students.

6. We have introduced a **life span perspective** in the chapters on relationships.

7. We have introduced the **theme of civility** in both interpersonal and public communication chapters, with coverage of topics such as bullying and civil discourse.

8. In the public speaking chapters, we have **reformulated our treatment of outlining** and **thesis development** and have introduced contemporary issues and concerns relevant to the creation and delivery of effective presentations.

9. With respect to the *e-Search* feature and the mediated communication content throughout the text, we have made sure to stress contemporary issues and concerns, such as online dating, online source credibility, and intergenerational mediated communication.

We continue to integrate examples from popular culture throughout the text and have expanded our discussion of contemporary ethical concerns to include lying in interpersonal relationships and in the public arena. We worked diligently to include activities that are adaptable to both large lecture and traditional class settings.

EIGHTH EDITION HIGHLIGHTS: SIGNATURE FEATURES AND THEMES

Our approach and organization reflect our commitment to helping students actively explore how and why communication works.

Skill Builders

Because we believe that people learn best when they participate, we continue to offer a wide selection of *Skill Builders*—learning activities that appear in the text, online, and in the instructor's resources—for use inside or outside of class. *Skill Builders* encourage students to observe and consider communication, to assess its effects, and to experience the insights and practice they need to become skillful communicators. Instructors report that these exercises make *Communication Works* a complete teaching

> *All of the book's features are designed to create a pedagogical environment that compels students to ask questions and become involved.*

and learning package and make the study of communication active, exciting, involving, and rewarding. We do not expect any instructor to use in a single course or semester all the *Skill Builders* or other exercises, or even all the chapters in the text. We purposely have built flexibility into the text, so that each instructor may easily choose those elements that fit the needs of his or her students and the available time frame.

Exploring Diversity, Ethics and Communication, and Thinking Critically

To reflect the needs and interests of an increasingly diverse student audience, and to encourage critical inquiry, we continue to pay significant attention to the influence of culture and the importance of communication ethics. Content related to culture and ethics is represented comprehensively throughout the narrative as well as in the **Exploring Diversity** boxes, the **Ethics & Communication** boxes, and the **Thinking Critically** exercises, all of which appear throughout the text.

e-Search, Media Wise, and Resources for Further Inquiry and Reflection

Because of the myriad ways in which communication and technology are linked, we have continued and improved the *e-Search* and *Media Wise* boxes. We also have updated the *Listen to Me, View Me,* and *Read Me* features and enhanced them by adding a *Tell Me* component. This feature encourages students to demonstrate and apply their understanding of chapter content to popular media, such as music, movies, and books. All of the book's features are designed to create a pedagogical environment that compels students to ask questions and become involved, and that launches individual assignments or group or class discussions. The text's special features—*Skill Builder, Exploring Diversity, Ethics and Communication, Media Wise, e-Search, Thinking Critically,* and *Resources for Further Inquiry and Reflection*—are clearly identified in the table of contents, so that instructors and students can locate them easily.

ORGANIZATION

We have made every effort to design and produce a book that students enjoy reading, because we believe that student interest and information presentation are equal partners. Thus, we were devoted to creating a book that exhibits clarity of language, encourages reader participation, and does so in a lively, colorful format. We have tested the text materials with students of different ages, cultures, and ethnic groups. Based on feedback, we have retained several popular pedagogical features from prior editions.

Each chapter begins with behavioral objectives, which illuminate the material, establish goals, and prepare the readers for the concepts that will be introduced. Within the chapters, students are periodically expected to complete self-assessment scales to evaluate their attitudes and reactions and to measure their mastery of skills. The marginal comments and questions, which juxtapose key content, are written to arouse curiosity and encourage thinking and questioning. The running glossary is meant to make terminology accessible. The **Wrap-Up,** which concludes each chapter, comprises a summary that reflects the chapter's behavioral objectives and recapitulates key content and

To reflect the needs and interests of an increasingly diverse student audience, and to encourage critical inquiry, we continue to pay significant attention to the influence of culture and to the importance of communication ethics.

skill-building; a list of key chapter terminology; and instructions for the *Test Your Understanding* self-quizzes.

COMMUNICATION WORKS CD-ROM AND ONLINE LEARNING CENTER WWW.MHHE.COM/GAMBLE8

The *Communication Works* CD-ROM and Online Learning Center are integral parts of this text. Both extend the concepts and pedagogical methods of the book and were produced to appeal to a variety of learning styles. In the book itself, icons in the text margin and in the end-of-chapter *Wrap-Up* sections prompt readers to view relevant video clips and to use relevant interactive tools. The CD-ROM is packaged free with every new copy of the book, and the Online Learning Center does not require students to use a password. The enthusiastic reaction of instructors and students who used these media resources with the previous edition of this text has been gratifying. Thanks to feedback from many of those students and instructors, both media have been revised and improved.

> *The Communication Works CD-ROM and Online Learning Center are integral parts of this text. Both extend the concepts and pedagogical methods of the book and were produced to appeal to a variety of learning styles.*

McGraw-Hill offers a Syllabus Service, whereupon after receiving an instructor's syllabus, it will integrate elements of the *Communication Works* CD-ROM and Online Learning Center alongside the book chapters assigned by the instructor and return its recommendations promptly. Instructors report that students who independently use these media resources perform better in the classroom and on examinations. The Syllabus Service promotes and enables usage of these media by all students.

The *Communication Works* CD-ROM and Online Learning Center feature the following:

Self-quizzes with feedback

Key terminology flashcards

Communication Concepts videos

Speech videos

Outline tutor

Outline exercises

Checklist for preparing and delivering a speech

Topic helper

Speech critique

PowerPoint tutor

BiblioMaker

Bibliography formats

We are especially proud of this edition and hope you enjoy its new information and features. We would love to hear from you. Please know we value your suggestions. You can reach us via e-mail at gamble@carroll.com.

ACKNOWLEDGMENTS

The eighth edition of *Communication Works* reflects a quarter century of effort and an astute awareness of incredible changes in our communication environment, our society, the students, and ourselves. As in previous editions, the improvements we have made are the result of input from students and the suggestions of colleagues; they truly represent a team effort.

Our editing team at McGraw-Hill deserve much credit. We are especially grateful to Phil Butcher for his good counsel and trust; Nanette Giles for her ability to take this project to new heights, commitment to quality, and vision; and Jennie Katsaros for her creative problem-solving skills and continued uncanny ability to know what we are thinking and feeling. We also want to thank the project manager, Rick Hecker, whose attention to detail and ability to keep ahead of schedule kept us all on our toes; Kim Menning, our designer, who ensured that the fresh design supported the content and revisions; and David A. Tietz, who oversaw the photo research, further enhancing the book's visual appeal.

We are especially grateful to our reviewers for their insightful suggestions:

Susan Andersen, *Valencia Community College*

Josh Compton, *University of Oklahoma*

Todd Frobish, *Iona College*

Karen Krumney-Fulks, *Lane Community College*

Kate Horowitz, *Central Washington University*

Donna Munde, *Mercer County Community College*

Carol Teaff, *West Virginia Northern Community College*

Finally, we have so much to thank Matthew and Lindsay, our children, for. Their communicative instincts and self-searches have helped us to learn so much. In fact, every new edition of this book is a testimony to their growth and maturation. They continue to amaze us and remain the best proof we can offer that communication works!

DIVERSITY

Thoughtful, balanced integration of diversity prepares students to meet the challenges of communicating in today's complex societies.

Exploring Diversity

Exploring Diversity boxes prompt students to consider the effects of diversity on communication, and facilitate classroom discussions of topics such as Culture, Gender, and Emotional Display, The Magic of Sign Language, and Leadership Styles in Men and Women.

EXPLORING Diversity

Side by Side

"The National Study of the Changing Work Force," a report issued by the Families and Work Institute, notes that, contrary to expectations, younger employees are unprepared to work in a diverse workplace.

The report, based on interviews with almost 3,000 workers, pointed out that employees under age 25 showed no greater preference than older employees for working with people of other races, ages, or ethnic groups. Just over half of the surveyed workers of all ages said they prefer working with people of the same race, gender, and educational level.

Despite this finding, according to diversity expert Robert Lattimer, when they are used, "diverse employee teams tend to outperform homogeneous teams of any composition. Homogeneous groups may reach consensus more quickly but are not able to generate new ideas or solve problems as well because their collective perspective is narrower."[18]

Compile a list of other reasons a diverse group might outperform a homogeneous one. How, for example, might diversity affect the group's perception of both the problem and its solution?

Diverse teams of employees frequently outperform homogeneous teams.

Hip Hop and Rap Talk

Hip hop is a social community that uses rap, a special language, to help express its culture.[26] Rap is a celebration of language that speaks to both the body and the brain. Since its introduction about a quarter of a century ago, rap has been maligned and praised, condemned and lauded. It has been blamed for promoting violence and misogyny, praised for promoting peace and minority influence. In 2003, the U.S. government began to broadcast raps on the airwaves of Radio Sawa in an effort to win over Arab youth.[27]

The rapper's words arrive in syncopated speech, which is peppered with both rapid-fire rhymed boasts and taunts. The subjects of rap range from sex, money, and guns to love, politics, the minutiae of our lives, and the American social experience. Rappers redefine the meanings of words. When someone attuned to the hip hop culture says, "I'm keeping it ghetto," he or she means "I'm keeping it real." The words in a rap mean something different than what most Americans have come to understand. Rap is an influence on American popular culture in music, fashion, and language, and it can be difficult to keep up with all the new words that hip hop adds to the national vocabulary. Consequently, journalist Alonzo Westbrook wrote *The Hip Hop-tionary: The Dictionary of Hip Hop Terminology*. Westbrook traveled the United States from coast to coast in order to capture the language as it is used around the country. Sometimes the meaning of a word is coded in order for the rapper to hide behind it. For example, according to Westbrook, hip hop artists code the word *nigger* as an acronym to mean "never ignorant, getting

Def Poetry Jam is the embodiment of a marriage between hip hop and the spoken word.

Integrated Diversity

Cultural Diversity is woven throughout the text and consistently is included in examples and sample speeches. The section on hip hop and rap talk discusses how rap, a special language, expresses hip hop culture.

What if you woke up tomorrow as a person of a race or ethnicity different from your own? How do you imagine your view of your life and the world would change? Would a change in age affect you the same way? What about a change in gender?

The book's features are designed to help students explore how and why communication works. Throughout the text, questions in the margins, boxes, headings, and picture captions encourage students to become actively involved with the course. Skill building, diversity, communication ethics, media and technology, and critical thinking are the five themes which unify the contents of *Communication Works* and synthesize the student's experience with the text.

Coverage of ethics throughout the text examines how ethics impacts communication in families, social groups, the workplace, and more.

ETHICS

Ethics and Communication

Ethics and Communication boxes present a range of the ethical quandaries communicators face as they work to define what the expression "ethical communication" means. Topics covered include, relationships and trust in the workplace, living in a gated community, the relationship of self-esteem to age and physical ability.

Ethics & COMMUNICATION

Relationships, Trust, and the Workplace

What do you perceive to be the advantages and disadvantages of workplace romances?

How do you feel about entering into a romantic relationship with a co-worker or boss? While people who work together probably already share a number of interests and the work environment provides a ready-made setting for meeting and getting to know a potential partner, do you think you can make a relationship work in which you spend not only your work-time but also your free-time together? How do you imagine the relationship you shared would affect others who work with you? How do you imagine it would affect you and your career?

What if you were not the person having such a romantic relationship? What if it were your boss and another co-worker? Or what if it were two of your co-workers? Do you think either relationship would impact you and your chances for career success? Which do you think would affect you more?

According to Dr. Robert R. Provine, laughs are rhythmic bursts of social glue.[66] He reports that much of what we laugh at in life is predominantly the stuff of social banter, not necessarily particularly funny or clever. Laughter, however, is contagious. When we hear laughter, we usually start laughing ourselves. Its infectious nature can have dramatic effects on our relationships. We not only our relationship partners, laugh at what we say; in fact, the average speaker laughs 46 percent more frequently than do those listening to him or her. While laughter does not intrude on speech, it does provide its punctuation. It helps us synchronize our moods and perhaps our actions. As such, it may also help solidify our relationships.

Like any relationship tool, laughter has a downside too. The opposite of joyful laughter is jeering, malicious laughter, laughter that is designed to punish, belittle, or exclude rather than include another. In this case, laughter rather than expressing our sociability, signals our disdain for and power over another person.

When it comes to the use of humor in our relationships, there are wide laughter variations based on sex. A man talking with a male listener laughs only marginally more than his interaction partner. A woman talking with a woman listener laughs somewhat more than her partner. And a male speaker with a female listener laughs less often than does the woman. However, when a woman speaks to a man, she laughs much more than her male partner.[67] Why do you think that is so?

Reports versus Reality

During 2003's Operation Iraqi Freedom, many of the initial reports made by journalists covering the war were not proven. For example, one news story reported that Saddam Hussein had been killed; another said that he had been injured and was last seen on a stretcher, blue-faced and gasping into an oxygen mask; and still another reported that he looked hale and hearty and had survived unscathed. The following reports versus reality inventory appeared in USA Today.[38] In your opinion, what are the dangers of merging fact and fiction when reporting on war?

Ethics & COMMUNICATION

Since the United States and its allies began the war March 19, many initial reports have not been proven. Some examples are:

Date	Initial Report	Reality
March 20	Saddam Hussein may have died in airstrike.	His fate remains unclear.
March 20	Banned Scud missiles were fired at U.S. troops.	False
March 21	The southern port city of Umm Qasr was controlled by the coalition.	Premature
March 23	A captured chemical plant produced banned weapons.	False
March 23	The southern city of Basra was taken by coalition forces.	Premature
March 24	Thousands of Iraqi Shiites revolted against Saddam in Basra.	False
March 25	A convoy of 1,000 Iraqi vehicles carrying Republican Guard troops headed south from Baghdad and was decimated by coalition forces.	No evidence that convoy ever existed.
March 30	British troops captured an Iraqi general in Basra.	Iraqi POW impersonated a general.
April 6	Bodies found in warehouse in southern Iraq were victims of Saddam's brutal regime.	Remains were from 1980s war against Iran.
April 7	Chemical warheads and other weapons of mass destruction were found.	Confirmation pending
April 7	The general nicknamed "Chemical Ali" was killed in an airstrike.	Confirmation pending

Source: "Reports vs. Reality," USA Today, April 8, 2003. Copyright © 2003 USA Today. Reprinted with permission.

Students are encouraged to consider ethics as it relates to communication. In "Reports versus Reality" the authors discuss the dangers of merging fact and fiction when reporting, in this case, the war in Iraq.

Imagine someone who writes 50 love letters but receives no answer. Has this person received feedback?

Communication
Works

online learning center

www.mhhe.com/gamble8

As integral as mediated and mass communication are to our communication behaviors, they also are a natural part of contemporary education. Consequently, Communication Works is not just a text; it is a learning system that comprises the book, the Communication Works CD-ROM and the Communication Works Online Learning Center. The media components are fully integrated in the text, with icons in the margins and at the end of each chapter, encouraging students to follow a variety of learning styles and to use a variety of formats to learn and explore course content. Page xii provides details about the features of the CD-ROM and Online Learning Center.

Media and Technology certainly play a key role in shaping the world. Communication Works examines how mediated and mass communication dramatically influence our interactions in all communication contexts.

Media Wise

Media Wise boxes are designed to develop media literacy skills and an understanding of issues such as the influence of media, and the ethics of media practitioners.

Topics include a discussion of the effect of TV shows like CSI on students' career choices, talk radio, stereotypes on film and TV, what our choice of clothing labels reveal about us, and family life and the internet.

Piquing Career Interest

Have you found that you and/or your friends are taking more of an interest in criminal justice and forensics? If so, you are not alone. Even a large number of universities report having increased the scope of courses they offer in criminal justice. To what is this surge in interest attributed? Many believe it is due to television.

The public appears fascinated with investigation and the justice system, as evidenced by the popularity of television shows such as *Crossing Jordan*, *Law and Order*, *Forensic Files*, and *CSI*. In fact, *CSI* (crime scene investigation-) based shows were the most highly watched shows on television in 2003. The popularity of media offerings has spilled over into the real world, sparking an increasing interest in criminology careers. Even the Nevada law enforcement agency Field Services Division has responded to popular interest in forensic science, changing its name to Crime Scene Investigations.[2]

In your opinion, to what extent, if any, is the portrayal of criminology careers on television and film contributing to unrealistic career expectations in those who now seek to become criminologists? For example, most of the crimes featured on CSI-type shows are solved in an hour, while they might take months or even years to solve in the real world. In addition, the programs on television rarely show the boring days, they reveal the staff working with state-of-the-art equipment that many cities cannot afford, and they have a crime solve rate that actual criminologists could never attain.

CSI-type programs have sparked interest in criminology careers.

...ay that the **interview** is the most common type of purposeful, planned, ...ecision-making, person-to-person communication. Thus, in the interview, ...teraction is structured, questions are asked and answered, and behavior is ...terchanged in an effort to explore predetermined subject matter and realize ... definite goal. This description is in keeping with a well-known and often

Interview
the most common type of purposeful, planned, decision-making, person-to-person communication

The Online Listener

Is having someone listen to you online the same as having someone listen to you in person? Even when cybercommunicators are using the same online language, because of the Internet's global reach, that language may not be their native language. As a result, the meanings given to the words used may differ drastically. As in face-to-face interaction, not all online listeners receive the same message. As you interact with persons from different cultures in cyberspace, ask yourself these questions:

1. Do they favor a direct or indirect style? While some cultures, including those in the United States, tend to exhibit a direct style in communicating—communicators tell it like it is—many Asian cultures use an indirect style, preferring to emphasize politeness and face-saving strategies rather than truth telling. Which style do you prefer?

2. Do they offer hard evidence or tell stories? In the United States, our decision making is influenced by logical reasons and

credible testimony. In contrast, members of other cultures tend to be influenced by stories other sources tell convincingly. What kind of substantiation do you tend to offer? Receive?

3. What kind of feedback do they offer? In the United States, we expect to receive honest feedback that reveals the feelings of those with whom we communicate. In Asian cultures, however, communicators believe it is more important to offer positive reactions than truthful ones. Not every culture perceives feedback the same way. What kind of feedback do you prefer?

4. How do opportunities for anonymity influence online listening behavior? Because we may remain anonymous, some of us tend to exhibit less ego involvement when listening online than when interacting face-to-face. How does the change in ego involvement affect you?

e-Search

e-Search boxes lead students to discover how the Internet affects their communication both on and off line.

Topics include moderating online conflicts, cybergroups, and cyperspace job searches.

To what extent, if any, does your use of media impede or enhance the time you spend communicating with other persons? Explain.

A focus on development and practice of communication and critical thinking skills is evident throughout the text, and students are encouraged to apply these skills to their current academic, personal, and professional lives.

Skill Builder

Skill Builder boxes help students look at communication, assess its effects, experience key insights about communication, and practice skill to become stronger communications. Skill Builder topics include problem solving in organizations, relationship skills, group culture, and conflict resolution.

Wake-Up Call

According to one résumé expert, "The biggest mistake that people are making is that their résumés have no real impact. . . . A good résumé won't get you a job, but it will get you in the door."[12]

Look at the cartoon that appears in this box. What steps can you take to ensure that your résumé doesn't end up as origami? Describe how you would market yourself to ensure that the person who receives your résumé actually opens it and spends some time reading it? For example, one applicant for a marketing position sent her résumé in a package of gourmet coffees, which she sent to the potential interviewer with the slogan "Lindsay will wake up your marketing" affixed to the package. Do you think her résumé was read?

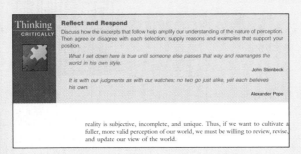

Reflect and Respond

Discuss how the excerpts that follow help amplify our understanding of the nature of perception. Then agree or disagree with each selection; supply reasons and examples that support your position.

What I set down here is true until someone else passes that way and rearranges the world in his own style.

John Steinbeck

It is with our judgments as with our watches; no two go just alike, yet each believes his own.

Alexander Pope

reality is subjective, incomplete, and unique. Thus, if we want to cultivate a fuller, more valid perception of our world, we must be willing to review, revise, and update our view of the world.

Thinking Critically: Reflect and Respond

Thinking Critically exercises promote higher-order thinking and class discussions about issues related to the text content. Examples include perception, conflict and conflict management, self-concept, and non-verbal cues.

Why would people who are competitive enjoy being surrounded by "yes people?" What dangers can such a mix pose?

For content review and test preparation

Self quizzes—Self-scoring quizzes allow students to assess their understanding of chapter concepts. ● and (online learning center)

Audio Flashcards—Students can hear how key terms are pronounced and study for exams. ● and (online learning center)

Crossword Puzzles—Students use key words and definitions to solve these chapter-specific puzzles. (online learning center)

For visualization of concepts and practice

Animations—Several animations illustrate elements of fundamental communication models. ●

Video Clips—17 brief video clips illustrate important chapter concepts. Nine of these, which are new to the 8th edition, provide sample student speeches (two informative, two persuasive, and five clips covering the use of statistics, examples, and images in a presentation). ●

For critical thinking and reflection

Self-Inventories—Chapter related surveys challenge students to examine their attitudes and feelings. Responses are included for each survey. ●

Internet Activities—Provide students with a wide variety of internet resources to further their understanding of chapter topics such as culture and diversity, non-verbal communication and sign language, and conflict resolution. (online learning center)

PowerWeb Sites: These password protected websites are offered free with new copies of the text. (Password card is bound into the inside front of the book.) They provide instructors and students with the following resources: (online learning center)

For *Public Speaking*—recent speeches from *Vital Speeches of the Day,* news and journal articles on topics such as speech anxiety, visual aids, and persuasion; articles on topics that students may use as source material for their speeches, and a newsworthy, annotated "speech of the week."

For *Communication*—primary source readings, course-specific study material, and current, relevant, validated Web content. PowerWeb helps students with online research by directing them to more than 6,000 high-quality academic sources.

The new Communication Works CD-ROM and the Online Learning Center are designed to appeal to a variety of teaching and learning styles by extending key course content into interactive and multimedia formats. These resources support the many ways students and instructors teach, study, work and practice. Icons in the text guide readers to specific applications on both resources.

For building confidence in public communication and managing speech projects

Audio Flashcards

17 Video Clips—Illustrate a number of communication concepts and offer sample student speeches.

Power Point Tutor—Presents the basic steps in effectively creating and using a Power Point presentation.

Outline Tutor—An interactive program and outlining template that shows the various parts of an outline and makes it easy for users to insert appropriate content into the parts.

Speech Critique—Enables students and instructors to evaluate speeches and generate written reports. Offers critiquing templates for informative, persuasive, and commemorative speeches.

Speech Preparation Checklist—Presents a list of steps to help students manage and prepare their speeches

Bibliomaker—After receiving bibliographic information from the user, BiblioMaker automatically formats the entry according to either APA or MLA style guidelines. and online learning center

Video

For work and career

Self-Inventory

Business Document Templates—Provides templates for resumes, cover letters, agendas, and memos.

Media Tours Videos—Provides behind-the-scenes tours of a small network-affiliated television station and Vibe Magazine.

The Essentials of Communication

Part One lays the foundation for your study of communication and introduces you to the communication concepts you will use as you study intrapersonal and interpersonal, group and organizational, presentational and public, and mass and machine-assisted communication. You will have the opportunity to examine what you believe about communication, identify steps you can take to avoid intercultural difficulties, consider how you view yourself, analyze when you are most comfortable interacting with others, assess the relationship that exists between words and their meaning, think about how language influences thought, determine how nonverbal cues influence communication outcomes, develop your skill in using nonverbal cues, and reflect on ways you can reduce listening and perceptual barriers. By the end of Part One, you'll begin to understand why communication works. Have fun!

Communication:
The Starting Line

1. Define *communication*.

2. List and explain the essential elements of communication.

3. Describe and explain representative models of communication, including one of your own creation.

4. Describe the characteristics and functions of communication.

5. Identify and provide examples of Watzlawick, Beavin, and Jackson's axioms of communication.

Whether clear or garbled, tumultuous or silent, deliberate or fatally inadvertent, communication is the ground of meeting. . . . It is, in short, the essential human connection.

—Ashley Montagu and Floyd Matson

Why did Beauty's disgust for the Beast turn to love? Why did Cinderella feel more beautiful when she was in the presence of the prince than at home? Why was the queen able to persuade Snow White to eat the poison apple? These timeless tales and characters illustrate both the simplicity and the complexity of human communication. Within these stories are messages about the effects of culture, self-concept, perception, the importance of listening, and the power of verbal and nonverbal language, as well as the specific nature of interpersonal, group, and public communication.

While we share much in common with the preceding characters, there are also important factors that differentiate us from them. First, we do not live in a fairy tale. Second, the twenty-first century finds us facing an array of new challenges, including globalization, the Internet, and gender role identity, challenges which we need to handle effectively in order to navigate our increasingly complex, persistently accelerating communication environment. Here are just a few of the questions we need to answer as we move between the personal and organizational, private and public, informational and persuasive, face-to-face and machine-assisted arenas of communication:

- What are the communication effects of growing up digitally?
- In what ways are evolving gender role identities affecting communication relationships?
- What impact do globalization and the diversifying of society have on our communication inputs and outcomes?
- What effects are media offerings having on our values and sense of self?
- To what extent do the contexts of communication—that is, whether we are interacting in professional, family, social, or romantic settings, for example—influence the nature of the communicative exchanges we have and the thoughts and feelings of the persons involved in the exchanges?

By answering questions like these, we may discover why communication works or fails. We may also come to understand that, while our study of communication will often extend to other people, the media, and even new technologies, it still needs to begin with you. Of all the knowledge and skills you possess, your understanding of and ability to use communication are of prime importance. Communication is your connection to your past, your present, and your future.

Communication is at the core of our humanness. How we communicate with each other shapes our lives and our world. We all rely on our communicative skills as we confront events that challenge our flexibility, integrity, expressiveness, and critical thinking skills. By making the effort to become more effective at interacting with persons from diverse backgrounds and by working at developing relationships based on mutual respect and a sense of ethical fairness, we increase our chances of leading more fulfilling personal and professional lives.

Our progress as a people depends on our learning to understand ourselves and others. To this end, we need to interact with each other to develop new ideas and solve problems. We need to participate in the exchange of information and ideas that we believe important to our well-being. And as we do this, we have to be able to weigh the benefits and the consequences of our expressed ideas and actions. Why do we place such a high value on communication? Because it is truly our bridge to the future, our link to the rest of humanity, and the tool we will rely on most as we make our way in the world.

THE IMPORTANCE OF COMMUNICATION

A college student. A corporate vice president. A teenager. An octogenarian. Two people in love. A doctor and a patient. A native and a foreigner. Parents. Children. Friends. Enemies. Decision makers. Speakers. You. All these people share at least one thing: a need to communicate.

This book is about you, about your need to communicate and how communication can help you relate more effectively to others. Possessing or developing the ability to communicate effectively with others is essential not only for your own success but also for the success of any organizations you work for, any groups you become part of, and any relationships you develop with people you come to know. In today's world, job-specific talent, technical expertise, and graduation from a prestigious school do not carry any guarantees for upward mobility or attainment of goals. Many of us get our jobs because of our social capital, that is, our social connections or social networks—whom we know—rather than our human capital—what we know.[1] Our workplaces are prime environments for connecting with others. The Internet has democratized information. Anyone with a modem can gather nearly as much intelligence as the CIA, access virtually as much data as exists in the Library of Congress, and contact people around the world at any hour.[2] One factor shared by people who are able to ascend both the professional and the personal ladders of success is superior communication skills. These people are promoted rapidly, are happy in their marriages and other relationships, and

Identify people you know personally or people you know of who have attained their positions because of their social capital and/or their human capital. Which form of capital do you believe is more important? Why?

Skill BUILDER

Contacts!

Identify five people with whom you recently had a sustained communication contact. (Note: The contact need not have been initiated by you.) For each contact, indicate the nature of your communication (the subject or message), the context or environment in which it occurred (classroom, office, home, voice mail, online, etc.), the type of interaction experienced (interpersonal, virtual, small-group, or public), and the outcome (what happened as a result of the interaction). Finally—and this is important—as an assessment of your communication effectiveness, rate each contact on a scale of 1 (extremely ineffective) to 5 (extremely effective), and give your rationale for each rating.

Extremely ineffective   1   2   3   4   5   Extremely effective

Now, how would you replay each contact if you were given the opportunity? If possible, would you prefer to increase or decrease the percentage of contacts you have that are virtual as opposed to face-to-face? Why?

For an example of the social, view clip 14 on the CD

in general view their lives as being rich and fulfilling. That is why this book can be of value to you. The topics we cover will help you as you go about your usual business of making friends, informing and persuading others, solving problems, falling in or out of love, and making your personal and professional relationships work.

We all depend on our communication skills to help us meet our needs, find happiness, and attain personal fulfillment. From birth to death, many types of communication are an integral part of your life. Whatever your sex, your occupation, and your goals, communication of one form or another plays a major role. The challenge is to communicate as effectively as possible—to build your communication skills so that communication works for you, not against you.

Whether you are 18 or 80, female or male, married or single, employed or unemployed, it is never too late to learn skills that will enrich and improve the quality of your life. Interpersonal, small-group, organizational, and public communication skills are not inborn. You have to develop them, a process that will continue throughout your life. That is why this book is designed to provide you with a program for lifelong learning. If you want to improve your ability to relate to people in your social life, your job, or your academic life, now is the time to start making communication work.

WHO IS A COMMUNICATOR?

A communicator is a person who enters into relationships with other people. Without communication, we would be unable to function. During the course of a single day we interact with others to share information and beliefs, exchange ideas and feelings, make plans, and solve problems. Sometimes this interaction is done interpersonally, sometimes in a team or small group, sometimes in a public forum, and sometimes through the media or via computer. However communication occurs, it is essential in helping us initiate, develop, control, and sustain our contacts with others.[3]

We all engage in intrapersonal (we communicate with ourselves), dyadic (one-to-one), small-group (one-to-a-few), public (one-to-many), and mass communication (communication that is shared across great distances with potentially large audiences through a technological device or mass medium). Many of us also participate in computer-assisted or online communication. Every time we knowingly or unknowingly send a verbal or nonverbal message to a friend, lover, relative, stranger, audience, acquaintance, supervisor, employee, co-worker, or group, communication takes place.[4] We can define **communication** as the deliberate or accidental transfer of meaning. It is the process that occurs whenever someone observes or experiences behavior and attributes meaning to that behavior. It doesn't matter whether the observed or experienced behavior is intentional or accidental, conscious or unconscious. As long as what someone does or says (his or her symbolic behavior) is interpreted as a message—as long as the behavior of one person affects or influences the behavior of another—communication is occurring. Thus, each facet of our lives from birth to death is dependent on and affected by our communication skills, especially the ability to create and interpret symbolic messages or behavior. Since we spend more time communicating than doing anything else, our communication skills help shape our personal, social, work, and professional relationships. Communication is our link to the rest of humanity.

> **communication**
> the deliberate or accidental transfer of meaning

The following examples illustrate the prevalence and importance of communication.

> *It's a mark of real leadership to take the lead in getting to know people. . . .*
> *It's always a big person who walks up to you and offers his/her hand and says hello.*
>
> —DAVID J. SCHWARTZ, *The Magic of Thinking Big*

> *The worst sin towards our fellow creatures is not to hate them, but to be indifferent to them; that's the essence of inhumanity.*
>
> —GEORGE BERNARD SHAW

> *Communication is the greatest single factor affecting a person's health and relationships to others.*
>
> —VIRGINIA SATIR, *The New Peoplemaking*

> *Computers don't just do things for us, they do things to us, including to our ways of thinking about ourselves and other people.*
>
> —SHERRY TURKLE, *Life on the Screen*

> *If my mind can conceive it and my heart can believe it, I know I can achieve it. Down with dope! Up with hope! I am somebody!*
>
> —JESSE JACKSON

> *To swallow and follow, whether old doctrine or new propaganda, is a weakness still dominating the human mind.*
>
> —CHARLOTTE PERKINS GILMAN

> *In study after study, most people agree that mass media influence attitudes— other people's attitudes, but not their own.*
>
> —STEVEN DUCK

Which of these observations do you agree with? Which do you find most applicable to your own communication experiences?

Media WISE

How Real Is Real?

In reality-based television shows such as *Survivor, American Idol, The Bachelor, Big Brother,* and *The Mole,* strangers are thrown together, filmed continuously, and either prevented from having or permitted to have only limited contact with the outside world as they compete against each other in an effort to win money, fame, and/or love.

As we watch shows like these on television or on the Internet, we enter the realm of voyeurism. We are peeking at people who have volunteered to live together for a period of time under constant surveillance by numerous cameras and microphones. In your opinion, do reality-based shows help us understand human interaction? How does the fact that these people can have no or only limited contact with the outside world influence their interactions with each other? To what extent, if any, does it concern you that television and the Internet are providing access to the potentially private, personal moments of others?

These shows also explore the nature of competition, our sense of ethics, and our communication competence. What do the popularity of shows like these reveal about our sense of competitiveness? What messages are shows that pit persons against each other in an effort to "win it all" send about the role competition plays in our lives? In your opinion, are shows like these symptomatic of an emerging **hyper-competitiveness,** the contention that one needs to defeat another to achieve one's goals? And what do they reveal about our communication ethics? Will people do anything to win? What do they suggest about whether or not people have the knowledge and skills they need to accomplish their communication objectives?

Finally, what, if anything, do we learn about the importance and nature of communication, in general, from watching such shows?

Reality-based TV shows such as American Idol *feed and reflect our hyper-competitiveness.*

hyper-competitiveness
the contention that one needs to defeat another to achieve one's goals

HOW GOOD A COMMUNICATOR ARE YOU?

When has insensitivity caused problems for you or others, on the job or at home?

Simply communicating frequently or having many person-to-person contacts each day does not mean that you are as effective a communicator as you could be. We frequently neglect problems that plague our communicative relationships—even though these issues are crucial in our lives. When we lack sensitivity and fail to consider the feelings of others, for example, our relationships suffer. There is no such thing as being too effective at establishing, maintaining, and controlling personal and public contacts with others.

We can all improve our communication skills. In the Skill Builder on page 6, you evaluated your proficiency during a variety of interpersonal, small-group, public, or computer-assisted communication experiences. Now let's consider steps you can take to improve or enhance your ability to relate to others in a variety of communication settings.

First, use the scale of 0 (totally ineffective) to 100 (totally effective) to rate your overall effectiveness as a communicator. Next, using the same scale, rate the communication skills of your best friend, an older relative, a fellow student, a boss or an instructor, and a boyfriend, girlfriend, or spouse.

| Totally ineffective | 0 | 10 | 20 | 30 | 40 | 50 | 60 | 70 | 80 | 90 | 100 | Totally effective |

According to the evaluations you have just completed, whose communication skills do you consider better than yours? Why? Whose communication skills do you consider equal to yours? Why? Whose communication skills do you consider inferior to yours? Why?

Now set a goal that indicates the extent to which you would like this course to improve your effectiveness as a communicator. If you are to realize this improvement, there are probably a number of skills you should work to maintain, a number of skills you should work to master, and a number of ineffective behaviors you should work to eliminate. To function effectively in interpersonal, small-group, public, mass, or computer-assisted communication, you will need to acquire certain skills and perceptions:

1. The ability to understand and communicate with yourself
2. Knowledge of how and why you and those with whom you relate see things the way you do
3. An appreciation of the extent to which gender, culture, the media, and new technologies affect communication
4. The capacity to listen and then process the information you receive
5. Sensitivity to silent messages that you and others send
6. Knowledge of how words affect you and those with whom you relate
7. An understanding of how relationships develop
8. An understanding of how feelings and emotions affect relationships
9. The ability to handle conflict by learning how to disagree without being disagreeable
10. An understanding of the behaviors that contribute to successful group decision making, leadership, and team building
11. An understanding of how beliefs, values, and attitudes affect the formulation and reception of messages and the development of speaker-audience relationships
12. The desire to apply all these skills and perceptions to each communication experience and arena

As we continue exploring and investigating what it means to experience effective interpersonal, small-group, mass, online or machine-assisted, and public communication, you will realize that the objectives just provided describe, in brief, the method and purpose of this book.

WHAT IS COMMUNICATION?

During **intrapersonal communication,** you think about, talk with, learn about, reason with, and evaluate yourself. In contrast, when you engage in **interpersonal communication,** you interact with another, learn about him or

intrapersonal communication
communication with the self

interpersonal communication
the relationship level of communication

group communication

interaction with a limited number of persons

public communication

communication designed to inform, persuade, or entertain audience members

---

Which type of communication do you use most? Least? Which do you enjoy most? Least? Why?

---

mass communication

the transmission of messages which may be processed by gatekeepers prior to being sent to large audiences via a channel of broad diffusion

online, or machine-assisted, communication

the building of relationships using computers and the Internet

essentials of communication

those components present during every communication event

senders

persons who formulate, encode, and transmit a message

receivers

persons who receive, decode, and interpret a message

her, and act in ways that help sustain or terminate your relationship. When you participate in **group communication,** you interact with a limited number of others, work to share information, develop ideas, make decisions, solve problems, offer support, or have fun. Through **public communication,** you inform and persuade the members of an audience to hold certain attitudes, values, or beliefs so that they will think, believe, or act in a particular way; on the other hand, you can also function as a member of an audience, in which case another person will do the same for you. During **mass communication,** the media entertain, inform, and persuade you. You, in turn, have the ability to use your viewing and buying habits to influence the media. During **online, or machine-assisted, communication,** you navigate cyberspace as you converse, research and exchange ideas, and build relationships with others using computers and the Internet. Whatever the nature or type of communication, however, the communicative act itself is characterized by the interplay of certain elements.

Elements of Communication

All communication interactions have certain common elements that together help define the communication process. The better you understand these elements, the easier it will be for you to develop your own communicative abilities. Let's begin by examining the **essentials of communication,** those components present during every interpersonal, small-group, public, and mass communication event.

People

Obviously, human communication involves people. Interpersonal, small-group, and public communication encounters take place between and among all types of **senders** (persons who encode messages) and **receivers** (persons who decode messages). Senders and receivers, respectively, are individuals who give out and take in messages. Although it is easy to picture an interpersonal, small-group, public, media, or computer-assisted communication experience beginning with a sender and ending with a receiver, it is important to understand that during communication the role of sender does not belong exclusively to one person and the role of receiver to another. Instead, the processes of sending and receiving are constantly being reversed. Reflecting this fact, in *That's Not What I Meant,* linguist Deborah Tannen writes, "Communication is a continuous stream in which everything is simultaneously a reaction and an instigation, an instigation and a reaction."[5] Thus, when we communicate with one or more people, we simultaneously send and receive.

If we were just senders, we would simply emit signals without ever stopping to consider whom, if anyone, we were affecting. If we were just receivers, we would be no more than receptacles for signals from others, never having an opportunity to let anyone know how we were being affected. Fortunately, that is not how effective communication works. The verbal and nonverbal messages we send are often determined in part by the verbal and nonverbal messages we receive.

Messages

During every interpersonal, small-group, or public communication encounter, we all send and receive both verbal and nonverbal messages. What you talk about, the words you use to express your thoughts and feelings, the sounds you make, the way you sit and gesture, your facial expressions, and perhaps even your touch or your smell all communicate information. In effect, a **message** is the content of a communicative act. Some messages we send are private (a kiss accompanied by "I love you"); others are public and may be directed at hundreds or thousands of people. We send some messages purposefully ("I want you to realize . . .") and others accidentally ("I had no idea you were watching . . . or 'lurking'"). Everything a sender or receiver does or says is a potential message as long as someone is there to interpret the behavior. When you smile, frown, shout, whisper, or turn away, you are communicating, and your communication is having some effect.

message
the content of a communicative act

Channels

We send and receive messages with and through all our senses; equally, messages may be sent and received through verbal and nonverbal modes, or **channels.** Thus, we are multichannel communicators. We receive sound messages (we hear noises from the street), sight messages (we see how someone looks), taste messages (we enjoy the flavor of a particular food), smell messages (we smell the cologne a friend is wearing), and touch messages (we feel the roughness of a fabric). Which channel are you most attuned to? Why? To what extent do you rely on one or more channels while excluding or disregarding others? Effective communicators are adept at switching channels. They recognize that communication is a multichannel experience.

channels
media through which messages are sent

The following dialogue between a husband and a wife illustrates the multichannel nature of communication:

> *Wife:* What's the matter with you? You're late again. We'll never get to the Adamses' on time.
>
> *Husband:* I tried my best.
>
> *Wife:* (Sarcastically) Sure, you tried your best. You always try your best, don't you? (Shaking her finger) I'm not going to put up with this much longer.
>
> *Husband:* (Raising his voice) You don't say! I happen to have been tied up at the office.
>
> *Wife:* My job is every bit as demanding as yours, you know.
>
> *Husband:* (Lowering his voice) OK. OK. I know you work hard too. I don't question that. Listen, I really did get stuck in a conference. (Puts his hand on her shoulder) Let's not blow this up. Come on. I'll tell you about it on the way to Bill and Ellen's.

Inventory each message you receive during a two-minute period, and note the channel through which it came.

What message is the wife (the initial source-encoder) sending to her husband (the receiver-decoder)? She is letting him know with her words, her voice, and her physical actions that she is upset and angry. Her husband responds in kind, using words, vocal cues, and gestures in an effort to explain his behavior. Both are affected by the nature of the situation (they are late for an appointment), by their attitudes (how they feel about what is occurring), and by their past experiences.

Noise

noise
anything that interferes with or distorts the ability to send and receive messages

In the context of communication, **noise** is anything that interferes with or distorts our ability to send or receive messages. Although we are accustomed to thinking of noise as a particular sound or group of sounds, the perceptive communicator realizes that noise can have both internal and external causes. Internal noise is attributed to the psychological makeup, intellectual ability, or physical condition of the communicators. External noise is attributed to the environment. Thus, noise includes distractions such as a loud siren, a disturbing odor, and a hot room; personal factors such as prejudices, daydreaming, and feelings of inadequacy; and semantic factors such as uncertainty about what another person's words are supposed to mean.

The following interplay between a husband and a wife reveals how each brings a field of experience or psychological frame of reference (a form of noise) to every interaction and how this influences the meaning each gives to received messages:

Wife: Hey, kids, don't bother Dad now. He's really tired. I'll play with you.
Husband: Don't isolate me from my own children! You always need to have all their attention.
Wife: I'm not trying to do that. I just know what it's like to have a really trying day and feel that I have to close my eyes to get back to myself.
Husband: I sure must be wound up.
Wife: I understand.

Context

context
the setting

Communication always takes place in a **context,** or setting. Sometimes a context is so natural that we hardly notice it. At other times, however, the context makes such an impression on us that it exerts considerable control over our behavior. Consider the extent to which your present environment influences the way you act toward others or determines the nature of the communication encounters you share with them. Consider as well the extent to which certain environments might cause you to alter your posture, manner of speaking, attire, or means of interacting. Take into account the fact that sometimes conditions of place and time—that is, context—can affect our communications without our consciously realizing it.

Feedback

feedback
information returned to a message source

positive feedback
a behavior-enhancing response

Whenever we communicate with one or more persons, we receive information in return. The verbal and nonverbal cues that we perceive in reaction to our communication function as **feedback.** Feedback tells us how we are coming across. A smile, a frown, a chuckle, a sarcastic remark, a muttered thought, or simply silence in response to something we did or said can cause us to change, continue, or end a transaction. Feedback that encourages us to continue behaving as we are is **positive feedback;** it enhances whatever behavior

Contact in Context

Compare and contrast the types of communication that would be most likely to occur in each of the following contexts. Include a description of the nature of each interaction, the probable attire of each interactant, and his or her demeanor.

1. The first few minutes of a party
2. A business meeting
3. A coffeehouse
4. A funeral home

5. A college classroom
6. A political rally
7. A football stadium
8. A computer chat room

is in progress. In contrast, **negative feedback** extinguishes a behavior; it serves a corrective rather than a reinforcing function. Thus, negative feedback can help eliminate unwanted, ineffective behaviors. Note that the terms *positive* and *negative* should not be interpreted as "good" and "bad"; these terms simply reflect the way the responses affect behavior.

Both positive and negative feedback can emanate from internal or external sources. **Internal feedback** is feedback you give yourself as you monitor your own behavior or performance during a transaction. **External feedback** is feedback from others who are involved in the communication event. To be an effective communicator, you must be sensitive to both types of feedback. You must pay attention to your own reactions as well as the reactions of others.

negative feedback
a response that extinguishes behavior in progress

internal feedback
a response you give yourself

external feedback
a response from another

Effect

As people communicate, they are changed in some way by the interaction, which in turn influences what follows. In other words, communication has an **effect** and can be viewed as an exchange of influences. This means that communication always has some effect on you and on the person or people with whom you are interacting.

An effect can be emotional, physical, cognitive, or any combination of the three. An interpersonal, small-group, or public communication contact can elicit feelings of joy, anger, or sadness (emotional); communication can cause you to fight, argue, become apathetic, or evade an issue (physical); or it can lead to new insights, increased knowledge, the formulation or reconsideration of opinions, silence, or confusion (cognitive). The result of a communication encounter can also be any combination of the three effects just mentioned. Since effects are not always visible or immediately observable, there is obviously more to a communication reaction than meets the eye, or the ear.

What positive and negative feedback have you recently given to others? What positive and negative feedback have you received?

effect
the communication outcome

SIX CRUCIAL CHARACTERISTICS OF COMMUNICATION

Besides having specific ingredients, or elements, in common, interpersonal, small-group, organizational, public, mass, and computer-assisted communication also share at least six general characteristics.

Communication Is Dynamic

When we call communication a dynamic process, we mean that all its elements constantly interact with and affect each other.[6] Since all people are interconnected, whatever happens to one person determines in part what happens to others.

Like the human interactants who compose them, interpersonal, small-group, and public communication relationships constantly evolve from and affect one another. Nothing about communication is static. Everything is accumulative. We communicate as long as we are alive, and thus every interaction we engage in is part of connected happenings. All our present communication experiences may be thought of as points of arrival from past encounters and as points of departure for future ones. (This is well illustrated by a spiral model of communication developed by Frank Dance, which is discussed in the section "Models of Communication" on pages 17 and 18.) Do your experiences support this premise?

Can you think of an interpersonal, small-group, or public communication encounter you had that affected a later encounter?

Communication Is Unrepeatable and Irreversible

Experience changes us forever.

Every human contact you experience is unique. It has never happened before, and never again will it happen in just the same way. Our interpretation of the adage "You can never step into the same river twice" is that the experience changes both you and the river forever. Similarly, a communication encounter affects and changes the interactants so that the encounter can never happen in exactly the same way again. Thus, communication is both unrepeatable and irreversible. We can neither take back something we have said nor erase the effects of something we have done. And although we may be greatly influenced by our past, we can never reclaim it. In the words of a Chinese proverb, "Even the emperor cannot buy back one single day." Do you think this proverb is right?

Can you describe a work-related or personal situation in which the irreversibility of communication caused difficulties for you?

Communication Is Affected by Culture

As we will learn in Chapter 2, how we formulate and interpret messages depends on our culture. Cultural diversity, including race, ethnicity, gender, and age, influences the meanings we attribute to communication. Cultural differences exist not only between persons who speak different languages but between persons who speak the same language as well. Every cultural group has its own rules or preferences for interaction. When these are ignored or

What does the following observation by Koji Yanase, a Japanese bar-association official, suggest about the nature of communication?

If an American is hit on the head by a ball at the ballpark, he sues. If a Japanese person is hit on the head he says, "It's my honor. It's my fault. I shouldn't have been standing there."

*Newsweek,
February 26, 1996*

unknown, we are likely to misinterpret the meaning of messages received and miscalculate the impact of messages sent.

Communication Is Influenced by Ethics

Every time we communicate we decide implicitly or explicitly whether we will do so ethically. Ethics are the moral principles, values, and beliefs that the members of society use to guide behavior. Since communication has consequences, it involves judgments of right and wrong. When the agreed-upon standards of behavior are violated, the behavior is judged unethical. For example, most of us expect those with whom we interact to be honest, play fair, respect our rights, and accept responsibility for their actions.

Communication Is Competence-Based

According to communication scholar Osmo Wiio, if communication can fail, it will.[7] The dilemma we face is, How can we prevent communication from failing?

While we all have different communication strengths and weaknesses, we can all benefit from getting better at communicating. When we add to our knowledge and make a commitment to develop the skills to apply that knowledge across an array of communication situations or contexts, we gain communication competence. For example, included among the skills necessary for effective communication is the ability to think critically. When we can think critically we have the ability to examine ideas reflectively and to decide what we should and should not believe, think, or do, given a specific set of circumstances.[8]

Communication Is Being Transformed by Media and Technology

As media critic Marshall McLuhan cautioned, "The medium is the message."[9] In McLuhan's view, different channels of communication affect the way a sender encodes a message and the way a receiver responds to a message. The same words delivered face-to-face, on paper, or via radio or television do not constitute the same message. The channel of communication changes things. For example, terminating a relationship via an answering machine or e-mail is very different from delivering such news in person. What channel would you use, for example, to say "good-bye"? Which channel would you use to tell someone "I'm sorry?" What about "I love you"?

Not just the medium, but also its content, changes communication. The content of books, newspapers, radio, television, and film, for example, also influence our cultural values, often reinforcing the stereotypes we have of gender, race, and ethnicity and contributing to the perceptions we have of various people and groups in society, including ourselves.

New forms of communication also alter our communication experiences. According to media scholar Neil Postman, a new technology does not merely add or subtract something; it changes everything. Postman contends that our culture is now a **technopoly**—a culture in which technology monopolizes the

Can you identify an experience in which the understanding or misunderstanding of culture contributed to your communication effectiveness or ineffectiveness?

Can you identify a communication experience that, looking back, you believe communication between you and another person was effective or ineffective because of the presence or absence of ethical behavior on your part?

Can you cite an example of how improving a specific communication skill enabled you to resolve a problem in your personal, academic, or professional life?

technopoly

a culture in which technology monopolizes the thought-world.

Are these changes increasing or undermining social contact? As Postman fears, are we becoming tools of our tools? Are technological innovations overwhelming us with information or underwhelming us with a lack of credibility? Are they freeing us or complicating our lives? Are they bringing us closer together or keeping us apart? What do you think?

thought-world.[10] Technology continues to speed up communication as it brings the world into our living rooms and bedrooms, offices and automobiles. Instead of valuing sequential understanding and careful logic, we now value immediate gratification and emotional involvement. Technology has also given us the ability to interact in more ways, more quickly, and with more people than ever before. We now experience events throughout the world as they happen. For example, we experienced the 2003 war in Iraq as it occurred, not after it was won. E-mail and digital cameras allow us to see, interact with, and visit people across the globe.

MODELS OF COMMUNICATION

Now that we have examined the basic components of communication—people, messages, channels, noise, context, feedback, and effect—we are ready to see how our understanding can be reflected in a picture, or model, of the communication process.

Through communication, we share meaning with others by sending and receiving messages—sometimes intentionally and sometimes unintentionally. Communication thus includes every element that could affect two or more people as they knowingly or unknowingly relate to one another.

At this point, we need to reiterate that communication occurs whenever one person assigns significance or meaning to the behavior of another. But, you might ask, will knowing this enable us to understand or establish better and more satisfying relationships with our friends, spouse, employer, parents? The answer is yes. If you understand the processes that permit people to contact and influence each other, if you understand the forces that can impede or foster the development of every kind of effective communication, then you stand a better chance of communicating effectively yourself. Models of communication like the ones in Figures 1.1 and 1.2 explain and help you visualize the process we employ to initiate and maintain communicative relationships with others. You will find these models useful tools in discovering how communication operates and in examining your own communication encounters.

FIGURE 1.1
Gamble and Gamble's Model of Communication.

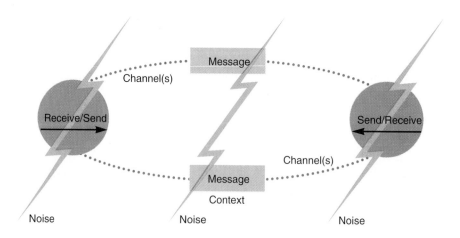

Modeling Communication

Skill
BUILDER

Draw or build something that represents your understanding of communication. You can focus on any or all of the components of the processes we have examined thus far. Your model can be lifelike or abstract. Be ready to present it to the class. Specifically, be sure to do the following:

a. Describe what your model suggests are the essential elements of the communication process (whether pictured or implied).

b. Explain what your model says about the communication process.

c. Develop a saying or an epigram that sums up your perception of the state of being in communication.

d. Explain how your model reflects one or more of the axioms of communication discussed in the section "Five Axioms of Communication," on pages 20–24, or identify how your model can be used to explain a communication interaction of your own choosing.

e. Suggest what insights into interpersonal, small-group, public, mass, or computer-assisted communication are provided by your model.

The model in Figure 1.1 shows that communication is a circle and that the sending and receiving responsibilities are shared by the communicators. A message or messages may be sent through one or more channels, and the interaction occurs in and is affected by a definite context. Note that noise can enter the interaction at any point and can affect either the sending or the receiving abilities of the communicators. Furthermore, noise can be caused by the context, can be present in the channel, or can pop up in the message itself.

Another model of communication, devised by communication theorist Frank Dance[11] (see Figure 1.2), depicts the communication process in a more abstract way. Dance's spiral, or helix, represents the way communication evolves or progresses in a person from birth to the present moment. This model emphasizes the fact that each person's present behavior is affected by his or her past experience and, likewise, that present behavior will have an impact on future actions. Thus, Dance's helix indicates that communication has no clearly observable beginning and no clearly observable end.

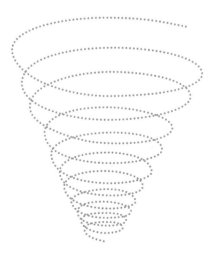

FIGURE 1.2
Dance's Communication Helix.

Source: From *Human Communication Theory: Original Essays* by Frank E. X. Dance. Holt, Rinehart & Winston. Copyright © 1967 by Frank E. X. Dance. Used by permission of the author.

FIGURE 1.3
Meeting of Helixes.

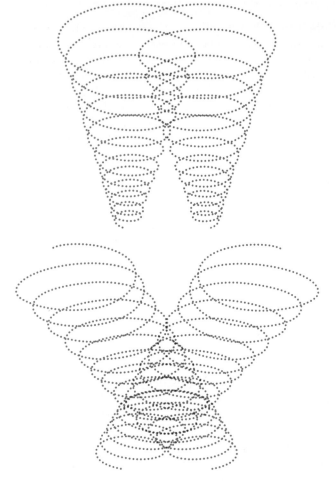

FIGURE 1.4
Model of Communication in Relationships.

By playing with Dance's model, we can picture two communication spirals as meeting in a number of different ways, as shown in Figure 1.3. The point where the spirals touch is the point of contact; each time a contact occurs, messages are sent and received by the interactants. Some helical spirals touch each other only once during a lifetime, whereas others crisscross or intertwine in a pattern that indicates an enduring relationship. Furthermore, the spirals (interactants) may sometimes develop in similar ways (grow together) and sometimes develop in different ways (grow apart; see Figure 1.4).

The understanding you now have should provide you with some of the background you will need as you work to increase your effectiveness as a communicator.

FUNCTIONS OF COMMUNICATION: WHAT CAN IT DO FOR YOU?

Every communication experience serves one or more functions. For example, communication can help us discover who we are, help us establish meaningful relationships, or prompt us to examine and try to change either our own attitudes and behaviors or the attitudes and behaviors of others.

Understanding and Insight

One key function of communication is self-other understanding: insight into ourselves and others. When you get to know another person, you also get to know yourself; and when you get to know yourself, you learn how others affect you. We depend on communication to develop self-awareness.

We need feedback from others all the time, and others are constantly in need of feedback from us. Interpersonal, small-group, public, and media communications offer us numerous opportunities for self-other discovery. Through communication encounters we are able to learn why we are trusting or untrusting, whether we can make our thoughts and feelings clear, under what conditions we have the power to influence others, and whether we can effectively make decisions and resolve conflicts and problems.

The one thing that unites all human beings, regardless of age, gender, religion, economic status or ethnic background is that deep down inside, we all believe that we are above average drivers.

—Dave Barry

In your opinion, are there other characteristics that unite us? If so, what are they?

Meaningful Relationships

In building relationships, we cannot be overly concerned with ourselves but must consider the needs and wants of others. It is through effective interpersonal, small-group, public, media, and computer-assisted communication contacts that our basic physical and social needs are met.

Psychologists tell us that we need other people just as we need water, food, and shelter. When we are cut off from human contact, we become disoriented and maladjusted, and our life itself may be placed in jeopardy. People who are isolated from others—people who lack satisfying social relationships—are more likely to experience health problems and to die early than people who have an abundance of satisfying relationships.

Communication offers each of us the chance to satisfy what psychologist William Schutz calls our "needs for inclusion, control, and affection."[12] The **need for inclusion** is our need to be with others, our need for social contact. We like to feel that others accept and value us, and we want to feel like a full partner in a relationship. The **need for control** is our need to feel that we are capable and responsible, that we are able to deal with and manage our environment. We also like to feel that we can influence others. The **need for affection** is our need to express and receive love. Since communication allows each of these needs to be met, we are less likely to feel unwanted, unloved, or incapable if we are able to communicate meaningfully with others.

need for inclusion
the need for social contact

need for control
the need to feel we are capable and responsible

need for affection
the need to express and receive love

In today's world, it is a given that we will need to interact with persons who are culturally different from us. To attempt to insulate ourselves from such intercultural contacts is virtually impossible, nor is it desirable. It is through communication that we can reveal to others what is important to us and what we stand for, as well as learn what is important to them and what they stand for.

Communication also gives us the chance to share our personal reality with people from our own culture, as well as people from different cultures. Whether we live in an East Coast urban area, a southern city, a desert community, a home in sunny California, a village in Asia, a plain in Africa, or a town in the Middle East, we all engage in similar activities when we communicate. We may use different symbols, rely on different strategies, and desire different outcomes, but the processes we use and the motivations we have are

"I Hate Him"

Over 24 years ago, researcher Gordon Allport wrote the following in his now classic *The Nature of Prejudice:*

> See that man over there?
> Yes.
> Well, I hate him.
> But you don't know him.
> That's why I hate him.

Why does lack of knowledge or familiarity breed hate? Why might we experience hate when encountering people from a new or unfamiliar culture or group? Although Allport was writing over two decades ago, his comments remain true today. Why? To what extent do you believe that enhanced self-other understanding can help resolve this predicament? Explain.

strikingly alike. Equally significant is the fact that insensitivity to another's needs and preferred ways of interacting can hamper our ability to relate effectively.

Influence and Persuasion

During interpersonal, small-group, public, mediated, and online communication, people have ample opportunities to influence each other subtly or overtly. We spend much time trying to persuade one another to think as we think, do what we do, like what we like. Sometimes our efforts meet with success, and sometimes they do not. In any case, our experiences with persuasion afford each of us the chance to influence others so that we may try to realize our own goals.

Go to the *Online Learning Center* at www.mhhe.com/gamble8 and answer the questions in the *Self Inventory* to evaluate your understanding of the five axioms of communication.

FIVE AXIOMS OF COMMUNICATION

Now that we have looked at elements, models, characteristics, and functions of communication, it will be useful to turn our attention to five basic axioms of communication (see Figure 1.5). These principles were described in a classic study by Paul Watzlawick, Janet Beavin, and Don Jackson.[13] Each axiom has functional implications and is essential to our understanding of the communication process.

FIGURE 1.5
Five Axioms of Communication.

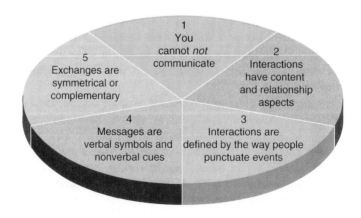

1 You cannot *not* communicate

2 Interactions have content and relationship aspects

3 Interactions are defined by the way people punctuate events

4 Messages are verbal symbols and nonverbal cues

5 Exchanges are symmetrical or complementary

Axiom 1: You Cannot Not Communicate

It is not uncommon to assume that we communicate only because we want to communicate and that all communication is purposeful, intentional, and consciously motivated. Obviously, this is often true, but just as often we communicate without any awareness of doing so—and at times even without wanting to.

Whenever we are involved in an interaction, we must respond in some way. Even if we do not choose to respond verbally, even if we maintain absolute silence and attempt not to move a muscle, our lack of response is itself a response and therefore constitutes a message, influences others, and hence communicates. In other words, we can never voluntarily stop behaving—because behavior has no opposite.

Watzlawick, Beavin, and Jackson identified four basic strategies that we usually employ when trying not to communicate—when we want to avoid making contact with someone. The first strategy is **rejection;** we may try to reject communication by making it clear to the other person that we are not interested in conversing. By doing this, however, we do not avoid communicating, and we probably create a strained, embarrassing, socially uncomfortable situation. (Furthermore, as a result of this action, a relationship now exists between us and the person we want to avoid.) The second strategy is **acceptance;** we may decide to accept communication. This strategy involves operating according to the "law of least effort," giving in reluctantly, and agreeing to make conversation in the hope that the person will go away quickly. The third strategy is **disqualification;** we may attempt to disqualify our communication.[14] That is, we communicate in a way that invalidates our own messages or the messages sent to us by the other person. We contradict ourselves, switch subjects, or utter incomplete sentences or non sequiturs in the hope that the other person will give up. The fourth strategy is **the symptom as communication;** we may pretend we would like to talk but because we are tired, nervous, sick, drunk, bereaved, deaf, or otherwise incapacitated, we simply cannot communicate at the moment. In other words, we use some symptom as a form of communication. To repeat, however, no matter how hard we try, we cannot *not* communicate, because all behavior is communication and therefore is a message.

rejection
communication that rejects communication efforts

acceptance
willingness to receive and respond to a message

disqualification
communication that invalidates a message sent

the symptom as communication
the use of an excuse as a reason for not wanting to communicate

Axiom 2: Every Interaction Has a Content Dimension and a Relationship Dimension

The **content level** of a communication is its information level, or data level; it describes the behavior expected as a response. In contrast, the **relationship level** of a communication indicates how the exchange is to be interpreted; it signals what one person thinks of the other. For example, "Close the door" is a directive whose content asks the receiver to perform a certain action. However, the communication "Close the door" can be delivered in many ways—as a command, a plea, a request, a come-on, or a turnoff. Each manner of delivery says something about the relationship between the source, or sender, and the receiver. Through such signals, we constantly give others clues about how we see ourselves in relationship to them.

content level
the information or data level

relationship level
the level of interpretation

confirmation
acknowledgment and
acceptance of another and
his or her self view

rejection
communication that rejects
another's self concept

disconfirmation
communication that shows
a lack of interest in another
person

*Describe communication
experiences in which you
were (a) confirmed,
(b) rejected, and
(c) disconfirmed by another
person. How did you respond
in each case?*

Watzlawick, Beavin, and Jackson identified three types of responses that we use to indicate our reactions to each other. First is **confirmation;** we can confirm other people's self-definitions, or self-concepts, and thus treat others as they believe they ought to be treated. For example, if your friend Mary believes she is competent and smart and if those around her reward her by asking for advice or seeking her help, her self-concept is being confirmed.

Second is **rejection;** we can reject other people's self-definitions by simply refusing to accept their beliefs about themselves. If your friend John imagines himself a leader but no one else treats him as if he has the qualities associated with leadership, he may be forced to revise his picture of himself.

Third is **disconfirmation;** we can disconfirm other people's self-definitions. Confirmation says, "I accept you as you see yourself. Your self-assessment is correct." Rejection says, "I do not accept you as you see yourself. Your self-assessment is wrong." Disconfirmation, on the other hand, says simply, "You do not exist. You are a nonentity." Disconfirmation implies that we do not care enough to let other people know how we feel and that we always treat people the same way no matter what they say or do. In other words, we do not offer people any clues whatever to indicate that we believe they are or are not performing well. In effect, we totally ignore them. Psychologist William James noted that consistent disconfirmation is perhaps the cruelest psychological punishment that a human being can experience: "No more fiendish punishment could be devised . . . than that we should be turned loose in a society and remain absolutely unnoticed."

Axiom 3: Every Interaction Is Defined by How It Is Punctuated

Even though we understand that communication is continuous, we often act as if there were an identifiable starting point or a traceable cause for a particular response. Actually, in many communication interactions, it is extremely difficult to determine what is stimulus and what is response. For instance, it is equally possible for a father to believe that he is reading or daydreaming to escape his small daughter's screaming and for the child to believe that she is screaming because her father is reading or daydreaming and won't play with her. The father sees behavior as progressing from screaming to retreating, whereas the child sees it as progressing from retreating to screaming. In other words, what is stimulus for one is response for the other. We all divide up, or punctuate, a particular experience somewhat differently because each of us sees it differently. Thus, whenever you suggest that a certain communication began because of a particular stimulus, you are forgetting that communication has no clearly distinguishable starting point or end point. Try to remember that communication is circular—it is a continuous, ongoing series of events.

Think of a recent argument you had that you believe was started by the other person. Describe the situation, and identify that person's stimulus behavior (the apparent starting point). Now, put yourself in the other person's place. How might he or she have answered this question?

digital
the word level of
communication

analogic
the continuous stream of
nonverbal cues

Axiom 4: Messages Consist of Verbal Symbols and Nonverbal Cues

When we talk to others, we send out two kinds of messages: (1) discrete, **digital,** verbal symbols (words) and (2) continuous, **analogic,** nonverbal cues that may contain sound but do not contain words. According to Watzlawick,

Beavin, and Jackson, the content of a message is more likely to be communicated through the digital system, whereas the relationship level of the message is more likely to be carried through the analogic system. Although words are under our control and for the most part are uttered intentionally, many of the nonverbal cues that we send are not. Thus, Watzlawick, Beavin, and Jackson write that "it is easy to profess something verbally, but difficult to carry a lie into the realm of the analogic." This means that, while you may lie with words, the nonverbal signals you emit are likely to give you away.

Axiom 5: Interactions Are Either Symmetrical or Complementary

The terms *symmetrical* and *complementary* do not refer to good (normal) or bad (abnormal) communication exchanges but simply represent two basic categories into which all communication interactions can be divided. Each type of interaction serves important functions, and both are present in a healthy relationship.

During a communication encounter, if the behavior of one person is mirrored by the behavior of the other person, Watzlawick, Beavin, and Jackson would say that a **symmetrical interaction** has occurred. Thus, if you act in a dominating fashion and the person you are relating to acts the same way, or if you act happy and the other person also acts happy, or if you express anger and the other person likewise expresses anger, for the moment the two of you have a symmetrical relationship.

In contrast, if the behavior of one interactant precipitates a different behavior in the other, Watzlawick, Beavin, and Jackson would say that a **complementary interaction** exists. In a complementary relationship, you and your partner engage in opposite behaviors, with your behavior eliciting the other person's behavior, or vice versa. Thus, if you behave in an outgoing manner, your partner might become quiet; if you are aggressive, he or she might become submissive; if you become the leader, he or she might become the follower.

Neither a symmetrical nor a complementary relationship is trouble-free. Parties to a symmetrical relationship are apt to experience what is termed **symmetrical escalation.** Since they believe they are equal, each also believes he or she has a right to assert control. When this happens, the interactants may feel compelled to engage in a battle to show how "equal" they really are. Since it is not uncommon for individuals sharing a symmetrical relationship to find themselves in a status struggle with each other, the main danger of this type of interaction is a runaway sense of competitiveness.

In contrast, the problem that surfaces in many complementary relationships is **rigid complementarity.** This occurs when one party to an interaction begins to feel that control is automatically his or hers and as a result the relationship becomes rigid or fixed. Control no longer alternates between the interactants; thus, both persons lose a degree of freedom in choosing how they will behave. For example, a teacher who never pictures himself or herself as a learner, a parent who cannot perceive that his or her child has reached adulthood, and a leader who can never permit himself or herself to act as a

symmetrical interaction
a relationship in which the behavior of one person mirrors the behavior of another person

complementary interaction
communication in which interactants engage in opposite behavior

symmetrical escalation
a relationship in which individuals compete for control

rigid complementarity
a relationship characterized by fixed, unchanging roles

How could the attitude expressed here affect the employer-employee relationship?

"Treat people as equals and the first thing you know they believe they are."

follower have all become locked into self-perpetuating, unrealistic, unchanging, and unhealthy patterns of behavior.

Imagine that you have a small daughter. Now imagine how you would feel if some years from now, while you are riding with your daughter in her car, she slams on the brakes and at the same time instinctively places her arm between the windshield and your body. Do you think you would be ready for this shift in power?

The five axioms of communication that we have just explained should provide you with the background knowledge you will need as you prepare to focus on how everything fits together.

COMMUNICATION, THE MEDIA, AND TECHNOLOGY

cyberspace

the digital world of computers and online communication

The media and new technologies are altering the nature of our communication experiences. The content of the media influences our thoughts and feelings about the world we live in. Of course, large numbers of us no longer rely merely on the more traditional media of television, music, radio, film, and print for information about ourselves, each other, and our world; millions of us now also interact with each other in **cyberspace**[15] (the digital world of computers and online communication; the term was first used in the science fiction novel *Neuromancer* by William Gibson). Thus, the media and emerging technologies are bringing us new ways of discovering ideas and information, new ways of relating with friends and strangers, and new ways of learning about our world, our identities, and our futures.

Cell phones and personal digital assistants keep us connected. In your opinion, are they facilitating or impeding human interaction?

The media and technology are also causing us to reexamine our relationships and redefine our notions of effective and meaningful communication. Because of their presence in our lives, we may think differently about ourselves, each other, and society in general.[16] Media and computers have the ability to influence our perceptions of communication, alter our interaction preferences, and reformulate our ways of thinking and knowing. As we expand our real and virtual communication repertoires, we need to continually ask the following questions: What changes are the media and technology creating in us? How are they influencing our social and emotional lives and cultural sensibilities? How are they altering our desire to relate to others—that is, our desire to communicate? In other words, what does it really mean to be a communicator today?

Exploring the World of the Cybercommunicator

First, describe the role that online interaction presently plays in your life. Next, interview three people to discover the role it plays in their lives. Then, identify the reasons you and those you interviewed have for seeking or avoiding the establishing of online relationships.

In what ways, if any, do you find that promoting or limiting online relationships is adding to or detracting from the richness of your life and the lives of those you interviewed? What does recent research on the effects of communicating online reveal? Be specific.

Finally, agree or disagree with the following statement; provide reasons for your response.

Too many observers of our new technologically wired society spout "cyberbole"—exaggerated claims about the effect the new technology has on society. In reality, the problems of social division in our society far outweigh what the Internet can bring to us. In the end, according to skeptic Steve Woolgar, the Internet will probably be like the telephone—"this huge new revolution that didn't make much difference to existing social structures."[17]

e-SEARCH

To what extent, if any, has your use of the Internet affected the time you have available for family and friends? How has it had an impact on your personal and professional relationships?

Like television in the 1950s, the Internet is a society-altering device that is affecting personal interaction. While the Internet and e-mail usage have increased some forms of human interaction, they may be limiting other forms of interaction. For example, 13 percent of Internet users say they spend less time with friends and family, 59 percent spend less time viewing television, 34 percent spend less time reading newspapers, and 25 percent spend more time working as a result of the time they spend online. (See Figures 1.6 and 1.7.) At the same

FIGURE 1.6
Connected.

Connected
A survey at the outset of this century concluded that 55% of Americans have access to the Internet. Of those, 36% said they were online at least five hours a week. Where do you fit into the graphs below?

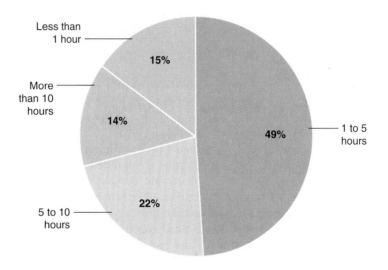

Source: "Stanford Institute for the Quantitative Study of Society." *New York Times,* February 16, 2000, p. A-1.

FIGURE 1.7
The Wired Life.

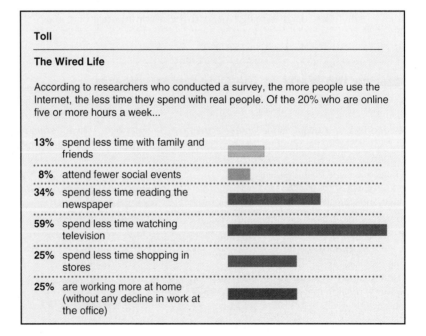

Source: "Stanford Institute for the Quantitative Study of Society." *New York Times,* February 16, 2000, p. A-18.

Reflect and Respond

Agree or disagree with the following statement; supply reasons and examples that support your position.

Communication is communication. If you can communicate effectively with persons who are similar to you, you can also communicate effectively with persons who are different from you. If you can communicate effectively with others when face-to-face, you can communicate equally well with them when online. In other words, neither the gender nor the nationality of the communicators, nor the means used to interact with others, should influence the satisfactions derived from or the outcomes of a communication experience.

Thinking
CRITICALLY

time, we realize that e-mail allows us to stay in touch with one another regardless of distance. It also allows us to communicate with one another regardless of time.[18] Thus, the question of whether the Internet is bringing us together or contributing to social isolation is worthy of our attention.

Another question worthy of our attention is the effect that the diffusion of cell-phones is having on our personal, social, and work lives. Since 2002, we have averaged more minutes talking on cell-phones than on traditional landline connections. The cell-phone with its text-messaging/video capabilities is a convergent social technology that is rapidly becoming an integral part of the mass media and technology mix. The cell-phone is no longer just a means of social interaction; it is also a source of news and public information, as well as a medium through which we express our social identity.[19]

IMPROVING YOUR EFFECTIVENESS AS A COMMUNICATOR

The major purpose of this book is to help you gain an understanding of communication and to assist you in developing your skills at interpersonal, small-group, public, mass, and online communication. To achieve these goals, you will need to accomplish the following preliminary tasks.

Become Actively Involved in the Study of Communication

The materials in this book will benefit you only if you make a commitment to try out and experience the principles discussed. First, each chapter opening lists targets, or objectives, that specify what you should have learned after completing your study of the chapter. Use these lists to clarify your personal communication objectives as you make your way through the book. Next, a plethora of boxes—Skill Builder, Exploring Diversity, Ethics & Communication, e-Search, Media Wise, and Thinking Critically—are included to help you explore communication and become aware of what you must know and do to become a more effective communicator. A number of these features contain self-analysis and assessment scales. Together, they give you an opportunity to process and apply your new knowledge to actual communication experiences.

Focus on Service Learning

Develop a two- to three-minute presentation promoting the importance of communication for delivery to an elementary school class and/or their parents and teachers.

If you use them as directed, you will increase your opportunities to grow because you will be actively using your own learning and diagnosing your own needs for self-improvement.

Believe in Yourself

Above all else, you must believe that you are worth the time and effort needed to develop your communication skills. You must also believe that developing these skills will immeasurably improve the quality of your life. We think you are worth it. And we know that communication works. Do you?

Revisiting Chapter Objectives

1. **Define *communication*.**   Communication is the deliberate or accidental transfer of meaning. Human communication takes place interpersonally (one to one), in small groups (one to a few), in public forums (one to many), via the media, or online.

2. **List and explain the essential elements of communication.**   The essential elements of communication are people, messages, channels, noise, context, feedback, and effect.

3. **Describe and explain representative models of communication, including one of your own creation.**   Models of communication have been developed to illustrate the communication process in action.

    All acts of communication share two general characteristics. First, since communication is a dynamic process, each interaction is part of a series of interconnected communication events. Second, every communication experience is unique, unrepeatable, and irreversible.

4. **Describe the characteristics and functions of communication.**   Communication serves a number of essential functions in our lives. It promotes self-other understanding, helps us establish meaningful relationships, and enables us to examine and attempt to change the attitudes and behavior of others.

5. **Identify and provide examples of Watzlawick, Beavin, and Jackson's axioms of communication.**   Watzlawick, Beavin, and Jackson have developed five basic axioms that further clarify the communication process. Axiom 1: You cannot *not* communicate. Axiom 2: Every interaction has both a content and a relationship dimension. Axiom 3: Every interaction is defined by the way it is punctuated. Axiom 4: Messages are digital and analogic (verbal and nonverbal). Axiom 5: Communication exchanges are either symmetrical or complementary.

    Developing communication skills is a lifelong process. This book explains the strategies you can use to assess your own communication abilities, improve the effectiveness of your communication relationships, and enhance the quality of your life.

Resources for Further Inquiry and Reflection

To apply your understanding of how the principles in Chapter 1 are at work in our daily lives, consult the following resources for further inquiry and

(side margin) THE Wrap-Up

reflection. Or, if you prefer, choose any other appropriate resource. Then connect the ideas expressed in your chosen selection with the communication concepts and issues you are learning about both in and out of class.

 Listen to Me

"You Outta Know" (Alanis Morrisette)
"Bohemian Rhapsody" (Queen)
"Cry Me a River" (Justin Timberlake)
"The Greatest Love of All" (Whitney Houston)

What message is the speaker sending regarding both the functions and the effects of communication?

 View Me

Traffic   *When a Man Loves a Woman*
The Matrix   *The Truth about Cats and Dogs*
Cast Away

What do the main characters in the selected film reveal about the nature of communication and how it has an impact on others?

 Read Me

Erma Bombeck. "When Did I Become the Mother and the Mother Become the Child?" In *If Life Is a Bowl of Cherries, What Am I Doing in the Pits?* New York: McGraw-Hill, 1978.
Edmond Rostand, Anthony Burgess, translator, *Cyrano de Bergerac,* Applause Books, 1998.
Toni Morrison, *Beloved,* NY: Knopf, 1998.

These authors identify certain understandings we must internalize if we are to be successful communicators. Identify and discuss the understandings conveyed by your selected author.

 Tell Me

Share with the class the insights you gained from your chosen Listen to Me, View Me, or Read Me selection.

React to the following statement with reasons justifying your stance: *More communication does not always make things better.*

Key Chapter Terminology

Use the Communication Works CD-ROM and the Online Learning Center at www.mhhe.com/gamble8 *to further your knowledge of the following terminology.*

acceptance 21	external feedback 13
analogic 22	feedback 12
channels 11	group communication 10
communication 7	hyper-competitiveness 8
complementary interaction 23	internal feedback 13
confirmation 22	interpersonal communication 9
content level 21	intrapersonal communication 9
context 12	mass communication 10
cyberspace 24	message 11
digital 22	need for affection 19
disconfirmation 22	need for control 19
disqualification 21	need for inclusion 19
effect 13	negative feedback 13
essentials of communication 10	noise 12

Communication Works

www.mhhe.com/gamble8

online, or machine-assisted, communication 10
positive feedback 12
public communication 10
receivers 10
rejection 21
relationship level 21

rigid complementarity 23
senders 10
symmetrical escalation 23
symmetrical interaction 23
symptom as communication, the 21
technopoly 15

Test Your Understanding

Communication
Works

www.mhhe.com/gamble8

Go to the *Self Quizzes* on the Communication Works CD-ROM and the book's Online Learning Center at www.mhhe.com/gamble8.

Notes

1. Robert D. Putnam. *Bowling Alone: The Collapse and Revival of American Community.* New York: Simon & Schuster, 2000.
2. Alan Murray. *The Wealth of Choices.* New York: Crown Business, 2000.
3. For a discussion of how the computer is altering communication, see David H. Rothman. *Networld!* Rocklin, CA: Prima, 1996.
4. See, for example, Stephen R. Covey. *The 7 Habits of Highly Effective People.* New York: Simon & Schuster, 1989, pp. 236–260.
5. See Deborah Tannen. *That's Not What I Meant!* New York: Morrow, 1986.
6. See, for example, Alan E. Ivey and James C. Hurse. "Communication as Adaptation." *Journal of Communication* 21, 1971, pp. 199–207. Ivey and Hurse reaffirm that communication is adaptive, like biological evolution—not an end in itself, but a process. For a more recent discussion of this topic, see J. F. Nussbaum, ed. *Life-Span Communication: Normative Processes.* Hillsdale, NJ: Erlbaum, 1989.
7. O. Wiio. *Wiio's Laws—and Some Others.* Espoo, Finland: Welin Goos, 1978.
8. C. Wade and C. Tarvis. *Learning to Think Critically: The Case of Close Relationships.* New York: HarperCollins, 1990.
9. Marshal McLuhan. *Understanding Media.* Cambridge, MA: MIT Press, 1994.
10. Neil Postman. *Technopoly: The Surrender of Culture to Technology.* New York: Vintage, 1992.
11. Frank E. X. Dance. "Toward a Theory of Human Communication." In Frank E. X. Dance, ed. *Human Communication Theory: Original Essays.* New York: Holt, Rinehart & Winston, 1967.
12. William Schutz. *The Interpersonal Underworld.* Palo Alto, CA: Science and Behavior Books, 1966.
13. Paul H. Watzlawick, Janet Beavin, and Don D. Jackson. *Pragmatics of Human Communication: A Study of Interaction Patterns, Pathologies and Paradoxes.* New York: Norton, 1967.
14. For additional information on disqualification, see Janet Beavin Bavelas. "Situations That Lead to Disqualification." *Human Communication Research* 9, 1983, pp. 130–145.
15. William Gibson. *Neuromancer.* New York: Ace, 1984.
16. For a discussion of identity in the age of the Internet, see Sherry Turkle. *Life on the Screen.* New York: Simon & Schuster, 1995.
17. John Markoff. "A Newer, Lonelier Crowd Emerges in Internet Study." *New York Times,* February 16, 2000, p. 1.
18. "Who Wins in the New Economy?" *Wall Street Journal,* June 27, 2000, p. B4.
19. J. E. Katz and M. Aakhus. *Perpetual Contact: Mobile Communication. Private Talk, Public Performance.* Cambridge, U.K.: Cambridge University Press, 2002.

Communicating in a Multicultural Society and World

1. Assess your ability to communicate effectively with persons from different cultures.

2. Discuss the kinds of problems the culturally confused face.

3. Define *intercultural communication*.

4. Compare and contrast culture and co-culture, ethnocentrism and cultural relativism, melting pot philosophy and cultural pluralism.

5. Compare and contrast the following: individualism and collectivism, high-context communication cultures and low-context communication cultures, high power distance cultures and low power distance cultures, masculine and feminine cultures.

6. Identify techniques you can use to reduce the strangeness of strangers.

7. Discuss how technology is bringing diversity into our lives.

If we don't speak out when people behave in a discriminatory manner, we are partly responsible for the consequences.
—**William Gudykunst**

Prejudice is the child of ignorance.
—**William Hazlitt**

Ours is the age of globalization. Our world is no longer in the process of becoming a global village. It is one. We are linked to people in all corners of planet Earth. Many of us, for example, travel regularly from one country to another. Migration across national borders occurs with increasing frequency. Corporations commonly cross national boundaries. Digital technology blurs the territorial boundary between countries, eroding the idea of nations. We have become neighbors, friends, and co-workers with people who were once strangers or considered beyond our reach. Because of this increased multiculturalism, diversity education is occurring on more and more college and university campuses. The practice has its critics and its supporters.

While some people believe that diversity education emphasizes our differences and creates conflict, others believe that it helps ease tensions between people and creates respect for difference. Which of these beliefs, if either, best expresses your position? While some people believe that more emphasis needs to be placed on teaching common American values, others believe that more emphasis needs to be placed on teaching us about each other's cultures.[1] To which of these beliefs, if either, do you subscribe?[2] Increased intercultural contact does not have solely interpersonal or educational implications. It also has economic and political ramifications. While some believe that the world benefits from globalization, others believe it is a cultural destroyer. While some say that globalization creates societies that are amalgams of colors and textures, others say globalization sacrifices cultural identity and autonomy.

Whatever our personal beliefs are, what we can all acknowledge is that communication is at the heart of both disputes over the effects of globalization and conflicts over the importance of diversity education. We need to be able to talk about different orientations toward globalization and the way it impacts cultures, just as we need to be able to talk about our differences and learn from them if diversity is to function as an asset rather than be perceived as a liability. Effective communication and the ability to understand cultural differences are skills that are too frequently deficient both in students and in educators.[3] With that in mind, answer these questions:

- Do you feel prepared to communicate in a society that is a nation of minorities?
- Do you have the understandings and sensitivity you need to interact in a global community in which other persons may look, act, and think differently than you do?
- In what ways, if any, do you find that the cultures of those with whom you relate both online and offline shape your own communication and vice versa?
- Are you willing to embrace globalization?
- Are you ready to embrace diversity?

PREPARING TO COMMUNICATE ACROSS CULTURES

To help you assess your personal preparedness to communicate effectively with persons of different cultures, respond to each of the following statements by labeling it true or false. Be sure to answer honestly.

1. I enjoy communicating with persons unlike me as much as with persons like me.
2. I am equally sensitive to the concerns of all groups in our multicultural society.
3. I can tell when persons from other cultures do not understand me or are confused by my actions.
4. I do not fear interacting with persons from minority groups any more than I fear interacting with persons from the dominant culture.
5. Persons from other cultures have a right to be angry at members of my culture.
6. Persons from other cultures who don't actively participate in a conversation, dialogue, or debate with others may act that way because of their culture's rules.
7. How I handle disagreements with persons from other cultures depends on the situation and the culture(s) they are from.
8. My culture is not superior to other cultures.
9. I am knowledgeable of how to behave with persons of different cultures.
10. I respect the communication rules of cultures other than my own.

Go to the *Online Learning Center* at www.mhhe.com/gamble8 and answer the questions in the *Self Inventory* to evaluate your understanding of cultural diversity.

In Japan, the word for "different" is the same as the word for "wrong." Compare and contrast a culture in which the goal is to become as much like others as possible with a culture in which the goal is to distinguish oneself from others. Which cultural attitude are you most comfortable with?

Developing insights into persons from different cultures facilitates communication. What steps have you taken to enhance your intercultural IQ?

How do you adapt when in the company of people who are more at home with an alternative cultural convention?

The greater the number of statements you labeled true, the more prepared you are to enrich your communication arena by welcoming people from different cultures into it.

Virtually every day, we find ourselves in situations that require us to communicate with persons culturally different from ourselves. Whether we are aware of it or not, culture influences our communication.[4] According to researchers, the effectiveness of the United States in the global arena depends on our ability to communicate competently with people from other cultures.[5]

THE COST OF CULTURAL IGNORANCE

culturally confused

lacking an understanding of cultural difference

Communicators who fail to realize that persons from different cultures may not look, think, or act as they themselves do run the risk of having those with whom they interact judge them to be insensitive, ignorant, or **culturally confused.** The culturally confused pay a high price. In fact, cultural misunderstandings often lead to lost opportunities and increased levels of tension between people. The following examples demonstrate the extent to which cultural ignorance affects communication:

Describe a cultural misunderstanding in which you or someone you know was involved. Was it resolved?

- While visiting Vietnam some years ago, an American official wanted to display his respect for the Vietnamese people by speaking to them in their own language. While the official intended to address the Vietnamese and say, "Vietnam for a thousand years," because he used the wrong tonal pronunciation when he spoke, the Vietnamese interpreted his statement as "The duck wants to lie down."[6]

- Crossing your legs in the United States is an acceptable practice and a sign of a relaxed attitude. In Korea, however, it is a social faux pas.

- McDonald's fast-food chain unintentionally offended thousands of Muslims when it printed an excerpt from the Koran on its throwaway hamburger bags.[7] Muslims saw this as sacrilegious. The mistake could have been avoided if McDonald's had displayed greater sensitivity and awareness.

- Also regarding McDonald's, corporate officers were surprised to learn that, in French-Canadian slang, "big macs" are large breasts.[8]

- To the Japanese, a business card is viewed as an extension of a person, while Americans view it as a business formality and a convenience. Consequently, while the Japanese handle business cards with great care, making certain to put them in safe places, Americans are quick to put them away and thus often end up insulting the Japanese.[9]

- Ming Us Dong, a textile manufacturing expert from China, reports that cultural differences between the United States and China often put him in awkward situations. After one three-hour job interview with the owner of an American company, Ming was asked the salary he wanted. Ming notes, "I couldn't say yet, because an honorable person in my culture doesn't take something unless he's producing."[10]

- While Arabs typically adopt a direct body orientation when communicating, Americans employ a stance that is somewhat less direct and thus often find the communication of Arabs aggressive and unnerving. Arabs and South Americans also tend to gesture vigorously when speaking to others, causing the less physical Americans to construe their behavior as inappropriate and unmannerly. It is common in Middle Eastern cultures for both males and females to physically exaggerate responses, while in the United States emotions are more likely to be suppressed. In Japan, individuals may try to hide or mask certain emotions. It is common among Asian cultures to exhibit reserve and emotional restraint.

- Eye contact preferences also differ across cultures. Americans place a high value on eye-to-eye communication and tend to distrust those who fail to look at them directly. The Japanese, in contrast, believe eye contact over a sustained period of time shows disrespect. Among Asian cultures, too much eye contact is deemed intrusive. Arabs, on the other hand, maintain direct eye contact with those they interact with for prolonged periods. Like Arabs, many African Americans use more continuous eye contact when speaking than do Whites. When listening, however, the opposite is true. Traditionally, African Americans are taught that looking away when someone is speaking to you reveals your respect for the speaker. Thus, when spoken to, African Americans typically do not look directly at the person addressing them, which can anger the speaker if he or she is not familiar with this practice.

- Americans tend to value personal achievement and individualism. In contrast, Asian and Native American cultures stress group cohesion and loyalty, placing greater emphasis on group rather than individual achievement.

Do you believe any of the following cultural practices are unethical?

- *Cockfighting*
- *The withholding of medical intervention, such as a blood transfusion*
- *Female circumcision*
- *The stoning of a rape victim*

If you answer yes to any, explain why. If you answer no to any, explain why not. To what extent do your answers support or negate the belief that every culture has a right to its own customs and beliefs?

As you can see, failing to develop insights into cultural nuances and differences can have its costs. In contrast, recognizing and responding to the differences among cultures can allow for more meaningful relationships. At the same time, we always need to be careful not to assume that everyone from a particular culture exhibits the same characteristics and communication traits.

This chapter is designed to sensitize you to the ways cultural values and habits influence interaction. As a result of learning about such differences, you should be better able to (1) appropriately respond to varied communication styles, (2) recognize the need to expand your choices as a communicator, and (3) increase the effectiveness of your interactions with persons of different cultures.

The challenge facing us today is clear: to learn to accept cultural, and therefore communication, differences. Those of us who insist on clinging to

Seeing Our Culture through the Eyes of Others

Since 9/11/01, Americans have been moved to ask, "Why don't people in other countries like us more?"[11] Global public opinion surveys reveal that, in increasing numbers, persons from foreign countries perceive Americans to be overbearing, aggressive, and domineering. While some blame such perceptions on foreign policy, others, such as communication researchers Melvin and Margaret DeFleur, blame the media. The DeFleurs surveyed 1,259 teenagers from 12 countries whose main contact with Americans was through the television programs and movies they watched and the music they listened to. Based on these vicarious experiences, in their judgment, Americans were violent, materialistic, sexually loose, disrespectful of people unlike them, unconcerned about the poor, and prone to criminal activity. The DeFleurs concluded that the exporting of American commercialized popular culture contributes to cultural imperialism and the creation of anti-Americanism.[12]

If imperialism is the expansion of dominion of one country over another country, then **cultural imperialism** is the expansion of dominion of one culture over another culture. Cultural imperialism's critics assert that the news, entertainment, and products of an industrialized country such as the United States overwhelm the national cultures of other countries. They contend that our ethnocentricity leads us to promote our way of life as superior.

On the other hand, there are some signs that the reign of American pop culture is beginning to erode. Foreign film successes such as "Crouching Tiger, Hidden Dragon," a film set in China starring Chinese actors speaking in Chinese, was wildly successful in the United States. U.S. music charts regularly feature vocalists from other countries who speak in Spanish or another language, and foreign news services such as al Jazeera are influencing coverage of the war on terrorism. Cross-fertilization of ideas inevitably leads to more diversity.

However, in order to consider how exposure to popular culture in the United States is affecting the opinions that people in other countries have of the United States and its people, try this: Select an issue of *TV Guide*. Imagine that you live in the Middle East, Africa, or any other Third-World country. Based on your perusal of our prime programming, what characteristics would you attribute to Americans? How many of your listed characteristics would you consider to be positive? Negative?

cultural imperialism

the expansion of dominion of one culture over another culture

the notion of a homogeneous melting pot, who refuse to take cultural diversity into account, will simply not be able to meet the communication needs of our society and our world. Most likely, we will not only fail to share meaning with others but also not understand why we fail. When we view the world myopically, we distort our ability to respond appropriately.

Intercultural communication is nothing new. It has been practiced for as long as persons of different cultures have interacted with one another.[13] In this age of increased global contact, however, it is essential that we become even more interculturally aware and competent. We need to learn how to communicate effectively with persons culturally different from ourselves—persons with whom we should still be able to freely share ideas, information, and feelings.

intercultural communication

interaction with individuals from different cultures

interracial communication

the interpreting and sharing of meanings with individuals from different races

DEFINING *INTERCULTURAL COMMUNICATION*

Whenever cultural variability influences the nature and the effects of communication, **intercultural communication** is at work. Thus, when we speak about intercultural communication, we are concerning ourselves with the process of interpreting and sharing meanings with individuals from different cultures.[14] In actuality, intercultural communication comprises a number of different forms. Among its many variations are **interracial communication** (which occurs when interactants are of different races), **interethnic communication** (which occurs when the communicating parties have different ethnic origins), **international communication** (which occurs between persons representing political structures), and **intracultural communication** (which includes all forms of communication among members of the same racial, ethnic, or other co- or subculture groups).[15]

Cultures and Co-Cultures

To become more adept at communicating with persons who are culturally different from ourselves, we need to learn not only about their cultures but also about our own. A **culture** consists of a system of knowledge, beliefs, values, customs, behaviors, and artifacts that are acquired, shared, and used by its members during daily living.[16] Within a culture as a whole are **co-cultures, or subcultures;** these are composed of members of the same general culture who differ in some ethnic or sociological way from the parent culture. In our society, African Americans, Hispanic Americans, Japanese Americans, the disabled, gays and lesbians, cyberpunks, and the elderly are just some of the co-cultures belonging to the same general culture.[17]

Have you ever felt like an outsider? Persons who believe they belong to a *marginalized group*—that is, a group whose members feel like outsiders—have a number of options to choose from regarding how they want to interact with members of the dominant culture or even if they want to interact with them at all. Have you or has anyone you know used any of the following strategies?

Co-culture members who use the strategy of **assimilation** attempt to "fit in," or join with, members of the dominant culture. They converse about subjects that members of the dominant group talk about, such as cars or sports, or they dress as members of the dominant culture dress. They give up their own ways in an effort to assume the modes of behavior of the dominant culture. In comparison, co-culture members who use the strategy of **accommodation** attempt to maintain their cultural identity even while they strive to establish relationships with members of the dominant culture. A gay or lesbian who takes his or her partner to an occasion in which members of the dominant culture will be present, such as a company or family celebration, is using the strategy of accommodation. On the other hand, when members of a co-culture resist interacting with members of the dominant culture, they employ the strategy of resistance, or **separation.** Because these persons, such as Hassidic Jews, prefer to interact with each other rather than have contact with persons they perceive to be outsiders, they tend to keep to themselves.

Members of co-cultures can practice *passive, assertive, aggressive,* or *confrontational communication* approaches in their efforts to accomplish their objectives relative to the dominant culture. Co-culture members who practice passive communication may use avoidance strategies as they seek to have as little to do as possible with the dominant group's members. They do not attempt to interact with or have contact with those outside of their own group. They passively accept their position in the cultural hierarchy. In contrast, co-culture members who employ an assertive communication approach seek to realize their objectives as well as meet the objectives of those with

---

interethnic communication
interaction with individuals of different ethnic origins

international communication
communication between persons representing different nations

intracultural communication
interaction with members of the same racial or ethnic group or subculture as yours

culture
a system of knowledge, beliefs, values, customs, behaviors, and artifacts that are acquired, shared, and used by members during daily living

co-cultures, or subcultures
groups of persons who differ in some ethnic or sociological way from the parent culture

Were you ever the only person of your age, race, ethnicity, or sexual preference in a group? How did the experience make you feel?

assimilation strategy
the means by which co-culture members attempt to fit in with members of the dominant culture

accommodation strategy
the means by which co-culture members maintain their cultural identity while striving to establish relationships with members of the dominant culture

separation strategy
the means co-culture members use to resist interacting with members of the dominant culture

whom they interact. One assertive technique is relating to the dominant group via liaisons, persons who share the same cultural identity or trusted members of the dominant group. In contrast, some co-culture members choose to exhibit a more aggressive communication approach whereby they become "hurtfully expressive" and "self-promoting" and attempt to control the choices the persons they are interacting with make.[18] Co-culture members who use a confrontational approach seek to make dominant culture members hear them, recognize them, and react to them by making it impossible for them to ignore their presence or pretend they do not exist.

In summary, co-culture members who opt for separation from the dominant culture typically use a passive communication approach (such as going to lunch alone, living in an area with similar people), those who seek accommodation use an assertive approach (such as wearing a yarmulke at work, wearing a sari to a party), and those who choose assimilation use an aggressive approach, often becoming confrontational, belligerent, or disruptive (such as the staging of a protest by a group such as Act Up (a group committed to direct action to combat the AIDS crisis) in their effort to demarginalize themselves and enter the world known to members of the dominant culture. See Table 2.1.

Many theorists believe that an understanding of both the general culture and its co-cultures is essential if one is to communicate effectively. Merely knowing another's language, jargon, or argot or sharing some but not all of a group's values does not necessarily ensure understanding. It is also necessary for you to become aware of the norms and rules of the culture or co-cultures that might influence the nature of interactions you have with its members, whether those interactions occur in public or in private.

Compare and contrast the lessons taught you by your culture with the lessons taught peers by other cultures.

Whenever a message generated by a member of one culture or co-culture needs to be processed by a member or members of another culture or co-culture, the interactants are communicating interculturally.[19] Thus, when you and the individuals with whom you are interacting belong to different cultures, for you to understand each other, you each need to consider the role culture plays in shaping your communication. According to cultural anthropologist Edward T. Hall, culture is communication and communication is culture.[20] It is your culture that teaches you how to think and what to think about. It is your culture that teaches you what is beautiful or ugly, helpful or harmful, appropriate or out of place. Culture is the lens through which you view the world; it is the mirror you use to reflect and interpret reality.[21]

TABLE 2.1 *Preferred Strategies and Communication Approaches of Marginalized Groups*

Strategy	Communication Approach	Example
Separation	Passive	Lunching alone, living in an area with similar people
Accommodation	Assertive	Wearing a yarmulke to work, wearing a sari to a party
Assimilation	Aggressive/confrontational	Staging a protest

Culture is the lens through which we see the world. Can you provide an example of how your culture has influenced your view of events?

Culture Guides Communication

Among the lessons taught by culture are how to say "hello" and "good-bye," when to speak or remain silent, how to act when you're angry or upset, where to focus your eyes when functioning as a source or receiver, how much to gesture during speech, how close to stand to another, and how to display happiness or rage at another's actions. By teaching you lessons like these, culture guides behavior and communication. It tells you who you are, how to act, how to think, how to talk, and how to listen.[22]

When cultures meet, when we interact with persons whose values are different from ours or whose behavioral norms differ from our own, we must first recognize and acknowledge our differences. We must come to accept diversity if we are to be able to process other cultures' influences and communicate with each other in a meaningful way. **Ethnocentrism,** the tendency to see your own culture as superior to all others, is a key characteristic of failed intercultural communication efforts. Persons who are ethnocentric experience great anxiety when interacting with persons from different cultures. Quick to utter statements like "They take our jobs," "They're everywhere," and "They're just not like us," those who embrace ethnocentrism lack cultural flexibility and are particularly unprepared to meet the challenges posed by our society and our world today.[23] The more ethnocentric you are, the greater your tendency is to view groups other than your own as inferior. As a result, you tend to blame others for problems and seek to maintain your distance from them.[24]

Cultural relativism is the opposite of ethnocentrism. When you practice cultural relativism, instead of viewing the group to which you belong as superior to all others, you work to try to understand the behavior of other groups based on the context in which the behavior occurs rather than from your own frame of reference.

Identify the extent to which ethnocentrism and/or cultural relativism affects you or those you know.

ethnocentrism
the tendency to see one's own culture as superior to all others

cultural relativism
the acceptance of other cultural groups as equal in value to one's own

TAKING THE DEMOGRAPHIC PICTURE: DIVERSITY IN FOCUS

The United States is the most demographically diverse country in the world. Have you taken advantage of the opportunities you have to interact with persons from different cultures?

To what extent has the amount of contact you have with persons of diverse cultural backgrounds changed since you were a child? When you were younger, you were more apt to interact with persons just like yourself. Your experience today most likely is different. Continuing developments in technology and changes in demography are influencing the nature of our interactions.

Society and the world have been transformed into a mobile, global village, much as Marshall McLuhan, a communication theorist, forecast over three decades ago. We now have a global economy, a global marketplace, and global media. Whether we travel abroad or stay at home, we are now regularly in contact with individuals who are significantly different from us.

Intercultural communication is fast becoming the norm. In fact, living in the United States gives you an incredible opportunity to interact interculturally without having to pay for international travel. But it hasn't always been that way. Years ago, the United States embraced a **melting pot philosophy.** According to that theory, when individuals from other countries came here, they lost or gave up their original heritage and became Americans. The national motto, *E pluribus unum*—a Latin phrase meaning "one out of many"—reflected this way of thinking. It was believed that diverse cultural groups should be assimilated into the parent, or dominant, culture. As a result, cultural differences were submerged and eradicated as quickly as possible rather than accepted by the parent culture and allowed to thrive.

melting pot philosophy
the view that different cultures should be assimilated into the dominant culture

Over time, this philosophy was replaced by one that stresses **cultural pluralism.** Cultural pluralists advocate respect for uniqueness, tolerance for difference, and adherence to the principle of cultural relativity. In a multicultural society, every group, it is believed, will do things differently, and that's OK.

Demographers tell us that diversity will shape our country's future. According to U.S. Census Bureau statistics, the five largest ethnic groups are composed of people who identify themselves as White (207.7 million), African-American (36.6 million), Hispanic (38.8 million), Asian-American (12.7 million), and Native American (3.5 million). Hispanics are now the largest minority group, followed by African Americans, Native Americans, and Hawaiian Pacific Islanders.[25]

The United States is now the most demographically diverse country in the world. Because of this and because of advances in communications and transportation, we will continue to experience an increasing number of contacts with members of other cultures. This alone makes it especially important for us to be able to understand and interact with persons of different backgrounds, nationalities, and lifestyles. We are truly interconnected with all of humanity.

THE INTERCULTURAL COMMUNICATION IMPERATIVE: REDUCE THE STRANGENESS OF STRANGERS

While intercultural communication is inevitable, we are neither as effective nor as successful at it as we could be. The reason is clear: Not all of us work hard enough to understand or to be understood by those with whom we differ.

According to intercultural communication theorists Larry A. Samovar and Richard E. Porter, there are too many of "us" who do not work as hard as we should at intercultural communication simply because we do not wish to live or interact with "them."[26] Too many of us have adopted an "us versus them" mentality, which prevents us from effectively meeting the challenges cultural diversity presents. To counter this, we need to conduct ourselves in a manner designed to reduce the strangeness of strangers; that is, we need to open ourselves to differences by adding to our storehouse of knowledge, by learning to cope with uncertainty, and by developing an appreciation of how increasing our cultural sensitivity will positively affect our communication competence. As you interact with persons from diverse cultures, watch for spoken and unspoken messages that provide clues about the values, norms, roles, and rules of those persons' cultures.

Exploring Cultural Differences

Let's continue by focusing on three variables used to distinguish cultures: (1) individualism versus collectivism, (2) high-context versus low-context communication, (3) high power distance versus low power distance, and (4) masculine or feminine culture.

Individualism versus Collectivism

The cultural dimension of individualism versus collectivism reveals how people define themselves in their relationships with others. In **individualistic cultures,**

---

cultural pluralism
adherence to the principle of cultural relativism

Statistics tell us an interesting story about diversity. The growth rate of the Caucasian population is lower than the growth rates for Asians, Hispanics, and African Americans. It is estimated that, by 2025, the Hispanic population will be about 25 percent of the total population. By 2025, the age distribution will also shift. More people will be very young (there will be a 21 percent increase in the people 14 or younger), fewer people will be middle-aged (there will be a 4 percent decrease in the people age 35–49), and more people will be very old (there will be a 14 percent increase in the number of people over 80). It is also expected that race and ethnic mixing will accelerate. What effects do you imagine that changes like these will have on the social and cultural landscape? How do you imagine they will personally affect you?

What steps have you taken to reduce the strangeness of strangers?

individualistic cultures
cultures in which individual goals are stressed

How Hard Do You Work?

Make a list of individuals whose cultural backgrounds differ from your own and with whom you have recently communicated. How many of the following questions can you answer with respect to each person on your list?

1. How do the individual's feelings about socialization differ from your own?
2. How does the individual's concept of self compare with yours?
3. To what extent do the individual's values and attitudes differ from yours?
4. Which of your behaviors did the individual have difficulty understanding or accepting? Which of his or her behaviors did you have difficulty with?
5. Which of the individuals you interacted with did you find most like you? Most

unlike you? Can you identify your points of similarity and difference?

6. To what extent was the individual more cooperative or competitive than you?
7. In what ways did the individual's use of verbal language differ from your own?
8. In what ways did the individual's nonverbal behavior differ from your own?
9. How did the individual's treatment of time and space differ from your own?
10. In what ways did the individual's thinking processes differ from yours?

For those questions you cannot answer, take the time to conduct research and answer them.

---

collectivistic cultures
cultures in which group goals are stressed

such as those of Great Britain, the United States, Canada, France, and Germany, individual goals are stressed, whereas in **collectivistic cultures,** represented by many Arab, African, Asian, and Latin American countries, group goals are given precedence instead. Individualistic cultures cultivate individual initiative and achievement, while collectivistic cultures tend to nurture group influences. This means that, while the "I" may be most important in individualistic cultures, the "we" is the dominant force in collectivistic ones. While in collectivistic cultures the individual is expected to fit into the group, in individualistic cultures emphasis is placed on developing a sense of self.

High Context versus Low Context

high-context communication
a tradition-bound communication system which depends on indirectness

low-context communication
a system that encourages directness in communication

A second way in which cultures vary in communication style is in their preference for high-context or low-context communication. Cultures with **high-context communication** systems are tradition-bound; that is, their cultural traditions shape the behavior and lifestyle of group members, causing them to appear to be overly polite and indirect in relating to others. In contrast, members of cultures with **low-context communication** systems generally are encouraged to exhibit a more direct communication style. Members of low-context cultures tend to gather background information when meeting someone for the first time. Thus, they will ask people they have just met where they went to college, where they live, and who they work for, while persons from high-context cultures are much less likely to ask such questions.[27] In addition, persons from low-context cultures are apt to feel that they have to explain everything rather than rely on nonverbal, contextual information as demonstrated by those who display a preference for high-context communication. In contrast, persons who believe that most messages can be understood without direct verbal interaction reveal their preference for high-context communication. Asian cultures typically emphasize high-context communication, whereas Western cultures typically represent low-context communication systems. For example, the Japanese have traditionally valued silence, believing that a person of few words is thoughtful, trustworthy, and respectable. Thus, the Japanese spend considerately less time talking than do people in the United States. This orientation also helps explain why the Japanese often perceive self-disclosures during interaction as socially inappropriate.

High Power Distance versus Low Power Distance

Power distance measures the extent to which individuals are willing to accept power differences. For example, individuals from **high power distance cultures,** such as Saudi Arabia, India, and Malaysia, view power as a fact of life and are apt to stress its coercive or referent nature. Superiors and subordinates in these countries are likely to view each other differently; subordinates are quick to defer to superiors. In contrast, individuals from **low power distance cultures,** such as Israel, Sweden, and the United States, believe power should be used only when it is legitimate; thus, they are apt to employ expert or legitimate power. Superiors and subordinates from low power distance countries emphasize their interdependence by displaying a preference for consultation; subordinates will even contradict their bosses when necessary.[28]

Masculine versus Feminine Culture

Cultures differ in their attitudes about gender roles.[29] In cultures that are highly masculine, members value male aggressiveness, strength, and material symbols of success. In highly feminine cultures, members value relationships, tenderness in members of both sexes, and a high quality of life. Among highly **masculine cultures** are Japan, Italy, Germany, Mexico, and Great Britain. Among highly feminine cultures are Sweden, Norway, Netherlands, Thailand, and Chile. The members of masculine cultures are socialized to be dominant and competitive. They tend to confront conflicts head-on and are likely to use a win-lose conflict strategy. In contrast, the members of **feminine cultures** are more apt to compromise and negotiate in order to resolve conflicts, seeking win-win solutions.

Interpreting Cultural Differences

Where a culture falls on the individualistic-collectivistic, low-context–high-context communication, and power distance scales affects the interactional preferences of its members. In Japanese and Chinese societies, for example, individuals tend to understate their own accomplishments and successes, while members of North American cultures typically are taught to be assertive and take credit for their personal achievements. It appears that individualistic cultures tend to use low-context communication, while high-context communication tends to predominate in collectivistic cultures. Thus, whereas members of low-context communication cultures interact in a direct way with each other, members of high-context communication cultures interact indirectly. For example, North Americans tend to speak directly on an issue, whereas individuals from Japan, Korea, and China prefer to avoid confrontation, to preserve a sense of harmony, and to make it possible for the individuals with whom they are speaking to save face, or maintain self-esteem. Similarly, rarely will one Saudi Arabian publicly criticize another; to do so would label the individual as disloyal and disrespectful.[30] When persons from diverse power distance cultures interact, unless these differences in orientation are acknowledged, interactions may well result in misunderstandings.

high power distance cultures

cultures based on power differences in which subordinates defer to superiors

low power distance cultures

cultures that believe that power should be used when legitimate

masculine culture

a culture that values aggressiveness, strength, and material symbols of success

feminine culture

a culture that values tenderness and relationships

Have you ever considered your culture superior to another culture? How did your feelings influence your relationship with members of that culture?

We take a giant step toward improving intercultural communication by accepting the fact that our culture is not superior to others. Nor should we base our behavioral expectations for the members of other cultures on our own culture's norms. To do so would cause us to label the responses of those who belong to other cultures as foreign or strange. To the extent that we are able to use our understanding of another's culture to reduce the number of misunderstandings between us, to the extent that we do not interpret the behavior of others based on our own frames of reference, we take further steps toward reducing the strangeness of strangers.

Media WISE

The Storyteller: Seeing through the Eyes of the Stereotyped

Over the years, some media producers have made the effort to remove stereotypes from films and television programs. Disney, for example, changed the sound of the original Bad Wolf in the *Three Little Pigs* from that of a heavy Jewish accent to a falsetto voice. Similarly, the lyrics to the opening song in *Aladdin* were revised after complaints by the American-Arab Anti-Discrimination Committee. In the film, however, both Jasmine and her father, though Arabian, speak unaccented, standard American English, while the "bad guys" speak with foreign accents.[31] If you were of Middle Eastern descent, how would you feel about having an accent associated with evil?

Latino advocates report that, while Black men seem to be getting meatier roles on television shows, they, Native Americans, and Asian Americans are not. They criticize the networks for a lack of racial and ethnic diversity in their schedules. Joining forces with the NAACP, the Asian Pacific American Media Coalition, and the American Indians in Film and Television, they negotiated agreements with the major networks to increase minority participation

both on and off the screen.[32] The problem isn't only minority representation, however. It's portrayal as well. Latino actor Martin Sheen (real name Ramon Estevez) plays a Caucasian character on TV's *The West Wing*. When minority representation is glaringly absent in media offerings, the roles minorities do appear in have more impact. The parts given Latinos, for example, often are reminiscent of pre-civil rights African-American portrayals such as the entertainer, the criminal, the crime victim, or the maid, or they are secondary roles with nonprofessional jobs. Were you to see yourself portrayed as a victim, or as subservient to the dominant Anglo society, how do you imagine that would affect your perceptions of the options that exist for you? How would they affect your view of your culture?

Like film, television has been called a cultural storyteller, an agent of norms and values. Watch a week's prime-time programming on a particular station. Count the number of characters in each program that are from another culture. What did you learn from each character about his or her culture? In your opinion, were cultural stereotypes used to develop each character from another culture? If so, describe them. To what extent, if any, did what you viewed reinforce and/or alter your existing attitudes toward members of that culture? What emotional reactions, if any, were triggered in you by each character? Did you find that the shows contributed to your having predominantly positive or negative attitudes toward the members of another culture? Finally, using one or two words, identify the key value of each show viewed. For example, the message of one show may focus on materialism, the message of another on force and violence.

TECHNOLOGY AND INTERCULTURAL COMMUNICATION

The Internet permeates national boundaries and erodes the now aging connection between location and experience. It enables us to interact more easily with people who have a different worldview than we do. We have the ability to become more personally connected to persons who would otherwise remain distant. Although a minority of the world's population currently uses the Web, computer connectivity is changing things. With a few clicks, you can locate a group of people with similar interests and form associations with a Web "tribe" or group independent of geography.[33]

Technology and computer networks are changing the traditional definition of a community. When we speak of a communication community today, no longer are we limited to real neighborhoods. Our concept of community has widened. **Virtual neighborhoods and communities** now also populate the communication landscape. Perhaps the neighborhoods in which we actually live are not delivering the person-to-person contact we seek. Seeking surrogate neighborhoods, millions of people communicate online. While we face increased electronic congestion, we appear, nonetheless, to have an insatiable hunger to connect with others via our networked world. For many of us, the Internet, with its worldwide reach, has become an integral part of our communication lives.[34] However, some critics contend that, rather than bring us together, computer networks are isolating. What's missing from online communities, they assert, is that which comprises the essence of a real neighborhood, including a sense of location and a feeling of permanence and belonging. They also believe that the culture of computing, especially when it comes to the Net's news groups, attracts extreme political positions and contributes to longstanding international conflicts.[35]

Being able to reach so many different people who live in so many different places so quickly gives us a new sense of communication power. Wherever we live, the Internet may also help bring diversity and culture into our lives. Over time, the Internet may help change our social and business lives. Through it, we may meet a wider array of people. It has the capacity to introduce us to new friends and contacts and to allow us to network with persons around the world. We can use it to compare experiences, find others who share similar interests and concerns, and elicit information and advice from experts in various countries. The question for us to ponder, however, is the form that these new alliances will take: Will they be shallow and short-lived or deep and enduring? Will we commit ourselves emotionally to them or keep our online interactions superficial? What kinds of relationships will we develop by conversing with diverse individuals in distant lands without actually meeting them? Will all voices really be heard? Will we be more or less tolerant of each other? For example, will we simply pull the plug, flame another person, or go offline when we don't like what we see on our computer screens? Will we be aware that words posted to global online groups have consequences, just as they do when delivered in person?

Our Western version of the Net is loaded with Western culture and advertising. Even most of us complain about the pop-ups and the advertising glut.

virtual neighborhoods and communities

online, surrogate communities

How this emphasis on consumerism is interpreted around the world is a source of controversy.

We also need to face the fact that, in some cultures and religions, technology is considered evil. Even in our own culture, we have over 100 million Americans who have no desire to get connected to the Internet.[36] In the past five years, over 30 million Americans chose to stop using the Internet. Why? Because they desired to lead a more simple life, asserting that technology was making their lives too complicated. These people are part of the digital backlash.[37]

There also is a question regarding who is represented on the Internet. Will we really be able to interact with diverse groups of people? Currently, African Americans, the elderly, and the poor are still underrepresented online. In time, however, increased access via libraries and schools may help change this trend.

HOW TO IMPROVE YOUR ABILITY TO COMMUNICATE INTERCULTURALLY

Having the desire to relate more effectively with persons of different cultures is critical to improving your ability to communicate interculturally. Also important is limiting your reliance on stereotypes that can diminish your success when you interact with others. In addition, you need to be able to reduce your uncertainty levels regarding the persons of different cultures with whom you communicate. Since you do not necessarily share the same communication rules, the degree of ambiguity you feel when interacting with them increases as your ability to predict their responses decreases. The following guidelines should help you increase your tolerance for ambiguity, enhance your ability to handle new situations, and better prepare yourself to meet the communication challenges of today and tomorrow:

Focus on Service Learning

Attend a local continuing education session for persons from other countries who want to learn English. Explore the stereotypes you have about the people there.

- Refrain from formulating expectations based solely on your own culture.

  When those you interact with have diverse communication styles, it is critical that you acknowledge the differences and accept their validity. By not isolating yourself within your own group or culture, you allow yourself to be more fully a part of a multicultural society and thus a better communicator.

- Recognize how faulty education can impede understanding.

  It is important to identify and work to eliminate any personal biases and prejudices you have developed over the years. Determine, for example, the

extent to which your family and friends have influenced your feelings about persons from other cultural groups. Do those you have grown up with appear comfortable or uncomfortable relating to persons of different cultural origins? To what extent have their attitudes affected your intercultural communication competence?

- Make a commitment to develop communication skills and abilities appropriate to life in a multicultural world.

While culture is a tie that binds, the creation of the global village makes it essential that you leave the comfort of your cultural niche, become more knowledgeable of other cultures, and strive to be culturally aware.

It is important to familiarize yourself with the communication rules and preferences of members of different cultures, so that you can increase the effectiveness of your communication encounters. Your ability to develop intercultural communication skills depends in large part on how many of the following promises you are willing to make:

I will make a commitment to seek information from persons whose cultures are different from my own.

I will try to understand how the experiences of persons from different cultures leads them to develop perspectives that differ from mine.

I will pay attention to the situation and the context when I communicate with persons from different cultures.

I will make every effort to become a more flexible communicator.

I will not insist that persons from other cultures communicate with me on my terms.

Intercultural communication will become increasingly important in the coming years. We hope you feel better prepared to meet your future.

Revisiting Chapter Objectives

1. **Assess your ability to communicate effectively with persons from different cultures.**   Ours is an age of increased global contact and diversity. Consequently, assessing and developing an understanding of and sensitivity to cultural differences is an essential component in each of our communication repertoires. To the extent we are able to reduce cultural ignorance and enhance cultural awareness, we increase our personal preparedness to communicate effectively.

2. **Discuss the kinds of problems the culturally confused face.**   By taking steps to eliminate cultural misunderstandings, we also facilitate the

THE Wrap-Up

development of more meaningful relationships between persons from different cultures whether these relationships occur face-to-face or online.

3. **Define *intercultural communication*.**　Intercultural communication is the process of interpreting and sharing meanings with individuals from different cultures.

4. **Compare and contrast culture and co-culture, ethnocentrism and cultural relativism, melting pot philosophy and cultural pluralism.**　To become more adept at communicating with persons who are culturally different from ourselves, we first need to understand the differences between the general culture and co-cultures, ethnocentrism and cultural relativism, and the melting pot philosophy and cultural pluralism.

5. **Compare and contrast the following: individualism and collectivism, high-context communication cultures and low-context communication cultures, high power distance cultures and low power distance cultures and masculine and feminine cultures.**　Interpreting cultural variations means learning to appreciate the differences between individualism and collectivism, high-context and low-context communication cultures, high power distance and low power distance cultures, and masculine and feminine cultures.

6. **Identify techniques you can use to reduce the strangeness of strangers.**　Although the lessons taught by culture influence our communication style preferences, there are techniques we can use to reduce the strangeness of strangers, adding to the storehouse of knowledge that underscores our communication competence and, as a result, increasing our ability to handle the communication challenges of today and tomorrow.

7. **Discuss how technology is bringing diversity into our lives.**　For many of us, the Internet is facilitating this task by helping to bring diversity and culture into our lives.

Resources for Further Inquiry and Reflection

To apply your understanding of how the principles in Chapter 2 are at work in our daily lives, consult the following resources for further inquiry and reflection. Or, if you prefer, choose any other appropriate resource. Then connect the ideas expressed in your chosen selection with the communication concepts and issues you are learning about both in and out of class.

 Listen to Me

"Born in the U.S.A." (Bruce Springsteen)
"Land Down Under" (Men at Work)
"My Woman from Tokyo" (Deep Purple)

What do the views of the song's speaker or speakers suggest about the ability they have to meet diversity's challenges?

 View Me

Bend It Like Beckham　　*Dances with Wolves*
Boys Don't Cry　　　　　*The Joy Luck Club*
The Chosen　　　　　　　*Jungle Fever*
Monsoon Wedding　　　　*Lost in Translation*

How does culture influence the interaction of the characters in the film? What lessons about the effects of culture can be taught through the film?

Read Me

 Tell Me

Harper Lee. *To Kill a Mockingbird*. Philadelphia: Lippincott, 1960.

Wen Ho Lee, *My Country Versus Me: The First-Hand Account by the Los Alamos Scientist Who Was Falsely Accused*, Hyperion Press, 2002.

Discuss how age, gender, ethnic affiliation, family ties, education, beliefs and religion, and/or nationality influence and shape attitudes.

Share with the class the insights you gained from your chosen Listen to Me, View Me, or Read Me selection.

Choose a side and discuss the arguments for and/or against using English as a universal language.

Key Chapter Terminology

Use the Communication Works CD-ROM and Online Learning Center at www.mhhe.com/gamble8 *to further your knowledge of the following terminology.*

 Communication **Works**

 online learning center

www.mhhe.com/gamble8

accommodation 37
assimilation 37
co-cultures, or subcultures 37
collectivistic cultures 42
cultural imperialism 36
cultural pluralism 41
cultural relativism 39
culturally confused 34
culture 37
ethnocentrism 39
feminine culture 43
high power distance cultures 43
high-context communication 42

individualistic cultures 41
intercultural communication 36
interethnic communication 37
international communication 37
interracial communication 36
intracultural communication 37
low power distance cultures 43
low-context communication 42
masculine culture 43
melting pot philosophy 40
separation 37
virtual neighborhoods and communities 45

Test Your Understanding

Go to the *Self Quizzes* on the Communication Works CD-ROM and the book's Online Learning Center at www.mhhe.com/gamble8.

 Communication **Works**

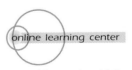 online learning center

www.mhhe.com/gamble8

Notes

1. See, for example, H. J. Whitlock Gyory and Diana D. Q. Tran. "Walking in Another's Shoes: A Reflective Diversity Exercise," *Journal of College Student Development*, January/February 2002, pp. 133–136.
2. Clarence Page. "Blurry Clarity on Diversity," *The Record*, October 13, 1998, p. L-9.
3. Gail L. Thompson. "Teachers' Cultural Ignorance Imperils Student Success," *USA Today*, May 29, 2002, p. 13A.
4. William B. Gudykunst. *Bridging Differences: Effective Intergroup Communication*, 3rd ed. Thousand Oaks, CA: Sage 1998, p. 40.
5. Guo-Ming Chen and William J. Starosta. "A Review of the Concept of Intercultural Sensitivity." *Human Communication* 2, 1997, p. 5.
6. Larry A. Samovar and Richard E. Porter. *Communication between Cultures*. Belmont, CA: Wadsworth, 1991, p. 154.
7. "Unhappy Meal for Muslims." *The Record*, June 8, 1994, p. C-3.

8. R. Armao. "Worst Blunders: Firms Laugh through Tears." *American Business,* January 1981, p. 11.

9. Wendy Griswold. *Cultures and Societies in a Changing World.* Thousand Oaks, CA: Pine Forge Press, 1994, p. 1.

10. Barrie Peterson. "Sometimes It's Rough Sailing the Cross-Cultural Job Currents." *The Record,* February 7, 1994, p. C-1.

11. Nicholas D. Kristof. "Why Do They Hate Us?" *New York Times,* January 15, 2002, p. A21.

12. Margaret H. DeFleur and Melvin L. DeFleur. "The Next Generation's Image of Americans: Attitudes and Beliefs Held by Teen-Agers in Twelve Countries" (www.bu.edu/news/releases/2002/defleur/report.pdf), October 3, 2002.

13. Larry A. Samovar and Richard E. Porter. *Intercultural Communication: A Reader,* 9th ed. Belmont, CA: Wadsworth, 2000.

14. William B. Gudykunst and Young Yun Kim, eds. *Readings on Communicating with Strangers.* New York: McGraw-Hill, 1992.

15. Larry A. Samovar and Richard E. Porter, *Communication between Cultures,* 4th ed. Belmont, CA: Wadsworth, 2001 pp. 5, 46–47.

16. Judith Cornelia Pearson and Paul Edward Nelson. *Understanding and Sharing: An Introduction to Speech Communication,* 6th ed. Dubuque, IA: Brown & Benchmark, 1994, p. 193.

17. Griswold, p. 57.

18. M.P. Orbe. "Laying the Foundation for Co-Cultural Communication Theory: An Inductive Approach to Studying 'Nondominant' Communication Strategies and the Factors That Influence Them." *Communication Studies* 47, 1996, pp. 157–176.

19. Samovar and Porter, *Communication between Cultures,* pp. 2, 46.

20. Edward Hall. *The Silent Language.* New York: Fawcett, 1959.

21. Griswold, pp. 22–24.

22. Carley H. Dodd. *Dynamics of Intercultural Communication,* 3rd ed. Dubuque, IA: Wm. C. Brown, 1991, p. 3.

23. Thomas Keneally. "Racism's as Human as Love." *The Sunday Record,* February 6, 1994, p. R-1.

24. William B. Gudykunst. *Bridging Differences,* 3rd ed. Thousand Oaks, CA: Sage, 1998, pp. 106–110.

25. U.S. Census Bureau; Haya El Nasser, "39 Million Make Hispanics Largest Minority Group." *USA Today,* June 19, 2003, pp. 1A, 2A.

26. Samovar and Porter, *Intercultural Communication: A Reader,* p. 5.

27. See Judith N. Martin and Thomas K. Nakayama. *Intercultural Communication in Contexts,* 2nd ed. Mountain View, CA: Mayfield, 2000, pp. 265–266.

28. G. Hofstede. *Cultures and Organizations.* London: McGraw-Hill, 1991.

29. See G. Hofstede. *Masculinity and Femininity: The Taboo Dimension of National Cultures.* Thousand Oaks, CA: Sage, 1998.

30. Robert R. Harris and Robert T. Moran. *Managing Cultural Differences,* 3rd ed. Houston: Gulf, 1991.

31. Fred E. Jandt. *Intercultural Communication: An Introduction.* Thousand Oaks, CA: Sage, 1998, pp. 90–91. See also F. Delgado. "Mass-Mediated Communication and Intercultural Conflict." In J. N. Martin, T. K. Nakayama, and L. A. Flores, eds. *Readings in Cultural Contexts.* Mountain View, CA: Mayfield, 1998, pp. 442–449.

32. Paul Shepard. "Latinos Seek More Featured TV Roles." *The Record,* July 4, 2000, p. A-10.

33. Josh Meyrowitz. "Media Theory." In Erik P. Bucy, ed. *Living in the Information Age.* Belmont, CA: Wadsworth, 2002, p. 32.

34. Clifford Stoll. *Silicon Snake Oil: Second Thoughts on the Information Highway.* New York: Doubleday, 1995, pp. 8–11.

35. Clifford Stoll. "Further Explorations into the Culture of Computing." In Erick P. Bucy, ed. *Living in the Information Age.* Belmont, CA: Wadsworth, 2002, pp. 210–215.

36. Edward Iwata. "Tech's Tyranny Provokes Revolt." *USA Today,* August 21, 2000, p. 1A.

37. Jan Samoriski. *Issues in Cyberspace.* Boston: Allyn & Bacon, 2002, p. 37.

Communication
and the Self-Concept:
Who Are You?

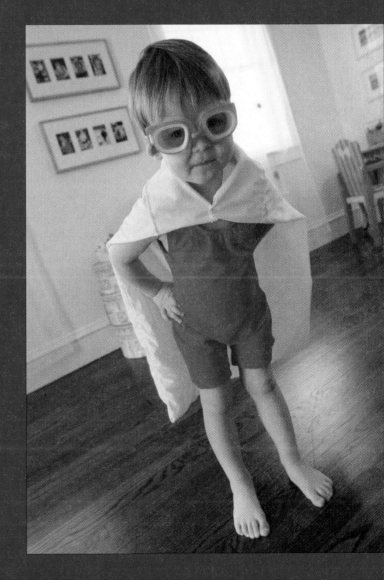

1. Define and explain the formation of the self-concept.

2. Identify how popular culture and technology help shape your self-concept.

3. Define *self-fulfilling prophecy* and explain how a self-fulfilling prophecy can influence behavior.

4. Compare and contrast the ways males and females as well as people from different cultures see themselves.

5. Identify the purposes and functions of the Johari window as a model of self-disclosure.

There are three things extremely hard, Steel, a Diamond, and to know one's self.

—Benjamin Franklin

. . . the self is not something that one finds. It is something that one creates.

—Thomas Szasz

D oes what you think about yourself matter? Would it help if your appraisal of yourself were more positive and supported by others? Should it be society's mission to help raise your self-esteem? If yes, why? If not, can you think of any good that can come from feeling bad about yourself? Do you ever want to wake up as someone else? How does who you are come to be?

Whomever we meet in life, whatever we do in life, is filtered through the self. Our sense of self is at the center of all we experience. We think about ourselves and what others think of us. The thoughts we have change as we change. We have the ability to reinvent ourselves. What we think about ourselves affects our communication with others. This leads us to ask a host of other questions: To what extent do you exhibit different selves and take on different roles when faced with different situations and people? How well do you really know and understand your identity? Can you see your identity reflected in the messages you send to others? These are just some of the questions that we will explore in this chapter.

WHAT IS THE SELF-CONCEPT?

Self-concept concerns us all. One sports coach, for example, notes, "If I single some out for praise, I would kill the others' self-esteem." One person praises another for a job that wasn't very well done, observing that "I didn't want to hurt his self-esteem."[1] Some school systems even believe that the promotion of self-esteem should be a central goal of education.[2] Others challenge the merit of a "feel-good curriculum" and distain the fact that we walk around on eggshells to avoid hurting another person's self-esteem. Why is self-esteem considered so critical? Consider this:

Have you ever been teased? How did it affect your sense of self?

> *Amy Hagadorn of Fort Wayne, Indiana, wanted only one day without teasing . . . On Tuesday, she reveled in festivities for Amy Hagadorn Day in Fort Wayne.*

Amy asked for Santa's help after hearing about a Letters for Santa promotion on a radio station. "I have a problem at school," she wrote in pencil. "Kids laugh at me because of the way I walk and run and talk. I have cerebral palsy. I just want one day where no one laughs at me or makes fun of me."

At school Friday, her classmates sang for her . . . A local nurse who has cerebral palsy offered to share with Amy the ways she has learned to strengthen her limbs and disguise her disability. A local man offered to send Amy and her sister Jamie on a $4,500 toy shopping spree. . . .

A delighted Amy said: "I think I had my Christmas today."[3]

According to The National Self-Esteem Association, it is important "to fully integrate self-esteem into the fabric of American society so that every individual, no matter what their age or background, experiences personal worth and happiness."[4] But does high self-esteem have a downside? While people with high self-esteem are happier, high self-esteem does *not* seem to offer immunity against bad behavior.[5] It appears that people with high self-esteem pose a greater threat to those around them than do people with low self-esteem.[6] Consider this: Some believe that an overemphasis on reinforcing self-esteem, especially in persons whose self-esteem is already high, has precipitated bullying in some segments of our culture. Why do people tease or bully others? What motivates one person to want to belittle another person? What is bullying? Who is a bully? Bullying is persistent teasing, name-calling, or social exclusion. A bully is likely to be among the most popular people, admired by others, and high among those persons others want to "hang" with.[7] Some researchers say the behavior of a person who bullies can be attributed to a self-appraisal that is unrealistically inflated.[8] A prime contributor to aggression in person-to-person interaction appears to be unusually high self-esteem combined with a sense of arrogance and narcissistic tendencies.[9] Consider the adulation in our society that is accorded our icons of popular culture, including professional athletes and music and movie stars. Our behavior helps precipitate the self-centered, egomaniacal characteristics they too often exhibit. Balance is needed in how much praise we give people, lest we help create in them a perception of their own self-importance that is out of whack with reality.

Rather than thinking that raising self-esteem is the panacea for the individual and social problems that exist in society, we need to work instead to develop our resilience, so that we become better at bouncing back from personal defeats and disappointments.[10] We have to help individuals build from their strengths in order to overcome or compensate for their weaknesses.

As humans, we have a unique ability to reflect on ourselves. Your **self-concept** is your self-appraisal. Included within it is everything you think and feel about yourself. It is the entire collection of attitudes and beliefs you hold about who and what you are. Self-concept is composed of two components: **self-image,** or the sort of person you perceive yourself to be, and **self-esteem,** your feelings and attitudes about yourself, including how well you like and value yourself. Included in your self-image are the roles you see yourself performing, the categories you place yourself within, the words you use to describe or identify yourself, and your understanding of how others see you. Self-esteem, on the other hand, usually derives from your successes and/or failures. Thus, it colors your self-image with a predominantly positive or negative hue. In other words, if you have a favorable perception of yourself, you

In your opinion, is self-control more important than self-esteem?

self-concept
everything one thinks and feels about oneself

self-image
the sort of person one perceives oneself to be

self-esteem
how well one likes and values oneself

Ethics & COMMUNICATION

Self-Concern and Concern for Others

In her book *The New Peoplemaking*, Virginia Satir notes:

> *Every person has a feeling of worth, positive or negative; the question is, Which is it?*
>
> *Every person communicates; the question is, How, and what happens as a result?*
>
> *Every person follows rules; the question is, What kind, and how well do they work for her or him?*
>
> *Every person is linked to society; the question is, In what way, and what are the results?*[11]

How would you answer each of these questions with regard to yourself? Your parents? Your friends? The people you work with? What does each set of answers reveal about self-concern and concern for others? How is this an ethical issue?

---

probably have high self-esteem; conversely, if your perception of yourself is unfavorable, you are more likely to have low self-esteem. According to researcher Chris Mruk, self-esteem has five dimensions, which affect your feelings about yourself and your communication with others: competence (your beliefs about your ability to be effective), worthiness (your beliefs about the degree to which others value you), cognition (your beliefs about your character and personality), affect (how you evaluate yourself and the feelings generated by your evaluation), and stability or change.[12]

No matter what your age or position, it is important that you spend some time considering who you are and what you intend to do with the rest of your life. The question "Who am I?" is a serious one. How you answer it is extremely significant, since who you think you are to a large extent determines what you choose to do, how you choose to act, whom you choose to communicate with, and even whether you choose to communicate at all.

Our self-concept is shaped by our experiences.

Describe Yourself

Is it possible to define yourself in just a single word? Can you sort out all the complicated connectors of public and private life, measure all the facets of your personality, cast off what's extraneous, and then name an essential, identifying characteristic? Try it.

When a *New York Times*/CBS News poll asked 1,136 adults to describe themselves in only one word, interviewers received a multitude of answers.[13]

Generally, the respondents seemed to resist labeling themselves as members of a special interest group or easily identifiable minority group; avoiding stereotyping, they chose instead either a broader affiliation or a narrower, more personal response.

For example, none of the 97 Black respondents said "Black," and none of the 967 Whites said that being White was the defining fact of their lives. Instead, the word given most often in the survey was *American.*

For those who answered, it was certainly a challenge. "You cannot reduce yourself to one word. It is too complicated," said Suzanne Keller, a sociologist at Princeton University. "People really feel multiple. They have multiple poses and attitudes and roles and one is no more important than the next. If they're forced to choose between family and work and leisure roles, which are not even roles but personas, they can't, really, because they live a multifaceted, multitudinous life, not a single track."

Author Margaret Atwood seemed to feel the same way when asked to define herself in one word. She picked *indescribable,* warning that "one must always resist the tyranny of adjectives."

Now ask 10 people to describe themselves in one word. How do their responses compare with the ones in the study?

If someone were to ask you on 10 separate occasions "Who are you?"—and if each time you had to supply a different answer—what types of responses do you think you would offer? What would you say about yourself? To what extent could your answers be grouped into categories? For example, you might see yourself in reference to your sex (male or female), your gender (masculine or feminine), your religion (Buddhist, Jewish, Christian), your race (African American, Caucasian, Asian), your nationality (U.S. citizen, Turkish, German), your physical attributes (fat, thin), your roles (wife, son, student, employee), your attitudes and emotions (hopeful, pessimistic, personable), your mental abilities (smart, slow), and your talents (musically or artistically gifted). The words you use to describe yourself reveal both to yourself and to others what you think you are like.

> *Part of knowing who we are is knowing we are not someone else.*
> —**Arthur Miller, *Incident at Vichy***

HOW IS YOUR SELF-CONCEPT FORMED?

How did your self-concept develop? The day you recognized yourself as separate from your surroundings, life began to change as you strove to fit into the world as you saw it. In short order, your concept of self—that relatively stable set of perceptions you attribute to yourself—became your most important possession.

While you are not born with a self-concept, you certainly do play a key role in building one.[14] Even though you are constantly undergoing change, once built, the theory or picture you have of yourself is fairly stable and difficult to alter. For example, have you ever tried to revise your parents' or friends' opinions about themselves? Did you have much luck? Our opinions about ourselves grow more and more resistant to change as we become older and presumably wiser. The statements we make are more or less accurate maps of the territory that is ourselves, but some of us map ourselves better than others do—that is, some of us have a more accurate mental picture of our personal strengths, weaknesses, and needs than others do.[15]

A number of forces converge to help create your self-concept. Among them are the image that other people have of you, which helps guide the way they relate to you; the way you experience and evaluate yourself; the roles you perform; the media messages you absorb; the expectations you and others have for you; and the gender, cultural, and technological messages you internalize.

How do your employer and your friends picture you?

To a large extent, your self-concept is shaped by your environment and by the people around you, including your parents, relatives, teachers, supervisors, friends, and co-workers. If people who are important to you have a good image of you, they probably make you feel accepted, valued, worthwhile, lovable, and significant, and you are likely to develop a positive self-concept as a result. On the other hand, if those who are important to you have a poor image of you, more than likely they make you feel left out, small, worthless, unloved, or insignificant, and you probably develop a negative self-concept as a consequence.

It is not difficult to see how people you value influence the picture you have of yourself and help determine the ways you behave. Nineteenth-century poet Walt Whitman recognized this:

> There was a child went forth every day,
> And the first object he look'd upon, that object he became,
> And that object became part of him for the day or a certain part of the day,
> Or for many years or stretching cycles of years.

ROLES, SELF-EVALUATIONS, BEHAVIOR, AND THE SELF-CONCEPT

What "masks" might people in business wear?

Self-concept, besides being your own theory of who and what you are, is a mental picture you have of yourself. This mental image is easily translated into the faces or masks you wear, the roles you play, and the ways you behave. For an illustration of this idea, see Figure 3.1. The top panel presents the self-image of a man who thinks of himself as a lowly cockroach. He has developed this image because he has felt he is performing a dull job in an impersonal work environment. However, when invited to attend a conference, he alters this perception and as a result changes his demeanor and adopts an "executive" appearance. The middle panel shows how this man views various colleagues who attend the conference. One is as proud as a peacock, another as close-mouthed as a clam; still others are ill-tempered (ram), loyal (dog), unforgetful (elephant), dangerous (wolf), and stubborn (mule). Finally, in the bottom panel we see what happens to this man once the meeting is over: He retreats into "roachhood" once more. He reemerges at one point to play the knight in shining armor. However, once he returns to what he perceives as mindless busywork, he views himself as a donkey. However, this man has not completely submerged his better self. When he is called on to make a business decision, he once again changes his self-image and pictures himself as an effective, capable individual.

FIGURE 3.1
How the Self-Image Can Change during a Single Day.

Source: Adapted from art by Paul Furlinger in *Psychology Today,* August 1972, p.5. Jules Power Productions.

If you feel you have little worth, you probably expect to be taken advantage of, stepped on, or otherwise demeaned by others. When you expect the worst, you usually get the worst. Similarly, if you feel you have significant worth, you probably expect to be treated fairly, supported, and otherwise held in esteem by others. When you expect to succeed, you usually find success.

We can conclude that the nature of the self at any given moment is a composite of all the factors that interact in a particular environment. Thus, how you look at yourself is affected by how you look at other people, how other people actually look at you, and how you imagine or perceive that other people look at you. We might say that self-concept is derived from experience and projected into future behavior. Of course, your self-concept may be realistic or unrealistic. Unfortunately, we never really come to know all there is to know about ourselves, so we keep searching for clues.

The language we use, the attitudes we display, and the appearances we present also change as we vary the masks we wear and the roles we perform. In effect, we become different selves as we move from one set of conditions to another. The more we attempt to be ourselves, the more selves we find. It is important to recognize that conditions and circumstances affect the nature

In "The Love Song of J. Alfred Prufrock," poet T. S. Eliot wrote, "Prepare a face to meet the faces that you meet." What do you think of such advice? Do you ever "prepare" your face when meeting or interacting with someone else?

Ethics & COMMUNICATION

Age, Physical Challenges, and Self-Esteem

Self-esteem may be related to age and physical ability. According to researchers Justine Coupland, John F. Nussbaum, and Nikolas Coupland, "elderly people are prone to assimilate society's devalued appraisals of their own social group, and so lower their self-esteem."[16] Similarly, researchers note that persons who are physically challenged often face myriad social barriers, primarily because they feel isolated from their peers and believe that their futures are limited and that their lives are less meaningful because of their disabilities.[17] On the other hand, in *Old Is Not a Four-Letter Word: A Midlife Guide,* author Ann E. Gerike notes that aging has advantages, bringing with it a more reliable inner voice, an acceptance that life is not always fair, and a willingness to shoulder responsibility instead of blaming others for what happens.[18] How do you feel about aging? What messages have you received from parents and older friends and relatives regarding their sense of self as they age? What messages do you send older or physically challenged people with whom you relate regarding your estimations of their worth and abilities?

How might online interactions with peers be used to transform the nature of self-concepts and lives? For example, if a person imagines that others view him or her negatively, low self-esteem can result. In contrast, when a person imagines that others find him or her interesting, self-esteem may be improved. Log on to *Ability Online.* Describe the extent to which sites such as this one can facilitate the strengthening of self-esteem by helping reduce the effect of a person's disability on his or her self-concept.

of the self. In every situation, how we see ourselves and how we think about ourselves in relation to others direct and modify our behavior.

According to developmental psychologist Jean Piaget, the construction of the self occurs as a person acts on his or her environment and figures out what he or she can and cannot do.[19] In cyberspace, for example, if you don't like how you are characterized or treated, you can adopt a new identity. According to FreeZone's Allison Ellis, "If you came into the chat room as one kind of kid and made some other kids angry by being rude, you can change your identity and come back as a different or better person." Online interaction lets you try again; it gives you a second chance to get it right. It lets you reinvent yourself to morph into different identities. This type of transformation is far different from being a student part of the day, an athlete another part of the day, an employee during the evening, and a child at home. In contrast, in cyberspace you can have parallel identities or parallel selves and use them to develop better relationships and to manage more effectively the many selves that exist within you.[20] In fact, the latest version of America Online offers the

Skill BUILDER

A Day in My Life

1. List the names of all the people with whom you interacted during a single day this week. For each, identify the environment in which you communicated.

2. Next, choose an adjective to describe your image of yourself during each interaction and an adjective to describe your image of the person with whom you spoke.

3. Finally, graph your perceptions on a chart like the one shown here, entering each of your responses in the appropriate box. (For example, you might see yourself as shy and "Person 1" as aggressive.)

4. Answer these questions: What does your chart tell you about the nature of your self-image? To what extent does your view of yourself change as you move from person to person? What factors can you point to in yourself, the individual with whom you were interacting, or the environment that help account for the changes?

5. Which, if any, of the people with whom you interacted made you feel positively about yourself? Which, if any, made you feel negatively about yourself? Which, if any, criticized you so harshly that they came close to destroying your self-esteem?

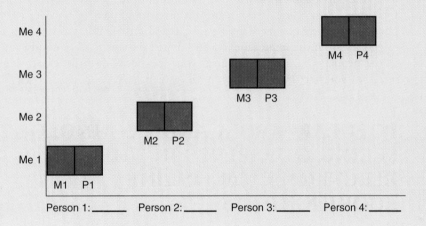

largest number of fictive identities per subscriber to date. Technological innovations not only encourage us to reinvent ourselves to find success or happiness but also provide us the tools to do so. Who do you want to be today?

When it comes to thinking about the self and who we want to be today, some of us categorize ourselves as optimists. If we suffer a defeat, we view it as a temporary setback brought about by circumstances, bad luck, or other people. Optimists are resilient; they do not view defeat as their own fault. Psychologist Albert Bandura tells us that an optimistic belief in our own possibilities and competence endows us with feelings of **self-efficacy.** (Note: We are talking about optimism, not unrealistic optimism based on overconfidence.) When we have strong feelings of self-efficacy, we are more persistent, less anxious, and less depressed. We don't dwell on our inadequacy when something goes wrong but instead seek a solution. Those of us who are persistent are apt to accomplish more. And when we accomplish more, our belief in ourselves grows.[21] Some of us categorize ourselves as pessimists. In contrast to optimists, pessimists lack resilience and believe that bad events are their own fault, will last a long time, and will undermine whatever they do. Instead of believing they can control their own destiny, they believe that

Pessimism is self-fulfilling. Pessimists don't persist in the face of challenges, and therefore fail more frequently—even when success is attainable.
—Martin P. Seligman

self-efficacy
an optimistic belief in one's own competence

According to the psychologist Martin P. Seligman, pessimists can learn to be optimists. How do you think optimism would enhance the self-concept?

outside forces determine their fate. In effect, they "can't because they think they can't," versus optimists, who "can because they think they can." Psychologist Martin Seligman tells this story:

> We tested the swim team at the University of California at Berkeley to find out which swimmers were optimists and which were pessimists. To test the effects of attitude, we had the coach "defeat" each one: After a swimmer finished a heat, the coach told him his time—but it wasn't his real time. The coach had falsified it, making it significantly slower. The optimists responded by swimming their next heat faster; the pessimists went slower on their next heat.[22]

Are you the person you think you are, the person someone else thinks you are, or the person you think someone else thinks you are? Why?

Clues to self-understanding come to you continually as you interact with others and with your real-world or online environments. If you are to understand yourself, you need to be open to information that other people give you about yourself. Just as we tend to categorize ourselves and others, so others tend to categorize themselves and us. For better or worse, the categorization process is a basic part of interpersonal communication. We classify people according to their roles, their status, their material possessions, their personality traits, their physical and vocal qualities, and their skills and accomplishments. Which of these categories are most important to you? Which do you think are most important to the people who are significant in your life? How do others help shape your image of yourself? How do they enhance or belittle your sense of self?

POPULAR MEDIA AND TECHNOLOGY: SEEING OURSELVES IN THE ELECTRONIC OR ONLINE LOOKING GLASS

Thus far we have established that your self-image is made up partly of information and feelings drawn from past experiences and partly from your interactions with others. At least five other important sources affect your opinion of who you are: television, film, radio and music, the print media (especially advertisements), and the Internet. We are all influenced by media images, including the personalities and characters that populate the media, to a greater extent than we may realize. Subtly but effectively, these visual and aural media shape our views of ourselves and our relationship to our world.

Let's consider some ways the popular media and the experience of "growing up digital" affect the picture you have of yourself. First, many media and Internet offerings expose us to a standard of living few of us can expect to achieve. Thus, our evaluation of ourselves as providers—or even as successful—may be seriously colored by what we see. Second, media and online offerings may affect the ways parents and children perceive themselves and each other. After all, both parents and children are exposed to a steady succession of media counterparts who appear either so perfect that even their mistakes become the raw material of a closer relationship or so absurd that their foibles can only constitute charming comedy. Third, the visual media can fill our need for a bigger, better, smarter, prettier, stronger personal image. When we were younger, it was easy and fun to try on television and film images. For example, we could become Harry Potter, a Power Ranger, Daredevil, Lara Croft, a Hobbit, the new Wonder Woman, or Xena. As we mature, however, this process becomes more subtle. As adolescents, we attempt to become like popular idols or heroes by imitating their fashions, by adopting their speech mannerisms, and by copying their movements and gestures. Thus, we communicate part of the picture we have of ourselves, or the picture we would like to have, through the way we dress, move, speak, and so on. When you put on a certain outfit, comb your hair in a new style, walk or speak in a particular way, or choose to wear a certain artifact, you are telling other people something about who you think you are, whom you would like to resemble, and how you would like to be treated. Fourth, today's teenagers and young adults are often smarter on cyber issues and have more digital expertise than those for whom they work or from whom they learn. You are users, not just viewers or listeners, as were your parents. You have new, powerful tools for self-expression. Among teenagers, being online is now perceived as on a par with dating and partying. The parting line "Call me" is being replaced by "Send me an e-mail"[23] or "I-M me."

The way the physically challenged are depicted in media offerings can affect their self-concept and the way persons without disabilities relate to them. Some years ago, the Mattel corporation introduced the first disabled fashion doll, Share a Smile Becky, as a new friend for Barbie. According to a Mattel marketing manager, "Some kids want a doll that looks like them, and we wanted to make that possible for kids in wheelchairs. But we hope all kids play with her."[24] It is hoped that the new doll will help break down barriers for children and others with disabilities, and that children who play with this new doll will also become more comfortable interacting with persons who are physically challenged.[25] In contrast, Drew Browning, an expert on portrayals of people with disabilities in the media, sees the introduction of such a doll differently. According to Browning, "It's telethon phraseology, implying people with disabilities need cheering up because they're so pitiful. It makes her sound like a Barbie poster child."[26] Browning believes that Beckie should have been Barbie, not merely her friend. What do you think?

Media and online offerings can support us or deflate us. They can cause us to feel good, adequate, or inferior.

If you could trade places with any television or film star or character, who would you be? What does this person, real or fictional, "do" for you? Do you have a more positive image of this person than you have of yourself? Why? Would you like to be more like the media image, or would you like the image to be more like you?

My Media Life

1. Divide your life into three approximately equal stages. (For example, if you are 18 years old, your life would be divided into these segments: ages 1 to 6, ages 7 to 12, and ages 13 to 18. If you are 24, it would be divided into these segments: ages 1 to 8, ages 9 to 16, and ages 17 to 24.) From each life period, select a media offering (broadcast or online) that you believe exerted some influence on the way you thought and felt about yourself, your daily existence, or the people with whom you interacted. Give specific examples.

2. Compare and contrast the image you have of each of the following with the image portrayed in the broadcast or online media. Which image do you prefer and why?

A doctor	The elderly	The rich
A teacher	Gays and lesbians	Business executives
A family	The police	African Americans
A teenager	The poor	Arabs
Marriage		

Media
WISE

EXPECTATIONS: THE SELF-FULFILLING PROPHECY AND THE PYGMALION EFFECT

Consider the following excerpt from *The People, Yes,* by poet Carl Sandburg:

> Drove up a newcomer in a covered wagon. "What kind of folks live around here?" "Well, stranger, what kind of folks was there in the country you come from?" "Well, they was mostly a lowdown, lying, gossiping, backbiting lot of people." "Well, I guess, stranger, that's about the kind of folks you'll find around here." And the dusty grey stranger had just about blended into the dusty grey cottonwoods in a clump on the horizon when another newcomer drove up. "What kind of folks live around here?" "Well, stranger, what kind of folks was there in the country you come from?" "Well, they was mostly a decent, hardworking, law-abiding, friendly lot of people." "Well, I guess, stranger, that's about the kind of people you'll find around here." And the second wagon moved off and blended with the dusty grey.[27]

self-fulfilling prophecy

a prediction or an expectation that comes true simply because one acts as if it were true

The speaker in this passage understands the significance of the self-fulfilling prophecy. A **self-fulfilling prophecy** occurs when an individual's expectation of an event helps create the very conditions that permit that event to happen (see Figure 3.2). In other words, your predictions can cause you and others to behave in ways that will increase the likelihood of an initially unlikely occurrence. For example, have you ever anticipated botching a presentation and then did so? Have you ever assumed you wouldn't like someone and you turned out to be correct? Have you ever had to perform a task that others

FIGURE 3.2
The Self-Fulfilling Prophecy in Action.

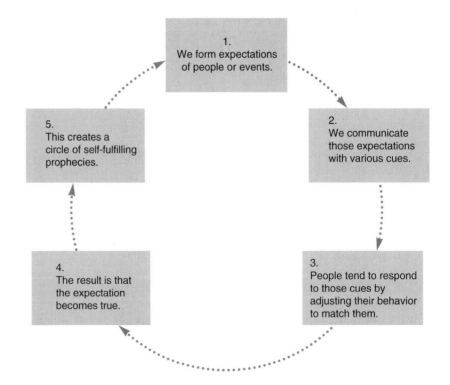

1. We form expectations of people or events.

2. We communicate those expectations with various cues.

3. People tend to respond to those cues by adjusting their behavior to match them.

4. The result is that the expectation becomes true.

5. This creates a circle of self-fulfilling prophecies.

told you would be dull? Was it? Why? In each instance, did it occur to you that you might have acted in a way that caused the prediction to come true?

Perhaps the most widely known example of the self-fulfilling prophecy is the **Pygmalion effect.** The term comes from the Greek myth of Pygmalion, a sculptor, who falls in love with a beautiful statue of his own creation. The goddess Aphrodite, moved by Pygmalion's obsession with the statue, comes to his rescue and brings it to life. George Bernard Shaw adapted the story to a more modern setting, and Shaw's version in turn served as the basis for the stage and film musical *My Fair Lady.* In this version, Henry Higgins (Pygmalion) seeks to transform a flower seller, Eliza Doolittle, into a refined, well-spoken lady of the upper class. The play illustrates the principle that we live up to labels. We, like Eliza Doolittle, learn to act like the sorts of people others perceive us to be.

A real-life example of the startling effects of self-fulfilling prophecies is a classroom experiment described by psychologist Robert Rosenthal.[28] In the experiment, teachers were notified that certain of their students were expected to bloom—that is, to do exceptionally well—during the course of the school year. What the teachers did not know was that there was no real basis for this determination. The experimenters had simply selected the names of the "bloomers" at random. Do you think the selected students actually bloomed? If you said yes, you are quite right. Those students did perform at a higher level than would otherwise have been expected and did improve their IQ scores.

Why did this happen? First, the teachers' expectations apparently influenced the way they treated the selected children. The teachers gave those students extra positive verbal and nonverbal reinforcement, waited patiently for them to respond if they hesitated, and did not react negatively when they offered faulty answers. Second, it seems that the way the teachers treated the students had a marked impact on the way the students perceived themselves and their own abilities. The bloomers responded to the prophecy that had apparently been made about them by fulfilling it.[29]

This treatment of students, choosing certain ones to succeed, continues. Researchers Myra and David Sadker describe their view of education in the book *Failing at Fairness: How America's Schools Cheat Girls:*

> Sitting in the same classroom, reading the same textbook, listening to the same teacher, boys and girls receive very different educations. From grade school through graduate school female students are more likely to be invisible members of classrooms. Teachers interact with males more frequently, ask them better questions, and give them more precise and helpful feedback. Over the course of years the uneven distribution of teacher time, energy, attention, and talent, with boys getting the lion's share, takes its toll on girls. Since gender bias is not a noisy problem, most people are unaware of the secret sexist lessons and the quiet losses they engender.
>
>   Girls are the majority of our nation's schoolchildren, yet they are second-class educational citizens. The problems they face—loss of self-esteem, decline in achievement, and elimination of career options—are at the heart of the educational process. Until educational sexism is eradicated, more than half of our children will be shortchanged and their gifts lost to society.[30]

You should recognize that the self-fulfilling prophecy has important implications, not only for education but also for our personal lives. Have you ever

---

Pygmalion effect

the principle that we fulfill the expectations of others

Do you have any beliefs that cause you to function in ways that are self-defeating? What are they? What can you do to eliminate them?

Identify people who have functioned as positive or negative "Pygmalions" in your life. Then complete these sentences: I work best for people who . . . ; I work least for people who . . . .

joined a group of people you were convinced would not like you? What happened? Very likely you were proved right. What you probably did was act in a way that encouraged them to dislike you. The self-fulfilling prophecy also plays itself out in families. If a parent tells a child that he or she can't do anything right, the child will soon incorporate this idea into his or her self-concept and fail at most of the tasks he or she attempts. In contrast, if a parent repeatedly demonstrates to a child that he or she is lovable or capable, the child will probably live up to that expectation as well.[31]

The Pygmalion effect is also at the root of many business problems.[32] Apparently, some managers treat employees in ways that precipitate superior performance, while many others unconsciously treat workers in ways that precipitate inferior performance. High expectations tend to result in increased productivity, whereas low expectations result in decreased productivity. Thus, subordinates more often than not confirm the expectations of their superiors. For this reason, when you assume a leadership role, you have the potential to function as both a positive and a negative Pygmalion. Which would be more effective?

What about the messages you send yourself? A variation of the Pygmalion effect is the **Galatea effect.** (Galatea is the name Pygmalion gave his statue once it was brought to life.) The *Galatea effect* refers to the expectations we have for ourselves rather than the expectations others have for us. We tend to realize the expectations we have for ourselves. We react to the internal messages we continuously send ourselves. Our feelings about our own competence and ability can exert an influence on our behavior in much the same way that our performance can be influenced by others' high or low expectations for us. Thus, how we and others answer the question "Who are you?" affects how we behave.

GENDER: DO MALES AND FEMALES SEE THEMSELVES DIFFERENTLY?

Do you think you would feel differently about yourself if you were of the opposite sex? If you answered yes, is it because you believe that others would treat you differently? Would they encourage you to exhibit certain behaviors while at the same time discouraging you from exhibiting others?

Research tells us that others do treat us differently because of our gender. For example, we dress male and female babies in different colors and styles. For the most part, our prevalent conceptions of masculinity and femininity are reinforced in the television shows we view, the films we watch, the books we read, the toys we play with, and the online sites we frequent. For instance, young girls are given Barbies that say, "Let's go shopping," while young boys are given G.I. Joes that say, "Attack." A group calling itself the Barbie Liberation Organization attempted to call attention to such sexual stereotyping and make a statement about the way toys can influence behavior by switching G.I. Joe voice boxes with Barbie voice boxes, thereby altering the dolls to say the unexpected. The result? "A mutant colony of Barbies-on-Steroids who roar things like 'Attack!' 'Vengeance is mine!' and 'Eat lead, Cobra!' The emasculated G.I. Joes meanwhile twitter, 'Will we ever have enough clothes?'"[33] The point is that the experiences we have during our formative years influence our later views of masculinity and femininity, thus affecting our identities.

As soon as our gender becomes integrated into our self-concept, we form a gender identity. Once we learn the attributes of maleness and femaleness,

Biologists have determined that, technically speaking, the bumblebee cannot fly. Fortunately, the bumblebee doesn't know this. Remember: People rise no higher than their expectations.

Galatea effect

the principle that we fulfill our own expectations

our perceptions of self are affected by what we have come to believe about our gender. When asked to describe their characteristics, for example, males mention qualities such as initiative, control, and ambition. Females, in contrast, lead with qualities such as sensitivity, concern for others, and consideration. Appearance plays a major role in the self-image of a woman but is not nearly as integral to the self-image of a man. Why is this so? Can it be because, since infancy, greater emphasis is placed on a female's looks? Can it be because women, more than men, are teased about how they look and how much they weigh?[34]

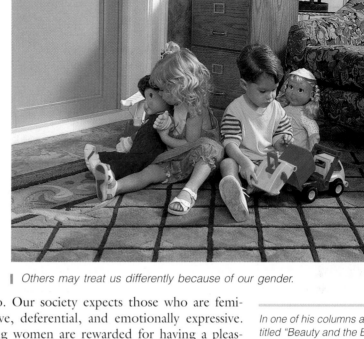

❙ *Others may treat us differently because of our gender.*

Many women develop a less positive self-concept than men do. Our society expects those who are feminine to be nurturing, unaggressive, deferential, and emotionally expressive. Because of this expectation, young women are rewarded for having a pleasing appearance, revealing their feelings, being forgiving, and being helpful to others. While women of all ages appear to value relationships, adolescent girls become so preoccupied with pleasing others that they metaphorically "bend themselves into pretzels."[36] Girls are more likely to be self-critical and self-doubting than are boys. In contrast, men are more apt to develop an independent sense of self. Since men are expected to be strong, resilient, ambitious, in control of their emotions, and successful and, unlike women, are reinforced for displaying these qualities, independence is central to their lives.[37] According to John Gray, a relationship specialist and best-selling author, "A man's sense of self is defined through his ability to achieve results. A woman's sense of self is defined through her feelings and the quality of her relationships."[38] What is noteworthy is that male characteristics typically are more highly valued by our society than are female characteristics. Thus, men often feel better about themselves than do women. And that may be why many women try harder and harder to attain success by attempting to be and do it all.[39] As Carol Leifer, a standup comic, expresses it: "I just had a baby an hour ago and I'm back at work already. While I was delivering, I took a course in tax-shelter options."

In one of his columns aptly titled "Beauty and the Beast," Miami Herald columnist and humorist Dave Barry reported that, for men, being considered average-looking is just fine; for women, being average is not good enough.[35] To what extent, if any, do your experiences support such findings and observations?

No one can make you feel inferior without your consent.
—Eleanor Roosevelt

DIVERSITY AND THE SELF-CONCEPT: HOW IMPORTANT IS THE "I"?

Diversity influences person-to-person interactions in both subtle and overt ways. It affects the way we look at the self, the expectations we have for ourselves and others, and our behavior. Our notion of "self" is shaped by our culture. Who we are, at least in part, emerges from participation in a culture.

In North American and Western European cultures, the self is considered paramount. People from these cultures tend to reflect the importance placed on individuals as they set and work toward the realization of personal goals. In contrast, people from Asia, Africa, Central and South America, places where collectivistic cultures are dominant, are more likely to downplay their own goals, emphasizing instead goals set or valued by the group as a whole.[40] Japanese parents, for example, do not lavish praise on their children because they are concerned that, if they do, the children will end up thinking too much about themselves and not enough about the group.[41] In Western cultures, the assumption is that your life will be enriched if you are able to define who you are—all your possible selves. Stress is placed on the power of personal control. There is an intra-individual focus.[42] Even in popular culture, the focus is on self-reliance ("I Did It My Way"), self-realization ("I Gotta Be Me"), and self-love ("The Greatest Love of All"). In the United States, for example, we emphasize self-determination. In contrast to the independence emphasized in Western cultures, the emphasis in collectivistic cultures is on the interdependent self. Identity is not defined individually but, rather, in relation to others. Thus, the focus is extra-individual.[43]

Go to the *Online Learning Center* at www.mhhe.com/gamble8 and answer the questions in the *Self Inventory* to evaluate your understanding of individualistic and collectivistic orientation.

For members of collectivistic cultures, the self is not of prime importance. In their view, the group, not the individual, is the primary social unit. Thus, whereas individualistic cultures link success with personal achievement, collectivistic cultures link it to group cohesion and loyalty. This basic difference is symbolized by the fact that the "I" in the Chinese written language looks very much like the word for *selfish*.[44] While Western cultures emphasize self-promotion, Asian cultures decry self-importance and reward cooperation with the group. No one is singled out; members share credit and blame. Members of collectivistic cultures gain a sense of identity via their group memberships, not by stressing their self-importance, as members of Western cultures tend to do.[45] Loyalties in collectivistic cultures are directed at others instead of the self. For members of those cultures, the "we" takes precedence over the "I"; the self is not developed at the expense of the group. Thus, culture influences our whole notion of self.

Researchers use the terms **idiocentric** to refer to an individualistic point of view and **allocentric** to mean a primarily collectivistic way of thinking and behaving.[46] Which term would you use to describe your standpoint?

As you can see, your self-concept—how you define yourself—is influenced by your unique personal experiences as well as by your membership in a group or groups. Together with culture, these influences play integral parts in helping you formulate a sense of self. According to **distinctiveness theory,** a person's own distinctive traits (red-headed, minority group member, left-handed) are more salient to him or her than are the more prevalent traits (Caucasian, brunette, right-handed) possessed by other people in the immediate environment. For example, persons who are members of groups that are a numeric minority in the United States are more mindful of their ethnicity. For this reason, a White person is much less apt than a minority group member to mention his or her ethnicity when asked to define himself or herself. As a result, an African-American woman in a large group of Caucasian women will probably be well aware of her race. When the same woman is with a large group of African-American men, she is more conscious of her gender and less conscious of her race.[47]

idiocentric

exhibiting an individualistic orientation

allocentric

exhibiting a collectivistic orientation

distinctiveness theory

a person's own distinctive traits are more salient to him or her than are the more prevalent traits possessed by others in the immediate environment

Idiocentric versus Allocentric

Assess the extent to which you exhibit an individualistic (idiocentric) or collectivistic (allocentric) orientation by evaluating the following statements. If the statement is very important to you, rate it a 5; somewhat important, a 4; neither important nor unimportant, a 3; somewhat unimportant, a 2; and very unimportant, a 1.

I Matter

_____ 1. I desire to prove my personal competency.

_____ 2. I've got to be me.

_____ 3. I want others to perceive me as having stature.

_____ 4. I need to achieve personal fulfillment.

_____ TOTAL

We Matter

_____ 1. If I hurt you, I hurt myself.

_____ 2. I desire harmony at all costs in my relations with others.

_____ 3. My goal is to preserve the welfare of others, even if it is at my expense.

_____ 4. I am loyal to tradition.

_____ TOTAL

To determine your score, total the numbers you entered for each category. Which score is higher? A higher "I Matter" score indicates greater idiocentric tendencies. A higher "We Matter" score indicates greater allocentric tendencies.

Your culture also feeds your self-concept. For example, African-American girls tend to have higher overall self-esteem during their adolescent years than do Caucasian or Latina girls. According to Peggy Orenstein, Latina girls experience the most serious self-esteem crisis. She notes that, between the ages of 9 and 15, the number of Latina girls who are happy with the way they are plunges by 38 percentage points.[48] Despite basic differences in orientation, however, young people throughout the world still share many attitudes regarding the self. Most are concerned about developing and maintaining social relationships, especially with their peers, and most are confident in their ability to assume responsibility for themselves in the future. However, despite this apparent optimism, about 25 percent of the teenagers described themselves as sad and lonely, emotionally empty, and overwhelmed by life's problems; these youngsters are burdened with the weight of poor self-images.

Young people are not the only group that describes themselves as lonely. The 2000 U.S. Census report found that 27 million Americans live by themselves—more than twice the number of single-person households reported in 1970. An editorial in the *New York Times* noted that, although solitary living cannot be equated with loneliness, it may certainly involve some loneliness:

> If [individuals are] elderly, they may take great pleasure in having the wherewithal to live on their own, especially if they remember when the old depended on relatives for meals and a bedroom off the hall. If they're young, they may rejoice that the pressure's off, that marriage is no longer regarded as the ceremony that separates the desirable from the unwanted. On the other hand, they may not. To some of them, a home empty of companions may be synonymous with an empty life.[49]

In fact, more and more people are reporting that they experience transitory, if not persistent, bouts of loneliness.[50] People who describe themselves as lonely typically have difficulty making connections with other people. The loneliness they experience seems attributable to a gap between what they want and what they achieve in their social relationships.

DEVELOPING SELF-AWARENESS

In order to enhance our ability to communicate with others, we need to use ourselves as a resource. By focusing on and acknowledging ourselves, we become more aware of ourselves and more sensitive to our own thoughts and feelings.

The Self-Concept versus the Self

One of the first things we need to become aware of is the difference between the self and the self-concept. The self-concept represents who you think you are, not necessarily the self you actually are. Sometimes your image of yourself may be more favorable than the image others have of you. For instance, you might view yourself as an extremely talented writer, but others might consider you a hack.

If men define situations as real, they are real in their consequences.
—**W. I. Thomas**

Many factors allow us to maintain pictures of ourselves that others may regard as unrealistic. For one thing, we might be so worried about our presentation of self that we fail to pay attention to feedback from others about how they see us. Or others might send us distorted information about ourselves in an attempt to spare our feelings. Or we might be basing our self-view on outdated, obsolete information that allows us to cling to the memories of the past rather than face the realities of the present.

Just as there are times when we view ourselves more favorably than we should, there are times when we view ourselves more harshly than we should. For example, a woman might be convinced that she is ugly despite other people's insistence that she is attractive. Why? This woman might be acting on the basis of obsolete data—that is, influences that are no longer accurate. Perhaps as a child she was gawky or clumsy, and even though she is now graceful and agile, those past traits are still part of her self-concept.

Focus on Service Learning
Choose an organization such as The American Cancer Society or a homeless shelter. Identify issues related to the purposes of the agency that could adversely affect the self-concept of the agency's clients. What strategies can be used to ameliorate harm to the clients' self-image?

Distorted feedback can also perpetuate a negative self-image. People who are strongly influenced by an overly critical parent, friend, teacher, or employer can develop a self-view that is far harsher than the view others hold. Another reason people often cheat themselves out of a favorable self-concept is the social customs of society. In the United States, at least, it is far more acceptable for people to downplay, underrate, and criticize themselves than it is for them to praise or boast about themselves or display self-appreciation.

In the poem "Song of Myself," Walt Whitman wrote: "I celebrate myself and sing myself." To what extent are you able to celebrate yourself? Do you have a predominantly positive or negative self-concept? Take some time now to inventory what you perceive to be your assets and liabilities. The practice of honestly reviewing your strong and weak points can help reshape your image of yourself.

Viewing Ourselves and Others: The Johari Window

You need to realize that self-understanding is the basis of self-concept. To understand yourself, you must understand your own way of looking at the world. To understand others, you must understand how they look at the world.

Yesterday, Today, and Tomorrow

1. Your instructor will divide the class into small groups.

2. Each group should use the incomplete sentences listed below as starters in three rounds of conversations. During the first round, indicate how you would have responded to each incomplete statement as a young child (between 5 and 8 years old). During the second round, indicate how you would have responded during later childhood and adolescence. Finally, during the third round, indicate how you would respond to these statements today.

   a. Other people want me to . . . .
   b. The best way to measure personal success is . . . .
   c. When I do what I really want to do, I . . . .
   d. I get frustrated when . . . .
   e. I want to be a . . . .
   f. I have fun when . . . .
   g. Marriage for me is . . . .
   h. People who are in charge should be . . . .
   i. I miss . . . .
   j. What I really like about myself is . . . .
   k. When I am with people who do a lot of talking, I . . . .
   l. Sometimes I feel like . . . .
   m. A decade from now, I . . . .

3. What do the responses tell you about yourself and your peers during these three stages of life? Were there discernible consistencies? Were there changes? Why?
   Can you identify some of the things you are hesitant to let others know about yourself? Why are these things easier to hold back than express?

Skill BUILDER

Some of your answers to the Skill Builder exercise "Yesterday, Today, and Tomorrow" may illustrate one of the ideas of psychiatrist Eric Berne. Berne believes that we sometimes pattern our transactions in such a way that we repeatedly reenact the same script with a different set of players. In other words, it is not uncommon for us to attempt to "stage" dramas with casts of characters drawn from different phases of our lives. We might, for example, repeatedly enact life scenes in which we express the belief that others are out to get us or that they are jealous of us. This urge to repeat transactions can become a problem if it leads us to failure rather than to success.

Take some time to examine the extent to which your three sets of responses in the Skill Builder demonstrate flexibility rather than rigidity. Attempt to determine to what degree you have eliminated behaviors you did not like. In addition, try to understand what each of your responses says about your past, present, and future needs.

At one time or another, we all wish that we knew ourselves or others better. The concept of self-awareness, basic to all functions and forms of communication, can be explored through a psychological testing device known as the **Johari window.** Joseph Luft and Harrington Ingham developed an illustration of a paned window to help us examine both how we view ourselves and how others view us.[51] Before proceeding further, let's look at the window (see Figure 3.3).

Pane I, the **open area,** represents information about yourself that is known to you and another. For example, your name, age, religious affiliation, and food preferences might all be found in this pane. The size and contents of the quadrant vary from one relationship to another, depending on the degree of closeness you share with that other person. Do you allow some people to know more about you than others?

Johari window

a model containing four panes that is used to explain the roles that self-awareness and self-disclosure play in relationships

open area

the part of the self containing information known both to the self and others

FIGURE 3.3
The Johari Window.

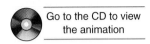
Go to the CD to view
the animation

	Known to self	Not known to self
Known to others	I Open	II Blind
Not known to others	III Hidden	IV Unknown

Source: From *Group Processes: An Introduction to Group Dynamics* by Joseph Luft. Copyright ©1984, 1970, 1963 by Joseph Luft. Reprinted by permission of The McGraw-Hill Companies.

blind area

the part of the self known to others but not known to oneself

hidden area

the part of the self that contains information about the self known to oneself but that is hidden from others

self-disclosure

the process of revealing to another person information about the self that this person would not otherwise know

What policy would you advocate the media follow regarding the disclosure of private information? Which in your opinion is more harmful: the media revealing a personal fact to the public that an individual did not want disclosed or someone whom you trusted revealing a personal fact about you to someone to whom you did not want to reveal the information?

Pane II, the **blind area,** contains information about you that others, but not you, are aware of. Some people have a very large blind area and are oblivious to their own faults and virtues. At times, people may feel compelled to seek outside help, such as therapy, to reduce the size of their blind area. Do you know something about a friend that he or she does not know? Do you feel free to reveal this information to your friend? Why? What effect do you think your revelation would have on your friend's self-image?

Pane III, the **hidden area,** represents your hidden self. It contains information you know about yourself but do not want others to find out for fear they will reject you. John Powell, author of *Why Am I Afraid to Tell You Who I Am?,* expresses the fear of rejection this way: "If I tell you who I am, you may not like who I am, and it is all that I have."[52] Sometimes it takes a great deal of effort to avoid becoming known, but at one time or another each of us feels a need to have people important to us know us well and accept us for what we are.

When we move information from Pane III to Pane I, we engage in the process of **self-disclosure.** Self-disclosure occurs when we purposely reveal to another person information about ourselves that he or she would not otherwise know. None of this is to suggest that the hidden area should not be allowed to exist within each of us. It is up to you to decide when it is appropriate for you to share your innermost thoughts, feelings, and intentions with others; it is also up to you to decide when complete openness is not in your best interest.

While self-disclosure is a process we normally control, what happens when this process is taken out of our control? What happens when another party, without our permission, takes information from our hidden area and reveals it in public? While anyone who knows us well can do this, some media practitioners have made a business out of forced disclosures. Tennis star Arthur Ashe, for example, was forced to reveal he had AIDS, although he and his family preferred to keep it private because otherwise the story of his condition would have appeared in a well-known tabloid. Florida Governor Jeb Bush's daughter had to deal with her drug problem under the scrutiny of the public eye. And because gay and lesbian groups threatened to go public with

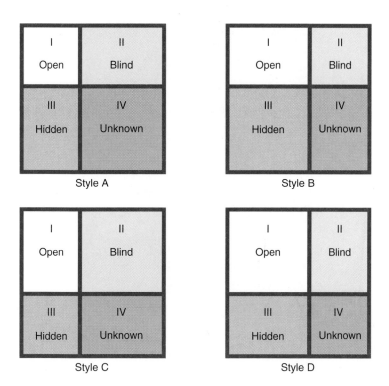

FIGURE 3.4
Interpersonal Styles, in Terms of the Johari Window.

the news, David Hope, the Bishop of London, was forced against his will to announce his homosexuality.

Pane IV of the Johari window is the **unknown area** in your makeup. It contains information about which neither you nor others are aware. Eventually, education and life experience may help bring some of the mysteries contained in this pane to the surface. Only then will its content be available for examination. Have you ever done something that surprised both you and the people close to you? Did you and a friend ever exclaim together, "Wow! I didn't know I could do that!" "I didn't know you could do that!"

People commonly develop a style that is a consistent and preferred way of behaving interpersonally. Figure 3.4 illustrates four representative styles. Style A is characteristic of people who adopt a fairly impersonal approach to interpersonal relationships. Dominated by their unknown areas, these people usually withdraw from contacts, avoid personal disclosures or involvements, and thus project an image that is rigid, aloof, and uncommunicative. In Style B, the hidden area, or facade, is the dominant window. Here we find people who desire relationships but also greatly fear exposure and generally mistrust others. Once others become aware of the facade, they are likely to lose trust in these people. Style C is dominated by the blind area. People who are characterized by this style are overly confident of their own opinions and painfully unaware of how they affect others or are perceived by others. Those who communicate with such people often feel that their own ideas or insights are of little concern. In Style D, the open area, or area of free activity, is dominant. Relationships involve candor, openness, and sensitivity to the needs and insights of others.

Communication of any depth or significance is difficult if the people involved have little open area in common. In any relationship you hope to

unknown area

the part of the self that is unknown to oneself and others

The media have participated in a number of "outings"—that is, exposing the homosexuality of persons who until then had kept their sexual preferences a secret. In effect, the media have moved information from the hidden area of these persons into the open area without the permission of the persons being "outed." In your opinion, should anyone other than you ever be in control of what you reveal to or conceal from others?

Which style appears to be most characteristic of you and the people you interact with?

Media images may influence dress and self-expression. What image do you think this person is attempting to portray?

Skill
BUILDER

Symbolizing the Self

Take four objects to class. The first object should reveal something about the way you see yourself, something you believe everyone recognizes about you. In other words, it should represent an aspect of your open area. The second object should reveal something about you that up until this point you believe resided in your hidden area. This second object could symbolize an attitude, feeling, desire, or fear that you had hoped to keep from others but are now willing to move into the open pane. The third object you bring to class should represent how you believe another person sees you. For example, do you believe that a friend or relative sees you as you see yourself? How do you

think your perceptions are similar? How are they different?

Finally, after selecting these three objects, ask someone else to choose an object that represents his or her perception of you. Take this fourth object to class along with the other three. Be prepared to discuss how your perceptions of yourself and the other person's perception of you conflict or coincide. For example, did the object selected by the other person help you move information from the blind area to the open area? To what extent has each phase of the experience altered the appearance of your Johari window?

sustain, your goal should be to increase the size of the open area while decreasing the size of the hidden, blind, and unknown areas. As human beings we are thinking about others and that they think about us. The question is whether we are able and willing to share what we are thinking.

MANAGING IMPRESSIONS

It is normal for us to want to present ourselves to others in desirable ways. However, this leads us to ask some questions: When we say something publicly, do we always feel it privately? Do we present a different self than we feel?

When we create a positive image of ourselves in order to influence what others think of us and how they view us, we are practicing **impression management.** Among the strategies we use to manage the impressions others have of us are *self-enhancement* (we bolster our own image) and *other-enhancement* (we bolster the image of others).

According to sociologist Erving Goffman, we use **facework** to present a public image, our *presenting self,* that is as favorable as possible to others. Our front-stage behavior, Goffman suggests, may contrast with our back-stage behavior, the behavior we exhibit when we are alone.[53] Does your experience support this?

SELF-CONCEPT AND TECHNOLOGY

If you're interested in honing the impression you make on others, computer-mediated communication might give you an advantage. After all, the computer gives you more control over what information you choose to reveal to others and what information you decide to keep hidden from others. For example, e-mail enables you to edit the messages you send until you create one that will succeed in communicating the impression you desire. It gives you the ability to correct what you say and take back a message by not sending it. "Some communicators just do better when they can push the delete key."[54] Online you can also deliver messages that it might be too difficult to deliver, were you face-to-face, especially if you are shy. And if the receiver doesn't like the message you send, he or she can ignore it rather than have to walk away or insult you, were she or he in your presence.

The Internet may also be a factor in influencing the way we think of ourselves. If we have a positive self-concept, we are probably better able to adapt to both the rapid changes and the technological innovations of our world. Some use the Internet to see themselves differently. Do you? The Internet makes it possible for us to inhabit virtual worlds, participate in simulations, and assume different personae. A Pew Internet and American Life Project survey revealed, for example, that teenagers in the United States typically have more than one e-mail address or screen name. Many adopt multiple personae to hide their real identity from friends or strangers. A large number of people experiment online by pretending to be those whom they are not. They provide fake personal data in their e-mails or instant messages. In effect, they use the Internet to try out new identities.[55] By constructing a number of imaginary selves and experimenting with different kinds of social relationships, they are able to explore unexplored aspects of themselves. They might, for example, pretend to be the opposite sex, conceal or reveal their culture or where they live, and gloat as they hide any number of physical or psychological characteristics. Who we are online can simply be whom we construct or who we want to be for the moment. Instead of playing the roles we play in real life when we make breakfast as a parent, go to work as an employee, or attend school as a student, when online we might simultaneously play a number of varied roles that facilitate our thinking about ourselves in different ways. Because we are able to remain anonymous, we feel freer to cycle through many selves in an effort to construct and reconstruct our identity and assume roles that we otherwise would consider not part of our "real self."[56]

impression management
the creation of a positive image designed to influence others

facework
the means used to present a public image

Do you ever find yourself doing things in private, such as making faces at yourself in a mirror, that you would never think about doing in front of other people?

What if you were given the opportunity to design a personal Web site whose function was to communicate you to all who accessed the site? The persons who opened your site might be friends you already know or faceless, anonymous strangers. What aspects of yourself would you focus on? What facets would you ignore? How much would you reveal about you on the site? Would you include pictures or leave them out? To what extent, if any, do you think that having a personal Web site enhances your ability to manage better the identity you present to others?

"On the Internet, nobody knows you're a dog."

Have you ever been anyone but yourself online? If so, what prompted you to adopt an alternative identity? If you spoke with people online whom you later discovered were not who they represented themselves to be, how did you feel? What did you do?

Psychologist Sherry Turkle notes that, in an online world, "The obese can be slender, the beautiful plain, the 'nerdy' sophisticated."[57] Thus, for some people, communicating online gives them an opportunity to feel more positive about themselves.[58] In addition, some researchers believe that online interaction can affect psychological health. While some researchers believe Internet use correlates positively with depression and loneliness, others contend that it decreases them and actually enhances self-esteem.[59] In your opinion, is an online persona an extension of who you are in real life? Is it part of the real you or completely separate and distinct from your real-life self?

e-SEARCH

Where Do You Feel Freer to Be You?

Consider the following comment by a woman who is about to come face-to-face with a man whom she met online:

I didn't exactly lie to him about anything specific, but I feel very different online. I am a lot more outgoing, less inhibited. I would say I feel more like myself. But that's a contradiction. I feel more like who I wish I was. I'm just hoping that face-to-face I can find a way to spend some time being the online me.[60]

To what extent, if any, is the computer changing the way you think and feel about yourself? In which environment, real or virtual, do you feel freer to experiment with who you are and who you can be? Why? What about that environment causes you to feel that way? Be specific. In your opinion, is the Internet an effective social laboratory for self-discovery? Explain with reference to specific sites and personal experiences.

IMPROVING SELF-AWARENESS AND AWARENESS OF OTHERS

Throughout this chapter, we have stressed that we all carry figurative pictures of ourselves and others with us wherever we go. Together, these pictures form a mental collage. Contained within the collage are past, present, and future images of ourselves—alone or interacting with other people. If you closely examine your various images, you probably will be able to discern that how you look in each is related to when the picture was taken, what environment you were in, and with whom you were communicating. Each picture reveals a somewhat different you, because you change and grow from moment to moment, situation to situation, and year to year.

We sometimes forget that our self-image and our images of others can change. Keeping "self-pictures" updated and current is a challenge. Sharpening a fuzzy image, refocusing an old image, and developing a new image are processes that can help you discard worn-out or inaccurate perceptions of yourself and others. The following guidelines can be used to improve the "picture-taking" skills you have gained while working your way through this chapter.

Take Pictures of Yourself and Others

You can increase your self-awareness by continuing to take the time to examine your self-image and your relationship to others. Developing a clear sense of who you are is one of the most worthwhile goals you can set for yourself. Be willing to watch yourself in action. Periodically examine your own self-perceptions—and your self-misconceptions.

Study the composite picture that emerges from your reflections. How close are you to becoming the person you would like to be? You should take enough time and develop enough courage and open-mindedness to engage in productive and worthwhile self-examination.

Encourage Others to Take Pictures of You

How others perceive you may be very different from how you perceive yourself. Obtaining information from others can help you assess how realistic your self-concept is. Others who come to know you may observe strengths you have overlooked, traits you undervalue, or weaknesses you choose to ignore. However, you do not have to accept all the pictures other people take of you.

No one can prevent you from adhering to your own beliefs and rejecting the opinions of others. Looking at other people's pictures of you does mean, however, that you are at least opening yourself to the possibility of change by attempting to see yourself as others see you.

Refocus, Refocus, Refocus

Carl Sandburg wrote, "Life is like an onion; you peel off one layer at a time." As you move from yesterday through today and into tomorrow, your self is in constant transition. Try not to let your view of yourself today prevent you from adapting to meet the demands of changing circumstances and conditions. Continually formulating new answers to the question "Who am I?" will allow you to discover the vibrant, flexible, and dynamic qualities of your self.

THE Wrap-Up

Thinking CRITICALLY

Reflect and Respond

First, agree or disagree with the following statement; state the reasons for your response.

I may not be what I think I am. I may not be what you think I am. I may well be what I think you think I am.

Then, consider this: Each of your friends, relatives, and co-workers probably sees you as a somewhat different person. Write a paragraph that describes your perception of how one person from each of these groups sees you. Who has the most positive view of you? Whose view, in your opinion, is most accurate? Why?

Revisiting Chapter Objectives

1. **Define and explain the formation of the self-concept.** Self-concept is the entire collection of attitudes and beliefs you hold about who and what you are. It is the mental picture you have of yourself. It can be positive or negative, accurate or inaccurate. Your self-concept influences all aspects of your communicative behavior—with whom, where, why, and how you choose to communicate.

2. **Identify how popular culture and technology help shape your self-concept.** You are not born with a self-concept. Rather, your self-concept is shaped by your environment, by its technology, and by those around you, including your parents, relatives, instructors, supervisors, friends, and co-workers. In addition, television and films, self-expectations and other people's expectations, gender, and culture can shape your opinion of who you are.

3. **Define *self-fulfilling prophecy* and explain how a self-fulfilling prophecy can influence behavior.** Your self-concept can also be affected by what is known as a self-fulfilling prophecy. A self-fulfilling prophecy occurs when prior expectations of an event help create the very conditions that permit the event to occur. The media, as well as other people, help determine which self-fulfilling prophecies you experience.

4. **Compare and contrast the ways males and females as well as people from different cultures see themselves.** Conditions and circumstances affect the nature of the self. Sometimes it seems that we become different selves as we move from situation to situation; our demeanor is affected by our perceptions of others and how we imagine they perceive us. Our culture and our gender also affect the way we see ourselves.

5. **Identify the purposes and functions of the Johari window as a model of self-disclosure.** You can change and improve your self-concept by developing greater self-awareness and self-understanding. The Johari window can help you identify the open, blind, hidden, and unknown areas of your self.

Resources for Further Inquiry and Reflection

To apply your understanding of how the principles in Chapter 3 are at work in our daily lives, consult the following resources for further inquiry and reflection. Or, if you prefer, choose any other appropriate resource. Then connect the ideas expressed in your chosen selection with the communication concepts and issues you are learning about both in and out of class.

 ### Listen to Me

"Beautiful" (Christina Aguilera)   "Hands" (Jewel)
"I'm a Loser" (Beck)   "Kim" (Eminem)
"Human Nature" (Madonna)   "Unpretty" (TLC)
"Eleanor Rigby" (The Beatles)

The speaker or speakers in these songs express beliefs about how communication affects the self. Choose a song, and use it to explain the interaction between communication and self-concept.

 ### View Me

Beautiful   *The Truth about Cats and*
Girl Fight   *Dogs*
Hoop Dreams   *American Beauty*
The Talented Mr. Ripley   *Shrek*

How do the incidents described in the film enhance your understanding of self-concept and its influence on person-to-person interaction?

 ### Read Me

What do the following two cartoons suggest about the self-concepts of males and females? Which do you believe is more accurate? Why?

Tell Me

Share with the class the insights you gained from your chosen Listen to Me, View Me, or Read Me selection.

Women and men spend more on cosmetics and body alterations today than was spent in 1970, yet the number of women and men unhappy with their appearance has increased and will probably continue to do so. In a brief presentation, agree or disagree with this statement, with reasons.

"I know I'm wrong, but I'm sure you can make me more wrong."

Key Chapter Terminology

Communication
Works

online learning center

www.mhhe.com/gamble8

Use the Communication Works CD-ROM and the Online Learning Center at www.mhhe.com/gamble8 *to further your knowledge of the following terminology.*

allocentric 66	open area 69
blind area 70	Pygmalion effect 63
distinctiveness theory 66	self-concept 53
facework 73	self-disclosure 70
Galatea effect 64	self-efficacy 59
hidden area 70	self-esteem 53
idiocentric 66	self-fulfilling prophecy 62
impression management 73	self-image 53
Johari window 69	unknown area 71

Test Your Understanding

Communication
Works

online learning center

www.mhhe.com/gamble8

Go to the *Self Quizzes* on the Communication Works CD-ROM and the book's Online Learning Center at www.mhhe.com/gamble8.

Notes

1. See Maureen Stout. *The Feel-Good Curriculum: The Dumbing Down of America's Kids in the Name of Self-Esteem.* New York: Perseus Books, 2000; and Mary Amoroso. "Is Self-Esteem Overrated?" *The Record,* April 27, 2000, pp. HF-1, HF-3.
2. Adam Bryant. "America's Latest Fad: Modesty It's Not." *New York Times,* February 9, 1997, p. E-3.
3. Kevin Kilbane. "This Girl Got Her Wish." Knight-Ridder News Service. December 23, 1993.
4. See www.self-esteem-nase.org.
5. Erica Goode. "Deflating Self-Esteem's Role in Society's Ills," *New York Times,* October 1, 2002, pp. F1, F6.
6. Lauren Slater. "The Trouble with Self-Esteem," *New York Times Magazine,* February 3, 2002, pp. 44–47.
7. Michele Orecklin, "Beware of the in Crowd," *Time,* August 21, 2000, p. 69.
8. R. Baumeister, L. Smart, and J. Boden. "Relation of the Threatened Egotism to Violence and Aggressions: The Dark Side of High Self-Esteem," *Psychological Review* 103, 1996, pp. 5–33.
9. B. Bushman and R. Baumeister. "Threatened Egotism, Narcissism, Self-Esteem, and Direct and Displaced Aggression: Does Self-Love or Self-Hate Lead to Violence?" *Journal of Personality and Social Psychology* 75, 1998, pp. 219–229.
10. R. Brooks and S. Goldstein. *Raising Resilient Children.* New York: Contemporary Books, 2001.
11. Virginia Satir. *The New Peoplemaking,* 2nd ed. Palo Alto, CA: Science and Behavior Books, 1988.
12. C. Mruk. *Self Esteem: Research, Theory, and Practice.* New York: Springer, 1995.
13. See James Baron. "Who Are You? If You Had to Choose One Word That Best Defined You and Your Life, What Word Would It Be?" *New York Times,* February 13, 1994, sec. 9, pp. 1, 7.
14. See D. Hamacheck. *Encounters with the Self,* 3rd ed. Fort Worth: Holt, Rinehart & Winston, 1992, pp. 5–8.
15. S. I. Hayakawa and Alan R. Hayakawa. *Language in Thought and Action,* 5th ed. San Diego: Harcourt Brace Jovanovich, 1990, pp. 217–218.

16. Justine Coupland, John F. Nussbaum, and Nikolas Coupland. "The Reproduction of Aging and Ageism in Intergenerational Talk." In Nikolas Coupland, Howard Giles, and John Wiemann, eds. *Miscommunication and Problematic Talk.* Newbury Park, CA: Sage, 1991, p. 85.

17. Don Tapscott. *Growing Up Digital: The Rise of the Net Generation.* New York: McGraw-Hill, 1998, p. 90.

18. A. Gerike. *Old Is Not a Four-Letter Word: A Midlife Guide.* Watsonville, CA: Papier Mache Press, 1997.

19. See Jean Piaget. *The Construction of Reality in the Child.* New York: Free Press, 1954.

20. See also Sherry Turkel. *Life on the Screen.* New York: Simon & Schuster, 1995.

21. See A. Bandura. *Self-Efficacy: The Exercise of Control.* New York: Freeman, 1997.

22. Martin E. P. Seligman. Interview in *Success,* July–August 1994, p. 41.

23. Don Tapscott. *Growing Up Digital: The Rise of the Net Generation.* New York. McGraw-Hill, 1998.

24. Linda Temple. "Is Barbie's Pal an Insult or an Inspiration?" *USA Today.* May 30, 1997, p. 7D.

25. Janelle Carter. "Barbie's Newest Friend Uses a Hot-Pink Wheelchair." *The Record,* May 22, 1997, p. A-17.

26. Temple.

27. Carl Sandburg. *The People, Yes.* New York: Harcourt Brace Jovanovich, 1936.

28. Robert Rosenthal and Lenore Jacobson. *Pygmalion in the Classroom.* New York: Holt, Rinehart & Winston, 1968.

29. R. Rosenthal in J. Aronson, ed. *Improving Academic Achievement: Impact of Psychological Factors on Education.* San Diego: Academic Press, 2002, pp. 25–36.

30. Myra and David Sadker. *Failing at Fairness: How America's Schools Cheat Girls.* New York: Scribner's, 1994, p. 1.

31. See, for example, P. Watzlawick. "Self-Fulfilling Prophecies." In J. O'Brien and P. Kollock, eds. *The Production of Reality,* 3rd ed. Thousand Oaks, CA: Pine Forge Press, 2001, pp. 411–423.

32. J. Sterling Livingston. Cited in video, *The Self-Fulfilling Prophecy.* CRM Films, 1992.

33. David Firestone. "While Barbie Talks Tough, G.I. Joe Goes Shopping." *New York Times,* December 31, 1993, p. A-12.

34. T. F. Cash. "Development Teasing about Physical Appearance: Retrospective Descriptions and Relationships with Body Image." *Social Behavior and Personality* 23, 1995, pp. 123–130.

35. Dave Barry, "Beauty and the Beast," *Miami Herald,* January 30, 1998.

36. Diane Hales. *Just Like a Woman.* New York: Bantam, 1999, p. 136.

37. Julia T. Wood. *Gendered Lives: Communication, Gender and Culture.* Belmont, CA: Wadsworth, 1994, p. 21.

38. John Gray. *Men Are from Mars, Women Are from Venus: A Practical Guide for Improving Communication and Getting What You Want in Your Relationships.* New York: Harper-Collins, 1992, pp. 16–22.

39. See Sally Quinn. "Look Out, It's Superwoman." *Newsweek,* February 15, 1993, pp. 24–25.

40. Richard Breslin. *Understanding Culture's Influence on Behavior.* Orlando, FL: Harcourt Brace Jovanovich, 1993, p. 47.

41. "Hey, I'm Terrific." *Newsweek,* February 17, 1992, p. 48.

42. Steven J. Heine. "Self as Cultural Product: An Examination of East Asian and North American Selves." *Journal of Personality* 69:6, December 2001, pp. 881–906.

43. Ibid.

44. Larry Samovar and Richard Porter. *Communication between Cultures.* Belmont, CA: Wadsworth, 1991, p. 91.

45. W. B. Gudykunst and S. Ting Toomy. *Culture and Interpersonal Communication.* Newbury Park, CA: Sage, 1988.

46. H. C. Triandis, K. Leung, and F. Clark. "Allocentric v. Idiocentric Tendencies." *Journal of Research in Personality* 19, pp. 395–415.

47. O. Appiah. "Americans Online: Differences in Surfing and Evaluating Race-Targeted Web Sites by Black and White Users." Paper presented at the annual meeting of the Association for Education in Journalism and Mass Communication. Miami, FL, August 2002.

48. P. Orenstein. *School Girls: Young Women, Self-Esteem, and the Confidence Gap.* New York: Anchor Books, 1994.

49. From "In Truth, Most of Them May Not Be Lonely." *New York Times,* May 9, 1991, p. A-24.

50. Robert A. Bell and Michael E. Roloff. "Making a Love Connection: Loneliness and Communication Competence in the Dating Marketplace." *Communication Quarterly* 39, no. 1, winter 1991, p. 58.

51. Joseph Luft. *Group Processes: An Introduction to Group Dynamics,* 2nd ed. Palo Alto, CA: Mayfield, 1970.

52. John Powell. *Why Am I Afraid to Tell You Who I Am?* New York: Tabor, 1982.

53. See E. Goffman. *The Presentation of Self in Everyday Life.* Garden City, NY: Doubleday, 1959, and *Relations in Public.* New York: Basic Books, 1971.

54. A. Markham. *Life Online: Researching Real Experience in Virtual Space.* Walnut Creek, CA: Alta Mira Press, 1998, pp. 202–203.

55. A. Lenhart, L. Rainie, and O. Lewis. *Teenage Life Online.* Washington, DC: Pew Internet and American Life Project, 2001.

56. Turkle, pp. 14, 178.

57. Turkle, p. 12.

58. John A. Bargh, Y. A. Katelyn McKenna, and Grainne M. Fitzsimons. "Can You See the Real Me? Activation and Expression of the 'True Self' on the Internet." *Journal of Social Issues* 58:1, January 2002, pp. 33–49.

59. See, for example, Larry M. Gant. "In Defense of the Internet: The Relationship between Internet Communication and Depression, Loneliness, Self-Esteem, and Perceived Social Support." *CyberPsychology and Behavior* 5:2, April 2002, pp. 157–172.

60. Turkle, p. 179.

CHAPTER 4

Communication and Perception: I Am More Than a Camera

1. Explain why a person is more than a camera.

2. Define and explain how the following affect perception: the figure-ground principle, selective exposure, selective perception, closure, stereotyping, open and closed orientation, and first impressions.

3. Describe how past experience, gender, cultural background, the media, and technology can influence perception.

4. Define and provide examples of allness, blindering, and facts and inferences.

5. Identify ways to increase the accuracy of your perceptions.

If, to people, crickets appear to hear with their legs, it is possible that to crickets, people appear to walk on their ears.

—**Anonymous**

As I am, so I see.

—**Ralph Waldo Emerson**

While the following geographically based descriptions of people are meant to be humorous, they do help us understand the perceptual differences that color communication. How many of these do you agree with? What do they suggest to you about the nature of perception?

You live in California when . . .

- The high school quarterback calls a time-out to answer his cell phone.
- You know how to eat an artichoke.

You live in New York when . . .

- You say "the city" and expect everyone to know you mean Manhattan.
- You think eye contact is an act of aggression.

You live in the Deep South when . . .

- "Ya'll" is singular and "all ya'll" is plural.
- After five years you still hear, "You ain't from 'round here, are ya?"

You live in the Midwest when . . .

- Your idea of a traffic jam is 10 cars waiting to pass a tractor.
- You've never met any celebrities, but the mayor knows your name.

Go to the *Online Learning Center* at www.mhhe.com/gamble8 and answer the questions in the *Self Inventory* to evaluate your understanding of perceptual differences.

As the preceding descriptions suggest, a perceptual gulf may exist among persons who live in different regions of the United States.

A perceptual gulf may also exist among persons living in different regions of the world or different countries. There may well be a "geography of thought."[1] Persons living in different countries interpret events differently. On September 11, 2001, not just people in the United States but people throughout the world watched the unbelievable news that terrorists had turned planes into bombs and crashed into the World Trade Center in New York City and the Pentagon in Washington, DC. After this occurred, the world media, including South and North Korean news agencies, reported on the attacks. Even though South and North Korea reported on the same attack, because of their very different relationships with the United States—only one is an ally—their perceptions of what had occurred differed. It appears that media companies tend to report international events from the same perspective as their government's foreign policy.[2] Like North and South Korea, Americans and residents of predominantly Islamic countries differ dramatically on everything from who carried out the September 11th terrorist attacks to whether the United States is a friendly nation. Although most Americans perceive their own country as trustworthy, friendly, caring about poorer nations, and respectful of Islamic values, many people living in Muslim countries perceive just the opposite.[3] This perceptual gulf also made itself apparent in news coverage of the war against Iraq. The United States and the Arab world watched and reported different wars. Press coverage of the war tended to mirror ideology.

Perceptual differences may also exist between people who were born into different generations. For example, if you were born after 1984, your lifetime has always included AIDS; "The Day After" is a pill to you, not a movie; the United States and Russia have always been partners in space; Ozzy's lifestyle has nothing to do with the Nelson family; cyberspace has always existed; the United States has always maintained that it has a "clear right to use force against terrorism"; hip-hop and rap have always been popular musical forms; and there has always been MTV.[4]

Like geography and time, race or culture can also influence perception. For example, the front cover of one major city's daily newspaper depicted 15 photos of fugitives wanted for murder by that city's police department. The suspects featured on the cover were all African-American, Hispanic, or Asian-American. Although there also were a number of Caucasians who were among the fugitives on the loose, none were pictured on the paper's cover. Why is this? Could racial profiling be a factor? Consider the advertisement on page 84 describing a contrast in perceptions that appeared in an array of publications. What does it reveal about perception? Unfortunately racial stereotypes precipitate racial profiling.[5] For too many years, police have stopped drivers based on their skin color rather than how they were driving. Consider that Aquil Abdullah, an American rowing champion, was not permitted to board his plane at Newark's Liberty International Airport because he had a common Muslim name.[6] What does it reveal about perception?

Although the Hispanic population of the United States has increased 58 percent since 1990 to over 35 million, Hispanics continue to be marginalized on evening news programs. Out of 16,000 stories that aired on four networks—NBC, ABC, CBS, and CNN—only 99 of them—less than 1 percent—were about Hispanics. Racially and ethnically insensitive news coverage patterns are all too common. Race and ethnicity influence interpretation.[7]

While African-American motorists represent a minority of the drivers and speeders on interstate highways, they have been stopped and searched by state police more often. What do you think accounts for this?

Which man looks guilty? If you picked the man on the right, you're wrong. Wrong for judging people based on the color of their skin. Because if you look closely, you'll see they're the same man. Unfortunately, racial stereotyping like this happens every day. On America's highways, police stop drivers based on their skin color rather than for the way they are driving. For example, in Florida 80% of those stopped and searched were black and Hispanic, while they constituted only 5% of all drivers. These humiliating and illegal searches are violations of the Constitution and must be fought. Help us defend your rights. Support the ACLU. www.aclu.org **american civil liberties union**

What if you woke up tomorrow as a person of a race or ethnicity different from your own? How do you imagine your view of your life and the world would change? Would a change in age affect you the same way? What about a change in gender?[8]

Complicating perception still further is the reality that, even when we witness an event, we don't all necessarily experience or see the same thing. When hundreds of people watched the crash of American Airlines Flight 587 near Kennedy International Airport in New York on November 12, 2002, they apparently saw hundreds of different things. Thus, according to the National Transportation Safety Board, which interviewed 349 eye witnesses of the crash, 52 percent of those interviewed said they saw a fire while the plane was in the air. Twenty-two percent of those said the fire was in the fuselage, but a majority cited other locations on the plane. While 20 percent of the witnesses said they saw the plane make a right turn, another 20 percent said it was a left turn.[9]

The realization that we operate from an array of disparate frames of reference may help us answer questions such as these: Why do the members of different groups see things so differently? How can we account for the gulf in perceptions? Why is it that "seeing isn't believing"? Can we ever believe our own eyes?

In this chapter, we will attempt to answer questions about perception as we explore how we perceive our world and the people in it. By learning more about the process of perception, we will prepare ourselves to better handle the continuing problems posed by perceptual variations. By exploring why stimuli appear different to each of us, we will better understand why we think and act differently as well. Only by getting behind the "I" of the eye do we put ourselves in a position to understand why "where we stand depends on where we sit."[10] Or, as a Chinese proverb suggests, "Two thirds of what we see is behind our eyes."

WHAT IS PERCEPTION?

Perception is a complex process. Certainly we use our senses to perceive, but perception includes more than just the eye alone, more than just the ear alone, more than just the nose alone, more than just the skin alone, and more than just the tongue alone. What occurs in the "real world" may be quite different from what we perceive to occur. During the process of perception, we make experience our own. Keeping this in mind, we can define **perception** as the process of selecting, organizing, and subjectively interpreting sensory data in a way that enables us to make sense of our world.

perception
the process by which we make sense out of experience

Perceiving Stimuli: The "Eye" and the "I"

In many ways, we all inhabit different worlds. We view reality from different angles, perspectives, or vantage points. Our physical location, our interests, our personal desires, our attitudes, our values, our personal experiences, our physical condition, and our psychological states all interact to influence our judgments or perceptions.

How do you absorb information from the world around you? Do you look and listen? Do you touch, taste, and smell your environment and those who interact in it? Certainly. Your senses function as perceptual antennae and gather information for you all the time.

However, it is impossible for you to internalize or process all the stimuli available to you. Without realizing it, you take steps to select or limit what you perceive. You will see this for yourself if you try the following test:

1. For the next 60 seconds, attempt to internalize everything that exists in the room you now inhabit. Make an effort to react to each sound, sight, smell, touch, and taste that is present in your environment.

2. Were you able to focus simultaneously on each stimulus or sensory experience, or did you find yourself skipping from one stimulus to another and back again?

Most probably, you found yourself switching between stimuli; thus, you are aware that you simply cannot effectively handle, or process, all the sensory experiences that compete for your attention. Information theorists tell us that the eye can process about 5 million bits of data per second; they also tell us that the brain can utilize only some 500 bits per second. We are therefore forced to identify or select those stimuli we will attend to or experience. By exhibiting **selective perception**—that is, by focusing on particular stimuli while ignoring others—we create a more limited but more coherent and meaningful picture of our world, one that conforms to our beliefs, expectations, and convictions.

selective perception
the means of interpreting experience in a way that conforms to one's beliefs, expectations, and convictions

Perceptual processes are not only highly selective but also personally based. For this reason, different people experience the same cues in very different ways. Thus, we never really come into direct contact with reality.[11] Instead, everything we experience is manufactured by the nervous system.

Organizing Stimuli: The "I" of the Beholder

We have said that perception provides each of us with a unique view of the world—a view sometimes related to, but not necessarily identical with, that held by others. Since we cannot actually become one with the world out there, we are forced to use our senses to help create a personal picture of the people

Do different people perceive you differently? Why?

"Wernock, here, sees your suit as half empty, but I see it as half full."

and objects that surround us. How do we make sense of our world? How do we process the stimuli that compete for our attention?

During the perception process, we are active, not passive, participants. We do not simply relax and absorb stimuli available to us, the way a sponge absorbs liquid. We select, we organize, and we evaluate the multitude of stimuli that bombard us, so that what we focus on becomes figure and the rest of what we experience becomes ground.[12] This is how the **figure-ground principle** functions.

figure-ground principle

a strategy that facilitates the organization of stimuli by enabling us to focus on different stimuli alternately

To experience the concept of figure and ground, examine Figure 4.1. What do you see? At first glance, you probably see a vase—or you may see

FIGURE 4.1

Figure and Ground. Do you see a vase or two people?

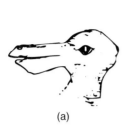

(a)

(b)

Source: Mitsuko Saito-Fakunage, "General Semantics and Intercultural Communication," *ETC,* Vol. 46, no. 4, Winter 1989, p.27. Reprinted by permission of the International Society for General Semantics.

FIGURE 4.2
Figure-Ground Illustrations:
(a) Duck or Rabbit?
(b) Eskimo or Indian?

two people facing each other. When stimuli compete for your attention, you can focus on only one, because it is simply impossible to perceive something in two ways at once. Although you may be able to switch your focus rapidly, you will still perceive only one stimulus at any given time. The same holds true for Figure 4.2. When you look at Figure 4.2(a), you may see a duck, a rabbit, or both alternately. In Figure 4.2(b), you may see the profile of an Indian, the back of an Eskimo walking away, or both alternately.

In addition to using the principle of figure-ground as an organizing strategy, we also use **closure**—the tendency to fill in missing perceptual pieces. Look at the stimuli pictured in Figure 4.3. What do you see? Most see a dog rather than a collection of inkblots and a rectangle, triangle, and circle rather than some lines and an arc. Because we seek to fill in gaps, we mentally complete the incomplete figures. We fill them in on the basis of our previous

closure

the means we use to perceive a compete world

FIGURE 4.3
Test for Closure.

experiences and our needs. We make sense of relationships and events in much the same way. We fill in what isn't there by making assumptions, or inferences—some of which are more accurate and valid than others.

Processing Stimuli: The "I's" Memories

As we see, perception involves a series of stages: (1) the selecting stage, during which we attend to only some stimuli from all those to which we are exposed; (2) the organizing stage, during which we give order to the selected stimuli; and (3) the interpreting/evaluating stage, during which we make sense of or give meaning to the stimuli we have selected and organized based on our life experiences (See Figure 4.4). Perception also involves a fourth stage, the responding stage, during which we decide what to think, say, or do as a result of what we have perceived. How we interpret and respond to selected stimuli also determines whether or not a particular person or experience enters our memory. If a perception does enter our memory, we can retrieve it at another point in time. Whether or not our memory is reliable, however, depends on whether our reconstruction of experience is accurate and clear. Our perceptual abilities influence how we interpret and remember events. For example, many Americans have memories of September 11, 2001. In interviews, when asked to recall those memories, many Americans spoke of watching television all morning, riveted to the TV by images of the two planes striking the twin towers. Their memory of what they think they witnessed is false. There was no video that day of the first plane hitting the World Trade Center. Despite this, 76 percent of New Yorkers surveyed said they saw

FIGURE 4.4
Stages of Perception.

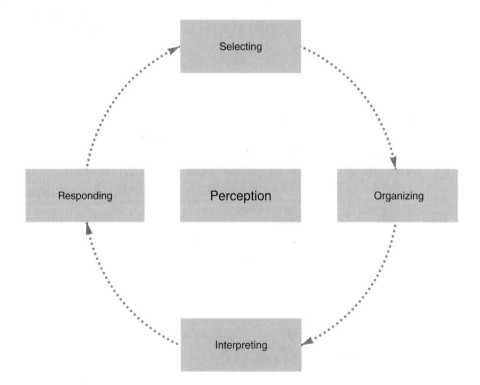

it on September 11, as did 73 percent of people nationwide. What is more, they were confident about their memories. Memory, however, is a human construct, an amalgam of what we experience, read, piece together, and want to be true. Again, we see that eyewitness recall may be fallible. There is little correlation between confidence and accuracy when it comes to memory. At least some of what we think is true is actually false.[13]

CULTURE, GENDER, AND PERCEPTION: INTERPRETING THROUGH DIFFERENT "I"S

There is more to perception than meets the eye. We see the world not necessarily as we are but as we have been conditioned to see it. Our culture, our gender, and our past experiences precipitate in us a preference for **perceptual constancy**—the desire to see exactly as we have seen in the past. Thus, many of our perceptions are learned. The more similar our life experiences, the more similarly we will perceive the world. The more dissimilar our life experiences, the wider the gap between us and others with respect to the way we view things.[14] Not everyone perceives things the same way we do. Cultural habits or selectivities see to that.

perceptual constancy
the desire to perceive experience exactly as we have perceived it in the past

Culture and Perception

Culture teaches us how to perceive. For example, when looking at configurations created by the craters on the moon, North Americans see a man, while Native Americans report a rabbit, the Chinese a lady fleeing her spouse, and Samoans a woman weaving.[15] Whether we are judging beauty, describing snow, or evaluating a child's behavior, our culture influences our assessment of reality. Individuals from different cultures are simply trained to regard the

Have you ever considered why the United States almost always appears in the center in our maps of the world? Is there any geographical reason for this? Or could it be an example of ethnocentrism on the part of mapmakers and users?

Through the Eyes of the Beholder

The defendant, 12-year-old Raymond Thomas, had shot 16-year-old Reggie Haines. How do you teach a 12-year-old defendant a lesson he will never forget? One judge devised a novel sentence in an effort to accomplish that objective. Circuit Judge Lynn Tepper imposed a sentence that required 12-year-old Thomas to get a feel for what life was now like for his gunshot victim. As punishment for shooting Haines point-blank in the forehead, Judge Tepper ordered that Thomas first serve time in a wheelchair, then that he use a walker, and finally that he walk with a cane. The judge told Thomas:

"You're going to be moving around in Reggie's world, which you created. You

will go to the bathroom in a wheelchair. You will get in and out of bed, eat, try to drink from the water fountain in a wheelchair." The judge continued, *"Perhaps you will appreciate what Reggie had to go through to get where he is today, which is a miracle."*[16]

What message is the judge's sentence designed to communicate? In your opinion, is the punishment ethical? Why or why not? Do you believe that Raymond Thomas will perceive the judge's message as intended? In addition, will the sentence enable Raymond Thomas to perceive what Reggie is really going through?

Ethics &
COMMUNICATION

same cues differently; they interpret what they perceive through a cultural lens. For example, some years ago, researchers used a binocular-like apparatus to compare the perceptual preferences of Native Americans and Mexicans. Each subject was shown 10 pairs of photographs—in each pair, one photo displayed a picture from U.S. culture and, the other photo, a picture from Mexican culture. After viewing the paired images through the binocular-like device, the subjects reported their observations. Results showed that both the Native Americans and the Mexicans were more likely to report having seen a picture from their own culture.[17]

Similarly, culture teaches us to expect others to behave in certain ways when faced with specific conditions. Misunderstandings can result, however,

Focus on Service Learning

What perceptional understandings must a local charity have in order to attract more diverse supporters?

EXPLORING

Diversity

Side by Side

"The National Study of the Changing Work Force," a report issued by the Families and Work Institute, notes that, contrary to expectations, younger employees are unprepared to work in a diverse workplace.

The report, based on interviews with almost 3,000 workers, pointed out that employees under age 25 showed no greater preference than older employees for working with people of other races, ages, or ethnic groups. Just over half of the surveyed workers of all ages said they prefer working with people of the same race, gender, and educational level.

Despite this finding, according to diversity expert Robert Lattimer, when they are used, "diverse employee teams tend to outperform homogeneous teams of any composition. Homogeneous groups may reach consensus more quickly but are not able to generate new ideas or solve problems as well because their collective perspective is narrower."[18]

Compile a list of other reasons a diverse group might outperform a homogeneous one. How, for example, might diversity affect the group's perception of both the problem and its solution?

Diverse teams of employees frequently outperform homogeneous teams.

when each party in an interaction is operating according to different assumptions and rules. Consider, for example, a European-American teacher questioning an African-American student. As she answers the teacher, the African-American student may not make eye contact with him. Because of deficient eye contact, the teacher may evaluate the student's behavior as disrespectful and conclude that the student is hiding something from him. On the other hand, the student believes that, by keeping her eyes downcast when responding to the teacher's questions, she is not being rude but is displaying respect. That is, after all, what she has been taught to do.[19]

We have not all experienced the same lessons, and thus we do not attribute the same meanings to similar behavioral cues. When we fail to understand this concept, we exhibit **cultural nearsightedness.** As a result, we misread cues and miss opportunities to use the differences between us as a means to help ourselves perceive each other more clearly.

cultural nearsightedness
the failure to understand that we do not attribute the same meanings to similar behavioral clues

Gender and Perception

Like ethnicity, gender influences the interpretation of experience. Men and women perceive different realities, have different expectations set for them, and exhibit different communication styles. Beliefs regarding gender-appropriate behavior not only influence how men and women see each other but also affect how they relate to each other. From childhood on, both men and women are conditioned to use behaviors that conform to their gender: While men are rewarded for displaying strength and independence, women are reinforced for expressing their feelings and being nice to others. While women are categorized as emotional, men are classified as rational.[20]

Through interaction with parents, teachers, peers, and others, we internalize the lessons of appropriate male and female behavior. These lessons frame our perceptions and teach us how society expects us to behave. These constructs, however, can limit the way each gender is perceived and may lead to males and females being judged on the basis of gender expectations rather than observed cues. Perceived differences in male/female behavior develop as a result of the expectations of others, the behavior exhibited by role models, the traditional educational institutions that promote stereotyped notions of sex roles, and the media that send repeated confirmation of male/female stereotypes.[21] If we want to change the perception of the kinds of behavior appropriate for males and females, then we need to change the way they are categorized by society.

As we defy gender-based definitions, we help redefine them. Which, if any, have you helped to redefine?

As we perceive, we sort stimuli, selecting some and rejecting others. What we select and store in our internal database determines our view of reality and gives our lives a sense of stability. If, for example, we conclude that men are more dominant than women, then we feel we can more readily predict their actions and thus recategorize them as such. When expectations lead to misperceptions, undesirable consequences can result. All too frequently, rigid categorizing precipitates communication problems. For example, a recent *New York Times Magazine* contained a series of full-page photographs depicting women soldiers. Titled "Warrior Women," the series acknowledged the change in the Pentagon's perception regarding what positions women could serve.[22] Although still barred from roles that have specific physical requirements and from units primarily involved with front-line battle, because modern warfare

Are these women redefining a gender prescription? Will their behavior change how others perceive them?

may have no perceptible front line at all, women can come under attack and easily become casualties. Thus, the list of women injured or killed in combat situations is likely to rise. Are you perceptually ready for this change? Why or why not?

Similarly, criticisms of mass media productions often include a discussion of how women and minorities are systematically excluded and/or relegated to minor roles or roles that are consistent with traditional stereotypes. These portrayals reinforce perceptions that perpetuate racism and sexism.[23]

Individual men and women, however, can reject cultural prescriptions, and when they do so, they can elicit changes in the behavior of others toward them. As we defy a gender-based definition, we also help redefine it. When, for example, one woman encourages another to be more independent, she may help her friend expand her definition of behavior appropriate for women. As women change their behavior and roles, men may perceive them and themselves differently and may change as well. As we widen our perceptions of each other by experiencing a greater variety of situations and people, our expectations for each other may be altered, and our views of what males and females can do may be revised as well. In the process, what masculinity and femininity mean is recast.

BARRIERS TO PERCEPTION

Many variables affect us during the perceptual process, interacting to guide us in making our perceptual selections. Some of these constitute "barriers" to perception.

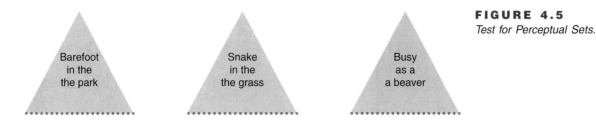

FIGURE 4.5
Test for Perceptual Sets.

Perceptual Sets: Is Your Past Following You?

Past experiences often provide us with expectations, or **perceptual sets,** that affect how we process our world. To better understand the concept of a perceptual set, quickly read the statements written in the triangles in Figure 4.5. Then examine the words more carefully. During your first reading, did you miss anything that you now perceive? Many people fail to see the second *the* or *a* in the statements on the first reading. Did you? Why? We are so accustomed to seeing words in familiar groups, or clusters, that often we simply fail to perceive a number of single words when we see them in such phrases. Faster, more accomplished readers make this mistake more readily than slower, less skillful readers.

Past experiences create perceptual sets in numerous ways. Sometimes culture is a factor. In Saudi Arabia, for example, the way women are raised influences how people both within that culture and outside it perceive them. In Saudi Arabia, women have few legal rights, are usually not permitted to drive a car, and need a man's permission to obtain a passport; clearly, the Saudis and Americans perceive women very differently.[24]

Motivation is another variable affecting our perceptual sets and thus our perception. Both hunger and poverty, for instance, can alter the way we interpret experience. In one study, researchers showed sailors some ambiguous pictures and asked them to describe what they saw. Sailors who were hungry "saw with the stomach"—to them, an elongated smudge looked like a fork, and a swirl looked like a fried onion. In a second study, rich and poor children were shown circles of various sizes and were asked which ones were the same size as certain coins. The poor children consistently chose circles that were much too large. Why? A quarter looks bigger to the poor than to the rich.[25]

Obviously, education is also an important part of our past experience. How much education and what kind of education we have had affect the way we process and perceive information.[26] For instance, you may find that your views of television and other media have changed since you were in grade school and that they will change again as you acquire additional education. (Young children, for example, view television commercials as absolute truths.) At times, education can become a barrier rather than a facilitator of or aid to perception. For example, when asked to interpret a stimulus as simple as a nursery rhyme or as complex as a world event, a sociologist, an economist, a political scientist, or a biologist might bring their specific professional bias to the assignment, which could blind them to other possible interpretations.

As is apparent, perceptual sets are the result of unique experiences. The lessons life has taught you necessarily differ from those life has taught others. As a result, people can perceive the same stimulus differently.

perceptual sets
expectations that produce a readiness to process experience in a predetermined way

Exploring Selectivities: Are You Open or Closed? Are You a Distorter?

selective exposure

the tendency to expose oneself to information that reinforces thinking

selective attention

the tendency to focus on certain cues and ignore others

selective retention

the tendency to remember those things that reinforce one's way of thinking and forget those that oppose one's way of thinking

Can you cite instances when you chose not to expose yourself to a certain stimulus or idea? Are there some subjects you would prefer not to know about? Are there some people you would just as soon avoid?

Four types of selectivity concern us: (1) **selective exposure**—the tendency to expose ourselves to information that reinforces rather than contradicts our thinking; (2) **selective attention**—the tendency to focus on certain cues and ignore others; (3) *selective perception*—the tendency to see, hear, and believe only what we want to; and (4) **selective retention**—the tendency to remember those things that reinforce our thinking and forget those that oppose our way of thinking.

A key factor in how we view our world is the extent to which we open ourselves to experiences. Although numerous sensory stimuli compete for our attention, we tend to practice selective exposure; we select only those experiences that reaffirm our existing attitudes, beliefs, and values. We likewise tend to ignore or diminish the significance of those experiences that are incongruent with our existing attitudes, beliefs, and values. Just as children sometimes place their hands over their ears to avoid hearing what a parent is saying, so we can select what we will perceive by deciding whether to expose ourselves to a variety of types and sources of information. When driving through poverty-stricken areas, for example, people often roll up their automobile windows. They tell themselves that they are doing this for self-protection, but rolling up the windows is also a means of self-deception that helps them avoid contact with some of the depressing sights and sounds of their society. Similarly, when it comes to selective exposure, conservatives are more apt to read the book *The Savage Nation* by radio talk show host Michael Savage than are liberals who are the favorite targets of the author. How difficult is it for you to expose yourself to certain new ideas, places, or experiences? As for selective attention, you are more apt to overhear someone seated near you speak of wanting to buy a home if you are a realtor than if you are in computer sales. Selective perception is a related concept. When it comes to selective perception, we tend to overlook negative qualities in persons we like, just as we tend to deemphasize the negative policies of institutions we support. We see what we want to see and hear what we want to hear. As a result of selective perception, different people may interpret the same message or event differently. Why do we distort stimuli until they conform to what we want or expect?

Each individual's perception of an event is influenced by his or her existing attitudes. Thus, out of the swirling mass of data available to us, we interpret and digest information that confirms our own beliefs, expectations, or convictions, and we reject information that contradicts them. Try viewing the same news broadcast with someone whose political views differ sharply from your own. How similar do you imagine your interpretations of the delivered information will be? Why?

Finally, our memories aid us in this process by enabling us to engage in selective recall—we recall better the positive qualities of persons we like and the negative qualities of persons we dislike. Perception is subjective. What we think about as well as what we think about one another are powerful forces.

As we see, these selective processes allow us to add, delete, or change stimuli, so that we can avoid dealing with certain information. Time and time again, past experiences, expectations, needs, and wants join forces to determine our present perceptions. Their effect is strengthened by our desire for closure, our desire to perceive a complete (and thus secure) world. What significance does this tendency to fill in missing information have for our everyday perceptions and interactions? How often do we find ourselves filling in "people gaps"? How often do we feel the need to make sense out of human actions and experiences by completing them as we would like to see them turn out? We all fill in the gaps about family members, friends, co-workers, and media personalities, such as sports personalities, film stars, and political figures, only to have our perceptions damaged or shattered by reality.

The reality is that we can bias the selection process and end up with quite a distorted view of the people in our lives as well as the world. For example, think about a relationship that has soured and that you are planning to terminate. Since making this decision, have you become more aware of qualities the person has that you do not like? Why do you suppose this is so? When we like or love someone, we tend to perceive primarily his or her positive qualities. This is called the **halo effect.** However, when our perception of another changes for the worse, we are more likely to see only his or her negative qualities. This is called the **horn effect.**

halo effect
the perceiving of qualities that are primarily positive

horn effect
the perceiving of qualities that are primarily negative

First Impressions: Do You Freeze Your Perceptions of Others?

It is important to realize that your perceptions of a person are a key determinant of the type of relationship you will share with him or her. On what basis do you form **first impressions,** or make initial judgments about the people you meet? What makes you decide if you like or dislike someone? Is it his or her economic status? Is it the job he or she holds? Perceiving others and the roles they play is an essential part of the communication process. We will explore how we form first impressions and why we sometimes stereotype other

first impressions
initial judgments about people

"You're not at all like your answering machine."

What's on First?

Person A. Read the following list of A's character traits to another person, in the order given:

1. Intelligent
2. Industrious
3. Impulsive
4. Critical
5. Stubborn
6. Envious

Ask that person to choose one word to represent his or her impression of A.

Person B. Next, read this list of B's character traits to another person, in the order given:

1. Envious
2. Stubborn
3. Critical
4. Impulsive
5. Industrious
6. Intelligent

Then, ask the person to choose one word to represent his or her impression of B.

people. We will attempt to determine why we often feel it is necessary to "freeze" our perceptions of people to conform to our expectations.

"You must make a good first impression" is a piece of advice frequently given to people who are starting a new job, preparing for an interview, or getting ready to participate in some other communication encounter. How important is the first impression?

If you analyze the responses you obtain for the Skill Builder entitled "What's on First?" (adapted from an experiment conducted by Solomon Asch[27]), you'll find that people usually attribute positive qualities to person A, selecting a descriptive word with very positive connotations. In contrast, person B is often perceived as possessing negative qualities, and for this reason the word chosen to describe B also has negative connotations. Why? The answer seems to be simply that the first list begins with positive traits and the second begins with negative traits; otherwise, each list is precisely the same. Thus, first impressions can dramatically affect perception. In addition, a first impression—or **primacy effect,** as it is sometimes called—can even affect the result of communication efforts. Trial lawyers, for example, depend to some degree on the primacy effect when selecting jurors. The first impression that potential jurors make on attorneys will often determine whether the attorneys accept them or use peremptory challenges to remove them from consideration.

Even if our first impressions are wrong, we tend to hold on to them. Doing this can cause a number of problems. For example, if the opinion we have of someone is erroneous, we can sustain our inaccurate perception by clinging to it and reshaping the conflicting information available to us until it conforms to the image we hold. Thus, we may never come to experience the real person—only our faulty conception of him or her. And it is this faulty conception that will influence the way we respond to that person. Suppose, for instance, you make a new friend, Kevin, at work. You tell an old friend about him. Your old friend tells you, "Yeah. I know that guy. Worked with him two years ago. He's nothing but trouble. Always looking to use people. He'll bleed you of your ideas, pass them off as his own, and leave you far behind as he makes his way to the top. Did it to me. And he'll do it to you. Watch and see." The danger here is that this evaluation may be unfair, biased, or simply wrong. Kevin might have changed during the past two years, or your friend's initial assessment of him might have been incorrect. But your friend's words will probably influence the way you interact with Kevin, and you will probably find reasons to substantiate your first impression, whether

primacy effect

the ability of one's first impression to color subsequent impressions or not such reasons are actually present. You simply may not be able to avoid a basic stumbling block to accurate perception—closing your mind after forming a first impression.

In a communication interaction, receivers' psychological states can affect their first impressions of senders. Sometimes receivers use cues provided by senders, mix those cues with their own preconceptions, and create perceptions based partly on myth or fiction. When such perceptions involve dividing people into groups, it is called stereotyping.

Stereotypes: Do You Squeeze Others into Niches?

A **stereotype** is a generalization about people, places, or events that is held by many members of a society. For example, when we go into a physician's waiting room for the first time, we carry with us a general idea, or stereotype, about what to expect and how to behave in that environment. In other words, we have developed an ability to identify and generalize about what we consider appropriate in a physician's office. For example, while waiting to be examined, we would not expect to find flashing laser lights or people dancing to loud music.

The stereotypes we hold affect how we process stimuli around us. For one thing, while we remember more favorable information about in-groups, we retain more unfavorable information about out-groups. Our stereotypes also cause us to disregard any differences individuals may have that set them apart from the stereotyped group. When we stereotype, instead of responding to the communication or cues of individuals, we create expectations, assume they are valid, and behave as if they had occurred. Thus, when we stereotype, we judge persons on the basis of what we believe about the group in which we have placed them. We emphasize similarities and overlook discrepancies. Stereotyping leads us to oversimplify, overgeneralize, and grossly exaggerate what we observe. Lazy perceivers develop prejudices; **prejudice** involves making a negative prejudgment based on membership in a social category. Lazy perceivers also rely on stereotyping as their key perceptual process. Because it discourages careful observation and encourages pigeonholing, it discourages the noting of differences and encourages categorization.

Sports reporter Jerry Bembry reports the following incident:

> At a basketball media day at the Naval Academy, a ranking Navy official was greeting the news media. Each journalist received a gracious hello, but when the Navy man got to me, I was asked a question.
>
> "So," the official said, extending his hand. "Where did you play ball at to get this job?"
>
> His assumption: Because I'm an athletic-looking African American male, my education must have come in combination with an athletic scholarship. It's a question I'm often asked, although I've never played collegiate sports.
>
> No matter how many times such instances happen to me, it's unsettling.[28]

In your opinion, what accounts for such behavior? What can we do to prevent ourselves and others from making such assumptions?

Experts believe stereotyping can be as big an issue among groups of minorities as it has been between Whites and minorities. In other words, stereotypes, unfortunately, are everywhere. In fact, a variety of ethnic groups

stereotype
a generalization about people, places, or events held by many members of a society

Has anyone ever stereotyped you? How did his or her doing so affect your relationship with that person?

prejudice
a biased, negative attitude toward a particular group of people; a negative prejudgment based on membership in a social category

share the same stereotypes as Whites.[30] Commonly held stereotypes about Hispanics include that they are foreign-born, have a lot of children, and speak only Spanish. Existing stereotypes about Asians include that they are inscrutable and disloyal and that they own restaurants and laundries. Americans are likely to be stereotyped as being boisterous and loud. African Americans are stereotyped as being of low intelligence.

Stereotypes are dangerous because, even at best, they are oversimplifications and overgeneralizations; often, they are gross exaggerations and misrepresentations. Stereotypes based on half-truths and derived from invalid premises pose major problems for us. Ralph Ellison, an African American and author of the book *Invisible Man,* noted:

> I am an invisible man. No, I am not a spook like those who haunted Edgar Allan Poe. . . . I am a man of substance, of flesh and bone, fiber and liquid . . . and I might be said to possess a mind. I am invisible, understand, simply because people refuse to see me. Like the bodiless heads you see sometimes in circus sideshows, it is as though I have been surrounded by mirrors of hard, distorting glass. When they approach me they see only my surroundings, or figments of their imagination—indeed, everything and anything except me.[31]

Stereotypes do a special kind of harm when groups believe their own caricatures. If, for example, African Americans believe the stereotype and think that they are good only at sports, music, and dance, then it's entirely possible for some group members to exhibit "internalized oppression," act on the stereotype, and harass achievers in the group who don't fit that stereotype.[32]

The term *stereotype* is derived from a printing practice in which the typesetter repeatedly uses the same type to print text. In effect, when we stereotype, we repeatedly use the same thoughts, or fixed mental images, to "print" the same judgment repeatedly. We use our knowledge, beliefs, and expectancies about a human group to make judgments about people and our potential interaction with them. We apply the judgment to all members of the group, failing to acknowledge the uniqueness of what we are describing. We use the stereotype as a means of rationalizing our behavior in relation to members of that group. Media theorist Peter Orlik notes:

> When ages, occupations, genders, religions, or racial groups are represented in stereotypical ways, the treatment becomes potentially more dishonest the longer it is allowed to remain on microphone or on camera. All Texans, all Native Americans, all Baptists, or police officers are not the same; and to depict each member of such groups as exactly the same is to be functionally dishonest and insincere . . . to the concept of individual human dignity.[33]

The practice of stereotyping can be extremely harmful. At one time or another, almost everyone forms fixed impressions of a racial, ethnic, religious, occupational, or socioeconomic group.[34] When we stereotype, we project our attitude toward a group of people onto one particular member of that group. By ignoring individual differences, persons who stereotype create perceptual inaccuracies.

What should be emphasized, of course, is that we are all individuals. Whenever we interact with another person, we must realize that we are communicating with a person, not with a stereotype. Furthermore, we need to understand that our stereotype of any group is necessarily based on incomplete information and that, although stereotypes may be partly true, they are never completely true. In fact, when we stereotype, categorize, or pigeonhole others, we are really stereotyping, categorizing, or pigeonholing ourselves.

To improve our perceptual capabilities, we must make an effort to see differences as well as similarities among people. To paraphrase communication expert Irving J. Lee, the more we are able to discriminate among individuals, the less we will actively discriminate against individuals.[35] We can be aware of stereotypes but reject them.

Allness: Do You Assume That's All There Is?

Have you ever noticed how some radio and television commentators speak with great finality? Several have based their careers at least partially on a parentlike image; that is, they seem to have all the answers about everything happening in the world. Is it possible for a commentator—or for any of us—to know, much less tell, all there is to know concerning a topic? Of course not. Knowledge of everything about anything is certainly an impossibility. In his book *Science and Sanity,* Alfred Korzybski coined the term **allness** to refer to the erroneous belief that any one person can possibly know all there is to know about everything.[36] Even if we are wise and do not assume that our favorite newscaster (or even our favorite friend) is telling us all there is to know about a topic, we often persist in believing that he or she is telling us all that is important about the topic. Did you ever ask someone to fill you in on the content of a class session you missed? Did you assume that the person was giving you all the important information? Did a later exam prove you wrong?

allness

the erroneous belief that any one person can know all there is to know about anything

How can we avoid allness? We can begin by recognizing that, because we can focus on only a portion of a stimulus or an event, we necessarily neglect other aspects of that stimulus or event. Another safeguard is to refrain from thinking of ourselves as the center of the world.

Allness can impede the development of effective relationships. To counteract allness, try to end every assessment you make with the words *et cetera* ("and others"). You can never know everything there is to know about anything, and these words remind you that you should not pretend to know it all.

FIGURE 4.6
Test for Blindering.

Blindering: Is Your Focus Too Narrow?

blindering

the process by which one unconsciously adds restrictions that limit one's perceptual capabilities

The concept of **blindering** as a factor in perception can be illustrated by the following exercise. Attempt to draw four straight lines that will connect each of the dots in Figure 4.6. Do this without lifting your pencil or pen from the page or retracing over a line.

Did you find the exercise difficult or impossible? Most people do. Why? The problem imposes only one restriction—that you connect the dots with four straight lines without lifting your pencil or pen from the page or backtracking over a line. Most of us, however, add another restriction: After examining the dots, we assume that the figure to be formed must be a square. Actually, no such restriction exists, and once you realize this, the solution becomes clear. (Check the answer in the Answer Key at the back of the text.) In effect, the image of a square "blindered" you in your attempts to solve the problem.

Just as we put blinders on a horse to reduce the number of visual stimuli it receives, we can also put blinders on ourselves. Blinders may help a horse, but they can drastically hinder human beings. Because it is a habit that forces us to see only certain things or to see things only in certain ways, blindering can lead to undesirable actions or prevent us from finding solutions. It can also impede needed actions or decisions.

Inferences: Do You Confuse What You Infer with What You Observe?

Another factor that affects our perception and evaluation of people and events in our world is the inability to distinguish what we have inferred from what we have observed. For example, if you plan to leave your home to drive to a friend's house about a mile away, you probably make some inferences: that when you put the key into the ignition, your automobile will start; that you will not have a flat tire; and that no construction will block your approach to the friend's home. Likewise, when a traffic light turns green, you usually infer that it is safe to cross the street.

fact

that which is known to be true based on observation

inference

an assumption with varying degrees of accuracy

It is important to distinguish facts from inferences. A **fact** is something that you know to be true on the basis of observation. You see a woman walking down the street, carrying a briefcase. The statement "That woman is carrying a briefcase" is a fact. If the woman with the briefcase has a frown on her face, you may state, "That woman is unhappy." This second statement is an **inference,** since it cannot be verified by observation. In the old crime TV series *Dragnet,* Jack Webb, in the role of police officer Sergeant Joe Friday, would often tell witnesses, "All I want is the facts, just the facts." Facts are not always easy to come by, and sometimes we mistakenly believe we have facts when we actually have inferences. Failing to recognize this distinction can be embarrassing or dangerous. For example, when actor and concert pianist Dudley Moore began flubbing lines, walking unevenly, and having difficulty playing the piano, he was mistakenly accused by entertainment industry insiders of being drunk, when in reality he was suffering from an incurable neurological disease.[37]

> *He laughed because he thought that they could not hit him; he didn't imagine that they were practicing how to miss him.*
>
> **—Bertolt Brecht**

Ethics & COMMUNICATION

Reports versus Reality

During 2003's Operation Iraqi Freedom, many of the initial reports made by journalists covering the war were not proven. For example, one news story reported that Saddam Hussein had been killed; another said that he had been injured and was last seen on a stretcher, blue-faced and gasping into an oxygen mask; and still another reported that he looked hale and hearty and had survived unscathed. The following reports versus reality inventory appeared in *USA Today*.[38] In your opinion, what are the dangers of merging fact and fiction when reporting on war?

Since the United States and its allies began the war March 19, many initial reports have not been proven. Some examples are:

Date	Initial Report	Reality
March 20	Saddam Hussein may have died in air-strike.	His fate remains unclear.
March 20	Banned Scud missiles were fired at U.S. troops.	False
March 21	The southern port city of Umm Qasr was controlled by the coalition.	Premature
March 23	A captured chemical plant produced banned weapons.	False
March 23	The southern city of Basra was taken by coalition forces.	Premature
March 24	Thousands of Iraqi Shiites revolted against Saddam in Basra.	False
March 25	A convoy of 1,000 Iraqi vehicles carrying Republican Guard troops headed south from Baghdad and was decimated by coalition forces.	No evidence that convoy ever existed.
March 30	British troops captured an Iraqi general in Basra.	Iraqi POW impersonated a general.
April 6	Bodies found in warehouse in southern Iraq were victims of Saddam's brutal regime.	Remains were from 1980s war against Iran.
April 7	Chemical warheads and other weapons of mass destruction were found.	Confirmation pending
April 7	The general nicknamed "Chemical Ali" was killed in an airstrike.	Confirmation pending

Source: "Reports vs. Reality," USA Today, April 8, 2003. Copyright © 2003 USA Today. Reprinted with permission.

Sharpen your understanding of facts and inferences by reading the following newspaper story:

Norwich, N.Y. (AP) They had arrested him for drunken driving, but he insisted he was sober.

Police said his eyes were glassy, his speech thick and his walk unsure.

Roswell Woods was given the usual tests. He was asked to blow up a balloon as a test. He couldn't do it.

He was taken to court. He pleaded not guilty and asked for an attorney.

Before a jury, the 47-year-old veteran heard himself accused. His attorney, Glen F. Carter, asked Woods to stand. He did.

"It has been testified that your eyes were glassy," the attorney said gently.

The accused pointed to his glass eye, placed there after he had lost an eye in battle.

"It has been testified that your speech was thick," the lawyer continued.

The defendant, speaking with difficulty, said he had partial paralysis of the throat. He said it resulted from one of the 27 injuries received in the line of duty in the South Pacific.

"It is also testified," Carter went on, "that you failed to pick up a coin from off the floor."

He brought out that Woods had been injured in both legs and had undergone an operation in which part of a bone in one leg was used to replace the shattered bone in the other. Woods was unable to stoop, he said.

"And now, the blowing-up of the balloon," the attorney said. "You couldn't blow it up, could you?"

The defendant replied, "I lost one of my lungs in the war. I can't exhale very well."

The jury returned its verdict quickly: "Not guilty."[39]

Skill BUILDER

The Detective

Read the following story. Assume that the information contained in it is true and accurate. Then assess each statement that follows the story. On a sheet of paper, indicate whether you think the statement is definitely true by writing *T*, definitely false by writing *F*, or questionable by writing a question mark. (Note: A question mark indicates that you think the statement could be true or false, but on the basis of the information in the story, you cannot be certain.) Respond to the statements in the order given. Do not go back to change any of your responses.

A tired executive had just turned off the lights in the store when an individual approached and demanded money. The owner opened the safe. The contents of the safe were emptied, and the person ran away. The alarm was triggered, notifying the police of the occurrence.

1. An individual appeared after the owner had turned off the store's lights.
2. The robber was a man.
3. The person who appeared did not demand any money.
4. The man who opened the safe was the owner.
5. The owner emptied the safe and ran away.
6. Someone opened the safe.
7. After the individual who demanded the money emptied the safe, he sped away.
8. Although the safe contained money, the story does not reveal how much.
9. The robber opened the safe.
10. The robber did not take the money.
11. In this story, only three persons are referred to.

Acting as if an assumption is a certainty can be risky. When we confuse facts with inferences, we are likely to jump to conclusions. Test your ability to distinguish facts and inferences by completing the Skill Builder on page 102, "The Detective." How did you do? (Check your answers against the Answer Key at the back of the text.) This test is not designed to discourage you from making inferences. Of necessity, we live our lives on an inferential level. It is designed, however, to discourage you from making inferences without being aware of doing so. It is also designed to help you stop operating as if your inferences were facts.

Are you aware of the inferences you make? As semanticist S.I. Hayakawa noted, the real question is not whether we make inferences but whether we are cognizant of the inferences we make. One of the key characteristics of a mature relationship is that neither party to it jumps to conclusions or acts on inferences as if they were facts.

The following list summarizes some of the essential differences between facts and inferences:

Facts	*Inferences*
1. May be made only after observation or experience	1. May be made at any time
2. Are limited to what has been observed	2. Extend beyond observation
3. Can be offered by the observer only	3. Can be offered by anyone
4. May refer to the past or to the present	4. May refer to any time—past, present, or future
5. Approach certainty	5. Represent varying degrees of probability

THE MEDIA AND PERCEPTION

The media also play a role in determining how we perceive experience. According to the book *Glued to the Set: The 60 Television Shows and Events That Made Us Who We Are Today,* we are defined by and, thus, become like what we watch.[40]

Judging the Accuracy and Inaccuracy of Media Perceptions

The more television people watch, the more accepting they become of social stereotypes, and the more likely they are to help perpetuate the unrealistic and limiting perceptions shown them.

What are some of the specific perceptual lessons we learn from the media? In part, because women and older people are underrepresented in the media, we come to believe that they are unimportant or invisible. In a review of prime-time television programming, for example, it was determined that viewers see three times as many White men as women.[41]

The media can limit our perceptions of males and females in other ways as well. Whereas the media often present men as active, independent, powerful,

Media
WISE

Frames of Reference and Fear

In February 2002, the media reported that the Department of Homeland Security had raised the risk assessment of a terrorist attack on the United States from yellow to orange. This set off a frenzy of duct tape and plastic wrap buying by worried citizens who wanted to prepare for such an attack by taping their windows and sealing their homes. Were you among them?

According to some researchers, the media can distort our perception of risk, inducing us to experience fear that is out of proportion with actual danger. The more attention the media pay to a particular risk factor, the worse we assume the risk to be. For example, Dr. Baruch Fischoll, a psychologist at Carnegie Mellon University and a leader in the study of risk perception, reports, "If scientists are studying it and the news reports it, people assume it must be worth their attention."[42] Another risk researcher, Dr. Paul Slovic, reports that adding to this effect is the finding "that people put more stock in reports of bad news than in reports that might increase their trust."[43]

Give an example of a media report that caused you to perceive a risk as greater than it was in reality. Did it involve weather? Traffic? Crime? Environmental issues? Political issues?

Films perpetuate inaccurate perceptions that induce fear in viewers. View one of the following films: *The Siege, True Lies, Rules of Engagement, Executive Decision,* or *Not Without My Daughter.* In what ways, if any, does the film perpetuate bias against Arabs? In your opinion, is the Arab-as-terrorist stereotype responsible for increasing our fear and arousing our suspicion regarding who may or may not be a potential terrorist? Keep in mind that the alert issued by the FBI after the 1995 bombing of the federal building in Oklahoma City cautioned officials to be on the lookout for a pickup truck carrying passengers described as "Middle Eastern with dark hair and beards," when the people ultimately arrested were two Caucasian males.[44]

and virile, women are frequently portrayed as passive, dependent, and incompetent and as the objects of male sexual desires. Whereas men are shown taking care of business, women are more typically shown taking care of their looks and other people, especially family members. From the point of view of the media, then, males dominate and females are subservient.[45] Males are providers. Females are caregivers.

For similar reasons, we might also come to perceive minorities inappropriately. Minorities have even less of a media presence than do women. For the most part, minorities occupy supporting rather than leading roles and often, instead of being depicted in complimentary ways, they are depicted as lazy, lawbreaking, or dumb. Writer David Evans criticized television for stereotyping Black males as athletes and entertainers. Doing this, wrote Evans, causes young Black males to conclude that success "is only a dribble or dance step away" and prevents them from developing more realistic expectations.[46] Critics believe that the depiction of African Americans not only reinforces and sharpens prejudices but also reconfirms the negative images African Americans may have of themselves.[47] As a result of media depictions, our perceptions of Native Americans also may be inaccurate. For example, the print media too frequently present an image of them that is negative and degrading, suggesting that "all American Indians are poor, greedy, corrupt alcoholics, who just cannot seem to succeed in American society."[48] Representing Native Americans in this way undermines their ability to act effectively or be taken seriously.

On the other hand, Leon E. Wynter, author of the book *American Skin: Pop Culture, Big Business and the End of White America,* notes that we are now witnessing the browning of mainstream commercial culture. In addition to superstars like Michael Jordan, Oprah Winfrey, and Tiger Woods, we also have Eddie Murphy playing Dr. Doolittle, former heavyweight champ George Foreman as an affable pitchman, and ads like the Budweiser "Whassup?!" commercial that feature basically anonymous Black men talking Black street talk. It appears that American pop culture is becoming increasingly transracial. Products that aspire to be perceived as "all-American" depict a racially diverse image. According to Wynter, American wants to perceive itself as a unified multiracial society.[49]

TECHNOLOGY AND PERCEPTION

According to social psychologist Kenneth Gergen, as new communication technologies continue to spread our relationships across the globe and as our knowledge of other cultures continues to revitalize our attitudes, depriving us of firm behavioral norms, we tend to exist in a state of flux, in which perceptions are partial and negotiated rather than complete and fixed.[50]

Computer-mediated communication raises a variety of perception-based issues involving the nature of communication and identity. We tend to perceive and interact with people differently when we relate to them online than when we talk to them face-to-face. A number of researchers even refer to communication that occurs in the world of cyberspace as unreal in order to differentiate it from communication that occurs in real life, also known as IRL, and without the aid of computer mediation.[51] Fantasy and playfulness play significant roles in online interactions, allowing people to experiment in ways that may be uncomfortable for them in real life. Thus, the Internet is precipitating perceptual revisions of the self and others.[52]

The Internet inspires some of us to feel larger than ourselves. In addition, the availability of the computer and virtual reality allows many of us to spend more time in our dreams. As sociologist Sherry Turkle reminds us, "In film and photography, realistic-looking images depict scenes that never took place between people who never met."[53] Anyone can create an image, import sections of pictures, and blend them into a new whole. Image processing and synthesis enable us to create illusions of reality. In effect, with digital media you never know what's real, what's the truth. As a result, Web users must develop the ability to look critically at what they perceive rather than simply accept what is on the screen as a given; it has become imperative for them to analyze, weigh, probe, and take stock of what they perceive. This practice differs from the experiences of the members of earlier generations, who would rarely perceive a picture and feel it was a fake. Back then, it was felt that a fact was a fact. Today, we all know better. We now see a photograph and realize that it could be a total fabrication.[54]

For example, during the Iraqi war, a photo that appeared in the *Los Angeles Times* of a British soldier standing over a group of Iraqi civilians near Basra was actually a combination of two photographs taken moments apart. How was this discovered? A reader noticed that some of the figures in the background appeared twice. Why did the journalists choose to merge the photos and deceive the public? One photo featured a dramatic pose of a British soldier, while the other photo featured an Iraqi man carrying a child. In the

Digital Image Processing

Examine the covers of the December 1997 issues of *Time* and *Newsweek*. Both display a picture of Bobbi McCaughey, the mother of sextuplets. While one of the news weeklies ran the image as it was taken, the other used a computer to retouch the shot and correct the imperfections on McCaughey's teeth. In your opinion, how did retouching McCaughey's teeth affect the reader's perception of her? Do you believe that the capabilities of digital image processing will undermine the perceptual principle that seeing is believing? Why or why not?

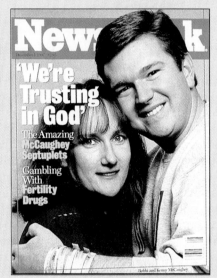

Photo editors can create illusions of reality. Notice how each photo changes the appearance of its subject, thus altering the way you feel and respond as well.

more powerful merged version, the soldier and the civilian appeared to be interacting. While the *Los Angeles Times* fired the journalist for his deception, what is noteworthy is that this kind of deception is not new. The E-Search features a picture of a mother of septuplets, Bobbi Ann McCaughey, which *Newsweek* retouched so that she would have nicer teeth. Unfortunately, the camera continues to lie. How long will it be before we consider real photos to be fake?[55]

Rather than inhabiting a culture of only what is real, we can now also reside in a culture of simulation. We may come to learn that people aren't always who they present themselves as or who they are presented to us as. The world of **virtual reality** contains visual, auditory, and tactile information about an environment that exists as data in a computer system rather than as physical objects and actual locations in the real world. However, these illusions are sustained for a time in the minds of the users. In other words, users treat these simulated environments as if they were real.[56]

We also need to understand how other factors, such as race, influence our attention to Web sites. For example, recent research reveals that African Americans are more attentive when visiting a Black-targeted site, while Caucasians are equally attentive to White- and Black-targeted sites. It appears that race

virtual reality

an environment that exists as data in a computer system

or ethnicity may be of more interest to people whose racial or ethnic group is in the minority of their social environment than to people of the majority group. Since they are in the majority, Caucasians may be less mindful of their race when browsing a Web site.[57]

We are also faced with a number of questions: Will emerging technologies help us become more flexible and resilient? Or will they cause us to think strictly logically and constrain us to prescribed, more conventional, thought channels? Will they facilitate our ability to use our virtual experiences to enrich our real experiences? Or will they contribute to our losing our sense of reality by enabling us to lose ourselves in a virtual world that disappears when we disconnect our modems?

One thought to keep in mind is that we can't disconnect the modem because we don't like the comments of a spouse we live with or of a co-worker with whom we have to work side by side.

HOW TO INCREASE THE ACCURACY OF YOUR PERCEPTIONS

Although our effectiveness as communicators is determined in part by our perceptual abilities, we rarely consider ways to increase our perceptual accuracy. Let's examine some suggestions for improving perceptual skills.

Be Aware That Your Perceptual Processes Are Personally Biased

By becoming aware of your role in perception, by recognizing that you have biases, by acknowledging that you do not have a corner on the truth market, you can increase the probability that your perceptions will provide you with accurate information about the world around you and the people who are a part of it.

Take Your Time

Effective communicators are not in a hurry; they take the time they need to process information fairly and objectively. When we act too quickly, we often make careless decisions that reveal poor judgment. In our haste, we overlook important clues, make inappropriate or unjustified inferences, and jump to conclusions. To combat this, we need to take time to be sure we have assessed a situation correctly. Delaying a response instead of acting impulsively gives us an opportunity to check or verify our perceptions.

Try to Be More Open

Frequently, we act like robots or computers that have been programmed to look at the world in a set way. But a person is neither a robot nor a computer. We can take steps to become more observant and broaden our expectations. We need to become willing to expect the unexpected and to expand the size of our perceptual window. This will happen if we recognize that our

Reflect and Respond

Discuss how the excerpts that follow help amplify our understanding of the nature of perception. Then agree or disagree with each selection; supply reasons and examples that support your position.

What I set down here is true until someone else passes that way and rearranges the world in his own style.

John Steinbeck

It is with our judgments as with our watches; no two go just alike, yet each believes his own.

Alexander Pope

reality is subjective, incomplete, and unique. Thus, if we want to cultivate a fuller, more valid perception of our world, we must be willing to review, revise, and update our view of the world.

Develop Your Ability to Empathize

Differing perceptions lie at the heart of an array of interpersonal and global communication challenges. If we can experience the world from a perspective other than our own—in effect, recreating it from the other party's perspective—we can help facilitate mutual understanding. Both cognitive and emotional behaviors are integral components of empathy. The cognitive component, perspective taking (the ability to assume the viewpoint of another person) requires that we take on the opinions of another, setting our own opinions away until we understand theirs. The second component of empathy, emotional understanding, requires that we step into the shoes of the other person and feel what they are feeling. The third component, caring, is "the icing on the cake." When you genuinely care about the welfare of another person and you combine this with the personal realization of what their situation is like, that is, you have made their experience your own thinking and feeling as they feel, at least temporarily, you gain a greater appreciation of what the world looks like through their eyes. The ability to empathize can make a difference in life.

Revisiting Chapter Objectives

1. **Explain why a person is more than a camera.**   Perception is the process of selecting, organizing, and interpreting sensory data in a way that enables us to make sense of our world. Perceptions are personally based. They are affected by the perspective we adopt, our sensory capabilities, our past experiences, and our level of motivation.

2. **Define and explain how the following affect perception: the figure-ground principle, selective exposure, selective perception, closure, stereotyping, open and closed orientation, and first impressions.**   The accuracy of our perceptions is affected by our inability to perceive two stimuli simultaneously (figure-ground principle). It is also influenced by our tendency to close ourselves to new experiences (selective exposure), our inclination to

distort our perceptions of stimuli to make them conform to our need for internal consistency (selective perception), our desire not to open ourselves to unfamiliar experiences, and our need to perceive a complete world (closure).

How we perceive another person is a key determinant of the kind of relationship we will share with that person. Thus, perceiving others and the roles they play is an essential part of the communication process. In this regard, a number of factors can prevent accurate perceptions. We frequently evaluate others on the basis of first impressions, and we tend to stereotype people—to divide them into groups and place them in niches. Stereotyping can be especially harmful by promoting prejudice, since it encourages us to emphasize similarities and ignore differences. Prejudice is an unfair or biased extension of stereotyping, which we must guard against.

3. **Describe how past experience, gender, cultural background, the media, and technology can influence perception.**   Past experience, culture, gender, the media, and technology influence how we perceive and interpret people and events. By serving as perceptual filters, they guide us in giving meaning to both our real and virtual experiences.

4. **Define and provide examples of allness, blindering, and facts and inferences.**   Other barriers to perceptual accuracy are allness (the habit of thinking we know it all), blindering (the tendency to obscure solutions to problems by adding unnecessary restrictions), and confusion of facts with inferences (the inability to distinguish between observations and assumptions).

5. **Identify ways to increase the accuracy of your perceptions.**   It is important that you work to increase the validity of your perceptions. As a first step, you need to recognize the role you play in the perceptual process.

Resources for Further Inquiry and Reflection

To apply your understanding of how the principles in Chapter 4 are at work in our daily lives, consult the following resources for further inquiry and reflection. Or, if you prefer, choose any other appropriate resource. Then connect the ideas expressed in your chosen selection with the communication concepts and issues you are learning about both in and out of class.

 Listen to Me

"Hurricane Eye" (Paul Simon)
"I've Seen It All" (Bjork)
"If I Could Turn Back Time" (Cher)
"Suspicious Minds" (Elvis Presley)
"Jenny from the Block" (Jennifer Lopez)
"Wonderful World" (Louis Armstrong)

These songs explore one or more aspects of perception. Choose a song and discuss how the speaker's perception affects his or her relationship with one or more other people.

 View Me

Big
Dancer in the Dark
The Doctor
Groundhog Day
Life Is Beautiful
Rashomon

American History X
Shallow Hal
The Cider-House Rules
Remember the Titans
A Beautiful Mind

In each of these films, perception plays a key role in the plot. Choose one film and identify the lessons we learn regarding how perception can alter one's reality and life experiences.

Read Me

James Thurber. "The Secret Life of Walter Mitty." In *The Works of James Thurber.* New York: Longmeadow Press, 1986.

Mark Medoff. *Children of a Lesser God.* New York: Dramatists Play Service, 1980.

Ralph Ellison. *The Invisible Man.* New York: Random House, 1989.

Laura Z. Hobson. *Gentleman's Agreement.* New York: Simon & Schuster, 1947.

How does the perception of the main character or characters in the work affect both their experiences and their interaction with others? To what extent, if any, does stereotyping play a role in limiting perception?

 Tell Me

Share with the class the insights you gained from your chosen Listen to Me, View Me, or Read Me selection.

Find examples that enable you to support or negate the following: Once you have a belief, it influences your perception of all other relevant information. Once you call a country hostile, you will interpret ambiguous actions on the part of its leaders as indicative of that hostility.

Key Chapter Terminology

Communication Works

www.mhhe.com/gamble8

Use the Communication Works CD-ROM and the Online Learning Center at www.mhhe.com/gamble8 *to further your knowledge of the following terminology.*

allness 99

blindering 100

closure 87

cultural nearsightedness 91

fact 100

figure-ground principle 86

first impressions 95

halo effect 95

horn effect 95

inference 100

perception 85

perceptual constancy 89

perceptual sets 93

prejudice 97

primacy effect 96

selective attention 94

selective exposure 94

selective perception 85

selective retention 94

stereotype 97

virtual reality 106

Test Your Understanding

Communication Works

online learning center

www.mhhe.com/gamble8

Go to the *Self Quizzes* on the Communication Works CD-ROM and the book's Online Learning Center at www.mhhe.com/gamble8.

Notes

1. R. E. Nisbett. *The Geography of Thought: How Asians and Westerners Think Differently . . . and Why.* New York: Free Press, 2003.

2. Jinbong Choi. "Between Friend and Enemy: News Coverage of the September 11th Event by South and North Korean News Agencies." Paper delivered at the annual convention of the Association for Education in Journalism and Mass Communication in Miami, FL, August 7–10, 2002.

3. Richard Benedetto. "Differences in Perceptions Fuel Mistrust," *USA Today,* March 5, 2002, p. 11A.

4. Kemba Dunham. "They Also Might Be Wondering Why People 'Dial' a Telephone." *Wall Street Journal,* February 19, 1999, p. B; and "Beloit College Releases Its Annual Guide for Understanding a New Group of Freshmen." *The Chronicle of Higher Education.* August 28, 2002.

5. See, for example, I. V. Blair. "The Malleability of Automatic Stereotypes and Prejudice." *Personality and Social Psychology Review* 6:3, 2002. pp. 242–262.

6. Ira Berkow. "Rower with Muslim Name Is an All-American Suspect." *New York Times,* February 21, 2003, pp. D1, D4.

7. "A Newspaper Apologizes for Photos." *New York Times,* August 31, 2002, p. A9.

8. For an in depth discussion of how race affects perception, see M. L. Hecht, R. L. Jackson II, and S. A. Ribeau. *African American Communication,* 2nd ed. Mahwah, NJ: Lawrence Erlbaum Associates, 2003.

9. Matthew L. Wald, "For Air Crash Detectives, Seeing Isn't Believing." *New York Times,* June 23, 2002, p. WK5.

10. Steven R. Covey. *7 Habits of Highly Effective People.* New York: Simon & Schuster, 1990, p. 28.

11. William V. Haney. *Communication and Organizational Behavior.* Homewood, IL: Irwin, 1973, p. 55.

11a. V. Manusov, A. R. Trees, L. A. Reddick, A. M. C. Rowe, and J. M. Easley. "Explanations and Impressions: Investigating Attributions and Their Effects on Judgments for Friends and Strangers." *Communication Studies* 49, 1998, pp. 209–223.

12. E. Rubin. "Figure and Ground." In D. Beardslee and M. Wertheimer, eds. *Readings in Perception.* Princeton, NJ: Van Nostrand, pp. 194–203.

13. Sharon Begley. "The Memory of Sept. 11 Is Seared in Your Mind; But Is It Really True?" *Wall Street Journal,* September 13, 2002, p. B1.

14. Marshall Singer. "Culture: A Perceptual Approach." In Larry A. Samovar and Richard E. Porter. *Intercultural Communication: A Reader,* 4th ed. Belmont, CA: Wadsworth, 1985, pp. 62–69.

15. Larry A. Samovar and Richard E. Porter. *Communication between Cultures.* Belmont, CA: Wadsworth, 1994, p. 105.

16. "Boy Who Shot Teen Ordered to Spend Time in Wheelchair." *Sunday Record* (Bergen, NJ), January 9, 1994, p. A-16.

17. J. W. Bagby. "A Cross-Cultural Study of Perceptual Predominance in Binocular Rivalry." *Journal of Abnormal and Social Psychology* 54, 1957, pp. 331–334.

18. Virginia V. Weldon. "The Power of Changing the Context." *Vital Speeches of the Day.* January 15, 1994, pp. 217–219.

19. L. S. Samovar and R. E. Porter. *Communication between Cultures,* 2nd ed., Belmont, CA: Wadsworth, 1995, p. 199.

20. Julia T. Wood. *Gendered Lives.* Belmont, CA: Wadsworth, 1994, pp. 21, 131.

21. See Judy Cornelia Pearson. *Gender and Communication.* Dubuque, IA: Wm. C. Brown, 1985.

22. Dan Winters. "Warrior Women." *New York Times Magazine,* February 16, 2003, pp. 23–34.

23. J. Long. "Symbolic Reality Bites: Women and Racial Ethnic Minorities in Modern Film." *Sociological Spectrum,* 22:3, July–September 2002, pp. 299–335.

24. Samovar and Porter, p. 81.

25. Paul Chance. "Seeing Is Believing," *Psychology Today,* January–February 1989, p. 26.

26. See Charles G. Russel. "Culture, Language and Behavior: Perception." *ETC.* 57:2, Summer 2000, pp. 189–218.

27. Solomon Asch. *Social Psychology.* New York: Oxford University Press, 1987.

28. Jerry Bembry. "The Pain That Whites Don't See." *The Record,* January 23, 1994, p. E-3.

29. Chance.

30. Maria T. Padilla. "Studying Stereotypes among Minority Groups." *The Record,* July 19, 1998, p. L-1.

31. Ralph Ellison. *Invisible Man.* New York: Random House, 1989.

32. Padilla, p.L-3.

33. Peter B. Orlik. *Electronic Media Criticism: Applied Perspectives.* Boston: Focal, 1994, p.23.

34. See, for example, Gordon W. Allport. *The Nature of Prejudice*. Garden City, NY: Double-day, 1958.

35. Irving J. Lee. *How to Talk with People*. San Francisco: International Society for General Semantics, 1982.

36. Alfred Korzybski. *Science and Sanity*, 4th ed. San Francisco: International Society for General Semantics, 1980.

37. As told on *20/20*, ABC Television, June 30, 2000.

38. See S. Marshall. "Accuracy of Battlefield News Often Hazy." *USA Today*, April 8, 2003, p. 7A.

39. Copyright Associated Press. Reprinted by permission of Associated Press.

40. See Steven D. Stark. *Glued to the Set: The 60 Television Shows and Events That Made Us Who We Are Today*. New York: Free Press, 1997.

41. S. A. Basow. *Gender: Stereotypes and Roles*, 3rd ed. Pacific Grove, CA: Brooks/Cole, 1992, p. 159.

42. See Daniel Goleman. "Hidden Rules Often Distort Ideas of Risk." *New York Times*, February 1, 1994, pp. C-1, C-10.

43. Goleman.

44. Nancy Beth Jackson. "Arab Americans: Middle East Conflicts Hit Home." In Paul Martin Lester, ed. *Images That Injure: Pictorial Stereotypes in the Media*. Westport, CT: Praeger, 1996, p. 63.

45. Wood, p. 238.

46. David Evans. "The Wrong Examples." *Newsweek*, March 1, 1993, p. 10.

47. B. W. Gorham and Eileen N. Gilligan. "The Linguistic Intergroup Bias in Interpretations of a Race-Related Crime Story." Paper delivered at the annual convention of the Association for Education in Journalism and Mass Communication in Miami, FL, August 7–10, 2002.

48. Autumn Miller and Susan Dente Ross. "They Are Not Us: Framing of American Indians by the Boston Globe." Paper delivered at the annual convention of the Association for Education in Journalism and Mass Communication in Miami, FL, August 7–10, 2002.

49. Leon E. Wynter. *American Skin: Pop Culture, Big Business and the End of White America*. New York: Crown, 2002.

50. Kenneth Gergen. *The Saturated Self: Dilemmas of Identity in Contemporary Life*, New York: Basic Books, 1991, p. 6.

51. Andrew F. Wood and Matthew J. Smith. *Online Communication: Linking Technology, Identity, & Culture*. Mahwah, NJ: Lawrence Erlbaum Associates, 2001, p. 18.

52. Susan B. Barnes. *Online Connections: Internet Interpersonal Relationships*. Cresskill, NJ: Hampton Press, 2001, p. 102.

53. Sherry Turkle. *Life on the Screen: Identity in the Age of the Internet*. New York: Simon & Schuster, 1995, p. 267.

54. Don Tapscott. *Growing Up Digital: The Rise of the Net Generation*. New York: McGraw-Hill, 1998, p. 100.

55. Russell Frank. "Altered Picture's Worth a Thousand Lies." *The Record*, April 9, 2003, p. L11.

56. Steven G. Jones. *Cybersociety: Computer-Mediated Communication and Community*. Thousand Oaks, CA: Sage, 1995, pp. 164–166.

57. Osei Appiah. "Americans Online: Differences in Surfing and Evaluating Race-Targeted Web Sites by Black and White Users." Paper presented at the annual convention of the Association for Education in Journalism and Mass Communication, Miami, FL, August, 2002.

Language and Meaning: Helping Minds Meet

After finishing this chapter, you should be able to

1. Define *language*.

2. Describe and explain the triangle of meaning.

3. Distinguish between connotative and denotative meanings.

4. Discuss how culture and gender influence language use.

5. Provide examples of bypassing and intensional and extensional orientation.

6. Identify two strategies to improve oral language abilities.

7. Explain how technology is affecting language use.

Whatever we call a thing, whatever we say it is, it is not. For whatever we say is words, and words are words and not things. The words are maps, and the map is not the territory.

—**Harry L. Weinberg, "Some Limitations of Language"**

Tact is . . . a kind of mind reading.

—**Sara Orne Jewett**

Go to the *Online Learning Center* at
www.mhhe.com/gamble8
and answer the questions in the *Self Inventory* to evaluate your understanding of communication terms.

Have you ever listened to babies babble? What does their babbling mean to you? When infants babble, they are actually learning the techniques of speech and attempting to master the sound system of language, something we have already accomplished. But what if we hadn't? Have you ever considered what kind of person you would be if you were unable to use words to express yourself? How would it feel to have certain ideas and not be able to communicate them? Without words, phrases, and sentences, it would be much more difficult to communicate meaning to another person.

Thus, as you read the words of this book, you are experiencing one of humanity's wonders—the fact that we share a remarkable, seemingly natural ability—the ability to use and interpret language. Language is so much a part of our lives that it is virtually impossible for us to imagine living without it.

Like so many other things of importance, however, the ability to communicate is frequently appreciated only when it is threatened or lost. We depend on language to help us transfer meaning to others, and meaning is what communication is all about. If we understand how language works, we will be better able to use words to help us share meaning with others.

WHAT LANGUAGE IS

language

a unified system of symbols that permits the sharing of meaning

symbol

that which represents something else

Language is a unified system of symbols that permits the sharing of meaning. A **symbol** stands for, or represents, something else. Words are symbols, and thus words represent things. Notice the words *represent* and *stand for* rather than *are*. This is a very important distinction. Words stand for, or represent, things but are not the things they stand for. Words are spoken sounds or the written representations of sounds that we have agreed will stand for something else. Thus, by mutual consent, we can make anything stand for anything.

The process of communication involves using words to help create meanings and expectations. However, as important as words are in representing and

Looking at Language

There is a joke among language scholars:

Q: What do you call a person who speaks three languages?
A: *A trilingual.*
Q: What do you call a person who speaks two languages?
A: *A bilingual.*
Q: What do you call a person who speaks one language?
A: *An American.*

In his book *Language Shock,* Michael Agar notes that a commonly held stereotype is that Americans find it particularly difficult to enter into the world that goes with another language because it requires them to adopt another point of view, another way of doing things.[1] In your opinion, to combat this stereotype and change the way Americans look at the world and at themselves, should they have to learn another language? Why or why not?

Ethics & COMMUNICATION

describing objects and ideas, the meaning of a verbal message is not stamped on the face of the words we use. Meanings are in people, not in words. Meanings are unique; you have your meaning and other people have theirs. Even a common word such as *cat* can bring to mind meanings ranging from a fluffy Angora to a sleek leopard. Your goal in communicating with another person is to have your meanings overlap, so that you can each make sense out of the other's messages and understand each other. Thus, to communicate, you translate the meaning you want to express into language, so that the other person will respond to it by forming a meaning similar to yours. Although language is obviously intended to aid communication, far too often language serves as an obstacle to communication.

HOW LANGUAGE WORKS: WORDS, THINGS, AND THOUGHTS

Language can fulfill its potential only if we use it correctly. The **triangle of meaning,** developed by two communication theorists—C. K. Ogden and I. A. Richards—helps explain how language works (see Figure 5.1).[2] In Ogden and Richards' triangle of meaning, the three points are *thought*, *word*, and *thing.* The broken line connecting word (a symbol) and thing (a referent, or stimulus) indicates that *the word is not the thing* and that there is no direct connection between the two. Thus, when you use words, you must constantly remind yourself that the only relationships between the words you use and

triangle of meaning
a model that explains the relationship which exists among words, things, and thoughts

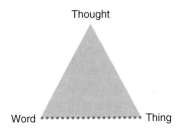

FIGURE 5.1
Triangle of Meaning.

Thought

Word ·········· Thing

The Triangle of Meaning at Work

Situation 1. "Congratulations. You've just given birth to a 3.5-kilogram baby." How do you respond? Your joy is momentarily muted if you don't know what a kilogram is. There is no information in bare facts; information comes from what you do with the facts and what you bring to them. If you've never stored a mental image of a kilogram, you can't generate a mental image of the baby's weight from the data.[3]

Situation 2. Imagine that you're at an old Western Union telegraph office. The telegraph operator hears a message on the wire and bursts into tears. You hear the same dots and dashes but have no reaction at all. Why not? If you don't know

Morse code, the information means nothing, even if you hear it quite clearly. Meaning is not in the cues reaching our senses but in the associations we attach to them.

Situation 3. Instead of referring to North Korea as "the imperialist aggressor," U.S. government officials have been instructed to refer to it as a "superpower of concern."[4] Then President George W. Bush included North Korea in the "axis of evil." In your opinion, will this make a difference in how we perceive and behave toward the North Korean people?

Situation 4. Provide your own example of the triangle of meaning at work.

the things they represent are those that exist in people's thoughts (including, of course, your own). Frequently, even the existence of an image (a physical object) does not establish meaning. Some years ago, a public service commercial depicting a rat and a child living in a tenement was shown on television. The child was seen beckoning to the rat as she repeated, "Here, kitty, kitty! Here, kitty, kitty!" Although this example may seem somewhat bizarre, its meaning is really quite clear: It is possible for two of us to look at the same object but give it different meanings. No one else will respond to a stimulus (a word or thing) exactly as you do, because the meaning of anything is inside each person who experiences it.[5] If you are to be a successful communicator, you should understand the relationships that exist between words and people's thoughts and reactions.[6]

THE COMMUNICATION OF MEANING

The communication of meaning from one person to another is a key function of language. The factors identified in this section relate to problems in the sharing of meaning.

Word Barriers

Words, like eyeglasses, blur everything that they do not make more clear.
—**Joseph Jourbert**

In talking to others, we often assume too quickly that they understand what we mean. There are many reasons, however, we may not be understood as we want to be and why the words we use can create barriers. In Lewis Carroll's *Through the Looking Glass,* Humpty Dumpty and Alice have the following conversation:

> "I don't know what you mean by 'glory,'" Alice said.
> Humpty Dumpty smiled contemptuously, "Of course you don't—till I tell you. I meant, 'There's a nice knock-down argument for you!'"

"But 'glory' doesn't mean 'A nice knock-down argument,'" Alice objected.

"When I use a word," Humpty Dumpty said in a rather scornful tone, "it means just what I choose it to mean—neither more nor less."

We can make words mean whatever we want them to mean. Nothing stops us—except our desire to share meaning with others.

Meanings Are Both Denotative and Connotative

Sometimes we forget that we may experience a problem in communication if we consider only our own meaning for a word. Although *we* know what we mean, the crucial question is, What does our word bring to mind for those with whom we are communicating? When we think about what language means, we must think in terms of both **denotative** (objective, or dictionary) **meaning** and **connotative** (subjective, or personal) **meaning.**

denotative meaning
dictionary meaning; the objective or descriptive meaning of a word

connotative meaning
subjective meaning; one's personal meaning for a word

Meaning and Time

Every noteworthy event, particularly catastrophes, catapult words into everyday speech and dictionaries. September 11, 2001, is no exception. When the American Dialect Society met to decide the top or newly reconditioned words of the previous year, 9/11 was voted the expression most likely to last. Also recognizing this, the editors of the *American Heritage College Dictionary's* fourth edition went back in after their editorial deadline and added an entry for 9/11.

Words come and go from dictionaries. For example, the word *wilding*, meaning the action or practice by a gang of youths of going on a protracted and violent rampage in a street, a park, or another public place, attacking or mugging people at random along the way, was included in a 1993 supplement to the *Oxford English Dictionary*, as well as the fourth edition of *The American Heritage Dictionary*, released in 2000. The word became popular after being used by suspects in the rape of a Central Park jogger to describe their behavior: "We were going wilding," one of them told police. The use of the word has since faded because it was intrinsically linked with that attack. When issues fade from consciousness, some words fade with them.[7]

Bad now has a new definition—"good." The word *gay*, now an acceptable term for "homosexual," is losing its former primary meaning of "happy," "bright," or "merry." Until the creation of the Apple Computer, when someone heard the word *apple*, they probably thought of the fruit. That's probably not the first thing you think of today when someone refers to an apple. (To get a good sense of how time affects meaning, try the Skill Builder "A Time Capsule for Words" on page 118.)

Time, then, is certainly an important element in determining meaning. Consequently, when we use a word that referred to a particular object at a particular time, we should attempt to determine if it still means the same thing now. Many "old" words acquire vivid new meanings every decade or so. It's often necessary to remember this when speaking with people who are older or younger than we are. Viruses today aren't just germs spread from person to person but malicious programs that can spread instantaneously from one computer to millions of other computers globally.[8]

Skill
BUILDER

A Time Capsule for Words

1. Briefly define each of the following terms:

Net _____

Radical _____

Pot _____

Swing _____

Straight _____

Crack _____

Rap _____

Grass _____

Mud _____

Hip _____

Dust _____

Joint _____

Stoned _____

Dude _____

AIDS _____

Spam _____

Cookies _____

2. Show the list, without definitions, to your parents, older relatives, or older friends, and ask them to write their definitions for the words.

3. Compare your meaning for each term with the meanings given by others. Why do you suppose their meanings differed from yours?

4. Pretend it is now the year 2020. On a separate sheet of paper, create a new meaning for each word listed.

Meaning and Place

Not only do words change meaning over time, but they also change meaning from one region of the country to another. For example, what would you envision having if you were to stop for a soda? For an egg cream? For a Danish? For some pop? What each word brings to mind probably depends on what region of the country you grew up in. In some parts of the United States, *soda* is a soft drink, but in others it refers to a concoction of ice cream and a soft drink. In some sections of the country, an egg cream is a mixture of seltzer, syrup, and milk, but elsewhere it conjures up the image of an egg mixed with cream. To people in certain parts of the United States, a Danish is any kind of breakfast pastry; in other regions, people expect to be served a particular kind of breakfast pastry. In still other places, the server might think that you were ordering a foreign specialty—or even a foreigner!

Meaning and Experience

The meanings we assign to words are based on our past experiences with the words and with the things they represent. Consider the word *cancer,* for example. If you were dealing with three people in a hospital—a surgeon, a patient, and a statistician—how do you imagine each would react to this word? The surgeon might think about operating procedures or diagnostic techniques, or about how to tell a patient that he or she has cancer. The patient might think about the odds for recovery and might well be frightened. The statistician might see cancer as an important factor in life expectancy tables.

Unlike denotative (dictionary) meanings—which are generally agreed to and are objective, abstract, and general—connotative (personal) meanings are individual, subjective, and emotional. Thus, your own experiences influence the meanings you assign to words; that is, your connotative meanings vary according to your own feelings for the object or concept you are considering.

Whether Language Is Concrete or Abstract Influences Meaning

The language we use varies in its specificity. Consider this family pet. We could call it:

Dog
Domesticated canine
Small, domesticated canine
A toy Poodle
Lucy

Lucy is a poodle with personality.

In each instance, our description becomes somewhat more specific. Alfred Korzbski and S. I. Hayakawa devised an abstraction ladder to describe this process.[9] The ladder is composed of a number of descriptions of the same thing. Lower items focus specifically on the person, object, or event, while higher items are generalizations that include the subject as part of a larger class. As the words we use move from abstract (less specific) to concrete (more specific), they become more precise in meaning and are more likely to appeal to our senses and conjure up a picture. Specific words clarify meaning by narrowing the number of possible images a person pictures. Were we to talk, for example, about our children's academic experience, we could say that one of our children is in college and the other in graduate school (rather high levels of abstraction), or we could get more concrete and say that our daughter is in the management school of a Big East university and our son is in the molecular biology Ph.D. program at Cornell at Sloan-Kettering.

Using high-level abstractions serves a number of functions. First, because high-level abstractions function as a kind of verbal shorthand, they enable us to generalize, and our communication becomes easier and faster. Second, when we believe it is necessary, because they also enable us to be deliberately unclear, high-level abstractions allow us to limit understanding and avoid confrontations. When, for example, a friend asks you what you think of a new outfit or your boss asks you what you think of a new corporate strategy, if telling the truth appears too risky to you, you can offer an abstract answer to the question and avoid being put on the line. On the other hand, relying on high-level abstractions can also cause meaning to become fuzzy—primarily because the words you use can be interpreted ambiguously. Thus, becoming aware of levels of abstraction reduces the likelihood of misunderstandings. For example, if individuals do not have a reservoir of shared experiences or interpretations, using more concrete language can enhance understanding between them. The goal is to use the level of abstraction that meets the needs of your communication objectives and the situation.

CULTURE AND LANGUAGE

Since culture influences language use, communication between members of diverse cultures can be a challenge.

Culture Influences the Words Used

dominant culture

the culture in power; the mainstream culture

Both the **dominant culture** (the culture in power, the mainstream culture composed of people who share the same values, beliefs, and ways of behaving and communicating and who pass them on from one generation to another) and co-cultures (groups of people such as African Americans, Hispanics, Asians, musicians, athletes, environmentalists, and drug users, who have a culture of their own outside the dominant culture) have different languages. Hence, usages vary from culture to culture. If a concept is important to a culture, there will be a large number of terms to describe it. For example, in our culture, the word *money* is very important and we have many words to describe it: *Wealth, capital, assets, backing, resources,* and *finance* are just a few. Similarly, the Inuit, or Eskimos, have a number of words for snow, because they need to be able to make fine distinctions when speaking of it. Thus, for the Inuit, *gana* refers to falling snow, *akilukah* to fluffy fallen snow. In contrast to the Inuit, Arabs have only one word for snow—*talg*—and it refers to either ice or snow. The Arabs are simply not very interested in snow, since it rarely affects them. Similarly, Mandarin (a Chinese language) reflects the interests and concerns of the Chinese people. There are, for example, at least 19 Chinese words for silk and 8 for rice. And because the Chinese care deeply for their families, there is a plethora of words for relations. The Chinese have 5 words they can use for uncle, depending on whose brother he is.[10]

Some cultures encourage minimal verbal communication. A Japanese proverb says, "By your mouth you shall perish." What do you think this proverb means?

Sapir-Whorf hypothesis

the belief that the labels we use help shape the way we think, our worldview, and our behavior

The world we experience helps shape the language we speak, and the language we speak helps sustain our perception of reality and our view of our world. This idea is contained in the **Sapir-Whorf hypothesis,** which holds that the labels we use help shape the way we think, or our habits of thinking; our worldview, or the way we perceive the world; and our behavior. According to the Sapir-Whorf hypothesis, people from different cultures perceive stimuli and communicate differently, at least in part because of their language differences. For this reason, you should not assume that the words you use and the words people from other cultures use mean the same thing, nor should you assume that you even see the same reality when viewing the same stimulus. Quite simply, our language and our perception are intertwined.[11]

The Sapir-Whorf hypothesis has two threads: linguistic determinism and linguistic relativity. **Linguistic determinism** suggests that, our language influences how we interpret the world. **Linguistic relativity** suggests that, since language affects thought, persons who speak different languages will perceive the world differently. In *When Cultures Collide,* Richard Lewis explains linguistic relativity by explaining why the Zulu language has 39 words for green, while English has but 1. According to a Zulu chief, before their national highway system exisited, the Zulu were required to make long trips across the savannah, or grasslands. Since no signposts or maps existed to facilitate their journeys, they had to rely on the descriptions of those who traveled the road before. Thus, the Zulu devised different words for tree leaves, bush leaves, leaves vibrating with the wind, river greens, pool greens, tree trunk greens, crocodile greens, and so on. The different greens functioned much as a map would in alerting the travelers to important route signposts.[12]

linguistic determinism
the belief that language influences how we interpret the world

linguistic relativity
the belief that persons who speak different languages perceive the world differently

Cultural Differences Can Lead to Confused Translations

Translating ideas from one language to another sometimes leads to problems. Oftentimes the situation produced by a bungled translation, while costly, is still amusing. For example, an English-speaking representative of an American soft drink company could not understand why Mexican customers laughed when she offered them free samples of Fresca soda. In Mexican slang, the word *fresca* can be translated as "lesbian." Similarly, Beck's beer has been translated into Chinese as *Bei Ke,* which means "shellfish overcome."[13] In like fashion, Ford attributes the failure of its car, the Pinto, in Brazil to that fact that *Pinto* in Brazilian slang means "tiny male genitals." Ford subsequently renamed the car Corcel, meaning "horse". Along the same lines, Dr Pepper no longer runs its "I'm a Pepper" ads in the United Kingdom, because *pepper* in British slang means "prostitute."

Other times, however, a poor translation can insult and confuse recipients. For example, one Spanish-language letter sent to welfare recipients about changes in New Jersey's welfare program contained numerous grammatical errors, suggested a lack of multicultural competency, and suggested a lack of knowledge of basic Spanish. In a reference to the recipient's ability to support himself or herself, the letter uses the word *soportarse.* But the common translation of the verb *support* in Spanish is *sostener* or *mantener.* In Spanish, *soportarse* means "to tolerate oneself." Another section translated *parole violator* as "rapist under oath."[14]

In 2001 the United States experienced a diplomatic crisis with China after a U.S. spy plane collided with the EP-3E, a Chinese fighter, that had been tailing it. It appears that the Chinese wanted a formal apology, while the U.S.

government did not want to offer them one. Instead, both sides found a solution in linguistic ambiguity, writing a note that was nuanced enough to be satisfactory to the United States and China. Using one "sincere regret" and two "very sorrys" for the loss of the Chinese pilot and making an unauthorized landing, the letter was crafted in a way that enabled both sides to say that they had won. The U.S. side maintains it did not apologize. The Chinese say it did. The Chinese news agency interpreted "very sorry" as *"shenbiao qianyi,"* implying an apology. A Chinese version of the letter released by the U.S. Embassy said that the president was feeling very *baoqian*. According to one China expert, Robert Ross, *baoqian* is colloquial for apologizing for a minor matter, while *daoqian* has a greater gravity.[15] What this shows is that, by using language that can be interpreted in a number of ways, you can get what you want by appearing to express regret while not accepting blame. Apologies can be tough business. Have you ever had a similar experience?

Culture Influences Communication Style

As noted in Chapter 2, anthropologist Edward Hall distinguished between two kinds of cultures: *low-context cultures* (cultures in which self-expression is valued and whose members use explicit verbal messages to communicate information directly) and *high-context cultures* (cultures whose members place less reliance on explicit verbal messages and more emphasis on indirectness as a means of preserving social harmony). Because members of Asian cultures practice the principles of *omoiyari* (listeners need to understand the speaker without the speaker's being specific or direct) and *sassuru* (listeners need to use subtle cues to infer a speaker's meaning), they are apt to keep their feelings to themselves and use language more sparingly and carefully than do Westerners.[16] Because Westerners value straight talk, prefer to speak explicitly, and use inductive and deductive reasoning to make points, they may interpret the roundabout expressions of Asians as evasive, manipulative, or misleading.

The way parents in both Western and Asian cultures handle a request from a child to whom they do not want to accede provides a prime example of the cultural differences in directness. When confronted with such a situation, most U.S. parents would simply say no. In Japan, however, the parent would give reasons for denying the child's request but will not say no directly.[17] Every culture teaches its members its preferred style. Whereas in the United States we prefer to be up-front and tell it like it is, many Asian cultures stand by the value of indirectness because it helps people save face and avoid being criticized or contradicted in public.

In contrast to direct-speaking Westerners and succinct-speaking Asians, members of Middle Eastern cultures tend to rely heavily on elaborate, expressive, emotional discourse, that includes frequent exaggerations and repetitions for effect.[18] Such clashes in cultural style may lead to misunderstandings and conflicts between people.

Prejudiced Talk

Sometimes members of a dominant culture use derogatory terms or racist language to label members of a co-culture, disparage them as inferior or undesirable, and set them apart from the mainstream group. In effect, the language that others use to describe members of a co-culture affects our perception of them. **Linguistic prejudice** or the use of **prejudiced language,** which may also communicate racist attitudes, often reflects the dominant group's desire to exert its power over other groups. Such language stresses the differences between people of different groups, downplays any similarities, claims that the persons who are different do not make an effort to adapt, and notes that they are involved in negative acts and that they threaten the interests of in-group members.[19]

The courts have ruled that managers who use racial **code words** (words that are discriminatory but are not literally racist), such as "you people" and "one of them," help create a racially hostile environment. As a result of this ruling, many businesses are banning the use of such phrases.[20] Additionally, corporate advertisers and educational institutions have long used Native American names such as "redskins" "braves," "Seminoles," and "Crazy Horse," as well as logos and images such as severed heads, tomahawk chops, and a Native American princess to sell products and events. At present, 88 colleges and universities use these labels.[21] Stereotypical chants, dances, and music offensive to Native American culture and tradition are also used. Sports fans spend multimillions of dollars on such professional and nonprofessional sports merchandise. In your opinion, are such practices racist? Should they be eliminated? Why or why not?

Culture and Globalization Influence the Language Used

Because of the popularity of Hollywood and the Internet, the use of English around the world is growing. In the era of globalization, even some companies, such as French telecommunications company Alcatel, now use English as their internal language.[22] Not everyone is pleased with this side effect of globalization, however. The fear among non-English–speaking nations is that, if their citizens use English, the use of their native languages will disappear, threatening national identity. For example, so many young Germans mix their language with English so freely that their speech is called Denglish, a blend of German Deutsch and English.[23] The same phenomenon is happening in Japan. Contemporary Japanese is filled with so many English-sounding words that it is almost incomprehensible to persons belonging to older generations. The Japanese government appointed a panel to stem the foreign word corruption in the language.[24]

The same is true for persons within the United States for whom English is not their first language. When people from different groups converge, they begin to straddle cultural worlds, with language acting as the bridge. For example, the influence of English on New York Spanish produced Spanglish, a blend of Spanish and English. This may suggest that Latinos who speak Spanglish think of themselves less as members of national groups than they did in the past and more as members of a wider community. Spanglish is also used in TV programs such as *Mucha Lucha* and in Hallmark greeting cards, signifying its growing prominence. Do you think this is a good thing?

On the other hand, in an effort to find new ways to reach the now largest minority group in the United States, at the 2003 Grammy awards held in

linguistic prejudice
the use of prejudiced language

prejudiced language
language which communicates a negative bias

code words
words that are discriminatory but not literally racist

New York City, Crest, Procter & Gamble's (P&G) oral care brand, became the first P&G consumer product to air a Spanish-language advertisement during a nationally broadcast television event that reaches a general audience. The tag (last line) for the Crest spot, entitled "Good-Bye Kiss" was in English.[25] Do you think this is a good thing?

Hip Hop and Rap Talk

Hip hop is a social community that uses rap, a special language, to help express its culture.[26] Rap is a celebration of language that speaks to both the body and the brain. Since its introduction about a quarter of a century ago, rap has been maligned and praised, condemned and lauded. It has been blamed for promoting violence and misogyny, praised for promoting peace and minority influence. In 2003, the U.S. government began to broadcast raps on the airwaves of Radio Sawa in an effort to win over Arab youth.[27]

The rapper's words arrive in syncopated speech, which is peppered with both rapid-fire rhymed boasts and taunts. The subjects of rap range from sex, money, and guns to love, politics, the minutiae of our lives, and the American social experience. Rappers redefine the meanings of words. When someone attuned to the hip hop culture says, "I'm keeping it ghetto," he or she means "I'm keeping it real." The words in a rap mean something different than what most Americans have come to understand. Rap is an influence on American popular culture in music, fashion, and language, and it can be difficult to keep up with all the new words that hip hop adds to the national vocabulary. Consequently, journalist Alonzo Westbrook wrote *The Hip Hoptionary: The Dictionary of Hip Hop Terminology*. Westbrook traveled the United States from coast to coast in order to capture the language as it is used around the country. Sometimes the meaning of a word is coded in order for the rapper to hide behind it. For example, according to Westbrook, hip hop artists code the word *nigger* as an acronym to mean "never ignorant, getting

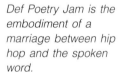

Def Poetry Jam is the embodiment of a marriage between hip hop and the spoken word.

goals accomplished." They flipped the word's meaning purposefully to make it less hurtful to African Americans.[28]

GENDER AND LANGUAGE

Language influences the attitudes we hold about males and females, as well as the way that males and females perceive each other.

Sexism in Language

Sexist language perpetuates negative stereotypes and negatively affects our communication. Frequently, the way we use language reflects the society in which we live.

The use of male generics, including *mankind, chairman, spokesman, manpower,* and *Man of the Year,* may cause men to be perceived as more important or significant than women, by suggesting that women can easily be ignored because they do not have the same status as men. To counter this perception, many companies and individuals no longer condone the use of male generics or other kinds of sexist language, preferring to use gender-neutral language instead.

Another way that language use may be sexist is the way words are used to address women. "Women, much more than men, are addressed through terms of endearment such as honey, cutie, and sweetie, which function to devalue women by depriving them of their name while renaming them with trivial terms."[29]

Finally, while the English language has more masculine terms than feminine terms, it has more negative feminine terms than masculine ones.[30]

Gender and Speech Style

Sometimes the sex of communicators affects not only the meaning we give to their utterances but also the very structure of those utterances. Women, for example, tend to use more tentative phrases, or **qualifiers,** in their speech than men do. Phrases like "I guess," "I think," and "I wonder if" abound in the speech patterns of women but not in those of men. This pattern is also passed on to the very young through their favorite cartoon characters. Just as their real-life counterparts are apt to do, female cartoon characters, more than

qualifiers
tentative phrases

Highlighting Who's Wed

Three decades ago, a survey of news stories revealed that a woman's marital status was mentioned 64 percent of the time, while a male's marital status was mentioned in only 12 percent of the stories.[31]

Pick up a copy of a recent English-language newspaper or magazine. Identify five male-centered and five female-centered news stories in it. Count the number of times the marital status of each person is referred to in each story. To what extent, if any, do the percentages of sexist references appear to have changed during the past three decades?

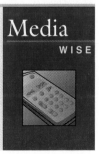

Media
WISE

Compile a list of differences you believe exist between men's and women's uses of language. Why do you think these differences have developed?

tag questions

a question that is midway between an outright statement and a yes-no question

disclaimers

remarks which diminish a statement's importance

male characters, use verbs that indicate lack of certainty ("I suppose") and words judged to be polite.[32] Is art mirroring life, or vice versa? When students were shown cartoon characters and asked to identify a character's sex on the basis of the words spoken by the character, students assigned the logical, concise, and controlling captions to male characters and the emotional, vague, and verbose captions to female characters.[33] Are cartoons helping to perpetuate stereotypes?

It appears that men and women rely on different conversational strategies. Women, for example, tend to turn statements into questions more than men do. Women typically ask something like "Don't you think it would be better to send them that report first?" Men, in contrast, typically respond with a more definitive "Yes, it would be better to send them that report first." According to Robin Lakoff, a researcher on language and gender, women do not "lay claim to" their statements as frequently as men do. In addition, women use more **tag questions** than men do. A tag is midway between an outright statement and a yes-no question. For instance, women often make queries like these: "Joan is here, isn't she?" "It's hot in here, isn't it?" By seeking verbal confirmation for their perceptions, women acquire a reputation for tentativeness. Similarly, women use more **disclaimers** than men do, prefacing their remarks with statements like "This probably isn't important, but . . . ." While male speech tends to be dominant, straightforward, and attention-commanding, female speech tends to be gentle, friendly, and accommodating.[34] Such practices weaken the messages women send to others.

Interestingly, according to communications researcher Patricia Hayes Bradley, even if men use tag questions, the perceptual damage done to them by this weaker verbal form is not as great as the damage done to women. Bradley found that, when women used tag questions and disclaimers, or failed to support their arguments, they were judged to be less intelligent and knowledgeable—but men were not. Simply talking "like a woman" causes a woman to be judged negatively.[35] Consequently, according to researchers Nancy Henley and Cheris Kramarae, females face a disadvantage when interacting with

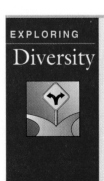

EXPLORING

Diversity

Language in Action

Interview five males and five females—if possible, from diverse cultural backgrounds. For each interviewee, in addition to identifying his or her sex, also identify his or her age, race, ethnicity, and social class. Ask each interviewee these questions:

1. In general, who tends to take turns more frequently when interacting, males or females?

2. In general, who tends to make reference to the comments of preceding speakers, males or females?

3. In general, who uses language more cooperatively, males or females?

4. In general, who makes more supportive comments, males or females?

5. In general, who is more polite, males or females?

To what extent, if at all, were the answers affected by sex? To what extent, if at all, were they affected by variables other than sex?

males: "Females are required to develop special sensitivity to interpret males' silence, lack of emotional expression, or brutality, and to help men express themselves. Yet it is women's communication style that is often labeled as inadequate and maladaptive."[36]

Gender-Lects

Gender affects how men and women use and process language in a number of other ways as well. According to linguist Deborah Tannen, men and women speak different **gender-lects.** While women speak and hear a language of connection and intimacy, Tannen finds that men speak and hear a language of status and independence.[37] As a result, when conversing with men, women tend to listen attentively rather than interrupt or challenge what a man is saying. Why? Tannen holds that it is because challenging the man could damage the established connection that most women believe must be preserved at all costs.

In addition, men and women tend to speak about different topics. Monica Hiller and Fern Johnson conducted a topic analysis of conversations held in two coffee shops, one frequented by young adults and the other by middle-aged and older customers. Their research revealed that, whereas men and women both talked about work and social issues, women talked about personal issues and the older men virtually never discussed personal issues.[38] Although men and women frequently talk to each other, their cross-gender talk differs topically from man-to-man or woman-to-woman talk. Women talk about their doubts and fears, personal and family problems, and intimate relationships, while, in general, men talk more about work and sports.

> **gender-lects**
> Deborah Tannen's term for language differences attributed to gender

LANGUAGE AND POWER

Both men and women have the potential to influence the way others perceive them by communicating in ways that make them appear more confident, more forceful, and thus more in control of a situation. The language people use helps us type them as having power or lacking power—as powerful or powerless.

Some people seem to announce their powerlessness through their language. It is assumed that, because they speak indirectly, they lack self-confidence and power. In contrast, persons perceived to be "powertalkers" make definite statements, such as "Let's go out to dinner tonight." Powertalkers direct the action; they assume control.

Typically, powertalkers also hesitate less in their speech. Instead of making statements filled with nonfluencies, such as "I wish you wouldn't, uh, keep me waiting so long," powertalkers enhance their sense of self-worth by projecting their opinions with more confidence. They eliminate fillers, such as "er," "um," "you know," "like," and "well," which serve as verbal hiccups and make a speaker appear weak.

Powertalkers also use fewer unnecessary intensifiers than more submissive talkers. "I'm not very interested in going" is a less forceful statement than "I'm not interested in going." Rather than strengthening a position, intensifiers actually deflate it.

| Flight crews are trained to express themselves in direct ways.

Powerful talk is talk that comes directly to the point. It does not contain disclaimers ("I probably shouldn't mention this, but . . .") or tag questions like those described in the section "Gender and Speech Style." If you succeed in speaking powertalk, your credibility and your ability to influence others will increase. Changing the power balance may be as simple as changing the words you use.

Talking powerfully may also be less risky. According to Deborah Tannen, speaking indirectly in specific situations can precipitate problems. She cites the following conversation about de-icing between a pilot and a copilot as an example of its dangers:

Copilot: Look how the ice is just hanging on his, ah, back, back there, see that? . . .

Copilot: See all those icicles on the back there and everything?

Captain: Yeah . . . .

Copilot: Boy, this is a, this is a losing battle here on trying to de-ice those things . . . .

Copilot: Let's check these tops again since we've been here awhile.

Captain: I think we get to go here in a minute.[39]

Has indirectness ever caused problems for you? What prevented you or the person you were speaking with from being more direct?

Less than a minute later, the plane crashed. While the copilot, probably because of his lower status, had tried to warn the pilot indirectly, the pilot failed to act on the cues. Indirectness, it seems, is easier for higher-status persons to ignore. As a result, flight crews today are trained to express themselves in more direct ways, and pilots are taught to pick up on indirect hints.

Tannen adds a note of caution by stating that indirect talk does not always reveal powerlessness. She finds that it is the prerogative of those in power to adopt either an indirect or a direct style to get something done. She also observes that the use of an indirect style is, in fact, the norm in many of the world's cultures. Japanese communication, for example, is judged to be good when meaning is derived without being stated directly. Again, this is in keeping with the key Japanese value *omoiyari,* or "empathy." The Japanese believe that people should be able to intuit each other's meaning.[40]

If you cry "Forward" you must be sure to make clear the direction in which to go. Don't you see that if you fail to do that and simply call out the word to a monk and a revolutionary, they will go in precisely opposite directions?
—Anton Chekhov

PROBLEMS WITH MEANING: PATTERNS OF MISCOMMUNICATION

If we do not make an attempt to analyze how people's backgrounds influence them in assigning meaning, we may have trouble communicating with them. For most of us, words have more than a single meaning. In fact, a commonly used word can frequently have more than 20 definitions. We know that a strike in bowling is different from a strike in baseball. We know that striking a match is not the same as striking up the band. For this reason, we must pay careful attention to the context of a message. Unfortunately, we frequently forget that words are rarely used in one and only one sense, and we assume when we speak to others that our words are being understood in only the way we intend them to be understood. Our receivers, however, may assume that their interpretation of our words is the meaning we intended. Let's explore what happens when this occurs.

Bypassing: Confusing Meanings

> All someone said was "Hi, Jack!" but at a suburban Detroit airport, those two words precipitated a crisis.
>
> A microphone happened to be open when an individual aboard a corporate jet greeted the co-pilot. Air traffic controllers in the airport's control tower equated those words with "hijack." The police, the SWAT team, and the FBI were alerted. The plane was ordered to return to the tower.[41]

Sometimes people think they understand each other, when, in fact, they are really missing each other's meaning. This pattern of miscommunication is called **bypassing,** because the interactants' meanings simply pass by one another.

We can identify two main kinds of bypassing.[42] One type occurs when people use different words or phrases to represent the same thing but are unaware that they are both talking about the same thing. For example, two urban politicians once argued vehemently over welfare policies. One held that the city's welfare program should be "overhauled," whereas the other believed that "minor changes" should be made. Far too much time passed before it was realized that the first politician's overhaul was actually equivalent to the second politician's minor changes. How many times have you argued unnecessarily because you were unaware that another person was simply using a different word or phrase to mean the same thing you were saying?

The second, and more common, type of bypassing occurs when people use the same word or phrase but give it different meanings. In such cases, people appear to be in agreement when they substantially disagree. Sometimes this type of bypassing is harmless. Semanticists tell a tall, but otherwise useful, story about a man who was driving on a parkway when his engine stalled. He managed to flag down another driver, who, after hearing his story, consented to push the stalled car to get it started. "My car has an automatic transmission," the first man explained, "so you'll have to get up to 30 or 35 miles an hour to get me moving." The other driver nodded in understanding, and the stalled motorist then climbed back into his own car and waited for the other car to line up behind him. After much more waiting, he turned around—to see the other driver coming at him at 30 miles per hour.

Developing an awareness that bypassing can occur when you communicate is a first step in preventing it from interfering with or needlessly complicating your relationships. If you believe it is possible for your listener to misunderstand you, then be willing to take the time needed to ensure that your meanings for words overlap. Try never to be caught saying, "It never occurred to me that you would think I meant . . ." or "I was certain you'd understand." To avoid bypassing, you must be "person-minded" instead of "word-minded." Remind yourself that your words may generate unpredictable or unexpected

bypassing
miscommunication that occurs when individuals think they understand each other but actually miss each other's meaning

Think of instances when bypassing caused problems for you.

reactions in others. Trying to anticipate those reactions will help you forestall communication problems.

Labeling: Confusing Words and Things

Sometimes we forget that it is people, not words, who make meanings. When this happens, we pay far too much attention to labels and far too little attention to reality. We can approach this phase of our study of meaning by considering the problem of labels and how strongly they can influence us.

After studying how labels affect behavior, linguistic researcher Benjamin Lee Whorf—who was one of the formulators of the Sapir-Whorf hypothesis— suggested that the way people define or label a situation has a dramatic impact on their behavior. According to Whorf, the words we use help mold our perceptions of reality and the world around us.[43] In other words, Whorf believes that our words actually determine the reality we are able to perceive. Thus, a person from a tropical country who has rarely, if ever, experienced snow and who simply calls snow *snow* probably sees only one thing (snow) when confronted with different kinds of frozen moisture falling from the sky. In contrast, skiers, who depend on snow, seek out snow, and diligently follow snow reports, are able to label and distinguish about six types of snow.

How important are labels in our culture? The Skill Builder "What's in a Name?" may help answer this question. A real-life judge faced with a similar case to skill builder ruled that the individual could not change his name to a number because a number was totalitarian and an offense to human dignity. What does a number, as opposed to a name, signify? Would we change if our names were changed?[44] In *Romeo and Juliet,* Shakespeare offered some thoughts on the significance of names when he had Juliet, of the Capulet family, say these words to Romeo, a Montague:

> 'Tis but thy name that is my enemy;
> Thou art thyself, though not a Montague.
> What's Montague? It is nor hand, nor foot,
> Nor arm, nor face, nor any other part
> Belonging to a man. O! be some other name;
> What's in a name? that which we call a rose
> By any other name would smell as sweet;
> So Romeo would, were he not Romeo call'd.

In an examination of the effect of labels, the concept of **intensional orientation** versus **extensional orientation** is useful. In his book *Influence,* Robert B. Cialdini provides an example that illustrates intensional orientation in action.[45] A friend of his had recently opened an Indian jewelry store in Arizona and wanted to move some turquoise jewelry she had been having trouble selling. She scribbled the following note to her head salesclerk: "Everything in this display case, price X ½." The owner then left for a business trip. When she returned to her jewelry store a few days later, she was not surprised to find that every piece had been sold. But she was surprised to discover that, because the employee had read the "½" in her scribbled message as a "2," the entire supply of turquoise jewelry had sold at twice the original price. The customers had displayed intensional orientation. In their minds, "expensive" meant "good," and the higher prices made them believe

---

What type of behavior would you exhibit around vats labeled "Gasoline Drums"? You would probably be careful not to light any matches; if you smoked, you would be certain not to toss away any cigarette butts. Would you change your behavior if the labels on the containers read "Empty Gasoline Drums"? Chances are, you might relax a bit and give less thought to the possibility of starting a fire— although empty drums are actually more dangerous because they contain explosive vapor.

What's in a name? Is who you are affected by what you are called? Do the names of your friends affect your opinions of them?

intensional orientation

preoccupation with labels

extensional orientation

focusing on the world of experience; not blinded by a label

What's in a Name?

First imagine that you are a district court judge and are faced with the following case. Simon Maynard Kigler would like to change his name to 1048. That is, Kigler would like to be called One Zero Four Eight, or One Zero for short. It is your task to decide whether to grant Kigler this requested name change. Justify your decision with specific reasons.

Judges in our country grant hundreds of name changes a year.[46] How do you imagine that your family and friends would react if you wanted to change your name? Do you think you should be required to have a legal basis, such as a divorce, an adoption, or a sex-change operation, to qualify for a name change? In your opinion, does changing your name really provide you with a new identity? Why or why not?

When it comes to the business world, an entire industry of namers has sprung up to coin new names for companies and products. Invented names are nothing new. Since the beginning of the twentieth century, companies have picked nebulous names, such as Amalgamated Holdings Limited and Consolidated Products Incorporated. Today's names, however, are heavier on mood—for example, the energetic-sounding Ajilon (an information technology consulting firm) and Motiva (a joint-venture oil refiner). Automakers and drug companies use the same tactic. The name of the sports car Miata and the drug Allegra could just have easily been mobile phone company names. Unlike the forthright names of older companies and brands that bore the name of the founder (Ford Motor, Hershey Foods) or the location (Hartford Property & Casuality, Alaska Airlines), today's names are ageless, placeless, and productless.[47] Imagine that you are a namer. It is your responsibility to come up with a name for a new computer company to rival Dell, Compaq, and IBM. What will you name the new company and why?

that the worth of the jewelry must be high. In other words, a dramatic increase in price led buyers to see the turquoise as valuable and desirable. But the customers were reacting to a label—the price—and labels don't always tell us all we have to know. The customers had failed to inspect the territory. If you react to a label without examining what the label represents, you are taking an intensional orientation. People who are intensionally oriented are easily fooled by words and labels. In contrast, when you take the time to look beyond a label, when you inspect the thing itself, you are taking an extensional orientation. People who are extensionally oriented are disposed to reality rather than to fantasy.

Evasive and Emotive Language

Frequently, our reaction to a person or event is totally changed by words, or by even a single word. If we are not aware of our responses, we can very easily be manipulated or conned by language.

Take some time to analyze the following sets of words to see how your reactions may change as the words used change:

1. Coffin　　　　Casket　　　　Slumber chamber
2. Girl　　　　　Woman　　　　Broad
3. Backward　　 Developing　　 Underdeveloped
4. The corpse　　The deceased　The loved one

A few years ago, the organization People for the Ethical Treatment of Animals asked the Federal Trade Commission to revise the fur label term

euphemism

the substitution of a pleasant word for a less pleasant one

"animal producing the fur" to read "animal slaughtered for the fur."[48] The word **euphemism** is derived from the Greek term meaning "to use words of good omen." When we use a euphemism, we substitute a pleasant term for a less pleasant one. Euphemisms can help conceal a communicator's meaning by making the message delivered appear more congenial than it actually is. For example, when First Fidelity Bancorp was sold to First Union Corporation, First Union (the bank) had to address the topic of lost jobs. In its press release, the bank announced: "First Union estimates expense savings of up to 5 percent from the combined operations, which reflects the expected consolidation of staff positions and the leveraging of technology expenses across a broader base."[49] Nothing was said about layoffs or job cuts. Employees who lose their jobs are "dehired," undergo a "vocational relocation," are left "indefinitely idling," or experience a "realignment" or "constructive dismissal."[50] When was the last time someone was fired? Knowing that the environment would be an issue in the 2004 presidential campaign, the Republican Party refocused its message on the environment by softening its language. Strategist Frank Luntz advised that Republicans use the term *climate change* in place of *global warming* because "while global warming has catastrophic communications attached to it, climate change sounds a more controllable and less emotional challenge."[51] He also suggested that *conservationist* be used instead of *environmentalist* because the former conveys a "moderate, reasoned, common sense position," while the latter has the "connotation of extremism."[52] Euphemisms, according to one expert on corporate doublespeak, are the "language of nonresponsibility."[53] The coiner of the term *doublespeak,* William Lutz, equates it with "linguistic fraud and deception."[54] Lutz believes that former president Ronald Reagan used doublespeak when he called the invasion of Grenada a "predawn vertical insertion," named the MX missile the "Peacemaker," and referred to taxes as "revenue enhancement." The Walt Disney Corporation did some verbal somersaults to make its Mr. Magoo character politically correct. Under fire by the National Federation of the Blind for resuscitating the nearsighted cartoon figure, a Disney spokesperson countered that Mr. Magoo is a "Forrest Gump"–like character who has a greater "intuitive ability to see what's going on" than does everyone else: "You see a flower, he sees a constellation. His visual limitation can impute poetic interpretation." According to Disney, Mr. Magoo isn't blind but, rather, "visually limited."[55]

In contrast to euphemisms, which disguise things we don't want to talk about and mask our feelings, are words we may use to editorialize on our feelings. For example, in 2002, President Bush started referring to countries that sponsored terrorism as belonging to an "axis of evil." How we feel about something or someone is revealed by the word choices we make. Thus, if we like an old piece of furniture, we might refer to it as an antique; if we don't like it, we might well call it a piece of junk. The words we use broadcast our attitude.

Politically Correct Language

The following definitions appear in Henry Beard and Christopher Cerf's tongue-in-cheek guide, *The Official Politically Correct Dictionary and Handbook:*

Lazy: motivationally deficient

Wrong: differently logical

Ugly: cosmetically different

Prostitute: sex-care provider

Fat: horizontally challenged[56]

What is politically correct language? Is it sensitive speech or censored speech? In what ways, if any, does its use sustain or violate our right of free speech?

Like so many other words, politically correct language means different things to different people. For some of us, being politically correct means making the effort not to offend by selecting words that demonstrate our respect for and sensitivity to the needs and interests of others. Politically correct language is meant to take the sting out of confrontations by blunting the sharpness of the words we use. For example, in the United States, over a period of time, the word *slow* was replaced by the word *retarded*, which was changed to *challenged* and then to *special*. Similarly, over a half century, the defining term for persons of African ancestry has shifted from *colored* to *Negro* to *Black* to *Afro-American* to *people of color* to *African American*.[57] When we use politically correct language, we adapt our language to reveal our sensitivity to the preferences of those we are conversing with.

For others, however, political correctness means that we feel compelled by societal pressures not to use some words—oftentimes referred to as taboo words—because we believe that doing so could cause others to label us as racist, sexist, homophobic, or ageist. For example, some years ago, a student at one Ivy League university was thought to be racist when he yelled, "Shut up, you water buffalo!" out a window at a noisy group of African-American

> *Each of us has learned to see the world not as it is, but through the distorting glass of our words. It is through words that we are made human, and it is through words that we are dehumanized.*
>
> **—Ashley Montagu,**
> ***The Language of Self-Deception***

Tug of Words

A news reporter for the *Washington Post,* Richard Cohen, ran into trouble with his paper when he suggested that store owners in Washington had reason to be wary of young Black men. A Long Island school decided to cancel a student production of *Peter Pan* because it was deemed offensive to Native Americans. The National Stuttering Project protested Nike ads that starred the cartoon character Porky Pig because the stuttering pig is often presented as a victim. It appears that the media are under pressure not to offend a single perceived interest group and, as a result, have begun to broadcast through a politically correct, sensitive lens.

Along the same lines, some people were outraged by the disparaging remarks made about civil rights icons Rosa Parks and Martin Luther King, Jr., in the 2002 film *Barbershop.* One of the film's characters, Eddie, says that Rosa Parks—the mother of the civil rights movement, who stayed in her seat on a segregated bus in Montgomery, Alabama, helping spark a boycott and modern civil rights movement—did so because she was tired. Eddie also refers to King as "a ho." In your opinion, are Eddie's comments meant to be humorous examples of social criticism and free speech, or should they have been cut from the film?

Where do you stand? In your opinion, does using politically correct language make its user appear more thoughtful? Or is the political correctness movement a form of thought control that threatens free speech and individuality and causes language to become content-free?

Media
WISE

women. Still others view political correctness and sensitivity training as a danger to free speech. Which of these three positions comes closest to the one you hold?

PROFANITY AND OBSCENITY: THE COARSING OF LANGUAGE

In 1995, Random House published a guide called *The F Word*. It seems that the use of the f-word had become so ubiquitous that such a book was judged justified. What this suggests is that the use of insults, vulgar expressions, and speech that degrades and encourages hostility in others is on the rise. It has become the language used to communicate.

In 2001, a female employee of a major construction company complained to the company's director of human resources about the cursing used in the company's facilities. The use of profanity distressed workers. The company countered by publishing "A Language Code of Ethics," separate and apart from its sexual harassment policy guide. It defined inappropriate language as "unwanted, deliberate, repeated, unsolicited profanity, cussing, swearing, vulgar, insulting, abusive or crude language." The company is now a cuss-free workplace. Workers who violate the policy are subject to disciplinary action.[58]

Profanity has become common, especially in high-stress jobs. Some policies differentiate between "casual" and "causal" swearing. Casual swearing is bad language we use for the fun of it, because we're too lazy to use other words and think we can get away with it. Causal swearing is profanity produced by the inability to control an aroused emotion, such as anger, frustration, or impatience.[59]

Why are we so comfortable using profanity? Might it be because profanity and speech that degrades have become so much a part of our mediated language landscape, used in virtually every crime/adventure television or cable program or film, that we hardly notice when a profane or an obscene expression occurs in real life?[60] Commonplace profanities now function as fillers—they slide off the tongue much as the words *you know* and *like* do. They have become part of the speech pattern—and not just for teenagers and adults. Even elementary school children use four-letter words when in and out of school. For some, this kind of speech is normative; it identifies them as a member of a group.

Students of popular culture observe that profanity has been increasing since the 1960s, when protesters used it to demonstrate their disdain for the establishment. Then, it was perceived as a liberating factor. Many of today's students are swearing, in part, because their parents did. A display of profanity used to be perceived as "macho." Women, for example, began to adopt it as they fought for equality of the sexes.

HBO's TV series *The Sopranos* gloried in profanity alternating between the f-word and the s-word. The opening of the movie spinoff of the *South Park* cable cartoon features the f-word approximately 30 times. Many Internet chat rooms contain pervasive profanity. It is a staple of the act of many stand-up comics. Entertainment media keep pushing the profanity envelope further and further making it a challenge to draw the line in either educational settings or the workplace. What do you think? Has profanity become an acceptable part of life, or should we develop the skill and discipline not to swear but to interact in a more civil manner?

Sometimes pejorative words that are used to stigmatize or degrade the members of a group are reclaimed by the group and redefined by group members as positive in nature. For example, gays and lesbians now use the term *queer* to make positive statements about who they are. Some women proudly refer to themselves as girls. And some African Americans, in an effort to invalidate the meaning that bigots attached to it, now use the racial epithet *nigger* among themselves.[61] In your opinion, does the reappropriation of words that were once used as slurs by members of the very groups that were the targets of the offensive language help ameliorate the damage done by those who used the same words in particularly offensive ways?

THINKING CRITICALLY ABOUT LANGUAGE: HOW TO MAKE LANGUAGE WORK FOR YOU

Whenever we communicate, we consciously or unconsciously select the level of language we will use. Normally, the words we select depend on the person with whom we are communicating and the situation in which we are communicating.

A Call for Common Sense

It should be apparent that, just as particular styles of apparel and behavior are appropriate for certain situations, so certain styles of language are appropriate at certain times and in certain places. Consider slang—a style of language used by special groups but not considered proper by society at large. Although we may use slang when conversing with our friends, it is inappropriate and unwise when speaking to an instructor or when delivering a speech to the town council.

A Call for Clarity

Simple language isn't so simple to use. Jacques Barzun said, "Simple English is no one's mother tongue. It has to be worked for."[62] In day-to-day communication, for any one of several reasons, we far too frequently use language that other people cannot easily understand. It doesn't matter how accurately a selected word or phrase expresses our ideas if the receivers cannot comprehend it. If you want to be understood, you must make every attempt to select words with meaning for your listeners. If you can accomplish this, you will have taken a giant step toward achieving understanding.

Another good rule to follow if you hope to achieve clarity is to keep jargon to a minimum unless your receiver is schooled in the jargon. In other words, speak the same language as your listener. Most of us who live in the United States share a common language, but many of us also frequently use one or more sublanguages. A sublanguage is simply a special language used

What kind of language do you find personally offensive? How does your language use change from person to person? Would you feel comfortable using obscenities with any of the following people: your best friend, your instructor, your employer? Why or why not?

"It's only fair to warn you that my conversation contains adult language that you may find offensive."

Jargon functions as shorthand for people who understand the use. In the war in Iraq, weapons of mass destruction were referred to in briefings the military had for the press and public as WMDs. Would you have understood this use?

by members of a particular subculture. We all belong to several subcultures—a national group, an occupational group, an educational group, an ethnic group, and perhaps a religious group. Having a common sublanguage helps members of the group attain a sense of identity.

However, since all sublanguages are intended to enable communication only within a particular group, a sublanguage is probably not readily understood by outsiders. As an example, consider the following brief dialogue between two doctors:

Doctor 1: How's that patient you were telling me about?

Doctor 2: Well, she's improving. But now she's suffering from cephalagia complicated by agrypnia.

In analyzing this interchange, you would probably not immediately guess that *cephalagia* is the medical term for a headache and that *agrypnia* refers to insomnia. Thus, people schooled in the technical language of a particular group should constantly guard against what may be an innate temptation to impress others rather than to communicate. In short, if we want our receivers to understand us, we must always ask ourselves, "Who am I talking to?"

Using readily understandable language need not keep you from aiming for accuracy. Never abandon your efforts to find the exact words that represent the ideas you want to communicate. Remember that a clear message is neither ambiguous nor confusing.

TECHNOLOGY AND LANGUAGE USE

Internet user Andrew Walker sometimes lapses into **onlinespeak** when writing offline: In one school paper, he wrote, "Surplus is an excess. But surplus can also mean 2 much." His instructor deducted 10 points. The protocol of informality that marks electronic communication for Andrew and millions of others has led to our using language in ways we never would have before and has set off a debate regarding whether the Internet invigorates language or strips it of its expressive power.[63]

onlinespeak
the protocol of informality that marks electronic communication

When linguists talk of dialects, by tradition, they are referring to the spoken word. The Internet, however, appears to have spawned a new written dialect, one in between speech and writing, in which punctuation is abandoned, uppercasing is used primarily if you are shouting, and an array of acronyms substitute for phrases. Knowing and using the dialect allows us to develop a sense of belonging to the group—a group that exists in cyberspace.

Currently, millions of us are writing letters, exchanging thoughts, and sharing meaning in a relatively new domain—a networked world, or online environment.[64] As we do so, we rely on our command and understanding of language to accomplish the encoding of our thoughts on a screen. We also become part of a virtual online community, or cybercommunity, that does not recognize national or linguistic borders. As members of a cybercommunity,

Educators believe that we should know where to draw the line between formal and conversational writing. Unthinkingly, "generation text" members mix rapid-fire Internet English and schoolwork.[65] Do you ever do this?

however, we probably share a special language, the equivalent of online jargon, as a strategy of connection. During our communications, for example, we may use truncated speech and acronyms for phrases, including *BTW* for "by the way," *TTFN* for "ta-ta for now," and *IMHO* for "in my humble opinion."

In addition to online truncation, the language of expedience has spread from the Internet to cell-phones.[66] Like the Internet, mobile phone text messaging has its share of short-hand expressions, including RUOK (Are you OK?), CUL8R (See you later), BHL8 (Be home late), TAH (Take a hint), A3 (Anytime, anywhere, any place), SPST (Same place, same time), XLNT (Excellent), U4E (Yours forever), and YTLKIN2ME (You talking to me?). One reason for the popularity of text messages is that they are cheap, although, as many of us know, their cost can add up. Text messaging caught on in the United Kingdom before the United States. Now, popular in the United States, the estimate is that over 15 million now use it, and a number of text-messaging shorthand dictionaries have been published to facilitate its use.[67]

Rules of the Internet—also known as **netiquette**—continue to evolve. Usually, the participants themselves work out conversational ground rules. The word *flame,* for example, is used to describe what occurs when one person online verbally attacks or denigrates another. Flaming, like intemperate speech during face-to-face interaction, is generally frowned upon. As an Internet user, you may *lurk,* or observe, before you actually enter into online dialogues with others. Doing so enables you to better understand and become sensitive to the nature of the online group before you plunge in.[68]

The online style of writers (how they say something) is equally as important as their message (what they say). When it comes to the sound, or tone, of online messages, e-mail writers frequently experience problems. Because of the volume of e-mail messages we send and receive, and the speed with which we fire them off, we may operate under the mistaken impression that we don't need to edit closely what we write. We should concern ourselves with tone, however, because what we write could end up being read by multiple readers.

Why has text messaging become so popular? It appears that people longing for private conversations enjoy communicating silently, especially in public places. Many use text messaging while at movies, at sports events, or on subways. Are you one of the many?

netiquette

rules of the Internet

e-SEARCH

Netiquette and Geek-Speak

Purely textual, online interaction does not work on its own. With this in mind, describe the positive norms of social language use that you believe should be promoted during online activity. Then discuss what language use taboos, if any, you think should be avoided. Finally, identify what sanctions, if any, you would recommend for violations of your established norms.

To what extent do you find that, the more time people spend online, the more they tend to talk about people as if they were machines? For example, to be "uninstalled" means to be fired, doing a "bit flip" means experiencing a disturbing personality alteration, engaging in "nonlinear behavior" (NLB) means acting irrationally, and taking a "bio-break" indicates a trip to the bathroom. Find other examples that demonstrate how technological developments have left their mark on online language. Discuss the degree to which you believe that such "geek-speak" disparages the real world and flesh-and-blood human beings and, as a result, gives credence to the unflattering stereotype of the computer geek as "withdrawn and relationally incompetent."

To this end, we should do our best to edit our e-mails for unintended meanings before clicking on "send."[69]

Instant messaging (IM) has also gone corporate, spreading to the workplace. It is helping reverse a trend attributed to e-mail and voice mail that had made it difficult for anyone to determine if businesspeople were in the office. It also facilitates telecommuting, because it can verify who is really working at home or at least is logged in. Since failing to respond quickly to an IM message is considered rude, workers typically sign out when they leave their office or show themselves as "too busy to chat" when they know their reply will be delayed in responding.[70]

Since members of online communities tend to be more concerned with what others think rather than what they look like, the presence of sexist and racist language tends to be rare. Nonetheless, one admonition warned: "We would like to remind the frequent posters here that what we say is going out to a potential readership of between 25,000 and 40,000 individuals. . . . So words do have meaning and what you write in haste or in anger may have more influence than you realize."[71] As we see, in many ways, language use on the Internet shares much in common with language use in society.

GUIDELINES FOR DEVELOPING LANGUAGE SKILLS

Throughout this chapter we have stressed that mastery of certain language skills will improve your ability to communicate effectively with others. Use the following guidelines to ensure that your words work for you rather than against you.

Identify How Labels Affect Your Behavior

We can state one of the most fundamental precepts of language simply and directly: Words are not the things they represent. Always remember that words are nothing more than symbols. No connection necessarily exists between a symbol and what people have agreed that symbol represents. In other words, symbols and their representations are independent of each other.

All of us at times respond as if words and things were one and the same—for example, when we make statements like these: "A bathroom is a bathroom. It's certainly not a water closet." "Pigs are called pigs because they wallow in mud and grime." Think of how often you buy a product such as Intimate, Brut, Bold, Caress, Secret, or Angel because of what the label seems to promise. How many times have you turned against a person because he or she is called liberal, conservative, feminist, chauvinist, intellectual, or brainless? Examine your behavior with others. Make certain that you react to people, not to the categories in which you or others have placed them.

Identify How the Words You Use Affect Your Feelings and Attitudes

It is important to recognize that few of the words you select to describe things are neutral. S. I. Hayakawa and Alan R. Hayakawa, authors of *Language in*

Thought and Action, noted this:

> We are a little too dignified, perhaps, to growl like dogs, but we do the next best thing and substitute series of words, such as "You dirty double-crosser!" "The filthy scum!" Similarly, if we are pleasurably agitated, we may, instead of purring or wagging the tail, say things like "She's the sweetest girl in all the world."[72]

snarl words

words with highly negative connotations

purr words

words with highly positive connotations

We all use **snarl words** (words with highly negative connotations) and **purr words** (words with highly positive connotations). These words do not describe the people or things we are talking about; rather, they describe our personal feelings and attitudes. When we make statements like "He's a great American," "She's a dirty politician," "He's a bore," "She's a radical," "He's a Wall Street sleaze," "She's a greedy conservative," "He's a male chauvinist pig," or "She's a crazy feminist," we should not delude ourselves into thinking that we are talking about anything but our own preferences. We are neither making reports nor describing conditions that necessarily exist. Instead, we are expressing our attitudes about something. Under such circumstances, if others are to determine what we mean by our descriptions, they are compelled to follow up and ask why.

Count the number of times you use purr words and snarl words each day. What do they reveal about your likes and dislikes? How do your words give you away?

It is also important to realize that a word that does not function as a snarl or purr word for you may function that way for someone else, even if you do not intend it to be given such an interpretation. All that matters is the response of the person with whom you are interacting. Therefore, become conscious of how others react to the words you use. Listen to people around you and attempt to read their responses to your words. Which words that incite them would not incite you? Which words do you find unacceptable or offensive? Why?

Identify How Experience Can Affect Meaning

Since we assign meaning on the basis of our experience, and since no two people have had exactly the same set of experiences, it follows that no two people have exactly the same meanings for the same word. This aspect of language should be neither lauded nor cursed; it should simply be remembered.

Focus on Service Learning

How can an understanding of language and meaning differences benefit the staff of a local health clinic?

Too frequently, we let our words lead us away from where we want to go; we unwittingly antagonize our families, friends, or co-workers. We are infuriated, for example, when an important business deal collapses because our position has not been understood, or we are terrified when the leaders of government miscommunicate and put their countries on a collision course.[73]

Thinking **CRITICALLY**

Reflect and Respond

Language expert Wendell Johnson was fond of noting that not only does the language we use put words in our mouths; it also puts notions in our heads.

On the basis of your personal understanding of language use and misuse, discuss the kinds of notions that language may promote.

In order to avoid or alleviate such problems, we must remember that meanings can change as the people who use words change. You might wear a sport jacket and slacks or a sweater and skirt if you are invited to a casual party, but this does not mean that everyone else who is invited to the party would interpret *casual* in the same way. One person might wear jeans and a sport shirt, another shorts and a T-shirt. Likewise, you may feel that the word *freak* has only positive connotations, but this does not exclude the possibility that another person thinks it has only negative connotations. The meanings people attribute to symbols are affected by their background, age, educational level, and work. Forgetting this can cause misunderstandings and lead to communication difficulties.

As John Condon, author of Semantics and Communication, advises, "Learning to use language intelligently begins by learning not to be used by language."

Be Sure That Meanings Are Shared

Since intended meanings are not necessarily the same as perceived meanings, you may need to ask people with whom you are speaking such questions as "What do you think about what I've just said?" and "What do my words mean to you?" Their answers serve two important purposes: They help you determine whether you have been understood and they permit the other people to become involved in the encounter by expressing their interpretations of your message. If differences in the assignment of meaning surface during this feedback process, you will be able immediately to clarify your meanings by substituting different symbols or by relating your thoughts more closely to the background, state of knowledge, and experiences of your receivers.

Revisiting Chapter Objectives

1. **Define *language*.**   Language is a unified system of symbols that permits a sharing of meaning. Language allows minds to meet, merge, and mesh. When we make sense out of people's messages, we learn to understand people.

2. **Describe and explain the triangle of meaning.**   There is no direct relationship between words and things, as Ogden and Richards' triangle of meaning illustrates. Words don't "mean"; people give meaning to words.

3. **Distinguish between connotative and denotative meanings.**   A serious barrier to communication occurs when we forget the fact that words have both generally agreed-to denotative (objective, or dictionary) meanings and highly individualized connotative (subjective, or personal) meanings. As a result, different people give different meanings to the same words.

4. **Discuss how culture and gender influence language use.**   Culture and gender influence the ways men and women experience, process, and use language. In part because language and perception are intertwined, language use varies from culture to culture. Words change over time and from place to place according to individual experience. Language also influences the attitudes we hold about males and females, as well as how males and females perceive each other.

THE Wrap-Up

5. **Provide examples of bypassing and intensional and extensional orientation.** Among the communication problems that result from changes in meaning are bypassing (when people think they understand each other but in fact do not) and mistaking a label for the thing itself (taking an intensional rather than an extensional orientation).

6. **Identify two strategies to improve oral language abilities.** There are two strategies we can use to improve our oral language abilities. First, we can use common sense to recognize that certain styles of language are appropriate at certain times and in certain places. Second, we can seek to make ourselves as clear as possible by selecting words with meaning for our listeners, taking into account their educational level and the sublanguages they understand.

7. **Explain how technology is affecting language use.** Technology is influencing language use. How we communicate online frequently differs from how we communicate in person. Some believe the Internet is invigorating language, while others believe it is stripping language of its expressive value.

Resources for Further Inquiry and Reflection

To apply your understanding of how the principles in Chapter 5 are at work in our daily lives, consult the following resources for further inquiry and reflection. Or, if you prefer, choose any other appropriate resource. Then connect the ideas expressed in your chosen selection with the communication concepts and issues you are learning about both in and out of class.

 Listen to Me

"Sweet Talkin' Guy" (The Chiffons)
"Snoop Dogg" (Snoop Dogg)
"Yakety Yak" (The Coasters)

Discuss the extent to which one's choice of words can influence the establishment and course of a relationship.

 Read Me

William Gibson. *The Miracle Worker.* New York: Bantam Books, 1975.
George Bernard Shaw. *Pygmalion.* New York: Dover, 1994.

Discuss how one of the preceding works illustrates the concept "meaning is in people, not in words."

 View Me

Nell   *Windtalkers*
What Women Want

In each of these films, the use of words either interferes with or facilitates a character's objective. Choose one film and discuss the role language plays in it to advance or impede the character's goals.

 Tell Me

Share with the class the insights you gained from your chosen Listen to Me, View Me, or Read Me selection.

Consider the following two statements made by one person: "I value freedom of speech." "I find hate speech and racist, sexist, and ageist speech objectionable." How do you reconcile the two positions? In your opinion, should any of the objectionable kinds of speech have First Amendment protection? In a brief presentation, explain why or why not.

Key Chapter Terminology

Communication
Works

online learning center

www.mhhe.com/gamble8

Use the Communication Works CD-ROM and the Online Learning Center at www.mhhe.com/gamble8 *to further your knowledge of the following terminology.*

bypassing 129
code words 123
connotative meaning 117
denotative meaning 117
disclaimers 126
dominant culture 120
euphemism 132
extensional orientation 130
gender-lects 127
intensional orientation 130
language 114
linguistic determinism 121

linguistic prejudice 123
linguistic relativity 121
netiquette 138
onlinespeak 137
prejudiced language 123
purr words 140
qualifiers 125
Sapir-Whorf hypothesis 120
snarl words 140
symbol 114
tag questions 126
triangle of meaning 115

Test Your Understanding

Communication
Works

online learning center

www.mhhe.com/gamble8

Go to the *Self Quizzes* on the Communication Works CD-ROM and the book's Online Learning Center at www.mhhe.com/gamble8.

Notes

1. Michael Agar. *Language Shock: Understanding the Culture of Conversation.* New York: Morrow, 1994.
2. C. K. Ogden and I. A. Richards. *The Meaning of Meaning.* Orlando, FL: Harcourt Brace Jovanovich, 1993.
3. Loretta Breuning. "Networking with Yourself: How the Brain Uses Information (Part 1)." *ETC.* 47:2, summer 1990, p. 106.
4. Steven Lee Myers. "A Kinder, Gentler Rogues' Gallery." *New York Times,* June 25, 2000.
5. Charles F. Vich and Ray V. Wood. "Similarity of Past Experience and the Communication of Meaning." *Speech Monographs* 36, pp. 159–162.
6. For a discussion of how the mindless use of language affects behavior, see Ellen Langer. "Interpersonal Mindlessness and Language." *Communication Monographs* 59:3, September 1992, pp. 324–327.
7. Robert F. Worth. "Horrific Crime Is Captured in One Word." *New York Times,* December 6, 2002, p. B4.
8. Michiko Kakutani. "When the Greeks Get Snide." *New York Times,* June 27, 2000, p. E1.
9. See, for example, S. I. Hayakawa and Alan R. Hayakawa. *Language in Thought and Action,* 5th ed. Orlando, FL: Harcourt Brace Jovanovich, 1990.
10. Nicholas D. Kristof. "Chinese Relations." *New York Times Magazine,* August 18, 1991, pp. 8–10.
11. B. L. Whorf. "Science and Linguistics." In M.J.B. Carroll, ed. *Language, Thought, and Reality.* Cambridge: Massachusetts Institute of Technology Press, 1956; and Paul Kay and Willet Kempton. "What Is the Sapir-Whorf Hypothesis?" *American Anthropologist* 86, 1984, pp. 65–79. Also, for a discussion of cultural diversity and political correctness, see Irving H. Bucher. "The Politics of Race, Gender and Sexual Orientation: Implications for the Future of America." *Equity and Excellence* 25:2–4, winter 1992, pp. 222–227.
12. R. Lewis. *When Cultures Collide: Managing Successfully across Cultures.* London: Nicholas Brealey, 1996, p. 16.

13. Liz Sly. "In China, the Right Name Is Crucial." *The Record,* October 6, 1996, p. A-31.

14. Elizabeth Llorente and Ovetta Wiggins. "Human Services Agency to Correct Letter." *The Record,* February 7, 1997, p. A-3.

15. Barbara Slavin. "U.S. Juggles Words, Finds Right Combination," *USA Today,* April 12, 2001, p. 3A.

16. See, for example, Deborah Tannen. *Talking from 9 to 5: How Women's and Men's Conversational Styles Affect Who Gets Heard, Who Gets Credit, and What Gets Done at Work.* New York: Morrow, 1994.

17. Tannen.

18. See, for example, A. Almaney and A. Alwan. *Communicating with the Arabs.* Prospect Heights, IL: Waveland Press, 1982.

19. See, for example, Carolyn Calloway-Thomas, Pamela J. Cooper, and Cecil Blake. *Intercultural Communication: Roots and Routes.* Boston: Allyn & Bacon, 1999, pp. 154–155: and William B. Gudykunst. *Bridging Differences: Effective Intergroup Communication,* 2nd ed. Thousand Oaks, CA: Sage, 1994, p. 83.

20. "Work Week." *Wall Street Journal,* p. A1.

21. J. J. Hemmer, Jr. "Exploitation of Native American Symbols: A First Amendment Analysis." Paper presented at the National Communication Association annual convention, New Orleans, LA, November 22, 2002.

22. Suzanne Daily. "In Europe, Some Fear National Languages Are Endangered." *New York Times,* April 16, 2001, pp. A1, A10.

23. Steven Komarow. "Some Germans Fear Language Is Being Infected by English." *USA Today,* May 16, 2001, p. 6A.

24. Howard W. French. "To Grandparents, English Word Trend Isn't 'Naisu.'" *New York Times,* October 23, 2002, p. A4.

25. See http://www.hispanicprwire.com/release_Crest_Ad_ENG.htm.

26. B. Kitwana. *The Hip Hop Generation: Young Blacks and the Crisis in African American Culture.* New York: Basic Books, 2002.

27. Jody Rosen. "Rap: A Celebration of Language." *The Record,* December 2, 2002, p. L15.

28. National Public Radio. Interview of Alonzo Westbrook by Tavis Smiley, November 5, 2002.

29. K. L. Schmidt. "Exit, Voice, Loyalty, and Neglect: Responses to Sexist Communication in Dating Relationships." Unpublished doctoral dissertation. Arizona State University, 1991, p. 30.

30. A. Nilsen. "Sexism as Shown through the English Vocabulary." In A. Nilsen, H. Bosmajian, H. Gershuny, and J. Stanley, eds. *Sexism and Language.* Urbana, IL: National Council of Teachers of English, 1977.

31. K. G. Foreit, T. Agor, J. Byers, J. Larue, H. Lokey, M. Palazzini, M. Paterson, and L. Smith. "Sex Bias in the Newspaper Treatment of Male-Centered and Female-Centered News Stories." *Sex Roles* 6, 1980, pp. 475–480.

32. A. Mulac, J. Bradac, and S. Mann. "Male/Female Language Differences and Attributional Consequences in Children's Television." *Human Communication Research* 11, 1985, pp. 481–506.

33. C. Kramer. "Stereotypes of Women's Speech: The Word from Cartoons." *Journal of Popular Culture* 8, 1974, pp. 624–630.

34. C. Kramer. "Male and Female Perceptions of Male and Female Speech." *Language and Speech* 20, 1978, pp. 151–161.

35. Patricia Hayes Bradley. "The Folk-Linguistics of Women's Speech: An Empirical Examination." *Communication Monographs* 48, pp. 73–90.

36. Nancy M. Henley and Cheris Kramarae. "Gender, Power and Miscommunication." In Nickolas Coupland, Howard Giles, and John Weimann, eds. *Miscommunication and Problematic Talk.* Newbury Park, CA: Sage, 1991, p. 42.

37. Deborah Tannen. *You Just Don't Understand.* New York: Ballantine, 1991, p. 42.

38. M. Hiller and F. L. Johnson. "Gender and Generation in Conversational Topics: A Case Study of Two Coffee Shops." Paper presented at the annual meeting of the Speech Communication Association, San Diego, CA, November 1996.

39. Cited in Craig Johnson and Larry Vinson. "Placement and Frequency of Powerless Talk and Impression Formation." *Communication Quarterly* 38:4, fall 1990, p. 325.

40. For these and other examples of the differences between direct and indirect style, see Deborah Tannen. "How to Give Orders Like a Man." *New York Times Magazine,* August 28, 1994, pp. 46–49.

41. "'Hi, Jack' Greeting to Co-Pilot Causes Stir." *The Record,* June 8, 2000, p. A-13.

42. See William V. Haney. *Communication and Organizational Behavior,* 3rd ed. Homewood, IL: Irwin, 1973, pp. 247–248.

43. Benjamin Lee Whorf. "Science and Linguistics." In John B. Carroll, ed. *Language, Thought and Reality: Selected Writings of Benjamin Lee Whorf.* Cambridge, MA: MIT Press, 1966.

44. For a discussion of names and how they affect us, see Mary Marcus. "The Power of a Name." *Psychology Today,* October 1976, pp. 75–76, 108.

45. For a more complete discussion of this incident, see Robert B. Cialdini. *Influence.* New York: Quill, 1993.

46. Eugenie Allen. "Changing Names." *Time,* July 10, 2000.

47. Daniel Altman. "What's in a Name? Today, Not Much." *New York Times,* August 23, 2001, p. A18.

48. "Washington Wire." *Wall Street Journal,* October 14, 1994.

49. Don Stancavish. "Companies Speaking in Euphemisms." *The Record,* February 19, 1996, p. B-1.

50. Louis Lavelle. "Canning the Gibberish." *The Record,* January 21, 2000, p. B-1.

51. Stancavish; William Lutz. *The New Doublespeak: Why No One Knows What Anyone's Saying Anymore.* New York: HarperCollins, 1996.

52. Jennifer Lee. "A Call for Softer, Greener Language." *New York Times,* March 2, 2003, p. 24.

53. Ibid.

54. See William Lutz. *Doublespeak Defined.* New York: Harper Resource, 1999; and National Council of Teachers of English. "The 1999 Doublespeak Awards." *ETC* 56:4, winter 1999–2000, p. 484.

55. Lisa Bannon. "The Vision Thing." *Wall Street Journal,* July 31, 1997, p. A1.

56. Henry Beard and Christopher Cerf. *The Politically Correct Dictionary and Handbook.* New York: Villard Books, 1992.

57. Donald G. McNeil, Jr. "Like Politics, All Political Correctness Is Local." *New York Times,* October 11, 1998, p. WK-5.

58. Rachel Emma Silverman. "On-the-Job Cursing: Obscene Talk Is the Latest Target of Workplace Ban. *Wall Street Journal,* May 8, 2001, p. B12.

59. See, for example, James O'Connor. *Cuss Control: The Complete Book on How to Curb Your Cursing.* Three Rivers, 2000.

60. J. B. Rusher. *Prejudiced Communication: A Social Psychological Perspective.* New York: Guilford Press, 2001.

61. Randall Kennedy. *Nigger: The Strange Career of a Troublesome Word.* New York: Pantheon Press, 2002.

62. Patricia T. O'Conner. "Plainspeak: Taking the Gobble Out of Gobbledygook." *New York Times Magazine,* August 23, 1999, sec. 6, p. 22.

63. Amy Harmon. "Internet Changes Language for :-) & :-(." *New York Times,* February 20, 1999, p. B-7.

64. T. K. Bikson and C. W. A. Panis. "Computers and Connectivity: Current Trends." Internet (http://www.rand.org/publication/MR/MR650/index.html), 1996.

65. Jennifer Lee, "I Think, Therefore IM." *New York Times,* September 19, 2002, pp. C1, C4.

66. Lini S. Kadaba. "4GET SPLLG & STRT MSGing!" *The Record,* August 25, 2002, pp. F1, F2.

67. Ibid.; and Sarah Ellison. "RU ReD 4 This? Text-Messaging Breeds a Brave New Dialect." *Wall Street Journal,* May 3, 2001, pp. A1, A4.

68. For a guide to Internet use, see Randy Reddict and Elliot King. *The Online Student: Making the Grade on the Internet.* Fort Worth, TX: Harcourt Brace College, 1996.

69. Philip Vassallo. "Beware the Seven Deadly Sins of Tone." *Etc: A Review of General Semantics* 57:1, spring 2000, pp. 100–114.

70. William M. Bulkeley. "Instant Message Goes Corporate; 'You Can't Hide.'" *Wall Street Journal,* September 4, 2002, pp. B1, B4.

71. Margaret L. McLaughlin, Keery K. Osborne, and Christine B. Smith. "Standards of Conduct on Usenet." In Steven G. Jones, ed. *Cybersociety.* Thousand Oaks, CA: Sage, 1995, p. 103.

72. Hayakawa and Hayakawa.

73. For more information, see *Time,* December 17, 1990, p. 114.

CHAPTER 6

Nonverbal Communication: Silent Language Speaks

After finishing this chapter, you should be able to

1. Define and distinguish among the following terms: *nonverbal communication, kinesics, paralanguage, proxemics, chronemics,* and *haptics.*

2. Explain why the face is an important source of information.

3. Explain how artifactual communication and color can affect interaction.

4. Distinguish among the following terms: *intimate distance, personal distance, social distance* and *public distance,* and *informal space, semifixed-* *feature space,* and *fixed-feature space.*

5. Explain why territoriality is an important concept in communication.

6. Identify the ways gender, diversity, and technology influence nonverbal behavior.

7. Explain the role nonverbal cues play in acception and truthtelling.

8. Identify how you can improve your nonverbal communication effectiveness.

What you are speaks so loudly that I cannot hear what you say.

—Ralph Waldo Emerson

It is easy to be wise after the event.

—Arthur Conan Doyle's Sherlock Homes

Some years ago, a youth by the name of Peter Reilly was convicted of a crime he did not commit. Years after his imprisonment, the court reversed Reilly's conviction because his written confession to police had not been videotaped. In the court's eyes, the lack of video substantiation of Reilly's written confession made it impossible to ascertain if his nonverbal cues would have supported or undermined the written message. It appears as if the court recognizes that nonverbal communication is a requisite part of the sharing and understanding of meaning. Whereas we can plan what we want to say before we write it, most nonverbal messages are neither planned nor deliberate.[1] The court's position confirmed that verbal messages are easier to fake and that *how* an individual says something provides a vital part of a message.

More recently, customs inspectors at John F. Kennedy Airport were carefully watching hundreds of passengers getting off a flight from South America. As people moved past them, they were on the lookout for telltale body language indicative of exceptional nervousness. One man caught their attention. His lips were so chapped and dry they appeared white and "his carotid artery was jumping out of his neck." They took the man aside and questioned him only to discover that he had paid cash for a business-class ticket, even though he was a low-paid service worker. X rays revealed that the man had swallowed several bags of heroin pellets.

Since 9/11, the science of spotting nervous or threatening behavior has gained respect. According to one security consultant, "well-trained body language profilers might have spotted and questioned some of the September 11th hijackers" using basic behavior pattern recognition work. In fact, security personnel positioned at airports and in office buildings are now trained to watch for darting eyes and hand tremors in addition to identifying other cues of suspicious behavior. For example, they are being taught that our lips get thinner when we become angry, and our blink rate increases when we become nervous. They now know that our nostrils flare when we are aroused, and our blood flow increases, reddening our skin when we prepare for a physical or mental fight.[2]

COMMUNICATING WITHOUT WORDS

Do you know anyone who has had trouble establishing and maintaining good relationships at work and in their personal lives, but they or you can't figure out why? The answer may be that they lack the nonverbal communication skills that are essential to social success.[3] Some of us, it appears, have trouble picking up on social cues that others of us use regularly and take for granted. The nonverbally skill-less are, for all practical purposes, communication clueless. For example, many gay men and lesbians possess the ability to identify other homosexuals accurately after only very limited interpersonal contact. They rely on eye contact, clothing style and fit, jewelry, facial expressions, posture, body type, and walk or gait, as well as the types and frequencies of gestures to provide them with needed information.[4] Given the vulnerability gays and lesbians face because of homophobia, their perceptual accuracy offers self-protection. Being able to understand and use nonverbal language is essential for developing and maintaining healthy, productive relationships.[5]

The founder of psychoanalysis, Sigmund Freud, once wrote: "He that has eyes to see and ears to hear may convince himself that no mortal can keep a secret. If his lips are silent, he chatters with his fingertips; betrayal oozes out of him at every pore." Our creative problem-solving abilities are often challenged as we seek to make sense out of communication situations. The following is a mystery that challenged many people:

> In turn-of-the-century Berlin, a man named Von Osten purchased a horse, which he named Hans. Von Osten trained Hans, not to jump, stand on his hind legs, or even dance, but to count by tapping a front hoof. To his master's astonishment the horse learned to count very quickly, and in a short time Hans also learned to add, multiply, divide, and subtract.
>
> Von Osten exhibited Hans at fairs and carnivals, and the crowds loved it when the horse would correctly count the number of people in the audience, the number of people wearing eyeglasses, or the number of people wearing hats. In addition, Hans thrilled observers by telling time and announcing the date—all by tapping his hoof. Von Osten later decided to teach Hans the alphabet: A was one hoof tap, B two taps, and so on. Once he learned this, Hans was able to reply to both oral and written questions, and his proficiency earned him the nickname "Clever Hans."

Go to the *Online Learning Center* at
www.mhhe.com/gamble8
and answer the questions in
the *Self Inventory* to evaluate
your understanding of
non-verbal communication.

Naturally, some people who heard about the feats of "Clever Hans" were skeptical and reasoned that no horse could do these things and so there must be some trickery involved. Eventually, a committee was charged with deciding whether there was any deceit involved in Hans's performances. On the committee were professors of psychology and physiology, the head of the Berlin Zoo, a circus director, veterinarians, and cavalry officers. Van Osten was not permitted to be present when the committee tested the horse, but despite the absence of his trainer, Hans was able to answer all the questions put to him. The committee decided that there was no trickery.

Some skeptics, however, were still not satisfied, and so a second investigation was conducted by a new committee. This time, however, the procedures were changed. Von Osten was asked to whisper [a number] into Hans's left ear; then another experimenter named Pfungst whispered a number into Hans's right ear. Hans was instructed to add the two numbers—an answer none of the observers, Von Osten, or Pfungst knew. Hans couldn't do it. It seems that Hans could answer a question only if someone in his visual field knew the answer to it.

Why do you suppose Hans had to see someone who knew the answer? Apparently, when the horse was asked a question that all the observers had heard, the observers assumed an expectant posture and increased their body tension. When Hans had tapped the correct number of hoofbeats, the observers would relax and move their heads slightly—cues Hans used in order to know when to stop tapping. Thus, somehow the horse had the ability to respond to the almost imperceptible movements of people around him. Much as you are able to sense when someone wants you to stop talking or when it is time for you to leave a party, Hans was able to interpret the nonverbal messages of onlookers.

We all communicate nonverbally. In a normal two-person conversation, the verbal channel carries less than 35 percent of the social meaning of a message; this means that more than 65 percent of the meaning is communicated nonverbally (see Figure 6.1).[6] By analyzing nonverbal cues, we can enhance our understanding of what is really being said when people talk. The nonverbal level can also help us define the nature of each relationship we share with someone else. With practice, we can learn to use the nonverbal mode to provide us with "ways of knowing" that would not otherwise be available to us.[7]

FIGURE 6.1
Communication of Social Meaning.

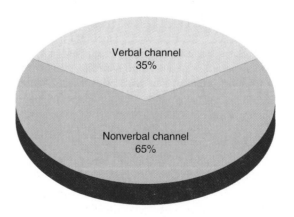

The Magic of Sign Language

Marilyn Daniels' book *Dancing with Words*[8] is an exploration of the dynamics of language acquisition through a special form of nonverbal communication. Daniels contends that the use of sign language not only makes hearing students bilingual but also increases the vocabulary learning, reading, and spelling skills of students in all subjects. She also believes that signing positively influences the self-assurance of hearing students, enhancing their ability to interpret and express ideas as well. According to Daniels, sign language is a natural language that, while strongly rooted in deaf communities throughout the world, also fulfills the diverse communicative needs of daily life, including facilitating communication in the home by allowing babies and young children to express their needs without becoming frustrated.

In your opinion, should we all be required to take a course in sign language? If so, why? If not, why not? Can you think of how the use of sign language might enhance your communication with hearing persons?

CHARACTERISTICS OF NONVERBAL COMMUNICATION: CUES AND CONTEXTS

What is nonverbal communication? How can you become a detective, perceiving and interpreting nonverbal cues? The term **nonverbal communication** designates all the kinds of human messages/responses not expressed in words.

The twinkle in his eye, the edge in her voice, the knowing look of his smile, the rigidness of her posture, the confidence in his walk, her dress, his hairstyle, where she sits, how closely he stands in relation to another, her eagerness to arrive early—each of these cues contains clues regarding the attitudes, feelings, and personality of the displayer. Often, however, we are virtually unaware of what we do with our body, our voice, or the space around us when we interact with others. We simply act and react, act and react, without considering how the way we act and the way we react modifies, reinforces, or distorts the messages we are communicating.

We communicate with our bodies and appearance. However, nonverbal content is even more extensive than this. We also communicate by sending messages through the environment we create and live in. If, for example, someone entered and walked through your house, apartment, or room at this very moment, what assumptions would he or she be able to make about you and your roommate or family? The spaces we inhabit broadcast information about us to others even when we are not in them. For instance, are you sloppy or tidy? Do you like roominess, or do you crave the security of cozy places? How you dress your environment and how you dress yourself provide clues about your role, status, age, and goals. Your voice also carries information about you.

Sometimes we consciously use nonverbal cues to send specific messages. Our use of nonverbal cues is then purposeful. For example, some years ago, during the Olympic games held in Mexico, some African-American athletes raised clenched fists to protest racial discrimination and symbolize Black

nonverbal communication
the kinds of human messages/responses not expressed in words

Toni Smith, the basketball player with her back to the flag, used her nonverbal behavior to express her attitude towards U.S. foreign policy.

power. It is all too common for professional athletes to make obscene gestures at officials, members of the opposing team, or fans. Even more to the point, in 2003, college basketball player Toni Smith elected to symbolize her displeasure with American policy by turning her back on the flag of the United States and looking down at the floor during the playing of the national anthem before every game. Others in Smith's presence signaled their support for American policy and expressed their patriotism by choosing to use different nonverbal cues: Some carried flags onto the court to counter Smith's actions. Others wore American flag lapel pins. Still others indicated their support or opposition to Smith's behavior with their cheers or boos.[9] Although U.S. laws enforcing freedom of speech protect the use of nonverbal cues, the principal of one high school told a student to remove an antiwar shirt that featured a picture of President George Bush with the legible label "International Terrorist."[10]

If, at this very moment, someone were to photograph you, what could others surmise by examining the photograph? How are you sitting? Where are you sitting? How are you dressed? What would your facial expression reveal about your reaction to this chapter?

For the next two minutes, face another person and try not to communicate anything to him or her. What happened? Did you look at each other? Look away? Giggle? Smile? Fidget?

Like verbal communication, nonverbal communication is ambiguous. (Think about the example we just gave—the photograph of yourself reading this chapter. Would different people interpret the photograph the same way?) Like words, nonverbal messages may not mean what we think they do. Thus, we have to be careful not to misinterpret them. Don't be surprised if you find that the real reason a person glanced at a clock, left a meeting early, or arrived late for class is quite different from what you assumed. It is simply not possible to develop a list of nonverbal behaviors and attach a single meaning to each. All nonverbal communication must be evaluated or interpreted within the context in which it occurs.

mixed message

message that occurs when words and actions contradict each other

Furthermore, verbal and nonverbal messages can be—and often are—contradictory. When we say one thing but do another, we send an incongruent or **mixed message.** As you become aware of the nonverbal cues you and others send, you will begin to recognize contradictory messages that impede communication. Whenever you detect an incongruity between nonverbal and verbal (word-level) messages, you will probably benefit by paying greater attention to the nonverbal messages. Researchers in communication believe that nonverbal cues are more difficult to fake than verbal cues—hence the importance of examining the nonverbal dimension. (Remember the case of Peter Reilly.)

Say, "I am really glad to be here," but meanwhile do everything you can to indicate the opposite. What means did you use? Tone of voice? Posture? Facial expressions?

FUNCTIONS OF NONVERBAL COMMUNICATION

Nonverbal communication serves an array of communicative functions that can work both independently of and in conjunction with verbal messages to clarify meaning. Knapp and Hall identify a number of these functions.[11]

Message Reinforcement or Complementation

Nonverbal cues reinforce the verbal message by adding redundancy. The woman who says, "I love you," to her fiancé and covers her partner's face with kisses. The friend who says, "Good to see you," and waves hello. When an instructor asks, "Did you complete the assignment?" and you reply, "Sure did!" and make an OK sign with your fingers. Message reinforcement occurs when the nonverbal and verbal messages complement each other.

Message Negation

Nonverbal cues can also contradict or negate a verbal message—such as a man who says to his lover, "I need us to spend more time apart," as he moves closer with each word spoken. Such a message is contradicted or canceled by the communicator's nonverbal cues. The interaction represents a double message—the nonverbal cues and the words spoken are at odds with each other. As we've noted, the nonverbal message is usually the more accurate reflection of meaning.

Message Substitution

Nonverbal cues can replace or substitute for verbal cues. Pointing at a person can single someone out. Another hand gesture lets everyone know you're OK. A shrug of the shoulders lets others know when someone doesn't care about something. Placing your finger over your lips can indicate that you'd like everyone in the room to stop talking. In each case, instead of words being spoken, an action is performed.

Message Accentuation or Intensification

Nonverbal cues also can be used to underscore or intensify parts of a verbal message. Slowing down speech to stress the meaning and importance of key words, smiling when you say, "It's nice to meet you," and clutching your hair when you say, "I'm so angry I could pull my hair out!" are nonverbal cues that accent or emphasize the verbal messages sent.

Message Regulation

Finally, nonverbal cues help regulate the back-and-forth flow of person-to-person interaction. We modulate conversational turn taking with nonverbal cues. With eye contact, posture, gestures, and voice, we signal that we have finished speaking or indicate who should talk next. Nonverbal cues help us manage and control communication. They provide the traffic signals for verbal exchanges.

If we are going to use nonverbal cues effectively, we must understand them. The section "Aspects of Nonverbal Communication" considers the important features of nonverbal communication.

ASPECTS OF NONVERBAL COMMUNICATION

While we use language to communicate explicit information and message content, we use nonverbal communication to convey relational messages, including how we feel about another person, as well as status, power, and deception.[12] To arrive at a better understanding of communication and develop skills that will permit us to both send and receive cues more accurately, we will examine the following areas:

Body language (kinesics)

Clothing and artifacts

Voice (paralanguage)

Space and distance (proxemic and environmental factors)

Colors (meanings and associations)

Time (communicative value of chronemics)

Touch (haptics)

The types of messages that fall within these categories do not occur in isolation; they interact, sometimes supporting and sometimes contradicting one another.

Body Language: Kinesics

kinesics

the study of human body motion, or body language

Kinesics—body motion, or body language, as it is popularly called—typically includes facial expression (particularly eyebrows, forehead, eyes, and mouth), posture, and gestures. Thus, hand movements, a surprised stare, drooping shoulders, a knowing smile, and a tilt of the head are all part of kinesics. The role of signing and gestures in learning garnered attention when it was reported that infants and toddlers who learn to use and read gestures may learn to read faster and do better on future IQ tests than children who do not.[13] Consciously using multiple channels facilitates communication.

Facial Expressions

Picture this: You play soccer. You have suffered a serious injury and have had a CAT scan. You are meeting with the doctor to discuss your prognosis for a full recovery. You search the doctor's face, looking for clues. Or consider this:

You are returning home 24 hours late from a business trip. Your significant other meets you at the door. As you approach, your eyes focus on the expression of the awaiting face. Within a very short span of time, each of the these faces can move us to tears of happiness or sadness, put us at ease or arouse our rage. To a large extent, we send messages with our facial muscles. Why is the face so important? First, it is our main channel for communicating our own emotions and for analyzing the feelings and sentiments of others. This is one reason motion picture and television directors use so many close-ups. Television is often referred to as the "medium of talking heads." The face is relied on to reinforce or contradict what is being communicated through dialogue. Likewise, in your personal relations, your face and the faces of those around you broadcast inner feelings and emotions.

How well do you read faces? Research has shown that many people are able to decipher facial cues with great accuracy, but others lack this ability. It has been proposed that unpopularity, poor grades, and a variety of other problems that plague schoolchildren may be attributed to an inability to read the nonverbal messages of teachers and peers. According to psychologist Stephen Norwicki, "Because they are unaware of the messages they are sending, or misinterpret how other children are feeling, unpopular children may not even realize that they are initiating many of the negative reactions they receive from their peers."[14] Your ability to read someone's face increases when you know the person, understand the context of the interaction, and are able to compare and contrast the person's facial expressions with others you have seen him or her make.

Of all the nonverbal channels, the face is the single most important broadcaster of emotions. You may be able to hide your hands, and you may choose to keep silent, but you cannot hide your face without making people feel you are attempting to deceive them. Since we cannot put the face away, we take great pains to control the expressions we reveal to others.

How do we do this? We can use **facial management techniques** to control our facial behavior. Among these techniques are intensifying, deintensifying, neutralizing, and masking. When we intensify an emotion, we exaggerate our facial responses to meet what we believe to be the expectations of others who are watching us. Have you ever pretended you loved a gift so as not to disappoint the giver, when in reality you couldn't stand it? When we deintensify an emotion, we deemphasize our facial behaviors so that others will judge our reactions to be more appropriate. Were you ever very angry with a professor but were compelled to restrain yourself because you feared the professor's response if you let your anger show? When we neutralize an emotion, we avoid displaying it at all. Sometimes neutralization is an attempt to display strength, as when we are saddened by the death of a relative but want to appear brave. In our culture, men neutralize fear and sadness more frequently than women do. This suppression, or internalization, may partly account for the fact that men have more ulcers than women do. Finally, when we mask an emotion, we replace it with another to which we believe others will respond more favorably. Thus, we sometimes conceal feelings of jealousy, disappointment, or rage. George Orwell spoke of the need for masking in his novel *1984:*

> It was terribly dangerous to let your thoughts wander when you were in any public place or within range of a telescreen. The smallest thing could give you

Did you know that the 80 muscles in the face can create more than 7,000 expressions?

The face is the single most important broadcaster of emotions. What message is your face sending right now?

facial management techniques
the means we use to control the expressions we reveal to others

Have you ever been guilty of facecrime? Were you punished? Should you have been? Why or why not?

affect blends

facial movements which accompany the communicating of multiple emotions

microfacial, or micromomentary, expressions

expressions 1/8 to 1/5 of a second in duration, that occur when an individual attempts to conceal an emotion

How can you use facial cues to determine if others—including your boss, co-workers, and friends—are being honest with you?

When the face assumes an expression of anger, fear, or sadness, the heart rate increases. According to psychologist Robert Levenson, this is because emotions are often associated with a need to behave in a certain way on very short notice. For example, anger and fear are associated with either fighting or fleeing—both of which start the heart pumping.

away. A nervous tic, an unconscious look of anxiety, a habit of muttering to yourself—anything that carried with it the suggestion of abnormality, of having something to hide. In any case, to wear an improper expression on your face (to look incredulous when a victory was announced, for example), was itself a punishable offense. There was even a word for it in Newspeak: facecrime, it was called.[15]

Facially, we may at any time—without realizing it—be communicating multiple emotions rather than one. Researchers Paul Ekman and Wallace Friesen call these facial movements **affect blends.**[16] The presence or absence of certain affect blends may help explain why we feel comfortable around some people but uncomfortable around others. It seems that some expressions appear on the face for only a fraction of a second. Thus, what begins as a smile may ever so briefly become a grimace and then may be transformed into a smile. These changes may last no more than one-eighth to one-fifth of a second. Researchers call these fleeting emotional displays **microfacial, or micromomentary, expressions.**[17] Microfacial expressions were discovered with slow-motion techniques. What escaped the naked eye at normal speed (24 frames per second) became visible when the film was slowed (to 4 frames per second). Micromomentary expressions are believed to reveal actual emotional states and usually occur when a person is consciously or unconsciously attempting to conceal or disguise an emotion or a feeling. Although microfacial expressions may be little more than a twitch of the mouth or of an eyebrow, they can indicate to observers that the message a sender is trying to transmit is not the message the sender is thinking.[18]

In addition, the appearance of a particular face is the most visible and reliable means of identifying a previously unidentified person.[19] Just as victims describe faces of the accused for police artists and aggrieved parents describe the faces of their missing children, so relatives, friends, and acquaintances describe your facial features to others. People use the face more frequently than any other bodily cue to distinguish one individual from another.

Besides identifying you, your facial appearance influences judgments of your physical attractiveness.[20] In addition, it affects others' assessment of you as being dominant or submissive.[21] Thus, we speak of a baby face, a face as cold as ice, a face as strong as a bulldog's, and so on. What words would you use to describe your own face?

By now you are probably beginning to realize the importance of observing facial expressions. But what should you watch for? For purposes of analysis, a person's face can be divided into three general areas: (1) the eyebrows and forehead, (2) the eyes, and (3) the mouth. Let us focus on each area separately.

Eyebrows and Forehead   If you raise your eyebrows, what emotion are you showing? Surprise is probably most common, but fear may also be expressed by raised eyebrows; when you are experiencing fear, the duration of the movement will probably be longer.

The brows help express other emotions as well. Right now, move your brows into as many configurations as you can. With each movement, analyze your emotional response. What do the brows communicate?

The forehead also helps communicate your physical and emotional state. A furrowed brow suggests tension, worry, or deep thought. A sweating forehead suggests nervousness or great effort.

Eyes   The second of the three areas is the eyes. Ralph Waldo Emerson noted, perceptively, "The eyes of men converse at least as much as their tongues." What do your eyes reveal to others?

Many expressions refer to the eyes—"shifty eyes," "the look of love," "the evil eye," "look me in the eye." Various eye movements are associated with emotional expressions: A downward glance suggests modesty; staring suggests coldness; wide eyes suggest wonder, naivete, honesty, or fright; and excessive blinking suggests nervousness and insecurity. Researchers have also shown that, as we begin to take an interest in something, our blinking rate decreases and our pupils dilate. As an example, consider this: Years ago anthropologist Edward T. Hall said PLO leader Yasir Arafat wore dark glasses to take advantage of the pupil response—to keep others from reading his reactions by watching the pupils of his eyes dilate. Hall is an authority on face-to-face contact between persons of different cultures. In an interview on understanding Arab culture, he said that a University of Chicago psychologist discovered the role pupils play as sensitive indicators. Eckhard Hess found pupils dilate when you are interested in something but tend to contract if something is said that you dislike.

> "The Arabs have known about the pupil response for hundreds if not thousands of years," Hall says. "Since people can't control the response of their eyes, which is a dead giveaway, many Arabs, like Arafat, wear dark glasses, even indoors."[22]

Although Arafat no longer appears in public wearing dark glasses, many celebrities and public figures still do.

Like pupil response, the direction of eye gaze provides interesting insights. For example, have you considered in what direction people look when they are not looking directly at you—and what that might signify? Richard Bandler and John Grinder, two of the founders of neurolinguistic programming, have developed a number of interesting theories. They suggest that people look in one direction when they try to remember something and in another direction when they try to invent something. To test their hypothesis, try this with a partner. Face each other. One person asks the following series of questions; the other person thinks of a response to each. When asking the questions, watch for any patterns in the direction your partner looks while thinking of a response.

Questions That Evoke Visually Remembered Images
What color are the carpets in your car?
What color are your mother's eyes?
What color is your instructor's hair?

Questions That Evoke Visually Invented Images
How would you look from my point of view?
How would you look in purple and green hair?
What would your home look like after it had been ravaged by fire?

Questions That Evoke Auditorily Remembered Images
Can you hear your favorite music?
Can you hear music you dislike?
What are the first four notes of Beethoven's Fifth Symphony?

How does eye contact or lack of eye contact affect your interactions with others? You can explore this by using the following experimental conditions when talking to others. (1) Keep your eyes on the floor. (2) Glance around continually. (3) Stare at the other person's face. (4) Look at the other person's waist. (5) Maintain comfortable eye contact. Report your findings to the class.

FIGURE 6.2
How Direction of Gaze Varies According to the Nature of the Item under Consideration.

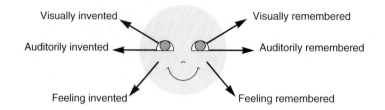

Questions That Evoke Auditorily Invented Images

How would your dog sound singing "Mary Had a Little Lamb"?

What would King Kong sound like tiptoeing through the tulips?

Bandler and Grinder suggest that a right-handed person will look in the directions shown in Figure 6.2. Do your experiences confirm their findings? Could a lawyer or negotiator ask questions and then use these findings to determine whether the person answering had invented the reply? Could a CIA agent use the technique to determine if a paid informant was telling the truth? If the findings are valid, presumably the answer is yes. The agent, for example, could inquire about where hostages were being held: "What does the house look like? Did you see terrorist members there?" If the informant looked up and to the right, he or she might be creating images rather than actually remembering; in other words, the informant might be lying.

Whatever your conclusions about the direction of eye gaze, it is important to maintain eye contact with others in order to recognize not only when others are not looking at you but where they are looking. Each cue provides you with potential information about people's unconscious processes and how they internally access data. When we communicate with others—whether in school, on the job, at home, or on a date—eye-accessing cues are a channel we can use to help make sense of their behavior. Because these cues are not consciously controlled, they will seldom mislead us.

Another eye cue that helps reveal what is on a person's mind is the eye blink. In an article titled "In the Blink of an Eye," Shawna Vogel notes:

> Someone should have told Richard Nixon that his eyelids were giving him away. On August 22, 1973, during his first nationally televised press conference since the Senate's Watergate investigation began six months earlier, the president maintained a calm, controlled tone of voice. But in answering such pointed questions as, "Is there any limitation on the president, short of impeachment, to compel the production of evidence?" Nixon's eyes became a blur. In an average minute he blinked 30 to 40 times. Unimpeachable adults blink only about 10 to 20 times a minute, and even that may be excessive; studies on infants show that the physical need to blink comes just once every two minutes.[23]

How long we look or gaze at a person or thing also communicates a message. In our culture, it is deemed acceptable to stare at animals and inanimate objects, such as paintings or sculptures, but rude to stare at people. (Julius Fast, author of the popular book *Body Language,* suggests that we stare at individuals we believe to be "nonpersons."[24]) Instead of staring at others, we are supposed to practice **civil inattention,** avoiding sustained eye contact and letting our eyes rest only momentarily on people (in other words, keeping our

civil inattention

the polite ignoring of others so as not to infringe on their privacy eyes to ourselves). Although it is permissible to look at someone we do not know for one or two seconds, after that we are expected to move our eyes along. Notice your own eye behavior the next time you walk down a street. Your eyes will probably wander from face to face. However, if you and a stranger happen to make eye contact while approaching one another from opposite directions, at least one of you will redirect his or her gaze before you actually get close. If we look at people for a long time, it may make them fidgety and uncomfortable or may seem to imply that we are challenging them. Have you ever innocently rested your eyes on a stranger who then demanded, "What are you staring at? You want to start something?"

The presence or absence of eye contact indicates whether a communication channel is open or closed. What does the eye contact of these people suggest about their relationship?

Despite civil inattention, in any gathering, the first thing most people do is eye one another. Eye contact is important in communication because it gives us certain information. It gives us feedback on how we are coming across to others in interpersonal and public situations. Eye contact can indicate that the communication channel is open. It is much easier to avoid talking or listening to people if we have not made eye contact with them. Eye contact between people can also offer clues to the kind of relationship they share. For one thing, it can signal a need for inclusion or affiliation. People who have a high need for affiliation will frequently return the glances of others. There is a high degree of eye contact between people who like each other. We also increase eye contact when communicating with others if the physical distance between us is increased.

For others to find us persuasive, we need to refrain from excessive blinking. We should maintain a steady gaze—that is, neither look down nor away from the individuals we are trying to convince and not exhibit eye flutter. In general, we judge persons who look us in the eye as more honest and credible than those whose eyes do not directly meet ours. When individuals avoid meeting our eyes or avert their gaze, we often assume that they have something to hide, that they lack confidence, or that they are unknowledgeable.[25] Visual dominance correlates with increased levels of looking, while increases in the frequency of eye aversions create an impression of submissiveness. Humans, like apes, can stare down each other to establish dominance. Look away first, and you may well find that you have unknowingly agreed to be the less powerful player in the interaction.

What is communicated if eye contact is missing? Lack of eye contact can cause others to think that we are trying to hide something or that we do not like them. It can also suggest that two people are in competition with each other. Others may interpret its absence as signifying either boredom or simply a desire to end an interaction. How do you rate your own eye contact? When are you a looker and when are you a nonlooker?

Of course, we must keep in mind that eye contact is influenced by culture. Some cultures use eye contact more than we do; other cultures use it less. Arabs, for example, engage in more direct eye contact, the Japanese in less eye contact, than is typical of Americans. The Japanese, in fact, believe that prolonged eye contact is a sign of disrespect. Japanese children learn at an early age to avoid direct eye contact and to direct their gaze to the area of the Adam's apple instead.[26]

The fact is, the eyes have much to tell us.

Mouth   A few years ago, a little girl born with a perpetually grumpy look underwent surgery that literally brought a smile to her face. According to surgeon Avron Daniller, "Just being unable to smile has numerous problems associated with it, social and psychological."[27] People who do not smile are perceived to be unfriendly, uninterested in others, or bored. People respond more favorably to those who smile.[28]

Like the eyes, the lower facial area has much to communicate. For example, some people smile with just the mouth and lips. For others, the smile appears to consume the entire face. As a child, were you ever told to "wipe that smile off your face"? Why? Besides happiness, what can a smile communicate?

How does your face look when you are not smiling—when it is at rest? Some faces have a neutral expression; others have a frown, snarl, or habitual smile—that is, the corners of the mouth seem to turn up normally.

When you choose to smile, how do people react to your smile? People often find that others will return a smile to those who smile at them but will look away from, or avoid stopping to speak to, a person whose lips are pursed in a frown. To what extent do your experiences confirm this?

Both men and women tend to smile when seeking approval, but in general women smile more frequently than men do. Women tend to smile even when given negative messages. Why do you think this is so?

Facial cues communicate a large portion of the messages you send to others. Researcher Albert Mehrabian has concluded that, while verbal and vocal cues are used extensively to help transmit meaning, the face is relied on to an even greater extent than either of these.[29]

Posture

How many times have you heard the following admonitions?

"Stand up straight!"

"Why are you hunched over that desk?"

What kinds of nonverbal messages does your posture send to others? The way we hold ourselves when sitting or standing is a nonverbal broadcast, giving others information that they use to assess our thoughts and feelings.

Research has provided us with enough information to reach some general conclusions about how others are likely to interpret our posture. Nancy

---

Even though women in general smile more than men do, young children think that the smile of a male is friendlier than the smile of a female. Do you agree? Explain.

Describe the posture you consider appropriate for a corporate president.

Ethics &
COMMUNICATION

Going Expressionless

An increasing number of men and women employed in jobs as salespersons, lawyers, bankers, and stockbrokers, afraid that betraying an emotion might cost them a sale, a jury verdict, or a deal, are using botox (a drug which temporarily paralyzes muscles) to freeze and sculpt their faces into semipermanent poker faces. With an injection, they are eliminating frowns, scowls, and signs of fatigue. Executives are having their brows deadened with botox to give them an advantage when negotiating. Although the most popular use of botox remains among mostly women and a growing number of men who want to erase the effects of age and turn back the clock, it is now extensively being used to give people a competitive edge in business.[30]

In your opinion, is it acceptable to use botox to address problems created by angry or otherwise revealing facial expressions or other nonverbal cues? If you are feeling one emotion, is it ethical to use an injected drug to help you communicate another emotion? If revealing nonverbal cues and expressions are taken away and you can't look at a person's expression to gauge his or her sincerity, how will you be able to tell who is a friend or a foe? What kind of statement do you think showing less expression really makes?

Henley, in her book *Body Politics,* suggests that "the bearing with which one presents oneself proclaims one's position in life."[31] Television and film support this premise by frequently contrasting the upright bearing of a wealthy person with the submissive shuffle of a servant or the slumped demeanor of a nobody. In line with this, Albert Mehrabian has found that, when people are compelled to assume inferior roles, they reflect this by lowering their heads. In contrast, when they are assuming superior roles, people often raise their heads.

Each of us has certain expectations regarding the postures we expect others to display. For instance, we might expect a high-ranking military officer to adopt an extremely straight and somewhat official posture. Henley suggests that standing tall, in and of itself, helps a person achieve dominance.

Recall an instance when posture affected your perception of someone else.

As a communicator, you will want to develop a posture appropriate to and supportive of your goals and aspirations. Stooped shoulders can indicate that you are heavily burdened or submissive; raised shoulders suggest that you are under a great deal of stress. To Americans, square shoulders usually suggest strength. Our emotions or moods and physical bearing are closely related. This relationship is expressed through the verbal idioms that have developed through the years. It is said that we "shoulder a burden," have "no backbone," keep our "chin up," or "shrug off problems." The way we carry ourselves can affect the way we feel and the way others perceive us, just as much as the way we feel can affect the way we carry ourselves.

Try on various postures and see what you feel like in each. To what degree does each posture affect your emotional state?

The last aspect of posture we will consider is the way we lean, or orient ourselves, when we communicate. If you were speaking to someone who suddenly turned or leaned away from you, would you consider that a positive sign? Probably not. We usually associate liking and other positive attitudes with leaning forward, not withdrawing. The next time an interesting bit of gossip is discussed in the cafeteria, notice how most of the listeners, if not all, will lean forward to ensure that they do not miss even one detail of the story. When you are communicating with others, a slight forward tilt of your upper body may indicate that you are interested in what they have to say. Mehrabian

Leaning forward communicates liking and interest. Are you aware when you do this? Is it always a conscious move?

found that we lean either left or right when communicating with a person of lower status than ourselves. This right or left leaning is a part of our more relaxed demeanor.[32]

Gestures

The movements of our arms, legs, hands, and feet constitute another important way we broadcast nonverbal data. For instance, the way you position your arms transmits information about your attitudes. Cross your arms in front of you. Do you feel closed off from the world? Stand up and put your hands on your hips. How does this stance make you feel? (You may remind yourself of the old stereotype of an army sergeant.) Next, clasp your arms behind your back in a self-assured manner. Then, hold your arms stiffly at your sides, as if you were a nervous speaker or a wooden soldier. Finally, dangle your arms at your sides in a relaxed fashion. Become aware of the arm positions that you habitually use. What message does each of these positions communicate?

Our legs also convey information about us. Try standing as a model would stand. Next, sit down and put your feet up on a desk or table. Then stand with your feet wide apart. Does this last stance make you feel more powerful? Why? The distribution of body weight and the placement of legs and feet can broadcast stability, femininity, masculinity, anger, happiness, or any number of other qualities. For a communication encounter, choose the stance that most accurately reflects your goals.

Nonverbal communication researcher Roger D. Masters notes that people have specific preferences and dislikes in the body language of their leaders. The greatest turnoff for receivers is fear. Leaders communicate fear by looking down; hesitating; making rapid, jerky movements; grimacing; or freezing their movements. In contrast, smiling, tilting their heads, or making the right amount of eye contact reassures observers.[33]

It is important to recognize, however, that gestures do not have universal meanings. The meaning one culture gives to a gesture may be very different from the meaning another culture gives it. Consider, for example, our "OK" gesture made by forming a circle with the thumb and forefinger. In Japan, the thumb and forefinger making a circle is used as a symbol for money. To most Americans, this joining of thumb and forefinger signifies that all is positive; the French and Belgians, in contrast, would interpret the gesture as meaning "you're worth zero."[34] Not understanding this cultural difference can have dire ramifications. For example, a traveler once took a hotel room in France, and when the concierge asked, "Is your room satisfactory?" the traveler replied with the "OK" sign. The concierge appeared irritated at the answer and said, "If you don't like it, we'll just have to find you another room."[35]

By the way, keeping your hands behind your back instead of gesturing will not automatically keep you out of trouble. Doing so is considered an impolite posture in Belgium, Indonesia, France, Finland, Japan, and Sweden.[36]

A lack of universality in gesturing can create problems for global advertisers, not just tourists. For example, for years, Allstate Insurance Company implied that it offers consumers security and protection by using in its advertisements the image of a person holding out his or her hands while a voice over intones, "You're in good hands with Allstate." The ad failed in Germany, however, because in that country hands held out symbolize begging rather than security and protection. We should keep in mind that crossing one's legs does not necessarily play well from country to country. In fact, it is perceived as highly offensive in Turkey and Ghana.[37]

Clothing and Artifacts

Since people make inferences about our age, social and economic status, educational level, group membership, athletic ability, personality, and relationships to others by the way we dress, our use of **artifactual communication** (the use of personal adornments, such as clothing, jewelry, makeup, hairstyles, and beards) provides important nonverbal cues.

> **artifactual communication**
> the use of personal adornments

How we dress is extremely important in creating a first impression. What kinds of clothing or jewelry do you like to wear? What do your appearance, hairstyle, and mode of dress suggest to others about who you are and what you are like? Are your choices of clothing or bodily adornments appropriate? To what extent do your choices meet with or disappoint the expectations of those with whom you interact?[38] Interestingly, from Mary Tyler Moore's Laura Petrie on the now classic *The Dick Van Dyke Show* to the T-shirts and unstructured jackets of Crockett and Tubs (Don Johnson and Philip Michael Thomas) on *Miami Vice* and from Sarah Jessica Parker's Carrie Bradshaw on *Sex and the City,* with her name necklaces and large flower pins, to Lauren Ambrose's artsy Claire Fisher on *Six Feet Under,* television also influences the way we dress and present ourselves to others. What impression would you like to create when you first meet someone? As the role you enact changes, your dress and chosen image often change as well.

> *Have you ever found yourself extremely overdressed or underdressed for an occasion? How did you feel? Were you able to augment your outfit or take off part of it to fit in with what everyone else was wearing? Have you ever been to a posh restaurant that requires men to put on ill-fitting jackets and out-of-style ties in order to partake of the food?*

How we dress influences how we behave. Consider singer Gwen Stefani. In your opinion, does Stefani's dress support her behavior? Given the kind of music she sings, could she just as easily wear more prim and proper attire? Why or why not? While Gwen Stefani purposefully wears such clothing to her job, could you wear the same or similar clothing to yours? Unless you're a singer or dancer, you probably answered this question with an "Are you

---

Media WISE

Do Labels Become You?

Much of the clothing we wear and the accessories we carry or use to adorn our bodies feature legible labels that announce to others our status or interest in something. For example, the Kate Spade or Tiffany label helps suggest something about financial status; FCUK, Armani Exchange, and Diesel say something about our style consciousness; while the logo of a professional sports team on a sweatshirt or cap says something about our interests. Similarly, some clothing features slogans that attest to a philosophy or belief the wearers hold. For example, at a recent Grammy Awards ceremony, singer Sheryl Crow appeared with the words "I Don't Believe in Your War, Mr. Bush"

emblazoned on her chest, and actor Viggo Mortensen, who appeared in the film *The Lord of the Rings,* showed up at a book signing with "War is not the answer" scrawled on his shirt. T-shirts are not mere articles of clothing. David Wolfe, a creative director, calls the T-shirt the new press conference or picket sign.[39]

Inventory the clothing and accessories you have that prominently display or advertise a brand name, a logo, or another visible message. What does each reveal about your beliefs and/or aspirations? Have any caused others to develop misconceptions about you? In your opinion, should such legible labeling be banned? Why or why not?

What message does the appearance of Gwen Stefani of No Doubt send?

kidding?" or "No way." The clothing we wear to work should support the job roles and functions we perform. Some years ago, businesses in the United States began to relax office dress codes by instituting a practice called "Casual Fridays," when employees could wear more relaxed attire to work. The one-day-a-week practice soon spread to the entire workweek. While it was expected that wearing more comfortable clothing would free worker creativity and unleash worker productivity, actually the opposite occurred. Casual dress led to reduced worker productivity, increased lateness, and increased rudeness.[40] It seems that casual dress fostered too much of a casual attitude. Most companies have since gone back to requiring workers to wear more formal clothing on the job.

John T. Molloy, author of *Dress for Success* and *The Woman's Dress for Success Book,* gathered data from numerous studies in which people offered their first impressions of the attire of others. Molloy identified the kinds of clothing he claims should be worn by people who want to become managers or executives. For men, he suggests dark blue pinstriped suits to add a feeling of authority. Dark gray is also acceptable as executive attire. Molloy also created a uniform for women in business. The basic outfit is summed up in this statement, which many of the women in Molloy's seminars adopted:

What is your reaction to Molloy's advice? Would this kind of attire be appropriate for you in your present job? In the future? To what extent is his advice contradicted by the casual attire practices of some major corporations? Use the exercise in the Skill Builder on page 165 to assess how the clothes you wear affect others.

> I pledge to wear a highly tailored, dark-colored, traditionally designed, skirted suit whenever possible to the office.[41]

It is clear that we react to people on the basis of their clothing. In the early stages of a relationship, clothing and appearance affect first impressions and exert influences that lead to acceptance or rejection. In addition, judgments regarding our success, character, dominance, and competence are made on the basis of the type of clothing and jewelry we wear.[42] Typically, we respond more positively to those we perceive to be well dressed than we do to those whose attire we find questionable or unacceptable. We are also more likely to respond to requests from or follow the lead of well-dressed individuals, including persons in uniform, than we are to listen to or emulate those whose dress suggests lower status or lack of authority.[43]

"You're right. It does send a powerful message."

Something Different

Tomorrow wear something different to school or work. Your change in dress style should be very noticeable to others. For instance, if you feel you are usually sloppily dressed, appear as meticulous as possible.

Assess the results. How did people respond to you? Did anyone seem surprised?

Did anyone ask you questions about your appearance? If so, what kinds of questions were you asked? Compare the reactions you received with the experiences of other people who tried this experiment.

Skill
BUILDER

Has technology become an accessory? Is it now a regular part of your wardrobe? Does wearing it help enhance your credibility?

Voice: Paralanguage

Your friend asks you a question, and you matter-of-factly reply, "Mm-hmm." Another person shares a revealing piece of gossip with you, and you shout, "Huh!" Reading about the ethical lapses of some politicians, you click your tongue: "Tsk, tsk, tsk." These elements of speech that are not standard words are a part of **paralanguage.** How good you are at using paralanguage determines whether or not you will be able to do your part to convey the meaning of a message to others.[44]

paralanguage
vocal cues that accompany spoken language

In many ways, you either play your voice—like a musical instrument—or are a victim of your voice. Albert Mehrabian estimates that 38 percent of the meaning of a message delivered during face-to-face conversation is transmitted by voice or vocal cues.[45] Frequently, *how* something is said is *what* is said. How effective are you at playing your voice?

Among the elements of paralanguage are pitch, volume, rate, and pauses. Wise communicators realize that the spoken word is never neutral, and they have learned how to use the elements of paralanguage to convey both the emotional and the intellectual meanings of their messages. Adept communicators know how to use vocal nuances to help their listeners appreciate and understand content and mood. Let us examine the elements of paralanguage more closely.

pitch
the highness or lowness of the voice

Pitch is the highness or lowness of the voice; it is the counterpart of pitch on a musical scale. We tend to associate higher pitches with female voices and lower pitches with male voices. We also develop vocal stereotypes. We associate low-pitched voices with strength, sexiness, and maturity and high-pitched voices with helplessness, tenseness, and nervousness. Although we all have what is termed a characteristic, or **habitual, pitch,** we have also learned to vary our pitch to reflect our mood and generate listeners' interest.

habitual pitch
the characteristic pitch one uses

Some people tend to overuse one tone to the exclusion of others. These people have monotonous voices characterized by too little variety of pitch. Other people speak at or near the upper end of their pitch scale, producing very fragile, unsupported tones. One way to discover a pitch that is not overly high is simply to yawn. Try it now. Permit yourself to experience a good

"I think I've finally found my own voice."

stretch; extend your arms to shoulder level and let out a vocalized yawn. Do it again. Now count to 10 out loud. To what extent does the pitch of your voice appear to have changed? Is it more resonant? It should be. If you indulge yourself and yawn once or twice before stressful meetings or occasions, you will be able to pitch your voice at a more pleasing level.

Volume, or degree of loudness, is a second paralinguistic factor that affects perceived meaning. Some people cannot seem to muster enough energy to be heard by others. Others blast through encounters. Have you ever sat in a restaurant and heard more of the conversation at a table several feet away than you could hear at your own table? Volume frequently reflects emotional intensity. Loud people are often perceived as aggressive or overbearing. Soft-spoken people are often perceived as timid or polite.

volume
degree of loudness

Volume must be varied if it is to be effective. Knowing how to use volume to control meaning is a useful skill. Try it by participating in the following exercise (adapted from Ken Cooper, *Nonverbal Communication for Business Success*[46]): Read the following sentence to yourself: How many animals of *each species* did Moses take aboard the ark? Then tell a friend or an acquaintance that you have a riddle. (Why is this a riddle? Moses, of course, never had an ark. Noah was the ark builder.) Read the sentence aloud, being careful to increase your volume for each of the italicized words. Keep a tally of the number of people who answer "two." Try the question again, this time increasing your volume only on the name Moses. How did your vocal change affect the reactions of the listeners?

The **rate,** or speed at which we speak, is also important. Do you, for example, expect high-pressure salespeople to talk rapidly or slowly? Most often, they speak very quickly. Similarly, those who are selling gadgets in

rate
speaking speed

department stores or on television also speak at a quick clip to retain the audience's interest and involvement. With regard to persons from other cultures, increased rate enhances judgments of credibility.[47]

Of course, more stately or formal occasions require slower speaking rates broken by planned pauses or silences. (Politicians at rallies typically punctuate their speeches with pauses that function almost as applause signs.) Goldman-Eisler, a communications researcher, has concluded that two-thirds of spoken language comes to us in chunks of fewer than six words.[48] Therefore, knowing when to pause is an essential skill. Pauses slow the rate of speech and give both sender and receiver a chance to gather their thoughts. Unfortunately, many people feel that all pauses must be filled and consciously or unconsciously seek ways to fill them. Frequently, we fill a pause with meaningless sounds or phrases: "Er—huh—uh—"; "You know? You know?" "Right! Right!" "OK! OK!" Such **nonfluencies** disrupt the natural flow of speech. Since pauses are a natural part of communication, we should stop trying to eliminate them. Instead, we should give pauses a chance to function.

Silence, the absence of both paralinguistic and verbal cues, also serves important communicative functions.[49] Silence, for example, can allow you time to organize your thoughts. It can also be used to alert receivers that the words you are about to share are important. In addition, choosing not to speak to someone at all can be a forceful demonstration of the indifference one person feels toward another and can be a very powerful message of disconfirmation. Silence can also be used as a form of punishment after an argument or a conflict to indicate that one person is still angry with the other. Silence, as we see, can communicate a number of meanings. For example, it can indicate that two people are so comfortable with each other that they do not feel a need to talk. In a different context, it can reveal a person's shyness, by suggesting discomfort or the inability to keep a conversation moving. On the other hand, silence may simply indicate that you, at the moment, agree with what is being said or simply have nothing to say.

How adept are you at employing the paralinguistic factors we have discussed? Try the Skill Builder "Alphabet Recital." This exercise, a variation of the classic study conducted by Joel Davitz and Lois Davitz, should prove that you do not always need to see people to tell whether they are happy, sad, angry, fearful, or proud.[50] Many of us can identify someone else's emotional

nonfluencies

meaningless sounds or phrases which disrupt the flow of speech

silence

absence of paralinguistic and verbal cues

Skill BUILDER

Alphabet Recital

Choose a partner. Each of you will try to convey one of the following emotions, without letting the other know beforehand which it is.

Happiness	Love
Sadness	Nervousness
Anger	Pride
Jealousy	Satisfaction
Fear	Sympathy

Your partner should close his or her eyes. Your task is to communicate the selected emotion to your partner by reciting the first seven letters of the alphabet (*A* to *G*). As you recite the letters, attempt to make your voice reflect the emotion. Your partner's goal is to identify the emotion by listening only to the paralinguistic cues you are sending.

To what extent did the various paralinguistic factors you used (pitch, volume, rate, and pauses) help your partner identify the emotion? If your partner was unable to determine the emotion you were projecting, what could you have done to make the message clearer?

state by voice alone. Of course, some of us encode emotional messages with our voices better than others, and some of us can decode these messages better than others. Accuracy in sending and identifying emotional messages appears to be related to one's own sensitivity and familiarity with the vocal characteristics of emotional expression.

Besides communicating emotional content, the voice also communicates personal characteristics. Listening to a voice can sometimes help you identify the speaker's individual characteristics. For instance, on the telephone we are frequently able to determine a speaker's sex, age, vocation, and place of origin even though we have never met him or her. We also tend to associate particular voice types with particular body or personality types. For example, what type of appearance would you expect in a person who has a breathy, high-pitched voice? How do you think a person who has a throaty, raspy voice would look? As a communicator, you should be aware that your voice suggests certain things about you. If receivers are interested in identifying your age, occupation, or status, they are likely to make assumptions based on what your voice says to them. Although the picture or stereotype they form may be far from accurate, your voice can influence their assessment of you as an individual and thus affect the way they interact with you.

How do the voices of 4-year-olds and teenagers differ? The voices of college-age men and retired men? Are there differences in vocal characteristics between, say, a corporate executive and a construction worker?

Space and Distance: Proxemic and Environmental Factors

How much of the space on our planet do you call your own? How much space do you carry around with you? Are there times when people encroach on your space? In his book *The Hidden Dimension,* Edward Hall uses the term **proxemics** for human beings' "use of space."[51] *Proxemics* refers to the space that exists between us as we talk and relate to each other, as well as the way we organize the space around us in our homes, offices, and communities. Seating patterns, for example, influence our communicative behavior. What does the seating pattern of persons in Figure 6.3 suggest to you about their relationship to each other and how they will work together?

proxemics
the study of the use of space

FIGURE 6.3
Seating Pattern.

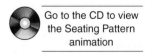
Go to the CD to view the Seating Pattern animation

Distances—Intimate, Personal, Social, Public

Hall identified four distances that we keep between ourselves and other people, depending on the type of encounter and the nature of the relationship:

Intimate distance: 0 to 18 inches
Personal distance: 18 inches to 4 feet
Social distance: 4 to 12 feet
Public distance: 12 feet to limit of sight

intimate distance

a distance ranging from the point of touch to 18 inches from a person

Intimate distance ranges from the point of touch to 18 inches from the other person. At this distance, physical contact is natural. We can wrestle, and we can make love. At this distance, our senses are in full operation. They are easily stimulated but also easily offended if we find ourselves in an uncomfortable situation. Have you ever had someone come too close to you and wanted that person to back off? Did you yourself back away? Sometimes we are forced to endure intimate distance between ourselves and strangers in crowded buses, trains, and elevators. How do you feel and respond in such situations?

personal distance

a distance ranging from 18 inches to 4 feet from a person

Hall's **personal distance** ranges from 18 inches to 4 feet. When communicating at this distance, you can still hold hands or shake hands with another person. This is the most common distance between people talking informally in class, at work, or at parties, and we are apt to conduct most of our conversations within this range. If you reduce personal distance to inti-

The amount of distance between us depends on the nature of our encounter and our relationship to each other. What do the distances between each of these interactants communicate to you about this relationship?

mate distance, you are likely to make the other person feel uncomfortable. If you increase it, the other person is likely to begin to feel rejected.

Hall's **social distance** ranges from 4 feet to 12 feet. At the social distance—in contrast to the personal distance—we are not likely to share personal concerns. By using social distance, we can keep people at more than arm's length. Thus, this is a safer distance, one at which we would communicate information and feelings that are not particularly private or revealing. Many of our conversations at meals and at business conferences or meetings occur within this space. In business, the primary protector of social space is the desk. Of course, the greater the distance between people, the more formal their encounters. (At a social gathering, you can normally tell how well people know one another by examining how close they stand to each other.)

Public distance (12 feet and farther) is commonly reserved for strangers with whom we do not wish to have an interaction. Distances at the farther end of the range are well beyond the area of personal involvement and make interpersonal communication very unlikely. People waiting in an uncrowded lobby for an elevator frequently use public distance. It can be assumed that, if a person opts for public distance when he or she could have chosen otherwise, that person does not care to converse.

What happens when we violate distance norms? Researchers tell us that the outcomes of such violations can be positive. For example, if the approaching person is perceived to be attractive or is viewed as a high-reward source, our evaluation of the approacher may become more favorable, especially if the distance violation is accompanied by other behaviors, such as compliments.[52]

Spaces—Informal, Semifixed-Feature, and Fixed-Feature

The nature of our environment affects the amount of distance we are able to maintain between ourselves and others. Researchers in nonverbal communication divide environmental spaces into three classifications: informal, semifixed-feature, and fixed-feature. These categories are based on the perceived permanence of any physical space.

Informal space is a highly mobile, quickly changing space that ranges from intimate to public (from no space between us and others to 25 feet or more). Informal space functions as a personal bubble that we can enlarge to keep people at a distance or decrease to permit them to get closer.

In contrast to the high mobility of informal space, **semifixed-feature space** uses objects to create distance. Semifixed features include chairs, benches, sofas,

social distance
a distance from a person of 4 feet to 12 feet

public distance
12 feet and farther from a person

Can you tell how interested people are in you by where they stand in relation to you? Explain. Think of an instance when you unconsciously expressed an interest in someone else by where you stood in relation to him or her.

informal space
space which is highly mobile and can be quickly changed

semifixed-feature space
space in which objects are used to create distance

Men and Space

According to communication researcher Dale Leathers, "men use space as a means of asserting their dominance over women." Leathers gives several examples:

1. Men claim more personal space than women.
2. Men more actively defend violations of their territories, which are usually much larger than women's territories.

3. Under conditions of high density, men become more aggressive in their attempts to regain privacy.
4. Men more frequently walk in front of a female partner than vice versa.[53]

In your opinion, is it appropriate for one sex to dominate the other as Leathers describes? How should the other sex respond?

Ethics &
COMMUNICATION

Mentally redesign your classroom to promote interaction. Next, redesign it to inhibit interaction. Then consider how you could design an office to promote— or inhibit—interaction.

fixed-feature space

space which contains relatively permanent objects

How are the chairs in your classroom arranged? Are they arranged in neat rows? Is the instructor partially hidden by a desk or lectern? Does he or she speak from a raised area or platform?

plants, and other movable items. (Some office walls and partitions can be classified as semifixed features, since they are designed to be relocated as spatial requirements change.) Researchers have found that barriers such as desks can reduce interaction. One study of doctor-patient relationships found that patients were more at ease speaking with a physician seated in a chair across from them than they were when the physician was sitting behind a desk.[54] Why do you think this was so? In many public places, if interaction is desired, the space will usually contain chairs facing each other. Such arrangements are found in bars, restaurants, and lounges. In contrast, the chairs in waiting rooms at airports and bus terminals are often bolted together in long parallel rows.

Fixed-feature space contains relatively permanent objects that define the environment around us. Fixed features include immovable walls, doors, trees, sidewalks, roads, and highways. Such features help guide and control our actions. For example, most classrooms are rectangular, with windows along one side, usually to the students' left. The window location also determines the front of the room. Apartment entrances that open onto a common rotunda increase the opportunity for communication among tenants, as do swimming pools and parks. Fences, on the other hand, can inhibit communication. Shopping malls and department stores rely on fixed features to help route pedestrian traffic in certain directions that will increase sales. The next time you shop in a carefully designed store, examine its fixed features. Can you walk, unimpeded, to any department, or are you carefully "directed" through the perfumes, lingerie, and knickknacks? Why?

Territoriality and Personal Space

Another aspect of proxemics is our need for a defined territory. Some animals mark their territory by urinating around its perimeter and will defend their

"Honest, Martha, I don't mean to crowd you."

area against invaders. Human beings also stake out space, or territory, and territoriality is an important variable in interpersonal communication. What examples of **territoriality**—the need to demonstrate a possessive or owner-ship relationship to space—can you remember encountering? Are you famil-iar with "Dad's chair"? "Mom's bureau"? How do you feel when someone invades your room—your territory? What happens when someone stands too close to you? How are you treated when you enter another person's territory?

territoriality

the need to demonstrate a possessive or ownership relationship to space

---

Guarded Territory and the New Need for Security

A majority of persons living in the United States would like to live in a gated community.[55] Gated communities require that someone al-low you to enter or that you have a permit that affords you the right of entry. They are typically protected by armed guards, gates, walls, or fences. As in Robert Frost's poetic line "Good fences make good neighbors," security de-vices and details in gated communities keep their members feeling safe by keeping out those whom the community does not want let in. Sometimes tire-piercing or other antiterrorist devices are used to guard against false entry into the community.

The prime motivator for living in a gated community is the desire for personal safety. On the other hand, because gated communities signal that outsiders should stay out, critics contend that social fragmentation is the cost society pays to allow those living inside them to feel secure. Thus, the fear is that gated com-munities precipitate in-groups and out-groups who compete for rights to use the same space.

Where do you stand? In your opinion, are gated communities a good idea? Are there other kinds of living arrangements that could produce security without closing off a commu-nity to the outside world?

Ethics &
COMMUNICATION

Places and Spaces

Entertainment programs present us with set-ting after setting in which material possessions and expensive furnishings are featured. While many programs and films highlight or revolve around people who are rich, even in those that don't, the furnishings and appearances of liv-ing quarters are probably beyond the means of those portrayed living in them. For the most part, the entertainment media present us with people who live in spacious, well-furnished homes or apartments.

1. Select a favorite program or film. Describe the set where one of more of the charac-ters live, including rooms featured, quality of furniture featured, and design aspects. To what extent does the set support or contradict the preceding thesis?

2. The Learning Channel's program *While You Were Out* involves the redesign of a room or garden area that is accomplished with-out the knowledge of one of the persons

who lives there, because his or her partner, roommate, or child slyly sent him or her away. On returning home, the person is surprised by the transformation that has occurred during his or her absence. The similar program *Trading Spaces* involves two sets of neighboring homeowners who, in two days' time, with a budget of $1,000, and with the aide of an interior designer, radically redo a room in each other's house. Select a friend's or relative's room to redesign. What changes would you make in the room's layout, furniture, and colors that you believe would be for the better? Share your plan with the room's owner(s). Are you surprised by the reac-tion(s) your plans elicit? Why or why not? How would you react were a friend or rela-tive to redesign your bedroom or another favorite space of yours while you were out?

Media
WISE

markers

items that reserve one's space

To establish territory, we use **markers,** items that reserve our space, set boundaries that help distinguish space, or identify a space as ours. At the library, for instance, you may spread your things out, over, and across the table, so that others will not find it easy to enter your territory. In large corporations, a person's status is often reflected by the size of his or her space. Thus, the president may be accorded a large top-floor territory, while a clerk is given a desk in a second-floor room amid a number of other desks and office machines. Regardless of the size of our location, however, we identify with it and frequently act as if we own it.

Colors: Meanings and Associations

Colors seem to have more than a passing effect on us. It has been found that color affects us emotionally and physiologically.

Max Luscher, in his book *The Luscher Color Test,* claims that, when people look at pure red for a long time, their blood pressure, respiration rate, and heartbeat all increase.[56] This is because red tends to excite the nervous system. In contrast, when researchers examined the effect of dark blue, they found just the opposite: Blood pressure, respiration rate, and heartbeat decreased, and people tended to become calmer.

In the past decade, an increasing number of U.S. companies have chosen to be associated with the color blue. Today 70 percent of Fortune 1,000 corporate logos are blue. There are "Big Blue" (IBM), JetBlue (an airline), BlueKite (a wireless technology company), Blue Martini (a software company), and Blue Nile and Bluefly (retail companies), just to name a few. According to the executive director of the Pantone Color Institute, "Blue is invariably connected with sky and water. The sky has never fallen and water has never gone away. It has dependability and constancy."[57] Some believe that, because the color blue also suggests "stature and professionalism," it is a safe choice.

During the uncertain, tension-filled times following 9/11, green became a hot color. Green, we are told, is safe and serene, and it makes people feel better. Even the Department of Homeland Security put green at the bottom of the terrorist alert code, meaning we're safe. According to color consultants, green is the color of harmony and balance.[58]

Diverse, top-selling, global brands such as Campbell's soup, Colgate toothpaste, and Coca-Cola are all packaged in red. A stroll down a supermarket aisle reveals an array of products, among them Kellogg, Nabisco, Del Monte, Jell-O, and Band-Aid, with red logos or names. According to John Steel, a senior executive at Colgate-Palmolive, "Red is warm and bright. It's not intimidating . . . . And red, of course, is the lifeblood."[59] Theories abound on why consumers are drawn to red. Some contend that red evokes feelings of warmth, passion, and sensuality. Others observe that people eat more often in the presence of red. Red provides a lift not only to human consumers; according to a report circulated over the World Wide Web, a company that markets red contact lenses for animals contends that chickens that spend the day wearing its lenses are happier and eat less food, and they have more time for laying eggs.[60] On the other hand, some people perceive red to be dangerous, associating it with stop signs and police car lights.

Color also helps persuade. Law enforcement officials, for example, know that, when suspects are questioned under green light, they talk more freely;

Keeping your own reactions in mind, examine the color schemes used in several public areas, including fast-food chains, stores, and terminals. What colors are used? Do they make you want to move quickly? Do the colors excite you, or are they designed to help you relax?

green helps get people to confess. One study, conducted by the Color Research Institute, was described by Vance Packard.[61] The institute was seeking to determine how the color of a package affected consumers' buying patterns. Women were given three boxes of detergent—one yellow, one blue, and one blue with yellow specks. Although the women thought the boxes contained different detergents, all three contained the same product. After using the products for three weeks, the women were asked which detergent they considered most effective for washing delicate clothing. The results of the study were revealing. The women reported that the detergent in the yellow box was too strong and that the one in the blue box was too weak. However, the detergent in the blue box with the splashes of yellow was felt to be just right. How do colors on packages affect you?

How do various colors make you feel? If you were a color consultant, what colors would you choose for a fast-food operation? An airline? Your classroom? Why?

Time: Communicative Value of Chronemics

Chronemics is the study of how we use time to communicate. The meaning of time differs not only around the United States but also around the world.[62] While some people are preoccupied with time, others regularly waste it. While some are typically early, others are chronically late. While some travel through life with a sense of urgency, others amble through it at a more leisurely pace. Some people function best in the morning (the early birds), while others perform best at night (the night owls). Chronemics expert Robert Levine notes that clock addiction is difficult to break. Because the West is becoming more devoted to the clock by the minute, altering the pace of your life poses numerous challenges. Table 6.1 depicts the countries and U.S. cities with the fastest and slowest paces of life.[63]

chronemics
the study of time use

Do you have enough time for most of your activities? Are you usually prepared for exams or assignments? Do you arrive for appointments on time, early, or late? For example, recent surveys reveal that tardiness is a chronic problem among chief executive officers of corporations who arrive late for 6 in 10 meetings.[64] Edward Hall says that "time talks."[65] What does your use or misuse of time say about you? To what extent do others communicate with

Some students have a habit of always being 15 minutes late to class—even when their previous class was just down the hall. What cues does such habitual lateness transmit to an instructor? Should the instructor conclude that the student is not interested in the class? That the student does not like the instructor? That the student is unable to organize activities to accomplish even the simplest goal?

TABLE 6.1 *The Rat Race*

Robert Levine timed pedestrians and postal workers to compare the pace of life around the world. His conclusions:

	Countries	U.S. Cities
Fastest	1 Switzerland	1 Boston
	2 Ireland	2 Buffalo
	3 Germany	3 New York
	4 Japan	4 Salt Lake City
	5 Italy	5 Columbus
Slowest	27 Syria	32 Memphis
	28 El Salvador	33 San Jose
	29 Brazil	34 Shreveport
	30 Indonesia	35 Sacramento
	31 Mexico	36 Los Angeles

Source: Robert Levine, "A Geography of Time," New York: Basic Books, 1997.

you by their use of time? Would you feel insulted if you were asked out for a date at the last minute by someone you did not know very well? (In the United States, at least, a last-minute invitation is often assumed to indicate that another date fell through or that the inviter is asking only as a last resort.)

Punctuality is an important factor in time communication. Misunderstandings, miscalculations, or disagreements involving time can create communication and relationship problems. Differences in interpreting the words *on time*, for example, reveal differences in individuals' understanding of and approach to the concept of punctuality. Being on time for a job interview, for instance, is different from being on time for a party. The latter usually allows for more flexibility than the former.

Many jobs demand that the worker be on time. To a military officer, being on time really means arriving 15 minutes early. Thus, the armed forces are characterized by the "hurry up and wait" mentality familiar to anyone in basic training. That is, everyone rushes to arrive, but then everyone stands around for a period of time with nothing to do.

Would you make real estate tycoon Donald Trump wait for a meeting with you, or would you arrive on time or even early? When negotiating a real estate transaction, a group of Chinese millionaires once made Trump wait for them—close to an hour. Do you feel that they were sending a message?

Another important factor in time communication is the allocation of certain activities to appropriate times. It is acceptable to call a friend for a chat at 3 P.M. However, one attorney goes to work at 5:30 A.M. and by 6:30 A.M. has already made phone calls to a number of people. (How would you react if you were called by a lawyer at 5:30 in the morning?) He does this, he reports, because it gets results: People's defenses are down at 5:30 A.M.; consequently, they often reveal things they would be prepared to cover up by 9 or 10 o'clock.

We are expected to structure time in certain ways to ensure that our activities and tasks are accomplished efficiently. American businesspeople, for instance, seek the greatest return on their time investment. In other countries, however, time is treated differently. In some cultures, people are accustomed to waiting several hours for a meeting to begin. In others, the meeting begins whenever the second party arrives. The following is an example of how the concept of structuring time is culturally determined:

> A Chinese official matter-of-factly informed an ARCO manager that China would one day be the number one nation in the world. The American said he did not doubt that, considering the size of the country and its population, and the tremendous technological progress that will be made, but he asked, "When do you think that China will be number one?" The Chinese responded, "Oh, in four or five hundred years."[66]

Even within the United States, people structure time differently. People from the Northeast, for example, usually walk and talk more quickly, provide change more quickly in shops, and are more likely to wear a watch than are people from other parts of the country. The authors come from two different regions of the country, and it has taken years of married life for them to adjust to each other's internal clock. (One of them can start and nearly complete a task before the other manages to be seated.) The phrase *a long time* can mean one thing to one person and something completely different to another.

How long we wait for something or someone is related, first, to the value we place on whatever it is we are waiting for and, second, to our own status. We are taught to value what we wait for. In fact, if something is too readily available, we may decide we don't want it after all. Status determines who waits. If we are "important," others usually have access to us only by appointment; thus, it is easier for us to make others wait—and difficult or impossible for others to make us wait. As psychologist Robert Levine writes:

> Time is power. With status, then, comes the power to control time, your own and others'. Those who control others' time have power and those who have power control others' time. There is no greater symbol of domination, since time cannot be replaced once it is gone.[67]

How well do you structure your time? In his book *The Time Trap*, Alex MacKenzie lists several barriers to the effective use of time:

Attempting too much (taking on too many projects at once)

Estimating time unrealistically (not realizing how long a project will take)

Procrastinating (putting it off, and off, and off . . .)

Allowing too many interruptions (letting yourself be distracted by telephone calls, friends, and so on)[68]

Do any of these apply to you? How might you go about improving your use of time?

Touch: Haptics

Our final category of nonverbal communication is touch, also referred to as **haptics.** According to researchers, touch is "one of the most provocative, yet least well understood" of nonverbal behaviors.[69] We have already mentioned touch in relation to space and distance. As we noted, Edward Hall suggests that intimate space ranges from the point of touch to 18 inches. How important is touch in your own communication encounters? As children, we were often admonished not to touch ourselves or things around us, yet all humans need to touch and be touched.[70] In fact, research reveals that a hug and 10 minutes of handholding with a romantic partner greatly reduce the harmful physical effects of stress. It appears that, because touch lowers stress hormones, such loving contact protects us throughout the day.[71]

How accessible are you to touch?

The amount of touching we do or find acceptable is, at least in part, culturally conditioned. Where do you touch your father? Your mother? Your brother? Your sister? A friend of the same sex? A friend of the opposite sex? In general, women are more accessible to touch than are men. Touch also correlates positively with openness, comfort with relationships, and the ability to express feelings.[72] Both men and women will often kiss women in greeting; men who meet usually shake hands. Usually, men touch women more than women touch men.[73] Physical contact between males is often limited to contact sports, such as football and soccer.

Touch can also reflect status. High-status people touch others and invade their space more than do people with lower status.[74] The person who initiates touch is usually the one with the higher status. Nancy Henley points out that

haptics
the study of the use of touch

You cannot shake hands with a clenched fist.
—Golda Meir

Whom have you touched today? Who has touched you?

Marasmus, *a Greek word meaning wasting away, was the term used in the nineteenth and early twentieth centuries to describe a disease babies placed in orphanages or hospitals died from. These infants suffered from a lack of physical contact. Today, in part because of the threat of sexual harassment, teachers refrain from touching students, and employers refrain from touching people with whom they work. In your opinion, is such a lack of touch contributing to people's thinking that the corporations they work for are cold and uncaring? Should warm and healing, as opposed to sexual, touching be put back into our schools and workplaces? What should be the rules of touch?*

we are unlikely to go up to our boss and pat him or her on the shoulder.[75] Would you put your arm around the president of your college or university? Why? Would your behavior change if you met the president at a party? Probably not. The president, however, might well put an arm around you or another student. The person who initiates touching usually also controls the interaction.

Touch, of course, functions importantly in sexual communication. If people hold hands, we assume they have a romantic interest in one another. Are we right? The shaving cream companies have made certain that American men shave every day in order to avoid stubble, which is presumably not touchable. Most American women shave their legs and underarms and use a variety of lotions to keep their hands soft to the touch. When you were growing up, did your parents touch in your presence? Many adults avoid any contact in front of their children. It is somewhat paradoxical that we spend a great deal of money on creams, razor blades, and other products designed to make us touchable and then avoid being touched.

How we use touch sends many messages about us. It reveals our perceptions of status, our attitudes, and even our needs. For example, in his book *The Broken Heart*, psychologist James L. Lynch establishes a correlation between many diseases—particularly heart disease—and loneliness.[76] Lynch tells the story of one man, hooked up to heart-monitoring devices, who was in a coma and near death. When a nurse would walk into his room and hold his hand for a few moments, his heartbeat would change from fast and erratic to slow and smooth.

Different cultures value touch differently. In Asian cultures, for example, very little touching behavior occurs because the members of Asian cultures adhere to norms that forbid public displays of intimacy or affection.[77] For the most part, cultures that encourage outward displays of affection touch more than cultures that stress emotional restraint and rigid status differences. Thus,

Touch facilitates the expression of feelings.

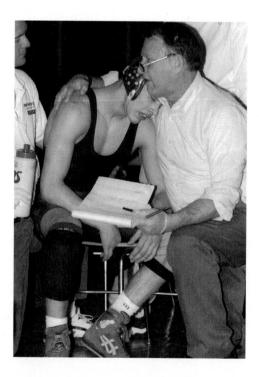

typically, German, Japanese, and English people touch less than people from the Middle East and Latin America. As a result, when a member of a culture that values touch interacts with a member of a culture that practices touching restraint, the person who is used to touching may perceive the person who rarely touches as aloof or cold, while he or she may be perceived by the other person as aggressive or overly familiar.[78]

TRUTH, DECEPTION, AND NONVERBAL COMMUNICATION

Actors and actresses use nonverbal cues to encourage us to suspend our disbelief and accept them as persons whom they are not. They carefully rehearse the parts they play, down to the smallest gestures and artifacts. As a result, they are able to control the nonverbal cues they exhibit, so that they present the characters being performed in exactly the way they desire.

What about the rest of us? We, too, may use nonverbal cues to create false impressions in others. While the aim of some deceptive communication is to help receivers save face (we try to appear calm when we are nervous) or to protect oneself from the embarrassment that bluntness can cause (" Yes, I love your new hairstyle," we say when we hate it), the goal of too many deceivers is to take advantage of those with whom they are interacting. Most of us, however, do not rehearse for every one of our person-to-person encounters. Our lives are not that plotted or planned. We do not map out the nonverbal cues we will use during our continuing interactions with others. But what if we could, and what if we did? Would others be able to discern our intentions? Would they be able to tell that we were not really feeling what we were expressing?

In general, people tend to pay closer attention to the nonverbal cues of persons whom they do not trust or whom they suspect may be lying than they do to the rest of the people with whom they interact.[79] Those who plan and rehearse the deceptive messages they are sending tend to be self-confident and experience no guilt about their deception. They are least likely to be suspected by others and, therefore, least likely to be uncovered as liars. This, to be certain, is not necessarily a good thing for those of us trying to detect deceptiveness in others.

Some of us are better at nonverbal deception than others. For example, persons whose occupations require that they sometimes act differently than they feel are most successful at deception. Included in this group are lawyers, diplomats, and salespersons.[80] Researchers also tell us that, as we age, most of us become better liars.[81] Those among us who are high self-monitors are also usually better dissemblers than those of us who possess less self-awareness.

Those of us who are better at nonverbal detection than others are more watchful. Unsuccessful liars are vulnerable to leakage, deception clues that careful observers pick up. Sometimes, it is a change in expression on the face, a movement of the body, a vocal inflection, a deep or shallow breath, a long pause, a slip of the tongue, a microfacial expression, or an ill-timed or inappropriate gesture.[82] How do you protect yourself from being lied to? While there are no specific nonverbal clues that indicate someone is lying, one book went so far as to provide readers with 46 clues to deception.[83] Although the context of the behavior must always be considered, among the nonverbal behaviors typically exhibited by deceivers are increased eye blinking, hand fidgeting, posture shifts, the making of speech errors, rising pitch, and hesitations.[84]

Researchers have reported the development of a facial imaging device that detects heat patterns in the skin of deceivers. Like the polygraph "lie-detector" test, however, the invention appears to measure anxiety rather than pure deception.[85] Being anxious and not being truthful are not the same things. Do you pride yourself on being a deception detector? What are the clues you rely on?

GENDER AND NONVERBAL BEHAVIOR: MASCULINE AND FEMININE STYLES

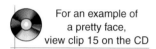

For an example of a pretty face, view clip 15 on the CD

visual dominance

a measure calculated by comparing the percentage of looking while speaking with the percentage of looking while listening

The ways men and women use nonverbal communication often reflect societal practices. While men, for example, are expected to exhibit assertive behaviors that demonstrate their power and authority, women are expected to exhibit more reactive and responsive behaviors. Thus, men often talk more than women and interrupt women more frequently than they are interrupted by women.[86]

During interactions, men also tend to be more visually dominant than women. **Visual dominance** is measured by comparing the percentage of looking while speaking with the percentage of looking while listening. When compared with women, men display higher levels of looking while speaking and lower levels when listening. Thus, the visual dominance ratio of men is usually higher than that of women and, again, reflects the use of nonverbal cues to reinforce perceptions of social power.[87]

Men can use space and touch to assert their dominance over women. They are much more likely to touch women than women are to touch them. Again, women are more typically the recipients of touching actions, rather than the initiators. Men also tend to claim more personal space than women usually do, and they more frequently walk in front of women than behind them. Thus, in general, males are the touchers, not the touchees, the leaders rather than the followers.

What kinds of nonverbal cues do women display more than men? They tend to smile and show emotion more often than men do. In general, they are more expressive than men are and exhibit higher levels of involvement when engaged in person-to-person interaction than men do. Women stand closer to one another than men do. Women also use nonverbal signals to draw others into conversations to a greater extent than men do. While women demonstrate an interest in affiliation, men generally are more interested in establishing the strength of their own ideas and agendas.[88] In addition, when tests are given to assess nonverbal decoding ability, including the ability to read another person's feelings by relying on vocal or facial cues, females usually outperform males.[89]

Of special interest when it comes to comparing the nonverbal behavior of men and women is a report that appeared on their reactions to the events of 9/11:

> It's an odd thing, probably not what one would predict or remember afterward, but when a person encounters true horror, the body's first response almost always occurs in the hands. With women, the hands tend to immediately come up to cover the mouth or press the cheeks. Among men, they tend to form a steeple over the nose and mouth or to clutch tightly onto the sides of the head. It is as if, in this moment of utter incomprehension and helplessness, the hands are trying to give comfort.[90]

In what other ways do you recall the reactions of men and women to the events of 9/11 differing, if at all?

DIVERSITY AND NONVERBAL BEHAVIOR: CULTURAL PATTERNS

People throughout the world use nonverbal cues to help them express themselves. In large measure, the culture of a people modifies their use of such cues. For example, people who belong to **contact cultures**—that is, cultures that promote interaction and encourage displays of warmth, closeness, and availability—tend to stand close to each other when conversing, seek maximum sensory experiences, and touch each other frequently. This is not the case, however, among members of **low-contact cultures,** where such behaviors are discouraged. Saudi Arabia, France, and Italy are countries with contact cultures; their members relish the intimacy of contact when conversing. In contrast, Scandinavia, Germany, England, and Japan are low- or lower-contact cultures, whose members value privacy and maintain more distance from each other when interacting.[91]

In similar fashion, people from different cultures may not display emotion or express intimacy in the same ways. Among the members of Mediterranean cultures, for example, it is normal for emotive reactions to be uninhibited and greatly exaggerated. Thus, it is common for the cultures' members to express a feeling like grief or happiness together with open facial displays, magnified gestures, and vocal cues that support the feeling. On the other hand, neither the Chinese nor the Japanese readily reveal their inner feelings in public, preferring to display less emotion, maintain more self-control, and keep their feelings to themselves; for these reasons, they often appear to remain expressionless.[92] In contrast, persons in the United States are likely to be emotionally expressive and to smile freely.

The cultural background of the individuals communicating also affects their use of personal space and touch. Americans stand farther apart when conversing than do persons from Middle Eastern cultures. Whereas Americans expect persons who live next door to them to be friendly and to interact with them, this expectation is not shared by the Japanese. Consequently, whereas the Japanese may view Americans as overly friendly, the Americans may conclude that the Japanese are unfriendly, cold, and distant. North Americans are also apt to do more touching of each other more than the Japanese are; in Japan, there is a taboo against strangers touching each other. In contrast, Middle Easterners are apt to do a significant amount of touching; they walk with their arms around each other and are apt to touch each other during conversations a lot more than are persons from noncontact cultures.

Even when the nonverbal cues displayed in different cultures are the same, they do not necessarily convey the same meaning. In the United States, for example, a head nod symbolizes agreement or consent, while in Japan it means only that a message was received. Hand signals can be confusing to those not tuned in to the culture. For example, people in the United States use their hand pointing at their chest when they talk about themselves. The Japanese use their forefinger pointed at their nose. In South Africa, an American trying to hitch a ride with his thumb backwards is telling the South Africans that he is seeking a homosexual encounter.[93] Similarly, diverse cultures feel differently

contact cultures
cultures that promote interaction and encourage displays of warmth, closeness, and availability

low-contact cultures
cultures that maintain more distance when interacting

Do you think you can teach nonverbal communication, the way you can teach a foreign language? Why or why not?

What kind of statement does a tatoo or a tongue or belly-button ring make? Do you believe such artifacts signal defiance, independence, or something else? What inferences are persons who do not use such personal adornments likely to make about those who do?

Is It Just Clothing and Makeup?

In some Middle Eastern countries, makeup has become a political weapon that women use to signal their defiance of authority. A journalist tells the following story. She and a female friend visited a bazaar and then decided to dine at a local restaurant. During their meal, the lights in the restaurant were suddenly turned off—a signal that the self-appointed morals police, who were obsessed with the dress code for women, had arrived. As the journalist watched, her friend wiped off her lipstick with a napkin. Other diners covered nail-polished fingers with gloves or put on socks to conceal their colored toenails. Before the lights were turned back on, the journalist and her friend escaped the restaurant, hailed a taxi, and made their escape. Once safe, her friend reapplied her lipstick as she explained that lipstick now transmits political messages; it is no longer just lipstick.[94]

Similarly, after the Western Alliance recaptured Kabul from the Taliban, images of Afghan women removing their burkas and revealing their faces in public for the first time in years flooded the airwaves. While Afghan women used their newly restored freedom to let the sun shine on their faces and show flecks of their hair, Afghan men also used their newly felt freedom to shave their faces of the beards, at least 4 inches long, that the Taliban had forced them to wear.[95]

Compare and contrast these examples with the following example closer to home. In the United States, every year for the past few years, the Victoria's Secret Fashion Show has broadcast a program that features women parading in thong panties, scanty nighties, and low-cut bras. In your opinion, what motivates this behavior? Is there any parallel between Muslim women shedding their burkas and showing their hair and American women shedding their clothes and showing their skin? Are American women demonstrating their hyper- or insecure femininity by revealing what some may perceive as their hyper-sexuality?

In addition, to what extent, if any, do you believe that in your own culture males and females use makeup and artifacts to make personal or political statements? What, for example, do you believe is communicated by body piercings and tattooing?

about silence. Whereas in the United States we are apt to perceive another person's silence as a negative and to infer that he or she is too self-absorbed, isn't listening, isn't interested, or has nothing of value to add to a conversation, other cultures interpret silence in a more favorable light. In Japan, for example, silence is frequently preferred to speech.

For us to experience more effective interaction with people from different cultures, we must make the effort to identify and understand the many ways each culture shapes nonverbal communication. We need to acknowledge that our communication style is not intrinsically better than others; that awareness will contribute to more successful multicultural exchanges.

TECHNOLOGY AND NONVERBAL COMMUNICATION

Nonverbal communication is alive and well in cyberspace. Just as those who communicate in cyberspace rely on established netiquette guidelines for the standards of behavior acceptable during their online interactions, so they have also evolved a system of written symbols to help reinforce those standards. Together, these symbols, called **emoticons,** replace physical gestures and facial expressions, substitute for nonverbal cues and help those engaged in online dialogues convey action, emotion, and emphasis.[96]

Emoticons, or relational icons, help add personalization and more expressive emotional exchanges to computer-mediated communication as a way to approximate the warmth and intimacy of face-to-face interactions. Thus, emoticons, are used also at times to indicate subtle mood changes.[97] In other words, emoticons function as social cues and fulfill the purposes served by facial expressions or vocal intonations. For example, a symbol called the smiley face looks like :-) and indicates the humorous intent of the sender. It may wink mischievously, ;-), or frown, :-(, depending on whether the online comment is to be interpreted humorously or sarcastically. Smiley faces may also suggest good spirits, disappointment, or surprise, as well as the general friendliness of the communicator.[98] Similarly, capitalizations and asterisks, such as GREAT and ***, convey a user's emphasis and enthusiasm. In addition, creative icons may be used to convey the identity of the user, as when an 8 is substituted for the colon in the preceding symbols to indicate that the person wears glasses.

The following list contains other emoticons that can be used to describe a communicator's physical or emotional condition or to depict feelings and actions that straight text alone could not depict. These symbols are commonly understood by online users.

:-P	someone sticking out the tongue
:-O	someone screaming in fright, their hair standing on end
:-&	someone whose lips are sealed
!#!^*&:-	a schizophrenic![99]

emoticons
symbols that replace nonverbal cues during machine-assisted communication

Do you think jokes play as well online as they do when delivered by someone in person? How does the loss of nonverbal cues influence the impact of a joke? How could you use emoticons to compensate for the loss of such cues?

It's Not What You Say . . . but the Emoticons You Use

Locate an Internet chat group on a subject of interest to you. Enter the group. Use a number of different emoticons to clarify the nature of your comments to your online peers. Print out a portion of the group's discussion. Examine the interaction and discuss the extent to which the emoticons are successful in replacing the nonverbal channel.

e-SEARCH

Of course, persons unfamiliar with online culture would more than likely be confused by the preceding keyboard symbols. Lacking more conventional social context cues, they would not be able to use the symbols to achieve understanding.

Since online communicators probably are not able to hear each other, they have also created a shorthand to describe their reactions. For instance, they may describe themselves as "rolling on the floor laughing" with the abbreviation ROFL.

Computer users have taken an active role in the codification of emoticons, even developing dictionaries that catalogue their use. Thus, the computer medium may become as expressive of gestures and emotions, intention and affect, as are nonverbal cues. Overall, when interacting with each other, women seem to use a considerably higher number of emoticons than men do when interacting with other men. In mixed-gender online conversations, however, men tend to use emoticons as much as women.[100]

Technological changes are affecting our nonverbal communication in other ways as well. According to Nelson Thall, the president and chief executive officer of the Marshall McLuhan Center on Global Communication, the current variety in fashion is an outgrowth of the electronic technological revolution. According to Thall, "Our clothing is an extension of our skin, just like a hammer is a technological extension of our hand."[101] Thall contends that, since computers and the Internet allow people to be nationless, sexless, and ageless, fashion now reflects that option. We now dress similarly across borders and wear clothing that is technologically friendly with room for cell phones, beepers, palm pilots, and so on. We even have a wearable computer, also known as a personal optical mobile appliance or personal multimedia appliance. While it may be a while before wearable computing is as socially commonplace as a cell phone or personal digital assistant (PDA), it was predicted that more than 60 percent of the U.S. population ages 15 to 50 will carry or wear a wireless computing and communications device at least six hours a day by the year 2007.[102] Are you wearing one today?

In addition, in our security-conscious age, training security personnel just to watch for darting eyes and trembling hands may not be enough. Technology is also being called into play to aid in person identification and behavior analysis by helping with the reading of nonverbal cues. The CIA, for example, has commissioned two research centers, the Salk Institute and Carnegie-Mellon University's Robotics Institute, to try to teach computers to watch for detailed facial-language clues. In addition, hidden computers are being used to pick up stress in the speech patterns of travelers when they check in at airports.[103]

ASSESSING YOUR EFFECTIVENESS AS A NONVERBAL COMMUNICATOR

Nonverbal communication includes body language (facial expressions, posture, and gestures), clothing, voice, distances and spaces, colors, time, and touch—all of which can either support or contradict the meaning of the words we speak. Use your knowledge of these variables to help you react to interactions you observe and to appropriate pictures in this text. For each picture you select, answer the following questions about the interactants and identify the cues that influenced your response:

1. Who is more trustworthy?
2. Who is more dynamic?
3. Who is more credible?
4. Who has more status?
5. Who is older?
6. Who is more intelligent?
7. Who is more powerful?
8. Who is more friendly?
9. What is their relationship to each other?
10. What can you predict about the course of their relationship?

Compare and contrast your responses with those of other students in your class. Discussing your observations will be valuable, since many of our judgments and decisions are based on nonverbal cues.

The following guidelines should prove helpful as you continue to develop your ability to make valid judgments and decisions on the basis of nonverbal communication.

Examine the Environment

For any nonverbal interaction, ask yourself if any environmental stimuli are likely to affect it. Determine if other people present could influence the communicators. Attempt to determine whether colors and decor will have an impact on the nature and tone of the communication. Analyze the amount of space available to the interactants. Determine whether architectural factors might alter the outcome. Where are chairs, tables, passageways, and desks situated? Why did the interactants situate themselves as they did? What type of behavior would we expect to see in this environment?

Observe the Communicators

Ask yourself if the sex, age, or status of the communicators will exert an influence on their relationship. Assess to what extent, if any, attractiveness, clothing, or physical appearance should affect the interaction. Determine if, in your own mind, the communicators' dress is appropriate to the environment. Decide if the communicators appear to like each other and to have similar goals.

Observe Body Language

What does each communicator's facial expression reveal? Are his or her facial expressions relatively consistent or fleeting? Do these expressions tend to fluctuate drastically? Assess the extent to which you believe the facial expressions are genuine.

Thinking CRITICALLY

Reflect and Respond

Agree or disagree with the following statement; supply reasons and examples that support your position.

Because of the important implications of nonverbal cues—in interviews, in adver-tising, and in interactions in general—the impressions we form are due more to the nonverbal signals displayed than to the words spoken by the communicators.

Analyze significant bodily cues. Attempt to decide if hand or foot movements suggest honesty or deception. Decide if either of the interactants moves too much or too little. Ask yourself if both are equally involved in the exchange. Is one more eager to continue the communication than the other? Would one prefer to terminate the communication? How do you know?

Assess the extent to which the interactants mirror each other's posture. Ask yourself how posture supports or contradicts their status relationship. Do the interactants appear to be relaxed or tense? Why? Determine if they have used their bodies to include or exclude others from their conversation. Analyze when and why the communicators alter their postures.

Watch the eye behavior of the participants. Determine if one looks away more than the other. Determine if one stares at the other. To what extent, if any, does excessive blinking occur? When is eye contact most pronounced? How does the eye contact of one participant appear to affect the other?

Listen for Vocal Cues

Assess whether the communicators are using appropriate vocal volumes and rates of speaking, given their situation. Determine if and how the way something that is said verbally supports or contradicts what is being said nonverbally. Analyze how and when silence is used. Be responsive to signals of nervousness and changes in pitch.

Observe Touching

Watch to see if the participants touch each other at all. Determine, if you can, why they touched. How did touching or being touched affect the interactants? Was the contact appropriate or inappropriate to the situation? Why?

Revisiting Chapter Objectives

1. **Define and distinguish among the following terms: *nonverbal communication, kinesics, paralanguage, proxemics, chronemics,* and *haptics.***
Nonverbal communication includes all the human responses that are not expressed in words. Over 65 percent of the social meaning of the messages we send to others is communicated nonverbally. Perceiving and analyzing nonverbal cues can help us understand what is really happening during a conversation.

Nonverbal messages fall into seven main categories: (1) body language, or kinesics (facial expressions, posture, eye gaze and eye contact, and gestures); (2) clothing and artifactual communication; (3) voice, or paralanguage (including pitch, volume, rate, and pauses); (4) space and distance, or proxemic factors (including both the space that exists between us when we talk to each other and the way we organize space in our homes, offices, and communities); (5) color; (6) time, or chronemics; and (7) touch, or haptics.

2. **Explain why the face is an important source of information.** Since the face cannot be easily hidden, it is an important source of nonverbal information and communicates a variety of emotions. In addition, eye contact, pupil size, and the smile provide additional cues to informed observers.

3. **Explain how artifactual communication and color can affect interaction.** Artifactual communication, another category of nonverbal cues, is an integral part of the nonverbal package. It includes the use of personal adornments, such as clothing, jewelry, makeup, hairstyles, and beards. People are apt to make inferences about us based on the way we dress.

4. **Distinguish among the following terms: *intimate distance, personal distance, social distance,* and *public distance* and *informal space, semifixed-feature space,* and *fixed-feature space.*** Proxemic cues, including the treatment of space and territory influence interaction and help define the communication experience. According to Edward Hall, there are four distances that we keep between ourselves and other people: intimate distance—0 to 18 inches; personal distance—18 inches to 4 feet; social distance—4 to 12 feet; and public distance—12 feet to the limit of sight. In addition, researchers divide environmental spaces into three categories—informal, semifixed-feature, and fixed-feature—based on the perceived permanence of the physical space.

5. **Explain why territoriality is an important concept in communication.** Typically, human beings stake out space, or territory. Territoriality is the need to demonstrate a possessive or ownership relationship to space. Markers are used to reserve space and set boundaries that help identify the space as belonging to someone.

6. **Identify the ways in which gender, diversity, and technology influence nonverbal behavior.** The use of nonverbal cues is affected by variables such as gender, culture, and technology. The ways men and women use nonverbal cues reflects societal practices. To a large degree, people modify their use of nonverbal cues depending on the culture they belong to or identify with. Nonverbal communication is also affected by whether communication is occurring online or offline.

7. **Explain the role nonverbal cues play in deception and truthtelling.** If we are watchful we can identify deception cues that leak when a person lies. High self-monitors emit fewer cues making detection more difficult.

8. **Identify how you can improve your nonverbal communication effectiveness.** You can improve your effectiveness as a nonverbal communicator by observing and analyzing both the physical environment of interactions and the body language, appearance, gestures, vocal cues, eye contact, and touching behavior of the participants.

Resources for Further Inquiry and Reflection

To apply your understanding of how the principles in Chapter 6 are at work in our daily lives, consult the following resources for further inquiry and reflection. Or, if you prefer, choose any other appropriate resource. Then connect the ideas expressed in your chosen selection with the communication concepts and issues you are learning about both in and out of class.

 Listen to Me

"Good Vibrations" (The Beach Boys)
"Your Body Is a Wonderland" (John Mayer)
"Superman" (Eminem)
"The Sound of Silence" Simon and Garfunkel
"You've Lost That Lovin' Feeling" (The Righteous Brothers)

Each song describes the effects of one or more non-verbal cues on an individual and/or a relationship. Identify and discuss the cue or cues emphasized, being certain to explain the impact on communication.

 View Me

The Mask   *Don't Say a Word*
Edward Scissorhands   *Look Who's Talking*

The characters in these films have a prime nonverbal channel either masked or unmasked. Discuss the extent to which the character is affected by his or her ability or inability to use a nonverbal cue effectively.

 Read Me

Arthur Conan Doyle. *Sherlock Holmes*. New York: Knopf, 1996.
Sister Souljah, *The Coldest Winter Ever,* NY: Pocket Books, 2000.
David L. Lieberman. *Never Be Lied to Again*. New York: St. Martin's Press, 1998.

On the basis of your reading of one of these books, discuss how nonverbal cues can be used to help identify someone who is guilty, select a jury, identify a real friend, or hire a business associate.

 Tell Me

Share with the class the insights you gained from your chosen Listen to Me, View Me, or Read Me selection.

According to baseball legend Yogi Berra, "Sometimes you can observe a lot by watching." Give an example of what you think Yogi meant.

Key Chapter Terminology

Communication Works

online learning center

www.mhhe.com/gamble8

Use the Communication Works CD-ROM and the Online Learning Center at www.mhhe.com/gamble8 to further your knowledge of the following terminology.

affect blends 156
artifactual communication 163
chronemics 175
civil inattention 158
contact cultures 181
emoticons 183
facial management techniques 155
fixed-feature space 172
habitual pitch 166
haptics 177
informal space 171
intimate distance 170

kinesics 154
low-contact cultures 181
markers 174
microfacial, or micromomentary, expressions 156
mixed message 152
nonfluencies 168
nonverbal communication 151
paralanguage 166
personal distance 170
pitch 166
proxemics 169

public distance 171
rate 167
semifixed-feature space 171
silence 168

social distance 171
territoriality 173
visual dominance 180
volume 167

Test Your Understanding

Go to the *Self Quizzes* on the Communication Works CD-ROM and the book's Online Learning Center at www.mhhe.com/gamble8.

Communication Works

online learning center

www.mhhe.com/gamble8

Notes

1. M. T. Palmer and K. B. Simmons. "Communicating Intentions through Nonverbal Behaviors: Conscious and Nonconscious Encoding of Liking." *Human Communication Research* 22, 1995, pp. 128–160.

2. Ann Davis, Joseph Pereira, and William M. Bulkeley. "Security Concerns Bring New Focus on Body Language." *Wall Street Journal,* August 15, 2002, pp. A1, A6.

3. See, for example, H. A. Elfenbein and N. Ambady. "Predicting Workplace Outcomes from the Ability to Eavesdrop on Feelings." *Journal of Applied Psychology* October 2002, pp. 963–972.

4. See, for example, L. Carrol and P. J. Gilroy. "Role of Appearance and Nonverbal Behaviors in the Perception of Sexual Orientation among Lesbians and Gay Men." *Psychological Reports,* 9:1, August 2002, pp. 115–122.

5. "Feeling 'Out of It' at Work and Socially?" *USA Today Magazine,* November 2002, p. 8.

6. Ray Birdwhistell. *Kinesics and Context.* Philadelphia: University of Pennsylvania Press, 1970; Mark L. Knapp and Judith A. Hall. *Nonverbal Communication in Human Interaction,* 3rd ed. Orlando, FL: Harcourt Brace Jovanovich, 1992; Albert Mehrabian. *Silent Messages.* 2nd ed. Belmont, CA: Wadsworth, 1981.

7. For some practical advice, see Dale G. Leathers. *Successful Nonverbal Communication: Principles and Applications.* New York: Macmillan, 1992.

8. Marilyn Daniels. *Dancing with Words: Signing for Hearing Children's Literacy.* Bergin & Garvey, Westport, CT: 2001.

9. Tom Pedulla. "Spurning Anthem Creates Rancor." *USA Today,* February 26, 2003, p. 4C.

10. Tamar Lewin. "High School Tells Student to Remove Antiwar Shirt." *New York Times,* February 26, 2003.

11. Knapp and Hall.

12. See, for example, Judith N. Martin and Thomas K. Nakayama. *Intercultural Communication in Contexts,* 2nd ed. Mountain View, CA: Mayfield, 2000, p.181.

13. Kathleen Fackelmann. "Look Who's Talking with Gestures." *USA Today,* July 5, 2000, p. 7D.

14. Quoted in Daniel Goleman. "Sensing Silent Cues Emerges as Key Skill." *New York Times,* October 10, 1989.

15. George Orwell. *1984.* New American Library ed. New York: New American Library, 1983.

16. Paul Ekman and Wallace Friesen. "The Repertoire of Nonverbal Behavior: Categories, Origins, Usage and Coding." *Semiotica* 1, 1969, pp. 49–98.

17. E. A. Haggard and K. S. Isaacs. "Micromomentary Facial Expressions as Indicators of Ego Mechanisms in Psychotherapy." In L. A. Gottschalk and A. H. Auerback, eds. *Methods of Research in Psychotherapy.* New York: Appleton-Century-Crofts, 1966.

18. See Klaus Fiedler and Isabella Walka. "Training Lie Detectors to Use Nonverbal Cues Instead of Global Heuristics." *Human Communication Research* 20:2, December 1993, pp. 199–223.

19. See H. D. Ellis and A. W. Young. "Are Faces Special?" In A. W. Young and H. D. Ellis, eds. *Handbook of Research in Face Processing.* Amsterdam: Elsevier, 1989, pp. 1–26.

20. M. D. Licke, R. H. Smith, and M. L. Klotz. "Judgments of Physical Attractiveness: The Role of Faces and Bodies." *Personality and Social Psychology Bulletin* 12, 1986, pp. 381–389.

21. D. S. Berry. "What Can a Moving Face Tell Us?" *Journal of Personality and Social Psychology* 58, 1990, pp. 1004–1014.

22. United Press International, 1979.

23. *Discover,* February 1989.

24. Julius Fast. *Body Language.* New York: Evans, 1970.

25. See C. L. Kleinke. "Gaze and Eye Contact: A Research Review." *Psychological Bulletin* 100, 1986, pp. 78–100.

26. Helmut Morsbach. "Aspects of Nonverbal Communication in Japan." In Larry Samovar and Richard Porter, eds. *Intercultural Communication: A Reader,* 3rd ed. Belmont, CA: Wadsworth, 1982, p. 308.

27. "Girl's Surgery Is Performed for a Smile, Doctors Hope." *New York Times,* December 16, 1995, p. 8.

28. V. Richmond. "Teacher Nonverbal Immediacy: Use and Outcomes." In J. L. Chesebro and J. C. McCroskey, eds. *Communication for Teachers.* Boston: Allyn & Bacon, 2002, pp. 65–82.

29. Mehrabian.

30. Susan L. Hwang. "Some Type A Staffers Dress for Success with a Shot of Botox." *Wall Street Journal,* July 31, 2002, p. B1.

31. Nancy Henley. *Body Politics: Power, Sex and Nonverbal Communication.* New York: Simon & Schuster, 1986.

32. For a summary of Mehrabian's work in this area, see his article "Significance of Posture and Position in the Communication of Attitude and Status Relationship." *Psychological Bulletin* 71, 1969, pp. 359–372.

33. Kim A. McDonald. "The Body Language of Leadership." *Chronicle of Higher Education,* January 5, 1996, p. A7.

34. Paul Ekman, W. V. Friesen, and J. Baer. "The International Language of Gestures." *Psychology Today,* May 1984, pp. 64–69.

35. "What's A-O.K. in the U.S.A. Is Lewd and Worthless Beyond." *New York Times,* August 18, 1996, p. 7E.

36. "What's A-O.K. in the U.S.A."

37. L. Samovar and R. Porter. *Communication between Cultures,* 4th ed. Belmont, CA: Wadsworth, 2001.

38. S. Kaiser. *The Social Psychology of Clothing: Symbolic Appearances in Context,* 2nd ed. New York: Macmillan, 1990.

39. Cheryl Lu-Lien Tan. "Stars Speak Loud and Clear without Even Opening Their Mouths." *The Record,* March 4, 2003, pp. F1, F5.

40. "New Wrinkles in Casual Dress Codes." *Kiplinger's Personal Finance Magazine,* November 1999, p. 28.

41. John T. Molloy. *New Dress for Success.* New York: Warner, 1990.

42. Molloy.

43. See, for example, M. S. Singer and A. E. Singer. "The Effect of Police Uniforms on Interpersonal Perception." *Journal of Psychology* 119, 1985, pp. 157–161.

44. See, for example, Scott Shane. "Language Help from, Um, Almost-Words." *The Sunday Record,* September 12, 1999, pp. L3, L7.

45. Mehrabian.

46. Ken Cooper. *Nonverbal Communication for Business Success.* New York: Amacom, 1980, p. 11.

47. For background on how culture affects rate, see Hyun O. Lee and Franklin J. Boster. "Collectivism-Individualism in Perceptions of Speech Rate: A Cross-Cultural Comparison." *Journal of Cross-Cultural Psychology* 23:3, September 1992, pp. 377–388.

48. F. Goldman-Eisler. "Continuity of Speech Utterance. Its Determinance and Its Significance." *Language and Speech* 4, 1961, pp. 220–231.

49. Adam Jaworski. *The Power of Silence: Social and Pragmatic Perspective.* Thousand Oaks, CA: Sage, 1993.

50. J. R. Davitz and L. Davitz. "The Communication of Feelings by Content-Free Speech." *Journal of Communication* 9, 1959, pp. 256–257.

51. Edward Hall. *The Hidden Dimension.* New York: Doubleday, 1969.

52. See J. K. Burgoon. "Privacy and Communication." In M. Burgoon, ed. *Communication Yearbook/6.* Beverly Hills, CA: Sage, 1982, pp. 206–249; J. K. Burgoon and L. Aho. "Three Field Experiments on the Effects of Violations of Conversational Distance." *Communication Monographs* 49, 1982, pp. 71–88; J. K. Burgoon and J. B. Walther. "Nonverbal Expectations and the Evaluative Consequence of Violations." *Human Communication Research* 17:2, 1990, pp. 232–265.

53. Dale Leathers. *Successful Nonverbal Communication: Principles and Applications.* New York: Macmillan, 1986, p. 236.

54. See, for example, A. G. White. "The Patient Sits Down: A Clinical Note." *Psychosomatic Medicine* 15, 1953, pp. 256–257.

55. D. Diamond. "Behind Closed Gates." *USA Today,* January 31, 1997, pp. 4–5.

56. Max Luscher. *The Luscher Color Test.* New York: Simon & Schuster, 1980. See also Luscher. *The Four-Color Person.* New York: Simon & Schuster, 1980.

57. Susan Carey, "More U.S. Companies Are Blue, and It's Not Just the Stock Market." *Wall Street Journal,* August 30, 2001, pp. A1, A2.

58. Craig Wilson. "Serene Color Gets the Green Light in Uncertain Times." *USA Today.* March 7, 2003, p. D1.

59. Meera Somasundaram. "Red Symbols Tend to Lure Shoppers Like Capes Being Flourished at Bulls." *Wall Street Journal,* September 18, 1995, p. A9.

60. Jennifer Steinhauer. "The Color Red Takes on a Youthful Look." *New York Times,* June 30, 1996, p. 42.

61. Vance Packard. *The Hidden Persuaders.* New York: McKay, 1957.

62. Robert Levine. *A Geography of Time, or How Every Culture Keeps Time Just a Little Differently.* New York: Basic Books: 1997.

63. See Alan Zarembo. "What If There Weren't Any Clocks to Watch." *Newsweek,* June 30, 1997, p. 14; and John Tierney. "Some Like It Fast." *New York Times Magazine,* July 20, 1997, p. 16.

64. Del Jones. "I'm Late, I'm Late, I'm Late." *USA Today,* November 26, 2002, p. B1.

65. Hall.

66. L. Copland and L. Greggs. *Going International: How to Make Friends and Deal Effectively in the Going Marketplace.* New York: Random House, 1985, p. 10.

67. Robert Levine. "Waiting Is a Power Game." *Psychology Today,* April 1987, p. 30.

68. Alex MacKenzie. *The Time Trap.* New York: McGraw-Hill, 1975.

69. J. Burgoon, J. Walther, and J. Baesler. "Interpretations, Evaluations, and Consequences of Interpersonal Touch." *Human Communication Research* 19, pp. 237–263.

70. Marilyn Elias. "Study: Hugging Warms the Heart, and Also May Protect It." *USA Today,* March 10, 2003, p. 7D.

71. An especially persuasive argument is made by Ashley Montagu in *Touching: The Human Significance of the Skin.* New York: Harper & Row, 1971.

72. See D. F. Fromme, W. E. Jaynes, D. K. Taylor, E. G. Harold, J. Daniell, J. R. Roundtree, and M. Fromme. "Nonverbal Behaviors and Attitudes toward Touch." *Journal of Nonverbal Behavior* 13, 1989, pp. 3–14.

73. Barbara Bales. *Communication and the Sexes.* New York: Harper & Row, 1988, p. 60.

74. See, for example, J. T. Wood. *Interpersonal Communication: Everyday Encounters,* 2nd ed. Belmont, CA: Wadsworth, 2002.

75. Henley.

76. James L. Lynch. *The Broken Heart.* New York: Basic Books, 1979. See also James L. Lynch. *The Language of the Heart.* New York: Basic Books, 1986.

77. M. S. Kim. "A Comparative Analysis of Nonverbal Expression as Portrayed by Korean and American Print-Media Advertising." *Howard Journal of Communication* 3, 1992, pp. 320–324.

78. Carolyn Calloway-Thomas, Pamela J. Cooper, and Cecil Blake. *Intercultural Communication: Roots and Routes.* Boston: Allyn & Bacon, 1999, p. 166.

79. M. G. Millar and K. U. Millar. "The Effects of Suspicion on the Recall of Cues to Make Veracity Judgments." *Communication Reports* 11, 1998, pp. 57–64.

80. R. G. Riggio and H. S. Freeman. "Individual Differences and Cues to Deception." *Journal of Personality and Social Psychology* 45, 1983, pp. 899–915.

81. D. B. Buller and J. K. Burgoon. "Deception: Strategic and Nonstrategic Communication." In J. Daly and J. M. Wiemann, eds. *Interpersonal Communication*. Hillsdale, NJ: Lawrence Erlbaum Associates, 1994.

82. Paul Ekman and Mark G. Frank. "Lies That Fail." In Michael Lewis and Carolyn Saarni, eds. *Lying and Deception in Everyday Life*. New York: Guilford Press, 1993, pp. 184–200.

83. David J. Lieberman. *Never Be Lied to Again*. New York: St. Martin's Press, 1998.

84. See, for example, T. H. Feeley and M. A. Turck. "The Behaviorial Correlates of Sanctioned and Unsanctioned Deceptive Communication." *Journal of Nonverbal Behavior* 22, 1998, pp. 189–204; A. Vrij, L. Akehurst, and P. Morris. "Individual Differences in Hand Movements during Deception." *Journal of Nonverbal Behavior* 21, 1997, pp. 87–102; and L. Anolli and R. Ciceri. "The Voice of Deception: Vocal Strategies of Naïve and Able Liars." *Journal of Nonverbal Behavior* 21, 1997, pp. 259–285.

85. J. Pavlidis, N. L. Eberhardt, and J. A. Levine. "Seeing through the Face of Deception." *Nature,* 415, 2002.

86. B. Veland. "Tell Me More: On the Fine Art of Listening." *Utne Reader,* 1992, pp.104–109; A. Mulac. "Men's and Women's Talk in Same Gender and Mixed Gender Dyads: Power or Polemic?" *Journal of Language and Social Psychology* 8, 1989, pp. 249–270.

87. J. F. Dovidio, S. L. Ellyson, C. F. Keating, K. Heltman, and C. E. Brown. "The Relationship of Social Power to Visual Displays of Dominance between Men and Women." *Journal of Personality and Social Psychology* 54, 1988, pp. 233–242.

88. Julia T. Wood. *Gendered Lives*. Belmont, CA: Wadsworth, 1994, p. 154.

89. N. G. Rotter and G. S. Rotter. "Sex Differences in the Encloding and Decoding of Negative Facial Emotions." *Journal of Nonverbal Behavior* 12:2, 1998, pp. 139–148.

90. Scott Anderson. "War Comes to America." *Esquire Magazine,* November 2001, pp. 107–113.

91. Peter Anderson. "Exploring Intercultural Differences in Nonverbal Communication." In L. Samovar and R. Porter, eds. *Intercultural Communication: A Reader,* 3rd ed. Belmont, CA: Wadsworth, 1982, pp. 272–282.

92. Edwin R. McDaniel. "Japanese Nonverbal Communication: A Review and Critique of Literature." Paper presented at the annual meeting of the Speech Communication Association, Miami Beach, FL, November 18–21, 1993.

93. B. Leighton. "Ewington, N.H., Trade Center Facilitates Multicultural Communication." *The Telegraph,* May 6, 2001.

94. Farzaneh Milani. "Lipstick Politics in Iran." *New York Times,* August 19, 1999, p. A23.

95. See Maureen Dowd. "Cleopatra and Osama." *New York Times,* November 18, 2001, pp. WK13.

96. Steven G. Jones. *Cybersociety: Computer-Mediated Communication and Community*. Thousand Oaks, CA: Sage, 1995, p. 116.

97. C. Consstantin, S. Kalyanaraman, C. Stavrositu, and N. Wagoner. "To Be or Not to Be Emotional: Impression Formation Effects of Emoticons in Moderated Chatrooms." Paper presented at the annual meeting of the Association for Education in Journalism and Mass Communication. Miami Beach, FL, August 7–10, 2002.

98. Jones, p. 152.

99. Jones, p. 172.

100. A. Wolf. "Emotional Expression Online: Gender Differences in Emoticon Use. *Cyberpsychology and Behavior* 3:5, 2000, pp. 827–833.

101. Karen De Witt. "So, What Is That Leather Bustier Saying?" *New York Times,* January 1, 1995, p. 2-E.

102. Edward C. Baig. "This 'Wearable Computer' Fits Like a Glove." *USA Today,* April 3, 2002, p. 6D.

103. Bret Lortie. "Your Lying Eyes." *Bulletin of the Atomic Scientists* 58:6, November/December 2002.

Listening and
Critical Thinking

After finishing this chapter, you should be able to

1. Define *hearing, listening,* and *critical thinking.*

2. Compare and contrast helpful and harmful listening and thinking habits.

3. Explain and use the listening level–energy involvement scale.

4. Define *feedback,* distinguish among and use different types

of feedback, and explain how each type affects communication.

5. Set appropriate listening goals.

6. Explain how technology influences listening.

To get what you want in your career, stop talking and start listening.

—Anonymous

Listening is not just hearing what someone tells you word for word. You have to listen with a heart.

—Anna Deavere Smith

Nothing new ever entered the mind through an open mouth.

—The Sperry Corporation (now part of UNISYS)

FIGURE 7.1

We do not listen with our ears alone, as the Chinese character for listening reveals.

The Chinese character for "listening" (see Figure 7.1) combines a number of symbols representing the ears, the eyes, and the heart, suggesting that when we listen we also need to give our undivided attention and that we should not rely on our ears alone but should use our eyes and our hearts as well. In your opinion, do most of the people you know accomplish this goal? Do you?

Famed American author Ernest Hemingway is said to have uttered the following words: "I like to listen. I have learned a great deal from listening. Most people never listen." On the basis of your personal experiences, do you think Hemingway's conclusion is right? Do most people never listen? Apparently, the corporate world believes there is some truth in Hemingway's words. Over the years, a number of American corporations have run advertising campaigns designed to promote awareness of the importance of listening.

Ear

Eyes

Undivided Attention

Heart

Do you believe that you listen well? One college student, Brett Banfe, convinced that he has failed miserably in listening to others, vowed to correct his failing by remaining silent for a year: "I noticed I wasn't really listening to people. I was just waiting for people to stop talking so I could chime in," Banfe said.[1] "I'd wait for them to stop talking, then I'd start talking. Because . . . my opinion was the right one anyway. It was like, 'Thanks a lot for your input, but here's how it really happened.'"[2] While you may think that the action taken by Brett Banfe seems extreme, far too often listening is something we take for granted. However, listening is a difficult, intricate skill and, like other skills, it requires training and practice.

LISTENING AND COMMUNICATION

Consider the following excerpt from Hannah Merker's book *Listening:*

> I noticed the world was getting quieter . . . a silence, a soundlessness was softening the edges of my sometimes strident life. The noticing did not appear in a single startling revelation. No, it was a slow astonishing surprise that I sensed the increasing hush around me, with no glimmer yet of the stunning reality: only my world was growing quieter. I was becoming deaf.
>
> When we are used to things, familiar with their presence, we often cease to see them. Or hear them. And silence was something I was becoming used to, an atmosphere once sought in retreat from a large noisy family. Now silence came unbidden, softly, unnoticed, creeping close and staying with me. I noticed the absence of things. My mini-house seemed hushed with the stillness present in a storm when power is cut off. We never hear the heating unit simmering slowly, the whirrings of refrigerators. Machinery around us never really registers in our minds as heard.[3]

Listening affects all kinds of communication. From the time the alarm clock rings until the late news winds up, we are inundated with things to listen to. As we proceed through our day and as we move from person to person, from class to lunch, from formal discussions to casual conversations, we are constantly called on to listen. We are expected to listen to others whenever we interact face-to-face with friends and acquaintances, use the telephone, attend meetings, participate in interviews, take part in arguments, give or receive instructions, make decisions based on information received orally, and generate and receive feedback.

The Ethics of Listening

While all of us continually engage in activities that require us to listen, some of us fail to pay enough attention to the role listening plays in these activities. The tragic shootings at educational institutions such as Columbine High School in Littleton, Colorado, and at Santana High School in Santee, California, however, should put us on notice that we need to listen to each other. Listening, as well as the failure to listen, has an impact on our relationships.

Effective listeners focus their attention. What difficulties do you have when attempting to focus?

Go to the *Online Learning Center* at www.mhhe.com/gamble8 and answer the questions in the *Self Inventory* to evaluate your understanding of critical thinking.

How Responsive a Listener Are You?

Although we expect others to listen to us, we sometimes fail in our ethical responsibility to listen to them. We may fake listening or not listen as carefully as we could. Consequently, problems due to ineffective listening occur.

At one time, a poll of American teenagers indicated that as many as half of them believed that communication between themselves and their parents was poor—and that a primary cause was poor listening. Parents, too, often feel that communication is failing. One woman was convinced that her daughter must have a severe hearing problem and took her to an audiologist. The audiologist tested both ears and reported back to the distraught parent: "There's nothing wrong with her hearing. She's just tuning you out."

A leading cause of the high divorce rate (approximately half of all marriages in the United States end in divorce) is the failure of husbands and wives to interact effectively. They don't listen to each other or respond to each other's messages.

Similarly, political scientists report that a growing number of people believe that their elected and appointed officials are out of touch with the constituents they are supposedly representing. Why? They don't believe these officials listen to them. In fact, it seems that sometimes our politicians don't

"I'm sorry, dear, I must have lost consciousness. What were you saying?"

even listen to themselves. Consider this true story: At a national legislative conference held in Albuquerque some years ago, a senator—Joseph Montoya—was handed a copy of a press release by a press aide shortly before he got up to deliver a speech. When he rose to speak, to the horror of his aide and the amusement of his audience, Montoya began reading the press release rather than his speech. He began, "For immediate release. Senator Joseph M. Montoya, Democrat of New Mexico, last night told the National Legislative Conference at Albuquerque . . . ." Montoya read the entire six-page release, concluding with "Montoya was repeatedly interrupted by applause."

Presidents of major companies also identify listening as one of their major communication problems.[4] One nationwide survey revealed that 14 percent of each work week is wasted due to poor listening. That amounts to about seven weeks of work per year.[5] A survey of personnel managers also identified listening as the skill most needed at work if work teams are to succeed.[6]

It is almost impossible to state a dollar value for the cost of poor listening. But since there are more than 100 million workers in the United States, just one $10 mistake by each of them in a single year would cost over $1 billion.

Are You Prepared to Listen?

Think back over the years you have spent as a student. Did you receive training in writing? Reading? Speaking? The answer to each of these questions is probably yes. In fact, many children now learn to read and write before they start school, and reading and writing skills are taught and emphasized throughout our educational careers. In addition, courses in writing and speed reading are popular in adult-oriented programs. We often take public speaking courses, and oral presentations are required in many of our classes. But what about listening? How much training have you actually received in listening? It is true that an International Listening Association now exists, and listening is taught in some schools and colleges. Still, of the four communication skills—reading, writing, speaking, and listening—listening has received the least attention from educators, yet listening is the fundamental process through which we initiate and maintain relationships, and it is the primary process through which we take in information. We need to learn to treat listening as if our very existence depends on it, because in many ways it does.[7]

How Well Do You Use Your Listening Time?

Studies show that, on average, we spend between 42 and 53 percent of our communicative time listening, 16 to 32 percent speaking, 15 to 17 percent reading, and only 9 to 14 percent writing.[8] Thus, we spend more time listening than engaging in other forms of communication. This holds true on the job as well. In fact, employees of Fortune 500 companies spend the majority of their day—approximately 60 percent of it—listening.[9] Despite these figures, we are not born knowing how to listen, or how to listen well. How efficient are your listening skills? Estimate the percentage of information you retain when you listen. This figure represents how good a listener you think you are. How good a listener are you really?

Take a moment to review your personal listening situation. Think of interactions you have had that were complicated because you or someone else failed to listen effectively. For example, when was the last time you jumped to a wrong conclusion? Missed an important word? Failed to realize you were not being understood? Reacted emotionally or let yourself become distracted? Far too often, instead of listening, we daydream our way through our daily contacts—we take side trips or otherwise tune out what is said to us. In other words, we adopt destructive "unlistening" behaviors.

Most people estimate that they listen with 70 to 80 percent accuracy. This means they believe that they can listen to others and accurately retain 70 to 80 percent of what is said. However, researchers like Ralph Nichols tell us that most of us actually listen at only 25 percent efficiency—that is, instead of retaining 75 percent of what we hear, we lose 75 percent.[10]

How Much of a Role Do You Play in Ensuring the Integrity of a Message?

Although most of us have supposedly had many years of practice in listening, errors are extremely common. According to communication theorist William

---

Ethics & COMMUNICATION

Asking Directions

Is it possible that men do not like to put themselves into a listening mode? Can it be that the male need for independence and control actually makes it harder for men to listen? What are the chances that women, used to seeking help from others, are better than men at listening to advice?

According to Deborah Tannen, author of *You Just Don't Understand: Women and Men in Conversation,* men desire dominance so strongly that they would prefer to drive right past a police officer than to stop and ask for directions. For men, listening to directions implies inferiority. But, according to Tannen, American women are so used to asking for help that they tend to ask strangers for directions even when they are well aware of where they are going.

What do you think? Do men and women listen differently? Should they? Explain.

"Are you telling me you won't even ask the computerized navigational system for directions?"

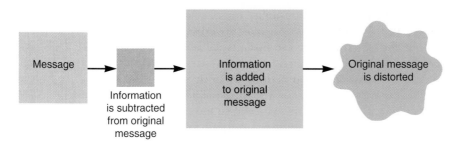

FIGURE 7.2
Serial Communication.

Source: William Haney.
Communication and Organizational Behavior. Homewood, IL: Irwin, 1973.

Haney, we frequently run into problems when we use **serial communication,** or chain-of-command transmissions, to relay messages (see Figure 7.2). In serial communication, person 1 sends a message to person 2; person 2 then communicates his or her perception of person 1's message (not person 1's message itself) to person 3, who continues the process.

serial communication
a chain-of-command transmission

Whenever one person speaks or delivers a message to a second person, the message occurs in at least four different forms:[11]

1. Message as it exists in the mind of the speaker (his or her thoughts)
2. Message as it is spoken (actually encoded by the speaker)
3. Message as it is interpreted (decoded by the listener)
4. Message as it is ultimately remembered by the listener (affected by the listener's personal selectivity and rejection)

According to sociologist Deborah Tannen, "Boys learn to hold center stage by talking; girls learn to listen." Do you agree or disagree? Why?

In traveling down this unwieldy chain of command from person to person, ideas can become distorted by as much as 80 percent. Several factors are responsible. First, because passing along complex, confusing information poses many problems, we generally like to simplify messages. As a result, we unconsciously (and consciously) delete information from the messages we receive before transmitting these messages to others. Second, we like to think the messages we pass along to others make sense. (We feel foolish if we convey a message we ourselves do not understand or deliver a message that appears illogical.) Thus, we try to make sense of a message before communicating it to someone else. We do this by adding to, subtracting from, or otherwise altering what we have heard. Unfortunately, as we see in Figure 7.2, once we make sense of the message, it may no longer correspond to the message originally sent. Such errors occur even though we have had years of practice in listening. Estimates are that a 20-year-old person has practiced listening for at least 10,000 hours; a 30-year-old, at least 15,000 hours; and a typical 40-year-old, 20,000 or more hours.[12] These figures are mind-boggling, but have we in reality been practicing listening or unlistening? Research suggests that we have been practicing unlistening.

By listening accurately and ethically, you help avoid communication difficulties and breakdowns and increase your chances of being well liked and appreciated by others.[13]

Listening requires we make an active, conscious effort to comprehend and remember what we hear.

Who has the primary responsibility for clear and effective communication—the speaker or the listener? An old proverb says, "Nature gave us two ears and one mouth so that we can listen twice as much as we speak." The effective communicator is not afraid to be two parts listener and one part speaker. Actually, since everyone functions as both sender and receiver, everyone must assume 51 percent of the responsibility for communication. This practice might not be mathematically sound, but it would certainly increase the effectiveness of our interpersonal, small-group, public, and mediated communication.[14]

Are You Ready to Collaborate with the Speaker?

Comedian George Burns once said, "I can't help hearing, but I don't always listen. "Describe an occasion when this statement might have been applied to your own behavior. What happened as a result?

There is a relationship between a speaker's acts and a listener's responses. Typically, speaker gaze coordinates this relationship. While listeners usually look more at the speaker more than the reverse, at key points a speaker will look directly at the listener, signaling that the speaker is seeking a response. If the listener is attentive, this creates a period of mutual gaze known as "the gaze window." When this occurs, listeners respond with a nod, a "mhm," or another verbal or nonverbal reaction that lets the speaker know they are listening and collaborating in the dialogue or conversation.[15]

Ethics & COMMUNICATION

Do We Need Listening and Noise Policies?

How do you answer the following questions?

Do you find yourself becoming more selective about what you are willing to listen to? For example, do you use caller I.D. to screen out callers with whom you do not want to speak?

Are you concerned that others might overhear a private conversation? Would you like to be able to make your voice unintelligible to eavesdroppers? Would you use a voice disguiser to realize this objective?

Do you think there should be cell-free zones, just as we have no-smoking zones?[16] Should cell phone users in public places be required to wear headgear, as cyclists and bikers are, only in this case the headgear would be a see-through hood with air holes so that their talk would be muffled?

Is your workplace too noisy? Due to the increasing number of cell phones, speaker phones, and fax machines, both the number of conversations and the noise level of offices have gone up. Often, it is a challenge for employees not to overhear very personal conversations. Recognizing that the modern workplace has gotten very loud, and in an effort to preserve "acoustical privacy," some employers are trying to subdue the noise by installing white noise machines, which produce low-level whooshing sounds akin to the hum of an air conditioner in order to help mute the noise.[17]

What do you think of using white noise to create a semblance of quiet? Some who oppose it do so because they fear that such sound masking may make it possible for the corporation to send workers subliminal messages. Others counter that low-tech solutions, such as creating small rooms that workers can frequent when they need to escape the noise and have a private conversation, are more appropriate. Others advise not pinning too many photographs or notices on cubicle walls, because doing so raises the decibel level by multiplying the number of surfaces that sound can bounce off of. Others simply snap their fingers or throw a crumpled piece of paper at the offending noisemaker.

After considering each of these problems, identify the policies that you think should be put into place.

Listening versus Hearing

Listening and hearing are not the same thing. Most people are born with the ability to hear. **Hearing** is a process that occurs automatically and requires no conscious effort on your part. If the physiological elements within your ears are functioning properly, your brain will process the electrochemical impulses received, and you will hear. However, what you do with the impulses after receiving them belongs to the realm of listening.

What is listening? **Listening** is a deliberate process through which we seek to understand and retain aural (heard) stimuli. Unlike hearing, listening depends on a complex set of skills that must be acquired. Thus, whereas hearing simply happens to us and cannot be manipulated, listening requires us to make an active, conscious effort to comprehend and remember what we hear. Furthermore, who we are affects what we listen to. In your environment, from minute to minute, far too many sounds bombard you for you to be able to pay attention to each one. Thus, in listening, you process the external sounds of your environment to select those that are relevant to you, your activities, and your interests. This is not to say that listening is just an external process. It is also an internal process. We listen to the sounds we hear, and we listen to what others say, but we also listen to what we say aloud and what we say to ourselves in response. (Do you ever talk to yourself? Are you your own best listener? Most of us are.)

hearing

the involuntary, physiological process by which we process sound

listening

the deliberate psychological process by which we receive, understand, and retain aural stimuli

Self-talk—listening to what you say to yourself—can help you make sense of the way you listen to and react to the people in your life.

Listening Levels

To help you begin to develop more effective listening skills, we have identified four levels of receiving. An understanding of these levels should help you assess your own effectiveness as a listener. Let's begin by examining the **listening level–energy involvement scale,** in Figure 7.3.

As the scale indicates, hearing requires little, if any, energy expenditure or involvement on your part. In contrast, listening to understand requires a greater expenditure of energy. In listening, you need to ensure that you comprehend what is being said. Remembering or retaining a message requires even more effort on your part, and working to analyze and evaluate what is said is

listening level–energy involvement scale

a scale identifying four levels of receiving

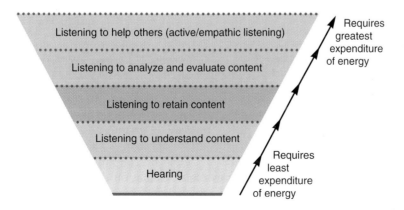

FIGURE 7.3
Listening Level–Energy Involvement Scale.

empathic listening
listening to help others

still more difficult and thus consumes more energy. Listening to help others, **empathic listening,** requires an even greater degree of involvement and even more energy.

A common problem of many poor listeners is the inability to determine the listening or involvement level appropriate to a situation. For example, in a course with large lecture sections, it is not uncommon to find some students tuning out—simply hearing when they should be listening to understand, retain, analyze, and evaluate content. All too frequently, these students will later assert adamantly that certain points were "never covered" in class ("I was sitting right there, and I never heard you say that!").

The following is an example of what can happen when people fail to listen effectively at the appropriate level:

> Kevin Daly, founder of Communispond, a company that helps train executives to communicate their ideas more effectively, reports that the president of a steel company in Pittsburgh had aides prepare a news release for him to read at a press conference. The release, as written by his speech writers, was eleven pages. The president did not have time to review the manuscript before arriving at the conference and taking his place on the podium. Nonetheless, he began to read the announcement confidently. As he continued reading the lengthy statement, he realized that page eight had been printed twice. Indeed, he was now reading page eight aloud for the second time. Somewhat flustered, he gazed out at the audience, only to observe that there was "no quiver of recognition" among his listeners. He finished reading the release certain that no one had picked up his error. He was right. The mistake was never reported.[18]

Why didn't the audience members—all of them educated people—listen more critically to what they were being told? How could they fail to perceive so blatant an error? How could they evaluate what was being said if they were not even aware of the content? Are you a more effective listener than the people in this story? (Are you sure?)

Listening versus Unlistening: Exploring the Unethical Behaviors of Ineffective Listeners

Of course, we do not—probably, we cannot—listen at full capacity all the time. But we should be aware of our ineffective listening behaviors if they prevent us from understanding what could be important to us or to someone else. While many factors might contribute to ineffective listening, and the following kinds of ineffective listeners are certainly not the only ineffective listeners we can identify, we have probably interacted with most of those identified here at some point in the past.

Fraudulent Listeners

How many of the ineffective listener categories are you familiar with? Would you ever place yourself in any of the groups?

Fraudulent listeners are pseudolisteners; they are also nodders. Persons who practice fraudulent listening and engage in nodding pretend that they are listening. They look at the speaker, nod their heads appropriately in agreement or disagreement, and utter remarks such as "mm" or "uh-huh" that imply they are paying attention. In actuality, the words are falling on deaf ears.

Fraudulent listeners adopt the outward appearances of listeners, but they are counterfeiters—pretenders who let no meaning through. Perhaps they fail to listen because they are thinking their own private thoughts, are bored with the conversation, or are otherwise occupied. Whatever their motivation, the outcome is similar—no listening occurs.

Monopolistic Listeners

Monopolistic listeners want you to listen to them, but they have neither the time nor the desire to listen to you. Frequently egocentric, and as a result, intrigued and obsessed with their own thoughts and ideas, monopolizers deny your right to be listened to while defending their right to express themselves, no matter what the cost.[19]

According to researcher Alfie Kohn, men are more likely than women to be monopolistic listeners, or ear hogs. Kohn finds that men interrupt women's statements more frequently than women interrupt men's statements; in fact, in his research 96 percent of the interruptions in male-female interactions were initiated by men.[20]

Completers

Completers are gap fillers; they never quite get the whole story when they listen. To make up for what they've missed or misinterpreted, they manufacture information to fill in the gaps. While the impression is that they got it all, nothing could be further from the truth.

Selective Listeners

Selective listeners are like bees going after the honey in a flower; they zero in on only those portions of a speaker's remarks that interest them or have particular importance to them. Everything else the speaker says is considered irrelevant or inconsequential and thus is rejected. Selective listeners, in their search for just the honey, often miss the flower.

Avoiders

Avoiders figuratively wear earmuffs; they close their ears to information they would rather not deal with. Sometimes they pretend not to understand what you tell them or act as if they did not hear you at all. Sometimes they simply forget, in short order, what you have told them.

Defensive Listeners

Defensive listeners tend to perceive the remarks of other persons as personal affronts or attacks. Usually insecure, they are apt to pounce when another person asks a simple question, or they are likely to perceive a threat in the comments of another, when none actually exists. When we listen defensively, we assume others are going to criticize or belittle us; we assume that they don't like, trust, or respect us. As a result, an innocent question such as "Did you file your expense account?" may be interpreted as criticism for having spent too much on a business trip.

We wear ear muffs when we close our ears to information we would rather not listen to.

Media WISE

Talk, Talk, Talk

Talk radio, a mediated form of interpersonal communication that is growing in influence, allows users a higher level of psychological comfort than does face-to-face interaction, because it allows them to remain relatively anonymous while interacting with another person. Often populated by loud talking, sometimes ranting and argumentative hosts such as Guardian Angels founder Curtis Slewa and conservative pundits Rush Limbaugh and Bill O'Reilly, talk radio programs often revert into yelling matches between the host and a guest who openly disagrees with an espoused position the host has taken or love fests between host and guest who support each other's views. Critics believe that talk radio hosts who attack those who do not agree with them incite antiliberal sentiments in listeners, so much so that nonconservative politicians are now attempting to fund their own liberal talk radio program, so that their voices may also be heard.

Listen to a talk radio program. What views did the host espouse? How many on-air callers shared and how many opposed the expressed opinions of the host? Determine whether the host gave the caller's comments an honest hearing or prejudged what the caller was saying. Count the number of times a host became loud and belittled or otherwise insulted a guest who did not agree with his or her views. How did the guest respond? Identify both the ineffective and effective listening behaviors of the host. How do you account for the talk show's popularity?

In The Argument Culture: Moving from Debate to Dialogue, *linguist Deborah Tannen discusses how the mindsets of people living in the United States predisposes them to attack rather than listen effectively to others.*[21] *Do you find this is true when it comes to relationships you share in your social and career life?*

Attackers

Attackers wait for you to make a mistake, so that they can undercut and challenge what you have to say. They lie in wait, hoping to gather ammunition they can use to diminish your effectiveness. They also are not above distorting your words to advance their personal goals. Attacking listeners are apt to precipitate defensiveness in the person they are listening to. Rather than working to understand your meaning and conducting a discussion with you that is open and fair, they compete with you in an effort to outdo you.

Feedback: A Prerequisite for Effective Listening

The feedback process is intimately connected with the listening process. Developing an understanding and appreciation of the way feedback works is essential to improving your listening skills.

What Is Feedback?

The term feedback implies that we are feeding someone by giving something back to him or her. Feedback consists of all the verbal and nonverbal messages that a person consciously or unconsciously sends out in response to another person's communication. As students, you continually provide your instructors with feedback. Many of you, however, are probably not completely honest when you send feedback. At times when you are confused or bored, you may nevertheless put on an "I'm interested" face and nod smilingly, indicating that you understand and agree with everything your instructor is saying. Unfortunately, such behavior tends to encourage the sending of unclear messages.

Imagine someone who writes 50 love letters but receives no answer. Has this person received feedback?

Whatever the circumstances, we must recognize that the nature of the feedback we give people will affect the communicative interactions we share with them.

Types of Feedback

We constantly provide others with feedback, whether we intend to or not. Everything we do or fail to do in a relationship or interaction with others can be considered feedback. Sometimes we send feedback consciously, intending to evoke a particular response. For example, if you laugh or chuckle at a speaker's joke or story, you may be doing so because you want the speaker to feel that you enjoyed the story and hope he or she will tell more jokes. In contrast, some of the feedback we transmit is sent unconsciously and evokes unintended or unexpected responses. Often, when our words or behaviors prompt a reaction that we never intended, we respond with useless phrases such as "That's not what I meant!" or "I didn't mean it that way!" or "What I meant was . . . ."

What we intend to convey by feedback, then, may not be what others perceive. Sometimes others intentionally choose not to perceive our messages. At other times, confusion results because feedback that we mean to be nonevaluative in tone is interpreted as evaluative. Distinguishing between these two categories of feedback will help us use both types effectively and appropriately.

Evaluative Feedback   When we provide another person with **evaluative feedback**—that is, an evaluative response—we state our opinion about a matter being discussed. For example, "How did you like my speech?" will almost always evoke a response that will be perceived as evaluative. A slight hesitation before the words "I loved it" might be perceived as connoting a negative response. When we give evaluative feedback, we make judgments—either positive or negative—based on our own system of values. As we go about the business of daily life, judgments about the relative worth of ideas, the importance of projects, and the classification of abilities are a necessity. By its very nature, the effect of evaluative feedback is either positive and rewarding or negative and punishing.

evaluative feedback
a positive or negative judgment

Positive Evaluative Feedback   Positive evaluative feedback tends to keep communication and its resulting behaviors moving in the direction they are already heading. If a company places an advertisement and achieves a tremendous growth in sales, the company will tend to place the same or a very similar ad in the same or very similar media in the future. If a person wearing a new hairstyle is complimented, he or she will tend to keep that hairstyle. If you are speaking to an instructor who appears receptive to your ideas and suggestions, you will tend to continue offering ideas and suggestions in the future. Thus, positive evaluative feedback makes us continue behaving as we are already behaving and enhances or reinforces existing conditions or actions.

Negative Evaluative Feedback   Negative evaluative feedback serves a corrective function in that it helps extinguish undesirable communicative behaviors. When we perceive feedback as negative, we tend to change our performance accordingly. For example, if you were to tell a number of off-color stories that your listeners found in bad taste, they might send you negative responses. They might turn away, attempt to change the subject, or simply maintain a cold, lengthy silence. Each cue would indicate that your message had overstepped the bounds of propriety; as a result, you would probably discontinue your anecdotes.

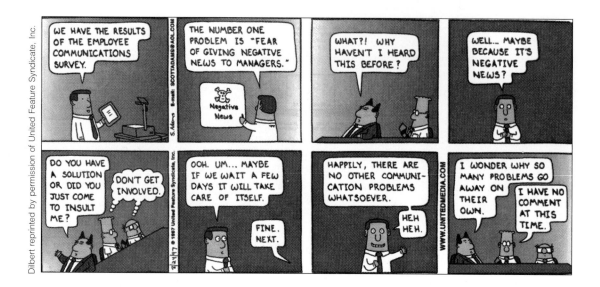

Dilbert reprinted by permission of United Feature Syndicate, Inc.

formative feedback

timed negative feedback

Formative Feedback **Formative feedback** is timed negative feedback. Don Tosti, an industrial psychologist, used timed negative feedback with some interesting results.[22] Tosti discovered that, in a learning situation, it is best to provide positive feedback immediately after someone has displayed a desired behavior. Thus, comments such as "You did a good job" and "Keep up the good work" should be offered immediately, because these responses give people a sense of pride and pleasure in themselves and their work. However, Tosti suggests that what he calls "formative negative" feedback should be given only just before an undesired behavior (or a similar behavior) is about to be repeated. Tosti believes that withholding negative feedback until the person can use it constructively makes the feedback seem more like coaching than criticism. Comments such as "OK, team, let's eliminate the errors we made last time" and "When you go out there today, try to . . ." reduce the extent to which negative feedback is perceived as harmful rather than helpful. Thus, giving formative feedback just before an activity is to be performed again can help eliminate the feelings of rejection that sometimes accompany negative feedback. (In contrast, it should be remembered that immediate positive feedback can do wonders for people's self-image and morale.)

Tosti's findings have many implications for communication. For example, if you handed in a paper to your instructor, following Tosti's guidelines, the instructor would hand you a list containing only positive observations. Not until the instructor had made the next assignment would you be offered formative or negative feedback in the form of a list containing errors to avoid. Formative feedback can also be used as a memory refresher or as a motivational tool to improve performance. With formative feedback, it is the timing that counts.

Unlike traditional negative feedback, formative feedback does not tend to discourage an individual from attempting to perform an activity again. Nor does it tend to demoralize the person. Test the theory behind formative feedback by using it in your own communication. Whenever you send evaluative feedback messages, whether positive or negative, preface your statements so

Feedback in Japan

Are you culturally sensitive when giving feedback? For example, many Japanese—unlike Americans—use an indirect style of communication. Thus, when interacting with someone from Japan, if you give feedback directly (for example, telling someone outright, "You are not working hard enough"), the feedback, instead of being viewed as helpful, might be viewed as a threat. And if it is perceived as a threat, it could well be ineffective. An American giving feedback to another American, however, can give feedback more directly.

Do you believe we ought to change the way we provide feedback to conform to the preferences of another culture? Explain.

as to make it clear that what you are offering is your opinion only. Such phrases as "It seems to me," "In my opinion," and "I think" are usually helpful, because they show your awareness that other interpretations and options are possible. Avoid using phrases like "You must" or "That's stupid." Such comments almost always elicit a certain amount of defensiveness. Expressing either positive or negative feedback in less than adamant terms tends to create a more favorable and receptive climate for the relationship.

Nonevaluative Feedback   In contrast to evaluative feedback, **nonevaluative feedback,** or nondirective feedback, makes no overt attempt to direct the actions of a communicator. Thus, we use nonevaluative feedback when we want to learn more about a person's feelings or when we want to help another person formulate thoughts about a particular subject. When we offer nonevaluative feedback, we make no reference to our own opinions or judgments. Instead, we simply describe, question, or indicate an interest in what the other person is communicating to us.

Despite its nonjudgmental nature, nonevaluative feedback is often construed as being positive. That is, other people's behaviors may be reinforced when we probe, interpret their messages, and offer support as they attempt to work through a problem. Nonevaluative feedback actually reaches beyond positive feedback, however, by providing others with an opportunity to examine their own problems and arrive at their own solutions. For this reason, carefully phrased nonevaluative feedback can be enormously helpful and sustaining to people who are going through a difficult period.

We will consider four kinds of nonevaluative feedback. Three—probing, understanding, and supporting—were identified by David Johnson. The fourth—"I" messages—was identified by Thomas Gordon.[23]

Probing   **Probing** is a nonevaluative technique in which we ask people for additional information to draw them out and to demonstrate our willingness to listen to their problems.[24] Suppose that a student is concerned about his or her grades in a particular course and says to you, "I'm really upset. All of my friends are doing better in geology than I am." If you use probing, you might ask, "Why does this situation bother you?" or "What is there about not getting good grades that concerns you?" or "What do you suppose caused this to happen?" Responding in this way gives the other person the chance to think through the overall nature of the problem while providing him or her with an opportunity for emotional release. In contrast, comments like "So

nonevaluative feedback
nondirective feedback

probing
a nonevaluative technique in which we ask for additional information

what? Who cares about that dumb class?" or "Grades don't matter. What are you worrying about?" or "You really were dumb when you stopped studying" would tend to stop the student from thinking through and discussing the problem and, instead, would probably create defensiveness.

Understanding   A second kind of nonevaluative response is what Johnson calls **understanding.** When we offer understanding, we seek to comprehend what the other person is saying to us, and we check ourselves by restating what we believe we have heard. Doing this shows that we care about other people and the problems they face.

Examine the following paraphrases to develop a feel for the nature of this kind of response:

> *Person 1:* I don't think I have the skill to be picked for the team.
>
> *Person 2:* You believe you're not good enough to make the team this year?
>
> *Person 1:* I envy those guys so much.
>
> *Person 2:* You mean you're jealous of the people in that group?

If we use understanding early in a relationship, in effect, we communicate that we care enough about the interaction to want to be certain we comprehend what the other person is saying to us. Such a response strengthens the relationship because it encourages the other person to describe and detail his or her feelings. By delivering understanding both verbally and nonverbally, we also provide support by showing that we are sensitive to the other person's feelings and are really willing to listen.

Supportive Feedback   A third kind of nonevaluative feedback is what Johnson calls **supportive feedback.** This response indicates that a problem the other person deems important and significant is also viewed by the listener as important and significant.

Suppose a friend comes to you with a problem she feels is extremely serious. Perhaps your friend has worked herself into a state of extreme agitation and implies that you cannot possibly understand the situation. In offering supportive feedback, you would attempt to calm your friend down by assuring her that the world has not ended and that you do understand the problem.

Offering supportive feedback is difficult. We have to be able to reduce the intensity of other people's feelings while letting them know that we consider their problems real and serious. Such comments as "It's stupid to worry about that" and "Is that all that's worrying you?" are certainly not supportive. A better approach might be to say, "I can see you are upset. Let's talk about it. I'm sure you can find a way to solve the problem." A friend who is upset because he or she has just failed an exam needs supportive feedback: "I can see you are worried. I don't blame you for being upset." This is certainly not the time to suggest that there is no valid reason for being upset or that your friend's feelings are inappropriate. It would be foolish to say, "Next time you'll know better. I told you that not studying wouldn't get you anywhere." When we use supportive feedback, we judge the problems to be important, but we do not attempt to solve them ourselves; instead, we encourage people to discover their own solutions.

---

understanding

a nonevaluative response that uses restatement to check comprehension

supportive feedback

a nonevaluative response indicating that the receiver perceives a problem as important

According to Doris Iarovici, a medical student at Yale, "One of the best things you can do for any patient is to listen and show that you care."[25] This, in a nutshell, is supportive feedback.

"I" Messages Certain nonevaluative feedback messages are called **"I" messages,** a term coined by Thomas Gordon. When we deliver an "I" message, we do not pass judgment on the other person's actions but simply convey our own feelings about the nature of the situation.

According to Gordon, when people interact with us, they are often unaware of how their actions affect us. We have the option of providing these people with either evaluative or nonevaluative feedback. Neither type is inherently good nor bad. However, far too often, the way we formulate our evaluative feedback adversely affects the nature of our interactions and the growth of our relationships. For example, do any of these statements sound familiar? "You made me angry!" "You're no good!" "You're in my way!" "You're a slob!" What do these statements have in common? As you have probably noticed, each one contains the word *you*. Each also places the blame for something on another person. When relationships experience difficulties, people tend to resort more and more to name-calling and to blaming others. Such feedback messages create schisms that are difficult and sometimes even impossible to bridge.

To avoid this situation, Gordon suggests that we replace **"you" messages** with "I" messages. If, for example, a parent tells a child, "You're pestering me," the child's interpretation will probably be "I am bad," and this interpretation will evoke a certain amount of defensiveness or hostility toward the parent ("I am not bad!"). But if the parent tells the child, "I'm really very tired and I don't feel like playing right now," the child's reaction is more likely to be "Mom is tired." Such an approach is more likely to elicit the type of behavior the parent desires than would name-calling and blaming ("You are a pest"). Which of the following messages do you believe would be more likely to elicit a favorable response?

> *Supervisor to Workers:* You lazy bums! We'll never meet the deadline if you don't work faster!
>
> *Supervisor to Workers:* I'm afraid that, if we don't work faster, we'll miss the deadline, and the company will lose a lot of money.

Obviously, the second statement would not produce the defensiveness that would be engendered by the first.

"I" messages have one other aspect you should be aware of. It is quite common to say "I am angry" to another person. Anger, however, is a secondary emotion. We are angry because of a stimulus or stimuli. In actuality, we develop anger. For example, if your child or a child you are watching ran into the street, your first response would probably be fear. Only after the child was safe would you develop anger, and then you would probably share your anger—rather than your fear—with the child. When formulating an angry "I" message, be certain to look beyond or beneath your anger and ask yourself why you are angry. Try to identify the forces that precipitated your anger— these are the feelings that should be expressed. Thus, if someone says something that hurts you, find ways to express the initial hurt rather than the resulting anger.

"I" messages

nonevaluative responses that convey our feelings about the nature of a situation

"you" messages

responses that place blame on another person

Using "I" messages as feedback will not always evoke the behavior you want from the other person, but it will help prevent the defensive, self-serving behaviors that "you" messages frequently elicit. At this point, ask yourself which of the types of feedback seem best. Which do you feel are most important? As you probably realize, the categories and types of feedback we have discussed are not necessarily good or bad. Each type can be put to good use. Thus, whether you choose to offer evaluative or nonevaluative responses depends on the person with whom you are interacting and on the nature of the situation in which you find yourself.

Effects of Feedback

How do you think feedback affects communication? Suppose that someone is telling you a funny story. What would happen if you should consciously decide to treat this person politely but neither smile nor laugh at the story? Such a reaction—polite but somber—can cause the best of storytellers to stop communicating. Sometimes in the middle of a story, the teller will notice that the listener is not amused. At this point, in an attempt to determine if the

---

Skill
BUILDER

Now You Have It; Now You Don't

Choose a partner. You and your partner should each draw on a card or slip of paper three designs consisting of a random series of straight, interconnecting lines (like the sample below). Do not show the diagrams to each other. The purpose of the exercise is to give verbal instructions that will enable your partner to reproduce your diagrams.

Deliver your instructions under three conditions:

1. *Zero feedback.* When you explain your first design, turn your back to your partner and neither watch nor comment on his or her efforts. Your partner is not allowed to speak to you or look at you during this phase. This situation approximates a zero feedback (no feedback) condition.

2. *Limited feedback.* When you describe the second design, you may turn and watch your partner work. You may comment on what he or she is drawing, but your partner may not speak to you or look at you. This approximates a limited feedback condition.

3. *Free feedback.* Finally, when you describe your third design to your partner, you may interact openly with each other. You may observe and comment on your partner's efforts, and your partner may interact with you by facing you and asking you questions to check on the accuracy of his or her drawing. This approximates a free feedback condition.

Next, if time permits, you and your partner should reverse roles and repeat the three steps.

Which condition produced the fastest replication? Why? Which condition produced the most accurate replication? Why? During which phase of the experience were you most confident? Least confident? Why? How did functioning as sender or receiver alter your feelings during each phase of the experience?

 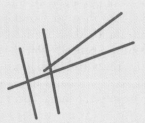 

receiver has heard what was said, the sender will repeat or rephrase key parts of the story: "Don't you understand? What happened was . . ." or "You see, what this means is . . . ." The feedback given by the respondent in any encounter strongly influences the direction and outcome of the interaction.[26] You might want to try the "no laugh" procedure the next time someone begins to relate a humorous incident or tale to you. If you do, note how not laughing affects the sender's ability to formulate a message.

The Skill Builder on page 210, adapted from an experiment designed by Harold Leavitt and Ronald Mueller, demonstrates how feedback affects the development of our relationships.[27] Feedback usually increases the accuracy with which information is passed from person to person. However, it also increases the amount of time required to transmit information. Under the "zero feedback" condition (phase 1 of the exercise), the speaker requires less time to transmit the information to the receiver than he or she would under either the "limited feedback" condition (phase 2) or the "free feedback" condition (phase 3). Still, most communicators feel that the added time is more than compensated for by the increased accuracy of the replications. In other words, under the free feedback condition, time is not wasted.

THE ROLE OF CRITICAL THINKING: ASSESSING THE CREDIBILITY OF WHAT YOU LISTEN TO

While you listen to information, you interpret and assign meaning to the spoken words. When you go the next step and engage in **critical thinking,** you think carefully about what another person has said to you, and you evaluate the believability of the spoken message. Just as speakers can get carried away with their message's urgency and importance, so listeners can end up believing false or dangerous ideas that have been made to appear reasonable. Consequently, it is essential for you as a listener to stay alert, so that you are ready to challenge and raise questions about what you are listening to. When functioning as a critical thinker, you make a commitment to think for yourself.

critical thinking
the careful and deliberate process of message evaluation

What Critical Thinkers Think About

What do critical thinkers think about? As a critical thinker, you determine if there is a logical connection between ideas and feelings. Rather than falling prey to strong emotional appeals, you examine the evidence on which conclusions are based and establish if they are valid or contain weaknesses and inconsistencies. Critical thinkers listen carefully in an effort to determine if what they are listening to makes sense and is worth retaining or acting upon.[28]

The Critical versus the Uncritical Thinker

The following characteristics differentiate a critical thinker from an uncritical one.

> *The Critical Thinker*
> 1. Knows what he or she does not know
> 2. Is open-minded and takes time to reflect on ideas

3. Pays attention to those who agree and disagree with him or her
4. Looks for good reasons to accept or reject expert opinion
5. Is concerned with unstated assumptions and what is not said, in addition to what is stated outright
6. Insists on getting the best evidence
7. Reflects on how well conclusions fit premises and vice versa

The Uncritical Thinker

1. Thinks he or she knows everything
2. Is closed-minded and impulsive; jumps to unwarranted conclusions
3. Pays attention only to those who agree with him or her
4. Disregards evidence as to who is speaking with legitimate authority
5. Is concerned only with what is stated, not with what is implied
6. Ignores sources of evidence
7. Disregards the connection or lack of connection between evidence and conclusions[29]

Critical thinkers do not rush to judge another's words. Instead of prejudging or evaluating the words of another prematurely, they exhibit a willingness to reexamine ideas. Thus, they withhold their evaluation until they have had sufficient opportunity to assess the information being given to them.

Questions to Facilitate Critical Thinking

You can ask yourself a number of questions to facilitate the critical thinking process:

1. Is the speaker's message plausible? Could it have reasonably occurred, or does it have a high probability of being true?
2. Does the support provided by the person speaking back up his or her claims? Are the claims he or she makes verifiable?
3. What do I know of the speaker's credibility or authority? Is the speaker reliable; that is, is she or he someone I should trust?
4. Is the speaker's message free of inconsistencies or contradictions?

It is apparent that, when you think critically about what other people say to you, you do much more than merely hear their words.

TECHNOLOGY'S INFLUENCE ON LISTENING AND THINKING

Although they have been working on it for about two decades, scientists have yet to devise a computer that functions as a virtual best friend—one that is able to listen sensitively and empathically to a user.[30] Diametrically opposed to the efforts of these scientists are people who believe that our connections to computers, e-mail, and the Internet are impeding our ability to listen. Focusing our attention on the visual rather than the aural, critics contend, causes us to emphasize the eye over the ear. Despite this perceived failure of the scientists (we wonder if not succeeding is really a benefit), and the objections of critics, our technological listening landscape continues to evolve rapidly.

Today, we listen globally—to radio, television, CDs, cellular telephones, videoconferences, beepers, personal message systems, and our computers. Indeed, our appetite for traditional media as well as for the computer and the Internet is eating into time spent listening to other people in face-to-face settings. In fact, even when we are face-to-face with another person, perhaps when at lunch, on a walk, or out for a drive, one of us may be conversing with a third person on a cell phone. Interpersonal etiquette appears to be at an all-time low. The world has become our phone booth. Perhaps we need cell-free zones, so that we can listen more attentively to the person we're with.[31] Perhaps we need cell-free zones for other reasons as well. More and more state legislatures have passed bills restricting car cell-phone use to headphone rather than hand-held models. While multitasking may seem like a necessity, it is hard to drive and speak on a cell phone at the same time. Using a headphone instead of a hand-held phone is probably as much of a distraction.

In addition to being surrounded by cell-phone users, according to David Shenk, author of *Data Smog,* we are being inundated with information: e-mail, net-to-phone, cell phones, pagers operating virtually nonstop, enveloping us within a toxic environment of continuous overstimulation.[32] According to the Institute for the Future, the typical American worker handles 201 messages a day.[33] It is probable that one outcome of this overload is a decrease in listening effectiveness.

Technology makes it possible for us to multitask when listening outside of our cars as well. How many of us check e-mail while talking to friends on the phone? When we multitask when interacting with another, we do not focus exclusively on one communication channel. As a result of doing this, we fail to give the other person our full attention. Do you think we need some rules about when multitasking is and is not socially acceptable? Try your hand at formulating some.

Advances in technology will continue to add listening wrinkles. For example, in the past when we listened, we were generally face-to-face with the speaker; we engaged in real-time, synchronous listening. Then came the telephone, and we had the option of not having to share the same space when we

---

Listening Gains and Losses

New technologies are changing our listening landscape. Online users spend less time listening to the radio, for example, than do nononline users. They also spend less time watching television. Consider this: How much more reading do you do today than in years past? Are you now reading more and listening less than you used to? In your opinion, what are the chances that e-mail use ultimately will wipe out voice contact?

On the other hand, we can now listen to radio over the Internet. With digital radio paired with the Internet, we can now personalize our listening stimuli. In effect, we can direct our own listening experience. In fact, we already have all-request radio, which enables us to hear the music we want and chat about it online with others. In your opinion, is being able to control what you listen to a good thing? Or did having your listening experience determined for you by others make it impossible for you to filter out what you didn't want to listen to and enable you to develop skills that will now deteriorate? Explain your responses.

Media
WISE

exchanged a real-time conversation. Finally, we are in the era of voice mail; we can now have serial conversations (asynchronous listening) with a person who is in a different location and doesn't hear our words as we speak them. More and more of our conversations are occurring asynchronously.[34] Continuing advances add to the listening challenge. We can now be more selective about our willingness to listen at all. Caller ID allows us to see who is calling and thus to decide who we want to listen to, while call waiting makes it possible for us not to miss a call from someone important to us. We can now line up our listeners.

Thus, we have to ask the following question: While we may be listening more to the sounds of new media, are we listening less to each other? How actively can we listen to another human being in our immediate environment when technological advances are absorbing our attention and propelling us across national boundaries and into settings far removed from the ones with which we are most familiar?

The real-time transmission of voice is possible over the Internet. Internet phones enable you to use your computer as a telephone. You can talk with another person anywhere in the world for as long as you want without the cost of a long-distance phone call. It is also possible to chat across the Internet using videoconferencing programs. Such programs make it possible for individuals to both hear and see each other.[35]

In addition, with the exception of films shown in theaters, media or computer-generated messages are usually processed by individuals viewing or listening to them alone or in small groups. Because we now process messages, CDs, and videos from around the world, our ears, habitually crossing national

---

e-SEARCH   **The Online Listener**

Is having someone listen to you online the same as having someone listen to you in person? Even when cybercommunicators are using the same online language, because of the Internet's global reach, that language may not be their native language. As a result, the meanings given to the words used may differ drastically. As in face-to-face interaction, not all online listeners receive the same message. As you interact with persons from different cultures in cyberspace, ask yourself these questions:

1. Do they favor a direct or indirect style?
   While some cultures, including those in the United States, tend to exhibit a direct style in communicating—communicators tell it like it is—many Asian cultures use an indirect style, preferring to emphasize politeness and face-saving strategies rather than truth telling. Which style do you prefer?

2. Do they offer hard evidence or tell stories?
   In the United States, our decision making is influenced by logical reasons and
   credible testimony. In contrast, members of other cultures tend to be influenced by stories other sources tell convincingly. What kind of substantiation do you tend to offer? Receive?

3. What kind of feedback do they offer?
   In the United States, we expect to receive honest feedback that reveals the feelings of those with whom we communicate. In Asian cultures, however, communicators believe it is more important to offer positive reactions than truthful ones. Not every culture perceives feedback the same way. What kind of feedback do you prefer?

4. How do opportunities for anonymity influence online listening behavior?
   Because we may remain anonymous, some of us tend to exhibit less ego involvement when listening online than when interacting face-to-face. How does the change in ego involvement affect you?

boundaries and opening wider and wider, are helping raze cultural, informational, and personal barriers.

While newer technology presents listening challenges, we also should not forget the listening challenges posed by radio and television. So much of what comes to us via radio and television is delivered in very abbreviated segments; consider, for example, the music videos MTV offers, as well as the average length of radio and TV news reports (shorter than 30 seconds). The fear is that such brevity keeps us from practicing the skills of concentration and focused attention, skills which must be honed for effective listening.

INCREASING YOUR EAR POWER: A PROGRAM FOR EFFECTIVE LISTENING

The first step in developing effective listening habits is to become aware of the importance and effects of listening. The second step is to become aware of the importance and effects of feedback. The third step is to realize that effective listening includes both nonjudgmental and critical responses. As a result, when necessary, you can make critical listening your partner, using it to help you determine the speaker's motivation and analyze and assess what you have listened to. At this point, you should have accomplished these three objectives.

The next step is to sharpen your listening skills by participating in a series of exercises and experiences. If you really want to improve your listening, these exercises should not merely be done once and put aside. Your listening skills will improve only if you return to them—and to similar experiences—repeatedly.

Focusing Your Attention

Let's begin our effective listening program by considering the need to be able to focus our attention. It is apparent that, if we are to listen effectively, we must be able to be mindful; we must be able to pay attention to what is being communicated in the present moment. While we make the effort to focus our attention and concentrate on what another person is saying, numerous internal and external stimuli bombard us and compete for our attention.

The difficulties we experience when attempting to focus attention are confirmed by how often, and in how many situations, we are admonished to "Pay attention!" When was the last time someone said something like, "He told us that in class. Weren't you paying attention?" All too frequently, the response is "Well, I thought I was." We will explore several ways you can work to improve your ability to attend consciously to information. Developing this ability will be a lifelong project.[36]

If you are to learn to focus your attention and improve your listening skills, one of your main tasks is to handle your emotions. Feelings of hate, anger, happiness, sadness, and anxiousness or apprehension can decrease your listening efficiency. As you become emotionally involved in a conversation, you are often less able or less willing to focus your attention accurately.[37]

Ralph Nichols, in the book *Are You Listening?* notes that certain words often cause us to react emotionally and thus reduce the extent to which we are able to pay attention. He calls these **red-flag words.** According to Nichols, red-flag words produce an emotional deafness, which sends our listening

red-flag words

words which trigger an emotional reaction and drop listening efficiency to zero efficiency down to zero.[38] Among the words known to function as red flags for some listeners are *AIDS, punk, mother-in-law, spastic,* and *income tax.* When some people hear these words, or other red-flag words, they abandon any effort to understand or perceive. Instead, they take side trips, dwelling on their own feelings and associations. In effect, the emotional eruption they are experiencing causes a listening disruption. It should be noted that, like words and phrases, certain topics can also make us react emotionally and lessen our ability to concentrate. For these reasons, it is important to identify words, phrases, or topics that tend to distract you emotionally. Your distraction words are personal and unique to you and change as you change. An issue that caused emotional deafness for you in the past may not even distract you momentarily in the future. Thus, it is a good practice to keep a record of all your distractors. If possible, list them on cards and reexamine them every three or four months. By keeping and updating your red-flag list, you will be better able to recognize and handle distractions during interpersonal encounters.

Physical factors can also be distractors. For example, the room you are in may be too hot or cold for your comfort, the space may be too small or too large, or the seating arrangement may be inadequate. (Have you ever tried to listen politely and efficiently when the springs in your chair were about to poke through the upholstery and pierce you?)

In addition to environmental factors, other people can also be a distraction. People you are relating to may speak too loudly or too softly. A person may have an accent you find difficult to comprehend or an appearance that interests or alarms you. (Have you ever been engaged in conversation with someone wearing such an unusual outfit that you found it difficult to focus your attention on what he or she was saying?)

speech-thought differential

the difference between thinking and speaking rates

One more factor should also be noted: the **speech-thought differential.** To put it simply, we can think faster than we can speak. When communicating, we usually speak at a rate of 125 to 150 words a minute. Researchers have found, however, that we can comprehend much higher rates of speech—perhaps even 500 words a minute. What does this mean for you, the listener? It means that, when someone speaks at a normal rate, you have time left over and may therefore tend to take mental excursions and daydream. Then, when you return your attention to the speaker, you may find that he or she is far ahead of you. We must make conscious efforts to use the speech-thought differential effectively. We can do this by internally summarizing and paraphrasing what is being said as we listen and by asking ourselves questions that help focus our attention instead of distracting us from the subject at hand. (Several speech-compression devices on the market can speed up the recorded rate of ordinary speech without distorting the speaker's voice.)

When you are mindful, you are fully engaged in the moment. You pay attention to the here and now. When you listen mindfully, you focus fully on what a person is saying and feeling. You do not judge the other but demonstrate your interest in understanding his or her ideas. Does that mean if you fail to listen that you are mindless?

Focusing or maintaining your attention is an act you must perform constantly. Smart communicators periodically check to see if their attention has wandered. Make an attention check an integral part of your effective listening program. Although the check itself can become an attention distractor, its benefits outweigh this potential deficit. Only after becoming aware that you are not listening can you begin to make the necessary corrections.[39]

Finally, attentive listeners adopt nonverbal behaviors that support listening. Ineffective listeners typically exhibit passive listening behaviors—they do not face the person they are interacting with; their posture is defensive and tense; they lean away from the other person; they avoid eye contact. Attentive listeners exhibit active listening behaviors—they face the other person directly, adopt an open posture, lean slightly toward the other person, and maintain comfortable eye contact.

We should be aware, however, that culture sometimes interferes with our ability to distinguish between attentive and inattentive listeners. The use of eye contact, for example, differs in traditional African-American and Caucasian cultures. Caucasians typically look away from a conversational partner when speaking and look directly at the partner when listening; African Americans, in contrast, usually look at the other person when speaking and away when listening. Consequently, Caucasians may perceive African Americans who look away while listening to them as not paying attention, when just the opposite is true.

Setting Appropriate Goals

Far too often, we find ourselves listening without really knowing what we are listening for; as a result, we become bored and irritated. One way to combat listening blahs is to set specific goals when listening. Research indicates that listening effectiveness increases when goals are identified.[40] How can you make this evidence work for you?

Before beginning an interaction, establish in your own mind one or more listening goals. After the interaction, analyze the extent to which you were able to attain your goal or goals.

Listening goals identify what you personally would like to gain during and after attending to a particular message. When you establish goals, you answer the question "Why am I listening to this?" Listening goals are closely related to the levels of listening. In general, we listen to understand, to retain, to analyze and evaluate content, and to develop empathic relationships with others. Thus, one way to set your listening goals is to identify which level of listening is most appropriate in a particular situation. For example, if you are an employee who is expected to internalize a series of directions for handling highly explosive materials, you will listen to understand and retain instructions. If you are listening to a series of lectures on types of computer operations and your objective is to select a computer for your company, you will listen to understand and retain but also to analyze and evaluate. In contrast, suppose your friend has lost a parent. In this situation, your goal is to listen empathically.

Just as trains switch tracks, so you should be able to switch listening goals. The goals you set are not meant to imprison you; they are meant to help you be flexible, able to adapt to the demands of each situation or experience.

Listening to Understand Ideas

After listening to information from another person, have you ever made a statement like "I'm sure I understand the main point" or "The central idea is crystal clear"? When we listen to understand, we listen for main ideas or central concepts. Let's examine how this works.

Listening to understand may be compared to a simple tooth extraction. When you visit the dentist to have a tooth pulled, you assume that the dentist will not simply reach into your mouth and pull any tooth at random. Instead, you assume that the dentist will locate the tooth that needs to be extracted, take hold of only that tooth, and remove it. When we listen to understand— a process that underlies all higher levels of listening—we, like the dentist, must locate the central concepts contained in the speaker's message and remove them (in this case, for further examination). Since it is almost impossible to remember every word that is said to us, we should work to recall the concepts that are most important—in other words, the ideas that constitute the main points of the message. Thus, when you listen to understand, you seek to identify key words and phrases that will help you accurately summarize the concepts being discussed. But remember that, unless the ideas you extract from the messages you receive are accurate representations of what was said, you are only hearing, not listening.

Listening to Retain Information

Robert Montgomery, a training expert who has developed a wealth of material on memory for the American Management Associations, says, "The art of retention is the art of attention."[41] If you are to retain what you hear, you must first learn how to focus your attention and then learn how to make certain that you understand what you have heard. Once you can focus your attention on what another person is saying and can understand what the person has said, you are ready to move up to the next level—listening to retain.

Our memory allows us to retain information and recall it when we need to. While our working memory is the part of our brain that assigns meaning to what we have paid attention to, let's start our discussion of memory by acknowledging that some forgetting may be essential for mental health. As the Barbara Streisand song "Memories" goes, "What becomes too painful to remember we simply choose to forget." That said, while we cannot and probably should not remember everything that we hear or have heard, memory and retention are important for sustained learning and personal growth. As such, memory is an integral part of the listening process. It is via memory that we create connections between newly heard information and what we already know.

While the instilling of a false memory is a possibility and has become a contemporary concern, especially when it comes to police investigations, most of our memories are not typically made-up. Memory requires the raw material produced by attention. Whenever we listen, we depend on our memory as a listening partner.

We have two key kinds of memory: short-term memory and long-term memory. Most of what we hear finds a brief resting place in our brain's memory motel, the short-term memory depository. It has limited room. Typically, unless we continually use and apply it, the information that we cram into our short-term memory is purged from its temporary home and forgotten before we can transfer it into our long-term memory bank for future reference. This helps explain why we only remember 50 percent of a message immediately after listening to it and approximately 25 percent after a brief period of time has elapsed. In contrast to short-term memory, long-term memory is like memory's primary residence—it is a more permanent home for the memories we may never lose and which play an important role in listening by providing us with connections to previous experiences, as well as to already known images and information. We tend to remember what is important to us or what is dramatic. For example, you probably remember the phone numbers of people you care about, as well as where you were when you found out about the terrorist attacks of 9/11.

Some of us remember more of what we hear *first;* you may recall that this is called the primacy effect. In contrast, the recency effect is the tendency to recall the last or most recent thing heard. There is no middle effect, because that's the part of a message we tend to recall least.

After receiving directions when traveling, did you ever find yourself saying to yourself, "Do I turn right or left here? What was I told?" After having a discussion with a friend and assuming that you understood the friend's point of view, did you ever find yourself wondering what that point of view was? Even worse, after being introduced to someone, did you ever find yourself asking, "What was that person's name?" We will now explore several techniques that you can use to help you retain what you hear. Such aids are commonly referred to as mnemonic devices. Use the ones that work best for you.

Repetition

Your basic tool for retaining the information you hear is repetition. The more you repeat a concept or an idea, the more likely you are to be able to recall it later. Repetition has two faces: We use repetition when we repeat a statement verbatim (exactly reproduce what was said) and when we restate what was said using other words.

One effective way to remember what others say is to reproduce their words verbatim in writing. The more proficient you are at note taking, the more information you are likely to be able to retain. Of course, in interpersonal situations, it is neither advisable nor practical to take notes. However, it is a good idea to keep a few index cards or a small notepad handy to record important names, numbers, appointments, and information.

Paraphrase

Paraphrasing can also be used to improve your retentiveness. By restating in your own words what a person has said to you, you not only check on your own understanding but also help yourself recall what was said. We will consider the art of paraphrasing in more detail when we discuss empathic listening. For now, it will suffice to realize that paraphrasing can help alleviate some of the problems created by the speech-thought differential. If you use some of your extra thinking time to replicate for yourself what has just been said, your mind will be less likely to wander.

paraphrasing
restating in your own words what another person has said

Visualization

Frequently, we are better able to recall information if we use **visualization**; that is, we picture something about it. For example, many people are able to associate names, places, and numbers with specific visual images. Often, the more outrageous or creative the image, the better it will help them recall a name. For instance, you might picture a person named John Sanderson as standing atop a large sand pile or sand dune, or a person named Susan Grant might be pictured as standing inside Grant's tomb.

visualization
the picturing of experience

Listening to Analyze and Evaluate Content

Being able to analyze and evaluate what you listen to calls for even greater skill than retention. When you learn to analyze and evaluate content effectively, you become adept at spotting fallacies in the arguments and statements you encounter during interpersonal discourse.

Often, we let our prior convictions prevent us from processing and fairly evaluating what we hear. Consider the following conversation:

Alice: Did you hear? Sandy was arrested by the police for selling drugs.

Jim: Sandy? I don't believe it. The police made a mistake. She isn't that type.

In this interchange, Jim is jumping to a conclusion. Instead of analyzing the information he has been given, he is reacting on the basis of his prior knowledge. How should Jim have reacted? Should he have agreed that the police were right to arrest Sandy? Jim should have asked what evidence the police had to support their claim and what evidence Sandy offered in her own defense. Effective listeners do not let their convictions run away with them; instead, they reserve judgment until the facts are in. In other words, they withhold evaluation until their comprehension of the situation is complete.

Attempts at persuasion often take the form of one person trying to make another believe something because "everyone else" believes it. If we accept such an approach, we may find ourselves swept away by emotion and overly influenced by others. For example, we might support a candidate simply because we imagine that everyone else does. Or we might join a pyramid scheme because we are convinced that everyone involved will become rich. Effective listeners realize they have a choice. They may join the majority, or they may choose to maintain their own opinion. Effective listeners do not feel compelled to follow the crowd.

For one week, keep a record of all the circular conversations you hear. Point out the fallacy in each instance.

If you become proficient at evaluating and analyzing the information you listen to, you will discover that people frequently argue or talk in circles—for example,

Elena: Divorce is wrong.

José: Why?

Elena: Because my minister told me it is wrong.

José: Why did he tell you that?

Elena: Because it is wrong!

We have a tendency to talk in circles when we are arguing without evidence, particularly if we feel an emotional tie to the topic under discussion or if we believe that our position is closely connected to our value system. When this occurs, we simply insist we are right: "That's all there is to it." We tell ourselves that we do not need reasons. Effective listeners perceive the fallacy inherent in circular reasoning and weigh a speaker's evidence by mentally questioning it. Effective listeners listen between the lines.

Listening Empathically, Listening Actively

When they are questioning witnesses, attorneys listen for contradictions or irrelevancies; that is, they listen to analyze. In contrast, social workers usually listen to help people work through a personal problem. This, too, is an important level of listening. It is referred to as empathic, or active, listening, and it is the last type of listening we will consider in our effective listening program.

The term *empathic listening* was popularized by psychotherapist Carl Rogers, who believed that listening can be used to help individuals understand their own situations and problems.[42] When you listen actively, or empathically, you do more than passively absorb the words that are spoken to you. Active listeners also try to internalize the other person's feelings and see life through his or her eyes.

The following poem by David Ignatow depicts the nonempathic listener in operation. Are you at all like this?

Focus on Service Learning

How might you use your understanding of listening to enhance the skills of persons who answer phones at local crisis centers?

Two Friends

I have something to tell you.
I'm listening.
I'm dying.
I'm sorry to hear.
I'm getting old.
It's terrible.
It is, I thought you should know.
Of course, and I'm sorry. Keep in touch.

I will. And you too.
And let me know what's new.
Certainly, though it can't be much.
And stay well.
And you too.
And go slow.
And you, too.[43]

How often do you put on an "I'm listening" mask, nod agreement, and utter the appropriate *oh*s and *I see*s, when in reality you are miles away and self-concerned?

We need to be willing to acknowledge the seriousness of other people's problems. We need to take the time required to draw others out, so that they can discuss a problem and come to terms with it. We need to show the other person that we understand the problem. We can do this by paraphrasing the person's statements and by reinforcing those statements with genuine nonverbal cues—eye contact, physical contact (touching), and facial expressions.

Active, empathic listeners put themselves in the speaker's place in an effort to understand the speaker's feelings. Active, empathic listeners appreciate both the meaning and the feeling behind what another person is saying. Thus, in effect, active, empathic listeners convey to the speaker that they are seeing things from the speaker's point of view.[44]

Active, empathic listeners rely heavily on paraphrasing:

Person 1: I am so mad at my mother.

Person 2: If I'm not mistaken, your mother is giving you trouble. Is that right?

Person 1: My boss is really trying to fire me.

Person 2: If I understand you, you believe your boss is out to replace you. Do I have it straight?

To paraphrase effectively, follow a three-step process:

1. Make a tentative statement that invites correction—for example, "If I'm not mistaken . . . ."
2. Repeat the basic idea or ideas in your own words.
3. Check your paraphrase with the other person; say, for example, "Is that correct?"

By paraphrasing a sender's thoughts, listeners accomplish at least two purposes. First, they let the other person know that they care enough to listen. Second, if the speaker's message has not been accurately received, they offer the other person the opportunity to adjust the message so that they can understand it as intended:

Person 1: I'm quitting my job soon.

Person 2: You're leaving your job tomorrow?

Person 1: Well, not that soon! But within a few weeks.

In summary, when you listen actively, or empathically, you listen for total meaning, and you listen in order to respond to feelings. When you listen empathically, the following statements do *not* appear in your conversation:

"You must do . . . ."

"You should do . . . ."

"You're wrong!"

"Let me tell you what to do."

"You sure have a funny way of looking at things."

"You're making a big mistake."

"The best answer is . . . ."

"Don't worry about it."

"You think *you've* got problems! Ha!"

"That reminds me of the time I . . . ."

Active, empathic listeners do not judge; they reflect, consider, and often restate in their own words their impressions of the sender's expression. Active listeners also check to determine if their impressions are acceptable to the sender. What kind of checker are you?

Findings from medical research underscore the importance of listening. Many medical school curricula now include courses and seminars that teach doctors how to listen, ask open-ended questions, and establish productive, caring relationships with patients. Not listening well—that is, failing to encourage patients to give relevant background on life circumstances and symptoms—can be a costly mistake. Far too often, doctors interrupt patients after allowing them to speak for a scant 18 seconds, erroneously assume they understand what patients mean, and they ask only questions they think important.[45]

Research also reveals that listening to family stories and reminiscing about the past may be both physically and emotionally healing. Listening to heartwarming or positive stories that recall meaningful moments has been shown to lower the heart rate and enhance a sense of overall well-being.[46]

At this point, you should realize why it takes "more than two good ears" to listen.

Listening to Culture's Influence

Knowledge is a product traded in world markets. In fact, the trading of knowledge is the central focus of many employees. With more global corporations, it is increasingly likely that we are trading knowledge with people who do not live in the same country or share the same language. Thus, the globalization of society is changing whom we will be listening to, and this means that we have to become more aware of how cultural differences influence listening.

According to C. Y. Cheng, the Chinese place greater emphasis on the receiving process and less emphasis on the sending process.[47] This is reflective of the East Asian concern for interpretation and anticipation. In Japan,

In what ways, if any, do you adjust your listening style to take cultural differences into account?

in fact, anticipatory communication is the norm. Speakers rarely tell or ask directly for something they want leaving receivers to guess and accommodate speakers' needs, which helps speakers and receivers save face in case what the speakers want done cannot be accomplished.[48] Thus, the Japanese use an indirect style of conversation and could be offended by the direct confrontations Americans are prone to. In comparison, German adults practice action-oriented listening. They are inquisitive and exhibit a direct style. Israelis, who carefully analyze information, prefer the content style of listening. Collective in orientation, they tend to deemphasize the personal aspects of interactions. The individually oriented Americans, on the other hand, exhibit a people-oriented style, which focuses more on the feelings and concerns of the people involved in an interaction and emphasizes the social aspects of interaction. At the same time, however, they are focused on the time that interaction consumes—a time-oriented style.[49]

Dialogic listening focuses on what happens between people as they respond to each other, work toward shared understanding, and build a relationship.[50] Too frequently, life's pressures appear to push us away from adopting an open-ended, tentative approach to conversation. We seem to prefer certainty, closure, and control. Whereas persons from Eastern cultures practice more speculative, metaphoric thinking, and believe that people should listen more than they talk, members of Western cultures are much less open and tentative in their listening behaviors, preferring specifically focused and concrete thinking instead.[51]

In addition, in the United States, listening rules vary depending on the racial and gender group to which you belong. African Americans, in general, display a more participative listening style than European Americans. When listening to a speaker, they are likely to shout out responses as a means of demonstrating their interest and involvement. Women and men also exhibit different listening styles. Women tend to search for relationships among message parts; they rely more on their feelings and intuitions. They listen to enhance

dialogic listening
the awareness of what happens between people as they respond to each other

Thinking CRITICALLY

Reflect and Respond

Agree or disagree with the father's thinking in the following excerpt from Steven R. Covey's *The 7 Habits of Highly Effective People.* Be sure to supply reasons and examples that support your stance.

> A father once told me, "I can't understand my kid. He just won't listen to me at all."
>
> "Let me restate what you just said," I replied. "You don't understand your son because he won't listen to you?"
>
> "That's right," he replied.
>
> "Let me try again," I said. "You don't understand your son because he won't listen to you?"
>
> "That's what I said," he impatiently replied.
>
> "I thought that to understand another person, you needed to listen to him," I suggested.
>
> "Oh!" he said. There was a long pause. "Oh!" he said again, as the light began to dawn. "Oh, yeah! But I do understand him. I know what he's going through. I went through the same thing myself. I guess what I don't understand is why he won't listen to me." [52]

their understanding as well as to establish personal relationships. They also demonstrate the ability to switch between competing messages; unlike men, who tend to focus on their reactions to only one speaker at a time, women appear able to split their focus. They are more receptive, in general, than are men to what is happening around them. Thus, women are more likely than men to be engaged in conversation with one person and still pick up on the words of another person who is conversing with someone else nearby. Women also use head nodding and facial expressions to indicate their interest in a conversation; because they view talk as a relationship developer, they also provide more vocal and verbal feedback to those they interact with. Women consider it important to be perceived as receptive and open. [53] In general, they listen to confirm the relationship as well as the person with whom they are communicating. [54] Women use more listening cues than men; they also excel at empathizing and at mood identification. Men, in contrast, are more at home with comprehensive listening and less at home with the emotional content of a message. When listening, men are more apt to focus on a message's structure or pattern. Their tendency is to direct their listening efforts toward a goal. Thus, they listen to receive facts; they want to get to the bottom line. They play up their expertise and use it to dominate a conversation. Men are more apt to listen to solve problems, rather than to provide support. [55]

Revisiting Chapter Objectives

1. **Define *hearing, listening,* and *critical thinking.*** Listening is a deliberate process through which we seek to understand and retain aural (heard) stimuli. Unlike hearing, which occurs automatically, listening depends on a complex set of acquired skills, including critical thinking. When you engage in critical thinking, you think carefully about what another person is telling you, and you evaluate the believability of the message. You also seek to determine if there is a logical connection between ideas and feelings.

2. **Compare and contrast helpful and harmful listening and thinking habits.** The average person listens at only 25 percent efficiency, losing 75 percent of what is heard. A graphic illustration of the results of inefficient listening is distortion of a message in serial communication (when a message is passed from one person to another in a series). A principal reason for poor listening is failure to determine the involvement level appropriate in a particular situation. Various behaviors we adopt cause us to unlisten—that is, they impede true understanding and critical reflection.

3. **Explain and use the listening level–energy involvement scale.** Understanding and using the listening level–energy involvement scale can help us develop more effective listening skills. The scale is comprised of five levels: hearing, listening to understand content, listening to retain content, listening to analyze and evaluate content, and listening to help others.

4. **Define *feedback,* distinguish among and use different types of feedback, and explain how each type affects communication.** A prerequisite of effective listening is effective feedback. Feedback consists of all the verbal and nonverbal messages that a person consciously or unconsciously sends out in response to another person's communication. Through feedback, we either confirm or correct the impressions others have of us and our attitudes. There are two main types of feedback. (1) Evaluative feedback gives an opinion, positive or negative, and attempts to influence the behavior of others. (2) Nonevaluative feedback gives emotional support. Probing, understanding (or paraphrasing), supportive feedback, and "I" messages are all forms of nonevaluative feedback that help sustain interpersonal relationships. When listening and giving feedback to people from other cultures, it is essential to be extremely sensitive to cultural norms.

5. **Set appropriate listening goals.** You can improve your listening skills by learning to focus your attention while listening and by setting appropriate listening goals. Listening to understand ideas, to retain information, to analyze and evaluate, and to empathize require progressively more effort and attention.

6. **Explain how technology influences listening.** Recognizing how culture, gender, and technology influence listening skills may further enhance our ability to develop more effective listening practices. New technological advances, while giving us the ability to listen globally, are also competing for our listening time.

Resources for Further Inquiry and Reflection

To apply your understanding of how the principles in Chapter 7 are at work in our daily lives, consult the following resources for further inquiry and reflection. Or, if you prefer, choose any other appropriate resource. Then connect the ideas expressed in your chosen selection with the communication concepts and issues you are learning about both in and out of class.

Listen to Me

"Bridge over Troubled Water" (Simon and Garfunkel)
"The Reason" (Celine Dion)
"Janie's Got a Gun" (Aerosmith)
"Don't Waste Your Time" (Mary J. Blige)
"She's Leaving Home" (The Beatles)
"The Sound of Silence" (Simon and Garfunkel)

Each of these songs describes a listening problem or skill. Choose one and use it to explain the role deficient or helpful listening plays in life.

 View Me

The Ring	*First Wives Club*
The Negotiator	*Good Will Hunting*
Analyze That	*Jerry McGuire*
Analyze This	

Listening, effective and/or ineffective, plays a central role in each of these films. Choose one, and discuss how the ability or inability to listen complicates or facilitates the life of one or more of the film's characters.

 Read Me

Edward Albee. *Who's Afraid of Virginia Woolf?* New York: Pocket Books, 1975.
Hannah Merker. *Listening.* New York: HarperCollins, 1995.

Discuss how the work contributes to our understanding of the role of listening in relationships and in other life experiences.

 Tell Me

Share with the class the insights you gained from your chosen Listen to Me, View Me, or Read Me selection.

Who is your best listener? Explain what this person has done to earn this title.

Key Chapter Terminology

Communication **Works**

www.mhhe.com/gamble8

Use the Communication Works CD-ROM and the Online Learning Center at www.mhhe.com/gamble8 to further your knowledge of the following terminology.

critical thinking 211
dialogic listening 223
empathic listening 202
evaluative feedback 205
formative feedback 206
hearing 201
"I" messages 209
listening 201
listening level–energy involvement scale 201

nonevaluative feedback 207
paraphrasing 219
probing 207
red-flag words 215
serial communication 199
speech-thought differential 216
supportive feedback 208
understanding 208
visualization 219
"you" messages 209

Test Your Understanding

Communication **Works**

www.mhhe.com/gamble8

Go to the *Self Quizzes* on the Communication Works CD-ROM and the book's Online Learning Center at www.mhhe.com/gamble8.

Notes

1. Cesar G. Soriano. "News Flash: Teen Stops Speaking!" *USA Today,* August 9, 2000, p. 1D.
2. Brendan Schurr. "Teenager Vows Not to Speak for a Year." *The Record,* August 16, 2000, p. A-5.
3. From Hannah Merker. *Listening.* New York: HarperCollins, 1995.

4. See Jane Allan. "Talking Your Way to Success (Listening Skills)." *Accountancy,* February 1993, pp. 612–663; and John W. Haas and Christina L. Arnold. "An Examination of the Role of Listening in Co-Workers." *Journal of Business Communication,* April 1995, pp. 123–139.

5. The Office Team Survey, 2000, was cited in *Sssh! Listen Up!* HighGain, Inc. Newsletter, June 2000, p. 4.

6. K. W. Hawkins and B. P. Fullion. "Perceived Communication Skill Needs for Work Groups." *Communication Research Reports,* 16, 1999, pp. 167–174.

7. See, for example, Wendell Johnson. "Do You Know How to Listen?" *ETC: A Review of General Semantics* 56, Spring 1999, p. 109.

8. See Tory Rankin. "The Measurement of the Ability to Understand Spoken Language." Ph.D. dissertation, University of Michigan, 1926, p. 43; Larry Barker, R. Edwards, C. Gaines, K. Gladney, and F. Hally. "An Investigation of Proportional Time Spent in Various Communication Activities by College Students." *Journal of Applied Communication Research* 8, 1981, pp. 101–109.

9. See A. D. Wolvin and C. G. Coakley. "A Survey of the Status of Listening Training in Some Fortune 500 Corporations." *Communication Education* 40, 1991, pp. 152–164.

10. For a detailed discussion, see Ralph G. Nichols and Leonard A. Stevens. *Are You Listening?* New York: McGraw-Hill, 1956. See also K. Watson and L. Barker. "Listening Behavior: Definition and Measurement." In R. Bostrom, ed. *Communication Yearbook/8.* Beverly Hills, CA: Sage, 1985, pp. 178–197; and Andrew Wolving and Carolyn Gwynn Coakly. *Listening,* 4th ed. Dubuque, IA: Wm. C. Brown, 1988.

11. John R. Freund and Arnold Nelson. "Distortion in Communication." In B. Peterson, G. Goldhaber, and R. Pace, eds. Chicago: Science Research Associates 1974, pp. 122–124.

12. Gerald Goldhaber. *Organizational Communication,* 4th ed. Dubuque, IA: Wm. C. Brown, 1988.

13. See L. Wheeless, A. Frymier, and C. Thompson. "A Comparison of Verbal Output and Receptivity in Relation to Attraction and Communication Satisfaction in Interpersonal Relationships." *Communication Quarterly,* spring 1992, pp. 102–115.

14. See, for example, Judi Brownell. *Listening: Attitudes, Principles, and Skills.* Boston: Allyn & Bacon, 1996.

15. Janel Beavin Bavelas, Linda Coates, and Trudy Johnson. "Listener Responses as a Collaborative Process: The Role of Gaze." *Journal of Communication,* 52:3, September 2002, pp. 566–579.

16. For example, see Sharon White Taylor. "Wireless and Witless." *New York Times,* July 5, 2000, p. A17.

17. Motoko Rich. "Shut Up So We Can Do Our Jobs!" *Wall Street Journal,* August 29, 2001, pp. B1, B8.

18. Kevin Daly, president of Communispond, New York. Press release report 1983.

19. See A. Vangelisti, M. Knapp, and J. Daly. "Conversational Narcissism." *Communication Monographs,* December 1990, pp. 251–271.

20. Alfie Kohn. "Girl Talk, Guy Talk." *Psychology Today,* February 1988, pp. 65–66.

21. D. Tannen. *The Argument Culture: Moving from Debate to Dialogue.* New York: Ballentine, 1998.

22. Don Tosti. "Operant Conditioning." Speech presented at Operant Conditioning Seminar, New York, fall 1983.

23. David W. Johnson. *Reaching Out: Interpersonal Effectiveness and Self-Actualization.* Englewood Cliffs, NJ: Prentice-Hall, 1972; and Thomas Gordon. *Leader Effectiveness Training.* New York: Wyden, 1977.

24. For a discussion of the benefit of questioning, see John F. Monoky. "Listen by Asking." *Industrial Distribution,* April 1995, p. 123.

25. Doris Iarovici. Quoted in "Making TLC a Requirement." *Newsweek,* August 12, 1991.

26. For a discussion of the kinds of information conveyed by verbal and nonverbal feedback, see Dale G. Leathers. "The Informational Potential of the Nonverbal and Verbal Components of Feedback Responses." *Southern Speech Communication Journal* 44, 1979, pp. 331–354.

27. H. Leavitt and R. Mueller. "Some Effects of Feedback on Communication." *Human Relations* 4, 1951, pp. 401–410.

28. See R. Boostrom. *Developing Creative and Critical Thinking.* Lincolnwood, IL: National Textbook, 1992.

29. Teri Gamble and Michael Gamble. *Public Speaking in the Age of Diversity.* Boston: Allyn & Bacon, 1994, p. 18.

30. See, for example, "Personality Typing." *Wired,* July 1999, p. 71.

31. Sharon White Taylor. "Wireless and Witless." *New York Times,* July 5, 2000, p. A-17; and "Cell Phone Rage: Helpful Hints." *New York Times,* July 8, 2000, p. A-14.

32. David Shenk. *Data Smog.* New York: Harper-Edge, 1997.

33. *The Commercial Appeal,* October 1, 1999, p. A-1.

34. Sheila C. Bentley. "Listening in the 21st Century." Paper presented at the annual convention of the National Communication Association, Chicago, November 1999.

35. Cynthia B. Leshin. *Internet Investigations in Business Communication.* Upper Saddle River, NJ: Prentice Hall, 1997, pp. 53–56.

36. See, for example, Vangelisti et al.

37. See Hauser, Barker and Hughes. "Receiver Apprehension and Listening Comprehension: A Linear or Curvilinear Relationship." *Southern Communication Journal* fall 1990, pp. 62–70.

38. Nichols and Stevens.

39. Ralph G. Nichols. "Listening Is a Ten-Part Skill." *Nation's Business* 45, 1957, p. 4.

40. For example, see Carol Roach and Nancy Wyatt. *Successful Listening.* New York: Harper & Row, 1988, pp. 39–44.

41. Robert Montgomery. *Memory Made Easy.* New York: Amacom, 1990.

42. See Carl Rogers. *Becoming Partners.* New York: Dell, 1973; and Carl Rogers. *On Becoming a Person.* Boston: Houghton Mifflin, 1972.

43. David Ignatow. "Two Friends." *Figures of the Human.* Copyright 1963 by David Ignatow. Wesleyan University Press by permission of University Press of New England.

44. See Michael Nichols. *The Lost Art of Listening.* New York: Guilford Press, 1995.

45. C. Crosen. "Blah, Blah, Blah." *Wall Street Journal,* July 10, 1997, pp. 1A, 6A; and Betsy A. Lehman. "Getting an Earful Is Just What the Doctor Needs." *The Record,* March 21, 1994, p. B-4.

46. Karen S. Peterson. "Sharing Memorable Moments Can Calm the Soul, Heal the Body." *USA Today,* February 15, 1999, p. 4D.

47. See, for example, C. Y. Cheng. "Chinese Philosophy and Contemporary Communication Theory." In D. L. Kincaid, ed. *Communication Theory: Eastern and Western Perspectives.* Academic Press, New York: 1987.

48. This was documented by T. S. Lebra in *Japanese Patterns of Behavior.* Honolulu: University Press of Hawaii, 1976.

49. C. Kiewitz, J. B. Weaver III, H. B. Brosius, and G. Wiemann. "Cultural Differences in Listening Styles Preferences: A Comparison of Young Adults in Germany, Israel, and the United States." *International Journal of Public Opinion Research* 9:3, fall 1997, p. 233.

50. John Stewart and M. Thomas. "Dialogic Listening: Sculpting Mutual Meanings." In J. Stewart, ed. *Bridges Not Walls: A Book about Interpersonal Communication,* 6th ed. New York: McGraw-Hill, 1995, pp. 184–201.

51. Larry A. Samovar and Richard E. Porter. *Communication between Cultures.* Belmont, CA: Wadsworth, 1995, pp. 211–212.

52. Stephen R. Covey. *The 7 Habits of Highly Effective People.* New York: Simon & Schuster, 1990, pp. 239–240.

53. S. Petronio, J. Martin, and R. Littlefield. "Prerequisite Conditions for Self-Disclosing: A Gender Issue." *Communication Monographs* 51, 1984, pp. 286–272.

54. Deborah Tannen. *You Just Don't Understand: Women and Men in Conversation.* New York: Morrow, 1990.

55. See also Michael Purdy and Deborah Borisoff. *Listening in Everyday Life: A Personal and Professional Approach,* 2nd ed. Lanham, MD: University Press of America, 1997.

2

Interpersonal Communication

The three chapters in Part Two are centered on interpersonal communication. We start by exploring relationship basics, expand our study to relational contexts, and end by focusing on the job interview. We explore how interpersonal relationships develop, consider the kinds of relationships you prefer sharing, and work to improve your relationship quotient in general and your interviewing skills in particular.

A special goal of Part Two's chapters is to demonstrate how culture, gender, and technology influence interpersonal communication. Few interpersonal interactions are not affected in some way by at least one of these variables. We hope that by the end of this section you'll be well on your way to making communication work even better for you.

Understanding Relationships

1. Explain why we need interpersonal relationships.

2. Define and discuss the following terms: *inclusion, control,* and *affection.*

3. Explain and distinguish among social penetration, cost-benefit theory, and relational dialectics theory.

4. Discuss and distinguish among 10 stages of relationships.

5. Discuss how deception, gender, and technology affect interpersonal communication.

6. Identify ways to enhance your satisfaction with your relationships.

People meet and separate. But funny things happen in between.

—**Mark L. Knapp**

. . . when you start out with someone, you're essentially driving a strange car for the first time and none of the controls are labeled.

—**Jerry Seinfeld**

Go to the *Online Learning Center* at www.mhhe.com/gamble8 and answer the questions in the *Self Inventory* to evaluate your understanding of relationship building.

During the 2002–2003 television season, we watched, Trista, *The Bachelorette,* marry Ryan, her chosen bachelor. We listened as *Joe Millionaire*'s Evan told his chosen one, Zora, that he had had to lie, that he really wasn't a millionaire at all, and then we "aahed" as Evan and Zora became an actual millionaire couple when presented with a reward of $1 million for choosing "love" over money. Good thing Evan and Zora were each given a $500,000 check; they are no longer together. We snickered as the Osbournes played out their familial and personal relationships before our eyes. We also watched the contestants on the latest version of *Survivor* interacting with and establishing relationships with an array of strangers, as each sought to be the one person not "voted off" by others.

What did these shows share with each other? In each of these "reality" shows, persons were unable to avoid developing interpersonal relationships. Many, in fact, experienced rather intense relationships. These shows were among the most highly rated shows of the year. Why did so many of us watch them? For some reason, we are fascinated watching people begin relationships, figure out the ground rules of their relationships, engage in interesting interactions, and then terminate or take a relationship to a new level. For many of us, there is nothing more important than having a meaningful relationship with another person. We long to make meaningful

Skill BUILDER

One Relationship, Indivisible

Make two lists of relationships. The first list should contain all the interpersonal relationships in which you have participated during the past month that you consider successful and likely to endure for at least another five years. The second list should contain the interpersonal relationships you experienced during the same time period that you expect will not continue much longer. Identify the differences in the relationships you shared that led you to draw your conclusions about each relationship's future. What do these differences tell you about the qualities necessary to sustain a relationship?

connections. Do these shows depict what we want and expect in our relationships? What do you think?

An **interpersonal relationship** is a meaningful dyadic person-to-person connection. When we share interpersonal relationships with another person, we become interdependent with that person. Over time, we engage in communication of a personal nature, such as friendship or romance, during which we interact with each other, develop a shared history, and attempt to meet each other's social needs. When one person withdraws from the relationship, and the other person is unable to work things out or convince the person to return, the relationship ends. An interpersonal dyad is indivisible. During our life span, we experience a wide array of social connections, some considerably more complicated, meaningful, and/or important to us than others. Some of our relationships will last a lifetime; others will be short-lived. Some will succeed and some will fail.

In *The New Peoplemaking,* Virginia Satir notes: "Once a human being has arrived on this earth, communication is the largest single factor determining what kinds of relationships she or he makes with others and what happens to each in the world. How we manage survival, how we develop intimacy, how productive we are, how we make sense . . . all depend on our communication skills."[1] This chapter explores the nature of the relationships we share with others, our satisfaction or dissatisfaction with them, and how we can improve them.

interpersonal relationship

a meaningful connection such as friendship

How would having the interactions of your close interpersonal relationships televised affect you?

THE ROLE OF RELATIONSHIPS

How important are relationships to us today? As our society places more and more emphasis on technology, it is feared that we will place less and less emphasis on personal relationships. Linguist John L. Locke, for example, argues that modern technology is robbing people of the inclination to speak meaningfully to one another. He believes that our social voices are disappearing, leaving us isolated from one another. He argues that, while new technologies such as e-mail have increased the amount of functional information we have access to, they lack the capacity for intimate talking. From his point of view, we now live in an **autistic society,** a society that is at home with computers but disadvantaged when it comes to establishing human intimacy.[2] Locke's critics, however, note that his fears may be unfounded. They believe that, while e-mail may strip away some of the intimacy of face-to-face conversation, it also strips away some of the fear, guilt, anger, and self-consciousness.[3] Other theorists reason that, to compensate for the alienation fostered by machine-made barriers, we, in fact, internalize a greater need to develop warm, personal relationships. As a result,

autistic society

a society at home with computers but disadvantaged when it comes to establishing human intimacy a major theme of our time is our desire for closer, more personal ties. It appears that forecaster John Naisbitt was right: Our high-tech society has precipitated in us an increasingly prevalent desire for "high-touch" contacts.[4] We now know that technology is not eliminating our need for relationships but, on the contrary, is helping foster friendships, even love. Thus, critics contend that we do not live in an autistic society but, rather, a **high-tech–high-touch society.**[5] In our society, traditional barriers of time and space no longer exist. Relationships now are begun across time zones and international borders.[6] Instant messages vie with phone calls as social glue.[7] In our technologically advanced world, meaningful relationships, while more difficult to maintain, are becoming even more precious.[8] Indeed, social contacts have a positive effect on mortality.[9]

Functions of Relationships: Three Basic Needs

A vast body of research spurred by the work of William Schutz consistently attests that we attempt to meet our needs for inclusion, control, and affection through our relationships.[10]

Inclusion has to do with the varying degrees to which we all need to establish and maintain a feeling of mutual interest with other people—a sense that we can take an interest in others and that others can take an interest in us. We want others to pay attention to us, to take the time to understand us. Wanting to be included is normal. We all remember how it feels to be left out—to be the last person asked to join a team, to not be invited to an important party, or to be ignored during a mealtime conversation. When our need for inclusion is met, we tend to feel worthwhile and fulfilled. If it goes unmet, we tend to feel lonely, and our health may even suffer.

Loneliness is an all too common affliction of our age.[11] Research reveals, for example, that men aged 50 and older who have no close friends or relatives are three times as likely to die after suffering high levels of emotional stress than are persons whose lives are less lonely.[12] What exactly is **loneliness?** A consensus has emerged that loneliness begins with a recognition that the interpersonal relationships we have are not the kinds we would like to have.[13] Thus, loneliness can be considered a result of a perceived discrepancy between desired and achieved social relationships.[14] Lonely people find it difficult to make connections with others. When our person-to-person contacts are deficient, we feel alone, and we seek substitutes for these contacts—sometimes, for example, opting for the company of professional contact people, such as radio talk show hosts and physicians. In order to help their patients handle feelings of isolation, physicians are spending course time learning how to deal with the more personal needs of patients.[15] Inclusion is so interconnected with our well-being that some years ago the California State Department of Mental Health mounted an advertising campaign designed to convince people that social rela-

high-tech–high-touch society
a technologically advanced society that values interpersonal relationships

inclusion
the need for social contact

We need to get close to each other to have a sense of community, to feel we're not alone in the world. But we need to keep our distance from each other to preserve our independence, so others don't impose on or engulf us.
—Deborah Tannen,
That's Not What I Meant

How do you navigate this duality in your own life? That is, how do you balance your need for individuality with your need for social contact?

loneliness
the perceived discrepancy between desired and achieved social relationships

Feelings of inclusion or loneliness can affect our health and the way we view ourselves.

tionships could enhance their physical and mental health and increase their life span.

Control deals with our need to establish and maintain satisfactory levels of influence and power in our relationships. To varying degrees, we need to feel that we can take charge of a situation, whereas at other times we need to feel comfortable assuming a more submissive role. When our control need goes unmet, we may conclude that others do not respect or value our abilities and that we are viewed as incapable of making a sound decision or of directing others' or our own future.

Finally, **affection** involves our need to give and receive love and to experience emotionally close relationships. If our need for affection goes unfulfilled, we are likely to conclude that we are unlovable and that therefore people will remain emotionally detached from us (that is, they will try to avoid establishing close ties with us). In contrast, if our experiences with affection have been more pleasant, we are probably comfortable handling both close and distant relationships, and most likely we recognize that not everyone we come into contact with will necessarily care for us in the same way.

These three basic needs differ from each other in a significant way. Inclusion comes first; that is, it is our need for inclusion that impels us to establish a relationship in the first place. By comparison, our needs for control and affection are met through the relationships we have already established. Thus, as psychologist William Schutz notes, "Generally speaking, inclusion is concerned with the problem of in or out, control is concerned with top or bottom, and affection with close or far."[16]

control

the need to feel we are capable and responsible and able to exert power and influence over our relationships

affection

the need to experience emotionally close relationships

Do you think men and women differ in their need for inclusion, control, or affection? Do they differ in the way they express their needs? Why or why not?

Relationships and Verbal and Nonverbal Conversations

In a news article on flirting, the author observed: "Woman spots man. Man spots woman. Woman smiles. Man looks away. Woman looks away. Man looks back." Will they speak to each other?[17] According to Robert E. Nofsinger, author of *Everyday Conversation*, "Almost everything we do that concerns other people involves us in conversation."[18] In effect, we talk to relate; we converse our way through our lives. Thus, talking is fundamental to our relationships—whether they are beginning, ending, or continuing.[19] We use talk as we attempt to manage both the light and the dark sides of our relationships.[20]

Some of our conversations help us accomplish our relationship goals; others end up impeding our ability to attain these goals.[21] For example, researchers report that rapport can be built nonverbally if the communicator exhibits nonverbal behaviors that others perceive positively rather than negatively.[22] Sometimes we embarrass ourselves in front of others; other times we embarrass the people we are with. Sometimes we find ourselves unable to participate in a conversation; other times we seem to be talking mainly to ourselves—no one else is paying attention. Sometimes we say what we know we shouldn't say; other times we listen when others wish we wouldn't. It is through verbal and nonverbal communication that we establish and strengthen—or weaken and terminate—every one of our relationships.[23] Typically, the more time we spend speaking with our relationship partners about our day, the healthier is the relationship we share.[24] As Nofsinger reminds us, "Our family life is created and enacted each day through conversation. And, in large part, we find employment (or fail to) through our everyday talk."

phatic communication
communication designed to
open the channels of
communication

Our conversations have outcomes; they produce results. Thus, as our conversations with others progress from **phatic communication,** surface clichés that are designed to open the channels of communication (like "What's up?" and "How are you doing?"), to statements of fact (like "Geography is my worst subject"), to statements of opinion (like "I really support Act Up"), to statements of feelings (like "I think Juana likes Joe and I'm jealous"), the better able we are to keep a conversation going, use self-disclosure techniques to draw others into conversation with us, and thereby increase the likelihood that we will develop friendships.[25] Thus, by taking turns or refusing to take turns—that is, through reciprocal turn taking or the lack of reciprocal turn taking—we influence the direction of our relationships. For this reason, some of our relationships go nowhere, while others are particularly effective—usually because we have worked to make them that way.

Whether or not we experience excessive levels of apprehension before or during interpersonal conversations can affect our effectiveness in initiating and maintaining relationships. For example, if we become very nervous when participating in conversations with persons we have just met, or overly tense in conversations with persons we know well, our willingness to begin or continue a conversation can be impeded. In contrast, if we remain calm and relaxed and evidence no fear of speaking up, for all practical purposes, we remove a key obstacle to person-to-person interaction.

GENDER, CULTURE, AND RELATIONSHIPS

Both gender and culture influence how we form and maintain relationships. Although we all have a need to connect with people, we may do so in different ways. When we don't know how to connect with others from diverse cultures, we may be left feeling that we remain unconnected strangers. Relationship misunderstanding can keep us apart.[26] Thus, it is important to recognize that people who grow up in different cultures have different ideas about what is natural and important in their relationships. Those who do not conform to gender or culture expectations can meet with negative responses.

Gender and Relationships

How do young men and women view the relationships they are likely to share in the future? In one recent poll of teenagers, responses revealed that the sexes hold different attitudes regarding their future relationships: Males, for example, are much more traditional than females regarding the kind of family life they hope to share. While 86 percent of teenage girls surveyed expect to combine work and family and are committed to having careers, only 58 percent of the boys said that they expected their wives to work outside the home. Male respondents expressed a desire for a traditional 1950s-style relationship in which the wife stays home, raises the children, and is a homemaker, while the husband is responsible for paying the bills and mowing the lawn. One teenage girl commented, "If [the male respondents] say they want their wives at home, I think it's because they want more power in the relationship."[27]

Males and females differ not just in their expectations of future relationships but also in their behavior during the preliminary stages of a relationship—for

| Because of the way they are socialized, men and women may share their feelings differently.

instance, when flirting. According to one educator, flirting is "a verbal power struggle between men and women."[28] For men "it is a form of foreplay," while for women it is more often "a way of making a connection."[29]

Researchers also affirm that women place a higher value on intimate relationships than do men, whose friendships frequently seem to lack emotional depth.[30] Because of the ways men are socialized, they often feel uncomfortable expressing their feelings directly with words, preferring instead to express them through shared activities like sports.[31] Thus, women use personal and disclosive talk to develop and sustain their relationships to a greater extent than do men. While women bond through talk, men bond through doing things together.[32]

In addition, women focus on the maintenance of relationships more than men do. They are eager to acquire personal information about their relational partners. They desire a partner who demonstrates care and concern and who is empathetic. As a result, they use more maintenance strategies than do men.[33]

This is not to imply that men and women do not share any commonalities in their views regarding relationships, because they do. Both men and women value same-sex friends and desire friends they can trust, who accept them and help them.

Culture and Relationships

Attitudes toward self and others influence the effectiveness of the relationships shared by persons from different cultures. Acceptance, for instance, is one

---

Women, Intimacy, and Isolation

According to sociologist Deborah Tannen, for women, life is a struggle to preserve intimacy and avoid isolation. Do you agree with Tannen? If so, do you believe this true only of American women? What about women from other cultures? What about men?

EXPLORING
Diversity

Source: Deborah Tannen. *You Just Don't Understand: Women and Men in Conversation.* New York: Ballantine, 1991.

necessary factor for relationship satisfaction. Researchers report that, to be satisfied in their relationships with Whites, both African Americans and Mexican Americans need to feel that Whites respect, confirm, and accept them.[34] Asians also practice the positive exchange of ideas, demonstrating care for the other person during the exchange. They value harmony as a means of relationship nurturance. Conformity and group well-being are especially important to them. Generally, they do not reach out to strangers, and they make great efforts to conceal unfavorable information about members of the group to which they belong from those whom they perceive to be outsiders.[35] Latinos, in contrast, tend to focus on relational support.[36]

While some cultures emphasize social relationships and instruct individuals to give preference to the interests of others over their own private interests, other cultures, including American culture, stress individualism. While Americans find it natural to begin and end relationships, Asian cultures believe that relationships should be long-lasting, characterized by loyalty and the fulfillment of obligations.

Across cultures, while points of difference influence the early stages of a relationship, as self-disclosures increase and uncertainty is reduced, our dissimilarities affect us less. To the degree we can accept members of other cultures as they are, avoid negative stereotyping, and make mutual behavioral accommodations, the relationships we develop stand a better chance of developing into real friendships.

There are other cultural understandings we should have about relationships as well. While in some cultures people voluntarily choose their relationship partners when it comes to romance and marriage, in other cultures, their relationship partners are selected for them by their parents, sometimes to bring two families together and other times to reap some financial reward. In addition, while in the United States, we typically assume that we have the right to terminate a relationship that makes us unhappy, in a number of other cultures, a relationship either may not be dissolved or is exceedingly difficult to dissolve.

DIMENSIONS OF RELATIONSHIPS: BREADTH AND DEPTH

breadth
the number of topics you discuss with another person

depth
a measure of how central the topics you discuss with another person are to your self-concept

social penetration theory
the theory that states that our relationships begin with relatively narrow breadth and shallow depth and develop over time

Every relationship—with a friend, a family member, a lover, or a co-worker—can be described in terms of two concepts: breadth and depth. **Breadth** has to do with how many topics you discuss with the other person. **Depth** has to do with how central the topics are to your self-concept and how much you reveal.

The relationship theory of social psychologists Irwin Altman and Dalmas Taylor can be schematized as shown in Figure 8.1.[37] Central to their **social penetration theory** is the idea that relationships begin with relatively narrow breadth (few topics are spoken about) and shallow depth (the inner circles are not penetrated) and progress over time in intensity and intimacy as both breadth and depth increase. Thus, our relationships may develop incrementally as we move from discussing few to many topics, and from superficial topics (the periphery of the circle) to intensely personal topics (the center of the circle). Figure 8.2 is an exercise using these concepts.

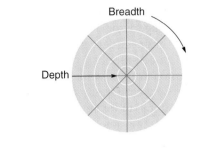

FIGURE 8.1
Breadth and Depth in Relationships.

Casual relationship
(a)

Intimate relationship
(b)

FIGURE 8.2
Casual and Intimate Relationships.
Use arrows with the segmented concentric circles to show the contrast between one of your casual relationships and one of your more intimate relationships.

The breadth of topics we discuss may be wide for casual as well as for intimate relationships, but the depth of penetration usually increases as a relationship becomes more intimate. Consequently, a highly intimate relationship will probably have both considerable breadth and considerable depth as the people involved extend the range of topics they discuss and reveal more about how they feel about those topics.

The social penetration model is useful for a number of reasons. First, it can help us visualize the nature of the relationships we share by indicating the range of topics we communicate about and the extent to which we reveal ourselves through our discussions. Second, the model can help explain why certain relationships seem stronger than others. For example, is there one person to whom you reveal more about a particular topic than you would reveal to anyone else? Is there someone with whom you would not even consider discussing a particular topic? Do you reveal more of yourself to some people at work than to others? Is the same true for members of your family? What about your friends? Although we may behave in ways that limit some people's access to certain portions of our relationship circle, others may have access to its entire scope; although we may keep some from straying too far from the periphery, we may let others venture close to the center. When your communication with another person lacks breadth, depth, or both, it should not surprise you that you feel little if any bond to that person; to enhance the strength of your relationship, you would have to alter the nature and extent of your interactions.

Sometimes, in an effort to get to know another person quickly, we may discuss topics at a depth that would normally be reserved for those with whom we are more intimate. When such disclosures occur too rapidly or prematurely in the development of a relationship, they may create a feeling that something is wrong, a signal that one participant was not ready for the relationship to

How do you feel when someone reveals more to you than you are ready for? Have you ever made anyone feel uncomfortable by revealing too much too quickly? What prompted you to do it? How did the other person react?

progress that quickly or to be that intense. For example, employees in one company complained when a supervisor discussed personal aspects of his marriage with them during the business day; noting that hearing such intimate disclosures made them feel uncomfortable, they requested that he limit the depth and scope of his communications with them.

When interactants are ready to deepen a relationship, they see increases in breadth and depth as a natural and comfortable development.

Together, the nature and the amount of information we share with another person affect the strength and the quality of our interpersonal relationship. When we deliberately reveal information about ourselves to another person, information that we consider significant and would otherwise not be known to that person were it not for our purposeful intervention, we take steps to increase both the breadth of information people have about us and the depth of understanding they have for what makes us tick. In other words, self-disclosure is the voluntary, purposeful revealing of confidential personal information about us that others would not otherwise have access to. Thus, the amount of disclosing we do with another person usually is a gauge of how close we feel to the person or how close we desire to become. On the other

"Let's go someplace where I can talk."

hand, when a relationship begins to wane, usually there are decreases in the breadth as well as the depth of our disclosures. We refrain from talking about some topics, and we discuss the topics we do talk about in less depth. Such changes signal that we are becoming less personal or intimate and have begun the depenetration, or pulling-away, process. Thus, self-disclosure reflects the health of a relationship. When disclosure between relationship partners is reciprocal and honest, partners feel more secure in the relationship. They become comfortable sharing their humanness.

DEVELOPMENT AND ANALYSIS OF RELATIONSHIPS

Relationships can be analyzed with reference to their stages, costs and benefits, or dialectical perspectives. As you read about each stage, consider how it applies to a close relationship of yours.

Stages of Relationships: From Beginning to Ending to Beginning . . .

All relationships we share are complex (each of us is a unique bundle of experiences, thoughts, fears, and needs) and ever-changing (as we change, our relationships change—they grow stronger or weaker over time). Relationships pass through a number of stages as they strengthen or dissolve.[38] We will explore them now.

Stage 1: Initiating

Stage 1, **initiating,** involves the things that happen when we first make contact with each other. At this time, we look for signals that either impel us to initiate a conversation or tell us that we have nothing to gain by interacting. If we decide to make contact, we search for an appropriate conversation opener—for example, "Nice to meet you" or "What's happening?"

What happens when we can't find an appropriate opener? The following passage from *Conversationally Speaking* by Alan Garner describes one such possibility:

> I decided to marry her. Courtship would be a mere formality. But what to say to begin the courtship? "Would you like some of my gum?" sounded too low-class. "Hello," was too trite a greeting for my future bride. "I love you! I am hot with passion!" was too forward. "I want to make you the mother of my children," seemed a bit premature.
>
> Nothing. That's right, I said nothing. And after a while, the bus reached her stop, she got off, and I never saw her again.
>
> End of story.[39]

Stage 2: Experimenting

Once we have initiated contact, we try to find out more about the other person; we begin to probe the unknown. This is the stage of **experimenting.** Often we exchange small talk—for example, we tell the other where we're from and whom we know—in an effort to get acquainted. Although many of

initiating
the relationship stage during which contact is first made

Relationships typically begin with small talk. What do you say to initiate communication with someone you'd like to get to know?

experimenting
the relationship stage during which we begin to probe the unknown

us may hate small talk, or cocktail party chatter, according to Mark Knapp it serves several useful functions:

1. It provides a process for uncovering integrating topics and openings for more penetrating conversations.
2. It can serve as an audition for a future friendship or a way to increase the scope of a current friendship.
3. It provides a safe procedure for indicating who we are and how the other person can come to know us better (reduction of uncertainty).
4. It allows us to maintain a sense of community with our fellow human beings.[40]

In an article on small talk, Michael Korda notes: "The aim of small talk is to make people comfortable—to put them at their ease—not to teach, preach, or impress. It's a game, like tennis, in which the object is to keep the ball in the air for as long as possible."[41]

At this stage, our relationships lack depth; they are quite casual and superficial. The vast majority of them never progress beyond this point.

Have you had some relationships that did not pass beyond the experimentation phase but that you now wish had gone further? What kept them from progressing?

Stage 3: Intensifying

intensifying

the relationship stage during which two people become good friends

When a relationship does progress beyond experimenting, it enters the third stage, **intensifying.** During this stage, people become good friends—they begin to share things, disclose more, become better at predicting each other's behavior, and may even adopt nicknames for each other or exhibit similar postural or clothing cues. In a sense, they are beginning to be transformed from an "I" and an "I" into a "we."

Stage 4: Integrating

integrating

the relationship stage in which two people are identified as a couple

The fusion of "I" and "I" really takes place in stage 4, **integrating.** Two individuals are now identified as a pair, a couple, or "a package." Interpersonal synchrony is heightened; the two people may dress, act, and speak more and more alike or share a song ("our song"), a bankbook, or a project.

Stage 5: Bonding

bonding

the relationship stage in which two people make a formal commitment to each other

In stage 5, **bonding,** the interactants announce that their commitment to each other has been formally contracted. Their relationship is now institutionalized, formally recognized. This recognition can be a wedding license or a business contract, for example. The relationship takes on a new character: It is no longer informal. It is now guided by specified rules and regulations. Sometimes this alteration causes initial discomfort or rebellion as the interactants attempt to adjust to the change.

Stage 6: Differentiating

differentiating

the relationship stage in which two people identified as a couple seek to regain unique identities

In stage 6, **differentiating,** instead of continuing to emphasize "we," the interactants attempt to reestablish an "I" orientation, to regain a unique identity. They ask, "How are we different?" "How can I distinguish me from you?" During this phase, previously designated joint possessions take on a more individualized character; "our friends" become "my friends," "our bedroom" becomes "my bedroom," "our child" becomes "your son" (especially when he misbehaves). Although an urge to differentiate the self from the other is

A wedding signifies the formal bonding of a couple.

not uncommon (we need to be individuals as well as members of a relationship), if it persists, it can signal that the relationship is in trouble or that the process of uncoupling has begun.

Stage 7: Circumscribing

In stage 7, **circumscribing,** both the quality and the quantity of communication between the interactants decrease. Sometimes a careful effort is made to limit areas open for discussion to those considered safe. Other times there is no actual decrease in breadth of topics, but the topics are no longer discussed with any depth. In other words, fewer and less intimate disclosures are made, signaling that mental or physical withdrawal from the relationship is desired.[42] Dynamic communication has all but ceased; the relationship is characterized by lack of energy, shrinking interest, and a general feeling of exhaustion.

circumscribing
the relationship stage in which both the quality and the quantity of communication between two people decrease

Stage 8: Stagnating

When circumscribing continues, the relationship stagnates. In stage 8, **stagnating,** the participants feel that they no longer need to relate to each other because they know how the interaction will proceed; thus, they conclude that it is better to say nothing. Communication is at a standstill. Only the shadow of a relationship remains: The participants mark time by going through the motions while feeling nothing. In reality, they are like strangers inhabiting the hollow shell of what once was a thriving relationship. They still live in the same environment, but they share little else.

stagnating
the relationship stage during which communication is at a standstill

Stage 9: Avoiding

During the stage of **avoiding,** the participants actually go out of their way to be apart; they avoid contact with each other. Relating face-to-face or voice-to-voice has simply become so unpleasant that one or both can no longer

avoiding
the relationship stage during which persons intentionally avoid contact

continue the act. Although communicated more directly at some times than at others (sometimes the "symptom" is used as a form of communication; at other times an effort is made to disconfirm the other person), the dominant message is "I don't want to see you anymore; I don't want to continue this relationship." At this point, the end of the relationship is in sight.

Stage 10: Termination

termination

the relationship stage during which the relationship ends

At stage 10, **termination,** the bonds that used to hold the relationship together are severed; the relationship ends. Depending on how the participants feel (whether or not they agree on termination), this stage can be short or drawn out over time and can end cordially (in person, over the telephone, with a letter or legal document) or bitterly. All relationships eventually terminate (by the death of one participant if not before), but this doesn't mean that saying good-bye is easy or pleasant.[43]

Summary

Identify relationships in your own life that have stabilized at one or more of Knapp's "coming together" stages: initiating, experimenting, intensifying, integrating, bonding.

A relationship may stabilize at any one of the stages. Many relationships never proceed beyond the experimenting stage; others stabilize at the intensifying stage, the bonding stage, and so on. When the participants disagree about the point of stabilization, difficulties can arise. Movement through the stages may be forward or backward. For instance, we may advance and then retreat, deciding that a more superficial relationship is what we really desire. Additionally, we proceed through the stages at our own pace. Some relationships, especially those in which time is perceived to be limited, develop more quickly than others; the rate at which the participants grow together or apart, however, usually depends on their individual needs. What is important to remember is that many relationships do not arrive at a stage and simply stay there. Rather, they can be recursive. Relationships may even terminate and then begin anew.

A Special Case: Relationship Termination Caused by Death

grief process

a mourning process composed of 5 stages: denial anger, guilt, depression, and acceptance

What happens when death takes a loved one or a relationship partner away? When this occurs, many of us experience feelings of loneliness and social isolation. Actually, the **grief process** (see Figure 8.3) entails a number of stages:

FIGURE 8.3
The Grief Process.

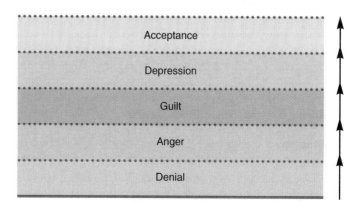

The first stage is denial—we deny what has happened. Denial diminishes as we acknowledge the impact of our loss and the feelings that accompany it. The second stage is anger—feeling helpless and powerless, we strike out and rail against the loss. The third stage is guilt—we turn our anger against ourselves. We feel bad about things we have said or done to hurt the person who has died. We find ourselves left with a sense of unfinished business. In the fourth stage, depression, we feel that nothing will be right again. Looking forward feels impossible. We feel lonely, empty, and isolated. The fifth stage is acceptance—while things will not be the same, we believe that we will make it through and be able to go on with life.[44] The question is, How do we get to stage 5?

The tendency in those who are closest to someone who has suffered a loss is to try to protect the person and shield him or her from sadness. Instead of trying to suppress and walk around sadness, however, we should work to help mourners experience it. For example, even though the death of a family member might make a family turn inward, for the person(s) grieving, expressing feelings to friends who are not directly affected by the loss can help.

Even very young children grieve, although their grief may be different from the grief experienced by adolescents and adults. With help and support, however, people of all ages can handle rather than submerge grief and, as a result, recover from grief's effects and go on with their lives. Part of the process involves constructing an image of the deceased loved one that the bereaved can take with them into their continuing lives.[45] It is the processing of feelings that appears to be key.

Research reveals that we do not simply replace a former partner but, rather, remain loyal to the deceased partner in almost all new relationships that we form, whether the relationship takes the form of a consummate partner, less intimate steady companion, or service provider. Still, reengagement in consummate partnerships and steady companionship is effective in reducing loneliness and helping us fulfill our relational needs.[46]

Men and women handle the death of a partner differently, especially when they are older. The myth is that, in widowhood, women grieve while men replace. Despite the fact that a significant percentage of men and women aged 50 and over attain new partner relationships after divorce or widowhood, older widowed men are more apt to remarry than older widowed women. For some widows, particularly those who, due to their partner's death, are living by themselves for the first time, being alone actually provides a sense of liberation. These women do not want to give this up or use it as trade-off for companionship and caring responsibilities. As a result, some establish living apart together (LAT) relationships, relationships that offer a fulfilling intimate relationship but also ensure a significant degree of autonomy and avoid the unequal demands of caring for a partner that may have previously been experienced. In contrast, widowers view the loneliness they experience after the death of a partner as a sense of deprivation, especially after a life of being cared for by a woman in whom they had entrusted their emotional existence.[47]

How does grief change when, instead of mourning a personal loss, we mourn a public loss? Lately in this country we have suffered a number of significant tragedies. In the course of a few years, we have participated in public mourning for the victims of 9/11, the victims of the second *Challenger* explosion, and the victims of the second Gulf War. How do we cope with

Personalization has hit the casket industry. You can now purchase a casket adorned with scenes of the last supper, your favorite flag, or your favorite musical group. Some critics see these "art caskets" as an expression of self-absorption and narcissism, while others see it as a meaningful way to have the last word in self-expression. What do you think?

❙ *9/11 Memorial.*

such shock and loss? Interestingly, scientists report that we appear to have been numbed by the series of stress inoculations. According to habituation theorists, repeated exposure to a particular stimulus, even a painful or horrific one, evokes less and less reaction with each subsequent exposure. Thus, for those of us who remember the first *Challenger* disaster and the first Gulf War, the subsequent losses were less shocking, and we responded with less intensity. In your opinion, is this a good thing, or does the muted nature of the response reflect a "hardening of the heart that speaks ill of us as human beings"?[48]

Cost-Benefit/Social Exchange Theory and Relationship Development

Though relationships may proceed through stages, they are not always predictable. No relationship is foreordained in heaven or hell for success or failure. Rather, our relationships develop as a consequence of the energy we are willing to commit to them and as a result of what we are willing to do with and for one another.

Unless the people who share a relationship are able to continue to grow together and adapt to their continually changing environment, the relationship may begin to deteriorate at any point. According to **cost-benefit/social exchange theory,** we will work to maintain a relationship only as long as the benefits we perceive for ourselves outweigh the costs.[49] These benefits include feelings of self-worth, a sense of personal growth, a greater sense of security, additional resources for accomplishing tasks, and an increased ability to cope with problems. In comparison, costs include the time spent trying to make the relationship work, psychological and physical stress, and a damaged self-image. We enter our relationships with a **comparison level** in mind; we have

cost-benefit/social exchange theory

the theory that we work to maintain a relationship as long as the benefits we receive outweigh the costs

comparison level

an expectation of the kinds of rewards and profits we believe we ought to derive from a relationship a general idea, standard, or expectation of the kinds of rewards and profits that we believe we ought to get out of the relationship. When the rewards we receive equal or surpass our comparison level, we usually feel satisfied with the relationship. However, we also have a **comparison level for alternatives;** we compare the rewards we get from a current relationship with the ones we think we are able to get from an alternative relationship. If we believe that present relationship rewards are below those we could receive from an alternative relationship, then we might decide to exit our present relationship and enter a new one.

In general, however, when we think of a relationship in economic terms, the greater our rewards or profits and the lower our costs, the more satisfying a relationship will be. Each relationship partner acts out of a self-oriented goal of profit taking.[50] When costs begin to outweigh benefits, we are more and more likely to decide to terminate the relationship. In contrast, when benefits outweigh costs, the relationship will probably continue to develop. Cost-benefit/social exchange theory predicts that the worth of a relationship influences its outcome. Positive relationships will probably endure, whereas negative relationships will probably terminate.

Relational Dialectics Theory

According to relational dialectics theorists, our relationships are not linear but, rather, consist of the oscillation between contradictory goals or desires. During relationship development, communicators seek to meet important goals, some of which may be incompatible. When opposing goals meet, **dialectical tensions** are created. Three central relational dialectical tensions exist between connection and autonomy, predictability and novelty, and openness and privacy.[51] Let us explore each in turn.

Connection versus Autonomy

We desire to be independent of our significant others and to find intimacy with them. We want to be close as well as separate. Perhaps you have found yourself saying the following about a partner. "He barely spent any time with me." "I have no time for myself." "She made me feel trapped." "He just wouldn't commit to being an 'us.'" "I need my freedom." If any of these statements sound familiar, then you and a partner had conflicting desires for connection and independence. Since we want to establish more intimate connections with others we care about, we cherish the sharing of experiences. At the same time, however, we need to preserve an independent identity. We don't want our relationships to destroy our individuality. Some relationships do not survive the connection-autonomy negotiations; instead of working out an acceptable balance that preserves individuality while creating intimacy, partners break up. On the other hand, as a result of resolving their connection-autonomy disagreements, relationship partners can redefine their relationship and become even closer.[52]

Predictability versus Novelty

We desire the excitement of change and the comfort of stability. We want both a routine and spontaneity. Too much routine becomes boring. Perhaps these words sound familiar: "We always do the same things." "I want to do

comparison level for alternatives
the comparing of rewards derived from a current relationship with ones we expect to get from an alternative relationship

dialectical tensions
tensions that occur when opposing goals meet

something different." "I know everything there is to know about her." Variety adds spice to normal routines. The challenge for relationship partners is to find the right mix between the desire for predictability and the need to keep the relationship fresh and interesting.

Openness versus Privacy

We wrestle with tensions between dislosure and silence or concealment. For many of us, complete openness is intolerable to contemplate. While we want to share our inner selves with people we care deeply about, there are times when we don't feel like sharing and desire the preservation of privacy instead. Desiring privacy some of the time doesn't mean a relationship is on the rocks. Our desires for openness and closedness wax and wane. We go through periods of disclosing and periods of withholding.[53] During every stage of our relationship, our desires for openness and privacy can fluctuate.

Resolving Dialectical Tensions

When a relationship is successful, partners are able to manage the dialectical tensions. They can use a number of strategies to accomplish this. First, they can negotiate a balance between connection and autonomy, predictability and novelty, and openness and closedness. Second, they can choose to favor one dialectic and ignore the other. Third, they can segment each of the dialectics by compartmentalizing different areas of their relationship and assigning each dialectic to different times or spheres. Fourth, they can reframe the dialectics by defining them as not contradictory at all.[54] One ineffective way of handing dialectical tensions is to deny that they exist. Instead of confronting the challenges that face the relationship, the partners ignore them.

DECEPTION AND RELATIONSHIP DEVELOPMENT

Are we living in the age of the lie?[55] Over the past few years, photos have been digitally altered to influence or mislead readers or viewers; major corporations, such as Enron, Global Crossing, and Arthur Anderson, have been charged with deceiving stockholders and the public; news reporters have staged stories; and the entertainment industry has based a number of new programs such as *Joe Millionaire* and *The Bachelor,* on a lie. For example, on the reality TV show *Joe Millionaire*, the first "Joe," Evan Marriott, pretended to be a millionaire, when he was actually a rather poorly compensated construction worker. His job was to deceive potential female partners into believing that he had inherited a vast sum of money and then see how his chosen partner reacted when faced with the truth.

While most of us would condemn lying, during the course of a typical week, nearly every one of us lies. How do you explain this?

A lie is the deliberate presentation of information you know not to be true. You can lie by omission or commission. When you lie by omission, you deliberately withhold relevant information, thereby causing people to draw an erroneous conclusion. When you lie by commission, you make a statement you know to be false. Although at times the motivation for lying is to avoid a confrontation or increase one's social desirability, there is no question that the speaker's intention is to deceive one or more receivers when a lie is told.[56]

Consider your feelings about lying. How do you define the word *lie*? To whom would you lie? What kinds of situations call for a lie? How many times in the past month have you lied to someone with whom you share a relationship? How many times were you caught? What happened as a result? While women appear to be more sensitive than men to relational deception, and develop more negative attitudes to the deceiver than do men, exposed instances of deception cause members of either sex to view the target significantly less favorably.[57]

Lying appears to be commonplace in our society. Some 91 percent of Americans confess that they regularly don't tell the truth; 20 percent admit they can't get through a day without telling a conscious, premeditated lie. Approximately a quarter of all serious lies are told to cover up an affair.[58] Thus, we lie not only to strangers but also to those we care about. For example, when dating his future wife, a man falsely told her that his middle name was Algonquin and that the middle names of his brothers and sisters were Iroquois, Dakota, and Mohawk, merely to make himself seem more interesting to her.

When we lie to someone, we do not merely deliver wrong information; we also intentionally seek to deceive him or her. Sissela Bok, the author of *Lying*, says that, when we lie, it is both our hope and our expectation that we will succeed in making the target of our efforts believe something we do not believe.[59] This description is supported by the communication theorists Steven A. McCornack and Timothy R. Levine, who note: "Deception is the deliberate falsification or omission of information by a communicator, with the intent being to mislead the conversational partner."[60]

It is rare to tell someone only one lie. To sustain our original lie, we usually need to tell more lies. As Bok writes, "The liar always has more mending to do." And the liar has to expend a great deal of energy remembering to whom he or she told what and why.

Why do people lie? Of course, the reasons are as numerous as the situations that precipitate a need to lie in the first place. However, two reasons appear to dominate: Most people lie to gain a reward or to avoid punishment. What kinds of reward are we after in our relationships, and what kinds of punishment are we trying to avoid?

According to some researchers, we lie to continue to satisfy the basic needs fulfilled by our relationships, to increase or decrease desired and undesired affiliations, to protect our self-esteem, and to achieve personal satisfaction.[61] Most often, when we lie, we benefit ourselves, although a percentage of our lies are designed to protect the person or persons we are lying to, and an even smaller percentage benefit a third party.

Why is lying a strategy we use? We may use lying as a strategy because lies help us manage what we perceive to be difficult situations, situations that make us more vulnerable than we would like to be.

Are we good at detecting lies? Research says we are not. In one study, a researcher had subjects watch their romantic partners describe another person as attractive or unattractive. Other subjects who did not know the romantic partner also watched the interaction. Results revealed that the subjects with the romantic attachment were considerably worse at spotting their partners' lies than were the strangers. If the romantic partners were asked indirect questions, however, such as how suspicious they were or if they received enough

Why are you lying to me who are my friend?
—**Moroccan proverb**

In Tennessee Williams's play A Streetcar Named Desire, *one of the characters—Blanche DuBois—says, "I don't tell the truth. I tell what ought to be truth." Does this practice help or hinder the development of relationships? Why?*

How is a liar like a counterfeiter?

information from their partners, the answers indicated that at some level they had picked up the deception, and picked it up better than strangers did. It seems, without being asked such questions, they were reluctant to call their partner a liar.[62]

How does a lie affect our relationships once it is uncovered? Imagine sharing a relationship, no matter how ideal in other aspects, in which you could never rely on the words or gestures of the other person. Information exchanged in that relationship would be virtually worthless, and the feelings expressed would be practically meaningless. No one likes to be duped. No one likes to appear gullible. No one likes to play the fool. When someone does deceive us, we become suspicious and resentful; we are disappointed both in the other person and in ourselves.

As Sissela Bok observed, people who discover they have been lied to "are resentful, disappointed and suspicious. They feel wronged; they are wary of new overtures." Further, Bok notes, people "look back on their past beliefs and actions in the new light of the discovered lies." While bending the truth to sustain a relationship may be a common practice, unless trust and truthfulness are present, it is only a matter of time before the relationship will die. Lying is likely to precipitate a relationship crisis. Many relationship breakups are attributed directly to the discovery of a major deception.

Quite simply, lies are fundamentally destructive and often kill a relationship. Few factors have more influence on a relationship than trust. In fact, the reason most commonly cited for terminating a relationship is a loss of trust in one's partner. And nearly all breakups due to deception are reported to be initiated by the recipient of the lie.[63]

Focus on Service Learning

Speak at a local Parents and Teachers meeting about the importance of honesty in relationships.

Trust and Relationship Development

Trust gives us the ability to rise above our doubts.

—**John K. Rempel, John G. Holmes**

There is a potential for trouble in any relationship. One cause of trouble is lying. Another, equally important, cause is misreading the other person's desires with regard to the depth of the relationship—that is, how much he or she trusts you at a particular point in time. Trust is an outgrowth of interpersonal communication. It is a reflection of how secure we are that a person will act in a predicted and desirable way. When we trust another person, we have confidence that he or she will behave as we expect and that the person will not use whatever personal information we have confided to him or her to harm us. Some of us are more trusting than others.

Skill BUILDER

Lies, Lies, Lies

1. Report on an experience of being lied to. Indicate who lied to you, the nature of the lie, and your reactions when you found out you had been lied to. How did the lie affect your relationship with the liar?

2. Report on an experience when you lied to someone else. Indicate whom you lied to, the nature of the lie, your reason for lying, and the other person's reaction when he or she found out you had lied. How did your lie affect the relationship you shared?

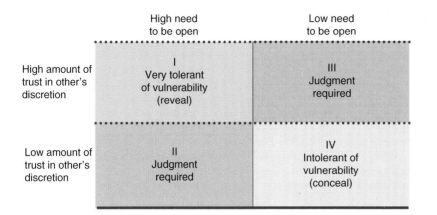

FIGURE 8.4
Rawlins's Trust Matrix.

Source: Matrix created by William K. Rawlins from "Openness as Problematic in Ongoing Friendships: Two Conversational Dilemmas," by W. K. Rawlins, *Communication Monographs* 50 (March 1983), p.11. Reprinted by permission of National Communication Association.

How trusting are you? Whether or not you trust another person depends on whether prior relationships have reinforced trusting behavior or consolidated your fears about the risks of exhibiting trusting behavior. Trust creates a paradox: To be able to trust, we must be willing to take the risk of trusting. When we take the risk, we risk being wrong. If we fail to take the risk, however, we can never be right.[64] The degree of trust you place in another person to accept information you disclose to him or her without hurting you or the relationship is your **tolerance of vulnerability.** Your tolerance of vulnerability varies from person to person, topic to topic, and situation to situation.

Researcher William Rawlins designed a matrix, shown in Figure 8.4, that we can use to analyze the amount of trust we place in different people at different times in a relationship's development. We can also use this matrix to determine which of our relationships have more stability or staying power than others. A relationship in which the partners have difficulty trusting one another is a troubled relationship.

tolerance of vulnerability
the degree of trust you place in another person to accept information you disclose without hurting you or the relationship

LAUGHTER AS AN INTERPERSONAL TOOL

Like trust, laughter is an interpersonal tool. Every day we give and receive social laughter while interacting with friends, co-workers, and lovers. Laughter punctuates our conversations so regularly that we are apt not to think about or notice it. However, if laughter disappeared from any of our important relationships, we would miss it.

In the section "A Special Case: Relationship Termination Caused by Death," we discussed the grief that accompanies the death of someone we love. Even in grief, however, humor can play a part. Humor can help us cope with anything. Once you are able to laugh again, you know that you are regaining control. For example, in the aftermath of the 9/11 terrorist attacks, it was then mayor of New York Rudy Giuliani's appearance on the TV show *Saturday Night Live* that signaled an end to the mourning.[65] Humor offers us a fresh perspective on events large and small.

Ethics & COMMUNICATION

Relationships, Trust, and the Workplace

What do you perceive to be the advantages and disadvantages of workplace romances?

How do you feel about entering into a romantic relationship with a co-worker or boss? While people who work together probably already share a number of interests and the work environment provides a ready-made setting for meeting and getting to know a potential partner, do you think you can make a relationship work in which you spend not only your worktime but also your free-time together? How do

you imagine the relationship you shared would affect others who work with you? How do you imagine it would affect you and your career?

What if you were not the person having such a romantic relationship? What if it were your boss and another co-worker? Or what if it were two of your co-workers? Do you think either relationship would impact you and your chances for career success? Which do you think would affect you more?

According to Dr. Robert R. Provine, laughs are rhythmic bursts of social glue.[66] He reports that much of what we laugh at in life is predominantly the stuff of social banter, not necessarily particularly funny or clever. Laughter, however, is contagious. When we hear laughter, we usually start laughing ourselves. Its infectious nature can have dramatic effects on our relationships. We, not only our relationship partners, laugh at what we say; in fact, the average speaker laughs 46 percent more frequently than do those listening to him or her. While laughter does not intrude on speech, it does provide its punctuation. It helps us synchronize our moods and perhaps our actions. As such, it may also help solidify our relationships.

Like any relationship tool, laughter has a downside too. The opposite of joyful laughter is jeering, malicious laughter, laughter that is designed to punish, belittle, or exclude rather than include another. In this case, laughter, rather than expressing our sociability, signals our disdain for and power over another person.

When it comes to the use of humor in our relationships, there are wide laughter variations based on sex. A man talking with a male listener laughs only marginally more than his interaction partner. A woman talking with a woman listener laughs somewhat more than her partner. And a male speaker with a female listener laughs less often than does the woman. However, when a woman speaks to a man, she laughs much more than her male partner.[67] Why do you think that is so?

Media WISE

Tracking Laughs and Laugh Tracks

Observe a favorite television talk show. Note when people laugh on the show and why, identify the kinds of comments that precipitate laughter, count whether women laugh more than men or vice versa, and notice whether a person laughs more while speaking or while listening. Also note where in the conversation laughter occurs and what its effect is.

Next, do the same for two main characters in a TV sitcom. In addition, identify where the major laugh-track laughs occur. In the sitcom you have chosen, are more of the laughs directed at men or at women?

TECHNOLOGY AND OUR RELATIONSHIPS

The Internet created a new social space for person-to-person interaction.[68] While men initially led the way into online communication, women are now estimated to constitute approximately 50 percent of online users. Thus, over time, it appears that male and female usage has equalized.[69] Technology is enabling men and women alike to initiate, sustain, and end relationships in new ways. We now have different options when it comes to developing or terminating our relationships. In fact, while we still have singles bars, singles cruises, parties, and personal ads, many relationships now begin on the Internet. In addition to an abundance of chat rooms, there has been a proliferation of commercial Web sites focused on helping people meet. In December 2003, for example, 26 million people visited online dating sites, and in 2002, the online personals category became the largest paid-content category on the Internet. Even Hallmark Cards has cards linked to Internet dating.[70] We appear to be using electronic places to look for love.

In addition, users of newsgroups also form friendships or relationships with persons they meet on line. In fact, approximately 25 percent of the people in one newsgroup study reported that they communicated with their partners a minimum of three or four times weekly.[71] While women are more likely than men to form personal relationships online, persons of both sexes establish both friendships and romantic relationships in cyberspace.[72] Although the computer probably will not replace face-to-face interaction, the relationships begun in cyberspace may transfer to real space. In fact, a number of relationships begun in cyberspace develop into extended romances and marriage.[73] Thus, the computer presents us with different options when it comes to developing or terminating our relationships.

There are a number of key differences between face-to-face and online communication that can impede relationship development. First, unless we exchange photographs or video, the person with whom we are connected in cyberspace remains invisible to us. Second, since we cannot see most of the nonverbal behavior that accompanies another person's message, we may misinterpret the message's meaning. Third, because we control the pace of online interaction, some of the spontaneity as well as the immediate feedback that characterize face-to-face communication making it interesting are missing. Fourth, because we do not have access to as much information (verbal and nonverbal) as face-to-face interaction provides, we may find it even more difficult to decide if we can trust the person with whom we are relating.

Despite these drawbacks, for many users, being able to develop relationships online complements face-to-face relationships and has certain benefits. One teenager even notes that it is easier to begin a relationship online: "It's easier to talk to girls on the Internet than in school. Sometimes I can't talk well in person. It doesn't come out like I want it."[74]

According to Sherry Turkle, author of *Life on the Screen: Identity in the Age of the Internet,* when people are online, they tend to express different aspects of themselves in different settings. They find ways to conceive of themselves not as single and unitary but, rather, as having many aspects. As people form new relationships, they come to see themselves as the sum of their distributed presence on the windows they open on their screens.[75]

In addition, as more and more people make their way online, they are discovering that the anonymity that characterizes cyberspace enables those who communicate on the Internet to disregard gender, race, and appearance. Instead, whether or not an online relationship continues depends on the ability to build rapport. At least until people meet face-to-face, looks are placed on the back burner.

On the other hand, simply because of the inelasticity of time, Internet use may substantially reduce face-to-face interpersonal interaction and communication, contributing to our sense of alienation.[76] Indeed, some observers note that heavy Internet users become alienated from normal social contacts, even cutting off such traditional interactions as the Internet becomes the predominate social factor in their lives. As a result, they believe that increased Internet use will ultimately lead to loneliness. In contrast, others counter that it is those people who are already lonely who spend the most time online.[77] What do your experiences with the Internet tell you?

Adding to this debate are those who wonder if e-mail makes contact less of an intrusion. For example, when compared with an e-mail, a telephone call may be perceived as an outright invasion. Now, rather than calling another person and wondering if it's a good time for that person to talk to us, we can send an e-mail and that person can get back to us when it's convenient.[78]

distance relating
relating with persons via e-mail, chat rooms, and instant messages

Many believe that e-mail, chat rooms, instant messages, and the Internet, in addition to enabling us to connect with our friends, are also strengthening family connections by facilitating our contact. They enable us to engage in **distance relating** with family members who live far away. What is more, they are also helping the homebound overcome conditions that make them feel isolated and lonely. While the homebound may not be able to meet in person with others because of their situation, they are now able to initiate and sustain a number of surrogate online contacts. Online relationships also have a dark side. Sometimes when clicking their way into online relationships and support groups, the people in need elicit outpourings of sympathy not only from the compassionate and from fellow sufferers but also from incorrigible fakes who lie their way into networks of people with real troubles who have come to care about one another. For example,

e-SEARCH

Meeting Online

In your opinion, does communicating over the Internet help build social skills? If so, how? If not, why not? How does the fact that you do not have to reveal who you really are or what your background is affect your ability to develop meaningful relationships with others in cyberspace? When interacting online, do you find that you are likely to confine yourself to meeting only those who share your interests? Do you prefer, for example, to hang out in chat rooms with virtual clones of yourself, or do you seek more diversity in the online relationships you establish? In which setting do you find it easier to speak to others—online or offline? Why?

If you had the choice to initiate a relationship online or face-to-face, which would you choose? What relationship stages, if any, do you find more conducive to online communication? Explain why.

"*You can access me by saying simply 'Agnes.' It is not necessary to add 'dot com.'*"

teenagers present themselves as adults, poor people present themselves as wealthy, and some adults who want to have relationships with children or teens present themselves as members of these groups.[79] In effect, the ease with which one can deceive another person online leads some users to abuse the benefits offered by anonymity. Unfortunately, in addition to the relational benefits it presents, the Internet also lends itself to personal misrepresentation and deception.[80]

What is more, a 2003 study from the Pew Internet and American Life Project revealed that 42 percent of American adults assert that they are not connected to the Internet. A large percentage of these (20 percent) are "Net evaders": people living in Internet-connected homes where others go online. Reasons given for remaining offline include limited free-time, fear that it will take over their lives, and a desire for face-to-face contact. The Pew study also revealed that 17 percent of nonusers are Net dropouts, persons who became disillusioned with the online world.[81] Are you a member of either of these two groups?

IMPROVING YOUR RELATIONSHIP SATISFACTION

Our relationships can contribute to feelings of happiness or unhappiness, elation or depression. They can enrich and stimulate us, or they can limit and harm us. To enhance your ability to develop relationships that satisfy, follow these guidelines.

Actively Seek Information from Others and Reinforce Others Attempting to Seek Information from You

People who fail to initiate contacts or fail to reinforce the conversational attempts of others are less likely to build stable foundations for effective relationships. Passive, restrained communicators are simply more likely to remain chronically lonely. Although we all experience short-term loneliness from time to time, sustained chronic loneliness leads to social apathy, which in turn increases loneliness.

Recognize the Characteristics of Friendship

friendships

relationships characterized by enjoyment, acceptance, trust, respect, mutual assistance, confidences, understanding, and spontaneity

People who share effective **friendships** report that the following qualities are present: enjoyment (they enjoy each other's company most of the time), acceptance (they accept each other as they are), trust (both assume that one will act in the other's best interest), respect (each assumes that the other will exercise good judgment in making life choices), mutual assistance (they are willing to assist and support each other), confidences (they share experiences and feelings with each other), understanding (they have a sense of what the

Our relationships can contribute to our feelings of happiness.

other thinks is important and why the other behaves as he or she does), and spontaneity (they feel free to be themselves).[83]

Recognize That Relationships Evolve

Ours is a mobile and increasingly technological society in which each change we experience has the potential to bring us different relationships. Be prepared for changes in relationships; recognize that in our lives we are likely to experience a certain amount of turnover and change. As we grow and develop, so will our relationships.

Know When to Sever a Relationship

While one party to a relationship may desire to sustain it, not all relationships or connections are meant to continue. When a relationship is draining our energies and our confidence, or when it becomes unhealthy, we need to extricate ourselves from it before it destroys us.

Recognize That Communication Is the Lifeblood of a Relationship

Without communication, relationships shrivel and die. Any relationship that is worth your time and energy depends on effective communication to sustain and nourish it. Your desire and motivation to communicate are key ingredients in the establishment and growth of a relationship.[84]

Revisiting Chapter Objectives

1. **Explain why we need interpersonal relationships.**   Communication is one variable common to all relationships. As a result of communication, we establish and nurture or withdraw from and end our relationships. Relationships play many roles in our lives. They fulfill our needs for inclusion, control, and affection.

2. **Define and discuss the following terms: *inclusion, control,* and *affection.*** We need to feel that others take an interest in us, that they view us as capable of exerting control over our lives, and that we are lovable. It is through conversation that we establish, maintain, and end our relationships.

THE Wrap-Up

3. **Explain and distinguish among social penetration, cost-benefit theory, and relational dialectics theory.**   Every relationship we share is unique and varies in breadth (how many topics we discuss with the other person) and depth (how much we are willing to reveal to the other person about our feelings). Most relationships develop according to a social penetration model, beginning with narrow breadth and shallow depth; over time, some relationships increase in breadth and depth, becoming wider, more intimate, or both. Social exchange theory holds that we work to maintain those relationships that yield the greatest personal profits and fewest costs. Relational dialectics explores the oscillation that occurs between conflicting relationship goals.

4. **Discuss and distinguish among 10 stages of relationships.**   Researchers have also identified a number of stages our relationships may pass through: initiating, experimenting, intensifying, integrating, bonding, differentiating, circumscribing, stagnating, avoiding, and termination. Note that a relationship may stabilize at any stage. When the participants disagree about the point of stabilization, problems are likely to arise.

5. **Discuss how deception, gender, and technology affect interpersonal communication.**   Relationships are also affected by gender and cultural preferences, lies or deception, vulnerability and trust, and even technological innovations.

6. **Identify ways to enhance your satisfaction with your relationships.**   It is important to recognize that how we communicate plays a key part in determining whether our relationships are as effective and rewarding for us as they could be.

Resources for Further Inquiry and Reflection

To apply your understanding of how the principles in Chapter 8 are at work in our daily lives, consult the following resources for further inquiry and reflection. Or, if you prefer, choose any other appropriate resource. Then connect the ideas expressed in your chosen selection with the communication concepts and issues you are learning about both in and out of class.

 Listen to Me

"Crash into Me" (The Dave Matthews Band)
"Don't Know Why" (Norah Jones)
"She's Leaving Home" (The Beatles)
"Your Song" (Elton John)
"You've Got a Friend" (James Taylor)

These songs explore close relationships. Choose one and discuss the speaker's beliefs about his or her role in the relationship.

 View Me

The Boiler Room   *Secrets and Lies*
Wall Street   *House of Kings*
Unfaithful   *When Harry Met Sally*
Sweet November

These films explore the stages of relationships and why we maintain or end a relationship, as well as the role honesty and deception play in relationship building or termination. Choose one film and use it to discuss the factors just identified.

Read Me

Edward Albee. *Who's Afraid of Virginia Woolf?* New York: Dramatist Play Service, 1962.

Robert Harling. *Steel Magnolias.* New York: Dramatist Play Service, 1998.

William Shakespeare. *The Taming of the Shrew.* Edited by Robert Heilman. New York: Penguin Books, 1998.

Deborah Tannen. *You Just Don't Understand: Women and Men in Conversation.* New York: Ballentine, 1991.

Tennessee Williams. *A Streetcar Named Desire.* New York: New American Library, 1947.

These works explore the nature of friendships and/or intimate relationships. Choose one and use it to describe how the nature of the communication shared by people contributes to the health or toxicity of their relationship.

 Tell Me

Share with the class the insights you gained from your chosen Listen to Me, View Me, or Read Me selection.

In a brief presentation, respond to the following questions. What do consider the most acceptable rationale for lying? Do you think it is more acceptable to lie if the lie will benefit you or if the lie will save others from hurt?

Key Chapter Terminology

Use the Communication Works CD-ROM and the Online Learning Center at www.mhhe.com/gamble8 *to further your knowledge of the following terminology.*

affection 235
autistic society 233
avoiding 243
bonding 242
breadth 238
circumscribing 243
comparison level 246
comparison level for alternatives 247
control 235
cost-benefit/social exchange theory 246
depth 238
dialectical tensions 247
differentiating 242
distance relating 254
experimenting 241

friendships 256
grief process 244
high-tech–high-touch society 234
inclusion 234
initiating 241
integrating 242
intensifying 242
interpersonal relationship 233
loneliness 234
phatic communication 236
social penetration theory 238
stagnating 243
termination 244
tolerance of vulnerability 251

Communication
Works

www.mhhe.com/gamble8

Test Your Understanding

Go to the *Self Quizzes* on the Communication Works CD-ROM and the book's Online Learning Center at www.mhhe.com/gamble8.

Communication
Works

Notes

1. Virginia Satir. *The New Peoplemaking.* Palo Alto, CA: Science and Behavior Books, 1998, p. 51.
2. John L. Locke. *The De-Voicing of Society: Why We Don't Talk to Each Other Anymore.* New York: Simon & Schuster, 1998.

www.mhhe.com/gamble8

3. Bruce Headlam. "Awash in All These Words, Will We Forget How to Talk?" *New York Times,* December 17, 1998, p. G-12.

4. John Naisbitt. *Megatrends.* New York: Warner, 1984, pp. 35–52.

5. See Debra Lynn Veal. "Electric Friendship, Information—Even Love." *Sunday Record,* April 3, 1994.

6. See Duane Stoltzfus. "Meeting á la Modem: Personal Computer Goes Interpersonal." *Sunday Record,* December 19, 1993.

7. Catherine Greenman. "From Yakety-Yak to Clackety-Clack." *New York Times,* November 5, 1998, pp. G-1, G-7.

8. See Judy Jeannin. "Sister Can You Spare a Moment?" *Sunday Record,* January 30, 1994.

9. J. O'Neil. "Help Others for a Longer Life." *New York Times,* November 12, 2002, p. F6.

10. William C. Schutz. *The Interpersonal Underworld.* Palo Alto, CA: Science and Behavior Books, 1966, pp. 18–20.

11. Steve Duck. *Human Relationships,* 3rd ed. Thousand Oaks. CA: Sage, 1999, p. 57.

12. *Time,* December 20, 1993, p. 15.

13. See, for example, Robert A. Bell. "Conversational Involvement and Loneliness." *Communication Monographs* 52, 1985 pp. 218–235.

14. Robert A. Bell and Michael Roloff. "Making a Love Connection: Loneliness and Communication Competence in the Dating Marketplace." *Communication Quarterly* 39:1, winter 1991, pp. 58–74.

15. Anna Quindlen. "The Human Touch." *New York Times,* May 14, 1994, p. 21.

16. Schutz, p. 24.

17. Andrea Heiman. "Flirting Still Has Its Attractions." *Sunday Record,* March 20, 1994.

18. Robert E. Nofsinger. *Everyday Conversation.* Newbury Park, CA: Sage, 1991, p. 1.

19. See Deborah Cameron. *Good Talk? Living and Working in a Communication Culture.* Thousand Oaks, CA: Sage, 2000.

20. S. W. Duck and J. T. Wood, eds. *Confronting Relationship Challenges,* vol. 5, *Understanding Relationship Processes.* Thousand Oaks, CA: Sage, 1995.

21. For a detailed discussion of difficult conversations, see Douglas Stone, Bruce Patton, and Sheila Heen. *Difficult Conversations.* New York: Viking, 1999.

22. Mark Heintzman. "Nonverbal Rapport-Building Behaviors." *Management Communication Quarterly* 7:2, November 1993, pp. 181–208.

23. See Sheila McNamee. *Relational Responsibility: Resources for Sustainable Dialogue.* Thousand Oaks, CA: Sage, 1998.

24. Anita L. Vangelisti and Mary A. Banski. "Couples' Debriefing Conversations: The Impact of Gender, Occupation, and Demographic Characteristics." *Family Relations* 42:2, April 1993, pp. 149–157.

25. Karen Shafer. "Talk in the Middle: Two Conversational Skills for Friendship." *English Journal* 82:1, January 1993, pp. 53–55.

26. William B. Gudykunst. *Bridging Differences: Effective Intergroup Communication,* 3rd ed. Thousand Oaks, CA: Sage, 1998.

27. Tamar Lewin. "Poll of Teen-Agers: Battle of the Sexes on Roles in Family." *New York Times,* July 11, 1994.

28. Heiman.

29. Heiman.

30. Julia T. Wood and C. Inman. "In a Different Mode: Recognizing Male Modes of Closeness." *Journal of Applied Communication Research,* August 1993.

31. Julia T. Wood. *Gendered Lives,* 3rd ed. Belmont, CA: Wadsworth, 1999, p. 201.

32. Deborah Tannen. *The Argument Culture: Moving from Debate to Dialogue.* New York: Random House, 1998, pp. 186–187.

33. J. D. Ragsdale. "Gender, Satisfaction Level, and the Use of Relational Maintenance Strategies in Marriage." *Communication Monographs* 63, 1996, pp. 354–369.

34. See M. Hecht, S. Ribeau, and J. Alberts. "An Afro-American Perspective on Interethnic Communication." *Communication Monographs* 56, 1989, pp. 385–410; and M. Hecht, S. Ribeau, and M. Sedano. "A Mexican-American Perspective on Interethnic Communication." *International Journal of Intercultural Relations* 14, 1990, pp. 31–55.

35. H. C. Triandis. *Culture and Social Behavior.* New York: McGraw-Hill, 1994, p. 30.

36. M. J. Collier. "Communication Competence Problematics in Ethnic Friendships." *Communication Monographs* 63, 1996, pp. 314–336.

37. I. Altman and D. A. Taylor. *Social Penetration: The Development of Interpersonal Relationships.* New York: Holt, Rinehart & Winston, 1973.

38. Mark L. Knapp and Anita L. Vangelisti. *Interpersonal Communication and Human Relationships,* 2nd ed. Boston: Allyn & Bacon, 1992, p. 33.

39. Alan Garner. *Conversationally Speaking.* New York: McGraw-Hill, 1981, p. 69.

40. Knapp and Vangelisti.

41. Michael Korda. "Small Talk." *Signature,* 1986, p. 78.

42. See Lawrence B. Rosenfield and Daniella Bordaray-Sciolino. "Self-Disclosure as a Communication Strategy during Relationship Termination." Paper presented at the national meeting of the Speech Communication Association, Denver, CO, November 1985.

43. Rosenfield and Bordaray-Sciolino.

44. See, for example, H. S. Kushner. *When Bad Things Happen to Good People.* New York: Schocken Books, 1981.

45. Erica Goode. "Experts Offer Fresh Insights into the Mind of the Grieving Child." *New York Times,* March 28, 2000, pp. F7, F12.

46. N. Stevens. "Re-engaging: New Partnerships in Late-Life Widowhood." *Aging International* 27:4, spring 2003, pp. 27–43.

47. See J. De Jong Gierveld. "The Dilemma of Repartnering: Considerations of Older Men and Women Entering New Intimate Relationships in Later Life." *Aging International* 27:4, spring 2003, pp. 61–79; S. G. Karlsson, and K. Borell. "Intimacy and Autonomy, Gender and Ageing: Living Apart Together." *Aging International,* 27:4, spring 2003, pp. 11–27; and K. Davidson. "Gender Differences in New Partnership Choices and Constraints for Older Widows and Widowers." *Aging International* 27:4, spring 2003, pp. 43–61.

48. See Sharon Begley. "How Humans React When Bad Things Occur Again and Again." *Wall Street Journal,* February 7, 2003, p. B1.

49. J. W. Thibaut and H. H. Kelly. *The Social Psychology of Groups.* New York: Wiley, 1959.

50. See Richard West and Lynn H. Turner. *Introducing Communication Theory: Analysis and Application.* Mountain View CA: Mayfield, 2000, pp. 180–190.

51. L. A. Baxter and B. M. Montgomery. *Relating: Dialogues and Dialectics.* New York: Guilford Press, 1996; and L. A. Baxter. "Dialectical Contradictions in Relationship Development. *Journal of Social and Personal Relationships* 7, 1990, pp. 69–88.

52. See also Sandra Petronio, ed. *Balancing the Secrets of Private Disclosures.* Mahwan, NJ: Lawrence Erlbaum Associates, 1999.

53. C. A. VanLear. "Testing a Cyclical Model of Communicative Openness in Relationship Development." *Communication Monographs* 58, 1991, pp. 337–361.

54. J. T. Wood, L. Dendy, E. Dordek, M. Germany, and S. Varallo. "Dialectic of Difference: A Thematic Analysis of Intimates' Meanings for Differences." In K. Carter and M. Presnell, eds. *Interpretive Approaches to Interpersonal Communication.* New York: State University of New York Press, 1994, pp. 115–136.

55. See, for example, L. Anolli, M. Balconi, and Rita Ciceri. "Deceptive Miscommunication Theory (DeMIT): A New Model for the Analysis of Deceptive Communication." In A. Luigi, R. Ciceri, et al. eds. *Say Not to Say: New Perspectives on Miscommunication. Studies in New Technologies and Practices in Communication.* Amsterdam, Netherlands Antilles: IOS Press. pp. 73–100.

56. See J. F. Roiger. "Using Expectations and Causes of Behavior: Naïve Perceptions of Differing Acts of Deception." Paper presented at the annual meeting of the National Communication Association, New Orleans, LA, November 2002.

57. See Erica Goode. "To Tell the Truth, It's Awfully Hard to Spot a Liar." *New York Times,* May 11, 1999, pp. F-1, F-9; and William G. Powers. "The Effects of Gender and Consequence upon Perceptions of Deceivers." *Communication Quarterly* 41:3, summer 1993, pp. 328–337.

58. Goode; Janny Scott. "Bright, Shining or Dark: American Way of Lying." *New York Times,* August 16, 1998, p. WK-3; and Bernice Kanner. "Americans Lie, or So They Say." *New York Times,* June 2, 1996, p. 43.

59. Sissela Bok. *Lying.* New York: Pantheon, 1978. See also Sissela Bok. *Secrets.* New York: Random House, 1989.

60. Steven A. McCornack and Timothy R. Levine. "When Lies Are Uncovered: Emotional and Relational Outcomes of Discovered Deception." *Communication Monographs* 57, June 1990, p. 119.

61. C. Camden, M. T. Motley, and A. Wilson. "White Lies in Interpersonal Communication: A Taxonomy and Preliminary Investigation of Social Motivations." *Western Journal of Speech Communication* 48, 1984, pp. 309–325.

62. Goode.

63. For an extended discussion of deception, see Dariusz Galasinski. *The Language of Deception.* Thousand Oaks, CA: Sage, 2000.

64. J. K. Rempel and J. G. Holmes. "How Do I Trust Thee?" *Psychology Today,* February 1986.

65. D. Howlett. "It Hurts Not to Laugh." *USA Today,* March 4, 2003, p. 9D.

66. Natalie Angier. "Laughs: Rhythmic Bursts of Social Glue." *New York Times,* February 27, 1996, pp. C-1, C-5.

67. Angier. Also see Regina Barreca. *They Used to Call Me Snow White . . . but I Drifted: Women's Strategic Use of Humor.* New York: Penguin Books, 1991.

68. I. Ibez. "Online Chat Rooms: Virtual Spaces of Interaction for Socially Oriented People." *CyberPsychology and Behavior* 5:1, February 2002, pp. 43–52.

69. "Readers Love the Net Effect." *USA Today,* May 22, 2000, p. 3D.

70. Patricia Winters Lauro. "Online Dating, a Hushed Subject but a Roaring Business, Goes Very Public in a Marketing Battle." *New York Times,* January 27, 2003, p. C9.

71. M. R. Parks and K. Floyd. "Making Friends in Cyberspace." *Journal of Communication* 46, winter, 1996, pp. 80–97.

72. Parks and Floyd; and M. L. Nice and R. Katzev. "Internet Romantics: The Frequency and Nature of Romantic On-line Relationships." *CyberPsychology and Behavior* 1, fall 1998, pp. 217–233.

73. A. N. Markham. *Life Online: Researching Real Experience in Virtual Space.* Walnut Creek, CA: AltaMira, 1998.

74. Scott McCartney. "Society's Sub Cultures Meet by Modem." *Wall Street Journal,* December 8, 1994, p. B1.

75. Sherry Turkle. *Life on the Screen: Identity in the Age of the Internet.* New York: Simon & Schuster, 1995; and Katie Hafner. "At Heart of a Cyberstudy, the Human Essence." *New York Times,* June 18, 1998, p. G-9.

76. N. H. Nie. "Sociability, Interpersonal Relations, and the Internet: Reconciling Conflicting Findings." *American Behavioral Scientist* 45:3, November 2001, pp. 420–426.

77. Y. Amichai-Hamburger and E. Ben-Artzi. "Loneliness and Internet Use." *Computers in Human Behavior* 19:1, January 2003, pp. 71–81.

78. See, for example, Esther Dyson. *A Design for Living in the Digital Age.* New York: Broadway Books, 1998.

79. See, for example, M. Lewis. "Faking It." *New York Times Magazine,* July 15, 2001, pp. 32–37, 44, 61–63.

80. Denise Grady. "Faking Pain and Suffering in Internet Support Groups." *New York Times,* April 23, 1998, pp. G-1, G-7.

81. Katie Hafner. "Eluding the Web's Snare." *New York Times,* April 17, 2003, pp. G1, G5.

82. Steve Duck. *Understanding Relationships.* New York: Guilford Press, 1991, pp. 1–2.

83. Keith E. Davis. "Near and Dear: Friendship and Love Compared." *Psychology Today,* February 1985, pp. 22–30.

84. For a discussion of how to enhance the teaching of relationships in the basic course, see Diane Tkinson Gorcyca. "Enhancing the Instruction of Relationship Development in the Basic Communication Course." Paper presented at the annual meeting of the Speech Communication Association, Miami Beach, FL, November 18–21, 1993.

Person to Person: Relationships in Context

After finishing this chapter, you should be able to

1. Identify and distinguish among the following relationship life contexts: acquaintanceship, friendship, and romantic, family, and work relationships.

2. Define and distinguish among the following terms: *emotional intelligence, emotion state,* and *emotion trait.*

3. Explain how attraction, proximity, reinforcement, similarity, complementarity, and the suppression and disclosure of feelings can affect the development of relationships.

4. Define *assertiveness, nonassertiveness,* and *aggressiveness* and explain how feelings can be handled effectively during conflicts.

5. Identify behaviors that foster or impede the development of a relationship based on assertiveness.

6. Draw and explain a relationship window.

7. Create and explain a DESC script.

There are no empty people, only people who have deadened their feelings and feel empty.
—Theodore Isaac Rubin

. . . many of our feelings in relationships are contextually and situationally driven.
—Steve Duck

emotional intelligence
the ability to motivate oneself, to control impulses, to recognize and regulate one's moods, to empathize, and to hope

For years, many of us have watched MTV's *The Real World,* a reality-type program in which a number of strangers are relocated into a comfortable home or apartment and agree to live there together for a period of time. A camera follows their every move as they get to know one another and establish a variety of interpersonal relationships. Some establish real friendships. Some date and end up lovers. Others dislike each other intensely and find themselves enemies. We observe as their layers of anonymity are peeled away, and we listen as the "houseguests" share some rather raw, emotionally intense interactions. We imagine what it would be like to be them. More recently, a new reality program competed for our attention. In *Married by America,* individuals gave up their right to select a romantic partner, opting instead to be united by a poll of viewers. Can you imagine yourself agreeing to have viewers select the person you might marry? In each of these shows, the persons involved displayed their emotions for all of us to witness. Over time, some participants demonstrated that they could handle their emotions, while others acted more like very young children, revealing an inability to control their emotions and a general lack of emotional intelligence. **Emotional intelligence** is a relatively recent concept. It can be defined as the ability to motivate oneself, to control impulses, to recognize and regulate one's moods, to empathize, and to hope.[1] Our success in our relationships depends to a great degree on how emotionally intelligent or mature we are. If, for example, we can understand and manage our emotions, such as anger and jealousy, and be sensitive to others' feelings as well, then we can also improve our ability to get along with a broad array of people in diverse contexts.

Thus, while this chapter explores relationships in context, it is also about emotions and feelings—your emotions and feelings and the emotions and feelings of people with whom you share relationships in different contexts.

As communication theorist Steve Duck writes, people talk in order to "express deeper emotion in relationships or to start a relationship in the first place."[2] Relationships involve a huge amount of emotional work.

RELATIONSHIP CONTEXTS: FROM FRIENDSHIP TO ROMANCE TO FAMILY TO WORK

Our relationships are colored by the life contexts in which they occur. By exploring the different kinds of relationships we share, we can come to understand how we strike a balance between intimacy and distance with the people we interact with regularly, whether that interaction occurs with friends, lovers, family members, or persons with whom we work. We will see how we have been socialized to express or limit our expression of emotions about relationships, depending on the relational context we find ourselves in.

Relationships, Uncertainty Reduction, and Predicted Outcomes

No matter how close we eventually become with another person, we start out as strangers. What is your goal when you meet someone for the first time? According to uncertainty reduction theory, when we initially meet someone, our relationship is characterized by uncertainty.[3] Because we prefer the known to the unknown, our communication goal is to reduce the uncertainty we have about that person.[4] In order to create understanding, we need to gain knowledge. We desire to find out what the other person is like and we want to figure out how to act. Do you agree? If so, how do you accomplish your objectives?

According to researchers, we rely on three key strategies to reduce uncertainty and increase predictability during an interpersonal relationship: (1) passive strategies, during which we unobtrusively observe the other person while he or she is engaged in doing something, preferably interacting with others; (2) interactive strategies, during which we communicate directly with the other person, asking probing questions that encourage the person to talk about himself or herself; and (3) active strategies, during which we get information about this person from a third party, manipulate a situation that enables us to observe another person, or set up a situation in which we can have someone else observe us as we talk with the other person. The more we interact with and converse with another person, the more our uncertainty decreases. The more we discover that we and the other person share things, the more our uncertainty wanes. The more we and the other person share a communication network—that is, interact with the same people—the more uncertainty is reduced. Since interpersonal ignorance is uncomfortable, the urge to reduce uncertainty motivates communication. If we are able to reduce uncertainty to the point that we become comfortable in the situation, our interaction will increase and the relationship may continue. Just as reducing uncertainty acts as a bridge to relational development, so it can also be used to bridge some culture gaps.[5]

Another factor that affects relationship development is the predicted outcome value of the potential relationship. Researchers believe that we formulate a personal hypothesis regarding whether or not a given relationship will be rewarding. Because we typically have limited information at the outset of a relationship, our initial judgment may be based on a person's physical appearance, the behaviors we observe, or the information we obtain from others.[6] As we reduce our uncertainty, our ability to make accurate predictions about a relationship's future increases. How accurate have you been at predicting the success of relationships at a first meeting?

Acquaintanceships

acquaintanceships

relationships with persons we know by name and with whom we converse when the chance arises

We have **acquaintanceships** with people we know by name, with whom we converse when the chance arises, but with whom our interaction is usually limited in scope and quality. Unless we want to turn an acquaintance into a friend, we rarely go out of our way to see that person, preferring instead to leave our meeting each other to chance.

Friendships

Do you agree with Frank Crane's definition of friendship?

What is a Friend? I will tell you. It is a person with whom you dare to be yourself.

A number of our acquaintanceships develop into friendships. Friends, in contrast to acquaintances, seek each other out, like being with each other, and exhibit a strong mutual regard for each other. Friends accept each other, confide in each other, trust each other to keep any confidences disclosed confidential, provide each other with emotional support, share interests, and expect their relationship to last.[7]

Of course, we might grow closer to some friends than others. It is to our very closest friends that we usually confide our most private thoughts and feelings. We share a greater degree of intimacy with the friends we feel closest to.

As friendships develop and become closer, we begin to increase our knowledge of and trust in each other, and both the breadth and depth of our relationship are enhanced. Bill Rawlins's six-stage model explains how friendships develop.[8] (See Figure 9.1.)

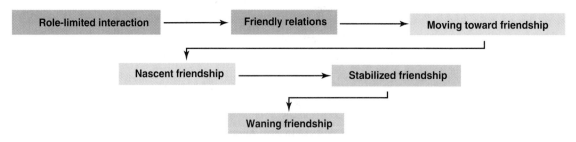

FIGURE 9.1 *Rawlins's Six-Stage Model of Friendship.*

Role-Limited Interaction

According to Rawlins, friendships begins with **role-limited interaction,** during which two individuals make initial contact in some context. Someone we meet at work, in a restaurant, on an airplane, or at a sports event can develop into a friend. The first stage of our potential friendship occurs when we first meet. At this point, we are unclear whether our relationship will develop, and we act tentatively in relating to each other. We lack personal knowledge about each other, and we are hesitant to reveal personal information. Typically, we trade polite exchanges and rely on standard scripts when conversing.

role-limited interaction
the beginning stage of friendship

Friendly Relations

The next interaction stage, **friendly relations,** finds us exploring whether we have enough in common to continue building a relationship. We engage in more small talk in an effort to see if our interest is reciprocated. We drop our guard somewhat and become more expressive, as we seek to discover if the other person is interested in us as well.

friendly relations
the friendship stage in which we explore whether we have enough in common to continue building a relationship

Moving toward Friendship

During the **moving toward friendship** stage, we step beyond conventional social rules and role playing and make small personal disclosures as a means of indicating that we'd like to expand our friendship. We invite the other person to interact with us in a context outside those that happen serendipitously. We might, for example, ask if the person might like to go out for a cup of coffee, to the movies, or to the library. Once in a different setting, we can reveal more of our attitudes, beliefs, and values to each other.

moving toward friendship
the friendship stage in which we make small personal disclosures demonstrating the desire to expand our relationship

Nascent Friendship

As the other person echoes our moves toward friendship, we enter the **nascent friendship** stage and begin to consider each other friends. We substitute our own rules in place of the social stereotypes and standards that regulated our interactions to this point. For example, we might decide to get together every Sunday afternoon to run in the park or every Friday night for a movie or to have dinner. We plan the activities we'll share together. Our interactions become more regular.

nascent friendship
the friendship stage that finds us considering each other friends

Stabilized Friendship

We enter the **stabilized friendship** stage once we decide that our friendship is secure and will continue. We now count on the other person to be there without our specifically planning to meet. We trust each other and respond to each other in ways that display our trustworthiness. We get together more frequently across a greater number of settings. We share more intimate information and reveal the fears and vulnerabilities that we keep hidden from most other people.

stabilized friendship
the friendship stage in which we decide that our friendship is secure and will continue

Waning Friendship

When friends begin to drift apart, they enter the **waning friendship** stage. Sometimes this happens when friends take their friendship for granted. Other times, for one reason or another, one or both make less of a personal effort to keeping the friendship going. Perhaps career, personal, or family obligations

waning friendship
the friendship stage during which friends begin to drift apart

get in the way. Perhaps a trust is violated or one person develops new interests that the other person doesn't share. Since friendships don't maintain themselves, when one or more of the preceding situations occur, the friendship may dissolve.

Romantic Relationships

Romantic love is different from the kind of love we feel for our friends or family members. Although statistics reveal that over half of all marriages in the United States ultimately fail, when we enter into marriage, we expect it to last. In fact, it is the expectation of permanence that helps distinguish a romantic relationship from other kinds of relationships.

Three additional characteristics unique to romantic relationships are commitment (the intention to remain in the relationship even if trouble occurs), passion (intensely positive feelings of attraction that make you want to be with the other person), and intimacy (sustained feelings of closeness and connection). Although any one of these can exist without the others, all three are essential to a romantic relationship.[9]

Romantic relationships, like friendships, develop in stages that reflect each party's perception of the amount of self-disclosing that is occurring and the kind of intimacy shared.

According to social historian and co-director of the National Marriage Project at Rutgers University, Barbara Dafoe Whitehead, we face "a contemporary crisis in dating and mating."[10] Most young men and women today want to be established in a career before they start looking for love. When ready for a true romantic relationship, they are not sure how to find it. The fast pace of our society leads some of us to expect instant relationships.

Not all romantic relationships are healthy. Some turn dark and become destructive. When a romantic relationship becomes dysfunctional, it is characterized by **toxic communication,** which includes the consistent use of verbal abuse and/or physical or sexual aggression or violence. Although spousal abuse is all too common, the highest incidence of violence occurs among unmarried cohabiting couples.[11] Relationship well-being is higher if a relationship we share develops in the way we think it should.[12]

Like romantic relationships, dysfunctional relationships move through a series of stages. During the first stage, relational tensions build in the abuser, who blames a partner for problems and seeks an excuse to vent anger. In the second stage, the tensions erupt into violence. In the third stage, the abuser apologizes and promises to make it up to the victim, assuring the victim that it will never happen again. In the fourth stage, there is a lull in violent activity, during which the victim again feels loved. Ultimately, however, relational tensions again build, and the cycle of abuse continues.[13]

Family Relationships

Most of our earliest relationships occurred within our family. Family members mutually influence each other as they work out the nature of their relationships. They are also expected to play certain roles in relation to each other and to the family as a whole. Among the roles family members perform are wage earner, homemaker, financial manager, and child care provider. These

toxic communication

the consistent use of verbal abuse and/or physical or sexual aggression or violence roles may be shared or may be the prime responsibility of a single family member. In healthy families, role relationships evolve as family members grow, develop, and enter different life stages.

Family members also have expectations for each other. They expect to receive emotional support from one another. They expect members to pull together to preserve the family unit. The rules that guide family interaction help regulate the behavior of family members. They reveal how family members divide tasks—who is in charge of what and the like. To thrive in a family, you need either to follow or to successfully renegotiate the rules that prescribe member behavior.

When a family practices healthy communication, members offer emotional and physical support to each other, reveal their feelings and thoughts to each other, meet each other's needs, and display flexibility and a willingness to adapt to change. On the other hand, when a family's communication practices become dysfunctional—that is, when they prohibit members from adequately expressing their feelings or needs or contain messages that are physically, sexually, or emotionally abusive—then family relationships suffer and deteriorate.[14]

Work Relationships

Friendships affect the well-being of both individuals and organizations. Even at work, we develop friendship networks that benefit us both in and out of the office.[15] When we work in an organization, we share interdependent relationships with the other people who work in the organization. When we are knowledgeable about how to build person-to-person on-the-job relationships, we put ourselves in a better position to nurture both our personal growth and the organization's growth. The notion of the rugged individual in the organization appears to be passé; replacing the rugged individual is the team player—a person who is effective working with one or more other employees both within and between groups. Team players realize the potential to work together to develop meaningful partnerships with many others in the organization.[16]

The relationship level is where most of the work of the organization gets done; it's also where many of the organization's difficulties are encountered.

In any organization, we find relationships in which some people are leaders and others are team members. Leaders and team members spend much of their time interacting. As with other relationships, when interactions are

TV, the Internet, and the Family

What lessons are we learning from television and the Internet regarding family life?[17]

First, consider this question: How do media images of family influence the image you have of your own family and the kind of family you would like to be able to create, were you free to do so? Select a television family and contrast it with your own. Describe the members of each family, their roles and relationships to each other, the factors that appear to hold the family together, the subjects family members discuss, the conflicts they handle, and the ways they resolve them. To what extent, if any, does your analysis of the television family contribute to your evaluating your own family as more or less positive? Explain.

Next, analyze how your use of the Internet is enhancing or detracting from life in your family.

Media WISE

perceived as supportive, open, and honest; when people operate in a climate that is trusting and confirming; when they feel part of a participative organization; and when leaders have a high tolerance for disagreement, job satisfaction is usually high. These aspects of communication will be discussed in greater depth in Part Three of this book.

YOU AND YOUR EMOTIONS

Emotions play a role in all our relationships. What is it really like to be angry? What does your body feel like when you get angry? What happens to your face? Can you identify the types of situations in friendships, in romantic relationships, in your family, and on the job that make you angry? Can you recall that you ever enjoyed being angry? Can you tell when a friend, family member, or co-worker becomes angry? How well do you read or express feelings when in a friendly, romantic, family, or work relationship?

An Emotions Survey

Consider the following emotions:

Anger
Happiness
Surprise
Fear
Sadness

Which of these feelings do you experience most frequently in each relationship context? Least frequently? Which of these feelings do you least enjoy

We unconsciously mirror and imitate the moods and emotions of individuals with whom we interact.

expressing? Which do you least enjoy observing in others? For each emotion, answer the following questions:

1. Identify an occasion when you felt this emotion.
2. On a scale ranging from 1 (mild) to 5 (intense), indicate the strength of the emotion.
3. Describe what you felt like and what you imagine you looked like when you experienced the emotion.
4. Describe how you attempted to handle the emotion.
5. Describe how others around you reacted to you.
6. Identify when you perceived an occasion that someone you were with was experiencing this emotion.
7. Describe your perceptions of how this person felt and looked.
8. Describe how he or she attempted to handle the emotion.
9. Describe your reactions to his or her behavior.

You can use the information you have just gathered in at least three ways: (1) to help you clarify how you feel about emotions, (2) to help you understand other people's emotions, and (3) to help other people understand your emotions.

Emotion States and Traits

Whether you realize it or not, at any given time, you are experiencing some emotion to some degree. In any particular context with any particular people, you will almost certainly have certain thoughts or attitudes about the situation. These thoughts or attitudes will give rise to a particular emotion state. According to theorist Carroll E. Izard, an **emotion state** is a particular emotional process of limited duration, lasting from seconds to hours and varying from mild to intense. One example is a state of sadness. Izard notes that "chronically intense emotions, or frequent episodes of intense emotion, may indicate psychopathology."[18] Thus a person who always feels an emotion intensely— who is always in an extreme state of joy, depression, or anger—is unusual.

emotion state
a particular emotional process of limited duration

In addition to emotion states (such as sadness), people may also exhibit **emotion traits**—that is, the tendency to experience specific emotions when interacting with others. For instance, if you were described as exhibiting a sadness trait, this would indicate that you had a tendency to experience sadness frequently in your daily interactions.[19]

emotion traits
the tendency to experience specific emotions when interacting with others

What emotion traits have you experienced or observed in others in the past 24 hours? Does any particular emotion trait punctuate either your own interpersonal behavior or the behavior of those with whom you habitually relate?

Every emotion you experience is accompanied by physiological changes in your body and physical changes in your appearance. Are you fine-tuned to the physiological and visual signals the body and face send as a person experiences an emotion? Let's find out.

What Do Feelings Feel Like?

Feelings can be accompanied by a wide range of physical sensations and changes. Sometimes, as with anger, blood rushes to your face, so that your face reddens; your heartbeat and pulse quicken; and you may experience an urge to wave your arms and legs, raise your voice, and use strong words to express what you are feeling. Likewise, when you are exposed to a threat or become anxious or frightened, your body will respond by releasing certain hormones into your bloodstream. According to David Viscott, in times of stress, the blood supply to the muscles is increased, while the supply to the abdomen and skin is decreased.[20] Thus, cold feet and pallor are two physical symptoms of the feeling of anxiety. In these and similar ways, your feelings let you know how people, ideas, and the environment affect you. In other words, they reveal to you what is important to you.

Not everyone experiences feelings in the same way. Your ability to accept the reactions of other people indicates an awareness that they can experience unique physical sensations—responses quite separate and distinct from your own. As Carroll Izard observes, "The joyful person is more apt to see the world through 'rose colored glasses,' the distressed or sad individual is more apt to construe the remarks of others as critical, and the fearful person is inclined only to see the frightening object (tunnel vision)."[21] Feelings are our reaction to what we perceive; they define and color our image of the world.

What Do Feelings Look Like?

Describe some of the ways face reading might affect the atmosphere of a workplace and the workers' productivity.

Your face is the prime revealer of your emotions. Although rules for displaying emotions vary from culture to culture, the facial expressions associated with certain emotions (specifically, fear, happiness, surprise, anger, and sadness) appear to be nearly universal and thus are recognizable anywhere in the world. As early as 1872, Charles Darwin, in *The Expression of the Emotions in Man and Animals,* observed that people the world over express basic feelings in similar ways. Without understanding a person's language, you can frequently determine whether he or she is angry, frightened, or amused. Moreover, it appears that these basic facial expressions are innate.

Both Paul Ekman and Carroll Izard have identified facial patterns (changes involving the facial muscles) that are apparently specific to basic emotions.[22] According to these researchers, surprise is a transient state and the briefest of all emotions, moving onto and off the face quickly. Surprise is typically expressed by lifted eyebrows that create horizontal wrinkles across the forehead, slightly raised upper eyelids, and (usually) an open, oval-shaped mouth. Surprise can turn to happiness if the event that precipitated it promises something favorable, but it can turn to fear or anger if the event poses a threat or foretells aggression.

Anger results most typically from interference with the pursuit of our goals. Being either physically or psychologically restrained from doing what you would like to do can produce anger. So can being personally insulted or rejected. Thus, an action that shows someone's disregard for our feelings and needs may anger us. When a person is angry, the eyebrows are usually lowered and drawn together, creating a frown. The eyes appear to stare at the object of anger, and the lips are tightly compressed or are drawn back in a squarish shape, revealing clenched teeth. Often the face reddens, and veins on the neck and head become more clearly visible. It can be noted, with regard

Angry, cynical people are five times as likely to die before 50 as people who are calm and trusting.

—**Dr. Redford B. Williams**

to anger and a closely related emotion, hostility, that these are potentially damaging states. For some time, a general personality type characterized by competitiveness, impatience, and aggression was believed to be strongly predictive of heart disease. More recently, the focus has shifted to hostility. According to Redford Williams, a professor of psychiatry, there is strong evidence that hostility alone damages the heart: "It isn't the impatience, the ambition or the work drive. It's the anger. It sends your blood pressure skyrocketing. It provokes your body to create unhealthy chemicals. For hostile people, anger is poison."[23] Some people have free-floating hostility, meaning that they are usually angry, often without real cause. These people are most at risk. Current research indicates that genes may account for 27 to 40 percent of a person's tendency toward anger.[24] This is not to say that all expression of anger is unhealthy. Indeed, for people who express some anger, versus a lot of anger, the risks for disease may be lower than for persons who express little or no anger. In fact, moderate expressions of anger, when compared with low expressions of anger, decrease the risk for heart attack and stroke by about 50 percent.[25] Anger that goes unexpressed can create other problems as well, including passive-aggressive behavior and a personality that is always negative and hostile. Consequently, demonstrating anger management—that is, learning to express anger constructively by expressing angry feelings in

What emotion is this man experiencing? Is his face easy to read?

Rants

Media WISE

On radio, on TV, on the Internet, on CDs, on MTV, and in books, Americans are ranting, engaging in name-calling, venting, and delivering tirades. We have turned listening to extremely angry human beings into entertainment.

For example, the best-selling album of 2002 was "The Eminem Show" in which Eminem vents his anger by writing lyrics that speak of a gun aimed at a woman and feces spread across the White House lawn. In the same song, he curses both Lynn Cheney, the wife of the Vice President Dick Cheney, and Tipper Gore, the wife of the former Vice President and Presidential candidate Al Gore. For writing lyrics containing such thoughts, Eminem was nominated for a Grammy.

Similarly, politically conservative spokesperson Ann Coulter, in her book *Slander,* denounced liberals as "venom-spewing haters" and "pathetic little parakeet males and grim quivering angry women" who "want to take more of our money, kill babies, and discriminate on the basis of race." On the other hand, speaking of conservatives, filmmaker Michael Moore, in his best-selling book *Stupid White Men,* described George W. Bush as "the thief-in-chief" and noted that "hard-core Republicans are desperately hoping that Big Dick Cheney can survive half a dozen more heart attacks and last long enough to oversee the raping and pillaging of everything west of Wichita."[26]

Is cacophony in the media drowning out reason? What functions, if any, do you believe mediated rants like these have? In your opinion, do we need to take steps to restore civility into the common discussion of social problems?

an assertive, not aggressive, way, redirecting anger, and calming oneself down—is a valuable skill. Anger management has also entered the technology age. Eudora, one of the oldest e-mail programs, allows users of its service to utilize a screening device, MoodWatch, software that analyzes incoming and outgoing messages for sentence structure and word usage that looks offensive or aggressive. By warning a receiver of a potentially anger-arousing message that could ruin the day, it allows the receiver to delete the e-mail before reading it.[27] Would you use such a screening service to avoid having your anger aroused?

What makes us happy? Why are some people happy, while others are not? The happiest people spend the least time alone, are not focused on materialism, and forgive easily—the trait most strongly linked to happiness.[28] After 9/11, for many Americans, happiness became "the new bottom line" as priorities were reordered.[29] Happiness is the easiest emotion for observers to recognize when expressed on the face. Happiness is the feeling that pulls the lips back and curves them gently upward. The raised cheek and lip corners create wrinkles, or dimples, which run down from the nose outward beyond the lips and from the eyes outward around the cheeks.

With sadness, the opposite of happiness, there is often a loss of facial muscle tone. Typically, the inner corners of the eyebrows are arched upward and may be drawn together. The lower eyelid may appear to be raised, the corners of the mouth are drawn down, and the lips may begin to tremble.

Are you able to decipher the look of fear?

When a person is experiencing fear, the eyebrows appear to be slightly raised and drawn together. The eyes are opened wider than usual, and the lower eyelid is tensed. The lips may be stretched tightly back, and wrinkles appear in the center of, rather than across, the entire forehead.

Think of an instance when you read and responded to someone else's feelings. Think of an instance when you failed to do so. How was the relationship you shared affected in each case?

According to research, putting on a sad, happy, or frightened face can actually produce the feeling that the expression represents. Facial expressions in and of themselves elicit feelings; they are not simply the visible sign of an emotion.[30] Thus, while our emotions may influence our facial expressions, our facial expressions may also influence our emotions.

Moods may also be contagious. If you've ever started your day in a great mood, gone to class, then ended up in a bad mood, you may want to consider that someone gave you that nasty mood. We can pick up moods as we pick up cold germs. What's most noteworthy is that, the more sensitive and

Ethics & COMMUNICATION

Emotional Contagion

According to a trio of researchers—Daniel Goleman, the author of *Emotional Intelligence;* Carl Jung, Swiss psychoanalyst; and Elaine Hatfield, a psychologist—our moods can be contagious. In fact, the more emotionally expressive people are, the more apt they are to transmit their moods when they talk with another person. In addition, the transmission of emotion appears to be both instantaneous and unconscious.

Assuming this is true, should a person who is experiencing a bout of sadness, or a similar depressive emotion, be kept isolated from others so as not to "infect" them with the same feeling? In other words, would we be better off if we were exposed only to people who were in a good mood? Why or why not?

empathetic we are, the more apt we are to be susceptible to **emotional contagion** and to catch someone else's mood. According to psychologist Elaine Hatfield, we do this by unconsciously mirroring and/or imitating the moods and emotions of those with whom we interact.[31]

emotional contagion
the catching of another person's mood

EMOTIONS AND RELATIONSHIPS: WORKING THROUGH FEELINGS

It is our feelings that make us human; that color our relationships by adding warmth, vitality, and spirit; and that cause us to move or be moved. In fact, feelings are at the heart of our relationships. Whether we are at work or at home, with a friend or a lover, to create liking, build trust, engage in self-disclosure, resolve conflicts, and influence others, we must communicate feelings.

Factors in Attraction

The first step in the study of how feelings affect our relationships is to recognize what causes us to seek out some people and not others. What is interpersonal attraction? Why are we attracted to one person and not to another? Why do we develop a positive attitude toward one person and a negative attitude toward another? A number of researchers have identified variables that influence how attracted people feel toward one another.[32] Attractiveness (not surprisingly), proximity, similarity, reinforcement, and complementarity are consistently named as determiners of attraction.

The first kind of information we process when we interact with someone is that person's outward attractiveness. We tend to like physically attractive people more than physically unattractive people, and we tend to like people who exhibit pleasant personalities more than those who exhibit unpleasant personalities. Of course, judgments of what is physically attractive and what constitutes a pleasant personality are subjective.[33] However, whatever we perceive as pleasing functions as an important element in creating and sustaining interpersonal attraction.

Proximity is the second factor influencing attraction. We usually find that, for the most part, we enjoy interacting with people with whom we work or people who live close to us. Apparently, physical nearness affects the amount of attraction we feel. Living physically close to another person or working near another person gives us ample opportunity to interact, talk, share similar activities, and thus form an attachment. For these reasons, the closer two people of the opposite sex are geographically, the more likely it is that they will be attracted to each other and marry. In all fairness, however, we should examine an opposite effect of proximity. According to Ellen Berscheid and Elaine Walster, the authors of *Interpersonal Attraction,* the closer people are located, the more likely it is that they can come to dislike each other. Berscheid and Walster note, "While propinquity may be a necessary condition for attraction, it probably is also a necessary condition for hatred."[34] What do you think?

Reinforcement is the third factor appearing in practically all theories of interpersonal attraction. We will feel positive about people who reward us or

Explore relationships you shared with a person who was critical of you, one who praised you, one who cooperated with you, and one who competed with you. Which relationship caused the most problems? Which was the most satisfying? Which was the most productive?

who are associated with our experiences of being rewarded, and we will feel animosity or dislike for people who punish us or are associated with our experiences of punishment. Thus, we are likely to like people who praise us, like us, and cooperate with us more than people who criticize us, dislike us, and oppose or compete with us. Of course, reinforcement can backfire: If people become overzealous in their praise and fawn over us too much, we will question their sincerity and motivation. But in general, as social psychologist Eliot Aronson notes, "We like people whose behavior provides us with a maximum reward at minimum cost."[35]

Similarity also affects our attraction to others. We are attracted to people whose attitudes and interests are similar to our own and who like and dislike the things we like and dislike. We usually like people who agree with us more than we like those who disagree with us, especially when we are discussing issues we consider salient or significant. In effect, similarity helps provide us with social validation: It gives us the evidence we need to evaluate the "correctness" of our opinions or beliefs. We also expect people who hold attitudes similar to our own to like us more than people who hold attitudes that are dissimilar to ours. Perhaps if we believed that everyone we met could not help liking us, we would more readily associate with unfamiliar people who held attitudes different from our own. By seeking the company of "similars," we play it safe.

Not all the evidence suggests that we seek to relate only to carbon copies of ourselves, however. In fact, **complementarity**—the last of the factors influencing interpersonal attraction—suggests just the opposite. Instead of being attracted to people who are similar to us, we frequently find ourselves attracted to people who are dissimilar in one or more ways. Both psychologist Theodore Reik and sociologist Robert Winch note that we often tend to fall in love with people who possess characteristics that we admire but do not ourselves possess. Thus, a dominant woman might seek a submissive man, and a socially awkward man might seek a socially poised woman.

complementarity

the attraction principle which states that opposites attract

The Role of Feelings in Relationships

Our relationships with most of the people we contact in the course of a lifetime will be transitory and will not amount to much. At times, however, we find that our interchanges continue; then it becomes quite important to be able to determine what the person with whom we are communicating is feeling. At that point, it is just as necessary for us to understand the world of the other person as it is for us to understand ourselves.

Feelings by themselves are not inherently good or bad. Feelings as such do not disrupt relationships, build walls, or add problems to your life. Rather, it is what you think and how you act when experiencing feelings that can affect a relationship for better or worse. For example, anger and fear are not necessarily harmful. As Izard notes, "Anger is sometimes positively correlated with survival, and more often with the defense and maintenance of personal integrity and the correction of social injustice."[36] Fear may also be associated with survival and at times helps us regulate destructive aggressive urges. Thus, it is not any emotion itself that is an issue but, rather, how you deal with the emotion and the effect it has on you and on those who are important to you.

Our feelings tell us about our needs and about the state of our relationships.[37] People who share healthy relationships are able to pay direct attention to the emotional reactions that occur during their interactions with others. They take time to become aware of these emotions by periodically asking themselves, "What am I feeling?" Once the feeling has been identified, their next step is to estimate its strength: "How strong is this feeling?" Next, they ask, "How did I get to feel this way?" "Where did the feeling come from?" "How did I contribute?" In healthy relationships, an emotion is reported as experienced—for instance, "I'm getting angry, and I'm beginning to say things I really don't mean."

Healthy relationships do not consist totally of positive feelings. Other feelings are also important. Unfortunately, many of us lack the commitment, courage, and skill needed to express our own feelings—particularly when those feelings are not positive—or to allow other people to express their feelings to us. Many people are reluctant to work their feelings through; instead, they ignore or deny a feeling until it eventually becomes unmanageable.

Thus, we often keep our feelings too much in check or, when we do express them, we express them ineptly and incompletely. Did you know that the majority of people who are fired from their jobs are asked to leave not because of incompetence but because of personality conflicts? Many of the problems we have with friends, parents, or employers are due to the inability to express or accept messages about feelings. Efforts to sacrifice or disregard feelings inevitably lead to problems with relationships or failures of relationships. In the section "Suppression and Disclosure of Feelings," we will examine how this happens.

Suppression and Disclosure of Feelings

Sometimes the way we handle feelings impedes our relationships with others.[38] For example, in any relational context, we may bury our real feelings, hesitate to express them, or unleash them uncontrollably.

Censoring Your Feelings

Feelings are not the enemy of healthy human relationships, yet at times we are taught to act as if they were. As a result, many of us grow up afraid of feelings.

Have important people in your life ever expressed sentiments similar to the following to you?

"You shouldn't feel depressed about what happened."

"If you can't tell me you're pleased with the way it looks, then don't say anything."

"Don't you scream at me! You have no right to get angry with me!"

"If you were strong, you would turn the other cheek and smile."

"There's nothing to be afraid of! Why are you such a baby?"

As these examples imply, feelings and emotions are frequently perceived as dangerous, harmful, and shameful. When this is the case, we censor our feelings and become overly hesitant to express our feelings to others or to let others express their feelings to us. We allow ourselves to exhibit only socially approved feelings for fear of being considered irrational or emotionally volatile. This leads to communication that is shallow, contrived, and frequently inappropriate.

Often, so as not to make waves or alienate others, both males and females act the part of the nice guy. At times people desperately want others to like them and so are willing to pretend to feel, or not feel, a particular emotion. People may also become what Theodore Isaac Rubin calls **emotional isolationists.**[39] That is, they may try to protect themselves from any exchange of feelings by minding their own business and avoiding entanglements or involvements. Or they may overintellectualize every experience in an attempt to render their emotions impotent. Each of these techniques is counterproductive and can ultimately cause problems with relationships.

emotional isolationists
persons who seek to avoid situations which may require the exchange of feelings

Display Rules

Various types of unwritten laws, or display rules, guide us in deciding when or when not to show our emotions. For instance, when we are young, we may be told not to cry at school, not to yell in front of strangers, or not to kiss in public. As adults, we may be advised not to flirt at office parties, not to display anger when disciplined, or not to be too outspoken during a meeting.

One determinant of display rules is gender. Although feelings do not discriminate between the sexes, and although members of both sexes obviously are equally capable of emotions of all kinds, our society for some reason deems it appropriate for men and women to behave differently with regard to their emotions. Theodore Isaac Rubin, author of *The Angry Book,* gives the following examples of confused ideas about anger:

> Big anger displays are not feminine.
> Big anger displays are only feminine and are not masculine.
> Gentlemen simply don't show anger.
> Ladies must not get angry at gentlemen.
> Gentlemen must not get angry at ladies.
> Very loud anger displays are evidence of homosexuality.[40]

As Rubin observes, "members of both sexes get equally angry" and "are equally expressive"; nevertheless, different rules and taboos regarding the expression of anger, and other emotions, have been internalized by males and females.

The two sexes may handle anger and aggression in strikingly different ways. While men and women are equally likely to experience anger, women are far more likely to suppress, repress, and deny it.[41] Only 9 percent of women report that they deal with anger by directly confronting the person who caused it, and 25 percent insist that they wouldn't express anger to a family member.[42] Instead, they keep it bottled up by enacting a "no anger" script.

In our society, men are generally viewed as more rational, objective, and independent than women. Women are perceived to be more emotional, subjective, and dependent than men. Women are also supposed to do more disclosing than men. When asked, people typically indicate that the "male" traits are more desirable than the "female" traits. But Kay Deaux notes in *The Behavior of Women and Men* that the supposedly female characteristics are not all seen as bad:

> There is a cluster of positively valued traits that people see as more typical of women than men; these traits generally reflect warmth and expressiveness. Women are described as tactful, gentle, aware of the feelings of others, and able to express tender feelings easily. Men in contrast are viewed as blunt, rough, unaware of the feelings of others, and unable to express their own feelings.[43]

"Do you know how masculine it is to risk crying?"

For the most part, women are perceived as warm and men as competent. Which do you feel is the more desirable trait? In general, because of the sharing of feelings and amount of disclosing involved, female friendships are perceived to be deeper and more enduring than the friendships of men. In addition, while women's willingness to verbalize their feelings is believed to improve their mental and physical health, prolonged ruminating about feelings can deepen depression and lead to anxiety and anger.[44]

The second important determinant of display rules is culture. For example, in some African societies, people will assume that you are friendly until you prove to them that you are not. When they smile, it means that they like you; if they don't smile, it means that they distrust or even hate you. The Japanese, on the other hand, often laugh and smile to mask anger, sorrow, or disgust. People from Mediterranean countries often intensify emotions such as grief, sadness, and happiness, whereas the British deintensify, or understate, these emotions.

The third determinant of display rules is personal values. In effect, we decide for ourselves under what conditions and with whom we will freely share or inhibit our emotional expressions. You might, for instance, feel it inappropriate to show anger before a parent, but you might readily reveal it to a boyfriend, girlfriend, or spouse. You might hesitate to express your innermost fears to an instructor or employer, but you might readily disclose them to a close friend.

Our personal display rules might also cause us to develop a characteristic style of emotional expression.[45] We might become withholders and try never to show how we feel, or we might become revealers and try always to show how we feel. Or we might become what Paul Ekman and Wallace V. Friesen call unwitting expressors, blanked expressors, or substitute expressors.[46] Unwitting expressors reveal their feelings without being aware that they have done so. (They then wonder how someone could read their emotions.)

To whom do you feel free to say, "I'm frightened of that," or "What you just did disappointed me," or "I really care about you"?

Culture, Gender, and Emotional Displays

When it comes to the display of emotion, our culture and our gender appear to compel us to act in accordance with societal norms. For example, Asians are less likely than Americans to express negative emotions publicly, and men generally tend to be more reticent in expressing emotions such as sympathy, sadness, and distress, while women are more inhibited when it comes to expressing anger and sexuality.

How are these cultural and gender expression differences sustained? Parents and society, in general, reinforce them. For example, recent studies reveal that, in the United States, we still treat boys and girls differently when it comes to their emotional lives. According to psychologist Virginia O'Leary, "The stereotypes of emotionality for men and women are as strong as ever, in spite of two decades of efforts to break them down." Some of the most compelling laboratory research shows, for instance, that, when provoked, men and women have equivalent reactions in terms of heart rate and other physiological responses, but, when questioned, men usually say they are angry, while women usually say they are hurt or sad.

In another study, men and women viewed scenes of accidents and their victims. Although physiological measures indicated that both the men and women were equally affected by the scenes, the men's faces showed no expression, while the women's faces expressed sympathy.

Consider the following questions:

1. To what extent does your own behavior confirm or contradict the preceding observations? Explain.

2. How might the different messages that men and women send about their emotions affect their ability to communicate honestly and effectively with each other?

Blanked expressors are certain that they are communicating feelings to others but, in fact, are not. (They are then confused or upset when people fail to pick up on their cues.) Substitute expressors substitute the appearance of one emotion for another emotion without realizing they have done so. (They then cannot understand why people react in unexpected ways.) Thus, personal display rules sometimes work to impede interpersonal relationships.

Effects of Suppressed Feelings on Relationships

As Jerry Gillies, the author of *Friendship,* writes, "You are not making contact if you are not putting out what you really are."[47] Interpersonal communication theorist Sidney Jourard noted that dissembling, concealing, and being hesitant to reveal feelings are "lethal" habits for men.[48] Jourard believed that men, because they are not as apt to express their feelings as are women, encounter stresses that actually cause them to have a shorter life span than women. Now that women are assuming what were traditionally male roles, will they, too, feel more compelled to keep their feelings to themselves? Whatever the answer, it is acknowledged that all people are likely to experience personal and interpersonal difficulties when they try to repress or disguise their feelings.

According to communication expert David Johnson, many people mistakenly assume that all we need to ensure the development of effective interpersonal relationships is rationality, logic, and objectivity. "To the contrary," writes Johnson, "a person's interpersonal effectiveness increases as all the relevant information (including feelings) becomes conscious, discussable, and controllable."[49] Thus, he holds, suppression of feelings results in ineffective interpersonal behavior. Psychologist Thomas Gordon notes that, besides reducing your interpersonal effectiveness, continually bottling up your feelings can cause you to develop ulcers, headaches, heartburn, high blood pressure, a spastic colon, and various psychosomatic problems.[50] There is also evidence linking emotion, disease, and the immune system. Researchers have found that strong emotional responses may bolster the immune system. For example, cancer patients who openly showed that they were upset and who exhibited a fighting spirit seemed able to marshal stronger immune defenses than patients who suppressed their feelings.[51] David Viscott, a medical doctor, states, "When we lose touch with our feelings, we lose touch with our most human qualities. To paraphrase Descartes, 'I feel, therefore, I am.'"[52]

If either person in a relationship attempts to suppress his or her feelings, one or more of the following consequences may result. First, it may become increasingly difficult to solve interpersonal problems. Research reveals that, in a relationship, the quality of problem solving improves when the participants feel free to express both positive and negative feelings. When the participants feel inhibited, the quality of communication is diminished. Second, unresolved feelings foster a climate in which misinterpretation, distortion, and nonobjective judgments and actions can thrive. Unresolved feelings create or enlarge blind spots in our interpretation of people and events. Third, repression of emotions can lead to serious conflicts and blowups. Intense feelings that are not dealt with fester beneath the surface until they erupt as a result of mounting internal (self) and external (other) pressures. (Holding in such feelings can make it impossible for participants to think clearly.) Fourth, maintaining an effective relationship means that participants are honest with each other. To penalize or reject a person for expressing emotions honestly is to tell that person that you deny him or her the right to reveal an authentic self. You also deny yourself the ability to know the person. Finally, continued repression of feelings can in time cause you to obliterate your capacity to feel anything.

Effects of Disclosed Feelings on Relationships

Certainly, there are people to whom you may not choose to reveal your feelings, and there are situations in which you decide that disclosure of your feelings would be inappropriate. Nevertheless, when you take the risk of revealing your feelings to others, your relationship is likely to reap definite benefits.

First, by honestly revealing your feelings, you make it less threatening for the other person to reveal his or her feelings. You demonstrate that you care enough to share your feelings; thus, risk taking becomes a reciprocal process. Second, you acknowledge that emotions are acceptable. You do not censor the feelings the other person experiences, nor do you decide which feelings he or she may and may not feel. You express an interest in the whole person; instead of using emotions as weapons, you show that you are willing to use them as tools. Third, by describing your feelings and by sharing your perceptions with others, you become more aware of what it is you are actually feeling. Fourth, you give yourself the opportunity to resolve difficulties and conflicts in a productive way. Fifth, by revealing your feelings, you can indicate to others how you want to be treated. In contrast, by keeping quiet—by saying nothing—you encourage others to continue behavior of which you may disapprove. Feelings, when respected, are friendly, not dangerous.

CONFLICTS AND RELATIONSHIPS

conflict
perceived disagreement

Conflict, or perceived disagreement about views, interests, and goals, is a part of every relationship. It is not so much the conflict or disagreement that creates problems in our relationships but the way we approach and handle it. Thus, while disagreements are normal and their presence does not signal relationship trouble, how we choose to manage conflict with another is an indicator of a relationship's health.

Managing Conflict: Handling Feelings during Conflict

One of our objectives in this chapter is to investigate conflict to see how we can learn to handle it effectively. You have been, and will continue to be, faced with conflicts all your life. Observing your own conflicts and giving more thought to them can be a positive experience.

Conflict develops for a multitude of reasons and takes a multitude of forms. It can arise from people's different needs, attitudes, or beliefs. Conflict tests each relationship we share with another person and in so doing helps us assess the health or effectiveness of the relationship. Handled well, conflict can help each participant develop a clearer picture of the other; thus, it can strengthen and cement a relationship. Handled poorly, conflict can create schisms, inflict psychological scars, inflame hostilities, and cause lasting resentments. Thus, conflicts can produce highly constructive or highly destructive consequences.[53]

Every relationship worth maintaining, every relationship worth working at, is certain to experience moments of conflict. As David Johnson notes, "A conflict-free relationship is a sign that you really have no relationship at all, not that you have a good relationship."[54] To say there should be no conflict amounts to saying that we should have no relationships. If a relationship is healthy, conflicts will occur regularly. If a relationship is healthy, conflicts will also be handled effectively. A survey by *Redbook* magazine suggests that how people express themselves in conflict situations is frequently more important than what they disagree about.[55] *Redbook* asked female readers how they were most likely to behave when displeased with their husbands and how their husbands were most likely to behave when displeased with them. Readers were asked whether they were most apt to "say nothing, brood about it, hint they were unhappy, express their feelings, or start an argument." They were also asked how they handled themselves when they did argue with their spouses. For instance, were they most likely to "leave the room, sulk, sit in silence, swear, shout, hit out, cry, or break things"? The results indicated that the most happily married women were those who said that both they and their husbands were able to reveal displeasure, discuss it, and try to resolve the problem calmly and rationally.

How we approach conflict can create problems. Handled poorly, conflict can destroy relationships and inflame hostilities.

They also noted that they rarely if ever felt compelled to resort to active aggressive fighting (swearing, shouting, hitting out, crying, or breaking things) or to passive-aggressive fighting (leaving the room, sulking, or keeping silent). Thus, it appears that avoiding conflicts, trying to settle them prematurely, or prohibiting the discussion of differences can lead to serious problems.[56]

Research also indicates that how your parents handled conflict may have influenced your early academic achievement and emotional well-being.[57] There is evidently a link between the emotional lives of your parents and your own emotional health.[58]

What conflicts have you been involved in recently—in class, at work, or at home? Why did you define each situation as a conflict?

Gender, Culture, and the Handling of Conflict

When women and men, and individuals from diverse cultures, communicate, they carry their assumptions, beliefs, and perceptions of each other with them. What soon becomes apparent is that the sexes, and different cultures, approach conflict in different ways.

From childhood on, males are typically more competitive and aggressive, while females adopt more cooperative behaviors. Since most males are more concerned with power, they tend to make demands, while most females, more concerned with relationship maintenance, tend to make proposals. Males often fail to provide rationales for positions, while females freely offer reasons.

As with men and women, different cultures socialize their members to behave in different ways when faced with conflict. Whereas members of individualistic cultures, such as the United States, are likely to exhibit a direct approach that emanates from the belief that individuals have a right to defend themselves, members of collectivistic cultures believe that such behavior is out of place or rude. Instead, they tend to value harmony, restraint, and nonconfrontation.[59] Hesitant to refuse a request directly, the members of a collectivistic culture might say, "Let me think about that" in place of "No."

By becoming sensitive to such differences, and recognizing the assumptions on which they are based, we can work toward developing a clearer understanding of how conflicts can be resolved.[60]

Reexamine your personal conflict inventory to identify your style of managing conflict. Do you or people you know use any ineffective methods of dealing with conflicts? Do you feel a need to deny that a conflict exists, withdraw, surrender, placate, or distract by introducing irrelevancies? Do you intellectualize, blame, find fault, or force the other person to accept your ideas by physically or emotionally overpowering him or her? Why? What elements of your relationship elicit irrational responses instead of a rational discussion of the disputed issues?

My idea of an agreeable person is a person who agrees with me.
—Benjamin Disraeli

Of the strategies available, only discussion, or leveling, can break impasses and solve difficulties. Thus, the fate of any conflict is related to the communication strategies employed. Conflict forces people to select response patterns that will forge an effective network of communication. We can choose either disruptive or constructive responses.

We see that, in any situation, problems can develop if we fail to deal with conflict appropriately. We can also see that there are certain definite benefits to be derived from handling conflict effectively. Alan Filley, in the book

Can you think of situations in your own life that illustrate the four values of conflict discussed here?

Interpersonal Conflict Resolution, identifies four major values arising from conflict. First, many conflict situations can reduce or even eliminate the probability of more serious conflict in the future. Second, conflict can foster innovation by helping us acquire new ways of looking at things, new ways of thinking, and new behaviors. Third, conflict can develop our sense of cohesiveness and togetherness by increasing closeness and trust. Fourth, it can provide us with an invaluable opportunity to measure the strength or viability of our relationships.[61] Conflict, after all, is a natural result of diversity.

How Conflict Arises: Categorizing Conflicts

We have examined what conflict is and how we feel about it. Now let us explore how and why it arises. Conflict is likely to occur wherever human differences meet. As we have seen, conflict is a clash of opposing beliefs, opinions, values, needs, assumptions, and goals. It can result from honest differences, from misunderstandings, from anger, or from expecting either too much or too little from people and situations. Note that conflict does not always require two or more people; you can sometimes be in conflict with yourself. **Self-conflict** occurs when we find ourselves having to choose between two or more mutually exclusive options—two cars, two classes, two potential spouses, two activities; the internal struggle in such a situation is called **intrapersonal conflict.** In contrast, **interpersonal conflict** is the same type of struggle between two or more people. Interpersonal conflict can be prompted by differences in perceptions and interests; by a scarcity of resources or rewards, such as money, time, and position; or by rivalry—situations in which we find ourselves competing with someone else. Those involved in an intrapersonal or interpersonal conflict usually feel pulled in different directions at the same time.

Consider the Skill Builder "Tied in Knots." How did that experience feel? Of course, when engaged in conflict, you do not have real ropes tugging at

self-conflict

the kind of conflict that occurs when we find ourselves having to choose between two or more mutually exclusive options

intrapersonal conflict

internal conflict

interpersonal conflict

conflict between two or more people

Skill
BUILDER

Tied in Knots

This exercise was suggested by an experience included in Virginia Satir's book *Peoplemaking.*

1. Think of some idea, belief, value, need, or goal that has involved you in a conflict situation.

2. Identify the relevant aspects of yourself or the other person or persons involved. Briefly summarize each position.

3. Choose class members to play the parts of those you perceived yourself to be in conflict with.

4. Cut heavy twine or rope into 10-foot lengths, one for each player. Also cut a

number of 3-foot lengths to tie around each player's waist, including your own. Next, tie your 10-foot lead rope to the rope around your waist. Then, hand your rope to the person with whom you perceive yourself to be in conflict, who will also hand his or her rope to you.

5. While tied to each other, begin to talk about the issue that is the cause of conflict.

Source: Virginia Satir. *Peoplemaking.* Palo Alto, CA: Science and Behavior Books, 1988.

you, but you sometimes feel as if you do. When you are able to handle a conflict, the ropes do not get in the way. At other times, however, a conflict escalates out of control. Before you know it, you are tied up in knots and unable to extricate yourself. Those who see themselves in conflict with each other are interdependent and have the power to reward or punish one another. Thus, whenever two or more people get together, conflicts serious enough to damage their relationship may develop.

We can categorize conflict in different ways. First, we can classify the goal or objective about which a conflict revolves. Goals or objectives can be nonshareable (for example, two teams cannot win the same basketball game) or shareable (your team can win some games and the other team can win some). Or they can be fully claimed and possessed by each party to the conflict. (You can each win everything—members of the rival Teamsters and Independent Truckers unions all get raises.)

Second, conflicts can be categorized according to their level of intensity. In a **low-intensity conflict,** the persons involved do not want to destroy each other; they devise an acceptable procedure to help control their communications and permit them to discover a solution that is beneficial to each. In a **medium-intensity conflict,** each person feels committed to win, but winning is seen as sufficient. No one feels that the opposition must be destroyed. In a **high-intensity conflict,** one person intends to destroy or at least seriously hurt the other. In high-intensity conflicts, winning as such is not necessarily sufficient; to mean anything, victory must be total.

A conflict can also be classified as a pseudoconflict, a content conflict, a value conflict, or an ego conflict. A **pseudoconflict** (as the term implies) is not really a conflict but gives the appearance of a conflict. It occurs when a person mistakenly believes that two or more goals cannot be simultaneously achieved. Pseudoconflicts frequently revolve around false either-or judgments ("Either I win or you win") or around simple misunderstandings (failing to realize that you really agree with the other person). A pseudoconflict is resolved when the people realize that no conflict actually exists.

A **content conflict** occurs when people disagree over matters of fact: the accuracy or implications of information, the definition of a term, or the solution to a problem. If the interactants realize that facts can be verified, inferences tested, definitions checked, and solutions evaluated against criteria, they can be shown that a content conflict can be settled rationally.

A **value conflict** arises when people hold different views on a particular issue. As an example, consider the American welfare system. A person who values individual independence and self-assertiveness will have opinions about public welfare very different from those of someone who believes that we are ultimately responsible for the well-being of others. The realistic outcome of such a conflict would be that the interactants would disagree without becoming disagreeable—that is, they would discuss the issue and learn something from one another, even though they might continue to disagree. In effect, they would agree that it is acceptable to disagree.

Ego conflicts have the greatest potential to destroy a relationship. An **ego conflict** occurs when the interactants believe that winning or losing is a reflection of their own self-worth, prestige, or competence. When this happens, the issue itself is no longer important because each person perceives himself or

low-intensity conflict
a conflict in which the persons involved work to discover a solution beneficial to each

medium-intensity conflict
a conflict in which each person feels committed to win, but winning is seen as sufficient

high-intensity conflict
a conflict in which one person intends to destroy or seriously hurt the other

pseudoconflict
the situation that results when persons mistakenly believe that two or more goals cannot be simultaneously achieved

content conflict
a disagreement over matters of fact

value conflict
a disagreement that arises when persons hold different views on an issue

ego conflict
a disagreement that occurs in which persons believe that winning or losing is tied to their self worth, prestige, or competence

herself to be on the line. Thus, it becomes almost impossible to deal with the situation rationally.

At this point, you should understand that conflict can develop for a number of different reasons, and you should be aware of the types of disagreements and problems that can arise during intrapersonal and interpersonal conflict. Particular conflict-generating behaviors affect each of us differently.

Some of us perceive ourselves to be involved in a conflict if we are deprived of a need; others do not. Some of us perceive ourselves to be involved in a conflict if someone impinges on our territory or disagrees with us about the way we define a role; others do not. Take some time to discover your own sources of conflict. Making such observations will help you understand the types of issues that draw you into disharmony with yourself and others. It will also let you see how you tend to respond when faced with a conflict situation. We will now examine constructive and destructive ways of handling conflict in greater detail.

When evaluating a conflict, Americans tend to see one side as right and the other as wrong. In contrast, the Chinese are more likely to see the validity of both sides. What do you see as the benefits and drawbacks of each orientation?

Resolving Conflict: Styles of Expression

As we have seen, our emotions and how we handle them can make or break the relationships we enter into. In other words, we can make our feelings work for or against us. There are three basic ways of handling emotionally charged or conflict-producing situations: nonassertively, aggressively, and assertively.

Nonassertiveness

Have there been moments in your life when you believed you had to suppress your feelings to avoid rejection or conflict, or when you felt unable to state your feelings clearly? Are you ever afraid to let others know how you feel? If you have ever felt hesitant to express your feelings to others, intimidated by another person, or reluctant to speak up when you believed you were being treated unfairly, then you know what it is to exhibit **nonassertiveness.** When you behave nonassertively, you force yourself to keep your real feelings inside. Frequently, you function as a weather vane or change colors as a chameleon does in order to fit the situation in which you find yourself. You become an echo of the feelings around you. Unfortunately, nonassertive people rarely take the steps needed to improve a relationship that is causing problems; as a result, they frequently end up with something they don't really want. With so much at stake, why do people refrain from asserting themselves?

nonassertiveness

the hesitation to display one's feelings and thoughts

Experience shows that we hesitate to assert ourselves in our relationships for a number of reasons. Sometimes inertia or laziness is a factor; the easiest response is simply no response at all. (After all, assertion can be hard work.) At other times, apathy leads us to be nonassertive; we simply do not care enough to become actively involved. Frequently, fear can lead to nonassertiveness. In particular, we may fear that rejection might result from active self-assertion. (We become convinced that speaking up may make someone angry.) Or we may simply feel we lack the interpersonal skills needed for assertiveness.

Why might you hesitate to protect your rights; that is, why would you be reluctant to assert yourself? Under what circumstances would nonassertiveness be most likely to occur?

Another important cause of nonassertiveness is shyness. Each of us feels inadequate from time to time. We may feel exploited, stifled, or imposed upon. These feelings manifest themselves in a variety of ways—as depression, as weakness, as loneliness—but most of all, according to psychologist Philip G. Zimbardo, as shyness. Shyness is embarrassment in advance. It is created by the fear that our real self won't match up with the image we want to project.[62]

According to Zimbardo and Shirley L. Radl, coauthors of *The Shyness Workbook,* few shy people consider their shyness a positive trait; they see it as evidence that something is wrong with them. Actually, Zimbardo and Radl note, "Shyness is not a permanent trait but rather is a response to other people evoked by certain situations. The unpleasant feelings of shyness come from having low self-esteem and worrying about what other people will think of you."[63]

According to Lynn Z. Bloom, Karen Coburn, and Joan Pearlman, authors of *The New Assertive Woman,* in our society shyness or nonassertiveness is often considered an asset for women but a liability for men.[64] To what extent do your experiences support this? Do you think women gain more from being nonassertive than men lose? Why?

There are many degrees of shyness. For example, shyness can take the form of mild bashfulness, or it can simply cause you to increase the distance you like to keep between yourself and others. Unfortunately, extreme shyness can make you fear all social relationships and can prevent you from expressing or even acknowledging your emotions.

Aggressiveness

Unlike nonassertive people, who often permit others to victimize them and are reluctant to express their feelings, persons who display **aggressiveness** insist on standing up for their own rights to the point at which they ignore and violate the rights of others. Although some people deliberately defy pushy people, in general, aggressive people manage to have more of their needs met than nonassertive people do. Unfortunately, they usually accomplish this at someone else's expense. The aggressor always aims to dominate and win in a relationship; breaking even is not enough. The message of the aggressive person is selfish: "This is the way I feel. You're stupid if you feel differently. This is what I want. What you want doesn't count and is of no consequence to me." In contrast to the nonassertive person, who ventures forth in communication hesitantly, the aggressive person begins by attacking, thereby precipitating conflict. It is therefore not surprising that a conversation with an aggressive person will often escalate out of control: The target of the aggressor frequently feels a need to retaliate. In such situations, no one really wins, and the result is a stalemated relationship.

People feel a need to act aggressively for a number of reasons. First, according to two assertiveness counselors, Arthur J. Lange and Patricia Jakubowski, we tend to lash out when we feel ourselves becoming vulnerable; we attempt to protect ourselves from the perceived threat of powerlessness.[65] Second, emotionally volatile experiences that remain unresolved may cause us to overreact when faced with a difficulty in a relationship. Third, we may firmly believe that aggression is the only way to get our ideas and feelings across to the other person. For some reason, we may think that people will neither listen to nor react to what we say if we take a mild-mannered approach. Fourth, we may simply never have learned to channel or handle our

Which situations and people in your life make you feel shy? What are the consequences of your shyness?

aggressiveness
the expressing of one's own thoughts and feelings at another's expense

Describe an interpersonal situation in which someone took advantage of you and you permitted it. What do you believe motivated the other person? What motivated you? Describe a situation in which you took advantage of someone else. Why do you believe the other person allowed you to victimize him or her?

Go to the *Online Learning Center* at www.mhhe.com/gamble8 and answer the questions in the *Self Inventory* to evaluate your understanding of assertiveness.

aggressive impulses. (In other words, we may not have mastered a number of necessary interpersonal skills.) Fifth, aggression may be related to a pattern of repeated nonassertion in the past; the hurt, disappointment, bewilderment, and sense of personal violation that resulted from nonassertion may have risen to the boiling point. No longer able to keep these feelings inside, we abruptly vent them as aggressiveness.

Damaged or destroyed relationships are a frequent result of aggression. Neither the nonassertive nor the aggressive person has many meaningful relationships. For this reason, we need to find a middle ground, or golden mean, between the extremes of nonassertion and aggression.

Assertiveness

The intent of nonassertive behavior is to avoid conflict of any kind; the intent of aggressive behavior is to dominate. By contrast, the intent of assertive behavior is to communicate honestly, clearly, and directly and to support your beliefs and ideas without either harming others or allowing yourself to be harmed. If we can assume that both nonassertion and aggression are due at least partly to having learned inappropriate ways of reacting in interpersonal encounters, we should be able to improve our interpersonal relationships if we work to develop appropriate ways of reacting. Understanding the nature of assertiveness will help us accomplish this goal.

assertiveness

expressing one's thoughts and feelings while displaying respect for the thoughts and feelings of others

When you display **assertiveness,** you protect yourself from being victimized; you meet more of your interpersonal needs, make more decisions about your own life, think and say what you believe, and establish closer interpersonal relationships without infringing on the rights of others. To be assertive is to recognize that all people have the same fundamental rights and that neither titles nor roles alter this fact. We all have the right to influence the way others behave toward us; we all have the right to protect ourselves from mistreatment. Furthermore, we all have the right to accomplish these objectives without guilt.

Assertive people have learned how to stop themselves from sending inappropriate nonassertive or aggressive messages. Thus, assertive people announce what they think and feel without apologizing but without dominating. This involves learning to say "no," "yes," "I like," and "I think." In this way, neither oneself nor the other person is demeaned; both are respected.

For an example of aggressive/assertive communication, view clip 2 on the CD

The focus of assertiveness is negotiation. Assertive people try to balance social power to equalize the relationships they share. Whereas aggressive people often hurt others and nonassertive people often hurt themselves, assertive people protect themselves as well as those with whom they interact. This means attending to feelings and using specific verbal and nonverbal skills to help solve interpersonal problems.

Remember that being assertive does not mean being insensitive, selfish, stubborn, or pushy. It does mean being willing to defend your rights and communicate your needs, and it does mean being willing to attempt to find mutually satisfactory solutions to interpersonal problems and conflicts. It is up to you to decide whether you would like to redefine some of the ways you relate to others. It is up to you to determine whether you need to shake off any inappropriate and unproductive ways of behaving in favor of assertiveness.

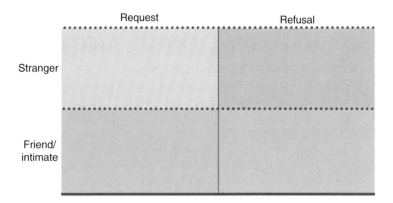

FIGURE 9.2
Relationship Window.

You may, of course, encounter difficulties as you attempt, through assertiveness, to promote more successful and open communication with others. Most assertion situations fall into at least one of four categories: (1) an interaction with a stranger, in which you are requesting something; (2) an interaction with a friend or an intimate, in which you are requesting something; (3) an interaction with a stranger, in which you are refusing something; (4) an interaction with a friend or an intimate, in which you are refusing something.[66] These situations may be represented as a relationship window (see Figure 9.2).

Most people will experience the majority of their difficulties with assertiveness in one or more of the quadrants shown in Figure 9.2. For example, some people may find it easy to refuse a stranger's request but difficult to deny that of a friend. For others, refusing close friends or strangers alike may pose few problems; instead, they may experience great anxiety when making requests of others. Where do you experience the most difficulty?

At one time or another, we will all have some difficulty in at least one of the quadrants. Once you have identified your own problem areas, however, you can begin to examine your behavior more closely. You can begin to recognize when you feel a need to fight, when you feel a need to flee, and when you feel a need to assert yourself. Fighting or fleeing makes sense for animals and is therefore characteristic of their behavior. These alternatives do not necessarily make sense for human beings in dealing with one another; still, we sometimes flee from each other, and we sometimes fight with each other. Sometimes we display these behaviors because we want to, sometimes because we feel we must, and sometimes because we don't know what else to do or may think we lack the social skills to do anything else. What we can do, however, is use our problem-solving ability to develop assertive ways to handle interpersonal difficulties. We can learn to be socially adept.

For any relationship to grow, the participants need to demonstrate at least a minimal level of assertiveness in their communication with each other. The important thing is to try to let your actions be dictated by the circumstances and the people. There is no single right way to act in every interpersonal encounter, and the choice of how you act should be your own. In general, however, we can all increase our feelings of self-worth by learning to be more assertive.[67]

TECHNOLOGY, RELATIONSHIPS, AND THE COMMUNICATION OF EMOTION

In a cyberaffair, one person carries on an interpersonal relationship that is not necessarily physical or intimate with another person online. In cybersex, which is anonymous and built on fantasy, persons talk about having sex, describing various sexual acts, with an online partner. If your significant other were to have a cyberaffair or engage in cybersex, would you consider him or her to be guilty of infidelity? Why or why not? What relational factors do you believe lead someone to have a cyberaffair and/or engage in cybersex?

flames
online insults

Can you read the emotions of people you interact with online? What cues do you use?

By using the Internet, we bring another social world into our offline lives, one in which we communicate with and maintain ties with people who live at a distance, some of whom we may never meet face-to-face.[68] How successful are we at managing the integration of this new world of relationships into our existing world? To what extent does our involvement with persons in cyberspace affect the relationships we already share with friends, family members, and people at work? Do you feel successful managing multiple interpersonal worlds?

The Internet has the potential to expand our relationship reach. The Net, in many ways, is the ultimate *noncontact* person-to-person network. For this reason, despite the fact that millions of people use Internet dating sites, unless they progress beyond the use of computers, cyber-relationships cannot become the developmental equivalents of real friendships or romances.[69] On the other hand, the Internet can be used to strengthen existing relationships and increase interaction with relatives and friends.

For some of us, the computer has freed us to express feelings and emotions we would be hesitant to express publicly. For example, e-mail and online chat groups are enabling shy persons to come out of their shells and interact with others. In addition, they allow those who are bedridden or isolated from others to find emotional support from online sources. They are also enabling those of us who have had limited contact with or experience interacting with persons from different backgrounds to have such opportunities. In the process, we are able to practice handling the conflict that can result when we converse with people who have different values or think differently than we do.

In addition to exposing us to differences, the bulletin boards we frequent can also function as electronic soapboxes, which we or others use to sound off or to vent our feelings. Chat rooms and e-mail may even function as virtual hotel rooms for friendly get-togethers into which you and one or more others may check into on a whim and interact.[70] When interacting online, in addition to interacting pleasantly, individuals can hurl insults, or **flames,** that feed interpersonal conflict. In fact, some people send computer-assisted messages to persons that they would never dare send if they were face-to-face with those individuals. Because there is neither rootedness to place nor danger of physical contact while interacting via computer, but there is the potential for anonymity, certain persons may even allow themselves the freedom to become verbally abusive or aggressive. How you react when you are the target of such flaming or verbal abuse is revealing. Some who are flamed withdraw, sit on the side, or turn away, while others counter the personal attack by replying immediately to the same audience. As with speech, the tone we imagine other persons to be using as they type their computer-mediated messages to us often becomes more important than what they actually write.[71]

The Expression of Emotion Online

Select an individual with whom you interact regularly both face-to-face and online. Compare and contrast the way you and your friend handle and express your emotions and feelings to each other when using each medium.

Also explore a selected chat room and bulletin board. Note how the people interacting or posting notices express their emotions. Are their emotions easily read, or does the reader have to make many more assumptions than if he or she were face-to-face with the other person?

As you complete your responses, also answer these questions:

1. Do people feel freer to self-disclose when face-to-face or online? Why?
2. Do people tend to be more blunt with each other when online or offline? Why?
3. Are conflicts more apt to surface between people when face-to-face or online? Why?
4. When a conflict surfaces, is it easier to handle when face-to-face with another person or online? Why?
5. Compare and contrast the techniques you use to resolve a conflict when offline with those you use when online. How are they similar or different?

Online journals are also gaining in popularity. Used primarily as a vehicle for pouring out emotions, members can inwardly focus as they publish journal entries or read and comment on the entries of friends and other journal keepers.[72] Researchers believe that pouring painful traumas out on a computer screen can also improve health and increase self-insight.[73]

In addition to changing the media we use to interact with each other, new technologies are redefining how and where we work. Greater and greater numbers of us spend significant parts of our day in front of computers (desk or laptop), on cellular telephones, and in general less tied to the notion of a traditional office. For many of us, the office is a relic. We telecommute, linked with others by a computer network. We have more virtual contact and less and less face-to-face contact. To combat the dearth of face-to-face interaction workers have with each other, some employers go out of their way to arrange opportunities for employees to meet face-to-face for casual exchanges.

New technologies are also changing how the boss delivers both good and bad news to workers. According to one study, people are more honest when using e-mail to communicate bad news than they are with other methods, such as phone or personal delivery. When negative feedback is delivered via e-mail, it contains less sugarcoating. According to managers, e-mail also lets them dole out praise more quickly. Managers now give workers virtual pats on the back.[74]

EXPRESSING YOUR FEELINGS EFFECTIVELY IN RELATIONSHIPS

Many of us have trouble expressing our feelings in person and online. Either we behave nonassertively and keep our emotions too much in check, or we behave aggressively and become excessively demanding or belligerent. The result is that our emotions impede the development of healthy relationships and foster the development of unhealthy relationships.

It is sad that we are rarely, if ever, taught to reveal our emotions in ways that will help our relationships. The key to using our feelings to promote effective relationships is learning to express them effectively. The following guidelines should help you communicate feelings in positive ways and thereby enrich the quality of your interpersonal encounters and relationships.

Work on Feelings You Have Difficulty Expressing or Handling

By now you should have a good idea of what feelings you have trouble expressing or responding to. Now concentrate on expressing or responding to these feelings when they arise. A first step is to let others know what feelings cause problems for you.

Stand Up for Your Emotional Rights

When we sacrifice our rights, we teach others to take advantage of us. When we demand rights that are not ours, we take advantage of others. Not revealing your feelings and thoughts to others can be just as damaging as disregarding the feelings and thoughts of others. The following is a bill of rights for every person:

1. The right to be treated with respect
2. The right to make your own choices or decisions
3. The right to make mistakes and to change your mind
4. The right to have needs and to have your needs considered as important as the needs of others
5. The right to express your feelings and opinions
6. The right to judge your own behavior
7. The right to set your own priorities
8. The right to say no without feeling guilty
9. The right not to make choices for others
10. The right not to assert yourself

These rights provide a structure on which you can build effective relationships. Internalizing them will enable you to learn new habits and formulate new expectations. Accepting your personal rights and the personal rights of others is an important step.

Check Your Perceptions

So far we've discussed *your* feelings, but what about the other person's feelings? Sometimes our interpretations of another person's feelings are determined by our own. Checking your perceptions requires that you express your assessment of others' feelings in a tentative fashion. You want to communicate to other people that you would like to understand their feelings and that you would like to refrain from acting on the basis of false assumptions that you might later regret. Sample perception checks include the following:

"Were you surprised at what Jim said to you?"

"Am I right in thinking that you feel angry because no one paid attention to your ideas?"

"I get the feeling that what I said annoyed you. Am I right?"

"I'm not certain if your behavior means you're confused or embarrassed."

Show Respect for Feelings

Don't try to persuade yourself or others to deny honest feelings. Comments like "Don't feel that way," "Calm down," and "Don't cry over spilt milk" communicate that you believe the other person has no right to a particular feeling. (You should avoid advising yourself or others to repress or ignore feelings.) Feelings are potentially constructive and should not be treated as destructive.

Use a Script to Handle Feelings Assertively

In their book *Asserting Yourself,* Sharon Bower and Gordon Bower present a technique you can use to handle interpersonal dilemmas effectively.[75] The approach utilizes what is called a **DESC script** (*DESC* stands for *d*escribe, *e*xpress, *s*pecify, *c*onsequences). A script contains characters (you and the person with whom you are relating), a plot (an event or a situation that has left you dissatisfied), a setting (the time and place the interaction occurred), and a message (the words and nonverbal cues of the actors).

DESC script
an acronym for *d*escribe, *e*xpress, *s*pecify, and *c*onsequences; a system for expressing one's feelings and understanding the feelings of another

You begin the script by describing, as specifically and objectively as possible, the behavior of another person that troubles you and makes you feel inadequate. By describing the bothersome occurrence, you give yourself a chance to examine the situation and define your personal needs and goals. Once you have identified what it is about the other person's behavior that you find undesirable, you are in a better position to handle it. Use simple, concrete, specific, and unbiased terms to describe the other's actions. For example, instead of saying, "You're always overcharging me, you dirty cheat!" try, "You told me the repairs would cost $50, and now you're charging me $110." Instead of saying, "You're ignoring me; you don't care about me," say, "You avoid looking at me when we speak." Instead of guessing at motives and saying, "You resent me and want Lisa," say, "The last two times we've gone out to eat with Jack and Lisa, you've criticized me in front of them."

After you have written a direct description of a behavior that bothers you (identifying the characters, the plot, and the setting), next add a few sentences expressing how you feel and what you think about the behavior. To do this, get in touch with your emotions and use personal statements. Using personal statements makes it clear that you are referring to what you are feeling and what you are thinking. The distinguishing feature of a personal statement is a pronoun such as "I," "me," or "my"; for example, use "I feel," "I believe," "my feelings," "it appears to me." Thus, when hurt by the behavior

Thinking
CRITICALLY

Reflect and Respond

Agree or disagree with the following quotation. Supply reasons and examples from a number of relationship contexts to support your stance:

In a sense we have two brains, two minds—and two different kinds of intelligence: rational and emotional. How we do in life is determined by both—it is not just IQ, but emotional intelligence that matters.[76]

Focus on Service Learning

Run a seminar on emotional intelligence or anger management for a local organization.

of an unthinking friend, you might say, "I feel humiliated and demeaned when you make fun of me." Realize that there are a number of ways feelings can be expressed. You can name a feeling: "I feel disappointed." "I feel angry." You can use comparisons: "I feel like a weeping willow" or "I feel like a rose whose petals have been ripped off, one by one." Or you can indicate the type of action your feelings are prompting you to exhibit: "I feel like leaving the room" or "I feel like putting cotton in my ears." By disclosing such feelings tactfully, you can make your position known without alienating the other person.

Once you have described the bothersome behavior and expressed your feelings or thoughts about it, your next step is to write down your request for a specific different behavior. That is, you specify the behavior you would like substituted. In effect, you are asking the other person to stop doing one thing and start doing something else. As before, make your request concrete and particular. It would be more effective to say, "Please stop playing the drums after 11 P.M." than to yell, "Stop being so damn noisy!"

Finally, note possible consequences—positive and negative—in terms of your own and the other person's behavior and feelings. Then review your script and rehearse it until you feel that your verbal and nonverbal cues support your goal.

Practice Four Basic Assertive Behaviors

Practice the following assertive behaviors:

1. Stop automatically asking permission to speak, think, or behave. Instead of saying, "Do you mind if I ask to have this point clarified?" say, "I'd like to know if . . . ." In other words, substitute declarative statements for requests for permission.

2. Establish eye contact with people with whom you interact face-to-face. Instead of looking down or to the side (cues that imply uncertainty or insecurity), look into the eyes of the person you are speaking to. This lets people know you have the confidence to relate to them honestly and directly.

3. Eliminate hesitations and fillers ("uh," "you know," "hmm") from your speech. It's better to talk more slowly and deliberately than to broadcast the impression that you are unprepared or lack self-assurance.

4. Say, "No" calmly, firmly, and quietly; say, "Yes" sincerely and honestly; say, "I want" without fear or guilt.

Revisiting Chapter Objectives

1. **Identify and distinguish among the following relationship life contexts: acquaintanceship, friendship, and romantic, family, and work relationships.** Our relationships occur in various life contexts. Among the different kinds of relationships we share are acquaintanceships, friendships, romantic relationships, family relationships, and work relationships. Our emotions have an impact on our inner life and on our relationships, regardless of the context in which they occur. Emotions can enhance or disrupt relationships. They can increase our understanding of other people, or they can prevent us from relating to other people effectively.

2. **Define and distinguish among the following terms: *emotional intelligence, emotion state,* and *emotion trait.*** We are experiencing some emotion to some degree at any given time. Our emotional intelligence, the ability we have to motivate ourselves, to control our impulses, to recognize and regulate our moods, to empathize, and to hope, determines how effective we are at handling feelings in our relationships. A temporary emotional reaction to a situation is an emotion state; a tendency to experience one particular emotion repeatedly is an emotion trait.

3. **Explain how attraction, proximity, reinforcement, similarity, complementarity, and the suppression and disclosure of feelings can affect the development of relationships.** Feelings can be accompanied by a wide range of physical sensations. A number of basic feelings (including surprise, anger, happiness, sadness, and fear) are also reflected by characteristic facial expressions that are similar around the world. We can improve our communication abilities by learning to read the facial expressions of others to discover their feelings and by letting our own expressions convey our emotions to others. It is believed that emotions are contagious—others frequently pick up an emotion displayed by one person during an interaction.

   Feelings are at the heart of our important interpersonal relationships. Among the factors that can cause us to establish relationships with some people but not others are attractiveness, proximity, reinforcement, similarity, and complementarity. How we deal with our emotions often influences the course of our relationships. When we censor or fail to disclose our feelings, we are likely to engage in interactions that are shallow or contrived rather than fulfilling and real. Sometimes we are simply obeying unwritten display rules—often based on gender or culture—when we decide which feelings we will reveal or conceal. Not expressing our feelings honestly can lead to misunderstandings and even to breakdowns in our relationships.

4. **Define *assertiveness, nonassertiveness,* and *aggressiveness* and explain how feelings can be handled effectively during conflicts.** Innovations in technology are enabling us to practice the management of our emotions in a variety of online settings. Whether we are interacting online or offline, there are three ways of expressing feelings in emotionally charged or conflict-producing interpersonal situations: nonassertively, aggressively, and assertively.

5. **Identify behaviors that foster or impede the development of a relationship based on assertiveness.** When we display assertiveness, we meet our

interpersonal needs, make our own decisions, and think and say what we believe without infringing on the rights of others. Only the assertive style enables us to express our beliefs and ideas without harming others or being victimized ourselves.

6. **Draw and explain a relationship window.**   We can use a relationship window—a model that analyzes how we interact with strangers, friends, and intimates—to identify the kinds of interactions in which we find it most difficult to be assertive.

7. **Create and explain a DESC script.**   We can analyze and learn to handle a typical situation by using a DESC script.

Resources for Further Inquiry and Reflection

To apply your understanding of how the principles in Chapter 9 are at work in our daily lives, consult the following resources for further inquiry and reflection. Or, if you prefer, choose any other appropriate resource. Then connect the ideas expressed in your chosen selection with the communication concepts and issues you are learning about both in and out of class.

 Listen to Me

"Happy Together" (The Turtles)
"Song Sung Blue" (Neil Diamond)
"You Can't Hurry Love" (The Supremes)
"What's Love Got to Do with It?" (Tina Turner)

Discuss the lessons the selected song teaches about how the feeling of interactants affect their relationships.

 View Me

The Story of Us	*Jungle Fever*
A River Runs through It	*Parenthood*
Disclosure	*Anger Management*

These films explore relationships in a specific context. Choose one and discuss the relationship's context, what we learn from the film about the effective and/or ineffective handling of emotions, how the suppression or expression of feelings affects relationships, and how conflict can influence a relationship's course.

 Read Me

Judith Guest. *Ordinary People*. New York: Viking Press, 1976.
Jacqueline Mitchard. *The Deep End of the Ocean*. New York: Viking Press, 1996.

These books are about families in crisis. Discuss how the untimely death or disappearance of a child affects family members. Identify the problems family members face as they try to cope with their tragedy. What, if anything, do family members do to improve their communication climate and get in touch with their emotions?

 Tell Me

Share with the class the insights you gained from your chosen Listen to Me, View Me, or Read Me selection.

Discuss your opinion regarding one of the following positions: Computer-mediated communication within virtual communities is a means of widening our social relationships. Computer-mediated communication within virtual communities is a means of diminishing the need for in-person relationships.

Key Chapter Terminology

Use the Communication Works CD-ROM and the Online Learning Center at www.mhhe.com/gamble8 to further your knowledge of the following terminology.

acquaintanceships 266
aggressiveness 287
assertiveness 288
complementarity 276
conflict 282
content conflict 285
DESC script 293
ego conflict 285
emotion state 271
emotion traits 271
emotional contagion 275
emotional intelligence 264
emotional isolationists 278
flames 290
friendly relations 267

high-intensity conflict 285
interpersonal conflict 284
intrapersonal conflict 284
low-intensity conflict 285
medium-intensity conflict 285
moving toward friendship 267
nascent friendship 267
nonassertiveness 286
pseudoconflict 285
role-limited interaction 267
self-conflict 284
stabilized friendship 267
toxic communication 268
value conflict 285
waning friendship 267

Test Your Understanding

Go to the *Self Quizzes* on the Communication Works CD-ROM and the book's Online Learning Center at www.mhhe.com/gamble8.

Notes

1. Daniel Goleman. *Emotional Intelligence*. New York: Bantam, 1995, p. 34.
2. Steve Duck. *Human Relationships,* 3rd ed. Thousand Oaks, CA: Sage, 1998, p. 36.
3. Charles Berger. "Uncertainty and Information Exchange in Developing Relationships." In Steve Duck, ed. *Handbook of Personal Relationships*. New York: Wiley, 1988, p. 244.
4. C. R. Berger and R. J. Calabrese. "Some Explorations in Initial Interactions and Beyond: Toward a Developmental Theory of Interpersonal Communication." *Human Communication Research* 1, 1975, pp. 98–112.
5. See, for example, W. Gudykunst. "Uncertainty and Anxiety." In Y. Y. Kim and W. Gudykunst, eds. *Theories in Intercultural Communication*. Sage: Newbury Park, CA: 1988, pp. 123–156.
6. M. Sunnafrank. "A Communication-Based Perspective on Attitude Similarity and Interpersonal Attraction in Early Acquaintance." *Communication Monographs* 51, 1984, pp. 372–380.
7. See, for example, Keith E. Davis. "Near and Dear: Friendship and Love Compared." *Psychology Today* 19, 1985, pp. 22–30; and Rosemary Blieszner and Rebecca G. Adams. *Adult Friendship*. Newbury Park, CA: Sage, 1992.
8. W. K. Rawlins. "Friendship as a Communicative Achievement: A Theory and an Interpretive Analysis of Verbal Reports." Doctoral dissertation, Temple University, Philadelphia, 1981.
9. Robert J. Sternberg. "A Triangular Theory of Love." *Psychological Review* 93, 1986, pp. 119–135; and Robert L. Sternberg. *The Triangle of Love: Intimacy, Passion, Commitment*. New York: Basic Books, 1988.
10. Karen S. Peterson. "Dating Game Has Changed." *USA Today,* February 11, 2003, p. 9D.

11. See Sally A. Lloyd and Beth C. Emery. *The Dark Side of Courtship: Physical and Sexual Aggression.* Thousand Oaks, CA: Sage, 2000; and J. D. Cunningham and J. K. Antill. "Current Trends in Nonmarital Cohabitation: The Great POSSLQ Hunt Continues." In Julia Wood and Steve W. Duck, eds. *Understanding Relationship Processes, 6: Off the Beaten Track: Understudied Relationships.* Thousand Oaks, CA: Sage, 1995, pp. 148–172.

12. D. Holmberg. "So Far So Good: Scripts for Romantic Relationship Development as Predictors of Relational Well-Being." *Journal of Social and Personal Relationships* 19:6, December 2002, pp. 777–796.

13. Julia T. Wood. *Gendered Lives,* 3d ed. Belmont, CA: Wadsworth, 1999, p. 340.

14. See Duck. *Human Relationships;* Virginia Satir. *The New Peoplemaking.* Mountain View, CA: Science and Behavior Books, 1988, p. 79; and D. Olson and H. McCubbin. *Families: What Makes Them Work.* Beverly Hills, CA: Sage, 1983.

15. D. Gibbons and P. M. Olk. "The Individual and Structural Origins of Friendship and Social Position among Professionals." *Journal of Personality and Social Psychology* 84:2, February 2003, pp. 340–352; and "The Power of Nice," *Workforce* 82:1, January 2003, pp. 22–24.

16. See, for example, Susan A. Wheelan. *Creating Effective Teams: A Guide for Members and Leaders.* Thousand Oaks, CA: Sage, 1999; and James R. Barker. *The Discipline of Teamwork: Participation and Concertive Control.* Thousand Oaks, CA: Sage, 1999.

17. See, for example, Gabriel Weimann. *Communicating Unreality: Modern Media and the Reconstruction of Reality.* Thousand Oaks, CA: Sage, 1999.

18. Carroll E. Izard. *Human Emotions.* New York: Plenum Press, 1977, p. 5.

19. Izard.

20. David Viscott. *The Language of Feelings.* New York: Pocket Books, 1976, p. 54.

21. Izard. p. 10.

22. Paul Ekman. *Darwin and Facial Expression.* New York: Academic Press, 1973. See also Paul Ekman. *Why Kids Lie.* New York: Scribner's, 1989.

23. Quoted in Earl Ubell. "The Deadly Emotions." *Parade,* February 11, 1990, pp. 3–5; and Jane E. Brody. "Controlling Anger Is Good Medicine for the Heart." *New York Times,* November 20, 1996, p. C-15.

24. See *The Record,* June 20, 1994, p. B-1; and Thomas Sancton. "Oedipus, Schmoedipus." *Time,* December 9, 1996, p. 74.

25. E. Nagourney. "Blow a Gasket, for Your Heart." *New York Times,* February 11, 2003, p. F6.

26. See P. Carlson. "The Angry Americans: It's All the Rage." *The Record,* February 16, 2003, pp. O1, O5.

27. "Flame Retardant for Hot E-Mail Messages." *Newsweek,* August 28, 2000, p. 62.

28. Martin E. P. Seligman. *Authentic Happiness,* New York: Simon and Schuster, 2003.

29. Stephanie Armour. "After 9/11, Some Workers Turn Their Lives Upside Down." *USA Today,* May 8, 2002, pp. A1, A2.

30. See Daniel Goleman. "A Feel-Good Theory: A Smile Affects Mood." *New York Times,* July 18, 1989.

31. Ellen O'Brien. "Moods Are as Contagious as the Office Cold." *The Record,* November 15, 1993, p. B-3.

32. For example, Ellen Berscheid and Elaine Hatfield Walster. *Interpersonal Attraction,* 2nd ed. Reading, MA: Addison-Wesley, 1978.

33. Emily Prager. "The Science of Beauty." *New York Times,* April 17, 1994.

34. Berscheid and Walster.

35. Eliot Aronson. *The Social Animal,* 3rd ed. San Francisco: Freeman, 1980, p. 239.

36. Izard.

37. John Powell. *Why Am I Afraid to Tell You Who I Am?* Niles, IL: Argus, 1969.

38. Sandra Petronio, ed. *Balancing the Secrets of Private Disclosures.* Mahwah, NJ: Lawrence Erlbaum Associates, 1999.

39. Theodore Isaac Rubin. *The Angry Book.* New York: Macmillan, 1970; and Theodore Isaac Rubin. *Emotional Common Sense.* New York: Harper & Row, 1986.

40. Rubin. *The Angry Book.*

41. Marilyn Elias. "The Traits of Wrath in Men and Women." *USA Today,* August 11, 1994, p. 1D.

42. Elias, p. 2D.

43. Kay Deaux. *The Behavior of Women and Men.* Belmont, CA: Brooks/Cole, 1976.

44. Carol Tavis. "How Friendship Was 'Feminized.'" *New York Times,* May 28, 1997, p. A-21.

45. See, for example, Michael Ryan. "Go Ahead—Cry!" *Parade,* January 5, 1997, p. 22.

46. Paul Ekman and Wallace Friesen. *Unmasking the Face.* Los Angeles: Consulting Psychology, 1984. For an intercultural perspective, see Stella Ting-Toomey. *The Challenge of Facework.* Albany: State University of New York Press, 1994.

47. Jerry Gillies. *Friendship: The Power and Potential of the Company You Keep.* New York: Coward-McCann, 1976.

48. Sidney Jourard. *The Transparent Self.* New York: Van Nostrand, 1971; and Sidney Jourard and Ted Landsman. *Health Personality.* New York: Macmillan, 1980.

49. David Johnson. *Reaching Out: Interpersonal Effectiveness and Self-Actualization.* Englewood Cliffs, NJ: Prentice-Hall, 1972.

50. Thomas Gordon. *Parent Effectiveness Training.* New York: Plume, 1988.

51. Daniel Goleman. "Strong Emotional Response to Disease May Bolster Patients' Immune System." *New York Times,* October 22, 1985.

52. Viscott.

53. See, for example, Denise H. Cloven and Michael E. Roloff. "The Chilling Effect of Aggressive Potential on the Expression of Complaints in Intimate Relationships." *Communication Monographs* 60:3, September 1993, pp. 199–219.

54. Johnson.

55. *Redbook,* June 1976.

56. See Bonnie Burman et al. "America's Angriest Home Videos: Behavioral Contingencies Observed in Home Reenactments of Marital Conflict." *Journal of Consulting and Clinical Psychology* 61:1, February 1993, pp. 28–39.

57. Susan Chira. "Study Finds Benefits in Emotional Control." *New York Times,* May 26, 1994.

58. See Myra Warren Isenhart and Michael L. Spangle. *Collaborative Approaches to Resolving Conflict.* Thousand Oaks, CA: Sage, 2000.

59. Also see J. W. Pennebaker, B. Rime, and V. E. Blankenship. "Stereotypes of Emotional Expressiveness of Northerners and Southerners: A Cross-Cultural Test of Montesquieu's Hypotheses." *Journal of Personality and Social Psychology* 70, 1996, pp. 372–380.

60. For additional information, see J. D. Pearson. *Gender and Communication,* 2nd ed. Dubuque, IA: Wm. C. Brown, 1991, pp. 183–184; and Stella Ting-Toomey. "Managing Intercultural Conflicts Effectively." In Larry A. Samovar and Richard E. Porter. *Intercultural Communication: A Reader,* 7th ed. Belmont, CA: Wadsworth, 1994, pp. 360–372.

61. Alan C. Filley. *Interpersonal Conflict Resolution.* Glenview, IL: Scott, Foresman, 1975.

62. Duck, *Human Relationships,* p. 54.

63. Philip Zimbardo and Shirley L. Radl. *The Shyness Workbook.* New York: A&W, Visual Library, 1979.

64. Lynn Z. Bloom, Karen Coburn, and Joan Pearlman. *The New Assertive Woman.* New York: Dell, 1975.

65. Arthur J. Lange and Patricia Jakubowski. *Responsible Assertive Behavior.* Champaign, IL: Research Press, 1976.

66. Sherwin B. Cotler and Julio J. Guerra. *Assertive Training.* Champaign, IL: Research Press, 1976, pp. 15–22.

67. For exercises related to topics covered, see Danny Saunders. "Exercises in Communicating." *Simulation/Games for Learning* 21:2, June 1991, pp. 186–200.

68. M. M. Kazmer and C. Haythornthwaite. "Juggling Multiple Social Worlds: Distance Students Online and Offline." *American Behavioral Scientist* 45:3, November 2001, pp. 510–530.

69. See, for example, K. Y. A. McKenna and A. S. Green. "What's the Big Attraction? Relationship Formation on the Internet." *Journal of Social Issues,* 2002; and M. Orecklin. "Are You with Anyone?" *Time,* February 5, 2001, pp. 31–35.

70. See, for example, Clifford Stoll. *Silicon Snake Oil: Second Thoughts on the Information Highway.* New York: Anchor Books, 1995, p. 219.

71. See Nicholas Negroponte. *Being Digital.* New York: Vintage Books, 1995.

72. David F. Gallagher. "A Site to Pour Out Emotions, and Just about Anything Else." *New York Times,* September 5, 2002, p. G6.

73. Marilyn Elias. "You've Got Trauma, but Writing Can Help." *USA Today,* July 1, 2002, p. 6D.

74. Stephanie Armour. "Boss: It's in the E-Mail." *Wall Street Journal,* April 10, 1999, p. B3.

75. Sharon Bower and Gordon Bower. *Asserting Yourself.* Reading, MA: Addison-Wesley, 1977.

76. Goleman, *Emotional Intelligence,* p. 28.

Interviewing:
From Both Sides
of the Desk

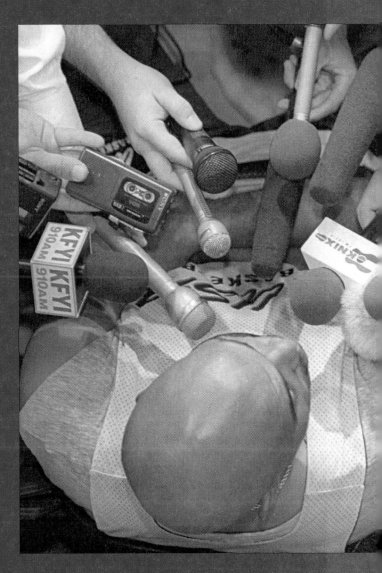

After finishing this chapter, you should be able to

1. Define *interview.*

2. Identify six types of interviews and the kind of information shared by participants in each interview.

3. Describe the stages of an interview.

4. Formulate closed, open, primary, and secondary questions.

5. Compare and contrast the roles and responsibilities of interviewer and interviewee.

Dear _____:
We enjoyed having you visit us here (last week) (last month) (recently). Everyone who talked with you was most impressed, and I personally feel that you are one of the most promising young (men) (women) I've seen in a long time. We all wish we could make you an offer at this time. However, ...

—From a corporation's
form letter

Twenty years from now, the typical American worker will have changed jobs four times and careers twice and will be employed in an occupation that does not exist today.

—Jeffrey Hallet

The employment interview is much like Match.com. The ultimate success of any corporation or business operation depends on the quality of the people it hires. How do employers find out who the best people are? They analyze résumés, call personal and professional references, and have interviews, during which they sit down with people who are strangers to draw conclusions whether a person is a "match" or not. The employment interview is a central tool in the search process.[1] At various points during the course of our lives, we will be expected to take part in interviews, assuming the role of interviewer or interviewee. The interview incorporates many of the characteristics and principles of communication that we have discussed. Culture, self-concept, perception, listening and feedback, nonverbal communication, language and meaning, and assertiveness all play a part in determining the effectiveness of communication in an interview setting. The time you spend interviewing or being interviewed can be critical. It can determine whether you give or get a loan, sell or purchase a product, hire the right person, get the job you want, or keep the job you have. By exploring the interview process, you can prepare yourself to participate in any interview—from either side of the desk.

Go to the *Online Learning Center* at www.mhhe.com/gamble8 and answer the questions in the *Self Inventory* to evaluate your understanding of interview apprehension.

WHAT IS AN INTERVIEW?

The Nature of Interviews: Beyond Conversation

Interviews, like other forms of communication, usually involve face-to-face interaction. However, in an interview—unlike ordinary person-to-person communication—at least one of the participants has a purpose that goes beyond interacting informally or simply talking for enjoyment. The conversation that occurs during an interview is planned and is designed to achieve specific objectives. Although sometimes three or more people are involved, you could

Piquing Career Interest

Have you found that you and/or your friends are taking more of an interest in criminal justice and forensics? If so, you are not alone. Even a large number of universities report having increased the scope of courses they offer in criminal justice. To what is this surge in interest attributed? Many believe it is due to television.

The public appears fascinated with investigation and the justice system, as evidenced by the popularity of television shows such as *Crossing Jordan, Law and Order, Forensic Files,* and *CSI.* In fact, *CSI-* (crime scene investigation–) based shows were the most highly watched shows on television in 2003. The popularity of media offerings has spilled over into the real world, sparking an increasing interest in criminology careers. Even the Nevada law enforcement agency Field Services Division has responded to popular interest in forensic science, changing its name to Crime Scene Investigations.[2]

In your opinion, to what extent, if any, is the portrayal of criminology careers on television and film contributing to unrealistic career expectations in those who now seek to become criminologists? For example, most of the crimes featured on CSI-type shows are solved in an hour, while they might take months or even years to solve in the real world. In addition, the programs on television rarely show the boring

CSI-type programs have sparked interest in criminology careers.

days, they reveal the staff working with state-of-the-art equipment that many cities cannot afford, and they have a crime solve rate that actual criminologists could never attain.

Media **WISE**

---

say that the **interview** is the most common type of purposeful, planned, decision-making, person-to-person communication. Thus, in the interview, interaction is structured, questions are asked and answered, and behavior is interchanged in an effort to explore predetermined subject matter and realize a definite goal. This description is in keeping with a well-known and often cited definition by Robert Goyer, Charles Redding, and John Richey, authors of *Interviewing Principles and Techniques: A Project Text.* They define an interview as a "form of oral communication involving two parties, at least one of whom has a preconceived and a serious purpose and both of whom speak and listen from time to time."[3]

No matter how an interview is defined, the participants are involved in a process of personal contact and exchange of information; they meet to give and receive information in order to make educated decisions. Ideally, the interview should be balanced: Both interviewer and interviewee should give themselves an opportunity to learn from the data given and received during the interchange.

interview
the most common type of purposeful, planned, decision-making, person-to-person communication

What types of information have you shared during interviews? What information have you received from the other participant in interviews? How do you think the information exchanged affected the decision-making process?

Skill
BUILDER

Talk, Talk, Talk

News shows, talk shows, and online interviews, in addition to allowing us to get to know news-makers and celebrities, often teach us about new topics, expose us to issues once kept private, and provide a platform to persons who, in general, would otherwise not be afforded such prominent exposure. The downside of such interviews is that, while some of the people interviewed are experts, others lack real knowledge, having no credentials or professional experience in the fields they are speaking about. Still, by experiencing them, we can learn about effective and ineffective interviewing techniques.

Select one news show, one talk show, and one online interview. For each, identify the interviewer and interviewee(s), the kinds of questions posed by the interviewer, the kinds of responses provided by the interviewee(s), the pace and tone of the interview, and any conflicts that occurred during the interview. Also discuss what you learned from the interview, whether or not you enjoyed it, and why.

Types of Interviews: Purposes and Goals

Interviews serve a variety of purposes. People engage in interviews to gather information (the information-gathering interview), to participate in an evaluation (the appraisal interview), to change someone's attitudes or behavior (the persuasive interview), to determine why someone is leaving a position (the exit interview), to provide guidance (the counseling interview), and to gain employment or select the right person for a job (the hiring or selection interview). Each of these types is characterized by different goals on the part of the participants.

Information-Gathering Interview

In an information-gathering interview, the interviewer's goal is to collect information, opinions, or data about a specific topic or person. It is the interviewer's

The interview is a popular format used by the media.

job to ask the interviewee questions designed to add to the interviewer's knowledge—questions about the interviewee's views, understanding, insights, predictions, and so on. Examples are interviews conducted with experts to complete an assignment and interviews conducted for the popular media. Whether the interviewer is Barbara Walters, Montel Williams, or you, the aim is to gather information from someone who has knowledge that you do not yet have.

Appraisal Interview

In an appraisal interview, the interviewee's performance is assessed by the interviewer, who is usually a superior from management. The goal is to evaluate what the interviewee is doing well and what he or she could do better. Through this means, expectations and behaviors are brought closer together. Interviewees gain perspective on how others view their work, and they reveal how they see themselves performing. In addition to reviews by supervisors, businesses also use what is called a 360 degree assessment. This means that an employee is not rated only by their superiors but by their peers and subordinates as well. In addition, some companies separate the performance review from the salary review process.[4]

Persuasive Interview

The goal of the interviewer in a persuasive interview is to change the interviewee's attitudes or behavior. It is hoped that, as the interview progresses, the interviewee will come to a desired conclusion or give a desired response. Salespeople typically conduct persuasive interviews with customers to close a sale.

Exit Interview

An exit interview is often conducted when an employee leaves an organization; it is an effort to determine why the match between employer and employee did not work or why the employee has decided to leave. Information obtained during an exit interview can be used to refine the hiring process, to help prevent other employees from leaving, or merely to make the departure a more pleasant experience for employer and employee.

Counseling Interview

A counseling interview is usually conducted by someone trained in psychology and is designed to provide guidance and support for the person being interviewed. Interviewees are helped to solve their problems, to work more productively, to interact with others more effectively, or to improve their relationships with friends and family members—in general, to cope more successfully with daily life.

There is only one person who can tell you whether any candidate is right for the job: the candidate him- or herself.
—Kevin J. Murphy,
Effective Listening:
Your Key to Career Success

Hiring or Selection Interview

A hiring or selection interview is conducted for the purpose of filling an employment position. The interviewer is an agent of the employer—perhaps a member of the personnel or human resources department or perhaps the person who would actually be the interviewee's supervisor. The interviewee, of course, is the person who is applying for the job. Because the hiring interview is experienced so commonly—and because it is so important—we will explore it in more detail.

For an example of an employment interview, view clip 3 on the CD

HOW DO YOU FEEL ABOUT INTERVIEWS? ASSESSING YOUR INTERVIEW ANXIETY

How do you feel about interviewing someone? How do you feel about being interviewed?

In the following list of fears commonly expressed by interviewers, circle the number beneath each statement that most accurately reflects your own level of apprehension: 0 = completely unconcerned; 1 = very mild concern; 2 = mild concern; 3 = more apprehensive than not; 4 = very frightened; 5 = a nervous wreck.

Interviewer

1. I won't be able to think of good questions to ask.
   0   1   2   3   4   5

2. I will appear very nervous.
   0   1   2   3   4   5

3. I will give the interviewee too little or too much information.
   0   1   2   3   4   5

4. I will not be considered credible.
   0   1   2   3   4   5

5. I will be asked questions about the company that I can't answer.
   0   1   2   3   4   5

6. I will be a poor judge of character.
   0   1   2   3   4   5

7. I will have poor rapport with the interviewee.
   0   1   2   3   4   5

8. I will not appear organized.
   0   1   2   3   4   5

9. I will be ineffective at probing for more information.
   0   1   2   3   4   5

10. I will not hire the right person for the job.
   0   1   2   3   4   5

Total the numbers you circled to arrive at your "interviewer's anxiety" score.

The following are some fears frequently expressed by interviewees. Circle the numbers that most accurately reflect your own level of apprehension: 0 = completely unconcerned; 1 = very mild concern; 2 = mild concern; 3 = more apprehensive than not; 4 = very frightened; 5 = a nervous wreck.

Interviewee

1. I will be asked questions I cannot answer.
   0   1   2   3   4   5

2. I will not dress properly for the interview.
   0   1   2   3   4   5

3. I will appear very nervous.
   0   1   2   3   4   5

4. I will not appear competent.
   0   1   2   3   4   5

5. The interviewer will cross-examine me.
   0   1   2   3   4   5

6. I will be caught in a lie.
   0   1   2   3   4   5

7. I will talk too much or too little.
   0   1   2   3   4   5

8. I will have poor rapport with the interviewer.
   0   1   2   3   4   5

9. I will undersell or oversell myself.
   0   1   2   3   4   5

10. I won't be hired.
    0   1   2   3   4   5

Total the numbers you circled to arrive at your "interviewee's anxiety" score.

Your scores indicate how frightened you are of assuming the role of interviewer or interviewee. If you accumulated 45 to 50 points, you are a nervous wreck; if you scored 35 to 44 points, you are too frightened; if you scored 20 to 34 points, you are somewhat apprehensive; if you scored 11 to 20 points, you are too casual; if you scored 0 to 10 points, you are not at all concerned—that is, you simply don't care.

Contrary to what you might assume, not being concerned at all about participating in an interview is just as much of a problem as being a nervous wreck, and being too casual can do as much damage as being too frightened. An interviewer or interviewee should be apprehensive to a degree. If you're not concerned about what will happen during the interview, then you won't care about making a good impression and, as a result, will not perform as effectively as you could.

THE HIRING OR SELECTION INTERVIEW

Some interviews are over before they begin. Why? Because the interviewer asks a question that he or she thinks is easy but that the interviewee cannot answer. For example, on being asked what she had to offer the company, all one interviewee could respond was "Hmmmmm, that's a toughie." Then she added, "I was more wanting to hear what you could do for me." The candidate did not get the job.[5] How would you have replied to that question?

The hiring or selection interview is among the best known and most widely experienced type of interview and probably is the next major interview you will face. In addition, the vast majority of organizations use the hiring interview as a primary tool for selecting employees.[6]

It is as a result of a hiring or selection interview that we find ourselves accepted or rejected by a prospective employer—an individual, a small business, a large corporation, and so on. The employment interview offers a unique opportunity for the potential employer and the potential employee to share meaningful information that will permit each to determine whether their association would be beneficial and productive. In a sense, the employment interview can be said to give both participants a chance to test each other by asking and answering relevant questions. Employers hope to gather information about

The hiring interview is the primary tool for selecting employees. Both interviewer and interviewee gain information during the interview.

you during the interview that your résumé, references, and any personality tests you may have been asked to take do not provide. They also believe the person-to-person approach is an effective way to sell their organization to you. As an applicant, you seek information about the employer and the job during the interview. You can deduce from your interaction with the interviewer what your long-term relationship might be and what life in that organization might be like if you are hired.

The better prepared you are for an employment interview, the better your chances will be of performing effectively and realizing your job objectives. Remember, an interview is certainly not "just talk."[7] Both the interviewer and the interviewee must plan and prepare to participate in an interview. Only with planning and preparation will important questions and answers be shared and interview anxiety reduced. Let's begin by familiarizing ourselves with some important aspects of the hiring or selection interview, most of which are also aspects of interviews in general.

Preliminary Tasks: Preparing the Cover Letter and Résumé

The job of the applicant is to be fully prepared for the interview. By completing two documents—a cover letter and a résumé—that are well written and register a positive impression, you provide the interviewer with a preview of who you are and why you are qualified for the position.

There are a number of facts to keep in mind as you do this. When asked how much time they spend reviewing résumés, 56 percent of executives surveyed admitted to reviewing them for five minutes or less.[8] Thus, you need to work to capture the attention of the person to whom you send your résumé.

The Cover Letter

The cover letter introduces you to the interviewer. It is a brief (usually one-page), well-written letter that fulfills the following six criteria: (1) It expresses your interest in a position; (2) it tells how you learned of the position; (3) it reviews your primary skills and accomplishments; (4) it explains why these

qualify you for the job; (5) it highlights any items of special interest about you that are relevant to your ability to perform the job; and (6) it contains a request for an interview. A résumé is always included with a cover letter. Figure 10.1 presents a sample cover letter.

FIGURE 10.1
Sample Cover Letter.

1616 River Road
New Milford, NJ 07646
April 10, 2004

Ms. Kelly Ames
Vice President, Human Resources
Stars and Strategies
1850 Broadway
New York, NY 10023

Dear Ms. Ames:

Your advertisement for a client representative in sports management appearing in last Sunday's *New York Times* immediately caught my attention and piqued my interest. My education and training uniquely qualify me to assist you in taking Stars and Strategies to the next level.

According to your advertisement, the job includes "assisting in the coordination and implementation of client services, as well as assisting in the identification and opening of new markets." It occurs to me that my background and experience in sports marketing parallel your needs. In addition, I am a highly motivated individual and a self-starter, with the following special qualifications to offer:

Four years of formal training in marketing
  and entrepreneurial studies
Proficiency in computers and Web site design

Once you have examined the enclosed résumé, I would like to talk with you about how I can put my skills and abilities to work for Stars and Strategies. I hope to have the opportunity to discuss in depth how my educational background and professional experience can contribute to your company's growth.

Sincerely,

John P. Garcia

John P. Garcia
Enclosure

The Résumé

The résumé summarizes your abilities and accomplishments. It details what you have to contribute that will meet the company's needs and help solve the employer's problems. Although formats differ, the résumé typically includes the following:

1. Contact information—your name, address, telephone number, and e-mail address
2. Job objective—a phrase or sentence that focuses on your area of expertise
3. Employment history—your job experience, both paid and unpaid, beginning with the most recent
4. Education—schools attended, degree(s) completed or expected, dates of completion, and a review of courses that relate directly to your ability to perform the job
5. Relevant professional certifications and affiliations
6. Community service
7. Special skills and interests you possess that are revelent to the job
8. References—people who agree to elaborate on your work history, capabilities, and character; reveal only that references are available on request unless you are asked to provide specific references at the time you submit your résumé

Figure 10.2 presents a sample résumé.

Structure: Stages of the Interview

Most effective interviews have a discernible structure; that is, they have a beginning, a middle, and an end. The beginning, or opening, is the segment of the process that provides an orientation to what will come. The middle, or body, is the longest segment and the one during which both parties really get down to business. The end, or close, is the segment during which the participants prepare to take leave of one another.

Just as the right kind of greeting at the start of a conversation can help create a feeling of friendliness, so the opening of an interview should be used to establish rapport between interviewer and interviewee.[9] The primary purpose of the opening is to make it possible for both parties to participate freely and honestly by creating an atmosphere of trust and goodwill and by explaining the purpose and scope of the meeting. Conversational icebreakers and orientation statements perform important functions at this stage. Typical icebreakers include comments about the weather, the surroundings, and current events—or a compliment. The idea is to use small talk to help make the interview a human encounter rather than a mechanical one. Typical orientation remarks include an identification of the interview's purpose, a preview of the topics to be discussed, and statements that motivate the respondent and act as a conduit, or transition, to the body of the interview.

In the body of the interview, the interactants really get down to business. At this point, the interviewer and interviewee might discuss work experiences, including the applicant's strengths, weaknesses, major accomplishments,

For the next few days, keep track of the verbal and nonverbal messages people use when they say hello or good-bye. Which beginnings and endings were particularly communicative? Which were ineffective? Did you observe any false starts or false endings? How could they have been avoided?

JOHN P. GARCIA

1616 River Road
New Milford, New Jersey 07646
201-836-4444
jpg@aol.com

EDUCATION
School of Management, Syracuse University
Bachelor of Science in Management, May 2001; GPA: 4.0
Concentration in Marketing and Entrepreneurial Studies

HONORS
Golden Key National Honor Society
Dean's List 1999–2004
President, Investment Club

EXPERIENCE
Steiner Sports Marketing, New York, New York
(Summer 1999, 2000) Marketing Intern
Assisted in the management of client relations
Solved client and customer problems
Represented the company at numerous special events

Shearson-Lehman Brothers, Stamford, Connecticut
(Summer 1998) Investment Intern
Assisted financial consultants
Analyzed trades
Evaluated financial securities options

KPM&G, Montvale, New Jersey
(Summer 1997) Accounting Intern
Assisted in analysis of weekly financial reports
Prepared daily cash activity records
Conducted interviews with clients to determine level of satisfaction

COMPUTER SKILLS
Proficient in HTML and Web site creation
Experienced in using Lotus, WordPerfect for Windows, Excel, PowerPoint, Quark Express, and PageMaker
Adept at mastering new programs and applications

ACTIVITIES
Student Council Representative, 2002–present
Peer Tutor, 2000–present
Orientation Leader, 2000–2002
Soccer Team, 1997–present

REFERENCES
Available upon request

FIGURE 10.2
Sample Résumé.

In your résumé, do you have the most important information first?

Ethics & COMMUNICATION

Résumé Padding and Résumé Poaching

1. Résumé padding has been around for a long time. Would you lie on your résumé to get your foot in the door? Would you "fix up" your résumé to help you look better on paper than you really are?

Not too long ago, Notre Dame's football coach, George O'Leary, had to step down from his head coach position after admitting that he had falsified the academic and athletic credentials listed on his résumé. In your opinion, should O'Leary have been fired for his résumé misrepresentations? Why or why not?

2. It is not merely some résumé writers who are ethically challenged. So are some recruiters. In fact, résumés posted on Internet job boards are not necessarily private or restricted to recruiters

and other employers who pay a fee for access. While some sites may sell their résumés, résumé poaching also threatens the privacy of job seekers. The employees of competitive sites have been known to pose as recruiters in order to download thousands of résumés without permission. Persons who post their résumés on supposedly "secure" sites find themselves harassed by readers who object to their professions. For example, one job seeker in chemistry found herself harassed by activists against animal research.[10] In your opinion, should Internet job-search sites be billboards for all to see, or should they be kept private and recruiters and employers adequately screened before given access?

"It has come to my attention, Pickarell, that you may have been somewhat less than forthcoming in your résumé."

difficult problems tackled in the past, and career goals. Educational background and activities or interests are relevant areas to probe during this phase of the interview. Breadth of knowledge and the ability to manage time are also common areas of concern.

During the close of the interview, the main points covered are reviewed and summarized. Since an interview can affect any future meetings the interactants may have, care must be taken to make the leave-taking comfortable.[11] Expressing appreciation for the time and effort given is important; neither interviewee nor interviewer should feel discarded. In other words, the door should be left open for future contacts.

Skill

BUILDER

Wake-Up Call

According to one résumé expert, "The biggest mistake that people are making is that their résumés have no real impact. . . . A good résumé won't get you a job, but it will get you in the door."[12]

Look at the cartoon that appears in this box. What steps can you take to ensure that your résumé doesn't end up as origami? Describe how you would market yourself to ensure that the person who receives your résumé actually opens it and spends some time reading it? For example, one applicant for a marketing position sent her résumé in a package of gourmet coffees, which she sent to the potential interviewer with the slogan "Lindsay will wake up your marketing" affixed to the package. Do you think her résumé was read?

Questions: The Heart of the Interview

How many times a day are you asked questions? How many times a day do you ask questions? Questions are obviously a natural part of our daily discourse.

Questions asked in the course of typical, everyday interpersonal encounters perform a number of functions. They help us find out needed information, satisfy our curiosity, demonstrate our interest, and test the knowledge of the person we are questioning; at the same time, they permit the person we are questioning to reveal himself or herself to us.

For these reasons, questions are the primary means of collecting data in an interview. Not only do questions set the tone for an interview, but they

> *The only way to get the accurate answers is to ask the right questions.*
> —**Kevin J. Murphy,**
> ***Effective Listening: Your Key to Career Success***

also determine whether the interview will yield valuable information or prove to be practically worthless. Asking the right questions opens the window into the personality of both the interviewer and the interviewee.[13]

The effective interviewer, like the effective newswriter, can benefit from this famous verse by Rudyard Kipling:

> I keep six honest serving-men
> (They taught me all I know).
> Their names are what and why and when
> And how and where and who.

The interrogatives *what, where, when, who, how,* and *why* are used throughout an interview because they lay a foundation of knowledge on which to base decisions or conclusions.

During the course of an interview, closed, open, primary, and secondary questions may all be used, in any combination.[14] **Closed questions** are highly structured and can be answered with a simple yes or no or in a few words. Following are examples of closed questions:

closed questions
highly structured questions answerable with a simple yes or no or in a few words

> How old are you?
> Where do you live?
> What schools did you attend?
> Did you graduate in the top quarter of your class?
> Would you accept the salary offered?
> What starting salary do you expect?

open questions
questions that offer the interviewee freedom with regard to the choice and scope of an answer

Open questions are broader than closed questions and are less restricting or structured; hence, they offer the interviewee more freedom with regard to the choice and scope of an answer. Following are examples of open questions:

> Tell me about yourself.
> What are your perceptions of our industry?
> How do you judge success?
> Why did you choose to interview for this job?
> What are your career goals?
> Describe a time you failed.
> Describe a time when you failed to solve a conflict.

Open questions give interviewees a chance to express their feelings, attitudes, and values. Furthermore, they indicate that the interviewer is interested in understanding the interviewee's perspective.

primary questions
questions used to introduce topics or explore a new area

Open and closed questions may be either primary or secondary. **Primary questions** are used to introduce topics or to begin exploring a new area. "What is your favorite hobby?" and "Tell me about your last job" are examples of primary questions—the first is closed; the second is open. A smart interviewer will prepare a list of primary questions before going to the interview, and smart interviewees will anticipate the primary questions they may be asked.

secondary questions
probing questions that follow up primary questions

Secondary questions—sometimes called probing questions—are used to follow up primary questions. They ask for an explanation of the ideas and feelings behind answers to other questions, and they are frequently used when answers to primary questions are vague or incomplete. Following are examples of secondary questions:

Go on. What do you mean?

Would you explain that further?

Can you give me an example?

What did you have in mind when you said that?

"Uh-huh" and "Hmm" are typical comments to the answers produced by secondary questions. The effective use of secondary questions distinguishes skilled from unskilled interviewers.[15]

To ask effective follow-up questions, you need to be an effective listener. You must be sensitive to and on the lookout for an interviewee's feelings and attitudes, in addition to the facts and opinions he or she states. You need to develop techniques that will permit you to see the world through the other person's eyes.

Just as skillful listening is essential if one is to be an effective conversationalist, it is also essential to the give-and-take that characterizes an effective interview. In fact, the key to the success of professional interviewers, such as Ted Koppel, Barbara Walters, Diane Sawyer, and Oprah Winfrey, is their ability to listen.[16] Of course, the interviewee must also be an effective listener.

Objectives: Roles and Responsibilities

Let's now examine the roles and responsibilities of each participant in an interview.

Both interviewer and interviewee come to the interview with certain goals in mind. Interviewers usually have a threefold objective. They hope to (1) gather information that will enable them to evaluate the interviewees' probable performance accurately, (2) persuade applicants that the business or organization is a good one to work for, and (3) ascertain whether the applicants and the people with whom they will work will be compatible. Interviewers also want to keep their own jobs. Remember that a company invests both time and money in hiring and training a new employee. If the employee doesn't work out, the investment is sacrificed, and some of the blame obviously falls on the original interviewer.

To fulfill their objectives, interviewers need to master the art of structuring a successful interview, use effective questioning techniques, and approach each interview with flexibility and sensitivity. Good interviewers work hard during an interview. They wear three hats: information seeker, information giver, and decision maker (see Figure 10.3). They recognize good answers, are aware of word choices, and pick up on silences and hesitations. They are active, not passive, participants as they seek to differentiate what is real from what is make-believe. They need to be patient observers and search for the inner truth that lies beneath the surface of a candidate.

You might be in demand for a job. And the potential employer might even be looking for someone with just your skills. But you still have to demonstrate that you're the right person for the job. Thus, interviewees also bear responsibility during an interview. They, too, need to speak and listen, provide

According to Mimi Collins, spokesperson for the National Association of Colleges and Employers, employers often cite good communication skills, both verbal and written, as important. Honesty and integrity are second, teamwork skills are third, interpersonal skills fourth, and strong work ethic fifth. How do you evaluate yourself against these criteria?

FIGURE 10.3
Responsibilities in an Interview.

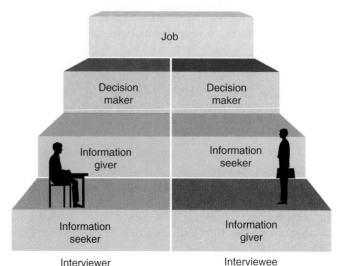

For an example of how to get a job in the TV and magazine industry, view clips 16, 17 on the CD

information, and at the same time collect information that will help them decide whether or not to accept the job. To accomplish these goals, interviewees need to research the organization to which they are applying and try to anticipate the questions they will be asked. They also need to plan to ask questions themselves. It's unfortunate and unproductive when only the interviewer gains information from an interview. The interviewee can often learn much about work conditions and the prospects for advancement by asking questions and probing for answers. To the extent that interviewees have a right to share the control of the interview, they can affect its direction and content. Like interviewers, interviewees need to be good listeners as well as adaptable and sensitive to the image they project.

Effective interviewees work hard at self-assessment. In effect, they take stock of themselves in order to determine who they are, what their career needs and their goals are, and how they can best sell themselves to an employer.

As a prospective interviewee, you will find it useful to prepare by thinking about and answering the following questions:

1. For what types of positions has my training prepared me?
2. What has been my most rewarding experience?
3. What type of job do I want?
4. Would I be happier working alone or with others?
5. What qualifications do I have that make me feel I would be successful in the job of my choice?
6. What type or types of people do I want to work for?
7. What type or types of people do I not want to work for?
8. How do I feel about receiving criticism?
9. What salary will enable me to meet my financial needs?
10. What salary will enable me to live comfortably?
11. What will interviewers want to know about me, my interests, my background, and my experiences?

In addition to conducting a self-survey, the interviewee needs to work to withstand the pressure of the interview situation. Are you prepared to maintain your composure while being stared at, interrupted, spoken to abruptly, or asked difficult questions? Have you practiced enough to keep cool when on the interview hot seat?[17] How do you think you would react if you were asked tough questions? The following questions are favorites among interviewers.[18] How would you answer them?

1. Tell me about yourself.
2. What do you think you're worth?
3. What are you good at?
4. If we hired you, what about this organization would concern you most?
5. What attributes do you think an effective manager should possess?
6. What are your short-term goals? How are they different from your long-term goals?
7. How has your background prepared you for this position?
8. What are your major strengths and weaknesses?
9. How would a former employer or instructor describe you?
10. Why did you leave your last job?
11. What do you consider your greatest accomplishment?
12. What's wrong with you?
13. What would you do if I told you that I thought you were giving a very poor interview today?
14. How long do you plan to remain with us if you get this job?
15. What would you like to know about us?

Some interviewers prefer to ask even more searching questions, such as the following:

Tell me about how you handled the last mistake you made.

Are there things at which you aren't very good.

At your weekly team meetings, your boss unexpectedly begins aggressively critiquing your performance on a current project. What would you do?

You're in a situation in which you have two very important responsibilities that both have deadlines that are impossible to meet. You cannot accomplish both. How do you handle that situation?[19]

Practice in answering questions like these—under both favorable and unfavorable conditions—is essential.[20] It is important that you know what you want to say during the interview and that you use the questions you are asked as an opportunity to say it. Along the way, you can flatter the interviewer by offering comments like "That's a really good question" or "I think you've touched on something really important."

The interviewer can, of course, consult a résumé to ascertain information about the applicant—about educational background and previous positions held, for example. However, gathering enough information to evaluate the personal qualities of an applicant is more difficult. Following is a list of personal qualifications, with the questions interviewers typically ask to evaluate them.

1. *Quality:* Skill in managing one's own career
   Question: What specific things have you done deliberately to get where you are today?
2. *Quality:* Skill in managing others?
   Question: What are some examples of things you do and do not like to delegate?
3. *Quality:* Sense of responsibility
   Question: What steps do you take to see that things do not fall through the cracks when you are supervising a project?
4. *Quality:* Skill in working with people
   Question: If we assembled in one room a group of people you have worked with and asked them to describe what it was like to work with you, what would they be likely to say? What would your greatest supporter say? What would your severest critic say?

Most employment interviews can be grouped into one of three categories: the behavioral, the case, and the stress interview. In the **behavioral interview,** an employer is looking for specific examples from the prospective employee of times when he or she has exhibited specific skills. When asked a question such as "Tell me about a time you acted in a leadership role," the interviewee might respond, "I was the director of a fund-raising group," or "I was an officer in Women in Communication." In the **case interview,** a company presents the interviewee with a business case and asks for him or her to work through it. To help prepare yourself for such an interview, check out the company Web site beforehand. Some companies post sample cases on their sites. The third type of interview, the **stress interview,** typically includes more than one interviewer firing questions at the interviewee to see how that person handles himself or herself during a stressful situation.

What other qualities do you believe interviewers look for in interviewees? If you were an interviewer, what questions would you ask to determine if a person possessed those qualities?

behavioral interview

an employment interview in which an employer looks for the employee to provide specific examples of specific skills

case interview

an employment interview in which the interviewee is presented with a business case by the employer and asked to work through it

stress interview

an employment interview in which more than one person fires questions at an interviewee

---

Skill BUILDER

Let's Get Tough

Human relations consultant and interviewer trainer Justin Menkes helps employment recruiters learn how to gather a lot of information in a brief period of time. To accomplish this, he suggests they ask questions like those identified in the text. Try your hand at answering one of those questions: You have two very important responsibilities that both have deadlines that are impossible to meet. You cannot accomplish both. How do you handle that situation?

Which of the following possible responses does your answer most resemble?

1. I'd focus on the project I'm most comfortable with and give it my all.

2. I'd plan carefully, assign segments of the project to others, and multitask so that I could complete both.

3. I'd ask my supervisor which project is most important to the company.

According to Menkes, the first response suggests that the interviewee's focus is on himself or herself, the second response does not answer the question asked, and the third response reveals an interest in the needs of the company and an interest in developing a collaborative relationship.[21]

To be effective, an interview requires both participants to work hard. Questioner and respondent constantly exchange information. While either the interviewer or the interviewee speaks, the other is conveying nonverbal information through posture, facial expression, gestures, and so on. You may stop talking during an interview, but that does not mean that you stop communicating. Know what you are trying to accomplish with your verbal and nonverbal messages.

Impression Management: Effective Interviewing

How well do we need to know someone before we believe we understand them? Experience says not very long. According to psychologists Nalini Ambady and Frank Bernieri, the power of first impressions arms us with a kind of prerational ability or intuition for making judgements about others that color the other impressions we gather over time.[22] It becomes a self-fulfilling prophecy. We assume that the way someone behaves in an interview is indicative of the way that person always behaves.

As an interviewee, what first impressions do you make? How do you know?

The adage that first impressions count apparently holds true for job interviews.[23] In fact, the word *interview* is derived from the French word *entrevoir*, meaning "to see one another" or "to meet." What happens when an interviewer and an interviewee meet for the first time? What variables influence the impressions the interviewer forms of the interviewee? For example, most interviewers make their decisions about an applicant during the actual course of the interview. In fact, although most decide in the last quarter of the interview whether or not to invite the applicant back, a bias for or against the candidate is established earlier in the interview, often during the first four to six minutes.

In *Your Attitude Is Showing,* Elwood N. Chapman notes:

> First impressions are important because they have a lasting quality. People you meet for the first time appear to have little radar sets tuned into your attitude. If your attitude is positive, they receive a friendly, warm signal, and they are attracted to you; if your attitude is negative, they receive an unfriendly signal, and they try to avoid you.[24]

Apparently, once interviewers form an initial impression, they selectively pick up on whatever information supports that impression. In effect, interviewers make self-fulfilling prophecies.

According to researcher Lois Einhorn, how much of the time allotted for an interview is actually used also sends an important message.[25] She found

Voices and Impression Management

People from different cultures use their voices differently, a fact that could lead to misunderstandings between interviewers and interviewees. People from the Middle East, for example, tend to speak louder than Westerners, causing Westerners to perceive them as overly emotional. In contrast, the Japanese tend to be much more soft-spoken, leading Westerners to believe that they are extremely polite and humble.

How could such habitual ways of speaking affect the interview process? What can interviewers and interviewees do to diminish such perceptual barriers?

EXPLORING
Diversity

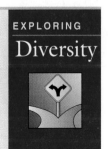

that interviewees who were not hired had participated in shorter interviews than successful applicants. She also found that successful interviewees spoke a greater percentage of the time than their unsuccessful counterparts. In fact, the successful applicants spoke for some 55 percent of the total interview time, whereas the unsuccessful applicants spoke only 37 percent of the time. Seeming to control the interview also leaves an impression. In Einhorn's research, successful applicants initiated 56 percent of the comments made during their interviews, whereas unsuccessful applicants were viewed as followers—they initiated only 37 percent of the comments. It is important for an interviewee to send messages that he or she is active, not passive.

The Job Applicant

It is important to realize that, as a job applicant, you will have to work to manage the initial impression you give. You will be evaluated on how you come across during the interview and on how you present yourself. What you say and how you say it are your basic resources—the key tools you have to work with. In effect, you are your own marketing manager; therefore, it's up to you to sell yourself to the interviewer. How you communicate your assets, your values, your attitudes, and your overall credibility will, at least in part, determine whether or not you are hired. Your resources and your ability to share what you are go with you to every interview.

Of necessity, interviewers need to find out a great deal about you in a short period of time. They want to evaluate your strengths as a communicator, your general personality, your social effectiveness, and your character. The interviewer also wants to determine your needs and wants—including your career and educational goals, interests, and aspirations. Interviewers will assess your appearance, your ability to use body language effectively, and your ability to maintain control during the interview.

To a large extent, the interviewer's assessment of you will determine whether or not you get the job. The following are some of the negative factors that turn off the interviewer and lead to applicant rejection:

Arrogance
Lack of motivation or enthusiasm
Immaturity
Poor communication skills
Unclear goals
Unwillingness to relocate or travel
Deficient preparation for the interview
Lack of experience
Too sloppy or too slick an appearance.[26]

Among the factors leading to your receiving job offers are the following:

A pleasant personality (likableness)
Enthusiasm

Interviewers will use dress and appearance in their assessment of you. Were you an interviewer, how would you assess the dress of these two candidates?

Your Marketing Profile

1. Identify the assets and talents you would bring to the position of your choice. In other words, enumerate the qualities and skills that would make you a good investment for an employer.

2. Identify your shortcomings and developmental needs. Enumerate the qualities and skills you wish to develop further and plan how you would do this.

3. Identify those personality strengths you will attempt to communicate during an interview.

4. Identify the communication skills you will use.

5. Using the information you gave in steps 1–4, compose a "Position Wanted" advertisement for yourself.

Skill
BUILDER

Interpersonal skills
Ability to function as part of a team
Knowledge of the field
Computer literacy
Creativity
Clear purpose and goals
Flexibility and the ability to handle change
Confidence in what you are doing and who you are
Integrity and moral standards
Global perspective
Sense of humor[27]

At least in part, interviewers will judge you on the basis of the nonverbal cues you send. Interviewers consistently give higher general ratings to applicants who are rated high in nonverbal expression than to applicants who are rated low. A highly rated nonverbal presentation includes (1) maintaining comfortable eye contact with the interviewer rather than looking away; (2) varying the pitch and volume of your voice rather than speaking in a monotone, whispering, or shouting; (3) eliminating hesitations ("uhs" and "ums"); (4) leaning forward from the trunk rather than slumping in your seat; and (5) communicating a high level of energy supported by smiles, hand gestures, and appropriate body movements. In like fashion, the avoidance of tightly held hands, twitching feet or fingers, and various other signs of physical tension will influence the interviewer positively.

Obviously, appropriate dress is also important to the impression you make during the interview. Most job applicants are aware that casual dress is out and conservative styles are in at job interviews. Ultraconservative is becoming the norm and the color gray, with its connotation of rock-solid dependability, the color of choice.[28] Consultant John Molloy reports that, when you interview for a job, it is advisable to dress as if you were a candidate for a position one or two steps higher than the one for which you are actually applying.[29] He notes that a man is safe if he wears a dark suit (navy blue, dark gray, or gray pinstripe); a white, light blue, or pale yellow shirt; and a conservative, nondescript tie. Molloy finds that gray suits worn with pale blue shirts and dark blue suits worn with pale yellow shirts increase likability. He

What type of clothing would you consider inappropriate for a job interview? What type of clothing would you wear to a job interview?

also comments that a solid gray or a conservative blue or gray pinstripe suit—preferably a three-piece suit—is the most powerful and authoritative suit and should therefore be saved for the crucial interview with the most important person you will see. Two decades ago, Molloy believed that a woman applying for a professional job should wear a dark-colored, skirted suit and a white or blue blouse. Today, however, he has softened his advice to women. Women no longer need to dress like men to succeed. Women may wear blazers instead of man-tailored coats, dresses with jackets, and pantsuits.[30] Why is there so much concern with dress? When all else is comparable—education, aptitude, experience—appearance may well be the deciding factor. The candidate who looks the most professional, competent, and confident will probably be the one who is hired.

You can cement a positive image in two ways. First, don't ask about vacation, company benefits, and personal days during your first interview.[31] Work instead to display your knowledge of the company and to understand its goals and how you can fit in. Ask questions that touch on strategic and tactical issues. Second, be sure to send a brief thank-you note to the person or persons who interviewed you. Richard Bolles, an interview specialist, writes: "This is one of the most essential steps in the whole job-seeking process—and the one most overlooked by job-seekers."[32] In fact, one of the authors was actually told that a person who interviewed her for a teaching position had recommended her because she was the only applicant to send him a thank-you note after the interview.[33]

The Interviewer

It should be remembered that, in any interview, the interviewer who judges is also judged by the interviewee. To the extent that this judgment is favorable, the interviewer can elicit the interviewee's fullest cooperation in accomplishing the aims and objectives of the interview.

The interviewer's ability to set the tone by reducing the interviewee's initial anxiety is an extremely important factor in the interviewee's first impression. During the body of the interview, the interviewer must work to (1) maintain control of the interchange, (2) deliver information so that it is clearly understood, (3) listen for both facts and feelings, (4) build trust, and (5) distinguish relevant from irrelevant information. Finally, at the conclusion, it is up to the interviewer to explain to the applicant the next course of action to be taken and to terminate the encounter smoothly and graciously.

Like interviewees, interviewers must be adept at using nonverbal cues. They must know when to pause and when to speak. For example, three- to six-second silences by interviewers have been found effective in getting interviewees to provide more in-depth information; this is one way the interviewer can increase the amount of time an applicant spends answering a question. Another way to increase the length of an applicant's response is for the interviewer to murmur "Mm-hmm" while nodding affirmatively. In fact, answers to questions posed by interviewers who say "Mm-hmm" have been found to be as much as two times longer than answers given to interviewers who offer no "Mm-hmms." When interviewees give a high rating of the interviewer's vocal communication and ability to listen, they tend to enjoy the interview more and rate the interviewer favorably in general.

DIVERSITY AND THE INTERVIEW

Our culture can influence how we conduct ourselves during an interview. For example, in collectivistic cultures such as those in China, Japan, and Korea, interviewees habitually display modesty. If Americans, who are used to stressing their positive qualities, were interviewing in any of those countries, they could be perceived as arrogant and self-centered. On the other hand, if persons from a collectivistic culture were to interview in the United States, they could be perceived as unassertive, lacking in confidence, and unprepared to assume leadership. While Western culture encourages people to be assertive and showcase strengths, Eastern culture traditionally teaches members to be more modest and humble about their personal achievements, qualifications, and experience. Similarly, Native American culture teaches that cooperation is a benefit and that one leads through deeds, not words. Thus, not wanting to appear boastful, Native Americans could also be hesitant to discuss their personal strengths.[34]

There are gender differences in what employees seek in a job. Survey results reveal that most men value compensation above all else, while most women put employee benefits first. Compensation is ranked third on most women's list, after opportunities for skill development.[35]

Age also correlates with what employees want most in a job. In contrast with all other groups, the under-thirties do not even rank benefits among their top five concerns. What is important to most persons in this age bracket are opportunities to develop skills, chances for promotion, compensation, vacations, and an appealing culture and colleagues.[36]

TECHNOLOGY AND THE JOB SEARCH

The Web is changing the way we find jobs. Persons with online savvy, who are able to demonstrate that they are technologically adept, can gain unexpected advantages over the competition because job openings are often posted online before they appear in newspapers.[37]

Applicants can also use a company's home page to get background information on the organization or to e-mail a résumé and cover letter. A company's Web site may be a good place to learn about the company's culture.

Many sites provide an overview of work-related policies and perks, including whether the firm encourages job sharing or telecommuting.[38] In addition, many companies post job openings on their own sites as well as on recruitment sites such as "The Monster Board," "Career Mosaic," and the "Online Career Center." In fact, there are an estimated 3,000 job-search sites that offer numerous vacancies, extensive résumé databases, and software programs that will e-mail you when job listings match your profile.[39] Following are Web sites you can consult for information on companies and jobs:

Company Information

> http://www.wsj.com
>
> http://www.nytimes.com
>
> http://www.bizweb.com
>
> http://www.companiesOnline.com
>
> http://www.adamsonline.com

Discussion groups about jobs and career opportunities

The web is revolutionizing the job search. Monster.com is a job search site. Log on and see if you can find a job opening of interest to you.

Job Information

http://stats.bls.gov

The Bureau of Labor Statistics Web site, which offers information on positions by state, listing the average salary being paid per position

http://www.careerbuilder.com

http://www.careersite.com

http://www.espan.com

http://www.monsterboard.com

http://www.careermosaic.com

Usenet newsgroups and listserv mailing lists are two other Internet resources you can use to learn about employment possibilities.

Some jobs seekers are creating their own home pages, featuring both their online résumé and business card.[40] A variety of online resources and computer programs exist to help you prepare your résumé. Many provide you with templates that you can complete as is or customize. You can also post your résumé on the Net by e-mailing it to a server.

In fact, more and more companies now request that potential employees submit an electronic résumé (a résumé that is obtained and analyzed electronically by the employer).[41] An electronic résumé should include key words that describe the person's competencies and skills. Once the employer scans the résumé into the company's computer tracking system, when a job becomes available, the employer can efficiently search the résumés contained in the database by key words that describe the characteristics a person qualified for the position should have. Electronic résumés require standard formats and block letters that are plain and simple. A résumé that is going to be scanned should not use boldface type, underlining, or bullets, because these special effects interfere with the scanning process. To facilitate the initial résumé screening, which will be done by a bias-free computer, an electronic résumé typically contains a block paragraph of key words, which immediately follows the identification information centered above it. Unlike your traditional résumé, which probably contains action verbs such as *communicates well,* your electronic résumé should contain nouns, such as *organizational skills.* A number of Internet sites can help you prepare an electronic résumé. By posting your résumé on a home page, you increase the likelihood that an employer looking for someone with your background and qualifications will access your résumé and contact you directly.

The Cyberspace Job Search

e‑SEARCH

Visit "Career Mosaic," "Yahoo!" and any other sites you discover to see what online résumés look like and to explore links to résumé posting resources.

Visit the home pages of companies that you are interested in working for. Record what is presented there. How does information on each Web site help you prepare your résumé and plan for an interview? Based on what you discover on the Web sites and in printed materials, such as annual reports about the company and its needs, identify what you would include in your online résumé to showcase your experience, education, and unique talents and skills.

A number of online career services offer job candidates listing enhancement. Careerbuilder.com, for example, has a "résumé upgrade" service, which lets users pay to have their résumés appear near or at the top of the list when an employer conducts a search. Users of Monster.com can pay for a premium service that presents their résumés in bold amid the plain-text search results.[42] Do you think job seekers should be able to buy themselves attention?

In addition, employers are using computers to add flexibility to currently available interviewing channels. By conducting a computer-assisted interview, for example, employers are able to conduct preliminary conversations with people geographically dispersed from them. In increasing numbers, in addition to telephones and videoconferences, interviews also are being conducted via e-mail and chat groups. Although these channels do not enable interviewer and interviewee to shake hands with each other, and despite the fact that such interviews will probably not replace face-to-face interviews, they do expand the information resources used by organizations and can be used to supplement face-to-face interviews.[43] There is at least one thing to be very cautious of when it comes to technology. Use a business-sounding e-mail address. Do not use an e-mail address such as "hotlips" or "imrbaby."

LOOKING AT THE LAW: ILLEGAL QUESTIONS IN INTERVIEWS

While we have seen that some interview questions are tough and probing, others concerning age, race, marital status, and other personal characteristics are protected under antidiscrimination statutes and are illegal to ask. The Equal Employment Opportunity Commission (EEOC) is the arm of the federal government responsible for monitoring discriminatory practices in hiring decisions. More than three decades ago, the EEOC initially issued employment interview guidelines. Over the years, these guidelines have been updated, and the laws of the EEOC apply in all 50 states.

According to the EEOC, criteria that are legally irrelevant to job qualifications are discriminatory. Interviewees in all states are protected from answering questions about race, ethnicity, marital status, age, sex, disability, and arrest records. It is important for both interviewers and interviewees to realize which questions are legally impermissible in employment interviews. Both parties to the interview have to be well versed in their rights to be able to protect them. The determining factor in whether a question is lawful is simple: Is the information sought relevant to your ability to perform the job? The following are among the most commonly asked illegal questions:

1. Are you physically disabled?
2. How old are you?
3. Are you married?
4. Do you have or are you planning to have a family?
5. What political party do you belong to?
6. Have you ever served time in prison?
7. Is English your native language?
8. What is your religion?
9. Will you need to live near a mosque?
10. Is it hard for you to find child care?
11. Are you a United States citizen?

12. Where were your parents born?
13. Who lives with you?
14. When did you graduate from college?
15. What was the last date of your physical exam?
16. To what clubs or social organizations do you belong?

17. Have you had any recent or past illnesses or operations?
18. How is your family's health?
19. Have you ever been arrested?
20. If you have been in the military, were you honorably discharged?

On the other hand, it is legal to ask the following questions:

1. Are you authorized to work in the United States?
2. What languages do you read or speak fluently? (if relevant to the job)
3. Are you over 18?
4. Would you relocate?
5. Would you be willing to travel as needed?
6. Would you be able and willing to work overtime as necessary?

7. Do you belong to any groups that are relevant to your ability to perform this job?
8. Are you gay?
9. Have you ever been convicted of [fill in the blank]? (The crime must be reasonably related to the performance of the job.)
10. In what branch of the armed forces did you serve?[44]

What if an interviewer asks you an illegal question? You can object diplomatically and remind the interviewer that the question is inappropriate. Doing so, however, can make that interviewer defensive and less willing to select you for the job. Another option is to respond to the illegal question with only information that the interviewer could have legally sought from you. That is, you handle the question by answering the part you don't object to without providing any information you don't wish to provide. For example, if the interviewer asks whether English is your native language, you can respond, "I am fluent in English." If he or she asks whether you belong to a political group, you can respond, "The only groups with which I affiliate that are relevant to this job are the Public Relations Society of America and the American Society for Training and Development."

GUIDELINES FOR INCREASING YOUR EFFECTIVENESS IN INTERVIEWS

As you can see, an interview, like any other interpersonal relationship, requires the cooperation, skill, and commitment of both participants to be effective. Both interviewees and interviewers can benefit from the following guidelines:

Focus on Service Learning
Share your understanding of interviewing with persons currently unemployed.

1. *Be prepared.* Understand the purpose of the interview; plan or anticipate the questions you will ask and be asked; understand your goals; and be able to communicate those goals clearly.

2. *Practice sending and receiving messages.* By its very nature, an interview demands skill at sending and receiving verbal and nonverbal messages. Not only must the interactants clearly encode their messages, but they must also be skilled at reading the reactions and checking the perceptions of the other.

3. *Demonstrate effective listening skills.* Problems occur in interviews when either the interviewer or the interviewee fails to listen closely to what the other is saying. As is noted in John Brady's *The Craft of Interviewing,* if participants listen carefully—rather than thinking about what they plan to say next—the interview has a better chance of being productive.[45]

4. *Have conviction.* Ask and answer questions and express your opinions with enthusiasm. If you aren't excited by your ideas, skills, and abilities, why should anyone else be?

5. *Be flexible.* Don't overprepare or memorize statements. Think things through thoroughly, and be prepared to handle questions or answers you didn't anticipate. Be able to adjust to the other person's style and pace.

6. *Be observant.* Pay attention to the nonverbal signals sent to you and by you. Be sure that the signals you send are positive, not negative. Give the other person your total attention.

7. *Consider the offer.* Both interviewer and interviewee need to consider the ramifications of a job offer. A typical 40-hour-a-week job done for approximately 50 weeks a year adds up to 6,000 hours in only three years. Be sure that your choice is one both you and the organization can live with.

8. *Chart your progress.* Each time you participate in an interview, fill out a copy of the following evaluation. Circle the number that best describes your response to each question.

a. How prepared were you for the interview?
   Not at all prepared   1   2   3   4   5   Fully prepared
b. What kind of climate did you help create?
   Hostile climate   1   2   3   4   5   Friendly climate
c. Were the questions you asked clear?
   Not clear   1   2   3   4   5   Clear
d. Were the responses you offered complete?
   Incomplete   1   2   3   4   5   Complete
e. How carefully did you listen to the other person?
   Not at all   1   2   3   4   5   Very carefully
f. How carefully did you pay attention to nonverbal cues?
   Not at all   1   2   3   4   5   Very carefully
g. To what extent were you distracted by external stimuli?
   Very much   1   2   3   4   5   Not at all
h. How self-confident were you during the interview?
   Not at all   1   2   3   4   5   Very confident
i. How flexible were you during the interview?
   Not flexible   1   2   3   4   5   Very flexible

j. Would you like to change or improve your behavior for your next interview?

Very much   1   2   3   4   5   Little, or not at all

If your answer to the last question is 1, 2, 3, or 4, consider how you would like to change.

Revisiting Chapter Objectives

1. **Define _interview_.** During the course of our lives, we all take part in a number of different types of interviews, as either interviewee or interviewer. The interview is the most common type of purposeful, planned, decision-making, person-to-person communication.

2. **Identify six types of interviews and the kind of information shared by participants in each interview.** We explored six different types of interviews including the information-gathering interview (designed to collect information, opinions or data), the appraisal interview (designed for evaluation purposes), the persuasive interview (designed to influence attitudes or behavior), the exit interview (designed to determine why someone is leaving a position), the counseling interview (designed to provide guidance), and the hiring or selection interview (designed to select the right person for a job).

3. **Describe the stages of an interview.** Effective interviews are well-structured interactions. They have a beginning, which provides an orientation to what is to come; a middle, when the participants get down to business; and an end, when the main points are reviewed and the participants take leave of one another.

4. **Formulate closed, open, primary, and secondary questions.** Questions are the heart of the interview and the primary means of collecting data. Four basic types of questions are asked in an interview: closed, open, primary, and secondary. Closed questions are highly structured and can be answered with a simple yes or no or in a few words; open questions are broader and offer the interviewee more freedom in responding. Primary questions introduce topics or begin exploring a new area; secondary questions (probing questions) follow up primary questions by asking for further information. Whatever the type of question, an interviewee must maintain honesty in answering.

THE Wrap-Up

5. Compare and contrast the roles and responsibilities of interviewer and interviewee. Good interviewers and interviewees work hard during an interview, functioning simultaneously as information seekers, information givers, and decision makers. To be a successful interviewee requires specific preparation. Honest self-assessment, practice in answering typical questions, and mastery of the techniques of impression management are of prime importance. To avoid misunderstanding, both interviewer and interviewee need to be aware of how cultural differences can affect the interview.

Resources for Further Inquiry and Reflection

To apply your understanding of how the principles in Chapter 10 are at work in our daily lives, consult the following resources for further inquiry and reflection. Or, if you prefer, choose any other appropriate resource. Then connect the ideas expressed in your chosen selection with the communication concepts and issues you are learning about, both in and out of class.

 Listen to Me

"From 9 to 5" (Dolly Parton)
"Let the River Flow" (Carly Simon)
"Get a Job" (The Silhouettes)

Each of these songs revolves around the world of work. What do the attitudes expressed in the song suggest about our eagerness and/or preparedness to interview for a job?

 View Me

A Few Good Men　　　*Disclosure*
The Caine Mutiny　　　*Kramer vs. Kramer*
Courage under Fire　　*Roger and Me*
Bowling for Columbine

Interviews play a key role in each of these films. How does the knowledge gleaned through one or more interviews advance the plot?

 Read Me

Moises Kaufman. *The Laramie Project*. New York: Dramatists Play Service, 2001.
Studs Turkel. *Working*. New York: Avon Press, 1992.

Interviews play a key role in each of these works. Identify the kinds of questions raised by the interviewer(s) that elicited the most useful information from the interviewee(s).

 Tell Me

Share with the class the insights you gained from your chosen Listen to Me, View Me, or Read Me selection.

Discuss the most unusual thing that you are aware of happening during an interview to either the interviewer or the interviewee.

Communication
Works

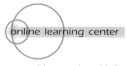

www.mhhe.com/gamble8

Key Chapter Terminology

Use the Communication Works CD-ROM and the Online Learning Center at www.mhhe.com/gamble8 *to further your knowledge of the following terminology.*

behavioral interview 318
case interview 318
closed questions 314
interview 303

open questions 314
primary questions 314
secondary questions 314
stress interview 318

Test Your Understanding

Go to the *Self Quizzes* on the Communication Works CD-ROM and the book's Online Learning Center at www.mhhe.com/gamble8.

Communication
Works

online learning center

www.mhhe.com/gamble8

Notes

1. See, for example, R. Bolles. *What Color Is Your Parachute?* 30th ed. Berkeley, CA: Ten Speed Press, 2000; and R. Bolles. *Job-Hunting on the Internet,* Berkeley, CA: Ten Speed Press, 1999.

2. Rick Bentley, "Interest in Forensic Science Has Surged during 'CSI,'" *heraldonline,* January 12, 2002, www.heraldonline.com.

3. Robert S. Goyer, W. Charles Redding, and John T. Richey. *Interviewing Principles and Techniques: A Project Text.* Dubuque, IA: Wm. C. Brown, 1968, p. 6.

4. Linda Martin. "Room with a Review." *New York Times,* March 31, 2002, p. 13.

5. Melinda Ligos. "Young Job Seekers Need New Clues." *New York Times,* August 8, 2001, p. G1.

6. William G. Kirkwood and Steven M. Ralson. "Inviting Meaningful Applicant Performances in Employment Interviews." *Journal of Business Communication* 36:1, January 1999, pp. 55–76.

7. For example, Lois J. Einhorn reports in "An Inner View of the Job Interview: An Investigation of Successful Communicative Behavior." *Communication Education* 30, 1981, pp. 217–228, that successful candidates were able to identify with the employer, support their arguments, organize their thoughts, clarify their ideas, and speak fluently.

8. "Résumés Get Only a Glance." *USA Today,* March 8, 2001, p. B1.

9. Leonard Zunin and Natalie Zunin. *Contact: The First Four Minutes.* Los Angeles: Nash, 1972, pp. 8–12.

10. Adam Geller. "Problem Postings." *The Record,* March 17, 2003; and Kris Maher. "Résumé Rustling Threatens Online Job Sites." *Wall Street Journal,* February 25, 2003, pp. B1, B10.

11. See Mark L. Knapp, Roderick P. Hart, Gustav W. Friedrich, and Gary M. Schulman. "The Rhetoric of Goodbye: Verbal and Nonverbal Correlates of Human Leave-Taking." *Speech Monographs* 40, 1973, pp. 182–198.

12. David Koeppel. "On a Résumé, Don't Mention Moon Pies or Water Cannons." *New York Times,* November 24, 2001, Section 10, p. 1.

13. Herbert M. Greenberg and Patrick J. Sweeney. *HR Focus* 76:10, 1999, p. 6.

14. Charles J. Stewart and William B. Cash, Jr. *Interviewing: Principles and Practices,* 6th ed. Dubuque, IA: Wm. C. Brown, 1991.

15. Stewart and Cash.

16. David Bianculli. "Nice Guys Can Interview, but 'Naturals' Get Results." *Baltimore Sun,* May 19, 1984, p. E3.

17. Amy Joyce. "Career Track: How to Keep Cool on the Interview Hot Seat." *Washington Post,* June 21, 1999, p. FO-8.

18. See also Joan E. Rigdon. "Careers: Starting Over." *Wall Street Journal,* February 27, 1995, p. R13.

19. Gladwell, p. 84.

20. Ibid.

21. For a study confirming that employers use a candidate's speech characteristics to judge competence and likability, see Robert Hopper. "Language Attitudes in the Employment Interview." *Speech Monographs* 44, 1974, pp. 346–351.

22. Gladwell, pp. 68–86.

23. "Initial Minutes of Job Interview Are Critical." *USA Today,* January 2000, p. 8.

24. Elwood N. Chapman. *Your Attitude Is Showing.* Chicago: Science Research Associates, 1987; see also Elwood N. Chapman. *I Got the Job!* Los Angeles: Crisp, 1988.

25. Einhorn.

26. Rachel Emma Silverman and Kemba J. Dunham. "Even in a Tight Market, Job Hunters Can Blunder." *Wall Street Journal,* June 20, 2000, p. B12.

27. Also see Malcom Gladwell. "What Do Job Interviews Really Tell Us?" *New Yorker,* May 29, 2000, pp. 68–72, 84–86; and C. J. Stewart and W. B. Cash, Jr. *Interviewing Principles and Practices,* 7th ed. Dubuque, IA: Wm. C. Brown, 1994.

28. Francine Parnes. "New Interview Uniform: Gray Means Business." *New York Times,* January 19, 2003, Section 10, p. 1.

29. See John T. Molloy. *Dress for Success.* New York: Warner, 1977; and John T. Molloy. *The Woman's Dress for Success Book.* New York: Warner, 1977.

30. John T. Molloy. *New Woman's Dress for Success.* New York: Warner, 1997.

31. Jay Levin. "Unforgettable Interviews." *The Record,* June 16, 1997, pp. H-8, H-12.

32. Richard Nelson Bolles. *The 1997 What Color Is Your Parachute?* Berkeley, CA: Ten Speed Press, 1997.

33. See Joan E. Rigdon. "Talk Isn't Cheap." *Wall Street Journal,* February 27, 1995, p. R13.

34. See, for example, F. Mahoney. "Adjusting the Interview to Avoid Cultural Bias." *Journal of Career Planning and Employment* 52, 1992, pp. 41–43.

35. Mary Williams Walsh. "Money Isn't Everything." *New York Times,* January 30, 2001, p. 10.

36. Ibid.

37. N'Gai Croal. "Want a Job? Get Online." *Newsweek,* June 9, 1997, pp. 81–82.

38. Maria Mallory and Margaret Steen. "Two-Way Interview: It's for You and the Employer." *Atlanta Journal,* April 2, 2000, p. R1.

39. Joann S. Lublin. "Web Sites Give Leads to Jobs, but You Still Have to Do Legwork." *Wall Street Journal,* July 11, 2000, p. B1.

40. For a discussion of online search techniques, see Cynthia B. Leshin. *Internet Investigations in Business Communication.* Saddle River, NJ: Prentice Hall, 1997, pp. 95–134.

41. See Zane K. Quible. "Electronic Résumés: Their Time Is Coming." *Business Communication Quarterly* 58, September 1995, pp. 5–9.

42. Susan Stellin. "New Economy." *New York Times,* January 20, 2003, p. C3.

43. Wallace V. Schmidt and Roger N. Conaway. *Results-Oriented Interviewing: Principles, Practices and Procedures.* Boston: Allyn & Bacon, 1999, p. 11.

44. "There Are Questions You Shouldn't Answer," *New York Times,* January 30, 2001, p. 2.

45. John Brady. *The Craft of Interviewing.* New York: Vintage, 1977.

Communicating in the Small Group

We are by nature a tribal people.

—Linda Ellerbee
Broadcast Journalist

Part Three centers on small-group communication. As you read each chapter, think about your roles as both group member and group leader. In addition to considering the best way for a group to approach problem solving, you'll also explore the potential limitations and strengths of groups, how to diffuse conflict, how to handle power issues, how to enhance the amount of influence you have in group decision making, and what action you can take to sharpen your skills at building, leading, and participating in effective teams.

Keep in mind that culture, gender, and technological innovations are influencing group life. Considering how you can develop your skills to improve the functioning of those groups you lead and belong to allows you to take a step forward in making communication work for you.

The Roles of the Group and Team in Decision Making and Problem Solving

1. Define *group*.

2. Enumerate the advantages and disadvantages of group decision making and problem solving.

3. Provide examples of how a group's climate affects its operations.

4. Compare and contrast various decision-making methods.

5. Apply the reflective-thinking framework to increase your effectiveness at problem solving.

6. Describe and use brainstorming.

Talented administrators know that they do not know all there is to know.

—Anonymous

Not even computers will replace committees, because committees buy computers.

—Edward Shepperd Mead

Go to the *Online Learning Center* at www.mhhe.com/gamble8 and answer the questions in the *Self Inventory* to evaluate your understanding of group interactions.

❙ *Employees spend extensive amounts of time in meetings.*

336

When it comes to your future, teamwork is one of the most important communication skills you can master.[1] Do you think that you could learn team-building skills by taking cooking classes? Apparently, a number of companies such as Sun Microsystems, Viacom, and Bank One Corp. think so. They have invested thousands of dollars in cooking classes for executives. The thinking is that, since a lot of things can go wrong in the kitchen, it is a good place to improve teamwork. Either "cooks" cooperate or they get in trouble.[2]

We profit from working together in teams or groups. While in prehistoric periods we may have divided into teams in order to hunt large game or increase our chances for survival, research suggests that teamwork can be its own reward. Researchers note that, just as desserts and money cause many of us to experience delight, so does cooperating with each other to achieve a goal. Using magnetic resonance imaging (MRI) to take portraits of the brain, researchers have shown that humans derive pleasure when they choose to forego immediate personal gain and opt instead to cooperate with others for the long-term common good.[3]

How important are groups to your future? Try to visualize what your personal and professional life would be like were there no groups for you to belong to. Some of the groups we belong to, such as the group of friends who meet for dinner once a week, are social. Some are more formally organized, such as the Parent-Teacher Association. Some, such as the Rotary Club, serve both public and private purposes. Others exist primarily to meet the needs of the organizations in which we work. Thus, groups provide much of the social fabric of our lives. In addition, they are also the basic building blocks of organizations, and when it comes to the world of work, team management is fast becoming the norm.

Over two-thirds of United States companies use formal work teams to accomplish their objectives.[4] Workers now participate in more groups and teams and attend more meetings than ever before. It is commonplace for committees of employees to make the kinds of decisions that were once handled by "dictatorial" executives. According to researchers, the majority of a manager's time is spent in meetings of one kind or another.[5] Thus, today's workers and managers are experienced at participating in different kinds of groups. **Quality circles,** for example, are small groups of employees who meet regularly to discuss organizational life and the quality of their work environment. During these meetings, employees make recommendations for improving products and work procedures. **Self-directed teams** are autonomous groups in which employees are empowered to make decisions and even supervise themselves. Among the major companies championing such approaches are Xerox, Procter & Gamble, and General Motors.[6] Do you feel prepared to become part of such groups?

You already spend a great deal of time in groups. A large part of your socialization—your adaptation to society—occurred in your family group. Much of your leisure time is spent in the company of groups of friends. If you attend a religious service, you become part of a group. If you participate in student government, a

quality circles
small groups of employees who meet regularly to discuss organizational life and the quality of their work environment

self-directed teams
autonomous groups of employees empowered to make decisions and supervise themselves

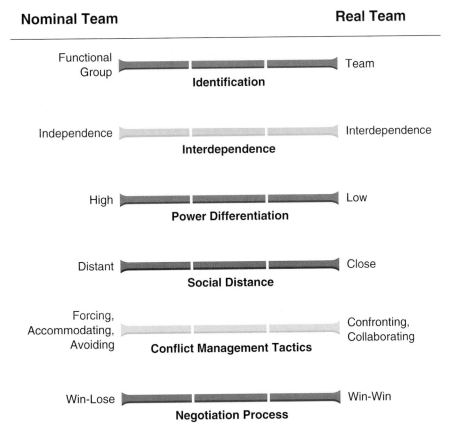

Nominal Team		Real Team
Functional Group	**Identification**	Team
Independence	**Interdependence**	Interdependence
High	**Power Differentiation**	Low
Distant	**Social Distance**	Close
Forcing, Accommodating, Avoiding	**Conflict Management Tactics**	Confronting, Collaborating
Win-Lose	**Negotiation Process**	Win-Win

Key Dimensions of Teams. Groups vary on each dimension from one extreme to the other. How would you describe a group you currently belong to? Is your group a real team?

 Go to the CD to view the animation

study group, or sports, you are part of a group. As a class member, you belong to a group. Thus, from your earliest days, you have been a member of a variety of groups.

Most of us belong to a number of different groups. Are you currently a member of two groups? Ten groups? Twenty groups? Take a moment to assess the nature of your group membership.

Our world contains over 6 billion individuals. It also contains hundreds of millions of formal and informal groups. How do the groups you belong to influence you as an individual?

GROUPS AND YOU

As we see, groups are everywhere. You belong to some groups for fun and to others for profit. You join some to increase your prestige; you join others simply because you have to. Some help you fulfill personal or professional objectives, and others meet your moral and ethical needs and give you a sense of well-being. Groups help you define who you are. The groups to which you belong or aspire to belong tell you about your own preferences and goals. The groups you refuse to join tell you about your dislikes, fears, and values. Groups have a great impact on your daily life, and you need to belong to a number of them to survive in today's world.[7]

Compile a list of groups to which you belong, groups to which you aspire to belong, and groups to which you would refuse to belong. Give your reasons for accepting, seeking, or refusing membership.

Some of your most important communication will take place in one group or another. It is estimated that over 11 million meetings are held each day and that at least 40 percent of your work life will be spent attending group meetings and conferences. A recent survey showed that the typical executive spends about 700 hours per year interacting in groups. That is the equivalent of two of every five days on the job.[8] Thus, knowing how to relate to others in a group setting is vital not only if you are to attain personal success but also if you are to attain professional success.[9] For this reason, although we realize that social groups are important, in these chapters we will focus on the work-related decision-making, problem-solving group, also called the task group.

 For an example of small group communication, view clip 5 on the CD

By the time you conclude your study of small-group communication, you will have the information you need to understand the forces that shape and modify group behavior. You will also have the skills you need to improve the quality of interactions in task groups. The knowledge and abilities you gain will be transferable to other areas of your life. We begin by looking into the characteristics of groups.

CHARACTERISTICS AND COMPONENTS OF GROUPS

Is it easy to explain what the word *group* means? Try your hand at it now. Generate five different ways of completing each of the following:

1. A group is . . . .
2. A group is not . . . .

Defining a group is tricky business.[10]

Evaluating Discussion Groups on Television

Just as you need to evaluate the effectiveness of your own information-seeking and problem-solving groups, so you also need to become an evaluator of televised discussions—their methods and their conclusions. Evaluate a television discussion show of your choice by answering the following questions:

1. To what extent was the program's topic well analyzed by the program's participants?

2. To what extent did the ideas and feelings of participants appear to be freely shared?

3. To what extent was the discussion monopolized by any member(s)?

4. What norms appeared to govern the discussion?

5. How did gender or cultural factors influence the discussion?

6. To what extent did a consensus emerge?

Media
WISE

Knowing how to relate to others in a group is important for personal and professional success. Are there some televised group discussions you enjoy watching more than others? Why?

Group Membership

A **group** is a collection of people. But it is not just a random assemblage of independent individuals; rather, it is composed of individuals who interact verbally and nonverbally, occupy certain roles with respect to one another, and cooperate to accomplish a definite goal. The members of a group recognize the other individuals who are part of the activity, have certain kinds of attitudes toward these people, and obtain some degree of satisfaction from belonging to or participating in the group. They acknowledge the do's and don'ts of group life, the norms that specify and regulate the behavior expected of members. Furthermore, communication within a group involves more than the casual banter that occurs between strangers at bus stops or in department stores.

The fact that a number of people are present in a particular space at the same time does not mean that a group exists. For example, under ordinary

group

a collection of individuals who interact verbally and nonverbally, occupy certain roles with respect to one another, and cooperate to accomplish a goal conditions, passengers in a train or an elevator are not a group. (However, should the train or elevator break down or experience some other difficulty, they might become a group in order to meet the demands of the new situation.) Rather, the members of a group consistently influence each other and are influenced by each other; that is, interaction in the form of mutual influence occurs. The individual members affect the character of the group and are affected by it.[11]

Group Size

While most group theorists and practitioners set the lower limit of group size at three members, researchers have found that, for most tasks, groups of five to seven people work best. This size enables members to communicate directly with each other as they work on a common task or goal, such as solving problems, exchanging information, or improving interpersonal relationships.

What is the optimal size for a group? In task-oriented groups, it is the smallest number of people capable of handling the assigned task.[12] The larger the group, the more difficult it becomes to schedule meetings, share information, and equalize opportunities for participation.

Group Goals, Structure, and Climate

group goals

a group's motivation for existing

group structure

group member positions and roles performed

group patterns of communication

patterns of message flow in a group

group norms

informal rules for interaction in a group

group climate

the emotional atmosphere of a group

Every group establishes its own **group goals** (motivation for existing, the end state desired), **group structure** (member positions and roles), **group patterns of communication** (patterns of message flow), **group norms** (informal rules for interaction), and **group climate** (emotional atmosphere). Every participant in the group usually has a stake in the outcome, will develop relationships with the other members of the group, and will assume roles and relationships that relate to group tasks and either foster or impede the group's effectiveness. Thus, the members' styles of interaction will have an impact on the kind of atmosphere, or climate, that develops in the group. Conversely, the climate will affect what members say to each other and how they say it. For example, have you ever belonged to a group that had too "hot" a climate—one in which members were intolerant of each other and tempers flared? Have you ever belonged to a group that had too "cold" a climate—one in which members were aloof, sarcastic, unconcerned about hurting one another's feelings, or too self-centered to notice that the needs of others were not being adequately met?

A group's climate tends to persist. If the group climate is cold, closed, mistrustful, or uncooperative, individual members will frequently react in ways that perpetuate those characteristics. In contrast, if the group climate is warm, open, trusting, and cooperative, members will usually react in ways that reinforce those characteristics. In the book *Communication within the Organization,* Charles Redding has suggested that an effective climate is characterized by (1) supportiveness, (2) participative decision making, (3) trust among group members, (4) openness and candor, and (5) high performance goals.[13] The healthier the group climate, the more cohesive the group.

Group climate affects group norms—the explicit and implicit rules that members internalize concerning their behavior. In some groups, we would exhibit certain behaviors that we would not dare exhibit in others. For example, in which groups that you belong to would you feel free to ask a question that might be considered "dumb," interrupt someone who is talking, express disagreement with another member, openly express support for an unpopular position, point out that someone isn't making sense, offer a comment unrelated to the topic, or simply not attend a meeting? In some groups, interaction is formal and stuffy; in others, it is informal and relaxed. Groups invariably create standards that they expect members to live up to. In this way, a group is able to foster a certain degree of uniformity.

In Chapters 12 and 13, we'll take a closer look at the communication patterns, roles, leadership behaviors, and problems that develop in groups. For now, let us recognize that certain attributes facilitate the group process, whereas others work against it. Douglas McGregor, an expert in organizational communication, summarizes the characteristics of an effective and well-functioning group as follows:

1. The atmosphere tends to be informal, comfortable, and relaxed.

2. There is a lot of discussion in which virtually everyone participates, but it remains pertinent to the task.

3. The task or objective is well understood and accepted by the members. There will have been free discussion of the objective at some point, until it was formulated in such a way that the group members could commit themselves to it.

4. The members listen to each other. Every idea is given a hearing. People do not appear to be afraid of being foolish; they will offer a creative thought even if it seems fairly extreme.

5. There is disagreement. Disagreements are not suppressed or overridden by premature action. The reasons are carefully examined, and the group seeks to resolve disagreements rather than dominate dissenters.

6. Most decisions are reached by a kind of consensus in which it is clear that everyone is in general agreement and willing to go along. Formal voting is at a minimum; the group does not accept a simple majority as a proper basis for action.

7. Criticism is frequent, frank, and relatively comfortable. There is little evidence of personal attack, either overt or hidden.

8. People are free to express their feelings and their ideas about the problem and the group's operation.

9. When action is taken, clear assignments are made and accepted.

10. The chairperson of the group does not dominate it, nor does the group defer unduly to him or her. In fact, the leadership shifts from time to time, depending on the circumstances. There is little evidence of a struggle for power as the group operates. The issue is not who controls but how to get the job done.

11. The group is self-conscious of its own operation.[14]

Select two groups you have belonged to that represent what you consider effective and ineffective climates. For each group, identify the types of behavior exhibited by members. How did each climate affect your participation in the group? How did each climate affect your relationship with other group members?

random thoughts *by archy*
i have noticed that when chickens quit quarreling over their food they often find that there is enough for all of them i wonder if it might not be the same way with the human race

—Don Marquis,
archy's life of mehitabel

FIGURE 11.1
Stages of Group Development.

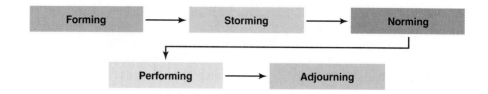

The Dynamics of Group Development

Once in place, a group's development occurs in stages. According to researchers, the key stages that a group moves through are forming, storming, norming, performing, and adjourning.[15] (See Figure 11.1.)

Upon joining a new group, we may experience some initial confusion or uncertainty, which results in what is called *primary tension*. We are unsure about how to behave or interact with others and unclear about the roles that we will have in the life of the group. We need to figure out who is in charge and why we were brought together. Thus, in the *forming stage* of a group, our primary objective is to fit in and be perceived as likeable. We also make an effort to find out about other group members and the group's task. Once we feel valued and accepted, we begin to identify with the group.

Invariably, members experience some conflict as they determine how to work together. Typically, groups experience both task and relational conflicts. During the *storming stage*, the group's members experience *secondary tension*—tension that results from members disagreeing and/or struggling to exert leadership as they work to clarify goals and the roles members will have in the life of the group. During this stage, rather than being concerned with fitting in, members now focus on expressing their ideas and opinions and securing their place in the group power structure.

Over time, a clear group structure emerges. Roles are firmed up and a leader or leaders emerge. During the *norming stage*, the group solidifies its behavioral norms, especially those relating to conflict management. In addition, the group forms a sense of identity as member awareness of their interdependence and need to cooperate with each other increases.

The emphasis of the group then switches to task accomplishment. During the *performing stage*, often perceived as the most important stage of group development, members combine their skills, knowledge, and abilities to overcome obstacles and reach the group's goals. Group members focus on problem solving.

Finally, during the *adjourning stage*, members review and reflect on their accomplishments or failures and determine how or whether to end the group and the relationships that have developed. Ending a group can involve having a party or simply saying good-bye to each other, or it can be more complicated and prolonged, with some groups opting to continue working together on a new or different task, and some members choosing to continue relationships that developed during the group's life.[16]

How a group develops through each of these stages determines how effectively it is able to function. Of course, there are a number of pros and cons to using groups.

Trace the development of a group to which you belong. Has it passed through each of the stages identified here?

If, as the saying goes, "A camel is a horse designed by a committee," why do we do so much of our work in groups?

USING GROUPS TO MAKE DECISIONS AND SOLVE PROBLEMS

We form small groups to share information that will permit us to solve common problems and make decisions about achieving certain identified common goals. But why use a small group instead of a single person? Working in groups can be both frustrating and rewarding; groups can facilitate or limit problem-solving effectiveness.

Advantages of the Small Group

In many ways, using a group to solve a complex problem is more logical than relying on one individual. Group problem solving offers a number of important advantages.

> *You know . . . everybody is ignorant, only of different subjects.*
>
> **—Will Rogers**

First, it permits a variety of people with different information and different points of view to contribute to the problem-solving, decision-making process. That is, a small group facilitates the pooling of resources. The broader the array of knowledge that is brought to bear on any problem, the more likely an effective solution becomes. Second, participating in a group apparently increases individual motivation. Group efforts often lead to greater commitment to finding a solution and then to greater commitment to the solution that has been arrived at. Third, group functioning makes it easier to identify other people's mistakes and filter out errors before they can become costly or damaging. Groups are frequently better equipped than individuals to foresee difficulties, detect weaknesses, visualize consequences, and explore possibilities. As a result, they tend to produce superior decisions and solutions. Fourth, the decisions or solutions of a group tend to be better received than those of an individual. As the adage says, "There is strength in numbers." The person or persons to whom a group solution is reported will tend to respect the fact that a number of people working together came to one conclusion. Fifth, working as part of a group is generally more pleasant and fulfilling than working alone. The group provides companionship, a chance to affirm ideas and feelings, and an opportunity for self-confirmation. It is rewarding to know that others respect us enough to listen and react to what we have to say. It is even more rewarding to have our thoughts and concerns accepted by others. (These advantages are summarized in Figure 11.2.)

> *There is a tendency to define one's own group positively in order to evaluate oneself positively.*
>
> **—John C. Turner**
>
> *Give an example of how you have enacted this quotation.*

Advantages	Disadvantages
Varied resources can be pooled.	Laziness is encouraged.
Motivation and commitment are increased.	Personal goals may conflict with group goals.
Errors are easier to identify.	A few, high-status members may dominate.
Decisions are better received.	Stubbornness leads to deadlock.
Rewards of working with others are provided.	Riskier decisions are made.
	Reaching a decision takes longer.

FIGURE 11.2
Why Use Teamwork?

Disadvantages of the Small Group

This is not to suggest that using a group does not have potential drawbacks. Several disadvantages of group problem solving have been identified.

As a new employee, what problems might you experience when interacting with others in a problem-solving group?

First, when we are working with a number of other people, it sometimes becomes very tempting to let someone else handle the duties and responsibilities. A lazy group member can maintain a low profile and simply coast along on the efforts of others. Second, personal goals sometimes conflict with group goals. As a result, people may try to use the group to achieve self-oriented objectives that might interfere with or even sabotage group objectives. Third, the decision-making, problem-solving process may be dominated by a few forceful, persistent members who do not take the time to ensure that all members have a chance to speak and be heard. Actual or perceived status plays a part here. Group members may be hesitant to criticize the comments of high-status people, and low-status people may be reluctant to participate at all. Consequently, position and power can affect whether ideas are offered, listened to, or incorporated into group decisions. Fourth, certain people who are set on having their ideas and only their ideas accepted may be unwilling to compromise. When this happens, the group decision-making machinery breaks down, and frequently no solution can be agreed on. In other words, the group becomes deadlocked. Fifth, the decisions reached and the actions taken after a group discussion are often riskier than the decisions individuals would have made or the actions individuals would have taken. This phenomenon has been called the risky shift. Sixth, it often takes longer to reach a group solution than an individual decision. In business and industry, where time is frequently equated with money, the group can be a costly tool. (See Figure 11.2 for a summary of these drawbacks.)

When to Use a Group for Decision Making and Problem Solving

Groups can bring out the worst as well as the best in human decision making.

Irving Janis

In view of these pros and cons, we may now ask: When does it make sense to use a group? At what point do the advantages outweigh the possible disadvantages?

Experience suggests that a group rather than an individual should be used to make decisions and solve a problem if the answer to most of the following questions is yes:

1. Is the problem complex rather than simple?
2. Does the problem have many parts, or facets?
3. Would any one person be unlikely to possess all the information needed to solve the problem?
4. Would it be advisable to divide the responsibility for problem solving?
5. Are many potential solutions desired, rather than just one?
6. Would an examination of diverse attitudes be helpful?
7. Are group members more likely to engage in task-related than nontask-related behavior?

In these complex times, it often makes sense for individuals of varied expertise to pool their knowledge and insight to solve problems. Group effort is futile if the members pool only ignorance and obstinacy. As we shall see, the kind of interaction that yields an array of relevant data is an essential ingredient in successful group work. The more information the members can gather and share, the more likely they are to rid themselves of bias, and in turn, the more objective their work becomes.[17]

DECISION MAKING IN GROUPS: REACHING GOALS

Thus far, we have established what a group is, the stages groups pass through during their development, and when and why it makes sense to use a group. In the process, we noted that every group has a goal—a reason for existing. We turn now to examining how groups reach their goals.

In our society, critical decisions are usually relegated to groups. Depending on the group, a wide variety of decision-making strategies or approaches may be used. In this section, we investigate the diverse methods members can adopt to arrive at a decision, as well as the advantages and disadvantages of each approach. Let's start by considering these questions: How do the groups to which you belong make decisions? Do different groups use different strategies? Why? Does the method any one group uses change from time to time? Why? Are you happy with each group's approach?

Identify the methods of decision making that are used most often in your class, at home, and at work. Are you satisfied with them? Why?

Strategies: Methods of Decision Making

Before we examine the different methods that groups use in making decisions, consider the following list to decide which decision-making strategy or strategies a group you belong to would employ most often if you had your way. Do this by ranking the possibilities from 1 (your first choice) to 8 (your last choice).

____ Ask an expert to decide.

____ Flip a coin.

____ Let the majority rule.

____ Let the group leader decide.

____ Stall until a decision no longer needs to be made.

____ Let the minority rule, because that's sometimes fair.

____ Determine the average position, since this is least likely to be offensive to anyone.

____ Reach a **decision by consensus;** that is, be certain all have had input into the discussion, understand the decision, can rephrase it, and will publicly support it.

Then consider the implications of your ranking.

As the preceding list suggests, the methods used by groups to make decisions include (1) decision by an expert, (2) decision by chance, (3) decision by

decision by consensus

a decision which all members understand and will support, reached as a result of members voicing feelings and airing differences

Ethics &
COMMUNICATION

Avoiding Problems

Group members face a number of problems that can influence the effectiveness of the decisions they make. How would you respond when faced with each of the following situations? What do your responses reveal about the nature of groups?

1. What consequences might your group face if instead of handling a problem, the members opted to run away from the problem, rationalize it, or otherwise avoid confronting it directly? Is running away from a problem ever a viable alternative to solving the problem?

PEANUTS reprinted by permission of United Features Syndicate, Inc.

2. Put yourself in the place of the character, Jim, in the following situation. What advice would you offer Jim?

Jim is, at heart, an investigative journalist who has considerable talent but who has been earning a living by writing restaurant reviews for a major magazine, which pays him very well, enabling him to support his wife and three young children. Despite this, Jim longs to return to his real vocation. Recently, he was offered a free-lance position with a well-known newspaper, which asked Jim to resign from his present position and go undercover in an effort to determine if there is collusion between U.S. government agencies and major companies that seek to influence policy decisions being made by the administration. If Jim is successful in his investigation, it could make his journalistic career. If he is unsuccessful, however, he will have expended considerable time and energy, possibly ruining his reputation and ending his journalistic career. Should Jim give up his current job to take the new assignment? Check the lowest probability that you would consider acceptable for Jim to take the new assignment:

____ 1 in 10	____ 6 in 10
____ 2 in 10	____ 7 in 10
____ 3 in 10	____ 8 in 10
____ 4 in 10	____ 9 in 10
____ 5 in 10	____ 10 in 10

the majority, (4) decision by the leader, (5) total deferral of decision, (6) decision by the minority, (7) decision by averaging individual decisions, and (8) decision by consensus. Each method has certain advantages and is more appropriate and workable than others under certain conditions. An effective group bases its decision-making strategy on a number of variables, including (1) the nature of the problem, (2) the time available to solve the problem, and (3) the kind of climate in which the group is operating or would prefer to operate.

Experience has shown that the various methods of group decision making vary considerably in their effectiveness. Majority vote is the method used most frequently. Most elections are decided and many laws are passed using this approach, and a large number of other decisions are made on the basis of the vote of at least 51 percent of a group's members. Lest we overlook the importance of the minority, however, we should note that it, too, can carry weight. Think of how often committees subdivide responsibilities, with the result that subgroups actually end up making the key recommendations and thus the key decisions.

Ethics &
COMMUNICATION

(Place a check next to 10 in 10 if you think Jim should take the new assignment only if it is certain that his investigation will be a success.)

After reaching your own decision, discuss the dilemma in a group. Determine if your group is likely to take a greater risk, be more cautious, or stay the same.

While some believe that groups are more cautious than individuals, in practice, the opposite actually is true. Decisions made in a group are usually riskier. This phenomenon is dubbed the *risky shift.* How do you imagine the risky shift phenomenon might affect the deliberations of juries? Business or military leaders?

3. There is another tendency in decision making that involves a movement toward *group polarization,* in which discussion is found to strengthen the average inclination of group members. For example, when business students were asked to imagine themselves having to decide whether to invest more money in the hope of preventing losses in various failing projects, individually 72 percent chose to reinvest money, while in groups 94 percent came to that decision.[18] Discussion with like-minded people strengthens existing views. How might such a trend influence the beliefs of prejudiced and unprejudiced persons when it comes to issues involving racial profiling, affirmative action, and who is responsible for increases in

crime? How might it influence the thinking of like-minded terrorist groups?

4. Look at the following cartoon. Based on your understanding of group polarization, would you agree with the advice the older sheep is giving the younger one? Why or why not?

"Now remember, 'just because everybody else is doing it' is a plenty good enough reason."

© Ann Telnaes, Margaret Shulock. Reprinted with special permission of King Features Syndicate.

Another popular decision-making strategy is averaging, by which the most popular decision becomes the group's decision.

Letting the expert member decide what the group should do is also fairly common. In this case, the group simply defers its decision-making power to its most knowledgeable member.

In many groups the leader retains all the decision-making power. Sometimes this is done after consultation with group members; at other times it is done without consultation.

Although each of these methods has been used successfully by a variety of groups, the most effective decision-making strategy is decision by consensus. When a group achieves consensus, all members agree on the decision. Even more important, all of them help formulate the decision by voicing their feelings and airing their differences of opinion. Thus, they all understand the decision and will support it.

Research shows that, the greater the involvement of members in the decision-making process, the more effective the decision will be. Of course, decisions by a leader, by an expert, or by a majority or minority vote all take less time than consensus; however, it should be remembered that, after all, it is the group that will usually be responsible for implementing the decision. If members disagree with a decision or do not understand it, they may not work very hard to make it succeed. A leader may make routine decisions or may be called on to make decisions when little time is available for a real discussion of the issues; however, under most circumstances, one person cannot be the best resource for all decisions. A drawback of the decision-by-expert method is that it is sometimes difficult to determine who the expert is. Also, decision by an expert—like decision by a leader—fails to involve other group members. Decision by averaging, on the whole, is superior to either decision by a leader or decision by an expert. With averaging, all members can be consulted and individual errors will cancel each other out, and an average position will usually not dissatisfy anyone too much. On the other hand, an average position usually doesn't satisfy anyone very much; thus, commitment to the decision tends to be rather low.

Under most circumstances, the quality of decision making and the satisfaction of the participants are higher when consensus is used. Consensus puts the resources of the entire group to effective use, permits discussion of all issues and alternatives, and ensures the commitment of all members. It is not the decision alone that is important in group interaction; we must also be concerned with the reactions and feelings of group members.

Personal Styles: A Decision-Making Grid

How do you behave when you are engaged in collective problem solving? The following list will provide you with a general indication of your own behavior in a problem-solving group. From the possibilities given, choose the approach that best characterizes your personal decision-making style. Rank your behavior from 1 (most characteristic) to 5 (least characteristic).

When my group is engaged in decision making, I

_____ Sit back and let others make the decision for me.

_____ Am concerned that a decision works, not whether others like it.

_____ Am concerned that members are satisfied with the decision, not whether it will work.

_____ Sacrifice my own feelings to reach a decision that can be implemented.

_____ Work so that everyone will discuss, understand, agree to, and be satisfied with a decision.

The decision-making grid in Figure 11.3, adapted from the work of Jay Hall, Vincent O'Leary, and Martha Williams, can help you understand your responses. It shows the relationship between concern that a decision works (concern for adequacy) and concern for the commitment of others to the decision (concern for commitment).[19] If you characteristically sit back and let others do the decision making, you exemplify the default style (you are a 1/1 with low concern for adequacy and low concern for commitment). If you insist that the quality of a decision is more important than the happiness of the group members, you represent the self-sufficient style. The exact opposite of

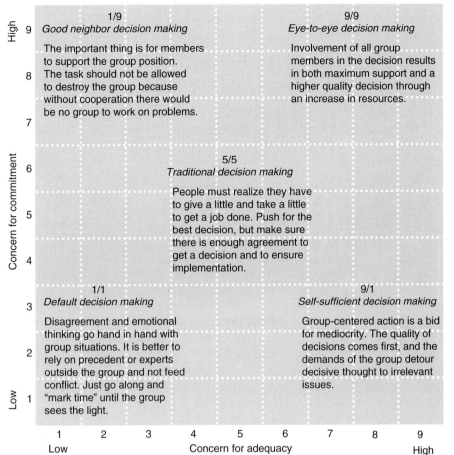

Source: "The Decision-Making Grid. A Model of Decision-Making Styles" by Hall, O'Leary and Williams. Copyright © 1964 by the Regents of the University of California. Reprinted from the *California Management Review*, Vol. 7, No. 2. By permission of The Regents.

FIGURE 11.3
Decision-Making Grid.

this type is the person who is more concerned about group support for a decision than about its quality or workability—the good neighbor style. The middle position, the traditional style, is typical of a sacrificer-compromiser, who is willing to give in to get a job done. Finally, if you characteristically employ an eye-to-eye style, you believe that consensus is possible if all group resources are used, if members feel free to express their opinions and ideas, and if consideration is given to the task itself and to the maintenance dimension of the decision-making process—that is, to social and emotional aspects and to members' satisfaction.

Gender, Culture, and Personal Styles

Communicating in groups and work teams calls for an understanding of how both the gender and cultural backgrounds of members can affect interaction. Each provides a set of unstated assumptions and rules that guides member behavior.[20]

Researchers suggest that, when working in groups, men and women focus on different aspects of the group's life. They also perceive and use power differently. While women appear to pay more attention to the relationships

Men frequently speak for longer periods of time when part of a group than do women.

shared by group members, men tend to be more focused on the group's task-related matters.[21] Similarly, women display more signs of liking or immediacy toward each other, while men display more signs of power or potency.[22] Unlike most men, who perceive power as finite, as something to be guarded for oneself and used to enhance personal status, most women perceive power as unlimited, as something to be shared, and as a resource for empowering others.[23] Researchers have also determined that, almost without exception, men speak more frequently and for longer periods of time than women. In fact, even the longest speaking turns of women are shorter than the shortest turns of men. In addition, men engage in interruptive behaviors more frequently than women, using the interruption as a means of conversational control.[24] Given this finding, how do you explain the stereotype that "women talk too much" and interrupt others frequently?

The cultural background of group members similarly affects the nature of communication in the work group or team. For example, since African-American culture in the United States is an oral culture, both verbal inventiveness and playfulness are highly valued. As a result, African Americans rely on back-channel responses (saying things such as "That's right," "Go on," or "Amen," to indicate their interest and involvement in the discussion). Because European Americans do not tend to use back-channel responses as frequently, African Americans may perceive them to be underreactive in the group's communication. In contrast, European Americans may perceive the African Americans as overreactive.

Persons from collectivistic cultures, such as those of Japan, China, and Pakistan, tend to be more conforming in groups than do persons from individualistic cultures, such as those of the United States, Great Britain, Australia, and Canada, who place a greater value on competition and dissent. In Japan, for instance, an organization's members have been taught to feel a sense of obligation to those who provide them with security, care, and support. When paired with the sense of dependency, a force called *on* results. *On* links persons in the group forever because the Japanese believe obligation continues throughout life. Hence, because nothing can be decided with a consideration of how the outcomes will influence everyone involved, consensus seeking, although not time efficient, becomes a priority.[25] Since collectivists let their participation be guided by group norms rather than their individual goals, they are also likely to be group players, stressing harmony and cooperation, more than individualists.[26] Individualists, on the other hand, are more apt to dominate group discussions and more prone to wanting to win in decision making. They are more apt to voice their disagreement, unlike collectivists, who prefer to slowly assess the feelings and moods of group members without verbalizing their objections or doubts. Consensus seeking doesn't come as easy to individualists as it does to collectivists.[27]

Questions for Decision Makers: Facts, Values, and Policies

The actual content of decision making is based on three key kinds of questions: questions of fact, questions of value, and questions of policy.

Questions of fact are concerned with the truth or falsity of a statement. Existing information may be inconsistent or contradictory, and group members are required to ferret out the truth. For example, a group might be asked to determine whether evidence proved beyond a doubt that John and Patsy Ramsey were involved in the murder of their daughter, JonBenet, or that former president Richard Nixon was taking mind-altering drugs without a prescription while in office. Questions of fact might be phrased like this: "What evidence supports the guilt or innocence of _____?" Similarly, a group might wrestle with questions like these: "What is the likelihood that a comet will hit the earth?" "What are the effects of depletion of the atmospheric ozone layer?" As you can see, answering questions like these requires that a group examine and interpret the available data carefully.

questions of fact
questions involving the truth or falsity of a statement

In contrast, **questions of value** are not factual; they involve subjective judgments. "Who was the best president to serve in the past 100 years?" is a question of value. So are the following: "To what extent is a college education valuable to all Americans?" "How desirable are physical fitness programs?" "To what extent, if any, is the use of laboratory animals for scientific research justified?"

questions of value
questions involving subjective judgments

Questions of policy are designed to help us determine what future actions, if any, should be taken. In fact, the key word in a question of policy is the word *should:* "What should colleges do to prevent student suicides?" "What should the United States do to discourage terrorism?" "What should federal policy be regarding the sale of semiautomatic military-style weapons to the general public?"

questions of policy
questions designed to help determine future actions

A Framework for Decision Making: Reflective Thinking

The quality of a group's decisions depends at least partly on the nature of its decision-making system. There is a generally agreed-upon structure, consisting of several stages, which, if used properly, can increase the problem-solving

reflective-thinking framework

a system for decision making and problem solving that is designed to encourage critical inquiry

effectiveness of most groups. This is called the **reflective-thinking framework.** It was first proposed by John Dewey in 1910. It is probably still the sequence most commonly used by problem-solving groups.[28]

The reflective-thinking framework has six basic components:

1. What is the problem? Is it clearly defined? Do we understand the general situation in which it is occurring? Is it stated so as not to arouse defensiveness? Is it phrased so as not to permit a simple yes or no answer? (For example, "What should the college's policy be toward final exams for seniors?" instead of "Should the college stop wasting the time of its seniors and eliminate final exams?" and "What should the government's policy be toward gun control?" instead of "Should the government restrain trigger-happy hunters?")

2. What are the facts of the situation? What are its causes? What is its history? Why is it important? Whom does it affect, and how?

3. What criteria must an acceptable solution meet? By which and whose standards must a solution be evaluated? What are the principal requirements of the solution? How important is each criterion?

4. What are the possible solutions? How would each remedy the problem? How well does each satisfy the criteria? What are the advantages and disadvantages of each?

5. Which is the best solution? How would you rank the solutions? Which offers the greatest number of advantages and the smallest number of disadvantages? Would some combination of solutions be beneficial?

6. How can the solution be implemented? What steps need to be taken to put the solution into effect?

EXPLORING Diversity

Culture, Gender, and Global Teams

Not only do we need to be able to work in teams in United States corporations, but because of the prevalence of multinational corporations and our developing global workforce, we also need to prepare ourselves to work in global teams in which diversity will be a given. For example, some members of the global team may believe in individualism and loyalty to the individual, while others may believe in collectivism and loyalty to the group. Some may believe that status is inherited, while others may believe it is achieved. Some may believe that members may confront one another when a disagreement occurs, while others may believe that a disagreement should never be discussed in front of others. Some may be monochromic, doing only one thing at a time and paying strict attention to deadlines and schedules, while others may be polychromic, doing many things at a time and not worrying about deadlines and schedules, believing that people are more important than work. Some may want a decision that delivers a quick payoff, while others may defer gratification in pursuit of long-term goals.

What do you believe you would need to learn and understand about yourself and others in order to function effectively as a member of a mixed-sex, global work team comprised of persons from the United States, Britain, Japan, Indonesia, and Saudi Arabia, whose cultures caused them to adhere to contradictory values? What specific problems would you need to overcome for the global team to become a productive unit? What steps would you take in order to find something that worked for everyone on the team? Finally, in your opinion, is it possible for a group of such diverse individuals to become a collaborative team?

To make this framework function, every member of the group must suspend judgment. Group members must be open to all available ideas, facts, and opinions. They must guard against early concurrence, which could force them to conclude the discussion prematurely. All data and alternative courses of action must be appraised thoroughly. Instead of insisting on your own position and closing yourself to new information, you need to explore all the major variables that contributed to the problem and investigate all the major issues that may be involved in producing a workable solution.

As you make your way through the framework, ask yourself if (1) the resources of all the group members are being well used, (2) the group is using its time to advantage, (3) the group is emphasizing fact-finding and inquiry, (4) members are listening to and respecting one another's opinions and feelings, (5) pressure to conform is being kept to a minimum while an honest search for diverse ideas is made, and (6) the atmosphere is supportive (noncritical), trusting (nonthreatening), and cooperative (noncompetitive). Remember, if group members are afraid to speak up, closed-minded,

The Individual in the Group

Ethics & COMMUNICATION

In the classic film *12 Angry Men,* 12 jurors file into a jury room on a hot, steamy day to decide on the guilt or innocence of a teenage boy accused of stabbing his father to death. Most of the jurors are exhausted and eager to reach a quick verdict. One dissenting juror, however, refuses to vote guilty. As jurors are forced to continue deliberating, the lone hold-out suc- ceeds in persuading all the other jurors, one-by-one, to change their minds until all the jurors reach a consensus vote of not guilty.

In your opinion, what makes one group member more persuasive than another group member? What behaviors should group members exhibit if they are to avoid drawing hasty and erroneous conclusions?

What can you do to promote a free flow of ideas during the problem-solving process? What steps can you take to guard against hasty decision making?

reluctant to search for information, or unmotivated, they will not perform effectively.

The Search for Better Ideas: Brainstorming

According to Jay Cocks, a business theorist and writer, "In an era of global competition, fresh ideas have become the most precious raw materials."[29] Where do fresh ideas come from? Betty Edwards, author of *Drawing on the Right Side of the Brain*, believes that fresh ideas come from developing creative problem-solving skills, as well as from encouraging creativity in the workplace.[30] To prepare students to meet the demands of the twenty-first century, colleges and universities across the country are offering entire courses on creativity. According to instructional technologist Jeff DeGroff, "The lesson of the twentieth century is that people must change patterns of thinking."[31] Thus, if you can come up with creative solutions, you may find yourself of great value to the companies and corporations of today and tomorrow. **Brainstorming** is one key technique used to thaw frozen patterns of thinking and encourage creativity. What is brainstorming?

A number of researchers have suggested that the best way to have a good idea is to have lots of ideas. Frequently, however, instead of suspending judgment and permitting ideas to develop freely, problem solvers tend to grasp at the first solution that comes to mind. Recognizing that this practice inhibits the search for new avenues of thought, Alex Osborn devised a technique called brainstorming.[32] This method is used primarily to promote a free flow of ideas and can be incorporated into the problem-solving process. For instance, although brainstorming is used most frequently when group members are attempting to identify a solution, it can also be used to help identify the factors that caused a problem, the criteria that a solution should meet, and the ways the solution could be implemented.

To ensure that brainstorming sessions are successful, group members need to adhere to certain guidelines:

1. Temporarily suspend judgment. That is, do not evaluate or criticize ideas. Instead, adopt a "try anything" attitude. This will encourage rather than stifle the flow of ideas.

2. Encourage freewheeling. The wilder the ideas that are offered, the better. It is easier to tame a wild idea later than it is to replace or invigorate an inert idea. At this point, the practicality of an idea is not of primary importance.

3. Think of as many ideas as you can. At this stage, it is the quantity—not the quality—of ideas that is important. The greater the number of ideas, the better the chance of finding a good one. Thus, in a brainstorming session, no self-censorship or group censorship is permitted. All ideas should be expressed.

4. Build on and improve or modify the ideas of others. Work to mix ideas until they form interesting combinations. Remember, brainstorming is a group effort.

5. Record all ideas. This ensures that the group will have available all the ideas that have been generated during the session.

6. Only after the brainstorming session is finished should group members evaluate the ideas for usefulness and applicability.

---

brainstorming

a technique designed to generate ideas

I had an immense advantage over many others dealing with the problem inasmuch as I had no fixed ideas derived from long-established practice to control and bias my mind, and did not suffer from the general belief that whatever is, is right.

—Henry Bessemer (discoverer of a new way of making steel)

Brainstorming is effective because it lessens the inhibitions of members and makes it easier for them to get their ideas heard; it promotes a warmer, more playful, enthusiastic, and cooperative atmosphere; and it encourages each individual's potential for creativity. But the unique aspect of brainstorming—and perhaps its most important benefit—is suspended judgment.

Too often, one or two group members stifle the creative-thinking effort of a brainstorming group. Despite the lip service they may pay to suspending judgment, they have come to the problem-solving experience with an evaluative mind-set. According to consultant Sidney Parnes, who studies creative thinking, this attitude surfaces in the form of **killer phrases,** like the

killer phrases
comments which stop the flow of ideas

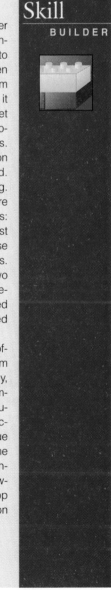

Skill BUILDER

Problem Solving in Organizations

While work groups use a variety of problem solving methods, including reflective thinking, three other frequently employed techniques include the nominal group technique, the Delphi method, and quality circles. How might your college use each of the following methods to solve a particular problem it faces? Be specific. Which method do you think you would find the most satisfying?

The nominal group technique uses limited discussion, reaching a group decision by secret vote. Especially valuable when group members are reluctant to voice their opinions, perhaps because the issue under discussion is extremely controversial and they do not want their idea attacked, this method enables each group member to contribute equally. The system involves a series of steps that alternates individual work and discussion. (1) The problem is defined for group members. (2) Without having any discussion, every group member writes down ideas for possible solutions to the problem. (3) Going in round robin sequence, each member, in turn, offers one idea on his or list. The offered ideas are recorded in order on a flip chart or an overhead, so that everyone can see them, until all ideas are exhausted. Duplicate ideas on the list are eliminated. Overlapping ideas on the list are combined. (4) Members clarify ideas. (5) Privately and in writing, every member rank orders the listed suggestions. (6) Member rankings are combined to produce a group ranking. (7) Discussion, clarification, and reordering, if necessary, ensue. (8) The ideas with the highest rankings are put into practice.

The Delphi method depends for its effectiveness on a selected group of experts, who do not communicate directly with each other but, instead, respond to a series of questionnaires. It is especially useful when you want to involve all members in finding a solution, when you want to prevent a dominant member from unduly influencing other members, and/or if it would be inconvenient or impossible to get participants physically together in the same location. It, too, contains a series of steps. (1) The problem is defined and the contribution needed from each member is specified. (2) Each member contributes ideas in writing. (3) The ideas provided by all members are combined and redistributed to the members: (4) Members choose the three or four best ideas. (5) Another list is created, using these contributions, and is distributed to members. (6) Members select and submit one or two ideas from the new list. (7) Using these responses, another list is created and distributed to members. (8) The solutions are identified and shared with all members.

A quality circle is a group of employees, often with different areas of expertise and from different levels in an organization's hierarchy, whose task it is to explore and make recommendations for improving the quality and usually the profitability of an organizational function. They use any problem-solving technique they desire to achieve their goal. At the same time, by becoming involved in the decision-making process, workers feel more empowered, bond to the organization, and develop better morale. The goal of any organization should be continual improvement.

following: "That won't work," "We tried that idea before," "You've got to be joking!" Comments like these stop the flow of ideas.[33]

This practice strikes at the heart and nature of brainstorming. It replaces the green light of brainstorming not so much with a yellow light of criticism or thoughtful evaluation as with a red light of frozen judgment. Killer phrases are often accompanied (or replaced) by **killer looks**—looks that discourage or inhibit the generation of ideas. (How often do killer phrases or looks intrude upon your group experiences?) By gaining insight into these types of killers and their effects, you can increase your ability to analyze your own behavior and change it if necessary.

The following example describes how creativity can be fostered in the workplace:

> Pamela Webb Moore, director of naming services (she helps companies figure out good names for their products at Synectics, a creativity consulting firm), uses a number of techniques to encourage creativity.
>
> One technique she uses to limber up the minds of tightly focused corporate managers is "sleight of head." While working on a particular problem, she'll ask clients to pretend to work on something else. In one real-life example, a Synectics-trained facilitator took a group of product development and marketing managers from the Etonic shoe corporation on an "excursion," a conscious walk away from the problem—in this case, to come up with a new kind of tennis shoe.
>
> The facilitator asked the Etonic people to imagine they were at their favorite vacation spot. "One guy," Moore says, "was on a tropical island, walking on the beach in his bare feet. He described how wonderful the water and sand felt on his feet, and he said, 'I wish I could play tennis barefoot.' The whole thing would have stopped right there if somebody had complained that while his colleague was wandering around barefoot, they were supposed to come up with a shoe. Instead, one of the marketing people there was intrigued, and the whole group decided to go off to play tennis barefoot on a rented court at 10 at night."
>
> While the Etonic people played tennis, the facilitator listed everything they said about how it felt. The next morning, the group looked at her assembled list of comments, and they realized that what they liked about playing barefoot was the lightness of being without shoes, and the ability to pivot easily on both the ball of the foot and the heel. Nine months later, the company produced an extremely light shoe called the Catalyst, which featured an innovative two-piece sole that made it easier for players to pivot.[34]

It is interesting to consider how brainstorming is related to what researcher Rosabeth Moss Kanter calls **kaleidoscope thinking.** According to Kanter,

> A kaleidoscope takes a set of fragments and forms them into a pattern. But when the kaleidoscope is twisted or approached from a new angle, the same fragments form a different pattern. Kaleidoscope thinking, then, involves taking existing data and twisting it or looking at it from another angle in order to see and analyze the new patterns that appear.[35]

Fishboning is a structured brainstorming technique groups use to aid the search for solutions to problems such as poor gas mileage. (See Figure 11.4.)

---

killer looks

looks that discourage or inhibit the generation of ideas

Do you see a problem as a game or as work? According to Mary Ann Glyn, who teaches organizational behavior at Yale University, people who see problems as games come up with more creative solutions than those who consider the same problems work.

kaleidoscope thinking

the taking of existing data and twisting it or looking at it from another angle

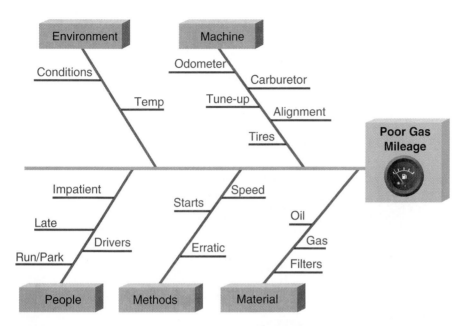

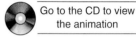

FIGURE 11.4
*Fishbone Technique.
Groups use the Fishbone
Technique to identify the
possible causes of a
problem however remote
they may seem. How can
such brainstorming help in
the search for an effective
solution?*

Go to the CD to view
the animation

TECHNOLOGY AND GROUPS: GROUPS IN CYBERSPACE

The growth of the Internet has led to the growth of virtual groups—people who interact with one another online without necessarily ever meeting face-to-face. Like groups in real places, groups in cyberspace fulfill both social and professional needs and functions. There are plenty of talkers online with forums and message board discussions for cancer survivors, parents who have lost children, persons in recovery, and running enthusiasts, just to name a few. For trust to develop among chat room members, numbers must be limited. Not anyone can enter the group. The chat room group, after all, is not a railroad station.[36]

Participants in chat rooms are free to talk about any subject—even those they would hesitate to talk about with others when in face-to-face meetings. Because rank is much less visible than in face-to-face meetings, a leveling of status differences tends to occur in online groups.[37] In addition, getting together with group or team members is more easily and more quickly accomplished than with a face-to-face meeting; in fact, a meeting can occur whenever members feel one is needed. Online groups are proliferating and are becoming a staple of group communication throughout the world; there is a drawback, however. According to Internet critic Clifford Stoll, popular online discussion groups also revolve around sex, bondage, and pornographic images.[38]

Networked communities give those who frequent them a sense of belonging to a neighborhood. In cyberspace, groups may meet in dungeons, or multiuser domains also known as virtual spaces; once they are at the site, individuals are able to play roles or to interact as themselves as they form a virtual

Getting together with group or team members is more easily and quickly accomplished online.

community and share, collaborate, or fantasize with each other as they play interactive role games. The environment they create offers them support during their participation in the online community. But no one is certain of anyone else's identity. Instead, they interact with online personae.

Professionals also sense that it is important to be online where they can interact in chat windows and beyond. Online work groups can edit shared documents, manipulate shared data, and take notes on shared "white boards." For example, small groups of doctors in different real locations, once in cyberspace, can at the same time look at the same CAT scan images on their screens and consult together about how to treat a patient's condition.[39]

In addition, especially since 9/11, businesses are holding virtual conferences that enable people separated by significant distance to interact with each other in real time. Whether the discussion is via teleconferencing that relies on telephones and speakerphones to connect people in different locations, via videoconferencing that makes it possible for people in different locations to see one another, or via interactive computer conferencing which occurs entirely via computers, technology is enhancing accessibility and changing the

e-SEARCH   The Cybergroup

Do you frequent or belong to any online groups? If yes, which ones, and what functions do they serve in your life? If no, why not?

In your opinion, is an online group able to perform as effectively as a group that meets in real space? Why or why not?

How might the ever-changing membership of online groups affect the group's climate and the nature of the site? Give examples.

group meeting landscape. Electronic brainstorming groups have similarly gained in popularity. So has the use of computer-mediated group decision support systems (GDSS), intended to promote participative, democratic decision making. Group members using GDSS each have a terminal and keyboard for each group member to provide input. GDSS groups demonstrate the ability to process more information more quickly and with greater, and more equal, member participation.[40]

In cyberspace, it is possible to chat with groups of people and not have gender, race, appearance, vocal qualities, age, or fear of how others will respond to the group influence your interactions.

MAKING GROUPS MORE EFFECTIVE

If a problem-solving group is to be effective in a real or an online setting, certain characteristics need to be present, and concerned members must work to develop these qualities. By becoming aware of the difference between optimal problem-solving behaviors and the actual behaviors of you and your fellow group members, you can begin to improve your group's method and style of operation.

An effective group exhibits the following characteristics:

1. *Group goals are clearly understood and cooperatively formulated by the members.* Goals are not merely imposed. If group members are confused about the nature of a problem, they will not be able to solve it. (As theorists Bobby R. Patton and Kim Giffin stress, "If we aim at nothing, we are pretty apt to hit it."[41])

2. *All members of the group are encouraged to communicate their ideas and feelings freely.* Ideas and feelings are valued; they are neither ignored nor suppressed. Keynote phrases are "I think," "I see," and "I feel." These phrases reveal a personal point of view and indicate that you recognize that someone else may feel, think, or see differently than you.

3. *Group members seek to reach a consensus when the decision is important.* Input from all members is sought. Each member's involvement is considered critical. Thus, the decision is not left to an authority to make on the basis of little or no discussion.

4. *Consideration is given to both the task and maintenance dimensions of the problem-solving effort.* Members look at the progress the group as a whole makes toward achieving its goal, as well as how successful members are at maintaining themselves as a group. In other words, both the quality of the decision and the well-being of the group members are considered important.

5. *Group members do not set about problem solving haphazardly.* A problem-solving framework is used, and an outline is followed that aids the group in its search for relevant information.

6. *Motivation is high.* Group members are eager to search for information, speak up, listen to others, and engage in an active and honest search for a better solution. They neither jump impetuously at the first solution that presents itself nor prematurely evaluate and criticize ideas.

Thinking CRITICALLY

Reflect and Respond

Agree or disagree with the following statement attributed to businessperson Arthur Jensen. Supply reasons and examples to support the position you take.

Most of the decisions that affect our lives are not made by individuals, but by small groups of people in executive boardrooms, faculty meetings, town councils, quality circles, dormitory rooms, kitchens, locker rooms, and a host of other meeting places.

Focus on Service Learning
How might you apply what you are learning in this chapter to help a local group solve a problem it faces?

---

7. An effort is made to assess the group's problem-solving style. Group members identify and alleviate factors that impede the group's effectiveness as well as identify and foster factors that enhance its effectiveness.

THE Wrap-Up

Revisiting Chapter Objectives

1. **Define *group*.**   In communication theory, a group is defined as a collection of people who interact verbally and nonverbally, occupy certain roles with respect to one another, and cooperate with each other to accomplish a definite goal. Some of our most important communication experiences take place in small groups. Today, groups are used, both online and offline, to solve common problems and make decisions by sharing information.

2. **Enumerate the advantages and disadvantages of group decision making and problem solving.**   The advantages of using a group instead of an individual are that resources can be pooled, motivation is increased, errors are more likely to be detected, decisions are more readily accepted by those outside the group, and group members can enjoy the companionship and rewards of working with others. There are, however, potential disadvantages to group problem solving: It may encourage laziness among some members; conflict may arise between personal and group goals; the group may be dominated by a few; one or two stubborn members may create a deadlock; the group may make an excessively risky decision; and the decision itself usually takes longer to reach.

3. **Provide examples of how a group's climate affects its operations.**   To operate effectively, group members need to be supportive; exercise participative decision making; show trust, openness, and candor; and set high performance goals. The healthier the group climate, the more cohesive the group. Keep in mind that in group meetings, men tend to speak more often, and longer, than women. Thus, women should make an effort to take the initiative, and men should give women the opportunity to air their views.

4. **Compare and contrast various decision-making methods.**   Groups use a number of methods to make decisions—decision by an expert, by chance, by majority, by the leader, by the minority, by the average of individual

decisions, and by consensus—or the group can defer a decision entirely. Making decisions by consensus is considered the most effective strategy. When a group achieves consensus, all members have helped formulate the decision, all have agreed on it, and all will support it.

5. **Apply the reflective-thinking framework to increase your effectiveness at problem solving.**   The behavior of group members can be plotted and analyzed on a decision-making grid, which provides a picture of the relationship between concern that a decision will actually work and concern that group members will be committed to the decision. Most groups can improve their problem-solving effectiveness by using the reflective-thinking framework, a systematic six-step approach to decision making.

6. **Describe and use brainstorming.**   A technique that is useful in some situations is brainstorming, which encourages each member's potential for creativity. Brainstorming can help you change your patterns of thinking and find new solutions.

Resources for Further Inquiry and Reflection

To apply your understanding of how the principles in Chapter 11 are at work in our daily lives, consult the following resources for further inquiry and reflection. Or, if you prefer, choose any other appropriate resource. Then connect the ideas expressed in your chosen selection with the communication concepts and issues you are learning about both in and out of class.

 Listen to Me

"We Can Work It Out" (The Beatles)
"You May Be Right" (Billy Joel)
"We Are the World" (Stevie Wonder)

How can problem-solving skills be put to work to resolve the problems identified in one of these songs?

 View Me

Oceans II   *The Full Monty*
ANTZ   *12 Angry Men*

All of these films focus on the role of the group in problem solving. Identify the decision-making and problem-solving lessons you learned from viewing any one of them.

 Read Me

George Orwell. *Animal Farm.* New York: Harcourt
  Brace, 1954.
Robert D. Putnam. *Bowling Alone: The Collapse and
  Revival of American Community.* New York: Simon
  & Schuster, 2000.

How do groups contribute to the establishment of a sense of community? What happens when the sense of community is stifled or disappears? Choose one of these books to use when answering these questions.

 Tell Me

Share with the class the insights you gained from your
  chosen Listen to Me, View Me, or Read Me
  selection.

Agree or disagree with this statement, with reasons: The major difference between a group meeting and a funeral is that the purpose of a funeral is perfectly clear.

Key Chapter Terminology

Use the Communication Works CD-ROM and the Online Learning Center at www.mhhe.com/gamble8 to further your knowledge of the following terminology.

brainstorming 354

decision by consensus 345

group 339

group climate 340

group goals 340

group norms 340

group patterns of communication 340

group structure 340

kaleidoscope thinking 356

killer looks 356

killer phrases 355

quality circles 337

questions of fact 351

questions of policy 351

questions of value 351

reflective-thinking framework 352

self-directed teams 337

Test Your Understanding

Go to the *Self Quizzes* on the Communication Works CD-ROM and the book's Online Learning Center at www.mhhe.com/gamble8.

Notes

1. See, for example, C. C. DuBois. "Portrait of the Ideal MBA." *The Penn Stater.* September–October 1992, p. 31; and J. Vice. "Developing Communication and Professional Skills through Analytical Reports." *Communication Quarterly* 64, 2001, pp. 84–93.

2. Eileen Daspin. "Memo to the Team: This Needs Salt!" *Wall Street Journal,* April 1, 2000, pp. B1, B14.

3. Natalie Angier. "Why We're So Nice: We're Wired to Cooperate." *New York Times,* July 23, 2002, pp. F1, F8.

4. See, for example, H. Lancaster. "That Team Spirit Can Lead Your Career to New Victories." *Wall Street Journal,* January 14, 1996, p. B1; and "Work Week." *Wall Street Journal,* November 28, 1995, p. A1.

5. Robert Gebeloff. "Oh No, Not Another Meeting." *The Record,* June 20, 1994, pp. C-1, C-4.

6. See M. A. Verespej. "When You Put the Team in Charge." *Industry Week,* December 1990, pp. 30–32; A. Versteeg. "Self-Directed Work Teams Yield Long-Term Benefits." *Journal of Business Strategy,* November/December 1990, pp. 9–12; and R. S. Wellins, C. W. Byham, and J. M. Wilson. *Empowered Teams: Creating Self-Directed Workgroups That Improve Quality, Productivity, and Participation.* San Francisco: Jossey-Bass, 1991.

7. See, for example, Robert D. Putnam. *Bowling Alone: The Collapse and Revival of American Community.* New York: Simon & Schuster, 2000.

8. Cheryl Hamilton and Cordell Parker. *Communicating for Results.* Belmont, CA: Wadsworth, 1990, p. 259.

9. Vincent DiSalvo. "A Summary of Current Research Identifying Communication Skills in Various Organizational Contexts." *Communication Education* 29, 1980, pp. 281–290.

10. There are numerous definitions of the word *group.* For a sampling, see David W. Johnson and Frank P. Johnson. *Joining Together: Group Theory and Group Skills,* 4th ed. Englewood Cliffs, NJ: Prentice-Hall, 1993; Gay Lumsden and Donald Lumsden. *Communicating in Groups and Teams.* Belmont, CA: Wadsworth, 1993; and J. Dan Rothwell. *In Mixed Company: Small Group Communication.* Fort Worth: Harcourt Brace, 1992.

11. See, for example, J. K. Brilhart and G. J. Galanes. *Effective Group Discussion,* 9th ed. Madison, WI: Brown & Benchmark, 1998.

12. J. Hackman. "The Design of Work Teams." In J. Lorsch, ed. *Handbook of Organizational Behavior.* Englewood Cliffs, NJ: Prentice-Hall, 1987, pp. 315–342.

13. Charles Redding. *Communication within the Organization.* New York: Industrial Communication Council, 1972.

14. Douglas McGregor. *The Human Side of Enterprise.* New York: McGraw-Hill, 1960.

15. B. Tuckman. "Developmental Sequencer in Small Groups." *Psychological Bulletin* 63, 1965, pp. 384–399; and S. A. Wheelen and J. M. Hockberger. "Validation Studies of the Group Development Questionnaire." *Small Group Research* 27:1, 1996, pp. 143–170.

16. See, for example, J. Keyton. "Group Termination: Completing the Study of Group Development." *Small Group Research* 24, 1993, pp. 84–100.

17. See, for example, Poole, Marshall Scott. "Do We Have Any Theories of Group Communication?" *Communication Studies* 41:3, 1990, p. 237.

18. See Y. Ohtsubo, A. Masuchi, and D. Nakanishi. "Majority Influence Process in Group Judgment: Test of the Social Judgment Scheme Model in a Group Polarization Context." *Group Process and Intergroup Relations,* 5:3, July 2002, pp. 249–262; and D. G. Meyers. *Social Psychology,* 7th ed. New York: McGraw-Hill, 2002, pp. 302–303.

19. J. Hall, V. O'Leary, and M. Williams. "The Decision-Making Grid: A Model of Decision-Making Styles." *California Management Review,* winter 1964, pp. 45–46.

20. See, for example, G. Hofstede. *Culture and Organizations: Software of the Mind.* New York: McGraw-Hill, 1997.

21. John E. Baird. "Sex Differences in Group Communication: A Review of Relevant Research." *Quarterly Journal of Speech* 62, 1986, pp. 179–192.

22. L. P. Stewart, A. D. Stewart, S. A. Friedley, and P. J. Cooper. *Communication between the Sexes: Sex Differences and Sex Role Stereotypes,* 2nd ed. Scottsdale, AZ: Gorsuch Scarisbrick, 1990.

23. S. Helgesen. *The Female Advantage: Women's Use of Leadership.* New York: Doubleday, 1990.

24. For a discussion of gender and group behavior, see T. and M. Gamble. *The Gender Communication Connection.* Boston: Houghton Miffin, 2003; Steward, Stewart, Friedley, and Cooper; E. Aries. "Gender and Communication." In P. Shaver and C. Hendricks, eds. *Sex and Gender.* Newbury Park, CA: Sage, 1987; and Julia T. Wood. *Gendered Lives,* 4th ed. Belmont, CA: Wadsworth, 2002.

25. Cathcart and Cathcart.

26. Harry C. Triandis, Richard Brislin, and C. Harry Hul. "Cross-Cultural Training across the Individualism-Collectivism Divide." *International Journal of Intercultural Relations* 12, 1988, pp. 269–289.

27. Delores Cathcart and Robert Cathcart. "The Group: A Japanese Context." In Larry A. Samovar and Richard E. Porter, eds. *Intercultural Communication: A Reader,* 8th ed. Belmont, CA: Wadsworth, 1997, pp. 329–339.

28. John Dewey. *How We Think.* Boston: Heath, 1910.

29. Jay Cocks. "Let's Get Crazy!" *Time,* June 11, 1990, p. 40.

30. Betty Edwards. *Drawing on the Right Side of the Brain.* New York: St. Martin's Press, 1979.

31. Jeff DeGroff. In Maryanne George. "Grab Your Textbook and Your Poker Cards." *The Record,* January 28, 1991.

32. A. F. Osborne. *Applied Imagination.* New York: Scribner's, 1957.

33. Sidney Parnes. *A Source Book for Creative Thinking.* New York: Scribner's, 1962.

34. Leslie Dorman and Peter Edidin. "Original Spin." *Psychology Today,* July 8, 1989, p. 46.

35. Rosabeth Moss Kanter. "How to Be an Entrepreneur without Leaving Your Company." *Working Woman,* November 1988, p. 44. See also Rosabeth Moss Kanter. *When Giants Learn to Dance.* New York: Touchstone, 1990.

36. Leslie Miller. "Chat Not Enough for Community Touch." *USA Today,* August 1, 2000, p. 3D.

37. S. L. Herndon. "Theory and Practice: Implications for the Implementation of Communication Technology in Organizations." *Journal of Business Communication* 34, January 1977, pp. 121–129.

38. Clifford Stoll. *Silicon Snake Oil: Second Thoughts on the Information Highway.* New York: Anchor Books, 1995, p. 57.

39. See, for example, Sherry Turkle. *Life on the Screen: Identity in the Age of the Internet.* New York: Simon & Schuster, 1995, p. 246.

40. A. F. Wood and M. J. Smith. *Online Communication: Linking Technology, Identity, and Culture.* Mahwah: NJ: Lawrence Erlbaum Associates, 2001, p. 120.

41. Bobby R. Patton and Kim Giffin. *Decision Making: Group Interaction.* New York: Harper & Row, 1978.

Group Networks, Membership, and Leadership

1. Explain how networks affect group interaction.

2. Define *group role* and distinguish among task, maintenance, and self-serving roles.

3. Define *leadership* and distinguish among various leadership styles: type X, type Y, autocratic, laissez-faire, and democratic.

4. Describe how trait theory, situation theory, and functional theory and transformational leadership contribute to our understanding of leadership.

5. Explain how cooperation versus competition and a defensive versus a supportive climate manifest themselves in group interactions and affect group climate.

I will pay more for the ability to deal with people than any other ability under the sun.

—**John D. Rockefeller**

When the best leader's work is done the people say, "We did it ourselves."

—**Lao-tzu**

Go to the *Online Learning Center* at www.mhhe.com/gamble8 and answer the questions in the *Self Inventory* to evaluate your understanding of leadership.

I n William Golding's *Lord of the Flies,* a group of schoolboys who survived a plane crash are marooned on an island. Since the island is uninhabited, the boys need to work together to create their own society. As they attempt to do so, they engage in a host of effective and ineffective examples of group membership and leadership. In this chapter, we will explore the various dimensions of group membership and the meaning of leadership; we will also elaborate on the characteristics of effective group communication. By gaining insights into the various roles performed by members and leaders, by familiarizing ourselves with the communication styles open to us, and by seeing how role expectations, leadership, and networks (communication patterns) affect group performance, we will be better equipped to analyze our own behavior in problem-solving groups.

Very few ideas and very few projects of any significance are implemented by one person alone.

—**Rosabeth Moss Kanter**

NETWORKS: PATTERNS OF COMMUNICATION

Any group's ability to accomplish its task is related to the interactions among its members. It is all but impossible for a small group to communicate well unless the members are comfortable in speaking with one another, feel free to express their ideas and feelings to each other, and have an opportunity to receive feedback about how they are coming across.

If you are able and willing to communicate with most, if not all, the members of your group, you can be said to occupy a central position in the group. In contrast, if you relate to only one person or at the most a few people in your group, you occupy a peripheral position. It is the group's networks, or patterns of communication, that determine the communication paths open to members and the effectiveness of their interactions. Figure 12.1 shows representative types of networks.

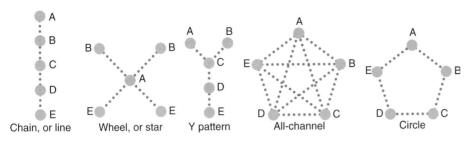

FIGURE 12.1
Communication Networks.

Network Effects

The first studies of group networks were conducted by sociological researchers Bavelas and Leavitt.[1] Bavelas studied four communication patterns: circle, line (or chain), star (or wheel), and Y. For each pattern, he measured the time it took group members to solve a simple problem and the satisfaction of group members with the operation of the group. Bavelas discovered that the Y pattern was the most efficient; that is, it enabled the members to solve the problem presented to them in the shortest time. However, he found that the circle pattern was associated with the highest morale. Bavelas also found that members who occupied central positions in group networks were more satisfied with the group's operation than members who occupied peripheral positions.

Leavitt studied the same four patterns of communication. In Leavitt's experiments, members of a circle group, a chain group, a Y group, and a wheel group had to discover a common symbol included on cards provided to them. He found that the network with the greatest degree of shared centrality—the circle—produced the highest morale among group members; the network with the lowest degree of shared centrality—the wheel—required the shortest time to come up with an accurate solution. In most of the groups Leavitt studied, the person who occupied the most central position was identified as the leader. The circle was described as having shared leadership; each of the other groups had one clearly emergent leader.

The particular type of communication network a group develops will determine which communication channels are open and which channels are closed, and thus the network will affect who talks to whom. Well-linked or connected persons tend to be the most influential.[2] The all-channel network, in which any group member can communicate with every other member, gives individuals equal opportunity to exert influence. The network also affects morale. When people are cut off from relating to each other, individual satisfaction decreases.

A network's members perform four kinds of communication roles: clique member, liaison, bridge, and isolate. A **clique** is a group of individuals who have a majority of their contacts with each other. Individuals who are not members of any one group or clique but link persons in one group with persons in another group are **liaisons. Bridges,** on the other hand, are persons in groups who have a predominant number of intragroup contacts and who communicate with one or more persons in another group or clique. Both liaisons and bridges tend to feel more strongly integrated in the group, are more team-oriented, and experience less frustration with the group's work

What position do you most like to occupy in the networks used by those groups in which you are a member? Does the position you occupy change as you change groups? Why or why not?

How do you react when you feel/find yourself isolated in a group? What steps, if any, have you taken to reduce feelings of alienation in either yourself or others?

clique

a group of individuals who have a majority of their contacts with each other

liaisons

individuals who are not members of any one group or clique but link persons in one group with persons in another group

bridges

persons in groups who have intragroup contacts and communicate with one or more persons in another group or clique

FIGURE 12.2
Network Roles.

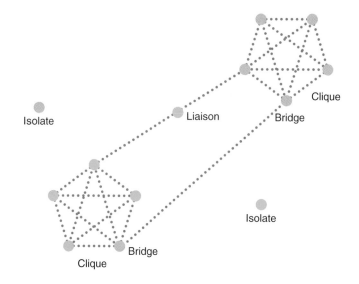

isolates

persons who have little, if any, contact with others

What type of network do you think would work best in the following situations: a family discussion about where to go on vacation, a football huddle, the issuing of a new company policy?

than others. In contrast, **isolates,** persons who have little, if any, contact with others, do not feel well integrated into the life of the group, fail to contribute to group functions, are less secure in their self-concepts, and are more likely to experience dissatisfaction. (See Figure 12.2.)

With the exception of the all-channel network, most communication networks are neither as formal nor as well defined as the ones we have examined. The impact that informal networks exert on a group's interaction dynamics, however, is just as real. Who talks to whom in a group is affected by a number of factors. In general, emergent networks reflect the relative power and attraction, roles, and relationships that exist among the group's members. In some groups, for example, there are some members we simply prefer to interact with. As a result, group members create the networks that, in turn, influence the ways members interact with each other.

One way to influence network development is by physically arranging furniture and seating in ways conducive to certain types of interaction. For example, if you want an all-channel network, arrange the chairs to ensure that members have equal centrality. On the other hand, if you want one person to be in control of the group, one person should sit in the most central position in the room.

A MODEL OF GROUP ROLE CLASSIFICATION

group role-classification model

a model that describes functions participants should seek to assume and avoid in groups

Even though their **group role-classification model** was formulated almost a half century ago, the system proposed by Kenneth Benne and Paul Sheats is still commonly used today. It describes the functions participants should seek to assume—and the functions they should avoid—during the life of a group.[3] Benne and Sheats considered goal achievement (completing the task) and group maintenance (building relationships) the two basic objectives of any group. They further reasoned that eliminating self-serving roles (nonfunctional behaviors) is a requirement or condition that must be met if the preceding goals are to be realized. Guided by these assumptions, Benne and Sheats identified three categories of roles:

1. Task-oriented roles
2. Maintenance-oriented roles
3. Self-serving roles

Task-Oriented Roles

The following are among the **task roles** that help the group realize its goals:

Initiating. The member defines a problem; suggests methods, goals, and procedures; and starts the group moving along new paths or in different directions by offering a plan.

Information seeking. The member asks for facts and opinions and seeks relevant information about the problem.

Opinion seeking. The member solicits expressions of feeling and value to discover the values underlying the group effort.

Information giving. The member provides ideas and suggestions and supplies personal experiences as well as factual data.

Opinion giving. The member supplies opinions, values, and beliefs and reveals his or her feelings about what is being discussed.

Clarifying. The member elaborates on the ideas of others, supplies paraphrases, offers examples or illustrations, and tries to eliminate confusion and increase clarity.

Coordinating. The member summarizes ideas and tries to draw various contributions together constructively.

Evaluating. The member evaluates the group's decisions or proposed solutions and helps establish standards for judgment.

Consensus testing. The member checks on the state of group agreement to see if the group is nearing a decision.

task roles
group roles designed to help the group achieve its goals

maintenance roles
group roles designed to ensure the smooth running of a group

Maintenance-Oriented Roles

The following **maintenance roles** help the group run smoothly:

Encouraging. The member is warm, receptive, and responsive to others and praises others and their ideas.

Gatekeeping. The member attempts to keep communication channels open; he or she helps reticent members contribute to the group and works to keep the discussion from being dominated by one or two members.

Harmonizing. The member mediates differences between participants and attempts to reconcile misunderstandings

Members in a group perform different roles. Which roles do you perform regularly?

or disagreements; he or she also tries to reduce tension by using humor or other forms of relief at appropriate junctures.

Compromising. The member is willing to compromise his or her position to maintain group cohesion; he or she is willing to admit error and modify beliefs to achieve group growth.

Standard setting. The member assesses whether group members are satisfied with the procedures being used and indicates that criteria have been set for evaluating group functioning.

Self-Serving Roles

self-serving roles

group roles that impede the functioning of a group by preventing members from working together effectively

Self-serving roles prevent the group from working effectively:

Blocking. The member is disagreeable and digresses in an effort to ensure that nothing is accomplished.

Aggression. The member criticizes or blames others and works to deflate the egos of other group members in an effort to enhance his or her own status.

Recognition seeking. The member attempts to become the focus of attention by boasting about his or her own accomplishments rather than dealing with the group task; he or she may speak loudly and exhibit behavior that is unusual.

Withdrawing. The member appears indifferent, daydreams, is lost in thought, or sulks.

Dominating. The member insists on getting his or her own way, interrupts others, and gives directions in an effort to run or control the group.

Joking. The member appears cynical or engages in horseplay or other inappropriate or irrelevant behaviors.

Skill
BUILDER

Role Call

Form groups of five to seven members. Designate two members of each group as group-process observers, who will chart the roles members perform during the life of the group.

Each group is to complete both of the following tasks.

Task A

Use materials such as cotton, pipe cleaners, construction paper, tape, glue, scissors, and string to build a container that will support and catch an uncooked egg dropped from a height of 5 feet without damaging the shell.

Task B

Choose a group name and design a group symbol to affix to your egg container. With the aid of your process observers, answer the following questions:

1. How did the group organize for work?
2. To what extent was the members' participation evenly distributed?
3. Which task or maintenance functions did various members perform?
4. Which task or maintenance functions were lacking or not sufficiently present, inhibiting the group's performance?
5. Which self-serving roles were present? How did they affect the group's operation?
6. Summarize what the group needs to do to enhance its ability to function in the future.

The Social Loafer

A common complaint expressed by students who have to work is groups is that some members end up having to do the work of other members who do not share a comparable level of commitment to the group or its task. Upon joining a group, members who function as social loafers reduce their work effort, miss meetings, or engage in otherwise dysfunctional behavior.

Why do you think that social loafers tend to be more prevalent in groups in individualistic cultures than in collectivist cultures? What steps should a group take to reduce the impact a social loafer has on other members and the group?

Ethics &
COMMUNICATION

Self-confessing. The member uses other group members as an audience and reveals personal feelings or insights that are not oriented toward group concerns.

Help seeking. The member tries to elicit sympathy or pity from other members.

Summary

Which roles do you find yourself performing most frequently? What conditions in the group, or what personal needs, do you think precipitate such behavior on your part?

Every group member affects the operation of his or her group; sometimes the members exhibit behaviors that improve task performance in specific ways, and sometimes they exhibit behaviors that reflect their general concern for human needs and feelings. Sometimes they exhibit helpful behaviors, and sometimes they exhibit behaviors that seem to announce a minimal regard for the group experience. Developing an understanding of membership roles and behavior is essential if we are to evaluate the effectiveness of the groups to which we belong. Developing an understanding of group leadership is also essential; after all, membership and leadership go hand in hand. Let's turn now to leadership.

APPROACHES TO LEADERSHIP: THE LEADER IN YOU

What is leadership? Are you a leader or a potential leader? What qualities does a good leader possess? Are effective leaders born or made?[4]

What is Leadership?

Leadership is the ability to influence others. Thus, every person who influences others can be said to exert leadership.[5] Leadership can be either a positive or a negative force. When its influence is positive, leadership facilitates task accomplishment by a group. But if its influence is negative, task

leadership
the ability to influence others

designated leader

a person given the authority to exert influence within a group

achieved leader

a person who exhibits leadership without being appointed

accomplishment is inhibited. Every group member is a potential leader.[6] Whether this potential is used wisely or is abused—or whether it is used effectively or ineffectively—depends on individual skills, on personal objectives, and on commitment to the group.

Groups, especially problem-solving groups, need effective leadership to achieve their goals. Effective leadership can be demonstrated by one or more of the members. Note that there is a difference between being appointed a leader—that is, serving as a designated leader—and exhibiting leadership behaviors. When you function as a **designated leader,** you have been dubbed the leader; this means that an outside force has given you the authority to exert your influence within the group. When you engage in effective leadership behavior without being appointed or directed to do so, you function as an **achieved leader;** that is, you are automatically performing roles that help a group attain task or maintenance objectives.

Effective leaders perform combinations of the task and maintenance roles; they demonstrate role versatility. Such leaders help establish a group climate that encourages and stimulates interaction; they make certain that an agenda is planned for a meeting; they take responsibility for ensuring that group communication proceeds smoothly. When group members get off the track, it is this type of leader who asks relevant questions, offers internal summaries, and keeps the discussion going. This is also the kind of leader who encourages continual evaluation and improvement by group members.

Leadership Styles

Theorists have identified a number of leadership styles. Among them are type X, type Y, autocratic, laissez-faire, and democratic leadership.

Type X and Type Y Leaders

The assumptions we make about how people work together influence the type of leadership style we adopt. The following are eight assumptions that a leader might make about how and why people work. Choose the four you are most comfortable with.

1. The average group member will avoid working if he or she can.
2. The average group member views work as a natural activity.
3. The typical group member must be forced to work and must be closely supervised.
4. The typical group member is self-directed when it comes to meeting performance standards and realizing group objectives.
5. A group member should be threatened with punishment to get him or her to put forth an adequate effort.
6. A group member's commitment to objectives is related not to punishment but to rewards.
7. The average person prefers to avoid responsibility and would rather be led.
8. The average person not only can learn to accept responsibility but actually seeks responsibility.

Media

Shakespeare et al. on Leadership

A number of the plays of Shakespeare offer insightful explorations of leadership. The lessons contained in them are as relevant in the twenty-first century as they were in the sixteenth century. For example, from the works of Shakespeare, we learn the importance of timing in achieving goals, the value of courage in facing challenges, the value of determination, and the need for establishing a firm, clear vision. While the artifacts of twenty-first-century corporate life are increasingly high-tech—dominated by cell phones, the Internet, and e-mail—the essence of leadership remains remarkably constant. The effectiveness of corporate teams and groups depends in large measure on the strengths or failings of the corporation's leadership, just as in

Shakespeare's day it depended on the strengths or failings of the king.[7]

While not up to the standard set by Shakespeare's plays, contemporary media offerings such as *West Wing* and *Survivor* also explore different types of leaders. As we recognize the types of leaders presented to us, we come to understand them and may even learn to deal with them more effectively.

Pick a recent film or television show. Identify and discuss one or more leadership lessons you learned from viewing the selected film or program, and explain how one or more of the characters in the film or program deepened your awareness of the people you work with or interact with every day.

A scene from the television show "West Wing." How do TV and real-life leaders differ?

If you picked mostly odd-numbered items in the preceding list, you represent what management theorist Douglas McGregor calls a **type X leader.** In contrast, if you checked mostly even-numbered items, you represent what McGregor calls a **type Y leader.**[8] The type Y leader is more of a risk taker than the type X leader. Y leaders are willing to let each group member grow and develop to realize his or her individual potential. X leaders, however, do not readily delegate responsibility; unlike Y leaders, X leaders are not concerned with group members' personal sense of achievement. (Are you satisfied with the set of assumptions you chose? What consequences could they have?)

type X leader

a leader who does not trust group members to work and is unconcerned with the personal achievement of group members

type Y leader

a leader who displays trust in group members and is concerned with their sense of personal achievement

EXPLORING

Diversity

Social Power and Leadership Behavior

Social power, like leadership, concerns the ability to influence others or to control the outcomes of their efforts. Currently, in the United States, more men than women occupy power positions. However, as is noted in the following excerpts from an article by Bettijane Levine, the leadership styles men and women use may cause this imbalance to change in the years ahead. After you read the excerpted article, answer the questions that follow.

Women, take heart. Men, take note. A new groundbreaking study shows that the two sexes differ dramatically when it comes to leadership—and that the feminine approach may be the wave of the future.

Male executives tend to lead the traditional way; by command and control, according to the study conducted by Judith B. Rosener at the University of California, Irvine. Men give an order, explain the reward for a job that's well done, and pretty much keep their power and knowledge to themselves.

Female executives, on the other hand, tend to lead in nontraditional ways: by sharing information and power. They inspire good work by interacting with the staff, by encouraging employee participation, and by showing how employees' personal goals can be reached as they meet organizational ones.

"The male leadership model of command and control is not necessarily better or worse than the female model," Rosener says. "If there is a fire, for example, you need a command-control-type leader to order everyone out, with no questions asked."

In fact, for years the traditional male leadership style has been the only style at top corporations. No other style was thought to exist. Rosener says it's still in place "at most Fortune 500–type" companies, where strict hierarchical structure means that all orders flow from the top, with everyone below following them.

But the hierarchical structure is starting to look anachronistic in a world where corporations have international headquarters and where decision making is required at lower levels, Rosener says.

It does not function as well in a global economy of multinational companies, service industries, and fast-changing technology businesses, where it's impractical to have only a few top people from whom all planning and orders flow.

The structure could actually be harmful to corporations in which far-flung, lower-level employees need to make quick, accurate decisions, backed by knowledge and power to make the decisions. . . .

The female tendency to share knowledge, power, and responsibility may be what's needed next, Rosener says.

Who would be more successful in leading a group that you were in—a man or a woman? A person from a collectivistic or an individualist tradition? Be sure to give reasons for your answers.

Source: From "(Wo)Men at Work," by Bettijane Levine, *Los Angeles Times*, October 29, 1990. Copyright 1990, Los Angeles Times. Reprinted by permission.

Autocratic, Laissez-Faire, and Democratic Leaders

In most discussions of leadership styles, three categories in addition to type X and type Y usually come up: the autocratic leader (the "boss"), the democratic leader (the "participator"), and the laissez-faire leader (the "do your own thing" leader).[9] Let's examine each briefly.

autocratic, or authoritarian, leaders
directive leaders

Autocratic, or authoritarian, leaders are dominators who view their task as directive. In a group with an autocratic leader, it is the leader who determines all policies and gives orders to the other group members. In other words, one boss typically assumes almost all leadership roles; in effect, this person becomes the sole decision maker. Although such an approach may be effective and efficient during a crisis, the usual outcome of this behavior is low group satisfaction.

The opposite of the autocratic leader is the **laissez-faire leader.** This type of leader adopts a "leave them alone" attitude. In other words, this person diminishes the leadership function to the point where it is almost nonexistent. The result is that group members are free to develop and progress on their own; they are indeed free to do their own thing. Unfortunately, the members of a laissez-faire group may often be distracted from the task at hand and lose their sense of direction, with the result that the quality of their work suffers.

The middle leadership position—and the one that has proved most effective—is that of **democratic leaders.** In groups with democratic leadership, members are directly involved in the problem-solving process; the power to make decisions is neither usurped by a boss nor abandoned by a laissez-faire leader. Instead, the leader's behavior represents a reasonable compromise between those two extremes. Democratic leaders do not dominate the group with one point of view, but they do attempt to provide direction to ensure that both task and maintenance functions are carried out. The group is free to identify its own goals, follow its own procedures, and reach its own conclusions. Most people prefer democratic groups. Morale, motivation, group-mindedness, and the desire to communicate all increase under the guidance of a democratic leader.

Although democratic leadership is traditionally preferred, all three leadership styles can be effective under the appropriate conditions. Thus, when an urgent decision is required, the autocratic style may be in the group's best interest. When a minimum of interference is needed for members to work together effectively, the laissez-faire style may be more effective. When commitment to the group decision is of greatest importance, the democratic style should be practiced.

laissez-faire leader
nondirective leaders

democratic leaders
leaders who represent a reasonable compromise between authoritarian and laissez-faire leaders

---

Divide into groups. Create a problem-solving situation and explain how an authoritarian, a laissez-faire, and a democratic leader might handle it. For example, imagine that a corporation needs to purchase data-processing equipment. What behaviors might each type of leader exhibit in a group discussion on this topic? In turn, each group will role-play each leadership style.

Theories of Leadership

Where does leadership ability come from? Why do some people exert more leadership than others? Why are some people more effective leaders than others? Are some people born to be leaders? Or does every situation create its own leader? Or is leadership a matter of learned abilities and skills? Over the years, theorists have given various answers to these questions.

Trait Theory

The earliest view of leadership was trait theory. According to **trait theory,** leaders are people who are born to lead.[10] (Do you know any men or women who seem to have been born to lead?) Trait theorists also believed there are special built-in, identifiable leadership traits. Accordingly, attempts were made to design a test that could predict whether a person would become a leader.

After many years of research, proof of trait theory is still lacking. Personality traits are not surefire predictors of leadership. For one thing, no one set of characteristics is common to all leaders, and leaders and followers share many of the same characteristics. Also, the situation appears, at least in part, to determine who will come forward to exert leadership. This is not to suggest, however, that trait research did not yield valuable findings. In fact, while the statement "Leaders must possess the following personality traits . . ." is not valid, the research does enable us to note that certain traits are indeed more likely to be found in leaders than in nonleaders.

trait theory
the theory of leadership that asserts that certain people are born to lead

---

Describe a person who you believe was born to be a leader. What attributes do you believe destined this person to lead?

TABLE 12.1 *Evaluating Your Leadership Traits*

Trait	Low				High
Dependability	1	2	3	4	5
Cooperativeness	1	2	3	4	5
Desire to win	1	2	3	4	5
Enthusiasm	1	2	3	4	5
Drive	1	2	3	4	5
Persistence	1	2	3	4	5
Responsibility	1	2	3	4	5
Intelligence	1	2	3	4	5
Foresight	1	2	3	4	5
Communication ability	1	2	3	4	5
Popularity	1	2	3	4	5

Use the scale in Table 12.1 to measure the extent to which you possess leadership attributes. Calculate your leadership score by adding up the numbers you have chosen. Next, use the scale to rate a person you definitely perceive as a leader. Finally, use the scale to rate a person you definitely perceive as not a leader. To what extent did you see yourself as having leadership traits? The highest possible score is 55. Such a score probably indicates strong leadership potential and means that a person perceives himself or herself as a leader or is so perceived by others. How does your total score compare with that of the person you considered a leader? With that of the person you considered a nonleader? If you are interested, you can compute an average score for men and women.[11] Which sex do you think would score higher? Why do you think each set of results turned out as it did?

According to researcher Marvin Shaw, the characteristics identified in Table 12.1 indicate leadership potential. Shaw notes that a person who does not exhibit these traits is unlikely to be a leader.[12] Of course, having leadership potential doesn't guarantee that you will actually emerge as a leader. A number of group members may have the qualities of leadership, but the final assertion of leadership will depend on more than potential.

Situational Theory

situational theory

the theory of leadership which asserts that leadership is situation dependent

The second theory of leadership is **situational theory.** According to this theory, whether an individual displays leadership skills and behaviors and exercises actual leadership depends on the situation.[13] The development and emergence of leadership can be affected by such factors as the nature of the problem, the social climate, the personalities of the group members, the size of the group, and the time available to accomplish the task. As organizational behavior theorist Keith Davis notes in *Human Relations at Work*, leader and group "interact not in a vacuum, but at a particular time and within a specific set of circumstances."[14] A leader is not necessarily a person "for all seasons."

Fred Fiedler's contingency theory and Paul Hersey and Ken Blanchard's readiness theory are both situational theories. Fiedler's theory contends that predicting a group's leader is contingent upon three situational factors: leader-member relations, task structure, and position power.[15] Hersey and Blanchard's

Keeping Down with the Competition

What problems are encountered when a group aspires to produce not the best work it possibly can but, rather, work that is only as good as that produced by competing groups?

Is a group as good as its strongest member? As bad as its weakest member? More than the sum of its parts? Explain.

Ethics & COMMUNICATION

"That's settled, then. We'll lower our standards to meet the competition."

theory contends that the readiness level of a group (the degree that members are willing and skilled enough to perform a task) determines the degree of task or relationship behavior a leader needs to emphasize.[16] Thus, the relationship behavior, task behavior, and maturity of the group members all come into play as a leader determines the style called for. For example, when groups are new, a *telling* style of leadership may be effective. The leader needs to provide direction, training, and instructions. When a group has some confidence in its skills, a *selling* style of leadership, one in which the leader uses both task and relational behavior to persuade members to accomplish tasks, is called for. In contrast, when group members take on more responsibility and become more independent, the leader becomes more equal to other group members. In this case, the leadership style of *participating* is used and decision making is shared. Finally, when the group is ready to provide its own leadership, a *delegating* style is appropriate.

Functional Theory

The third theory of leadership is **functional theory.** In contrast to trait theory and situational theory, which emphasize the emergence of one person as a leader, functional theory suggests that several group members should be ready to lead because various actions are needed to achieve group goals.

functional theory

the leadership theory which suggests that several members of a group should be ready to lead because various actions are needed to achieve group goals

Functional theorists believe that any of the task or maintenance activities can be considered leadership functions. In other words, when you perform any needed task or maintenance function, you are exercising leadership. Thus, according to functional theory, leadership shifts from person to person and is shared. Of course, sometimes one or two group members perform more leadership functions than others do. Consequently, one member might become the main task leader, whereas another might become the main socioemotional leader. However, the point is that we can enhance our leadership potential by learning to perform needed group functions more effectively.[17]

From the functional viewpoint, then, leadership is not necessarily a birthright; nor is it simply a matter of being in the right situation at a critical juncture. Instead, we are all capable of leadership, and what is required is that we have enough self-assertion and sensitivity to perform the functions that are needed as they are needed. In effect, this theory is asserting that good membership is good leadership. And the converse is also true: Good leadership is good membership.

Transformational Leadership

transformational leader

a leader who gives a group a new vision strengthens its culture or structure

A **transformational leader** transforms a group by giving it a new vision strengthening its culture or structure. The transformational leader does not merely direct members, elicit contributions from members, or wait for members to catch up with his or her thinking. Instead, the transformational leader helps group members imagine and visualize the future they can build together. Transformational leaders inspire, motivate, and intellectually stimulate group members to become involved in achieving the group's goals. They function as the group's guiding force.[18]

DIVERSITY, GENDER, AND THE GROUP

Groups operate within a society. Thus, the culture in which the members exist and the gender of the group's members influence the group's operation.

Skill
BUILDER

Thinking about the Culture of a Group

A group's culture is "the pattern of values, beliefs, norms, and behaviors that are shared by group members and that shape a group's individual 'personality.'"[19] The culture of a group provides the foundation for the rules followed, standards of behavior adhered to, actions undertaken, and behaviors exhibited or prohibited by group members. Organizational theorists believe that every organization evolves a unique group culture, which guides its behavior and the behavior of its members.

Describe the culture of an organization in which you would like to work. What makes the organization's culture and especially its norms attractive to you? How do employees use communication to perform the culture? For example, if a person wants to be successful in this organization, what should he or she do? What should he or she not do? What specifically does this organization make possible for its members?

Culture and Group Interaction

Your culture influences the way you communicate when you are part of a group. While cultural variations can enhance a group's operation, at times cultural clashes can impede it. For example, when Corning and the Mexican company Vitro made a cross-border alliance, their communication efforts were hurt by cultural misunderstandings. According to business analysts, problems developed in the relationship because of stereotypes as well as different decision-making and work-style approaches employed by the two companies. While the Americans were accustomed to eating during meetings, the Mexicans were used to going out for leisurely meals. The Mexicans typically put in much longer work-days because of their longer lunches and conducted evening meetings, whereas the Americans wanted to hold business to daytime hours. The Mexicans saw the Americans as too direct, while the Americans viewed the Mexicans as too polite. The decision-making methods of the two companies posed the toughest problem: Because Mexican businesses tend to be much more hierarchical, the decisions were made by the top executives, which slowed down the decision-making process. The Mexicans, unlike the Americans, also displayed an unwillingness to criticize. As a result, their conversations were more indirect.[20]

Like the Mexican style, the Japanese decision-making style differs from the American approach. While Americans tend to value openness in groups, the Japanese value harmony. While Americans emphasize individual responsibility, the Japanese stress collective responsibility.[21] Thus, there is a tendency among the Japanese to lose individual identity within the group.[22] While Americans believe that the individual is the most important part of a group, that the individual is free to choose the roles that he or she will perform in a group, and that it is an individual's right to remain as part of a group, the Japanese believe in the submergence of the individual within the group and demand complete loyalty. Group orientation is so pervasive that members do not usually assume self-serving roles, such as blocker or recognition seeker, because to do so would jeopardize the success of the group. To leave a group in Japan is to risk losing one's identity. Since Japan is a collectivistic culture, the group, not the individual, is the significant entity. In individualistic cultures such as the United States, the individual group member is accorded significant importance.

Native Americans, like the Japanese, refrain from competing publicly with others in a group for fear of causing embarrassment. Humiliating a fellow group member to prove a point is alien to them.

Even though group membership and group identity are highly valued in collectivistic cultures, participating in decision-making groups does not appear to give group members actual decision-making power. In one study of 48 Japanese organizations, while members were encouraged to contribute ideas, the decision-making power remained with the CEO and managers higher in the organization hierarchy.[23] Thus, culture influences both membership and leadership style.

Gender and Group Interaction

Besides studying cultural differences, researchers have investigated the interaction of men and women in groups. Results indicate that men and women

The 20 Percent Solution

It has been found that discrimination in groups decreases when minorities and women comprise at least 20 percent of a group's members.[24] If increasing the representation of women and ethnic minorities can reduce the bias against persons in these groups, including whether they have a chance to be chosen or emerge as a leader in major corporations, organizations, and government agencies, what steps should be taken to sensitize persons to the need for greater diversity, and what should be done to help women and minorities improve their chances to occupy such leadership positions?

have different goals for communicating. Women tend to pay more attention to the relationships among group members, while men tend to be more instrumental; they focus more on the task.[25] Women tend to analyze problems holistically, whereas men tend to analyze problems in a more linear fashion, looking for cause-and-effect relationships. Studies of mixed-sex groups indicate that, because men and women contribute in unique ways to a group, having men and women work together enhances group productivity.[26]

Who would you rather have as the leader of your group, a man or a woman? While responses to the question vary, men usually come out ahead. However, there is a greater likelihood today that you will be working with members of both sexes in the workplace. And when it comes to leadership, while both men and women enjoy being leaders, when part of a group, women are often more motivated to help others than are men and thus exhibit a much more personal leadership approach.[27] Women are also more

Who would you rather have as the leader of your group or team, a man or a woman? Why?

likely to employ a more participatory or collaborative communication style; men, in contrast, display a more directive style.[28] Thus, women tend to excel at relationship building and participative leadership, while men exhibit more work-directed and assertive behaviors.

Research reveals that sex-role stereotypes influence how the behaviors of leaders are perceived. The same messages are evaluated differently, depending on whether they are delivered by a male or a female. For this reason, while women delivering some messages are considered bossy or emotional, men delivering the same messages are seen as responsible and as exercising leadership. Too frequently, the leadership efforts of women are misinterpreted.[29]

GROUP MEMBER RELATIONSHIPS: A LOOK AT GROUP INTERACTION

Other variables also affect the quality of group interaction. Most important, the nature of the relationships shared by the members of a group is highly significant in determining whether the group will operate effectively. For this reason, the following questions deserve our attention: To what extent do members of a group cooperate or compete with one another? To what extent do the members foster a defensive or a supportive environment?[30]

Cooperation versus Competition

Obviously, the personal goals of each member have an impact on the operation of a group. If individual members view their goals as congruent or coinciding, an atmosphere of cooperation can be fostered. However, if individual members see their goals as contradictory, a competitive atmosphere will develop. Too frequently, group members attempt to compete with one another when cooperating would be more beneficial to the group. Psychologists Linden L. Nelson and Spencer Kagen believe that it is irrational and self-defeating to compete if cooperating would make better sense.[31] When a group experience develops into a dog-eat-dog situation, all the members may go hungry.

Few factors do more to damage a group's ability to maintain itself and complete a task than competition among members, yet highly competitive individuals do belong to groups and do, in fact, affect the group's communication climate and emergent goal structure. The term *goal structure* describes the way members relate to each other. Under a **cooperative goal structure,** the members of a group work together to achieve their objectives, and the goals of each person are perceived as compatible with or complementary to those of the others. Group members readily pool resources and coordinate their efforts to obtain what they consider common aims. In contrast, when a group develops a **competitive goal structure,** members do not share resources, efforts are not coordinated, and, consciously or unconsciously, individuals work to hinder one another's efforts to obtain the goal. According to psychologist Morton Deutsch, group members who have a competitive orientation believe that they can achieve their goals only if other members fail to do so.[32]

Certain requirements need to be met if the members of a group are to cooperate with each other. First, the members need to agree that each has an equal right to satisfy needs. Second, conditions must be such that each person in the group is able to get what he or she wants at least some of the time. Third, plays for power that rely on techniques such as threatening, yelling, or demanding are viewed with disdain and are avoided. Finally, members do not attempt to manipulate each other by withholding information or dissembling. Consequently, when you cooperate as a group member, you do not aim to win or to beat or outsmart others. Unlike competition, cooperation does not require gaining an edge over the other members of your group; for this reason, unlike competition, cooperation does not promote defensiveness.

How do you act in group situations you define as cooperative? In situations you define as competitive? To what extent does the sex of the other group members appear to make a difference?

cooperative goal structure

a goal structure in which the members of a group work together to achieve their objectives

competitive goal structure

a goal structure in which members hinder one another's efforts to obtain a goal

Supportiveness versus Defensiveness

defensive behavior

behavior that occurs when one perceives a threat

When was the last time you behaved defensively in a group? What precipitated such a response from you? How did your response affect others?

For an example of a defensive/supportive communication, view clip 1 on the CD

Defensive behavior can be said to occur when a group member perceives or anticipates a threat. When you feel yourself becoming defensive, you may experience one or more of the following symptoms: a change in voice tone (as you become nervous, your throat and vocal mechanism grow tense and your vocal pitch tends to rise), a tightening of your muscles and some degree of rigidity throughout your body, and a rush of adrenaline accompanied by an urge to fight or flee. Now let us examine the behaviors that can precipitate such reactions.

In general, we tend to become defensive when we perceive others as attacking our self-concept. In fact, when we behave defensively, we devote a great amount of energy to defending the self. We become preoccupied with thinking about how the self appears to others, and we become obsessed with discovering ways to make others see us more favorably. When a member of a group becomes overly concerned with self-protection, he or she may compensate either by withdrawing or by attacking the other members. When this happens, the conditions necessary for the maintenance of the group begin to deteriorate. In short, defensive behavior on the part of one group member gives rise to defensive listening in others. The postural, facial, and vocal cues that accompany words can also raise the defense level. Once the defensiveness of a group member has been aroused, that person no longer feels free to concentrate on the actual meaning of messages others are trying to send. Instead, the defensive member feels compelled to distort messages. Thus, as group members become more and more defensive, they become less and less able to process each other's emotions, values, and intentions accurately. For this reason, the consequences of defensiveness include destroyed or badly damaged individual relationships, continuing conflicts and increased personal anxiety within the group, wounded egos, and hurt feelings.

Before we can work to eliminate or even reduce defensiveness in our group relationships, we must understand the stimuli that can cause us to become defensive in the first place. Sociological researcher Jack R. Gibb identified six behaviors that cause defensiveness and six contrasting behaviors that allay or reduce the perceived level of threat (see Table 12.2).[33]

Gibb's first pair of contrasting behaviors is evaluation versus description. Group relationships can run into trouble if a member makes judgmental or evaluative statements. As Gibb notes in the article "Defensive Communication," "If by expression, manner of speech, tone of voice, or verbal content

TABLE 12.2 *Behaviors Characteristic of Defensive and Supportive Climates*

Defensive Climate	Supportive Climate
1. Evaluation	1. Description
2. Control	2. Problem orientation
3. Strategy	3. Spontaneity
4. Neutrality	4. Empathy
5. Superiority	5. Equality
6. Certainty	6. Provisionalism

the sender seems to be evaluating or judging the listener, then the receiver goes on guard."[34] Far too often, we offhandedly label the actions of others "stupid," "ridiculous," "absurd," "wonderful," or "extraordinary" because we simply are predisposed to use judgmental terms. Although it is true that some people do not mind having their actions praised, it is also true that most of us do mind having our actions condemned; moreover, whether judgment is positive or negative, the anticipation of judgment can hinder the creation of an open communication climate. In contrast to evaluative statements, descriptive statements recount particular observable actions without labeling those behaviors as good or bad, right or wrong. When you are descriptive, you do not advise changes in behavior. Instead, you simply report or question what you saw, heard, or felt.

Gibb's second pair is control versus problem orientation. Communication that group members see as seeking to control them can arouse defensiveness. In other words, if your intent is to control other group members, to get them to do something or change their beliefs, you are likely to evoke resistance. How much resistance you meet will depend partly on how openly you approach these people and on whether your behavior causes them to question or doubt your motives. When we conclude that someone is trying to control us, we also tend to conclude that he or she considers us ignorant or unable to make our own decisions. A problem orientation, however, promotes the opposite response. When senders communicate that they have not already formulated solutions and will not attempt to force their opinions on us, we feel free to cooperate in solving the problems at hand.

Gibb's third pair is strategy versus spontaneity. Our defensiveness will increase if we feel that another group member is using a strategy or is trying to put something over on us. No one likes to be conned, and no one likes to be the victim of a hidden plan. We are suspicious of strategies that are concealed or tricky. We do not want others to make decisions for us and then try to persuade us that we made the decisions ourselves. Thus, when we perceive ourselves as being manipulated, we become defensive and self-protective. In contrast, spontaneous behavior that is honest and free of deception reduces defensiveness. Under such conditions, the receiver does not feel a need to question the motivations of the sender, and trust is engendered.

Gibb's fourth pair is neutrality versus empathy. Neutrality is another behavior that can increase defensiveness in group members. For the most part, we need to feel that others empathize with us, that we are liked and are seen as worthwhile and valued. We need to feel that others care about us and will take the time to establish a meaningful relationship with us. If, instead of communicating empathy, warmth, and concern, a group member communicates neutrality or indifference, we may well see this as worse than rejection. We feel that he or she is not interested in us; we may even conclude that he or she perceives us as a nonperson.

Gibb's fifth pair is superiority versus equality. Our defensiveness will be aroused if another group member communicates feelings of superiority about social position, power, wealth, intelligence, appearance, or other characteristics. When we receive such a message, we tend to react by attempting to compete with the sender, by feeling frustrated or jealous, or by disregarding or forgetting the sender's message altogether. On the other hand, a sender who communicates equality can decrease our defensive behavior. We perceive him or her as willing to develop a shared problem-solving relationship with us, as willing to trust us, and as feeling that any differences between us are un-important.

Gibb's sixth pair is certainty versus provisionalism. The expression of absolute certainty or dogmatism on the part of a group member will probably succeed in making us defensive. We are suspicious of those who believe they have all the answers, view themselves as our guides rather than as our fellow travelers, and reject all information that we attempt to offer. In contrast, an attitude of provisionalism or open-mindedness encourages the development of trust. People who communicate a spirit of provisionalism—instead of attempting to win arguments, to be right, and to defend their ideas to the bitter end—are perceived as flexible and open rather than rigid and closed.

Gibb described behaviors associated with defensive and supportive climates; Linda Heun and Richard Heun, in *Developing Skills for Human Interaction,* and Anita Taylor, in *Communicating,* identified nonverbal cues that usually accompany such behaviors. Table 12.3 is adapted from their work. Take some time to examine the ways you feel you elicit defensiveness or support in the groups to which you belong.

TECHNOLOGY AND GROUPS: THE INTERNET AS ARENA FOR GROUP INTERACTION

Groups no longer have to meet in real space. They now also regularly meet in cyberspace. The Internet has made it possible for people to participate actively in an array of electronic groups. For example, "The Court of Last Resort" is a Web site to which individuals may submit their personal grievances

Groups at the Speed of Light

According to Don Tapscott, author of *Growing Up Digital,* today if you question some aspect of government policy, business practice, or anything else, you can instantly find others online who share your concerns. You can present your views, listen to others, and organize to take action. You have a powerful global medium as a tool. And it operates at the speed of light.[35]

With this in mind, identify groups who are using the Internet to expose unethical or socially dangerous practices. Then discuss whether or not you have used the Internet to solve problems of concern to you. If you have, what steps did you take to identify groups who shared your views?

How do group members compensate for the limitations imposed by written communication? To what extent is communicating in online groups more or less satisfying than communicating in real-space groups?

In what ways, if any, do you believe that the spontaneous and unedited conversations of cyberspace group members mirror real-space conversations? Does the written medium permit the personality of each member to come through the cycle of statement and response that constitutes group interactions?

Does a lack of direct knowledge of who a group member really is affect the productivity or safety of the group? Why or why not?

TABLE 12.3 *Nonverbal Cues Can Help Establish a Defensive or a Supportive Climate*

Defensive Nonverbal Cues	Supportive Nonverbal Cues
1. **Evaluation** Prolonged eye contact Pointing gestures Hands on hips Shaking the head Shaking the index finger	1. **Description** Comfortable eye contact Forward lean
2. **Control** Sitting in a focal position Hands on hips Shaking the head Prolonged eye contact Entering the other person's personal space	2. **Problem orientation** Maintaining comfortable personal distance Legs crossed in the direction of the other person Forward lean Comfortable eye contact
3. **Strategy** Prolonged eye contact Shaking the head Exhibiting forced gestures	3. **Spontaneity** Comfortable eye contact Legs crossed in the direction of the other person Animated, natural gestures Forward lean
4. **Neutrality** Legs crossed away from the other person A monotone voice Staring elsewhere Leaning back Establishing a greater body distance (4 1/2 to 5 feet)	4. **Empathy** Legs crossed in the direction of the other person Comfortable eye contact Establishing close personal distance (20 to 36 inches) Head nodding Forward lean
5. **Superiority** Extended eye contact Hands on hips Maintaining a higher elevation than the other person Entering the other person's personal space	5. **Equality** Comfortable eye contact Forward lean Maintaining oneself at the same elevation as the other person Comfortable personal distance
6. **Certainty** Extended eye contact Arms crossed Hands on hips Dogmatic voice tone	6. **Provisionalism** Comfortable eye contact Head nodding Head tilted to one side

Sources: Adapted from Linda Heun and Richard Heun. *Developing Skills for Human Interaction,* 2nd ed. Columbus, OH: Merrill, 1978; and Anita Taylor, Teresa Rosengrant. Arthur Meyer, and Thomas B. Samples, *Communicating.* Englewood Cliffs, NJ: Prentice-Hall, 1977.

against others. Then other persons who visit the Web site have the opportunity to read the registered complaints, discuss them with each other, and vote on the verdict. They function much as a jury. Internet users can also become members of various mainstream or alternative discussion and self-help groups. There are online groups for people who suffer drastic mood swings, victims of child abuse, persons with weight-control problems, political activists, parents and teachers, sports enthusiasts, and so on.

Online groups experience many of the same problems that groups experience in general. For instance, when using "Internet Relay Chat," which is like a huge group partyline, far too many people may talk (type their messages) at one time. In other words, the natural turn taking that occurs in many groups becomes a challenge.

Research reveals that computer-mediated communicators perceive the tone of their group meetings to be social:

> Members of electronic virtual communities act as if the community met in a physical public space. The number of times that on-line conferencees refer to the conference as an architectural place and to the mode of interaction in that place as being social is overwhelmingly high in proportion to those who do not. They say things like, "This is a great place to get together" or "This is a convenient place to meet."[36]

Cyberspace group members perform roles much as real-space group members do. Included among the roles performed by online group members are hackers, phreakers, moderators, and Net police. The specific rules adhered to by a group become part of the group's netiquette, or standards of conduct. Since there is an absence of physical proximity and traditional nonverbal cues, members may tend to be less inhibited in expressing themselves. However, if members consistently violate the standards and practices of the group, they can be reproached for their improprieties and may even be deprived of their access to the group. Group members may be reproached for violating ethical standards (revealing personal information about another group member without his or her permission); using inappropriate language (using language that is demeaning, insulting, or sexist); and wasting bandwidth (failing to edit a message judiciously).[37]

Unlike groups that meet in real space, groups that meet in cyberspace tend to undergo a process of continuous membership evolution. Thus, they are not as able to sustain and maintain themselves with the same group membership over a period of time. Despite the increasing prevalence of online group interaction, research reveals that computer-mediated communication leads to decreased group effectiveness, efficiency, and member satisfaction.[38] Nonetheless, the online setting is a unique laboratory we can use to study emergent forms of group life.

HOW TO IMPROVE COMMUNICATION AMONG GROUP MEMBERS

There are four things you can do to help ensure that the members of your group communicate and function effectively.

Encourage an Open, Supportive Environment

Group members must feel free to contribute ideas and feelings. They must also believe that their ideas and feelings will be listened to. Unless members feel free to exchange information and feelings, they are unlikely to achieve their objectives. It is only through the transmission and accurate reception of task- and maintenance-related content that groups progress toward their goals. Thus, experienced group members realize how essential it is to elicit contributions from all members and to encourage communication among all members.

Establish a Cooperative Climate

A competitive goal structure can impede effective group interaction. Members of a cooperative group deal honestly with each other, while members of a competitive group sometimes begin to dissemble and deliberately mislead each other. To guard against destructive competition and foster a cooperative orientation, members need to work to demonstrate mutual trust and respect. Thus, participative planning is essential. The key is coordination, not manipulation.

Be Ready to Perform Needed Leadership and Membership Roles

Members can help the group accomplish its tasks if they contribute to rather than detract from effective group functioning. To the extent that (1) task roles

Thinking
CRITICALLY

Reflect and Respond

On the basis of your knowledge of effective groups as well as your own experience working in groups, agree or disagree with the thoughts contained in the following excerpt from William Golding's *Lord of the Flies*. Supply reasons and examples from both research and your own life to support your position.

"What are we? Humans? Or animals? Or savages? What's grownups going to think? Going off—hunting pigs—letting fires out—and now!"

A shadow fronted him tempestuously.

"You shut up, you fat slug!"

There was a moment's struggle and the glimmering conch jigged up and down. Ralph leapt to his feet.

"Jack! Jack! You haven't got the conch! Let him speak."

Jack's face swam near him.

"And you shut up! Who are you, anyway? Sitting there telling people what to do. You can't hunt, you can't sing."

"I'm chief. I was chosen."

"Why should choosing make any difference? Just giving orders that don't make any sense—"

"Piggy's got the conch."

"That's right—favor Piggy as you always do—"

"Jack!"

Jack's voice sounded in bitter mimicry.

"Jack! Jack!"

"The rules!" shouted Ralph. "You're breaking the rules!"

"Who cares?"

Ralph summoned his wits.

"Because the rules are the only thing we've got!"[39]

are present and accounted for, (2) maintenance roles are effectively carried out, and (3) negative, individual, or self-centered roles are deemphasized, members' satisfaction with the group experience will increase and the group will prosper.

Encourage Continual Improvement

Focus on Service Learning
Use your understanding of networks, membership, and leadership to organize a social action group on campus.

Since there is no such thing as being too effective at communicating with others in a group setting, we should continually make every effort to improve our communication ability. Become a communication-process observer within your group. Pay careful attention to how your behavior affects others and how theirs affects you. Only in this way can you develop the insights needed to facilitate more effective group interaction.

Revisiting Chapter Objectives

1. **Explain how networks affect group interaction.** A group's ability to complete a task depends on how its members interact. The five most common kinds of communication networks in groups are the chain (or line), star (or wheel), circle, Y, and all-channel networks. The all-channel network is usually the most effective and satisfying, since each group member communicates directly with all the others and no one occupies a peripheral position.

2. **Define *group role* and distinguish among task, maintenance, and self-serving roles.** Every group member performs specific group roles. We contribute to the group's objective when we assume a task-oriented role (behaving in a way that promotes the accomplishment of the task) or a maintenance-oriented role (helping maintain the relationships among group members). However, we can undercut the group's effectiveness by playing a self-serving role—seeking to satisfy only our own needs or goals.

3. **Define *leadership* and distinguish among various leadership styles: type X, type Y, autocratic, laissez-faire, and democratic.** To achieve their objectives, groups need effective leadership. Leadership is simply the ability to influence others, and there are many leadership styles. A type X leader believes group members need to be closely controlled and coerced to work. A type Y leader believes members are self-directed and seek responsibility as well as opportunities for personal achievement. The autocratic leader dominates and directs all the other members of the group, whereas the laissez-faire leader lets them do their own thing. In most situations, the democratic leader, who encourages all the members to be involved constructively in decision making and problem solving, is preferred.

4. **Describe how trait theory, situation theory, and functional theory and transformational leadership contribute to our understanding of leadership.** There are four principal explanations of how people become leaders. Trait theory holds that some men and women are simply born to lead; situational theory holds that the situation itself—the nature of the problem and the characteristics of the group—determines who assumes leadership;

functional theory holds that a number of group members can and should share the various leadership functions that need to be performed if the group is to achieve its goals. A transformation leader helps group members imagine and visualize a future, strengthening the group's culture. Some research suggests that women tend to share power and information, while men tend to keep power and information for themselves.

5. **Explain how cooperation versus competition and a defensive versus a supportive climate manifest themselves in group interactions and affect group climate.** In addition to effective leadership, a group needs cooperation rather than pure competition among its members and a supportive rather than a defensive group climate to be able to work toward achieving its objectives. In effect, whether it operates in real space or cyberspace, a group creates its own culture in which to function.

Resources for Further Inquiry and Reflection

To apply your understanding of how the principles in Chapter 12 are at work in our daily lives, consult the following resources for further inquiry and reflection. Or, if you prefer, choose any other appropriate resource. Then connect the ideas expressed in your chosen selection with the communication concepts and issues you are learning about both in and out of class.

 Listen to Me

"Abraham, Martin, and John" (Dion)
"Only the Good Die Young" (Billy Joel)
"Hero" (Mariah Carey)

Each of these songs explores the nature of a hero or a leader. What concepts about leadership are illustrated in any one of these songs?

 View Me

Mutiny on the Bounty   *Flight of the Phoenix*
Lifeboat   *Chicken Run*

These films focus on a group in crisis. In the process of watching the group work through the crisis, we also learn about leadership and membership. Choose one of the films and discuss how the group sought to resolve its crises and the roles group members performed that facilitated or impeded the group's functioning.

 Read Me

Norman Augustine and Kenneth Adelman. *Shakespeare in Charge*. New York: Hyperion, 1999.
Wes Roberts. *The Leadership Secrets of Attila the Hun*. New York: Warner Books, 1991.
Tom Wolfe. *The Right Stuff*. New York: Bantam Books, 1983.
Oren Harari. *The Leadership Secrets of Colin Powell*. New York: McGraw-Hill, 2001.

These books explore the nature of leadership. Choose one and discuss those leadership lessons contained in it which you consider the most important.

 Tell Me

Share with the class the insights you gained from your chosen Listen to Me, View Me, or Read Me selection.

Agree or disagree, with reasons, to the following statement: Leadership is a popularity contest.

Key Chapter Terminology

Communication **Works**

www.mhhe.com/gamble8

Use the Communication Works CD-ROM and the Online Learning Center at www.mhhe.com/gamble8 to further your knowledge of the following terminology.

achieved leader 372

autocratic, or authoritarian, leaders 374

bridges 367

clique 367

competitive goal structure 381

cooperative goal structure 381

defensive behavior 382

democratic leaders 375

designated leader 372

functional theory 377

group role-classification model 368

isolates 368

laissez-faire leader 375

leadership 371

liaisons 367

maintenance roles 369

self-serving roles 370

situational theory 376

task roles 369

trait theory 375

transformational leader 378

type X leader 373

type Y leader 373

Test Your Understanding

Communication **Works**

www.mhhe.com/gamble8

Go to the *Self Quizzes* on the Communication Works CD-ROM and the book's Online Learning Center at www.mhhe.com/gamble8.

Notes

1. See A. Bavelas. "Communication Patterns in Task-Oriented Groups." *Journal of the Acoustical Society of America* 22, 1950, pp. 725–730; and H. J. Leavitt. "Some Effects of Certain Communication Patterns on Group Performance." *Journal of Abnormal and Social Psychology* 46, 1951, pp. 38–50.

2. D. Brass. "Being in the Right Place: A Structural Analysis of Individual Influence in an Organization." *Administrative Science Quarterly* 29, 1984, pp. 518–539.

3. Kenneth Benne and Paul Sheats. "Functional Roles of Group Members." *Journal of Social Issues* 4, 1948, pp. 41–49.

4. For a creative idea on how to use film to better understand leadership, see Roy V. Leeper. "Mutiny on the Bounty: A Case Study for Leadership Courses." Paper presented at the joint meeting of the Southern States Communication Association, Lexington, KY, April 14–18, 1993.

5. For a summary and critique of 114 studies on small groups, focusing on leadership, discussion, and pedagogy, see John F. Cragan and David W. Wright. "Small Group Communication Research of the 1970s: A Synthesis and Critique." *Central States Speech Journal* 31, 1980, pp. 197–213; and Michael S. Frank, "The Essence of Leadership." *Public Personnel Management* 22:3, fall 1993, pp. 381–389.

6. For a discussion of how to develop leadership skills, see Stephen S. Kaagan. *Leadership Games.* Thousand Oaks, CA: Sage, 1999.

7. Norman Augustine and Kenneth Adelman. *Shakespeare in Charge.* New York: Hyperion Books, 1999.

8. Douglas McGregor. *The Human Side of Enterprise.* New York: McGraw-Hill, 1960.

9. For a classic study on leadership style, see K. Lewin, R. Lippit, and R.K. White. "Patterns of Aggressive Behavior in Experimentally Created Social Climates." *Journal of Social Psychology* 10, 1939, pp. 271–299.

10. For an early study on trait theory, see Frederick Thrasher. *The Gang: A Study of 1313 Gangs in Chicago.* Chicago: University of Chicago Press, 1927.

11. For more information on this topic, see Nancy A. Nichols. "Whatever Happened to Rosie the Riveter?" *Harvard Business Review* 7:4, July–August 1993, pp. 54–57, 60, 62.

12. Marvin Shaw. *Group Dynamics: The Psychology of Small Group Behavior,* 3rd ed. New York: McGraw-Hill, 1981.

13. See Fred Fielder. *A Theory of Leadership Effectiveness.* New York: McGraw-Hill, 1967.

14. Keith Davis. *Human Relations at Work.* New York: McGraw-Hill, 1967.

15. See, for example, F. E. Fiedler. "Personality and Situational Determinants of Leadership Effectiveness." In D. Carwright and A. Zander, eds. *Group Dynamics: Research and Theory,* 3rd ed. New York: Harper & Row, 1968, pp. 389–398.

16. P. Hersey and K. Blanchard. *Management Organizational Behavior: Utilizing Human Resources.* Englewood Cliffs, NJ: Prentice Hall, 1988.

17. See Stephen R. Covey. *The 7 Habits of Highly Effective People.* New York: Simon & Schuster, 1989.

18. See, for example, M. Z. Hackman and C. E. Johnson, *Leadership: A Communication Perspective,* 3rd ed., Prospect Heights, Illinois: Waveland Press, 2000.

19. J. K. Brilhart, G. J. Galanes, and K. Adams. *Effective Group Communication Theory and Practice,* 10th ed. New York: McGraw-Hill, 2001, p. 124.

20. Anthony De Palma. "It Takes More Than a Visa to Do Business in Mexico." *New York Times,* June 26, 1994.

21. Lea P. Stewart. "Japanese and American Management: Participative Decision Making." In Larry A. Samovar and Richard E. Porter. *Intercultural Communication: A Reader.* Belmont, CA: Wadsworth, 1985, pp. 186–189.

22. Dolores Cathcart and Robert Cathcart. "Japanese Social Experience and Concept of Groups." In Larry A. Samovar and Richard E. Porter. *Intercultural Communication: A Reader,* 7th ed. Belmont, CA: Wadsworth, 1994, pp. 293–304.

23. Maire Brennan. "Mismanagement and Quality Circles: How Middle Managers Influence Direct Participation." *Employee Relations* 13, 1991, pp. 22–32.

24. T. Pettigrew and J. Martin. "Shaping the Organizational Context for Black American Inclusion." *Journal of Social Issues* 43, 1987, pp. 41–78.

25. John E. Baird. "Sex Differences in Group Communication: A Review of Relevant Research." *Quarterly Journal of Speech* 62, 1986, pp. 179–192.

26. Julia T. Wood. *Gendered Lives.* Belmont, CA: Wadsworth, 1994, p. 277.

27. P. W. Lunneborg. *Women Changing Work.* Westport, CT: Glenwood Press, 1990.

28. J. Rosener. "Ways Women Lead." *Harvard Business Review,* November–December 1990, pp. 119–125.

29. D. Butler and F. L. Geis. "Nonverbal Affect Responses to Male and Female Leaders: Implications for Leadership Evaluations." *Journal of Personality and Social Psychology* 58, 1990, pp. 48–59.

30. For a discussion of supportive leadership, see Peter G. Northouse. *Leadership: Theory and Practice,* 2nd ed. Thousand Oaks, CA: Sage, 2001.

31. Linden L. Nelson and Spencer Kagen. "Competition: The Star-Spangled Scramble." *Psychology Today,* September 1972, pp. 53–56, 90–91.

32. Morton Deutsch. "A Theory of Cooperation and Competition." *Human Relations* 2, 1949, pp. 129–152.

33. Jack R. Gibb. "Defensive Communication." *Journal of Communication* 2, 1961, pp. 141–148.

34. Gibb.

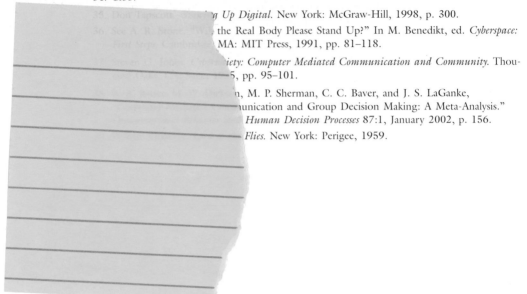

35. Don Tapscott, *...ng Up Digital.* New York: McGraw-Hill, 1998, p. 300.

36. See A. R. Stone, "...the Real Body Please Stand Up?" In M. Benedikt, ed. *Cyberspace: First Steps.* Cambridge, MA: MIT Press, 1991, pp. 81–118.

...Steven G. Jones, *...iety: Computer Mediated Communication and Community.* Thou-...5, pp. 95–101.

...n, M. P. Sherman, C. C. Baver, and J. S. LaGanke, ...unication and Group Decision Making: A Meta-Analysis." ...*Human Decision Processes* 87:1, January 2002, p. 156.

...*Flies.* New York: Perigee, 1959.

Handling Group Conflict: How to Disagree without Becoming Disagreeable

After finishing this chapter, you should be able to

1. Define *conflict* and explain how you feel when involved in a group conflict.

2. Define *groupthink* and explain its consequences.

3. Distinguish between competitive and cooperative conflict orientations.

4. Identify how to use the conflict grid and the benefits and problems that can result from effective and ineffective handling of group conflict.

5. Identify behaviors that can be used to resolve conflicts effectively.

Man is the only animal that can remain on friendly terms with the victims he intends to eat until he eats them.

—**Samuel Butler**

You can't eat your friends and have them too.

—**Budd Schulberg**

Go to the *Online Learning Center* at www.mhhe.com/gamble8 and answer the questions in the *Self Inventory* to evaluate your understanding of conflict.

On January 28, 2003, just a few days before the space shuttle *Columbia* broke apart (*Columbia* disintegrated during reentry and fell to earth on February 1, 2003), a NASA safety engineer warned of "a world of hurt," including the possibility of "catastrophic" consequences if foam insulation that broke off from the shuttle and struck it during its lift-off caused damage that allowed the heat of reentry to penetrate the shuttle's wheel well and burst the shuttle's tires. Other NASA officials and engineers, disagreeing with this "worst case scenario" came to conflicting conclusions, deciding that the foam which fell off was not a risk, and as a result, no one acted upon the engineer's warning. The engineer's warning never even made it up the chain of command. The rest, unfortunately, is history.[1]

Ignoring a conflict, or diminishing its importance, can be dangerous. The culture of effective decision making reveals that conflict is an inevitable part of the life of any group and sooner or later touches all group members. It is how group members handle conflict that makes a difference. The handling of conflict is one of the variables contributing to a group's success or failure.

A conflict can be started by anyone and can occur at any point in a group's existence. Opposed, or contradictory, forces within us can create inner conflicts, or we can find ourselves experiencing tension as

An unresolved labor conflict can lead to a strike.

external forces build and create interpersonal conflicts. Thus, a conflict can originate within a single group member or between two or more group members. It exists whenever persons who are interdependent have seemingly incompatible views, interests, or goals.

A **group conflict** also exists whenever a member's thoughts or acts limit, prevent, or interfere with his or her own thoughts or acts or with those of any other member. If you think about your recent group experiences, you will probably discover that you have been involved in conflicts. Some involved only you; some involved you and another. Probably, some were mild and subtle; others were intense and hostile. In any case, probably all of them were interesting.

Our goal in this chapter is to explore what conflict is, how it arises, how it affects us as group members, and how we can handle it productively. In doing so, we will develop skills to help us deal more effectively with group problem solving and decision making.

group conflict
conflict that occurs when a group member's thoughts or acts limit, prevent, or interfere with his or her own or another group member's thoughts or acts

Former Supreme Court Justice Arthur Goldberg is credited with saying, "If Columbus had an advisory committee he would probably still be at the dock." How has conflict among group members impeded the decision making and action taking of a group you have been in?

WHAT DOES GROUP CONFLICT MEAN TO YOU?

The word *conflict* means different things to different people. What does it mean to you? The following test will help you find out.

1. State your personal definition of *conflict* and indicate how you feel when involved in a conflict.
2. Next, use the scale in Table 13.1 to measure the extent to which you consider conflict in a small group positive or negative. For each item, circle the number that best reflects your attitude.
   a. Add your circled numbers together. If your score is 10 to 14, you believe that conflict is definitely positive. If your score is 15 to 20, you believe that conflict can be helpful. If your score is 21 to 30, you do not like to think about conflict; you have very ambivalent feelings. If your score is 31 to 40, you believe that

What high school groups did you belong to? Were you and your group(s) part of the "in-group?" In your opinion, might the presence of in- and out-groups in high school contribute to the kind of atmosphere that provides the context for school violence, such as the massacre that occurred at Columbine High School?

TABLE 13.1 *Conflict: Positive or Negative?*

Good	1	2	3	4	5	Bad
Rewarding	1	2	3	4	5	Threatening
Normal	1	2	3	4	5	Abnormal
Constructive	1	2	3	4	5	Destructive
Necessary	1	2	3	4	5	Unnecessary
Challenging	1	2	3	4	5	Overwhelming
Desirable	1	2	3	4	5	Undesirable
Inevitable	1	2	3	4	5	Avoidable
Healthy	1	2	3	4	5	Unhealthy
Clean	1	2	3	4	5	Dirty

conflict is something to try to avoid. If your score is 41 to 50, you believe that conflict is definitely negative.

    b. Determine the average scores for men and for women in the class. How do they compare? If they differ, what do you believe causes the difference? How does your score compare with the average for your sex?

    c. Compute the average score for your class as a whole. How does your score compare with the class average?

3. Complete these sentences:

    a. The time I felt worst about dealing with conflict in a group was when . . . .

    b. The time I felt best about dealing with conflict in a group was when . . . .

    c. I think the most important outcome of group conflict is . . . .

    d. When I am in conflict with a group member I really care about, I . . . .

    e. When I am in conflict with a group member I am not close to, I . . . .

    f. When a group member attempts to avoid entering into a conflict with me, I . . . .

    g. My greatest difficulty in handling group conflict is . . . .

    h. My greatest strength in handling group conflict is . . . .

How would being in conflict with others affect your ability to function on the job?

The dictionary defines *conflict* as "disagreement . . . war, battle, and collision." These definitions suggest that conflict is a negative force that of necessity leads to undesirable consequences. To what extent does your score suggest that you support this premise? To what extent do you believe that conflict is undesirable and should be avoided at all times and at all costs? Do you feel that conflict is taboo? Why? Unfortunately, many of us have been led to believe that conflict is evil—one of the prime causes of divorce, disorder, and violence—and that to disagree, argue, or fight with another person will either dissolve whatever relationship exists or prevent any relationship from forming. Somehow, many of us grow up thinking that nice people do not fight, do not make waves. Some believe that, if they do not smile and act cheerful, people will not like them and they will not be accepted or valued as group members.[2]

AVOIDING CONFLICT: GROUPTHINK

A body of research suggests that "smart people working collectively can be dumber than the sum of their brains."[3] As we noted at the outset of this chapter, investigators are now questioning the quick analysis by Boeing engineers that NASA used to conclude early in space shuttle *Columbia*'s mission that falling foam did not endanger its safety. Some are now saying that the conclusion reached by the engineers reveals that the problem turns out to be the culture of decision making at NASA that is indicative of **groupthink.** This is not the first time NASA has been accused of exhibiting a predilection toward groupthink. The agency suffered from the same criticism in 1986 after the loss of space shuttle *Challenger* and its crew on January 28 of that year. The official inquiry into that disaster revealed that the direct cause was a malfunction of the O-ring seal on the solid-rocket booster that caused that

groupthink

a dysfunction in which some group members attempt to preserve group harmony by suppressing the voicing of dissenting opinion shuttle to explode 73 seconds after it was launched. It seems that concerns about the O-rings had circulated within the agency for quite a while prior to the accident but that nothing was done about them. Groupthink has also been targeted as a cause of numerous fiascos, including the sinking of the *Titanic* by an iceberg, the surprise attack on Pearl Harbor, the foiled Bay of Pigs invasion of Cuba, and the escalation of the Vietnam War.

What is groupthink? How does it come about? According to Irving Janis, author of *Victims of Groupthink,* it occurs when groups let the desire for consensus override careful analysis and reasoned decision making.[4] In effect, then, groupthink is an extreme way of avoiding conflict. While cohesiveness is normally a desirable group characteristic, when carried to an extreme, it can become dysfunctional or even destructive.

Are you a groupthinker? To find out, answer yes or no to each of the following questions and explain your answers.

1. Have you ever felt so secure about a group decision that you ignored all warning signs that the decision was wrong? Why?

2. Have you ever been party to a rationalization justifying a group decision? Why?

3. Have you ever defended a group decision by pointing to your group's inherent sense of morality?

4. Have you ever participated in feeding an "us versus them" feeling— that is, in depicting those opposed to you in simplistic, stereotyped ways?

5. Have you ever censored your own comments because you feared destroying the sense of unanimity in your group?

6. Have you ever applied direct pressure to dissenting members in an effort to get them to agree with the will of the group?

7. Have you ever served as a "mind guard"? That is, have you ever attempted to preserve your group's cohesiveness by preventing disturbing outside ideas or opinions from becoming known to other group members?

8. Have you ever assumed that the silence of other group members implied agreement?

In groups characterized by groupthink, members try to maintain harmony by forgoing critical decision making. Did you or anyone you know ever feel a need for self-censorship at a meeting because it seemed dangerous to challenge the leader or boss? Did you ever feel the need to twist facts to please a boss or leader or to agree with whatever he or she said? If so, how did this influence the course of the meeting? If not, why not?

Each time you answered yes to one of these questions, you indicated that you have contributed to an illusion of group unanimity. In effect, you let a tendency to agree interfere with your ability to think critically. In so doing, you

"We're looking toward the Pacific Rim, Greenfield. What the hell are you doing?"

Could groupthink be to blame for demise of the space shuttle Columbia? What do you think?

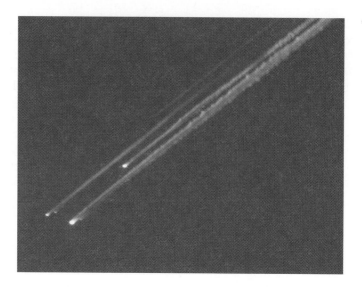

became a groupthinker. Groupthink impedes effective group functioning; when all group members try to think alike, no one thinks very much.

Groupthink is the triumph of concurrence over good sense. It is the primacy of authority over expertise. In order to prevent the flawed group dynamics that characterize decisions made when in a groupthink mode, group members would be well served to consider the merit of ideas rather than the titles of persons who express ideas. They should encourage critical evaluation, even assigning a devil's advocate, an individual who argues against a widely held position, to spur the airing of differences. Group members should also welcome critiques from persons both in and outside of the group. They should reward independent, critical thinking. The goal is to ensure that all the pros and cons of proposed solutions are considered, conflicting opinions are given a voice, and lingering doubts are aired.

Conflict as such is neither a positive nor a negative phenomenon. For this reason, we will not discuss how to avoid it. However, how you view conflict and how you handle it in any group to which you belong will determine the nature of the group's experience and your satisfaction with it. Conflict can be productive if you meet its challenge, but it can be counterproductive if you deal with it improperly. In other words, whether a group conflict is helpful or harmful, destructive or facilitative, depends on how constructively you cope with it.

GENDER AND CONFLICT: COMPARING APPROACHES

Women and men have been socialized to approach conflict situations differently. While most males have been socialized to be demanding and competitive, females have been taught to practice cooperativeness, compromise, and accommodation instead. While males tend to become verbally aggressive and adopt a fight mentality, women are more likely to engage in protracted negotiation in an attempt to avoid a fight.[5] Males are apt to give orders and assert themselves, while females are more prone to make proposals, give reasons for their positions, and attempt to resolve disagreements nonaggressively. When asked to describe how their style of handling conflict differed from that of men, women noted that men are overly concerned with power and content issues and underconcerned with relational issues. When compared with men, women place more emphasis on preserving their relationships during conflict; instead of focusing on content, they focus on feelings.[6]

Men, however, are more likely to withdraw from a conflict situation than are women. Researchers believe this may occur because men become substantially psychologically and physiologically aroused during conflict and may opt to withdraw from the conflict rather than risk further arousal.[7] Women, in contrast, prefer to talk about conflict in an effort to resolve it.[8] Women, when compared with men, are more likely to reveal their negative feelings and become emotional during conflict. Men, on the other hand, are more apt to keep their negative feelings to themselves and argue logically instead.[9]

Have you ever observed gender differences during conflict? Do you think you handle conflict more like the typical man or the typical woman? Why?

DIVERSITY AND CONFLICT: COMPARING VIEWS

Cultural values can influence attitudes toward conflict. In cultures that value individualism (such as the United States and Australia), the importance of the individual over the group is emphasized; conflict is viewed as a way of airing differences. As a result, conflict is usually not repressed but is handled openly and directly. In contrast, in cultures that value collectivism (such as Japan and Korea), the importance of group unity over individual desire is stressed; group conflict is perceived as a threat, and efforts are made to suppress it in public.[10]

The Japanese, for example, are apt to reveal false fronts, or *tatemae,* when interacting in meetings. This helps all participants save face. The importance of saving face is revealed in the following example. For years the automaker Mitsubishi hid complaints about defects in a file known to workers as "H," for the Japanese word for "secret" or "defer." The defects, including failing brakes, fuel leaks, malfunctioning clutches, and fuel tanks prone to falling off, were fixed on a case-by-case basis to avoid any humiliating recalls.[11]

In general, members of African-American and Asian-American cultures are also more collective than are members of the European-American culture—especially male members.[12] In fact, for African Americans, success in mixed-race groups is more related to building and maintaining relationships than it is for European Americans.[13]

While individualistic cultures view conflict as a step along the problem-solving path, collectivistic cultures see it as dysfunctional, distressing, and dangerous. The Japanese proverb "The nail that sticks out shall be hammered down" contrasts sharply with "Do your own thing," a well-known motto of American society. Consequently, while individualists see the potential for conflict to yield positive results, collectivists instead visualize the time that experiencing conflict will require them to invest in face-saving work.[14] As a result, collectivists refuse to put their own personal interests before those of other group members, believing instead that the team's collective state of mind is what is crucial.

Win-Win

A new teacher—let's call her Mary—arrived at a Navaho reservation. Each day in her classroom, something like the following would occur. Mary would ask five of her young Navaho students to go to the chalkboard and complete a simple mathematics problem from their homework. All five students would go to the chalkboard, but not one of them would work the problem as requested. Instead, they would all stand, silent and motionless.

Mary, of course, wondered what was going on. She repeatedly asked herself if she might be calling on students who could not do the assigned problems. "No, it couldn't be that," she reasoned. Finally, Mary asked her students what the problem was. Their answer displayed an understanding not many people attain in a lifetime.

Evidently, the students realized that not everyone in the class would be able to complete the problems correctly. But they respected each other's uniqueness, and they understood, even at their young age, the dangers of a win-lose approach. In their opinion, no one would win if anyone was embarrassed or humiliated at the chalkboard, and so they refused to compete publicly with each other. Yes, the Navaho students wanted to learn—but not at the expense of their peers.

Where do you stand? Would typical American schoolchildren behave similarly? Why or why not? Should they behave like the Navahos?

RESOLVING CONFLICTS

Conflict must be managed effectively if a group is to benefit from it. Whether conflict facilitates or debilitates group functioning depends directly on the orientations members bring to the conflict situation and how they define it.

Cooperative versus Competitive Conflict: Win-Win or Win-Lose

A lion used to prowl about a field in which four oxen dwelled. Many a time he tried to attack them; but, whenever he came near, they turned their tails to one another, so that whichever way he approached them he was met by the horns of one of them. At last, however, they fell a-quarreling among themselves, and each went off to the pasture alone in a separate corner of the field. Then the lion attacked them one by one and soon made an end to all four.

How does this story from *Aesop's Fables* apply to our study of conflict? Unlike the oxen, you can learn to handle your conflicts constructively; you can learn to disagree without becoming disagreeable. To do this, you need to put conflict into a mutual, noncompetitive framework. Unfortunately, sometimes this is more easily said than done. In many conflict situations, we are too quick to view our own position as correct or true while condemning and misperceiving the other person's position. Also, besides causing us to be too hasty in defending our own position and condemning someone else's, conflict in and of itself can make us compete when we should cooperate. When a conflict first develops, one of the key variables affecting the outcome is whether the participants' attitudes are cooperative or competitive. Will one person achieve victory by destroying the positions of others? Will the participants argue to a draw? Or will they share the goal?

"Let Us Sit Down and Take Counsel"

Woodrow Wilson once said:

If you come at me with your fists doubled, I think I can promise you that mine will double as fast as yours; but if you come to me and say, "Let us sit down and take counsel together, and if we differ from one another, decide just what points are at issue," we will presently find that we are not so far apart after all, the points on which we differ are few, and the points on which we agree are many, and if we only have the patience and the candor and the desire to get together, we will get together.

Where do you stand? Are patience, candor, and desire all that is necessary for the resolution of conflicts? Would such an approach work between nations? Co-workers? Friends? Family members?

When it comes to family relations, some families actually hold meetings, with an agenda that ranges from appreciations to concerns to conflict negotiations, adopting techniques that work in business meetings held around conference tables or in board rooms and transferring them to the dining room table or living room. Sitting together, family members hash out everything from disputes about toys and where to go on vacation to schedules and to-do lists.[15] Would such a strategy work in your family? Why or why not?

Ethics &
COMMUNICATION

Conflict Corner: Can You See It My Way?

Choose a current issue that is significant and controversial (for example, abortion, the war on drugs, capital punishment, nuclear energy). You will be assigned to defend or oppose it. Defenders and opposers will have a chance to meet and prepare their cases. Each defender (A) will be paired with an opposer (B). Person A will have five minutes to present the defense's position to person B. Person B then will have five minutes to present the opposition's position to person A.

Players will then switch roles, so that B presents A's case and A presents B's case.

1. To what extent did reversing roles help you understand and appreciate another point of view?
2. How could such a procedure help a person change from a win-lose orientation to a win-win orientation?

Skill
BUILDER

In general, we can say that people enter a conflict situation with one of two orientations, or perspectives: competition or cooperation. People who have a **competitive set** perceive a conflict situation in all-or-nothing terms and believe that, to attain victory, they must defeat the other participants. They do not believe that their own interests and those of others are compatible. By contrast, people with a **cooperative set** believe that a way to share the rewards of the situation can be discovered.

If people bring a competitive orientation to a conflict, they will tend to be ego-involved and will see winning as a test of personal worth and competence. In contrast, if people bring a cooperative orientation to a conflict, they tend to look for a mutually beneficial way to resolve the disagreement.

For a conflict to be defined as cooperative, each participant must demonstrate a willingness to resolve it in a mutually satisfactory way. In other words, each person must avoid behaving in any way that would escalate the conflict. If the people involved in a conflict are treated with respect by all the others

competitive set
a readiness to perceive a conflict in all-or-nothing terms

cooperative set
a readiness to share rewards to resolve conflicts

Media WISE

On-Air Conflicts

Talk show programs such as those moderated by Jerry Springer, Rikki Lake, and Jenny Jones feature groups of individuals discussing conflict-arousing topics, such as "Girls and Gang Life," "Opposing Interracial Dating," "Out-of-Control Teenagers," "Pressured to Lose Her Virginity," "Sleeps with Her Mom's Boyfriend," "Dresses Like a Slut," and "Needs to Tell Her Boyfriend She's a Lesbian." "Talk culture," however, appears ill-suited to deal with the controversial and complicated subjects being discussed. Even more significantly, many of the guests, who for the most part are drawn from lower socioeconomic groups, appear to be poorly educated, lacking in self-esteem, and in dire need of social support.[16]

Divide into groups and choose a talk show to view. Identify the techniques the host and guests use to handle the conflict that results during the discussion of the conflict-producing situation. Was enough time allowed to present the problem in its full context? To what extent did guests become aggressive or abusive? What role did the host and audience members play in escalating or defusing the conflict? What positive outcomes, if any, resulted from the exchange of comments among the guests, the host, and audience members? What kinds of lessons did the show teach about effective or ineffective conflict-resolution techniques?

❙ *Conflict arousing topics are a staple of talk shows.*

With whom have you had to negotiate recently: friend, spouse, co-worker, boss? Over what: money, goods, services, information, rules, prestige? What was the outcome?

involved, if they are neither demeaned nor provoked, and if communication is free and open instead of underhanded and closed, the disagreement may be settled amicably.

If a conflict is defined as competitive, the participants become combatants: they believe that, to attain victory, they must defeat the other side. Unfortunately, competing with or defeating another person with whom we are interacting is characteristic of encounters in our society. Many phrases we use reflect this orientation: We speak of "outsmarting" others, of putting people "in their place," of getting ourselves "one up" and someone else "one down."

We can define a conflict as a win-lose situation, or we can define it as a win-win situation. If we define it as win-lose, we will tend to pursue our own goals, misrepresent our needs, attempt to avoid empathizing with or understanding the feelings of others, and use threats or promises to get others to go along with us. If we define a conflict as win-win, we will tend to view it as a common problem, try to pursue common goals, honestly reveal our needs to others, work to understand their position and frame of reference, and make every effort to reduce rather than increase defensiveness.

To transform a conflict from competitive to cooperative, you must use effective communication techniques.[17] You can discover workable strategies and practice them until you can use them for yourself. You should aim to become a conflict processor and develop the ability to view a conflict from the standpoint of other people.

Role reversal—that is, acting as if you were the person(s) with whom you are in conflict—can help people involved in a conflict understand each other, find creative ways to integrate their interests and concerns, and work toward a common goal. Reversing roles helps you avoid judging others by enabling you to see things from their perspective. Once you can replace a statement like "You're wrong" or "You're stupid" with one like "What you believe is not what I believe," you will be on your way to developing a cooperative orientation.

Interview a manager. Ask about the nature of a conflict he or she had to resolve and the strategies he or she used to handle it.

role reversal

a strategy in which persons in conflict act as each other in order to understand each other's position

GOALS AND STYLES: A CONFLICT GRID

A number of paradigms, or models, have been proposed to represent the ways we try to resolve conflicts. Among them is Robert Blake and Jane Mouton's **conflict grid** (see Figure 13.1).[18] This grid has two sides. The horizontal scale represents the extent to which a person wants to attain personal goals. The vertical scale represents the extent to which the person is concerned for others. The interface between the two scales indicates how strongly the person feels about these concerns—that is, how his or her concern is apportioned.

Both scales range from 1 (low) to 9 (high), representing increasing importance of personal goals ("concern for production of results") and of other people ("concern for people"). On the basis of this measure, Blake and Mouton identified five main conflict styles. As you consider their grid and the following descriptions of their five styles, try to identify your own conflict style.

A person with a 1/1 conflict style can be described as an **avoider;** the avoider's attitude can be summed up as "lose and walk away." If you have a 1/1 style, your goal is to maintain neutrality at all costs. You probably view conflict as a useless and punishing experience, one that you would prefer to do without. Rather than tolerate the frustrations that can accompany conflict, you physically or mentally remove yourself from the conflict situation.

A person with a 1/9 style is an **accommodator,** whose attitude is "give in and lose." If you are a 1/9, your behavior demonstrates that you overvalue the maintenance of relationships and undervalue the achievement of your own goals. Your main concern is to ensure that others accept you, like you, and coexist in

conflict grid

a model portraying the styles individuals use to resolve conflicts

avoider

a person who, when faced with a conflict, does his or her best to remove himself or herself from the conflict situation

accommodator

a person who, when faced with a conflict, overvalues the maintenance of relationships and undervalues the achievement of his or her own goals

FIGURE 13.1
*Blake and Mouton's
Conflict Grid.*

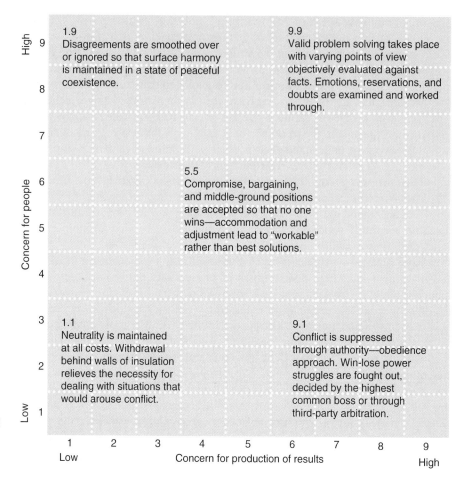

Source: Reprinted with permission
of NTL, "Conflict Grid" "The Fifth
Achievement" by Robert Blake and
Jane Srygley Mouton, *Journal of
Applied Behavioral Science* 6,
no. 4, © 1970 NTL Institute.

*Why would people who are
competitors (9/1) enjoy being
surrounded by "yes people"
(1/9)? What dangers can
such a mix pose?*

compromiser

a person who, when faced
with a conflict, tries to find a
middle ground

competitive forcer

a person who, when faced
with a conflict, adopts a win-
lose orientation in which the
attaining of personal goals is
paramount

peace with you. You are afraid to make others angry, and you will do anything
to avoid being perceived as a troublemaker. Although conflicts may exist in your
world, you refuse to deal with them. You feel a need to maintain the appearance of harmony at all costs. This discrepancy leads to an uneasy, tense state
characterized by a great deal of smiling and nervous laughter.

A person with a 5/5 style is a **compromiser,** whose attitude is "find a
middle ground." If you are a 5/5, your guiding principle is compromise.
Thus, you work to find a way to permit each participant in a conflict to gain
something. Compromise is, of course, a valid strategy in some cases. But it
can be a problem if you always settle for a workable solution because you are
afraid the conflict may escalate if you try to find the best solution. It is unde-
niable that "half a loaf is better than none," and this conflict style will leave
participants half satisfied, but it can also be said to leave them half dissatisfied. Thus, compromise is sometimes referred to as the lose-lose approach.

A person with a 9/1 style is a **competitive forcer,** who takes a win-lose
attitude. If you are a 9/1, attaining your personal goals is far more important to you than concern for other people. You have an overwhelming need
to win and dominate others; you will defend your position and battle with
others, whatever the cost or harm to them.

A person with a 9/9 style is a **problem-solving collaborator,** who takes a win-win attitude. If you are a 9/9, you actively seek to satisfy your own goals (you are result-oriented) as well as those of others (you are also person-oriented). This, of course, is the optimum style when you are seeking to reduce conflict. As a problem solver, you realize that conflicts are normal and can be helpful; you also realize that each person in a conflict holds legitimate opinions that deserve to be aired and considered. You are able to discuss differences without making personal attacks.

According to Alan Filley, effective conflict resolvers rely to a large extent on problem solving (9/9) and smoothing (1/9), whereas ineffective conflict resolvers rely extensively on forcing (9/1) and withdrawal (1/1).[19]

If we are to develop and sustain meaningful group relationships, we need to learn to handle conflicts constructively. A conflict has been productive if all the participants are satisfied with the outcomes and believe they have gained something.[20] In other words, no one loses; everyone wins. In contrast, a conflict has been destructive if all the participants are dissatisfied with the outcomes and believe that they have lost something. Perhaps one of the most important questions facing each of us is whether we can turn our conflicts into productive rather than destructive interactions.

We will be most likely to create constructive rather than destructive interactions if our conflicts are characterized by cooperative problem-solving methods, attempts to reach mutual understanding, accurate and complete communication, and a demonstrated willingness to trust each other. We will be most likely to fail if our conflicts become win-lose encounters characterized by misconceptions and misperceptions; inaccurate, sketchy, and disruptive communication; and a demonstrated hesitancy to trust each other. It is apparent that in a conflict situation the best approach to a constructive resolution is cooperation.

problem-solving collaborator

a person who, when faced with a conflict, adopts a win-win orientation, seeking to satisfy his or her own goals as well as those of others

Which conflict-resolving strategies do you use? Why?

GROUP CONFLICTS IN CYBERSPACE

Electronic discussion groups exist for virtually all academic subjects and topics of interest. On the Net, when persons are involved in newsgroups in which controversial issues surface and are discussed, the conflict that inevitably results among group members sometimes gets out of hand and escalates into an attack called a **flame war.**

Not all flame wars are fought over major issues. Some are fought over relatively minor ones, such as spelling, semantics, or grammar disagreements. Whatever their source, however, flames tend to be directed at specific persons, are usually argumentative or vituperative in tone, and frequently develop into disagreements that are unrelated to the original controversies that provoked them. Because flames are extremely personal, persons who are flamed may react reflexively by encoding insults that are even more offensive than the ones that initially elicited a disruptive response from them. Group members who are flamed perceive their reputations to be on the line and feel a need to defend them.[21]

Flame wars that get out of hand end up interfering with the discussion of persons who are not involved in them. Thus, if not extinguished quickly, flame wars can reduce the usefulness of the usenet or newsgroup discussion

flame war

a conflict that occurs in cyberspace

In what ways, if any, is online conflict different from face-to-face conflict?

Should Online Conflicts Be Moderated?

If someone flamed you online, how would you react? Would you flame the person back? Why or why not? Should flames be headed off at the pass? That is, should someone put them away before we see them, even if they are directed at us?

Sometimes, in an effort to decrease the amount of flaming that occurs online, cyberspace groups have moderaters. The person who acts as group moderator is sent all messages first, screens them, and decides which, if any, messages are inappropriate for distribution to other group members. Would you want to serve as a moderator? Why or why not? If you were the moderator of a group, what kinds of messages, if any, would you filter? Is moderating a form of censorship or just a means of keeping the contentiousness of some members under control? What other suggestions, if any, do you have for handling cyberspace conflicts?

itself. Sometimes group members decide to take their flame war to a conflict room—a place where they can participate in a flame war without disrupting the discussions of others in the group. Thus, when in the midst of a conflict, someone writes, "Let's take this discussion to 'alt. flame,'" that is what they are suggesting.[22]

Online conflicts also result because of spamming—the sending of repeated unsolicited e-mail or posting of the same message on numerous bulletin boards even though the message is inconsistent with the focus of the group. Spamming causes its recipients to consume valuable time and energy reading something they never wanted to receive. It also clogs systems and slows them down.

THE ETHICAL MANAGEMENT OF CONFLICT: SKILLS AND STRATEGIES

Conflict can be resolved productively by applying the principles of effective communication. When you use effective communication techniques, you reduce the likelihood that your comments will escalate a conflict by eliciting angry, defensive, or belligerent reactions. Learning to handle conflict successfully is an attainable goal that can lead to increased self-confidence, improved relationships, and a greater ability to handle stressful situations. All that is required is a commitment to practice and apply the necessary skills. Anyone who is willing can learn creative and effective ways of managing conflict— ways that will increase the likelihood of future harmony and cooperation.

Let us now examine the behaviors that can turn conflict situations into problem-solving situations. The following suggestions are a basic guide to conflict resolution.

Recognize That Conflicts Can Be Settled Rationally

A conflict stands a better chance of being settled rationally if you avoid certain unproductive behaviors, such as the following:

Pretending that the conflict simply does not exist
Withdrawing from discussing it

What does this photo suggest to you regarding the handling of conflict? Why is the President pointing at both participants?

Placating or surrendering to the people with whom you are in conflict

Trying to create distractions so that the conflict will not be dealt with

Overintellectualizing the conflict or rationalizing the conflict

Blaming or finding fault with the other people

Attempting to force the others to accept your way of seeing things

Recognizing unproductive behaviors is a first step in learning to handle conflicts more effectively. Being willing to express your feelings openly, directly, and constructively without resorting to irrational techniques that destroy trust and respect is a prerequisite for becoming a productive conflict manager. Thus, instead of insulting or attacking others or withdrawing from a conflict, be willing to describe whatever action, behavior, or situation you find upsetting. Do this without evaluating other people negatively or causing them to become defensive. Focus on issues, not personalities. Be willing to listen to and react to what the other person is saying.

Conflicts can be settled rationally if you act like a capable, competent problem solver and adopt a person-to-person orientation.

Define the Conflict

Once you have recognized that conflicts can be handled rationally, you are ready to ask, "Why are we in conflict? What is the nature of the conflict? Which of us feels more strongly about the issue? What can we do about it?" Here again, it is crucial to send "I" messages ("I think it is unfair for me to do all the work around here"; "I don't like going to the library for everyone else") and to avoid sending blame messages ("You do everything wrong"; "You are a spoiled brat"; "You'll make us fail"). Be very clear that you would like to join with the other group members in discovering a solution that will be acceptable and beneficial for all of you—a solution whereby none of you will lose and each will win.

Check Your Perceptions

A situation is a conflict when it is perceived as a conflict. In conflict-ripe situations, we often distort the behavior, position, or motivations of the other person involved. We prefer to see one set of motivations rather than another because it meets our own needs to interpret the situation that way. When we do this, we deny the legitimacy of any other position. Thus, it is not uncommon for each person in a conflict to believe, mistakenly, that the other person is committing underhanded and even vicious acts. It is not extraordinary for each person to make erroneous assumptions about the other's feelings, nor is it unusual for people to think they disagree with each other simply because they have been unable to communicate their agreement. For these reasons, it is important for each person to take some time to explain his or her assumptions and frame of reference to the others. It is also important for all the people involved to feel that their contributions are listened to and taken seriously.

After each of you has identified how you feel, it is time to determine whether you understand one another. This calls for active, empathic listening. Each of you should be able to paraphrase what the other has said in a way the other finds satisfactory. Doing this before you respond to the feelings expressed can help avert escalation of the conflict. Along with active listening, role reversal can help people in conflict understand one another. Like active listening, role reversal permits you to see things as others in the group see them. If you are willing to listen to and experience another person's point of view, that person will be more likely to listen to and experience yours.

Suggest Possible Solutions

The goal during the "possible solutions" phase is for group members to put their heads together and come up with a variety of solutions. Most important, neither you nor anyone else in the group should evaluate, condemn, or make fun of any of the suggestions. You must suspend judgment and honestly believe that the conflict can be resolved in a variety of ways.

Assess Alternative Solutions and Choose the One That Seems Best

After possible solutions have been generated, it is time to see which solution each person considers best. It is legitimate to try to determine which solutions will let one side win at the other's expense, which will make everyone lose, and which will let everyone win. Your objective is to discover which solutions are totally unacceptable to each side and which are mutually acceptable. (It is crucial to be honest during this stage.) Once all the solutions have been assessed, you are in a position to determine if one of the mutually acceptable solutions is clearly superior to all the others—that is, if it has the most advantages and the fewest disadvantages. Also, be sure to explore whether it is the most constructive solution.

Try Your Solution and Evaluate It

During the "tryout" stage, we see how well the chosen solution is working. We try to ascertain who is doing what, when, where, and under what

Reflect and Respond

On the basis of your understanding of the value of conflict and conflict management, agree or disagree with this excerpt from Deborah Tannen's *Talking from 9 to 5.* Supply reasons and examples from both research and your own life that support the stance you are taking.

When decisions are made by groups, not everyone has equal access to the

decision-making process. Those who will take a position and refuse to budge, regardless of the persuasive power or intensity of feeling among others, are far more likely to get their way. Those who feel strongly about a position but are inclined to back off in the face of intransigence or very strong feeling from others are much less likely to get their way.[23]

Thinking
CRITICALLY

conditions, and we ask how all this is affecting each person in the group. We want to know if the people involved were able to carry out the job as planned, whether the solution we adopted has solved the problem, and whether the outcome has been rewarding to everyone. If not, we know it is time to begin the conflict-resolution process again.

Focus on Service Learning
Work with your college or university's residence hall managers to see what topics related to group conflict they would like students living on campus to discuss.

Summary

Remember that conflict situations can be learning experiences. If handled properly, they can help you discover ways of improving your ability to relate to others. Thus, your goal should be not necessarily to have fewer conflicts but, rather, to make the conflicts you do have constructive. Instead of eliminating conflicts from your group relationships, you simply need to learn how to use them.

Revisiting Chapter Objectives

1. **Define *conflict* and explain how you feel when involved in a group conflict.**   Conflict is an inevitable part of the life of any group. A group experiences conflict whenever a member's thoughts or acts limit, prevent, or interfere with his or her own thoughts or acts or with those of another member.

2. **Define *groupthink* and explain its consequences.**   Conflict is not always a negative force. In fact, the absence or avoidance of conflict can result in groupthink, a problem that occurs when a group allows the desire for consensus to override careful analysis and reasoned decision making.

3. **Distinguish between competitive and cooperative conflict orientations.**   When a conflict is handled constructively, no one loses and everyone wins. A conflict can be destructive if all the participants are dissatisfied with its outcomes and believe they have lost something. Using cooperative problem-solving methods instead of creating win-lose encounters facilitates constructive conflict resolution.

4. **Identify how to use the conflict grid and the benefits and problems that can result from effective and ineffective handling of group conflict.**   Whether a conflict helps or hinders a group's operation depends on how the members react to it. If they resort to strategies such as blaming, withdrawing, intellectualizing, distracting, and forcing, their effectiveness will

THE Wrap-Up

be impaired. However, if they discuss the issues calmly, they can break impasses and solve difficulties. Various styles of handling conflict can be plotted on Blake and Mouton's conflict grid. The most effective style is that of the problem-solving collaborator, who takes a win-win approach and has high concern both for results and for the feelings of other people. It is essential to take into account the various cultures that people may reflect in their approaches to conflict and conflict resolution.

5. **Identify behaviors that can be used to resolve conflicts effectively.** A number of communication techniques can help us resolve conflicts that occur both online and offline. The first step is simply to recognize that conflicts can be settled rationally—by focusing on the issues, not on personalities. Next we should define the conflict and check the accuracy of our perceptions, using "I" messages, empathic listening, and role reversal, as appropriate. Then we should suggest and assess a variety of solutions to the conflict, choose the best one that is mutually acceptable, and try it.

Resources for Further Inquiry and Reflection

To apply your understanding of how the principles in Chapter 13 are at work in our daily lives, consult the following resources for further inquiry and reflection. Or, if you prefer, choose any other appropriate resource. Then connect the ideas expressed in your chosen selection with the communication concepts and issues you are learning about both in and out of class.

 Listen to Me

"Try to See It My Way" (The Beatles)
"The In Crowd" (Ramsey Lewis Trio)
"Leader of the Pack" (The Shangri-Las)
"Ohio" (Crosby, Stills, Nash, and Young)

How might the desire to be part of an in crowd or the leader of a pack influence one's sense of what is right or wrong?

 Read Me

William Golding. *Lord of the Flies.* New York: Penguin Books, 1999. (Original work published 1954.)
Irving Janis. *Victims of Groupthink: A Psychological Study of Foreign Policy Decisions and Fiascos.* Boston: Houghton Mifflin, 1972.

These books explore the role of the individual in a group, including the role the individual plays in precipitating or preventing bad group decisions. Choose one work and use it to discuss those aspects of group life as well as the role conflict plays in effective decision making.

 View Me

Apollo 13   *Lord of the Flies*
Titanic   *Almost Famous*

These films explore group forces that can impede and/or foster the handling of group conflict. Choose one film and use it to discuss both the dangers of groupthink and effective conflict management techniques.

 Tell Me

Share with the class the insights you gained from your chosen Listen to Me, View Me, or Read Me selection.

Agree or disagree with the following statement, with reasons: Truth springs from conflict.

Key Chapter Terminology

Use the Communication Works CD-ROM and the Online Learning Center at www.mhhe.com/gamble8 *to further your knowledge of the following terminology.*

Communication Works

online learning center

www.mhhe.com/gamble8

accommodator 403

avoider 403

competitive forcer 404

competitive set 401

compromiser 404

conflict grid 403

cooperative set 401

flame war 405

group conflict 395

groupthink 396

problem-solving collaborator 405

role reversal 403

Test Your Understanding

Go to the *Self Quizzes* on the Communication Works CD-ROM and the book's Online Learning Center at www.mhhe.com/gamble8.

Communication Works

online learning center

www.mhhe.com/gamble8

Notes

1. John Schwartz and John M. Broder. *New York Times,* February 13, 2003, pp. A1, A37.
2. For an interesting discussion of how conformity pressures can hamper decision making, see Russel F. Proctor. "Do the Ends Justify the Means? Thinking Critically about 'Twelve Angry Men.'" Paper presented at the annual meeting of the Central States Communication Association, Chicago, April 11–14, 1991.
3. John Schwartz and Matthew L. Wald. "NASA's Curse?" *New York Times,* March 9, 2003, p. WK5.
4. Irving Janis. *Victims of Groupthink: A Psychological Study of Foreign Policy Decisions and Fiascos.* Boston: Houghton Mifflin, 1972.
5. Deborah Tannen. *The Argument Culture; Moving from Debate to Dialogue.* New York: Random House, 1998, pp. 170, 194.
6. J. F. Benenson, S. A. Ford, and N. H. Apostoleris. "Girls' Assertiveness in the Presence of Boys." *Small Group Research* 29, 1998, pp. 198–211.
7. See, for example, Daniel Canary, William R. Cupach, and Susan J. Messman. *Relational Conflict.* Thousand Oaks, CA: Sage: 1995.
8. Marjaana Lindeman, Tuija Harakka, and Liisa Keltikangas-Jarvinen. "Age and Gender Differences in Adolescents' Reactions to Conflict Situations: Aggression, Prosociality, and Withdrawal." *Journal of Youth and Adolescence* 26, 1997, pp. 339–351.
9. Canary, Cupach, and Messman.
10. See Stella Ting-Toomey, C. Gab, P. Trubisky, Z. Z. Yang, H. S. Kim, S. L. Lin, and T. Nishida. "Culture, Face Maintenance, and Styles of Handling Interpersonal Conflict: A Study in Five Cultures." *International Journal of Conflict Management* 2, 1992, pp. 275–296.
11. Yuri Kageyama. "Mitsubishi Admits Coverup." *The Record,* August 23, 2000, pp. B-1, B-3.
12. See, for example, Anita K. Foeman and Gary Pressley. "Ethnic Culture and Corporate Culture: Using Black Styles in Organizations." *Communication Quarterly* 35, fall 1987, pp. 293–307.
13. Hal Lancaster. "Black Managers Often Must Emphasize Building Relationships." *Wall Street Journal,* March 4, 1997, p. B1.
14. P. Trubisky, S. Ting-Toomey, and S. L. Ling. "The Influence of Individualism-Collectivism and Self-Monitoring on Conflict Styles." *International Journal of Intercultural Relations* 15, 1991, pp. 65–84.
15. N. A. Jeffrey. "'Kids, Come to Order': Families Try Business-Style Meetings." *Wall Street Journal,* August 16, 2001, pp. W1, W4.

16. See, for example, Larry K. Leslie. *Mass Communication Ethics: Decision Making in Post-modern Culture.* Boston: Houghton Mifflin, 2000, pp. 263–266; Barbara Ehrenreich. "In Defense of Talk Shows." *Time,* December 4, 1995, p. 92; and Howard Kurtz. *Hot Air.* New York: Basic Books, 1997.

17. For a description of how to promote a win-win approach to conflict, see Deborah Weider-Hatfield. "A Unit in Conflict Management Communication Skills." *Communication Education* 30, 1981, pp. 265–273; and Joyce L. Hocker and William W. Wilmot. *Interpersonal Conflict,* 3rd ed. Dubuque, IA: Wm. C. Brown, 1991.

18. Robert Blake and Jane Mouton. "The Fifth Achievement." *Journal of Applied Behavioral Science* 6, 1970, pp. 413–426.

19. Alan Filley. *Interpersonal Conflict Resolution.* Glenview, IL: Scott, Foresman, 1975.

20. Morton Deutsch. "Conflicts: Productive and Destructive." *Journal of Social Issues* 25, 1969, pp. 7–43; H. Whitteman. "Group Member Satisfaction: A Conflict-Related Account." *Small Group Research* 22, 1992, pp. 24–58; and R. C. Pace. "Personalized and Depersonalized Conflict in Small Group Discussion: An Examination of Differentiation." *Small Group Research* 21, 1991, pp. 79–96.

21. Steven G. Jones. *Cybersociety: Computer-Mediated Communication and Community.* Thousand Oaks, CA: Sage, 1995, pp. 129–131; and Tannen, pp. 238–240.

22. Tannen, p. 130.

23. Deborah Tannen. *Talking from 9 to 5.* New York: Morrow, 1994.

Communicating to the Public

Part Four will introduce you to public presentations, discuss the breadth of public speaking opportunities, and explore factors you need to consider as you develop your skill as both speech maker and evaluator. The questions to consider as you read the six chapters are the following: How apprehensive are you about speaking in public? How do you limit a topic and adapt it to an audience? How competent are you at researching and supporting a topic? How do you respond to ideas with which you disagree? At what point does a speech and/or a speaker become unethical? What causes you to label a speaker a credible source? Can you be equally effective at informing and persuading others? What can you personally do to enhance your effectiveness as a presenter?

Consider how you can use the knowledge and experience you gain to improve your personal public presentation skills.

The Speaker and the Audience: The Occasion and the Subject

1. Identify the characteristics of effective public speakers.

2. Approach public speaking systematically—that is, select a topic, develop a topic, present a speech, and analyze its effectiveness.

3. Explain how the nature of the occasion influences a speech.

4. Formulate clear and precise purpose statements for yourself and behavioral objectives for your audience.

5. Formulate the thesis statement.

In the United States there are more than twenty thousand different ways of earning a living, and effective speech is essential to every one.

—**Andrew Weaver**

Public speaking can be a horror for the shy person, but it can also be the ultimate act of liberation.

—**Susan Faludi**

Violence is, essentially, a confession of ultimate inarticulateness.

—***Time* magazine**

Go to the *Online Learning Center* at www.mhhe.com/gamble8 and answer the questions in the *Self Inventory* to evaluate your understanding of public speaking.

public speaking

the act of preparing, staging, and delivering a presentation to an audience

Can you stand before an audience without fear? Can you discover content that personalizes a message, wins the ears of receivers, and draws them into your message? Can you organize a message so that you are able to stay on course without getting unnerved or derailed? Can you deliver a message so that audience members leave the experience richer for having listened to you? And can you have fun doing it? Even in our technologically rich environment with its e-mail, voice-mail, personal digital assistants, beamed messaging, and instant messaging, we still turn to public speaking as a key means of sharing ideas, expressing concerns, and making our voices heard.

In our age of electronic connections, public speaking is booming. Membership in the National Speakers Association, a professional speakers trade group, continues to grow. In addition, the number of platforms available for speakers has also increased. Everyone seems to want a speaker these days.[1] Perhaps, because now more than ever, everyone needs to be a speaker. In some ways, public speaking functions as a form of currency, only, instead of providing its users with access to the marketplace of goods and services, it provides access to the marketplace of ideas. Becoming effective at communicating ideas in a public forum is a skill that is equally important for women and men to develop. Public speaking is sure to play an important role in your future. Are you prepared for the challenge? (See video reference #5.)

Public speaking—these are two seemingly harmless words. **Public speaking** is the act of preparing, staging, and delivering a presentation to an audience. We speak every day. Under ordinary circumstances, we rarely give speaking, or our skills in speaking, a second thought—that is, until we're asked to deliver a speech or simply to speak in public. Once we know that is what we're going to have to do, if we're like most Americans, we fear it more than we fear bee stings, accidents, heights, or our own death.[2]

Just as we can learn to handle ourselves more effectively in our interpersonal and group relationships, if we take the time that is needed to analyze and practice successful behaviors, we can also learn to handle ourselves more effectively as public speakers. With practice, we can develop the understanding and master the skills that will make us articulate speakers who are organized, confident, and competent and can communicate ideas in such a way that others will be interested in them and persuaded by them.

Unfortunately, far too few of us ever bother to analyze our effectiveness in speaking until after we have stepped into the spotlight. It is time to correct this error. With that end in mind, the chapters in Part Four help you gain the understanding and master the skills you need to speak like a pro and to feel like a winner after addressing an audience.

APPROACHING SPEECH MAKING SYSTEMATICALLY

People respond to the challenge of public speaking in a variety of ways. Some believe that speech making is an inborn skill: "I talk a lot, so this public speaking business poses no difficulty for me." Others view it as torture: "I'm scared stiff! This will be traumatic!" These attitudes represent two extremes, and both can cause problems. Overconfident people run the risk of being inadequate speakers because they conduct little research and thus are ill prepared. People who are overly anxious or fearful may find it terribly trying and nerve-racking to stand before an audience and deliver a talk. The most effective speakers are those who display a healthy respect for the challenges involved in speaking before others and who work systematically to create, prepare, and deliver an admirable presentation.

How can you become an effective speaker? You must work at it. To help you, this chapter will put the entire speech-making process into a logical format that you can examine and follow in detail. The process should serve as a road map—one you can use to prepare every public presentation you will ever make. You will also learn to control your nervous energy, to make it work for and not against you as you deliver a speech. Then it will be up to you to supply the material and the creative energy that will help you develop your material into an effective presentation.

> *There is just no way around it—you have to do your homework. A speaker may be very well informed, but if he hasn't thought out exactly what he wants to say today, to this audience, he has no business taking up other people's valuable time.*
>
> **—Lee Iacocca, *Iacocca: An Autobiography***

Report Talk and Rapport Talk

According to researcher Deborah Tannen, men are more comfortable speaking in public than women are, while women are more comfortable speaking in private. Tannen finds that men excel at "report talk," while women excel at "rapport talk."

Do your experiences confirm or contradict this? If this disparity exists, what, if anything, do you think should be done to change it?

EXPLORING
Diversity

It is important to realize that public speaking is a creative undertaking—not something that just happens when you stand up to speak. The process actually begins when you first consider addressing a group of people, and it is not finished until you have completed a postpresentation analysis of your work. This creative process can be approached systematically, as shown in Figure 14.1. This chart divides speech making into four main stages: topic selection, topic development, presentation, and postpresentation analysis.

FIGURE 14.1
Systematic Speaking Process.

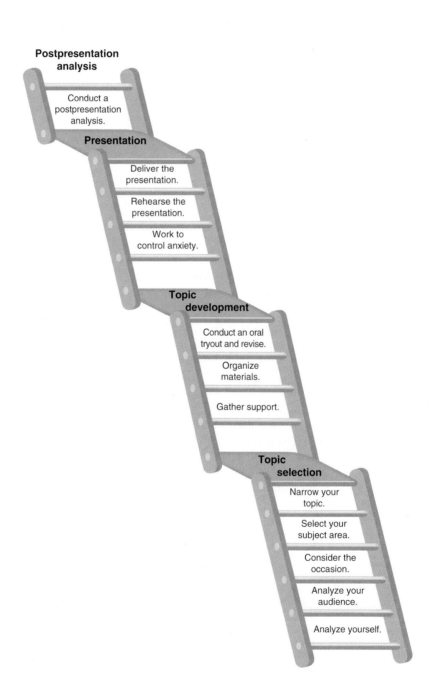

Postpresentation analysis

Conduct a postpresentation analysis.

Presentation

Deliver the presentation.

Rehearse the presentation.

Work to control anxiety.

Topic development

Conduct an oral tryout and revise.

Organize materials.

Gather support.

Topic selection

Narrow your topic.

Select your subject area.

Consider the occasion.

Analyze your audience.

Analyze yourself.

During stage 1, the topic selection stage, your job is to analyze yourself, your audience, and the nature of the occasion; choose a general subject area; focus on the subject; and narrow its scope until you hit on a particular aspect of the topic that you can handle in the time allotted. This becomes your purpose, or reason, for speaking. During stage 2, the topic development stage, you gather your evidence, organize the evidence according to your purpose, prepare visuals, and rehearse. During stage 3, the presentation stage, your main task is to control your anxiety so that you will be able to deliver your ideas clearly and effectively. During stage 4, the postpresentation analysis stage, you determine (with the aid of others—such as your instructor or fellow class members—or on your own) the strengths and weaknesses of your presentation to be better prepared to meet the challenge when the next occasion arises.

Not every phase of this sequence consumes the same amount of time, and the time you will need for each stage will vary from speech to speech. Sometimes you will need to spend a great deal of time analyzing your audience and identifying the needs of your listeners. At other times you will know your audience well and will need to spend relatively little time determining whether your speech is appropriate. Sometimes the subject of your talk will be provided for you. At other times you will be required to come up with your own topic. Sometimes you will be asked to fill a brief time period. At other times you will be allotted as much time as you need to share your ideas effectively with others. For example, as a manager, you may be required to deliver a detailed report on work that your unit has been doing and may be instructed to "take as much time as you need to inform us of your progress." On the other hand, you may find yourself asked to "say just a few words" or to "give a brief progress report." For some speeches you may find that you need to spend a great deal of time researching and gathering material. For others the primary problem will lie not in gathering materials but in organizing them so that the speech will flow smoothly and accomplish its objectives.

Because circumstances and occasions vary so widely, you should consider each step of the systematic speaking process for every speech you prepare. Skipping over any phase without at least being certain that you have adequately considered it can lead to embarrassing and uncomfortable moments for you and your audience.

Let's begin now to work our way through the speech-making process.

CONSIDERING THE SPEAKER

When you listen to a speaker—either in person or through the media—how do you expect him or her to behave? What do you want the speaker to do for you? It is helpful to view the process of speech making from the standpoint of the listeners. After all, without listeners, we would be speaking to ourselves—and that is not what public speaking is all about.

Speech . . . preserves contact—it is silence which isolates.
—Thomas Mann

Expectations for Speech Makers: Criteria

Good speakers have certain characteristics, which you may want to keep in mind as you prepare your own presentations. First, good speakers have insight. They know their own strengths and limitations. They understand and have considered the reservoir of experience on which they may draw. Second, good speakers know their audiences. They work to understand the nature and concerns of the people they have been called on to address. They are able to feel the pulse of this public, to stand in the shoes of the audience members, and to view the event or occasion through the audience's eyes so that they are able to share something that will be of value. Third, good speakers believe that what they are doing is important; they know why they are speaking, and they know what they hope to accomplish by speaking. They are clear about their purpose and about the main ideas they want to communicate. In addition, they are adept at formulating and delivering a message that is organized to support their purpose. Fourth, good speakers always practice. They conduct dry runs of the presentation, adapting it to potential changes in the audience and the audience members' needs. They also prepare well for questions audience members may ask. Fifth, good speakers think of the speech as if it is a performance. They know that they will need to work hard to keep the audience interested in what they have to say; they understand the essential fickleness of audiences, so they make it easy and pleasurable for listeners to stay tuned to their ideas. Finally, good speakers make a critique, or postpresentation analysis, of the speech. They know that there is much to learn from each experience, much that they may be able to apply the next time they are in the spotlight.

As a result of the media explosion, our society has grown accustomed to high-quality speeches. Talk shows, television news programs, and entertainers bring professional speech making into our homes every day. Newscasters, for example, have had years of training and practice in speaking. Public relations practitioners are often carefully schooled in public speaking to ensure that they know how to communicate a positive image to an audience. Many corporate executives employ speechwriters and speech coaches to help them communicate with diverse audiences. The need to deliver a high-quality presentation creates a difficult, though not an impossible, task for the student who is about to step into the spotlight. The communication environment you find yourself in is challenging. You will need to add the skills of sharing information and persuading audiences to your credentials, for only then will you have the expertise to communicate effectively in our multifaceted environment. From the classroom to the corporation, from the boardroom to the television studio, from the steps of city hall to the podium in a local auditorium, your challenge is to develop the skills and confidence you need to deliver—clearly and persuasively—the messages that are important to you and important to the people you represent.

Skill BUILDER

From the Listener's Point of View

1. Describe the behaviors exhibited by the most effective speaker you have had the good fortune to hear.

2. Contrast that description with a description of the most ineffective speaker you ever had the misfortune to hear.

Self-Analysis: You and Your Topic

Thorough self-analysis is a prerequisite for effective speech making. Although at times topics may be assigned, under many circumstances the choice will be left to you, the speaker. Even when a topic is specified, it is recommended that you conduct a self-analysis to help you uncover aspects that you may find particularly interesting or appealing. Such an analysis can also become the basis for personal stories or anecdotes that can eventually be integrated into your presentation.

There are more topics for speeches than you could possibly exhaust in a lifetime.[3] Still, "I just don't know what to say" is an all-too-familiar lament.

> But where was I to start? The world is so vast, I shall start with the country I know best, my own. But my country is so very large. I had better start with my town. But my town, too, is large, I had best start with my street. No: my home. No: my family. Never mind, I shall start with myself.[4]

At the outset of your preparation, you should take some time for what corporate trainers call a front-end analysis—a preliminary examination of possibilities. Following are five useful forms that a front-end analysis can take.

Review Your Life: Your Autobiography

You can begin by reviewing your life in terms of potential topics:

1. Divide your life (thus far) into thirds: early, middle, more recent. Compose one sentence to sum up what your life consisted of during each segment (for example, "I lived in Gary, Indiana, with my two brothers and mother, and went to elementary school").

2. Under each summary statement, identify your main interests and concerns at that time of your life.

3. Examine the interests and concerns you listed. Which of them recur? Which have you left behind? Which have you developed only recently?

Consider the Moment: This Moment

A second approach is to consider this very moment as a source of potential topics:

1. On the left side of a sheet of paper, list sensory experiences; that is, list everything you are able to see, hear, taste, smell, or touch from your present vantage point.

2. When you have listed 10 to 15 items, go back over the list and note topics that might be suggested by each observation or experience. Arrange these in a corresponding list on the right side of the paper. For example, if you list "passing train" in the left column, you might enter "mass transportation" in the right column. Note: If you are not satisfied with the topics you have identified, move to another location and begin the process again.

Search the News: Newspapers, Nightly News, and News Magazine Shows

A third approach is to work with a newspaper to find potential topics:

1. Take today's newspaper and, beginning with the front page, read a story and compile a list of topics suggested by it.

2. Do not prejudge your ideas. Simply work your way through the paper, looking for possibilities. For example, the June 8, 2003, issue of the *New York Times Magazine* was a special issue devoted to the coverage of money. What potential speech topics does such a subject area suggest to you? A speech on how money corrupts? The growing gap between the rich and the poor? Why we need to understand the relationship among international monetary systems? The relationship between deficit spending and the future of today's college students?[5]

A variation on this approach calls on you to view a nightly local or national news broadcast or news magazine program with pen and paper in hand. Divide the paper into two columns. Label the first column *"Stories Presented."* Label the second column *"Ideas Generated by This News Story."* Work your way through the program, looking for possibilities. The same methodology will work for news magazine programs such as *60 Minutes, 20/20,* and *Nightline.*

Use an Online Topic Generator

A number of Web sites can help with topic generation. Try using the following topic generators:

www.yukoncollege.yk.ca/~agraham/guides/tpgen.htm
www.lib.odu.edu/research/idea/index.htm

The Alphabet Technique

You can also use the letters of the alphabet to prompt you in developing a list of potential speech topics. You can work alone or with one or more partners to create your list—for example,

A age, advertising, animals, athletics
B babies, birth defects, boxing
C college life, culinary skills, cults
D drugs, diets, debt

The Topoi System

When searching for an idea, you can also use the Topoi system of topic development, derived from the ancient Greeks.[6] When using a Topoi approach, you select a possible topic and ask the following questions about it: Who? What? When? Where? How? Why? and So? For example, if you decided to speak on the Branch Davidians, you might ask the following questions:

Who were the cult's leader and members?
Where was the cult located?
What prompted the crisis at Waco?
When did the crisis occur?
Why did members remain inside the cult's compound?
How was the crisis resolved?
So, what does it mean?

CONSIDERING THE AUDIENCE

Having conducted a search of yourself, it is now time to determine where your audience fits in. A pitfall for many speakers is speaking to please themselves—approaching speech making with only their own interests and their own points of view in mind and neglecting the needs and interests of their audience. These speakers will often choose an inappropriate topic, dress improperly, or deliver a presentation that is either too simple or too technical for the audience. We have all heard medical experts address general audiences using such complex language that their listeners were baffled and bored. We have also heard speakers address highly educated groups in such simple language and about such mundane topics that everyone was not only bored but insulted. There's a catchy acronym for describing speeches that bore or confuse audience members; it's **MYGLO,** for "my eyes glaze over"—which is exactly what happens when you lose the audience's attention.[7]

Your focus during the initial stages of speech preparation should not, therefore, be solely on yourself. Be prepared to consider a potential topic from the point of view of your audience. Just as you bring your own background and experiences to a presentation, the audience members will bring theirs. Thus, it is important to consider what your listeners are thinking about, what their needs and hopes are. You may start by considering where you are, but you must not be so self-centered as to stop there. Successful communicators, in a sense, enlarge the area of the spotlight to include the audience.

To pay proper attention to your audience, you must know something about it. For example, how familiar are the audience members with what you are going to talk about? What is their attitude toward your topic? What are they anxious about? What would they like to know? What are their expectations? If you don't find out the answers to questions like these, you run the risk of having your words fall on deaf ears. Unfortunately, of all the steps in

Make a list of 10 subjects you believe would be inappropriate for delivery to your class. Discuss how each topic might be approached to make it appropriate.

MYGLO

an acronym for "my eyes glaze over"

Poor preparation may cause audience members to stop paying attention—a direct result of MYGLO—"my eyes glaze over."

the process of public speaking, audience analysis is most often overlooked. Speaking to hear yourself speak is a trap you will want to take steps to avoid every time you must speak before others. Making a speech without considering the audience is like talking to yourself. It is from behind the eyes of your audience that you must approach speech making.

Beginning Your Audience Analysis: Who Are They?

How can you know, or how can you try to determine, precisely who will attend your presentation? For example, can you expect certain interested groups or individuals to come? Will others whom you do not expect surprise you by showing up?

The Makeup of Your Audience

Finding information about the people you will be speaking to can often seem difficult or even impossible. But it is important to make educated guesses about the makeup of your intended audience. Actually, this is a simple task. What you are doing at this stage of the process is creating a mental picture of the people to whom you are going to speak.[8] Once you have created such an image, or snapshot, for yourself, you will be better able to continue planning your presentation.

Fortunately for most speakers, audiences seldom just happen. Unless people are in a park or a shopping mall or walking down a street when someone—such as a politician—begins to speak out about some issue, they tend to gather to hear a speaker for specific reasons. People meet to listen to speakers in a number of different settings, including lecture halls, auditoriums, parties, and houses of worship, as well as in front of radios and televisions. And they meet for a number of different purposes: to gain information, to evaluate ideas and proposals, to praise or pay homage to others, to assess

Ethics & COMMUNICATION

The Magic Bullet of Speech Making

What is the magic bullet of speech making? Practitioners and consultants offer varied answers to this question. George W. Bush, for example, believes a speech has to involve receivers on an emotional level. When reading and reworking the drafts of speeches presented to him by his staff of speechwriters, the president's comments and notes include such thoughts as "tugs at heartstrings" and "an emotional call to arms."[9]

On the other hand, Roger Ailes, chairman of Ailes Communication Inc. and a communications consultant to many corporations and their chief executive officers, says that being likable is the magic bullet of communication. Ailes writes: "With it, your audience will forgive just about everything else you do wrong. Without

it, you can hit every bull's-eye in the room, and no one will be impressed."

What do you think the magic bullet is? Is it being emotionally involving, likable, or something else? For example, is being able to emotionally arouse receivers more or less important than having something significant to say? Should it be? Is being likable more or less important than giving receivers information they need to have but may not enjoy hearing? Should it be? What happens when you have something significant or necessary to say but you fall short when it comes to involving receivers or motivating them to like you? What hurdles does a speaker whom you dislike have to overcome or who fails to involve you emotionally have to overcome?

attitudes and beliefs, to be entertained, to be spiritually uplifted, and to be comforted in sorrow. The primary emphasis in this book is on the first two of these purposes: speech making for audiences who have gathered to listen to either an informative or a persuasive address.

Sources of Audience Information

Information about your audience should come from two key sources:

1. Your personal experience with the group
2. Original research

Let's consider each of these.

Personal Experience   The best source of information about your audience is your personal experience with the group—either as a speaker or as an audience member. If you have attended several functions or are a member of the class or organization you are expected to address, you have personal knowledge of the audience members. Thus, you will probably be able to formulate reasonably accurate predictions about the appropriateness of your material for that group.

Research   What if you have had no previous contact with the group you are to address? If that is the case, you might ask the program planner to provide you with relevant information. For instance, if you have been asked to speak at a professional convention, you would be concerned with specific information about the makeup of the audience: How many will attend the lecture? Will there be students present? Government officials? All these factors would have to be taken into account in preparing and customizing the presentation.

Another way to gather information about a group is to obtain copies of public relations material. Recent news releases highlighting the organization may help put you on the same track as your audience. Corporate newsletters can also be valuable, as can a trip to the local library for information describing the organization.

Original research often takes the form of discussions with members of the potential audience. Robert Orben, a speech consultant and writer for former president Gerald Ford, tells the following story.[10] A presidential address had been planned for a college campus in Minnesota. The speechwriters knew that many of the students were not supporters of the president. They therefore spent a great deal of time on the telephone with students and school officials in an effort to obtain specific bits of information that could be included in the speech to help create a bond between the president and his audience. Finally, a somewhat disgruntled student provided the writers with the "gem" they felt they needed. They completed the speech, confident that they had done their job well—and they had. Ford began his address by saying, "Washington may have the new subway, Montreal may have the monorail, but this campus has the Quickie!" The students in the audience laughed and applauded warmly. Why? The drinking age was 21 in Minnesota but 18 in a neighboring state. And the 15-mile trip students often took to get to the first bar across the state line was known as "the Quickie." In this instance, talking at length to potential members of the audience provided information that helped establish an atmosphere in which the listeners, although not necessarily in agreement with the speaker, were at least rendered friendly enough to listen to his views.

Demographics of Audiences: What Are They Like?

Since the background and composition of your audience are important factors to consider in planning a speech, every effort must be made to determine audience demographics: age, gender, family orientation, religion, cultural background, occupation, socioeconomic status, educational level, and additional factors (such as membership in organizations). Despite the fact that no one audience will be entirely uniform in all these categories, you should consider each one during your initial planning sessions.

Age

Choose a topic of current interest. How would you approach the topic for a presentation to people your own age? How would you change your approach to appeal to an older or a younger audience?

Would you give precisely the same presentation to a group of children that you would give to your class? Almost certainly not. How might your presentations differ? Could you even deal with the same subject? The adult students would bring many more years of experience to your presentation than the children would. Adults may have been through economic hassles and even a war, for instance—experiences that children have probably not yet faced. Of course, the maturity of the two audiences would also differ. These contrasts may seem obvious, but age is a factor often overlooked in planning speeches. You might choose to speak on abortion or birth control to a college audience, but you might fail to realize that the same material would probably have less intrinsic appeal to an audience of senior citizens.

It's also wise to consider how your own age will affect your presentation. How close are you to the mean, or average, age of your anticipated listeners? If you are about the same age as the audience members, your job may be a little easier. If you are much older or much younger than the audience members, you will need to attempt to see your topic through their eyes and adjust it accordingly.

The background and composition of the audience need to be taken into account when planning a speech.

Your goal is to be sensitive to the references you employ, the language you use, and the rate at which you speak so that you shrink rather than enlarge the age gap that may exist between you and your receivers. Only if the receivers are able to comprehend your words, identify with your examples and illustrations, and recognize the persons and events you refer to will they be in a position to respond as you hope. When you close whatever age gap exists, you increase the likelihood of audience understanding. The point is that the average age of your audience matters. Research shows that, while younger listeners are more open to new ideas, older ones are less receptive to change. You can use information like this to judge how difficult it will be for you to attain your speech-making goal.[11]

Gender

Gender can also influence an audience's reaction to your speech. There are, admittedly, some myths and misconceptions about the effects of gender. (For example, in the past, researchers believed that women could be more easily persuaded than men.[12] Do you think this is a valid viewpoint today?) Still, you need to consider gender differences, especially if you speak to an audience composed entirely or mainly of one sex. Study your potential audience before drawing any conclusions. Although the same topics may appeal to both men and women, gender may affect the ways male and female audience members respond. For example, a discussion of rape may elicit a stronger emotional reaction from the women in your class, whereas a discussion of vasectomy may elicit a stronger response from the men. Be aware, though, that the so-called traditional roles of men and women are changing and that stereotypes once attributed to both groups are crumbling.

Family Orientation

Are most of the members of your audience single? Married? Divorced? Widowed? From one-parent or two-parent homes? These factors might influence your audience's reactions to your presentation. The concerns of one group are not necessarily the concerns of another.

Religion

If you are speaking to a religious group with which you have little familiarity, make a point of discussing your topic in advance with some group members. Some groups have formulated very clear guidelines regarding issues such as divorce, birth control, and abortion. It is important for you to understand the audience and its feelings if you are to be able to relate effectively to its members.

Cultural Background

Use your knowledge of an audience's culture and mind-set to create a bond with your listeners. Because our society is becoming increasingly multicultural, it is more important than ever that you attune yourself to beliefs held by audience members.[13] As you plan your speech, keep in mind how potential misunderstandings can result from racial, ethnic, religious, or cultural differences. Once you are aware of the makeup of your audience, you will be in a better position to predict how audience members will feel about your topic or the position you are advocating. Take time to consider how the presence or

On the Web site www.greatspeaking.com, accessed on May 20, 2003, it was suggested that, in order to appeal to the diverse backgrounds and interests of receivers, the speaker might "bounce around" rather than spend too much time catering to the interests and concerns of any one type of audience member. The subtext was that, if a speaker spent too much time attempting to involve only one audience member type, he or she would lose the interest of all the others in the audience. To what extent, if any, do you agree with such advice? On the other hand, do you see any potential dangers in "bouncing around"?

absence of receiver diversity might influence the reaction both to you and to your speech.

Occupation

People are interested in issues that relate to their own work and the work of those important to them. Consequently, if possible, relate your subject to the occupational concerns of your audience. Also, if you are speaking before an audience whose members belong to a particular occupational group, you must attempt to find or create examples and illustrations that reflect their concerns.

Socioeconomic Status

Researchers have found that there are psychological as well as economic differences among upper-class, middle-class, and lower-class people. Having or lacking discretionary income, power, and prestige evidently influences our attitudes and beliefs. Since our society is socially mobile, with a "move-up" philosophy, as a speaker, you can usually assume that your audience members want to get ahead and improve their position in life, and you can adjust your presentation to appeal to that desire.

Educational Level

Although it is important to determine your listeners' educational level, you cannot let your findings trap you into making unwarranted assumptions—either positive or negative—regarding their intellectual ability. Still, in general, you will probably find that the higher people's level of education, the more general their knowledge and the more insightful their questions. In addition, the more knowledgeable members of your audience may have specific data to dispute your stand on controversial issues. An educated and sophisticated audience may be far more aware of the impact of various political and social programs than, say, a group of high school dropouts. A less educated audience may need background information that a more educated audience may consider superfluous.

Whatever the educational level of your listeners, the following are three precepts to keep in mind:

1. Don't underestimate the intelligence of your listeners; don't speak down to them.
2. Don't overestimate their need for information; don't try to do too much in the time that is available to you.
3. Don't use jargon if there's a chance that your listeners are unfamiliar with it; listeners will quickly tune out what they don't understand.

Additional Factors

You may find that you need to consider several additional variables as you prepare your presentation. For example, if your audience is your class, do class members belong to a particular campus organization? Do members of the class involve themselves in any particular types of projects? Do the interests of the class relate in any way to your speech? Do class members have any identifiable goals, fears, frustrations, loves, or hates that could be tied in? How has their environment influenced their perception of key issues?

TABLE 14.1 *Audience Demographics*

Average age of audience members: _____

Gender makeup: _____

Family orientation: _____

Religious preference: _____

Cultural background: _____

Occupation: _____

Socioeconomic status: _____

Educational level: _____

Additional relevant factors: _____

Your topic: _____

Examples of ways to use the demographic information: _____

_____

_____

Summary

If used wisely, your knowledge of audience demographics can help you achieve your purpose as a speech maker. It can permit you to draw inferences about the predispositions of audience members and their probable responses to your presentation. Thus, when planning your next presentation, fill out a chart like the one in Table 14.1.

Attitudes of Audiences: What Do They Care About?

Once you have considered audience demographics, your next step is to try to predict the attitudes your listeners will have toward you and toward your presentation. You should consider whether or not the audience members are required to attend, whether the audience is homogeneous or heterogeneous, and whether the audience members favor your stand or are actively opposed to it.[14]

Motivation: Is Attendance Optional or Required?

People may attend a presentation because they want to (that is, they do so willingly), because they have to (they are required to do so), or simply because they are curious. You might attend a town council meeting because a proposed increase in property taxes is being considered; you might attend a parents' meeting at school out of a sense of duty or because your spouse insisted that you go; you might attend a lecture on the fur industry because you are curious about what might be discussed.

Try to rate your audience on the following scale with respect to audience members' overall motivation:

Required to attend   1   2   3   4   5   Strongly desire to attend

Since the audience's willingness to attend can affect how your presentation is received, it is important to make an educated guess regarding its probable level of enthusiasm. (Of course, it's also important to remember that, just because audience members want to attend your talk, they will not necessarily agree with what you have to say.)

Values: Is the Audience Homogeneous or Heterogeneous?

A second factor for consideration is the degree of homogeneity—that is, the extent to which everyone in the audience has similar values and attitudes. Of course, it is easier to address a homogeneous audience than a heterogeneous one. In addressing heterogeneous groups, speakers need to vary their appeals to ensure that all segments of the audience spectrum are considered.

Use the following scale to measure the extent to which the members of your audience share similar characteristics and values:

Homogeneous   1   2   3   4   5   Heterogeneous

We like to hear what makes us feel comfortable and self-assured. Yet this is exactly what we have no need of hearing; only those who disturb us can improve us.
—Sydney J. Harris

Level of Agreement: Does the Audience Agree with Your Position?

Whatever your topic, you must attempt to predict your audience members' reaction to the stance you take. For example, they may oppose you, they may support you, or they may be neutral or uninterested. The accuracy of your prediction will determine to some extent how your presentation is received.

Skill BUILDER

Attitude Check

1. For practice, select three to five current, controversial topics.
2. Each member of the class should fill out the following scales for each topic.
   a. If a speech were being given on this topic, which would you do?
      Attend only if required to   1   2   3   4   5   Have a great desire to attend
   b. Do you feel that your attitudes and values are similar or dissimilar to those of other members of your group?
      Dissimilar (heterogeneous)   1   2   3   4   5   Similar (homogeneous)
   c. Do you support this issue?
      Do not support   1   2   3   4   5   Support
   d. Is your involvement in or commitment to your position active or passive?
      Passive involvement   1   2   3   4   5   Active involvement
3. Using your knowledge about the class members, estimate where on each scale the average response will fall. Then add up the scores for each issue and divide by the number of class members participating to determine the actual class average for each issue.

How accurate were your predictions? Would you have been off base if you had spoken to the class on one or more of the identified topics? Why? How can the information you gathered help you become a more effective speaker?

Use the following scale to help you assess your audience's position in terms of its similarity or dissimilarity to your own:

Agrees with me   1   2   3   4   5   Disagrees with me

Your objective when speaking to an audience that agrees with your position is to maintain its support. Your objective when speaking to a neutral audience is to gain your listeners' attention and show them how your presentation can be of value to them. When facing an audience that disagrees with you, you need to be especially careful and diplomatic in your approach. In this case, your objective is to change your listeners' minds—to move the audience closer to the "agrees with me" side of the continuum. This task becomes easier if you establish a common ground with audience members—that is, if you first stress values and interests that you share. Keep in mind that your goal is to increase the likelihood that a voluntary audience will attend to your message and that a captive audience will give you a fair hearing.

Level of Commitment: How Much Do They Care?

Finally, you need to consider how much the audience members care about your topic. Is it very important to them? Do they feel strongly enough to be moved to action? Or are your concerns irrelevant to your listeners?

Use the following scale to represent your audience's commitment:

Passive   1   2   3   4   5   Active

Together, the four attitudinal scales will indicate how much background and motivational material you need to include in your presentation.

Predicting the Audience's Reaction

Once you have completed your audience research, you will be in a position to predict your listeners' reception of any topic you select. Consider the following questions:

1. What do the audience members now know about my topic?
2. To what extent are they interested in my topic?
3. What are their current attitudes toward this topic?

As you develop your presentation, you must keep in mind the audience's knowledge of, interest in, and attitude toward the subject matter. These important factors will help you select and shape material specifically for the audience members. If you have been unsuccessful at gathering information about how your audience feels about your topic, you may find it helpful to take the pulse of public opinion, in general, by familiarizing yourself with the results of several public opinion polls on your chosen subject. For example, you can log onto a Web site that features public opinion polls, such as www.gallup.com or www.washingtonpost.com, in an effort to get the information you seek.

In addition to focusing on yourself and your receivers, whenever you give a speech, you should also have a clear idea of the nature of the speech-making occasion and how your topic relates to it. Both the occasion and your subject will affect the way you develop your presentation, stage it, and deliver it. We focus on these considerations next.

CONSIDERING THE OCCASION

If asked to speak before a group—including your own class—your first response might well be "Why? What's the occasion?" Identifying the occasion and your role in it is also an essential step in the process of preparing a speech. Fortunately, much, if not all, of what you need to know about the occasion is relatively easy to determine. Essentially, only the following need to be specified:

Date and time of the presentation
Length of the presentation
Location of the presentation
Nature of the occasion
Size of the audience

Date and Time: When and How Long?

Date and time are the most obvious—and among the most important—bits of information you need to acquire. On some occasions, student speakers and professional speakers have arrived an hour early, an hour late, and even a day early or a day late. (Of course, it's far better to be early than late, but being a day early is surely excessive.)

Timing can influence a speaker's effectiveness. For example, one well-known speaker arrived late at a New York college and found a hostile audience that had waited nearly an hour. Some professional speakers schedule their engagements so close together—two or three a day—that they must rush out the door rudely, almost before they have completed their talks. In a situation like that, the audience may react angrily.

The length of the presentation can also influence its effectiveness. For instance, one student speaker was supposed to deliver a 10-minute informative speech, "The History of the Corvette." Although it was suggested that he limit his consideration of the topic to two or three major model changes, he attempted to discuss every minute body and grill alteration in the Chevrolet Corvette from 1954 to the present. The instructor made several attempts to stop him, but 40 minutes into the speech he was still going strong. At this point, the instructor announced a class break. The student responded, "That's fine. I'll just continue." And he did—although the majority of his audience had departed.

Sometimes we are not actually given as much speaking time as we have been led to expect. For example, lunch or after-dinner speakers are often told that they will have 45 minutes to fill, but after introductions and comments by preliminary speakers, they suddenly find themselves left with 30 minutes or less. Are you able to plan a presentation to ensure that you will not run over or under your time limit?

Location and Participants: Where and Who?

Reminding yourself of the location of your presentation and of the people directly connected with it is an important aspect of preparing a speech. This may seem obvious, but it is sometimes neglected, with absurd and embarrassing results. For example, at a speech by a world-famous psychologist whose audience consisted of members of the host college and the surrounding community, early in his speech, the eminent Dr. M———— mumbled what seemed to be the name of another college, although most of his listeners failed to notice. The second time, however, he clearly announced how happy he was to be at X————, mentioning the wrong college again. (Doubly unfortunate was the fact that college X was a rival of the host college.) By then, some members of the audience appeared embarrassed for the speaker, and others appeared hostile. The third time, the psychologist mentioned not only the wrong school but the wrong town as well. At this point, there was sufficient commotion in the audience for him to realize his error, and in evident confusion he turned to the college president to ask where he was.

During a state visit to South America, former president Ronald Reagan delivered a few words at the airport: "It was so nice to be here in Bolivia." Unfortunately, he was in Brazil. Realizing his mistake, he noted, "Bolivia is my next stop." Unfortunately, Bolivia wasn't on his itinerary.

How can you avoid such problems? The minister who officiated at this book's authors' marriage had a possible solution. During the wedding rehearsal, a page in his Bible was marked with a paper clip that held a slip of paper, and later we asked him about it. The minister showed us that it had our names clearly written on it. He explained that, because he was somewhat nervous when conducting a wedding, he frequently tended to forget the names of the bride and groom, even if they had belonged to the congregation for years. The slip of paper provided an unobtrusive reminder. Taking our cue from this experience, we now attach a slip of paper to the first page of our notes whenever we address a group. The slip bears the name of the organization, its location, the name of the person introducing us, the names of the officers, and other important information. Thus, we have at our disposal the data we need, to be integrated as appropriate. You may also want to adopt this simple procedure to avoid unnecessary embarrassment or loss of credibility.

Of course, there are other aspects to location besides merely the site where you are and the people who are present. Also of concern is the nature of the physical space you are to speak in. Is the space nicely or shabbily decorated? Hot, cold, or comfortable? Quiet or noisy? If appropriate, you might refer to the environment in your talk, as did one student who was speaking on the effects of AIDS (acquired immune deficiency syndrome):

> Take a look around you. What do you see? Desks, chairs, fluorescent lights, a chalkboard, your friends? Sights you take for granted every day. Eight-year-old Jane Doe doesn't take these sights for granted, though. Not any more. Jane has AIDS and has been barred by a court order from attending a public school. No more will she sit at a desk as you are sitting, glance at the board as you do, share the fun of learning with friends. AIDS is changing her life.

Type of Occasion: Why and How Many?

Why have you been asked to speak? Although every occasion is unique, you can ask some general questions to clarify the situation in your own mind. For example, is it a class session? Right now it probably is, but in the future it could well be a sales meeting, a management planning session, a convention, or a funeral. Is your presentation part of the observance of a special event? For example, is the occasion in honor of a retirement? A promotion? Is it some other type of recognition? Who else, if anyone, will be sharing the

Speakers need to be prepared to address sales meetings and management planning sessions.

program with you? Factors like these can affect the nature of your presentation. An appropriate topic for a retirement party, for instance, might be considered inappropriate for a more formal occasion.

Determining how many people will show up to listen to any particular presentation is difficult. In a classroom situation, for example, on one day the room may be filled, but on another day a speaker may arrive and find that a number of students are out sick or off on a special project for another course. The same problem confronts the professional speaker. It is a good idea to multiply and divide the sponsor's estimate by 2. Thus, you can be prepared to speak to a small group—that is, possibly 20—if 40 are expected—or to a large group—possibly 100—if 50 is the estimate.

Since you are not likely to have an advance person at your disposal when preparing to deliver your presentation—at least not yet—you must do all the advance thinking for yourself. Make it a habit to complete an analysis of both your audience and the occasion before completing work on any presentation. The predictions you make will serve you well as you continue preparing your speech.

CONSIDERING THE TOPIC

To continue preparing your speech without having selected a subject—on the basis of self-analysis, audience analysis, and occasion analysis—would be like trying to buy an airline ticket without knowing your destination.

Selecting a Topic: Criteria

You must carefully examine the list of possible topics you generated during the self-analysis and audience-analysis phases of your preparation. During this

Topic Evaluation Time

1. Working individually or in groups, develop a list of criteria by which you believe a topic for a class speech should be assessed.

2. Share your criteria with others. Which criteria seem to be most important in the selection process? Which appear to be least important? Why?

3. Compare the criteria you developed with those identified in the text. How are they similar or different?

examination, you evaluate your ideas according to specific criteria: (1) apparent worth, (2) appropriateness, (3) interest, and (4) availability of material. When you keep these criteria in mind, selecting a topic will be easier—if only because few of your choices will meet each of the criteria equally well with regard to the needs of particular audiences.[15]

Is the Topic Worthwhile?

You need to determine if the topic is important to you and to the people who will listen to you. Many speakers—including college students and business-people—often fall into the trap of choosing topics that are of little value to the audience. One of the authors recalls a time in a military training institute when he heard one colonel tell another, "After 25 years as an officer, I'm expected to waste my time hearing how to inspect a fork!" To that audience of high-ranking officers, the topic "Fork Inspection Techniques" was clearly trivial. You may also find that some topics chosen by others are trivial from your perspective. They may be so commonplace—how to set a table, for example—that they don't merit the time and energy you must expend in listening to them. Many subjects that are acceptable for interpersonal discourse may be inconsequential when presented in a public setting where the speaker's purpose is to inform or persuade. Which topics do you judge to be worth your time? Which, in your opinion, are unworthy of consideration?

Is the Topic Appropriate?

We have already discussed how important it is to determine if a topic is appropriate to you and your personal interests. Two additional facets of this criterion must also be considered: (1) Is the topic appropriate to the audience? (2) Is it appropriate to the occasion? Let's examine each in turn.

By this time, you should have developed a profile of your audience. That is, you have either determined precisely or made educated guesses about the age, gender, and educational level of the majority of the people who are going to hear your speech. It then becomes imperative for you to ask which of your possible topics is most appropriate for such a mix of people. Sometimes this determination is easy. For instance, you would not ordinarily give a talk about the evils of television to a group of network representatives. Nor, ordinarily, would you opt to speak on the advantages of a women's college to an audience already attending a women's college. You might not choose to speak on baseball trivia to an audience of highly educated professional women. Or would you? Is there a way to make seemingly inappropriate topics appropriate?

Every subject area must be seen through the eyes of its intended audience. Just as an automobile is customized for a particular owner, so a subject area must be customized to reflect the needs of a particular group of listeners. Just as the automobile is painted, detailed, and upholstered with an owner or a type of owner in mind, so you as a speaker must "outfit" your topic to appeal to the audience members you hope to reach. This takes work, but it can be done.

The appropriateness of the topic to the occasion must also be considered. For example, you can probably think of any number of occasions on which a humorous topic would be ill-conceived. Can you think of occasions when a humorous topic would be an asset? For example, a humorous topic would be inappropriate for an event commemorating servicemen and -women who have given their lives for their country, whereas it would be welcomed at a roast.

Is the Topic Interesting?

Speech makers often make the mistake of selecting topics they think they should speak about rather than topics they want to speak about. Student speakers, for instance, will sometimes turn to a newspaper or newsmagazine and, without further thought, select a story at random as the basis for a speech. One student insisted on talking about labor-management relations. Why? He thought it sounded like an important subject. Unfortunately, he had spent little time in the labor force and no time in management. And because he did not care enough to do much—if any—research, the entire subject remained foreign to him. Not surprisingly, the speech he delivered was dull and disjointed. A lazy, unenthusiastic speaker can make almost any topic uninteresting—even a potentially fascinating or exciting one.

John Silverstein, a spokesman for General Dynamics, put it this way: "You need to believe in your idea. This is very important. What a listener often gauges is how convinced the speaker is. If he has lived it, breathed it, and is himself really sold on it, it generally is enough to sell the argument."[16] Of course, selecting a topic that is appealing to you is a personal matter and can be relatively simple, but determining what will interest your audience can be somewhat more challenging.

Here, students have an advantage. As a student, you know your fellow students, and you should be able to identify topics that will interest them. When addressing less familiar audiences, however, you should feel free to return to your audience analysis and make some educated guesses. Determining an audience's interests is a never-ending challenge—one that some unadventurous speech makers prefer not to tackle. One corporate executive, for example, once delivered a speech that was gratifyingly well received. Unfortunately, he then delivered essentially the same speech for the next five years, although times and needs kept changing. Needless to say, his current audiences are not interested in his topic. As times change, people's interests change, and so should the topics selected by speakers. Topics must be updated to match the moods, needs, and concerns of listeners; only by updating can you ensure that your topic treats an issue of interest to your audience.

Advertising executives discovered long ago that people are interested primarily in themselves and in how products relate to them. Speech makers are in an analogous position. Keep this in mind when considering the interests of your audience members. Ask yourself how your subject relates to them. Ask yourself what they stand to gain from listening to you. Create an inventory for each of your possible subjects. If you are unable to identify significant ways your audience will benefit from hearing about a topic, there is good reason for you not to speak on that topic.

Is Sufficient Research Material Available?

Before choosing a topic, be certain that material on the subject exists and that you can find it readily—on the Internet, in a library, or somewhere else. Many speakers fall into the trap of requesting material that is unavailable in a school or local library, only to have it arrive too late or turn out to be unpromising. Such an experience can cause last-minute panic, and the result is an inadequately prepared speech maker and an inadequate presentation. Avoid this pitfall by giving careful attention to your library and other nearby sources during the selection phase of your preparation.

Narrowing the Topic

It is essential to consider how much time is available for your speech. For example, an army chaplain more than once demonstrated how adept he was at handling time constraints. The chaplain's job was to address groups of recruits during basic training, and on each occasion he was given only three minutes to get his message across. One day his objective was to persuade soldiers not to use foul language. (It was his belief that such a practice degraded both individuals and the service.) Realizing that he could accomplish only so much in the time permitted, he chose to focus on a single word—the particular word that he found most offensive. During his three-minute talk, he suggested that the troops avoid using just that one term. By doing this, the chaplain demonstrated that he understood how important it is to narrow a topic to manageable proportions and, incidentally, succeeded in realizing his objective. (After his speech, the abused word was heard much less frequently around the base.)

Far too many speakers attempt to give audiences "the world" in five minutes. It is essential to narrow your topic to fit the constraints imposed by the situation. Don't try to take on too much. Five minutes is not sufficient time to discuss the history of Russia, the industrial revolution, or even pedigreed dogs.

There is a strategy you can use to avoid biting off more than you can chew—or talk about. Select a topic and place it at the top of a "ladder." Then subdivide the topic into constituent parts; that is, break it down into smaller and smaller units, as shown in Figure 14.2. The smallest unit should appear on the lowest step of the ladder. This process is like whittling or carving a stick of wood. The more you shave off, the narrower the topic becomes. Like the carver, you decide what shape to give your topic and when to stop shaving.

For example, assume that you want to speak on the need to save the rain forest. One way to narrow your topic would be to focus on how indigenous people can save the rain forest. Your topic could be focused even further. You might explore how their harvesting of native plants can stop deforestation or, more specifically, how their harvesting of fruit can help preserve the ecological balance. Here's another example: If you want to talk on the current

FIGURE 14.2
Ladder Technique for Narrowing a Topic.

technology revolution, you might focus on how the use of multimedia has revolutionized education or, more specifically, on how computers are used to teach writing skills.

Formulating a Purpose Statement and Behavioral Objectives

Once you have identified a topic and narrowed its scope, reexamine exactly why you are speaking. What is your purpose? What do you hope to accomplish?[17] What kind of response would you like from your audience? What do you want your listeners to think or do as a result of your presentation? What is your ultimate objective?

Most speakers have one of two general objectives when they prepare to deliver a speech: They aim either to inform listeners (to share new information or insights with the audience) or to persuade listeners (to convince audience members to believe in or do something). However, in actual speaking situations, the purpose is not always so clear. Persuasive speeches usually contain informative material, and informative speeches may sometimes include elements of persuasion.

The Informative Speech

If your purpose is to inform, your primary responsibility is to relay information to your audience in an interesting, well-organized, and professional manner. Informative speakers may explain something, demonstrate how something functions, or describe how something is structured. When speaking informatively, you hope to provide a learning experience for your listeners, sharing information they did not possess before your talk. In other words, if your main goal is to inform an audience, you must be certain that the data you provide will enhance your listeners' understanding, and you must find ways to help the audience remember what you say.

To ensure that your purpose is clear—initially to yourself and ultimately to your listeners—you will find it helpful to develop a purpose statement. What this means is that you commit to writing a summary of what you want to accomplish; you describe what you hope to do with your speech. The purpose statement of an informative speech often contains such words as *show, explain, report, instruct, describe,* and (not surprisingly) *inform.* The following are examples of purpose statements for various kinds of informative speeches:

> To explain how selected Chinese character letters evolved
>
> To describe how a tornado forms
>
> To inform class members about current Internal Revenue Service (IRS) regulations that affect them
>
> To instruct class members on how to reduce personal debt
>
> To report on efforts to prevent human cloning

Notice that each example takes the form of an infinitive verb phrase; thus, each begins with *to.* Notice also that each statement contains only one idea and that it is written from the speaker's perspective.

Sometimes, in addition to developing a purpose statement, it is helpful to view the speech from the perspective of the listeners. To facilitate this process, you can formulate behavioral objectives. Objectives identify what you want the audience to take away after hearing your presentation; that is, they describe the behavior or response you want the audience to exhibit as a result of listening to your speech. For instance, you may want your listeners to be able to list, explain, summarize, state, or apply certain information. The following are examples of behavioral objectives:

> After listening to this presentation, the audience will be able to explain the process of photographic development.
>
> After listening to this speech, the audience will be able to name three kinds of questions that are unlawful in employment interviews.
>
> After listening to this presentation, the audience will be able to discuss the three main reasons college students fail to graduate.

The Persuasive Speech

The same principles used for an informative speech may be applied in formulating a purpose statement and behavioral objectives for a persuasive speech. In a persuasive speech, your main goal is to reinforce or change an audience's beliefs or to make the audience behave in a certain way. The words *convince, persuade, motivate,* and *act* commonly turn up in purpose statements for persuasive speeches. The following are some examples:

> To persuade audience members to ensure they get more sleep
>
> To motivate listeners to contribute money to the American Cancer Society

To persuade class members to become actively involved in the conservation of global resources

To convince class members that racist speech should be exempt from First Amendment protection

With regard to behavioral objectives, you might want your audience to support a plan or take an overt action. The following are examples of behavioral objectives:

After listening to my presentation, audience members will write their representatives, asking them to seek legislation that bans the sale and manufacture of air guns that shoot projectiles at speeds greater than 350 feet per second.[18]

After listening to my presentation, students will sign up to will their eyes to an eye bank.

After listening to my speech, students will boycott stores that sell products made of ivory.

In summary, formulating precise purpose statements and behavioral objectives makes good sense. Both can help you focus your efforts and clarify your goals.

Formulating the Thesis Statement

In recent years, public speaking theorists have begun to look more closely at guidelines for writing. As a result, speakers are now often encouraged to develop theses for their speeches, just as writers do for papers. A thesis simply divides a topic into its major components. Thus, once you have formulated a specific purpose, the next step is to prepare a declarative sentence that summarizes the thesis of your speech. When your speech is an informative one and not intended to persuade, the thesis statement is phrased in a relatively objective and neutral manner and is sometimes referred to as the central idea or topic statement of your speech. Its focus is on what you want audience members to understand or learn—for example, *"Nuclear power plants have three major parts: the reactor core, vessel, and control rods."* When your speech is persuasive, it is simply called the thesis statement or the claim. A thesis for a persuasive speech expresses an arguable opinion or point of view; for example, a thesis for a persuasive speech against the use of nuclear energy plants might be *"Nuclear power plants should be decommissioned."* Whether your speech is informative or persuasive, the thesis statement can be a powerful rhetorical device for setting your agenda as a speaker.

The thesis statement is the core idea or bottom line of your speech; it is your speech in a nutshell. It is a statement of the overriding concept of your speech that all the facts, quotations, and ideas in your speech are designed to support. In effect, the specific statement is the steering wheel of your speech; it directs the course of your speech and determines the content in it. The thesis helps you derive the main ideas or major propositions your speech will explore. Everything you say should support the thesis. In and of itself, the thesis statement does not present all the information you will offer in your speech; instead, it efficiently focuses that information into a brief summarizing statement.

An effective thesis statement fulfills three guidelines. First, it is a single sentence that conveys the essence of the speech. Second, it focuses the attention of the audience members on what they should know, do, or feel after experiencing your speech. Third, it supports the specific purpose. The following are examples:

Thesis: Traditional Muslim clothing represents the key values of Muslim culture.

Thesis: Sleep deprivation costs business billions of dollars a year in employee accidents and avoidable mistakes.

Thesis: Criminalizing the use of hand-held cell phones when driving will decrease accidents and save lives.

Thesis: Getting a good night's sleep will enhance your personal and professional life in four key ways.

Thesis: Zero coupon bonds can provide you with three significant benefits: income, security, and tax savings.

As you can see from these examples, the thesis brings you a step closer to the structure of the speech itself.

TECHNOLOGY AND TOPIC SELECTION

The Internet is a huge, rich source of information and an excellent resource for both speakers and speech critics alike. A multitude of online services currently exist on virtually any subject. You can find just about anything you want on the Net—if you know how to use it. By using a **search engine,** a program that allows you to look through an entire database of information quickly, such as "Google," "Yahoo!" "AltaVista," "HotBot," "Infoseek," and "Excite," you can probe for and find information on selected topics easily and quickly. The results of the search will be a set of links to all the Web pages in that database that match the key word(s) you selected.

In addition, the Net has thousands of mailing lists, forums for the discussion of particular topics. Once you subscribe to a mailing list, the messages posted to the list are sent to your mailbox, too.

search engine
a program that allows you to look through an entire database of information quickly

Speakers use the Internet as a resource. How have you used the Net to facilitate your speech research?

Cybersearch

Use Internet resources to conduct a search for information on the following general subjects or a subject of your own choosing:

   E-mail
   High-tech presentations
   Workforce diversity
   Male/female communication styles

Make notes about what you found and how you found it. Then select one of the topics researched and narrow it so that it becomes possible for you to use the topic as the basis for a three-minute speech you could deliver to your class. Compare and contrast your topics with those formulated by other students.

Reflect and Respond

Agree or disagree with the following statement; supply reasons and examples that support your stance.

Effective public speaking is nothing more than one side of an extended conversation.

With the exception of preparation time, public speaking and conversation demand the same skills.

usenet newsgroups

a conference system of computer bulletin boards devoted to different topics in which people with similar interests across the world can interact with each other

Usenet newsgroups are another resource. These constitute a huge conference system of computer bulletin boards devoted to different topics in which people with similar interests across the world can interact with each other.[19]

One group of students decided to see what information they could find on infant mortality rates. Entering this subject produced hundreds of articles. The Division of Vital Statistics, for example, produced infant mortality rates from around the world. An accompanying abstract summarized the major conclusions observers could draw from the data, including the fact that over half of all infant deaths in the United States each year are attributed to sudden infant death syndrome. Another group decided to investigate day care for young children. An examination of the National Public Radio (NPR) site provided several features about day care—including one on the subject of Chinese day care in the United States. It appears that many young Chinese couples send their children back to China to be with their grandparents.[20] The NPR site is particularly interesting because the features contained in it are available in downloadable audio formats.

Accessing the online sites of major and local newspapers can also be worthwhile. Thus, logging onto www.washingtonpost.com, www.usatoday.com, www.nytimes.com, or the Web site of your local paper can facilitate the research process.

USING ANALYSIS EFFECTIVELY

Effective speech makers do not approach their task haphazardly. As we have seen, careful thought precedes the actual speech. Every speaker, from novice to professional, can benefit from following these suggestions:

1. *Focus your attention on the characteristics of people you consider good speakers.* Assess the extent to which you measure up to the standards they represent. Begin to identify ways of improving your speaking skills.

2. *Conduct a systematic self-analysis as a preparation for speech making.* Take the time you need to survey your own likes, dislikes, and concerns. Effective speakers know themselves well. They know what they care about, and they know what ideas they would like to share with others.

3. *Analyze your audience.* Effective speakers adapt their ideas to reflect the needs and interests of their listeners. Speeches are not meant to be delivered in an echo chamber or a vacuum. Rather, they are delivered with the specific purpose of informing or persuading others—of affecting others in certain specific ways. The degree to which you will succeed is directly related to how well you know your listeners and how accurately you are able to predict their reactions.

4. *Analyze the occasion.* It is essential that you learn why, when, where, and for how long you are expected to speak. Without this information, your preparation will be incomplete and insufficient.

5. *Determine if your topic is supported by your own interests, your audience's interests, and the demands of the occasion.* Be certain to evaluate your subject according to the following criteria: Is the topic worthwhile? Is the topic appropriate? Is the topic interesting? Is sufficient research material available? Have I sufficiently narrowed my focus?

Focus on Service Learning

How can you apply what you have learned in this chapter to help a community group enhance its understanding of sudden acute respiratory syndrome (SARS)?

Revisiting Chapter Objectives

1. **Identify the characteristics of effective public speakers.** Public communication, unlike interpersonal communication, occurs in a somewhat formal setting and requires the communicator to be well prepared. Effective speakers understand the challenges involved in speaking before others and work in a systematic manner to create, prepare, and deliver their presentations.

   The public speaking process begins when you first consider addressing a group of people. Four main stages of speech making follow: topic selection, topic development, the presentation itself, and the postpresentation analysis.

2. **Approach public speaking systematically—that is, select a topic, develop a topic, present a speech, and analyze its effectiveness.** A thorough analysis of yourself and a thorough analysis of your audience are the essential preliminary steps in topic selection. Information about your audience should come from your personal experience with the group, from original research (for example, news releases and interviews), or both. First, you need to determine audience demographics, including such factors as age, gender, family orientation, religion, cultural background, occupation, economic status, educational level, and additional factors (such as membership in organizations). Then you should try to predict the attitudes the listeners will have toward you and your presentation. It will help you to know whether audience members are required to attend, are homogeneous or heterogeneous in their attitudes, are favorably or unfavorably disposed toward your position, or are uninterested in your topic altogether.

THE Wrap-Up

3. **Explain how the nature of the occasion influences a speech.** Identifying the occasion and your role in it is another essential step in the process of preparing a speech. Once you have determined the date, time limit, and location of the speech, as well as the nature of the occasion and the audience, you can start thinking about a suitable topic. Choosing a topic usually involves two steps: selecting a general subject and narrowing it down to a manageable topic. You can evaluate your topic by answering the following questions: Is the topic worthwhile? Is it appropriate for the intended audience? Is it interesting? Is sufficient research material available? Will there be enough time to cover the topic adequately?

4. **Formulate clear and precise purpose statements for yourself and behavioral objectives for your audience.** After you have chosen your topic, you need to reexamine your purpose for speaking. Most speakers have one of two general objectives when they prepare to deliver a speech: to inform listeners (to share new information or insights) or to persuade listeners (to convince the audience to believe or do something). To ensure that your purpose is clear, you should formulate a purpose statement—a summary of what you want to accomplish, expressed as an infinitive phrase. For example, you may want to inform your audience about something, to describe something, or to explain how something is done. You can also list behavioral objectives—abilities you want the audience to have internalized after listening to your presentation.

5. **Formulate the thesis statement.** The thesis statement is the central idea or claim of your speech. It is your speech in a nutshell. A declarative sentence, the thesis statement directs the course of your speech, helping you to determine the main ideas or major propositions your speech will explore.

Resources for Further Inquiry and Reflection

To apply your understanding of how the principles in Chapter 14 are at work in our daily lives, consult the following resources for further inquiry and reflection. Or, if you prefer, choose any other appropriate resource. Then connect the ideas expressed in your chosen selection with the communication concepts and issues you are learning about both in and out of class.

 Listen to Me

"What's Going On?" (Marvin Gaye)
"We Didn't Start the Fire" (Billy Joel)

What speech subjects come to mind as you listen to each recording?

 View Me

The Boiler Room   *Patch Adams*

How does the sales manager in the boiler room apply lessons relevant to speech topic selection, development, presentation, and evaluation when making his pitch to the members of his sales team? How does Patch Adams use his knowledge of the audience to reach a group of terminally ill patients?

Read Me   **Tell Me**

To what extent, if any, does this cartoon reflect your feelings about public speaking before reading this chapter? After reading this chapter? Explain.

Share with the class the insights you gained from your chosen Listen to Me, View Me, or Read Me selection.

The National Opinion Research Center (NORC) and the Gallup Poll are two well-known and respected polling organizations. Both conduct polls on a broad array of topics from attitudes toward the presidency and government to attitudes toward the trustworthiness of the press and the military. To access NORC, go to http://www.norc.uchicago.edu/. To access the Gallup Poll, go to http://www.gallup.com/poll/index/asp. In your opinion, should speakers use public opinion polls such as these solely in order to find out valuable information about audience attitudes prior to developing their own speeches, or should they use them to decide what topics to speak on or what opinions to support when preparing to speak before audiences because that way at least they know they'll receive a favorable hearing?

Key Chapter Terminology

Use the Communication Works CD-ROM and the Online Learning Center at www.mhhe.com/gamble8 *to further your knowledge of the following terminology.*

MYGLO 423   search engine 441
public speaking 416   usenet newsgroups 442

 Communication Works

 online learning center

www.mhhe.com/gamble8

Test Your Understanding

Go to the *Self Quizzes* on the Communication Works CD-ROM and the book's Online Learning Center at www.mhhe.com/gamble8.

 Communication Works

 online learning center

www.mhhe.com/gamble8

Notes

1. Leslie Wayne. "Leaping to the Lectern." *New York Times*, September 8, 1995, p. D-1.
2. David Wallechinsky, Irving Wallace, and Amy Wallace. *The Book of Lists*. New York: Morrow, 1977, p. 469.

3. For an overview of the speech selection process, see Teri Gamble and Michael Gamble. *Public Speaking in the Age of Diversity*, 2nd ed. Boston: Allyn & Bacon, 1998; and Stephen Lucas. *The Art of Public Speaking*, 7th ed. New York: McGraw-Hill, 2001.

4. Elie Wiesel. *Souls on Fire*. New York: Summit, 1982.

5. See, for example, *New York Times Magazine*, June 8, 2003.

6. For a more detailed discussion of Topoi, see Joseph Devito. *The Elements of Public Speaking*, 7th ed. New York: Longman, 2000.

7. See Charles Francis. "How to Stop Boring Your Audience to Death." *Vital Speeches of the Day*, February 15, 1996, p. 283.

8. The following sources expand on our discussion of audience analysis: Bruce Gronbeck, Douglas Ehninger, and Alan Monroe. *Principles of Speech Communication*, 12th ed. New York: HarperCollins, 1995; and Steven R. Brydon and Michael D. Scott. *Between One and Many*. Mountain View, CA: Mayfield, 1994.

9. D. T. Max. "The Making of the Speech: The 2988 Words That Changed a Presidency: An Etymology." *New York Times Magazine*, October 7, 2001, p. 36.

10. Robert Orben. "Speech Writing for Presidents." Presentation delivered to the Speech Communication Association in Washington, DC, April 1983.

11. W. McGuire. "Attitudes and Attitude Change." In G. Lindsley and E. Aronson, eds. *The Handbook of Social Psychology*, Vol. 2. New York: Random House, 1985, pp. 287–288.

12. Thomas M. Scheidel. "Sex and Persuasability." *Speech Monographs* 30, 1963, pp. 353–368.

13. W. A. Henry. "Beyond the Melting Pot." *Time*, April 9, 1990, p. 29.

14. See Lawrence R. Wheeless. "The Effects of Attitude Credibility and Homophily on Selective Exposure to Information." *Speech Monographs* 41, 1974, pp. 329–338.

15. For a look at the topics recently treated in public speeches by the leaders of the largest corporations in the United States, see 1999–2001 issues of *Vital Speeches of the Day*.

16. Thomas Leech. *How to Prepare, Stage and Deliver Winning Presentations*. New York: Amacom, 1982, p. 11.

17. For a step-by-step explanation of how to establish your purpose, see Leon Fletcher. *How to Design and Deliver a Speech*, 5th ed. New York: HarperCollins, 1995.

18. See Avril Johnson. "Air Guns: Weapons or Toys?" *Winning Orations*, 1993, pp. 87–89.

19. For additional information on Internet resources, see Carol Clark Powell. *A Student's Guide to the Internet*, 2nd ed. Upper Saddle River, NJ: Prentice Hall, 1998; and Randy Reddick and Elliot King. *The Online Student*. Fort Worth, TX: Harcourt Brace, 1996.

20. Jennifer Ludden. "Chinese Daycare." WBUR, Boston. Internet (www.npr.org), 2000.

Developing Your Speech: Supporting Your Ideas

After finishing this chapter, you should be able to

1. Identify and use the various online and offline research resources available to you.

2. Conduct an informal survey and a personal interview.

3. Identify various types of supporting material, including

definitions, statistics, examples, illustrations, and testimonials.

4. Use comparison and contrast, repetition and restatement.

5. Explain how visual and audio aids can enhance a presentation.

Research is the process of going up alleys to see if they are blind.

—**Marston Bates**

The world is already full of speakers who are too busy to prepare their speeches properly; the world would be better off if they were also too busy to give them.

—**William Norwood Brigance**

Basic research is what I am doing when I don't know what I am doing.

—**Wernher von Braun**

Now that you have considered your choice of subject from both your point of view and the point of view of your audience, and you have taken the nature of the speech-making occasion into account, it is time for you to focus on researching and developing support for your speech topic. In fact, your first step in the topic development stage of speech preparation is to gather material, such as illustrations, statistical evidence, expert opinions, and quotations, to integrate into your speech. How do you do this?

If you're like many people in America today, you are likely fascinated with crime scene investigation (CSI) television programs and films that demonstrate the painstaking effort that goes into solving crimes. Like forensic pathologists, whose task it is to take nothing for granted and to leave no stone unturned in the search for clues and the analysis of evidence, so the public speaker also needs to investigate a topic very carefully in an effort to discover appropriate supporting material with which to build the substance of a speech.

THE RESEARCH PROCESS: FINDING SUPPORTING MATERIAL

Go to the *Online Learning Center* at www.mhhe.com/gamble8 and answer the questions in the *Self Inventory* to evaluate your understanding of investigation.

If your speech is to be worthwhile and effective for both you and your receivers, you need to research it. Thus, during the process of preparing a speech, one of your chief tasks is the gathering of information. Potential sources available to you include published works, other people, and, of course, yourself. For example if you are planning to speak on the topic of hazing, you may share experiences you had in pledging a sorority or fraternity, or as a junior member of a sports team. Most of the time, you will have some personal knowledge of your topic. If you are discussing some aspect of sports medicine, for instance, you may rely on your experience of being injured in football, baseball, track, tennis, or swimming. If your topic has to do with business or technology, you may use examples from your work in an industry that relates directly to the topic. Far too often, speakers fail to realize that their personal experiences can be used to establish credibility and add interesting and pertinent examples.

Conducting Online and Offline Research

Suppose you were going to speak on the role of spin in our society, and you wanted to focus on how both government supporters and dissenters used spin during the waging of the Iraqi war. Where would you go for information? What sources would you turn to in order to learn what spin is, how it functions, why it is used, what its effects are, and whether it is ethical and/or legal and to find examples of spin in action? For example, both adherents of the Iraqi war effort and those opposed to the war effort spun their stories of the rescue of Private Jessica Lynch in the waning days of the Iraqi war. Would this serve as a good example to use in your speech? Through conducting research, you become able to answer such questions.

Libraries contain information storage and retrieval systems—resources that are invaluable for every type of research. Whatever your topic, the odds are that a library has relevant information. The library is one of the few real bargains left in our society. A huge array of material is available free; other materials and services (those available through a variety of photographic and electronic systems) are yours for only a minimal cost. In addition, every academic and public library has on its staff knowledgeable people who have been trained to aid you with your investigative work. In addition to your college library, you can also consult the following Internet libraries: the Internet Public Library (www.ipl.org), the Library Spot (www.libraryspot.com), and the Reference Desk (www.refdesk.com).

When you begin library research, you will need to consult several reference sources—sources you may have already encountered during your educational career. Your goal during this phase of research is to compile a preliminary bibliography. Thus, your first stop may well be the library's electronic catalog. Next, you will move on to a variety of newspaper, magazine, and journal indexes. Depending on your subject, you may also consult bibliographical sources, encyclopedias, and almanacs. And you will almost certainly encounter forms of computer-assisted searches.

Using the Library's Online Catalogs

In lieu of the card catalog system, now banished from most libraries, today's libraries usually contain a computerized catalog. Libraries, in increasing numbers, now offer computer or online catalogs that enable you to run more productive Boolean searches. When you run a **Boolean search,** instead of needing to know a specific author or title, you can merely enter two or three key words into the computer and it will search the library's collection for you. No longer do you need to go from card catalog drawer to card catalog drawer, searching for source materials. The computer has made the search process much more efficient.

Boolean search
a key word search

Using Reference Works

Since magazines, newspapers, and scholarly periodicals may contain information valuable to you, indexes are critical resources. One of the first indexes you will consult will probably be the *Reader's Guide to Periodical Literature.* It can lead you to a variety of popular and mass-distribution magazines, including *Time, Newsweek,* and *U.S. News & World Report,* all of which may contain information relevant to your subject. The *New York Times Index* and the *Wall Street Journal Index* are also high on the list of indexes you should consider. If your topic warrants it, you may also need to explore issues of *Education Index, Psychological Abstracts,* and *Sociological Abstracts.* These sources will offer you leads to articles that have appeared in a number of scholarly journals.

The *World Almanac, Statistical Abstract of the United States,* and *Information Please Almanac* are only three of many such reference works that can provide the speech maker with interesting factual and statistical evidence. Multivolume encyclopedias, such as the *Britannica* and the *Americana,* and one-volume versions, such as the *Random House Encyclopedia* and the *Columbia Encyclopedia,* may also be consulted. Specialized encyclopedias, such as the *McGraw-Hill Encyclopedia of Science and Technology,* may be useful for technologically oriented topics.

Biographical materials can be located in the *Dictionary of National Biography,* the *Dictionary of American Biography,* and even the *New York Times Obituary Index.* Similarly, *Current Biography* can help you research the lives of contemporary public figures.

Computer-Aided and Online Searches

Were it not for online catalogs, libraries would find it difficult, if not impossible, to process all the materials that need to be cataloged. Nor would it be as convenient to research catalogs from a wide array of libraries. The library research you conduct today can be done electronically rather than manually as in years past. What is required is that you master the proper commands that enable you to conduct an online subject search or author and title search so that you will be able to locate the information you are seeking.

A variety of reference tools, such as the *Reader's Guide to Periodical Literature* and *Facts on File,* and a number of encyclopedias are now available online. *Magazine Index* (a database that indexes hundreds of American and Canadian magazines) and *InfoTrac* (a resource covering general publications and government documents) are available on laser disk. See Figure 15.1 for

---

Skill
BUILDER

CSI: It's Your Turn

1. Working individually within groups, choose one well-known criminal case to investigate. Possibilities for investigation include the Jeffrey Dahmer, Scott Peterson, Mumia Abu-Jamal, Oklahoma City bombing, and JonBenet Ramsey cases.

2. Using the resources available in the local or college library, compile a bibliography of relevant materials.

3. Rank the entries in your bibliography: 1 (what seems to be the most useful source), 2 (the next most promising source), and so on.

4. Compare your list with the lists developed by the other members of your group. Discuss the number of sources cited by each individual in your group, the most unusual material located, and the decisions you made in ranking your references.

FIGURE 15.1
Sample Google Search.

Reprinted with permission from Google.com.

a sample search using Google, an online database. *Business Index,* another computerized resource, indexes the *New York Times* financial section and the *Wall Street Journal.*

There are also more sophisticated databases that you can consult via computer. Among them are *ERIC,* a comprehensive research system that indexes published and unpublished materials on a wide array of educational topics, and *ASI (American Statistics Index).* While you do not need extensive computer knowledge to conduct most online research, when you consult more complex databases, you may want to seek help from a research librarian. Since many of these searches require the payment of a fee, you'll want to be certain of your topic and of the specific information you need before using them.

You can also use the Internet as a well-equipped international library of information resources.[1] Among the major Internet resources you'll want to use when researching a speech are e-mail, newsgroups, and the World Wide Web.

E-Mail   You can use e-mail to write to knowledgeable potential sources, a group, or a **listserv,** an e-mail list of several to over hundreds of people who have interest in and knowledge of a particular topic—potentially one that you are researching. Go to www.liszt.com, a directory containing information about numerous listservs and whether new members are welcomed, to explore potentially useful listservs. Before joining a listserv, try to identify the types of messages members send and their usefulness to you. Also read the frequently asked questions (FAQ) file so that you don't ask questions that have already been answered.

Using e-mail, you can also create a listserv for your class. Once you have one in place, you can use it to ask your potential audience members to fill

listserv

an e-mail list of people who have interest in and knowledge of a particular topic

Almost any kind of content is available on the World Wide Web.

Which search engine is your personal favorite? Why?

out questionnaires that reveal their attitudes toward your chosen topic. You can also use the class listserv to seek and receive feedback after your speech.

Newsgroups Newsgroups facilitate the exchange of ideas on a broad array of topics through discussion forums. The Internet contains a multitude of newsgroups, also known as usenet. In a newsgroup, you can post messages, read the posts of others, and respond to them. Like listservs, newsgroups bring together people interested in sharing ideas about a topic. As with a listserv, before joining a newsgroup, be sure you read through the FAQ file; doing so will ensure you receive maximum benefits from the newsgroup.

You can use a search engine such as "Defa News" to search newsgroups for information on requested topics. Newsgroups that receive news feeds from news services such as the Associated Press are especially useful. You can also use the newsgroup to ask questions and poll people for opinions for a speech.

World Wide Web Almost any kind of content you can find in print is also available on the World Wide Web. The World Wide Web links all the individual Web sites and contains a vast collection of written, graphic, audio, and video documents. Just as a library offers you books, periodicals, news, and so forth, so does the Web. You can subscribe to various special interest groups or use a search engine to browse for information on your selected topic. A search engine is a program that makes it possible for you to search a database or index of Internet sites for information on topics of interest to you. Popular Internet browsers, such as "Netscape" and "Internet Explorer," include search functions as a part of other home pages, thereby providing ready links to popular search engines and directories. While browsing, you might visit CNN or the Associated Press online, peruse copies of historical documents or the *Congressional Record*. With the Internet, you have easy access to the information that exists on numerous campuses and every continent.[2]

A directory such as "Magellan" (http://www.mckinley.com) contains a list of subjects or categories of Web links. It operates much as a search engine does. Among search engines are "Google" (www.google.com), the most popular search engine with a 46.5 user share; "Yahoo!" (http://www.yahoo.com), the next most popular with a 20.6 percent user share; MSN Search (http://www.msn.com) with a 7.8 percent share; Alta Vista (http://www. altavista. digital.com) with a 6.4 percent share; and Terra Lycos (http://www. terralycos.com) with a 4.6 percent share.[3] These, together with Excite (http://www.excite.com), Infoseek (http://www.infoseek.com), and "HotBot" (http://www.hotbot.com), are search engines as well as directories. Newcomers in the search engine arena include Alltheweb (www.alltheweb.com), Teoma (www.teoma.com), and Wisenut (www.wisenut.com).

It is becoming easier to predict the Web site addresses of potential sources. When you know an address, or a uniform resource locator (URL), you are able

Ask Jeeves

One way to research a potential topic is to access www.askjeeves.com and ask a question about your topic. Based on the question you ask, you will receive a series of sources and Web sites to check out. In your opinion, is it ethical to have "jeeves" do your legwork? If "jeeves" locates sources, what is left for you to do? The answer is to separate the "wheat" from the "chaff"—that is, the useful and relevant from the useless and irrelevant. As you evaluate each potential source, answer the following questions:

1. Who wrote the material? Is the author a qualified and reliable source?

2. Who is the site's sponsor? To what sites, if any, is this site linked? What is the connection between the site and the links? What clues does the Internet address of the site provide? Is it, for example, a military site, a college or university, a business or commercial enterprise, a government agency, or someone's personal page?

3. How recent is the Web page? How often is information on it updated?

4. Why is the site on the Web? Is its primary purpose to provide information or to sell something?

to access the Web site by simply entering it in your Web browser. Corporate Web sites, for example, usually accessed by www.nameofcorporation.com, will provide you with access to annual reports, copies of speeches, and other information. You can also save your favorite sites as bookmarks, a Web browser feature that allows you to save your favorite links in a file to facilitate future access.

While the information contained in traditional research sources, including books, magazines, and journal articles, is typically reviewed and checked by others before being published, virtually anyone can post information in a Web site or to a newsgroup. Thus, verifying and thinking critically about the quality of the information you find online is a serious responsibility. As you decide what and what not to include in your speech from your Web search, ask yourself who a site's sponsor is. For example, CNN, MSNBC, and Fox are established news organizations, and you can weigh the information you find on their sites in the same way as you would weigh the information you use from their cablecasts. The same goes for major newspapers that also operate Web sites. As you evaluate Web-based information from other sources, it is important to determine if the source has an apparent or hidden bias. Ask yourself if postings are specific or general. Do the claims they make seem justifiable? Don't value a source simply because it is published on the Internet. Seek out confirming sources for what you discover.

Conducting Primary Research

You may also want to use primary information to support or flesh out your presentation. Three primary research techniques are (1) personal observation and experience, (2) informal surveys, and (3) interviews.

Personal Observation and Experience

One of the best ways to research a topic is to examine what you know about it. Search your own background and experiences for materials you might want to integrate into your presentation.

Informal surveys and formal interviews provide a speaker with statistical information, testimonials, and examples to use in his or her speech.

If your topic is one for which direct observation of an event, a person, or a stimulus would be appropriate, then by all means go out and observe. An observational excursion might take you to a biology laboratory, an airport, a supermarket, or a construction site, for example. Direct observation can provide you with a better understanding of your topic and enable you to incorporate new personal experiences into your presentation in the form of examples, illustrations, or quotations. When conducting a direct observation, be sure to take careful notes. If possible, arrive at the location with tape recorder or video recorder in hand. Sit down immediately after the experience and record your thoughts and feelings. File your firsthand notes with the materials gathered during your library research.

Informal Surveys

Developing a reliable scientific survey instrument is complicated. However, informal surveys can be used to provide the speech maker with useful and often entertaining information. For example, if you are investigating the possibility of adding online courses to the curriculum, a survey at your school may produce data you can use. (For instance, you may be able to discover the percentage of students interested in enrolling in such courses.)

Informal surveys normally consist of no more than 5 to 10 questions. To conduct an informal survey with a prospect, you need to identify yourself first and state the purpose of your survey: "Hello, I'm _____. I'm investigating the feasibility of incorporating online courses into the regular curriculum of the college." The survey can be conducted either orally, in writing, or over the Internet. A sample of 25 to 50 people and some simple mathematical calculations should provide adequate statistical information to integrate into your presentation. When you conduct an informal survey, you may gain more than expected. While running the survey or examining the results, you may find interesting off-the-cuff remarks to incorporate in your speech.

Interviews

An interview is similar to a survey except that it is usually more detailed and assumes that the person being interviewed is in some way an expert on the topic under consideration. On your campus, in your community, or in an online usenet discussion group, you will probably find knowledgeable people to interview about current issues and many other topics. Political, business, and religious leaders, for instance, can often be persuaded to talk to student speakers. And, of course, faculty members of a college are often eager to cooperate.

Be sure to record accurately the information gathered during an interview. Take careful notes and repeat or verify any direct quotations you intend to use in your presentation. Also be certain during the speech to credit the interviewee as your source, unless he or she has asked not to be mentioned by name.

A Note on Recording Information

It is important to organize the information you collect so that it is easily retrievable and usable. You should buy a pack of 5- by 7-inch note cards to record the information you gather. You might record the source of your data at the top of the card and write below it a direct quotation or summary of the information gathered. This procedure can be used for material derived from print, nonprint, survey, and interview sources. Also, since it's impossible to "make appointments" with ideas, you should plan to record any of your own thoughts in the same way. For instance, an idea about a possible format for your speech may occur to you. If so, write it down. Don't rely on your memory.

INTEGRATING YOUR RESEARCH: TYPES OF SUPPORTING MATERIAL

Taken together, your research and your experiences should yield a wealth of information to integrate into your presentation. But making your research and experiences come to life for an audience is not an easy task; in fact, it is a key challenge facing the speech maker. Following are some major ways to make research and experience understandable and believable for an audience.[4]

Definitions

Definitions explain what a stimulus is or what a word or concept means. It is especially important to use definitions when your listeners are unfamiliar with terms you are using or when their associations for words or concepts might differ from yours. Only if you explain how you are defining a term can you hope to share your meanings with your listeners. Thus, the purpose of a definition is to increase the audience's understanding.

For example, in a famous speech, "On Woman's Right to Suffrage," Susan B. Anthony took pains to define what she believed was meant by "we, the people": "It was we, the people, not we, the white male citizens; nor yet we the male citizens; but we, the whole people who formed the union."

In a speech he gave in 1999, Robert L. Dilenschneider defined *spin* as "mankind's attempt to put its best foot forward."[5] Do you think today's receivers would find his definition acceptable? In a speech on hazing, a student used the following definition of the behavior: "any humiliating or dangerous activity expected of you to join a group, regardless of your willingness to participate." The student then went on to flesh out the definition with specifics: ". . . Hazing activities include eating excrement, receiving physical beatings, coerced consumption of alcohol, using illegal drugs, vandalizing property, stealing, and even sexual attacks like rape."[6]

Statistics

Statistics are simply facts expressed in numerical form. They may be cited to explain relationships or to indicate trends. To be used effectively as support, statistics must be honest and credible. If used appropriately, they can make the ideas you are presenting memorable and significant.

definitions
the explanation of what a stimulus is or what a word or concept means

Choose a word for which people have different associations—for example, an abstract concept like honesty, jealousy, freedom, justice, or love. Write your own definition and share it with the class.

For an example of a vivid image, view clip 13 on the CD

statistics
facts expressed in numerical form

For an example of statistics, view clip 10 on the CD

For example, in a speech on the danger of tattoos, student Chandra Palubiak of Berry College used a series of statistics to make the point that "adding a little artwork" to one's epidermis can be dangerous to one's health: "The *Milwaukee Journal Sentinel* from April 6, 2001 says getting a tattoo could cause Hepatitis C, the most widespread chronic viral illness touching almost 2 percent of the United States population. Two percent doesn't seem that significant until you realize that it is nearly 4,500,000 people in the U.S. . . . 33 percent of those with tattoos contract Hepatitis C, which is nearly one in every three people."[7]

In a speech on why the World Trade Center must be rebuilt, the *New Yorker*'s Jonathan Hakala also relied on statistics to demonstrate the number of people who would be willing to work on the highest floors of the rebuilt edifaces: CBS News and the *New York Times* recently conducted a poll of more than 1,000 people and asked them, "Would you be willing to work on one of the higher floors of a new building at the World Trade Center site? Almost two of every five people said yes, we are indeed willing to work on the higher floors . . . . The Census Bureau says New York City has a labor force of more than 4.2 million people . . . . More than 1.6 million people are willing to work on the higher floors . . . . If you take the entire New York metropolitan area, more than 3 million would be willing to work on the higher floors. And that's enough people to fill the top half of more than 200 new towers."[8]

Examples and Illustrations

examples

representative cases

Illustrations

stories, narrative pictures

For an example of an example, view clip 12 on the CD

Examples are representative cases; as such, they specify particular instances.[9] **Illustrations,** on the other hand, tell stories and thus create more detailed narrative pictures. Both examples and illustrations may be factual or hypothetical.

Solomon D. Trujillo, chairman, president, and CEO of US West, Inc., used a series of examples to demonstrate for audience members that one idea can make a difference:

> We've seen how the idea that all people are created equal can find expression in an African-American woman on a bus in Alabama, or [in] a student on a

Ethics & COMMUNICATION

Hypothetical Examples and Illustrations

Speakers use both factual and hypothetical examples and illustrations to involve audience members in a presentation. Examples and illustrations help make a speaker's material specific, personal, and compelling. During the 2000 presidential election, both candidates were criticized for embellishing their successes via the anecdotes and examples they used in their public presentations. Some contend that candidates make a habit of exaggerating as they try desperately to connect with their receivers. For example, in one anecdote that then presidential candidate Al Gore told, he noted that the arthritis medicine his mother took cost three times as much as the animal version of the same medicine taken by his dog, Shiloh. According to the *Boston Globe,* however, Mr. Gore's information didn't come from his family's drug bills but, rather, from figures contained in a congressional report.

Must speakers let audience members know when they are using hypothetical examples or illustrations? Do speakers have an obligation to let listeners know when material is not factual but merely possible? As an audience member, would you feel betrayed if a speaker used an example to add human interest and you discovered later that the example was not real?

soda-fountain stool in North Carolina, or even in a young Hispanic business-man in Cheyenne, Wyoming.

A few weeks back, I was at the University of Colorado talking to a group of business students, and I told them that I would not be in the job I have were it not for Affirmative Action.

When I joined the old Bell system, AT&T had just entered into a consent decree with the government. Before I joined the company, people like me . . . for some reason . . . weren't likely to get hired. Those who were hired . . . for some reason . . . weren't in management jobs.

But people with courage and foresight knew that our nation's promise of freedom and justice for all was an empty one if you had the wrong color of skin, if you were female, if you spoke with an accent, or if your last name ended in a "z" or a vowel.[10]

University of South Dakota student Tony Martinet used a series of brief examples to add impact to a speech on the extent of incivility by parents of children participating in organized sports games:

> A book entitled *The Dark Side of Youth Sports* by sports psychologist Shane Murphy offers three examples of emotional abuse that almost everyone has witnessed:
>
> - A mortified child whose mother is screaming at the referee about a "blown call"
> - The embarrassed child whose dad is yelling at the coach about "getting my kid into the game"
> - The despondent child who is being verbally attacked by their parent or coach for a perceived lack of effort or for making a "dumb" mistake.[11]

Similarly, student Rebekah Olson of Alderson-Broddus College used the following example of the tragic slaying of homosexual student Matthew Shepard in her speech entitled "Cherish Diversity":

> The world has heard about Matthew Shepard, a young college student who was brutally murdered because of his homosexuality. Brutally beaten by two high school dropouts and left for dead overnight, he was found eighteen hours after the vicious attack by two bicyclists who believed him to be a scarecrow.
>
> Many of you who are familiar with Matthew Shepard's murder case might think the hate ends there. Unfortunately, the hate only begins with Shepard's murder. While Shepard lay dying in a Colorado hospital, a college homecoming parade that passed near the hospital included a scarecrow proclaiming "I'm gay" in bold letters. Anti-gay picketers turned out for Shepard's funeral. They held posters saying, "Matt's in Hell," "No Tears for Queens," and "AIDS Cures FAGS."[12]

Testimony

Whenever you cite someone else's opinions or conclusions, you are using **testimony,** or a testimonial. Testimony gives you an opportunity to connect the ideas in your speech with the thoughts and attitudes of respected and competent people. The testimony you include in a presentation need not be derived exclusively from present-day sources; words of people from the past may also be used to tie today and yesterday together. When using testimonials, be sure to consider whether the people you cite as authorities are credible sources, whether their ideas are understandable, and whether their comments are relevant to your purpose.

testimony
someone else's opinions or conclusions

University of Northern Iowa student Sara Gronstal used the following examples of testimony to enhance her credibility when speaking of the dangers of *Stachybotrys charatarum,* a.k.a toxic or killer mold:

> Toxicologist Richard Linsey reports that mold is hard to find because it's hidden inside walls and isn't detectable in air sample tests until the concentration is terribly high. "Stachy is tricky," he says. "It's not what's on the surface that hurts you, it's what's below that hurts you." Dr. James Craner told the *Today Show* that "very often, mold is not visible in the occupied space, and nevertheless, the mold spore can go from behind a wall or above a ceiling and get into the occupied area where people are exposed to those spores."[13]

Similarly, in a speech on the implication of The Patriot Act, Newman University student Stacy Champagne used an unusual mixture of testimony sources to make a point about the act's dangers:

> The . . . *Baltimore Sun* points out, "Anti-terrorism legislation passed by the House as the 'Patriot Act' and in the Senate as the 'Uniting and Strengthening Act' implying that opponents to the legislation are unpatriotic or opposed to uniting America." Chilling! Perhaps Hitler's second in command, Hermann Goering explained it best in the Nuremberg Trials when he said, "The people can always be brought to do the bidding of the leaders. That is easy. All you have to do is tell them they are being attacked, and denounce the pacifist for lack of patriotism and exposing the country to danger."[14]

As we see, testimony reinforces a speaker's claims. It may be quoted directly, as in the preceding example, or it may be paraphrased, as illustrated by Theresa McGuiness in her speech advocating that fraternities be abolished:

> Bernice Sandler, executive director of the Project on the Status and Education of Women at the Association of American Colleges, said that 90 percent of the gang rapes reported to her office involved fraternity members. According to Sandler, fraternity members have a word for gang rape: they call it "pulling train." She adds that charts of how many beers it took to seduce sorority women are common in fraternity houses. And if a woman actually does press charges against a fraternity, Sandler says, "Their excuse is, 'she asked for it'— even if she was unconscious."[15]

Use direct quotations when you believe that the language and the length of an expert's remarks are appropriate for your audience. Use a paraphrase when you need to summarize an expert's opinion in fewer words, or when you need to simplify its language.

EXPLORING

Diversity

Experts and Cultural Groups

If the testimony of others influences us in making decisions and assessing situations, then an audience's judgments about a public speaker—and about his or her speech—ought to be influenced by people the speaker quotes or refers to, who presumably have special knowledge or experience relevant to the topic.

Does it matter whether a speaker uses experts from the same cultural group as the audience, or would experts from other cultural groups serve just as well in adding strength and impact to the speaker's ideas? Explain your position.

Comparisons and Contrasts

Comparisons stress similarities between two entities; contrasts stress differences. Both are employed by speakers to help audiences understand something that is unknown, unfamiliar, or unclear.

William L. Laurence combined comparison and contrast when he described the atomic bombing of Nagasaki:

> As the first mushroom floated off into the blue, it changed its shape into a flower-like form, its grand petals curving downward, creamy white outside, rose-colored inside. . . . Much living substance had gone into those rainbows. The quivering top of the pillar was protruding to a great height through the white clouds, giving the appearance of a monstrous prehistoric creature with a ruff around its neck, a fleecy ruff extending in all directions, as far as the eye could see.

Kelly Sonderup of Hastings College used comparison and contrast to point out the insidious danger of soft plastic or phthalates:

> Recently, city health officials ordered the Kennedy Center to remove asbestos from its Opera House. Asbestos, once a friend because of its amazing heat resistance, is now a well-known foe because exposure can cause cancer. Similarly, a new friend turned foe is on our doorstep. Phthalates, a softening agent in plastic, is now feeling the heat. But, unlike asbestos, no one really knows how harmful phthalates can be.[16]

U.S. President George W. Bush used comparison and contrast when referring to the space shuttle tragedy which occurred in 2003; he said, "The crew of the shuttle Columbia did not return safely to earth; yet we can pray that all are safely home."[17]

Repetition and Restatement

When a speaker uses repetition, the same words are repeated verbatim. When a speaker uses restatement, an idea is presented again, but in different words. If used sparingly, these devices can add impact to a speech maker's remarks and thereby increase memorability.[18]

One of the most famous examples of successful use of repetition is the speech delivered by Martin Luther King, Jr., in 1963 at the Lincoln Memorial:

> I say to you today, my friends, so even though we face the difficulties of today and tomorrow, I still have a dream. It is a dream deeply rooted in the American dream. I have a dream that one day this nation will rise up . . . live out the true meaning of its creed—we hold these truths to be self-evident, that all men are created equal. . . .
>
> I have a dream that my four little children will one day live in a nation where they will not be judged by the color of their skin but by the content of their character. I have a dream today. . . .
>
> I have a dream that one day every valley shall be exalted, and every hill and mountain shall be made low, the rough places shall be made plain, and the crooked places shall be made straight and the glory of the Lord will be revealed and all flesh shall see it together.[18a]

For an example of an analogy, view clip 11 on the CD

Earnie Deavenport, retired chairman and chief executive officer of the Eastman Chemical Company, used repetition and restatement to emphasize the need for new role models for youth:

> They need more Madame Curie and less Marilyn Manson. They need more of Elijah McCoy and less of Eminen. They need more of George Washington Carver and less of Bad Boy Bobby Brown.[19]

Hillary Rodham Clinton, senator from New York and former first lady of the United States, used repetition and reinforcement when she spoke of the first women's rights convention and the importance of telling, retelling, learning, and relearning women's stories:

> Every time we vote, let us thank the women and men of Seneca Falls, Susan B. Anthony and all the others, who tirelessly crossed our nation and withstood ridicule and the rest to bring about the Nineteenth Amendment to the constitution.
>
> Every time we enter an occupation—a profession of our own choosing—and receive a paycheck that reflects earnings equal to a male colleague, let us thank the signers and women like Kate Mullaney, whose house I visited yesterday, in Troy, New York.
>
> Every time we elect a woman to office—let us thank groundbreaking leaders like Jeannette Rankin and Margaret Chase Smith, Patti Caraway, Louise Slaughter, Bella Abzug, Shirley Chisholm—all of whom proved that a woman's place is truly in the House, and in the Senate, and one day, in the White House, as well.
>
> And every time we take another step forward for justice in the nation—let us thank extraordinary women like Harriet Tubman, whose home in Auburn I visited yesterday, and who herself escaped from slavery, and then risked her life, time and again, to bring at least two hundred other slaves to freedom as well.[20]

ILLUSTRATING YOUR RESEARCH: PRESENTATION AIDS

The first question to ask yourself about audio and visual aids is. Do I need them? Many speakers make the mistake of not using such aids when the content really demands them. Other speakers use too many audio and visual aids; they clutter the content so much that the presentation becomes confusing and loses momentum. Of late, visual aids have become a weapon of choice of speakers in the public arena. In fact, when he laid out the U.S. case before the UN for going to war against Iraq, Secretary of State Colin L. Powell used a series of evidentiary visual aids, including satellite photographs, to build his case.[21]

In this section, we consider (1) how you can determine whether your presentation can be improved by audio and visual aids and (2) how you can select and prepare such aids when they are needed.

Why Use Presentation Aids?

Presentation aids have several functions. Ideally, they make it easier for the audience to follow, understand, respond to, and remember your speech. Thus, when deciding whether to use an audio or visual aid, begin by asking yourself if it will serve at least one of those purposes.

If your presentation contains highly technical information, the use of an appropriate aid may help reduce your listeners' confusion. If the presentation needs additional impact, using an audio or visual aid can help increase listeners' motivation. If you want to highlight an important point, an audio or visual aid can add emphasis. A three-dimensional model of the molecular structure of a virus, for instance, might evoke more interest than would words alone. The damage smoking does to a human lung can be depicted with visuals to capture the attention of smokers and nonsmokers alike. Audio and visual aids can also help an audience remember what you have said. A chart can dramatize statistical data, indicating, for instance, the number of infants who fall prey to sudden death syndrome each year or symbolizing a decline in real income. By providing your audience with an additional channel, audio and visual aids give needed reinforcement to key points and ideas.[22]

Visual aids reinforce a speaker's spoken message. A visual that is tangible can add drama to a presentation.

Selecting and creating materials to help accomplish your speech-making goals is not easy.[23] Once you decide to use audio or visual aids, there are a number of serious decisions to be made. Initially, you will need to identify precise points in your presentation when aids will be effective. One way to prepare yourself to make such judgments is to examine how producers of newscasts select audio and visual aids to complement the work of on-camera reporters. After all, in many ways you are the "producer" of your speech.

Another strategy is brainstorming. Examine the information you have and repeatedly ask yourself the following question: Which specific pieces of information could be improved with audio or visual aids? Keep a record of each idea that comes to mind, being sure to indicate how the audio or visual support would actually be used.

Once you have analyzed your needs for audio and visual reinforcement, it is time to reconsider the possibilities you have identified.

Visual Aids

One of the prime reasons for using visual aids is to increase audience comprehension and retention. Visuals reinforce and help communicate the speaker's spoken message, enabling receivers to understand what words alone cannot transmit.

Types of Visual Aids

Let's now examine a sampling of the types of visual aids at your disposal.

Objects and Models   In your brainstorming session, you may have decided that you would like to use an object to illustrate a certain concept. The object you choose can be the real thing—for example, a set of earphones, a food processor, or a computer.

However, using an actual object is often impractical: Objects like automobiles are obviously too large, and objects like microelectronic chips may be too small. In such cases, it may be necessary to use a model instead. A model

Ron D. Dittemore of NASA with a visual aid, sample of foam, which he said could not have caused sufficient damage to lead to the shuttle's loss.

pie, or circle, graph

a circle with the various percentages of the whole indicated by wedges; a means of showing percentage relationships

bar graph

a graph used to show the performance of one variable over time or to contrast various measures at a point in time

can be made of clay, papier-mâché, wood scraps, or other materials. If used creatively, inexpensive materials can serve your purpose very well. Your aim is simply to make a reasonable facsimile of the object—something that will enable you to share information more meaningfully.

In the accompanying photograph, a NASA spokesperson, Ron Dittemore, used an actual sample of foam when expressing doubts that its falling off the external fuel tank during the shuttle *Columbia*'s lift-off could have precipitated the destruction of the ship.[24] (In time, Mr. Dittemore was proven wrong.)

Objects and models make it easier for you to pull your audience into your speech. Since they are tangible, they can make your points more realistic, and they can add drama to your presentation.

Graphs You can use graphs to make an effective presentation even more successful. The most commonly used graphs are pie, or circle, graphs; bar graphs; line graphs; and pictographs.

A **pie, or circle, graph** is simply a circle with the various percentages of the whole indicated by wedges. By focusing on relationships, pie graphs show how items compare with each other and with the whole. Since the entire circle represents 100 percent, the pie graph is an effective way to show percentage relationships or proportions. In a speech on how to use the Web to find romance, for example, one student used a pie graph to provide a snapshot of persons in various age groups who are using online personal ads to look for love (see Figure 15.2).[25]

If your goal is to show the performance of one variable over time, a **bar graph** might be appropriate. A bar graph is used to compare quantities or magnitude. For example, in a speech on the dangers of nuclear proliferation, a student used the bar graph in Figure 15.3 to compare and contrast the size of nuclear weapons.[26] A bar graph can also be used to show the

FIGURE 15.2
A Pie Graph.
Who is using online personal ads to find romance?

Source: "Who Is Using Online Personal Ads?" from *Newsweek*, May 12, 2003, p. E20. Copyright © 2003 Newsweek, Inc. Reprinted by permission.

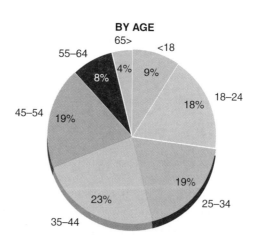

BY AGE

65> 4%
<18 9%
55–64 8%
18–24 18%
45–54 19%
25–34 19%
35–44 23%

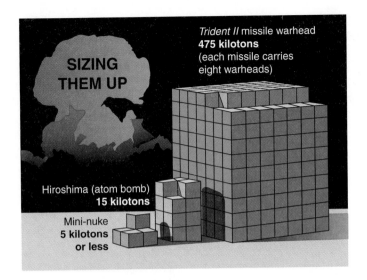

FIGURE 15.3
Creative Bar Graph.

Source: "Sizing Them Up" from
Time, May 26, 2003. Copyright
© 2003 Time, Inc. Reprinted by
permission.

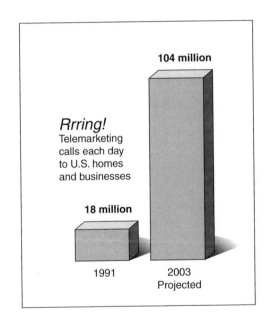

FIGURE 15.4
Bar Graph.

Source: "Rrring" from *Time,* April 28,
2003. Copyright © 2003 Time, Inc.
Reprinted by permission.

performance of one variable over time. For example, in a speech on the need to regulate telemarketers, a student used a bar graph to demonstrate the increasing prevalence and intrusiveness of telemarketers by contrasting the number of telemarketing calls made in 1991 with the number made in 2003 (see Figure 15.4).[27]

Like bar graphs, **line graphs** can illustrate trends, relationships, or comparisons over time. For example, in a speech describing how a virus such as SARS spreads today, a student used a line graph illustrating the quickness with which a virus can be spread around the world.[28] A line graph can show whether or not a perceptible trend is visible, as does the graph in Figure 15.5. The line graph is one of the easiest types for audiences to follow.

line graphs

graphs used to illustrate trends, relationships, or comparisons over time

pictographs

graphs that use sketches to represent concepts

Pictographs use sketches of figures to represent concepts (see Figure 15.6). During your research, you may discover sketches or pictures that could be integrated into a pictograph to help vitalize your content.

The general rule to follow in making and using graphs is that a single graph should be used to communicate only one concept or idea. Consider the line graph in Figure 15.7. This graph is far too cluttered for an audience to

FIGURE 15.5
Line Graph Depiciting a Trend.

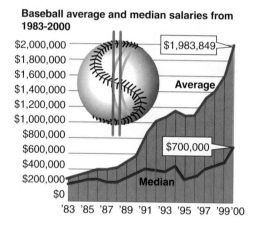

Source: USA TODAY research, Sam Ward, USA TODAY.

FIGURE 15.6
Pictograph.

Source: United Nations Population Fund. *The New York Times,* August 18, 1994. Copyright © 1994 by The New York Times Company. Reprinted by permission.

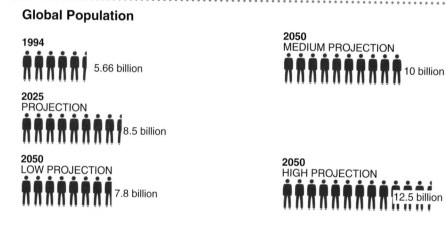

FIGURE 15.7
Poorly Designed Line Graph.

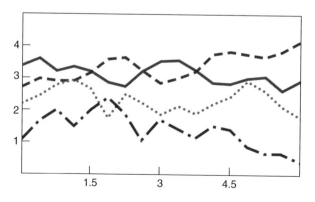

read easily and quickly. Your goal in devising a graph is to eliminate extraneous information and to focus, rather than diffuse, the audience's attention. Emphasize the essentials.

Photographs and Drawings You may find photographs or drawings that can add interest to your presentation and provide greater reality. For example, one student juxtaposed a photograph of deceased gymnast Chrisy Heinrich (taken from an article in a national weekly magazine) with one of her own sister to illustrate that anorexia nervosa is a disease afflicting both famous and ordinary people. Another used a photograph of the sheep named Dolly, the world's first reported clone of an adult mammal, to help illustrate a speech on the cloning process.

Drawings, like photographs, can help generate a mood, clarify, or identify. In explaining a sequence of plays that led to a success for his football team, one speaker used a drawing like the one in Figure 15.8. Would you recommend simplifying this sketch?

If possible, use a variety of dark, rich colors, such as red, black, blue, and green, to add contrast to a drawing. But remember, unless a drawing is large enough to be seen, it will not increase your audience's attention or strengthen your presentation.

Computer Graphics Advances in computer technology have made it possible for speech makers to use computer-generated visual aids. Most college speakers have traditionally used poster board and marking pens to enlarge charts and graphs so that they can be seen easily, but now computer graphics hardware and software are making it easier for students to develop professional-looking charts and graphs.

To prepare a computer graphic, begin by organizing your data. Next select the type of graphic you want—for example, pie chart, bar chart, or some other graphic. Many programs automatically generate legends for the visual.

For IBM systems, "Harvard Graphics" is one of the more sophisticated programs available. The program provides model charts and graphs; you input your own data and then make a printout. You can print on a transparency and

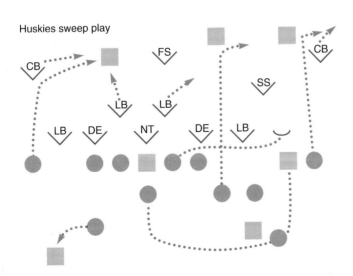

FIGURE 15.8
Drawing.

Huskies sweep play

The Proper Prop

Read this article by media relations practitioner Merrie Spaeth.

"Prop" Up Your Speaking Skills

When Moses came down from the mountain with clay tablets bearing the Ten Commandments, it was perhaps history's first example of a speaker using props to reinforce his message. It wouldn't have had the same impact if Moses had simply announced: "God just told me 10 things, and I'm going to relay them to you."

Props can be an invaluable tool in business presentations. They drive home the point in ways words alone cannot. A partner from a Big Six accounting firm showed clients an article criticizing executive compensation. "We're going to see more and more of this," he said, "and that's why it's important to look at how you executives stack up against industry standards." Seeing the article dramatized the topic's importance.

President Reagan loved to use letters as props. Once, at a briefing for editors of women's magazines, he was emphasizing that overregulation is a women's issue. He held up a letter from a small-business woman that described the burden of time and money that Occupational Safety and Health Administration rules imposed on her. It made his message credible and underscored his interest in women.

Pictures or illustrative objects make great props. A Texas banker was speaking to potential clients—treasurers of companies that were doing business in dozens of countries—about his bank's expertise in foreign exchange. He held up various foreign bills. Most of the treasurers recognized Dutch guilders, French francs and German marks, but were at a loss to identify currencies from places like Liberia and Turkmenistan. The bank, he made clear, had specialized knowledge that could help improve its clients' profits.

Props make a wonderful tool to introduce humor, especially if you aren't naturally funny. To point out how difficult it is for executives to juggle all their responsibilities, one CEO juggled three small beanbags. He got them going, looked up to acknowledge the applause—and lost his rhythm. As he grabbed for the beanbags, he said, "I said it was hard. Now, I proved it."

The new CEO of a large insurance company used props to make a vivid statement of his commitment to change. At his first speech to 250 top managers and agents, he eschewed traditional black-and-white overheads in favor of a variety of props—from a McDonald's bag to a large garbage can. He began by discussing how industries had changed. Holding up the McDonald's bag, he commented that the fast-food industry, which didn't exist until a few decades ago, had thrived because it met the needs of its customers. He talked about what new technology was going to mean for the agent on the street. He dragged the trash can to center stage and threw in a pile of receipts and bookkeeping forms. He got a standing ovation.

Even a seemingly outlandish prop can succeed in lightening a tough message. Three years later, that same CEO needed to get across the point that his agents weren't adapting quickly enough. He began by holding up a lobster. When the colonists arrived, he said, lobsters were plentiful: "No longer." The environment had changed, but lobsters hadn't. The audience leaned forward in their seats as he plopped the lobster into a pot of boiling water. Pacing up and down the stage, he explained how the business environment had changed—and periodically checked the pot. At the end of his speech, he hoisted aloft the now-cooked lobster, and said that companies and people who resist change are destined to become someone's lunch. "But we *will* change," he announced. Long pause: "Ladies and gentlemen, let's have lunch." All adjourned for lobster bisque.

The audience loved it. More important, the message that came through was a positive one: Change means opportunity. Speeches in which management must convey to employees that "you're not doing it right" or "you're not doing enough" are among the hardest to deliver successfully.

The message is intimidating unless the tone is just right. In this case levity made a tough speech into a morale builder.

The use of props isn't without its pitfalls. For one, a prop that doesn't really relate to what's being said only makes the speaker look foolish. One CEO, talking about lousy industry conditions, took a rubber chicken and threw it into the audience. Get it? Neither did the audience.

And if you don't rehearse, the best-conceived idea can go wrong. You don't want to be the executive whose letter gets stuck in his lapel pocket, or who pulls out a picture upside down, or who can't get the whip to crack. Executives don't practice enough, and we always hear the same excuse: "I don't have enough time."

But if you do make time for props, you'll likely find that they're an inexpensive and effective way of ensuring that the audience remembers your message.

Now, using the following general speech topics, identify props you might use to ensure the audience remembers your speech:

Cell phones and driving

Privacy and the Internet

Child beauty pageants

Product safety

Defibrillators

Finally, what lesson about props and speech making is contained in the following cartoon?

"Thank you, Barbara. Next, David Lombardo will give his presentation on the ancient city of Pompeii."

Source: From "'Prop' Up Your Speaking Skills" by Merrie Spaeth in *The Wall Street Journal,* July 1, 1996, p. A14. Copyright © 1996 Dow Jones & Co. Reprinted by permission of Dow Jones & Co. via Copyright Clearance Center.

FIGURE 15.9
*Computer-Generated
Graph.*

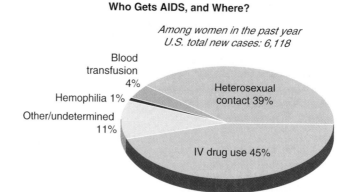

Who Gets AIDS, and Where?

*Among women in the past year
U.S. total new cases: 6,118*

Blood transfusion 4%

Hemophilia 1%

Other/undetermined 11%

Heterosexual contact 39%

IV drug use 45%

FIGURE 15.10
*Computer-Generated
Image.*

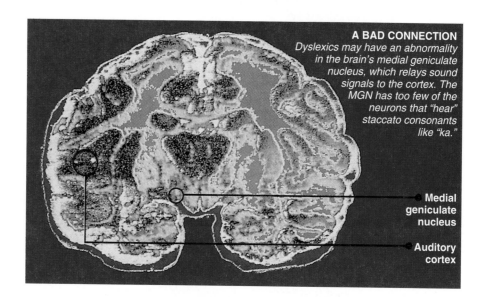

A BAD CONNECTION
*Dyslexics may have an abnormality
in the brain's medial geniculate
nucleus, which relays sound
signals to the cortex. The
MGN has too few of the
neurons that "hear"
staccato consonants
like "ka."*

**Medial
geniculate
nucleus**

**Auditory
cortex**

Source: Howard Sochurek-Medichrome-stock shop.

use the graphic with an overhead projector. The leading programs available for Macintosh users are "PowerPoint" (also available for IBM users) and "Persuasion." They work much as "Harvard Graphics" does and produce high-quality graphics. Figure 15.9 shows a sample of a computer-generated graph. "PowerPoint," "Persuasion," and "Harvard Graphics" can produce such graphs. Each of the systems takes some up-front time to learn. If you are computer-literate and learn quickly, you can probably experiment with graphics programs that your school has available. But be sure to have a backup plan with poster board and markers in case the computer program turns out to be too time-intensive. You can also use graphics generated by a professional, as one student did when delivering a speech on dyslexia (see Figure 15.10), and as another student did when explaining how the Ebola virus works (see Figure 15.11).[29]

Guidelines for Using Visual Aids

Speakers can justify the use of visual aids by showing how they contribute to audience understanding of the message.

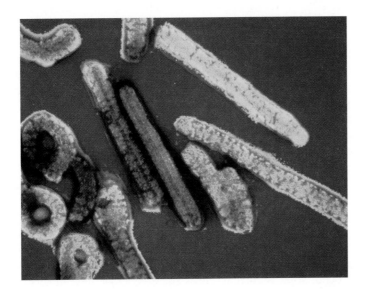

FIGURE 15.11
Speakers often Use Professional Graphics.
The Ebola virus at work.

Criteria When evaluating visuals, remember that they must be appropriate to the audience, the occasion, the location, and the content of your speech—and to you yourself.

In developing visual materials, keep three criteria in mind: (1) simplicity, (2) clarity, and (3) visibility. *Simplicity* means that the visuals should be as transportable as possible (so that you can easily take them with you to the presentation) and as easy as possible to use. Give careful consideration to the size and weight of large items. Ask yourself if a visual can be displayed without disrupting the environment. Ask yourself if it can be set up and taken down in a minimal amount of time. With regard to clarity, remember that the purpose of a visual aid is to enhance understanding, not to cause confusion. Ideally, each visual should depict only one idea or concept, or at least should be displayed so that only the relevant portions are visible at the appropriate point in your speech. Visibility is the third criterion. Since a visual aid obviously serves no purpose if it cannot be seen and read, you must determine if your audience will be able to see and read it. Make sure that the lettering is tall enough (3 by 4 inches high or larger) and that photographs or pictures are large enough.

Methods and Equipment One way to present flat visuals is to display them on a chart board or on oaktag. With variously colored markers, a yardstick, and a little time, you should be able to create appealing and functional visuals. If you are willing to invest a bit more time, energy, and money, use the press-on letters that are widely available in stationery stores to give your work a professional look. You may also use more sophisticated equipment to present visuals—overhead projectors, film, videotape, and 35-mm slides. Overhead projectors are often used by training professionals and salespeople. Transparencies can be created from almost any 8½- by 11-inch original of a photograph, an illustration, or a graph. Then the image can be projected onto a screen or a light-colored wall (if no screen is available). The room need not be completely darkened to use an overhead projector, but you should rehearse with transparencies to be sure they are clearly visible. (Setup time is about 10 minutes.)

Film clips can also be used to add life and motion to a presentation. For film, you need a screen or light-colored wall in a room that can be darkened. It will take about 15 minutes to prepare the room and equipment. Without adequate setup time, a film clip can become more of a hindrance than a help.

Slides are easier to use than film. However, unless you have been trained in multimedia or multi-image production, the number of slides you use should be kept to a minimum. (Also, be prepared to deal with jammed slide trays and burned-out bulbs.)

Videotape and DVD recorders have improved greatly in recent years and make it much easier for speakers to use videos and film clips. Video stores have many tapes or DVDs that can be used to arouse an audience's interest. One speaker used a clip of Abbott and Costello's "Who's on First?" routine to introduce the topic of language. A speaker on real estate used examples from a local real estate program on cable television. A company president regularly uses clips from the various *Rocky* films to motivate the sales force. The cable channel C-Span makes it convenient to incorporate current events into speeches. If your topic is current, check the C-Span listings—if C-Span is available in your area—to determine if and when the topic will be covered. Then, in addition to quoting a public official, you can actually have him or her as a video guest to briefly illustrate a point.

When using videotape, carefully edit the segment to 30 seconds or less and cue up the tape before you begin the speech. Far too many speakers press the "play" button only to find that they have no picture or sound on the monitor. One speaker had scarcely begun his presentation before he had to call a coffee break while repairs were done on the video equipment. Audiences today are simply not willing to sit while you and others tinker with electronic gadgetry. Prepare it carefully in advance, and rehearse.

Audio Aids

Audiotape is readily available and easy to use as an accompaniment to a speech. Cassette and CD players come in a variety of forms and sizes, many of which

What is this cartoon suggesting about the use of visuals?

Visuals should enhance a presentation.

are easily portable. Since speech makers often find it advantageous to integrate a brief excerpt from a song or a segment from an interview or a newscast into their presentations, audiotape has become a popular support medium. One student, for example, reinforced an informative presentation entitled "The Speech Capabilities of Dolphins" with a few moments of dolphin sounds that she had recorded during a visit to an aquarium. Another added impact to a speech called "Teenage Runaways" by using a segment of the Beatles' now classic song "She's Leaving Home."

If you decide to use audiotape, cue the tape to the precise point at which you want to begin. Do this before you arrive at the front of the room, so that finding the right spot on the tape will not bring your presentation to an untimely halt.

Computer-Assisted Presentations: PowerPoint

As we have noted, existing computer programs can help make visual aid production quicker and easier than ever before. In fact, of all the visual aids mentioned, computerized presentations are increasing the most in popularity.[30] You cannot only create various types of charts but also build effective online slide shows from your speech outline. You can also use a computer to display video clips, text, photographs, drawings, and charts. "PowerPoint," for example, contains a clip art library that enables you to select images that enhance the meaning of your words. It also allows you to generate backgrounds, formats, layouts, and colors that you believe best reflect the purpose of your presentation. The computer-generated visuals you create can be run directly from a computer projector, converted to 35-mm slides, printed out in handout form, or blown up for display to the audience. (See the sample computer-assisted slide presentation on the next page.)

When planning a "PowerPoint" presentation, you need to think in bullets (see sample slide presentation). Supporting your spoken speech, "PowerPoint" slides illustrate your talk. Pictures and charts, as well as animated graphics and talking points, are projected onto a screen, which both the speaker and receivers use.

Although computerized presentations are rapidly becoming the standard in business and education, you do need to be selective when deciding whether or not to create one. If not prepared with care or if allowed to upstage the speaker and overpower the message, computer presentations can drain a speech of its vitality.[31] Reflecting the growth in "PowerPoint" presentations, the current chairman of the Joint Chiefs of Staff issued the following order, although not in these exact words, to U.S. military bases around the globe: "Enough with the bells and whistles—just get to the point." One senior defense department official noted: "The chairman basically told everyone that we don't need Venetian-blind effects or fancy backdrops. All we need is the information."[32] To what extent do you agree or disagree with this advice? Whatever your position, the point is that a piece of technology that is supposed to facilitate communication should not be used in such a way that it becomes an obstacle to it.

One fear is that dazzling "PowerPoint" presentations can be used to cover up weak content.[33] Another is that the number of words and slides used will be out of control. In fact, one U.S. computer company has distributed guidelines

Sample Computer-Assisted Slide Presentation

Here is a speech that is supported by a computer slide program.

1.

2.

3.

4.

1. This slide introduces the topic to the audience. Speakers usually keep the title slide simple but provocative in order to draw receivers into the presentation. The speaker's task is to find a background for the slide that reflects the tone of the presentation. What do you think of the background provided here?

2. The second slide introduces the first main point of the speech. The speaker uses the slide to ask and answer a question, clarifying the subject for receivers. How did the speaker add credibility to the definition provided? In your opinion, should the speaker have done more to orient receivers visually to the topic prior to defining this key term?

3. This slide introduces the second main point of the speech by summarizing how tornadoes work. In your opinion, will this slide help sustain receiver interest? Why or why not?

5.

6.

7.

8.

4. This slide introduces the third point of the speech by revealing the warning signs of an approaching tornado.

5. In the fifth, sixth, and seventh slides, the speaker develops the fourth main point of the speech by describing how tornadoes are rated, explaining the size of the average tornado, and offering dramatic examples of tornado damage.

6. In the eighth and ninth slides, the speaker develops the fifth main point of the speech by summarizing where and when tornadoes are likely to occur and the kind of people who track them. In your opinion, are these slides too wordy? What should the speaker do to enhance receiver involvement in this phase of the speech?

9.

10.

11.
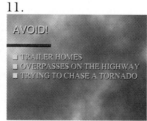

12.

7. The tenth and eleventh slides focus on the speaker's last main point—what receivers can do to protect themselves from tornadoes.

8. The final slide wraps up the speech by supporting the speaker's concluding words. It also provides a sense of closure by reflecting the very first slide the speaker used when beginning the presentation. In your opinion, did the speaker need to use a slide prior to this one, summarizing what the speech had accomplished? If so, what should that slide have contained?

9. Are there any other slides you think the speaker should have added to this presentation, or are there any that you felt the speaker could have done without?

to its employees about "PowerPoint" presentations that require them to adhere by the "Rule of Seven": seven bullets or lines per slide, seven words per line.[34] On the other hand, MIT psychology professor Steven Pinker notes that "PowerPoint" gives visual shape to an argument. Says Pinker, "Language is a linear medium: one damn word after another. But ideas are multidimensional . . . . When properly employed, PowerPoint makes the logical structure of an argument more transparent. Two channels sending the same information are better than one."[35]

TECHNOLOGY AND SPEECH RESEARCH: THE DANGERS OF INFORMATION OVERLOAD AND THE ETHICS OF VISUAL MANIPULATION

According to Sandy Sparks of Lawrence Livermore Laboratories, "We are, all of us, being drawn into the electronic world, and we can't stop it. It's like being given a car without anyone telling you how to drive it, and you don't have a road map. We're driving blind." Again, the point is that, if you don't know where you're going, you won't know when you actually get there. Yes, having access to the Internet can facilitate the speech research process, but such access also carries risks.

How much information is too much information? How do we avoid being overwhelmed with information or overwhelming others with information? What steps can we take to minimize the effects of information overload or "data smog"?[36]

The temptation the Internet creates to keep piling on more and more information is something we have to watch out for. According to David Shenk, author of *Data Smog: Surviving the Information Glut,* "With a majority of American workers now paid to churn out data, we have generated a morass of expert information that has started to undermine logical approaches

---

Can Too Many Experts Spoil the Clarity?

What do the experts think? Is nuclear power safe or unsafe? Does affirmative action work or not? Do vitamins prevent cancer? Using one of the preceding controversial issues or another of your choice, surf the Internet in search of studies and arguments on both sides of the question. Does your search lead you to agree or disagree with the *New York Times,* which noted that the "volleys of data" result in endless argumentation but no decision? Explain.

How can the public speaker solve such a dilemma?

e-SEARCH

Reflect and Respond

Agree or disagree with the following observation. Give reasons and examples that support your position.

According to Aristotle, "Of the three elements in speech making—speaker, subject, and person addressed—it is the last one, the hearer, that determines the speech's end and object."

To this observation, we can also add that it is the last one, the hearer, that also determines the supporting materials and visual and audio aids to be used.

Thinking
CRITICALLY

to deliberation and problem solving."[37] For example, more than 100,000 studies have been done on depression. What this produces is an overabundance of information and so many competing expert opinions that it becomes virtually impossible to draw a conclusion, which leads one to suffer the consequences of "paralysis by analysis."

When it comes to deception, computer graphics now make it possible for us to distort actual images. Unethical speakers can manipulate what receivers see by altering their visuals to conform to the point they are seeking to make. For example, because it was seeking an image of diversity in its recruitment literature, the University of Wisconsin at Madison admits to making an "error in judgement" when it doctored a photo on a brochure cover by inserting a Black student in a crowd of White football fans.[38] Because presenters now have the technological ability to doctor their visuals to make their points, the question that cries to be answered is the following: At what point does the touching up or retouching of a visual put you onto ethical thin ice? Just because a visual you have doctored works doesn't mean it is ethical to use that visual.

Ethics & COMMUNICATION

Diversity and the Visual

The following commentary on the retouching of a visual for a university's recruiting brochure appeared in *The Record*. Explain the extent to which you agree or disagree with the position taken by the article's author.

A University's Awkward Effort to Do Better

The University of Wisconsin found itself embroiled in controversy recently when graphic artists used computer technology to alter a photo in an attempt to make the school appear racially diverse.

The photo, used on the cover of the 2000 undergraduate application form, features a crowd of white football fans. An image of a black student was digitally inserted into that scene; creating the impression that he was also in the stands at that 1993 Badgers game.

Moral watchdogs took umbrage at this manipulation of history.

"They cheated!" shouted one newspaper headline this week. "A lie is a lie" clucked a Chicago Tribune *editorial. "Tsk, tsk," fumed one radio commentator, who wondered whether the university's research could be trusted and used the gaffe as yet another example of how society has lost its way.*

Spare me the hand-wringing. The university may be guilty of clumsiness, but moral bankruptcy? Not even close.

The flap made me realize how far we've come since I was a features editor at the Gary Post-Tribune *in the mid-1980s. Before my arrival, it was standard practice to replace the city wedding announcements with pictures of white couples for suburban zones because "people who live outside of Gary don't want to see black faces." All that color, management thought, might scare off white advertisers.*

I wonder whether those editors, stripping and sanitizing the paper because "it's good business," could have envisioned a world so dramatically changed that future editors would add minorities instead of hiding them?

To me, the inevitable backlash about academic integrity is much ado about nothing. Just as a newsroom has different standards than the advertising department, a university uses a different measure for a promotional brochure than for a medical journal. For starters, if this controversy were really about journalistic accuracy, the university wouldn't be using an image from seven years ago—but nobody is complaining about that.

IMPROVING YOUR ABILITY TO SUPPORT YOUR IDEAS

A speech devoid of support is like a skeleton; the structure is there, but the flesh is missing. By developing an understanding of the way support functions to flesh out ideas, you increase your chances of becoming a proficient speaker. Speakers who are adept at finding and using support realize the following:

1. *Support rarely, if ever, surfaces on its own.* You need to search for it by examining yourself, other people, and published materials.

2. *For ideas to affect listeners, the audience's imagination must be stirred.* Supportive devices can serve this function. Definitions, statistics, examples and illustrations, testimonials, comparison and contrast, and repetition and restatement can all be used to make spoken words more understandable and more believable, as well as to give them greater impact.

Focus on Service Learning
How can you use your researching to facilitate the work of a community group of your choice?

Ethics & COMMUNICATION

Flip through any college recruiting material (or corporate report, for that matter) and you will see a black, a white, and an Asian together—preferably in autumn, when the campus is dappled in sunlight. No one sports a Mohawk, tattoo, or triple piercing. Every dorm room is worthy of Martha Stewart, and cafeteria food is just one star short of the Michelin guide.

Anyone who thinks that recruiting publications are not carefully staged is naive, said Alan Cubbage, vice president of university relations at Northwestern University: "High school juniors understand that they are being marketed to . . . . This is about an institution wanting to put its best face forward."

It was a sentiment echoed throughout the Big Ten. Other calls to administrators revealed that they manipulate images, too, whether it's zapping a trash bin out of a landscape or showcasing a woman professor at the front of a crowded lecture hall.

Clearly, Wisconsin was more interested in projecting its hopes for the future than documenting the present. The 40,000-member student body is 10 percent minority but only 2 percent African-American, lagging behind other Big Ten schools.

Is it unethical? Wisconsin's graphic manipulation is different than if it had been done by, say, the University of Vermont, which has no black students at all. And its motive is certainly different than in Time magazine's digital darkening of the image of O.J. Simpson on its cover, which made him appear more ominous and sinister.

To me, the most troubling result of Wisconsin's tweaking is that the "doctored" student, senior Diallo Shabazz, will now know that whatever else he accomplished in his four years at Madison, he was most prized for his pigmentation.

The university has apologized to Shabazz and recalled the brochures. Even without that mea culpa, though, I was willing to cut the Badgers some slack—unlike the mail-order retailer that delivered a jacket that looked nothing like the one in the catalog or the frozen-foods company that sold me a lasagna that bore no resemblance to what was in the box.

The goal here is so much loftier than merely boosting sales and pleasing stockholders. It's about an institution, and a society, aspiring to be better than they were before. Along the way, there are bound to be missteps.

Source: Bonnie Miller Rubin. "A University's Awkward Effort to Do Better." The Record, October 3, 2000, p. L-7. Reprinted with permission.

3. *Audio and visual aids can also be used to enhance the effectiveness of a presentation*. If appropriately designed and integrated, they will increase listeners' comprehension, retention, and motivation.

IMPROVING YOUR ABILITY TO EVALUATE SUPPORTING MATERIALS

How credible is the support you include in your speech? The following Supporting Material Analysis System is a tool you can use to test the effectiveness of the information/evidence you use to build your speech. Simply ask yourself each of the following questions about the materials you incorporate:

1. How recent is the information/evidence?
2. How accurate is the information/evidence?
3. How reliable is the information/evidence?
4. How sufficient is the information/evidence?
5. How appropriate is the information/evidence?

In order to assess recency, ask yourself when the information/evidence used was written or produced. While some topics require you to locate very recent sources, others are not time-based and allow for more flexibility.

Ask the following questions to assess accuracy: Do other sources contain similar data? Does the source of this information provide specific information or does he or she make unsupported claims?

When assessing reliability, determine if the information cited appeared in a major book, newspaper or news show, magazine, or Web site. If, for example, the source is a Web site, determine who is responsible for information that appears on that site. If, for instance, the site address includes ".com," ask who supports the site. If includes ".org," ask who the site's sponsoring organization is. Your goal is to determine if the site's administrators or founders are biased or unbiased, supportive of particular social or political agendas or neutral.

When assessing the sufficiency of your information, you are seeking to determine whether or not you have enough data to support the point(s) you are making.

Finally, when assessing appropriateness, you evaluate whether the information you offer is supportive of your topic and used in good taste.

The following rating scales, in which 9/10 represents excellent, 8 represents good, 7 represents adequate, 6 represents poor, and 5 and below represent unacceptable, can facilitate your assessment:

RECENCY

Outdated   1 2 3 4 5 6 7 8 9 10   Current
Reason:

ACCURACY

Inaccurate   1 2 3 4 5 6 7 8 9 10   Accurate
Reason:

RELIABILITY

Unreliable   1   2   3   4   5   6   7   8   9   10   Reliable
Reason:

SUFFICIENCY

Insufficient   1   2   3   4   5   6   7   8   9   10   Sufficient
Reason:

APPROPRIATENESS

Inappropriate   1   2   3   4   5   6   7   8   9   10   Appropriate
Reason:

Evidence Score
Total _____ × 2 = _____ Evidence Score

Revisiting Chapter Objectives

1. **Identify and use the various online and offline research resources available to you.**   The first step in the topic development stage of preparing a speech is to gather a variety of effective research materials to integrate into your presentation. The materials you gather may come from online or offline sources. For example, when working offline, you may consult published works, including books, journals, magazines, and newspapers available in the library. When working online, you have the Internet and its many resources, including e-mail, listservs, newsgroups, and the World Wide Web at your disposal.

2. **Conduct an informal survey and a personal interview.**   In addition, you may be able to draw on your personal observations and experiences. You can, for example, conduct an informal survey and/or a personal interview.

3. **Identify various types of supporting material, including definitions, statistics, examples, illustrations, and testimonials.**   Depending on the nature of your topic, you can make your research interesting and understandable to your audience by using various kinds of verbal support: definitions, statistics, examples and illustrations, and testimonials (quotations).

4. **Use comparison and contrast, repetition and restatement.**   You can also increase the impact and memorability of your speech by using comparisons and contrasts, as well as repetition and restatement.

5. **Explain how visual and audio aids can enhance a presentation.**   Many speeches can be enhanced with visual and audio support. Objects, models, graphs, photographs, drawings, slides, videotapes, and audiotapes can be incorporated into the presentation to reinforce, clarify, and dramatize concepts. Computer graphics programs are now making professional-looking graphics available even to student speakers.

Resources for Further Inquiry and Reflection

To apply your understanding of how the principles in Chapter 15 are at work in our daily lives, consult the following resources for further inquiry and

THE Wrap-Up

reflection. Or, if you prefer, choose any other appropriate resource. Then connect the ideas expressed in your chosen selection with the communication concepts and issues you are learning about both in and out of class.

 Listen to Me

"Fight," "Have You Seen Me?" and "The Morality Squad" from *Live from Antarctica* (GWAR)
"Scenes from an Italian Restaurant" (Billy Joel)

What topics are explored in the music of GWAR and/or Billy Joel? For example, how does the explicitness and threatening nature of the band's rhetoric affect you? What meanings do receivers derive from the violent language and profane imagery contained in GWAR's songs? What means of support are used to target the central negative force in the band's message? What organizational pattern does Billy Joel use to convey the nature of the relationship between Brenda and Eddie?

 View Me

Other People's Money   *The Net*

What means of support does either Danny DeVito's or Sandra Bullock's character use to make his or her case?

 Read Me

David Slayden and Rita Kirk Whellock, eds. *Soundbite Culture: The Death of Discourse in a Wired World*. Thousand Oaks, CA: Sage, 1999.

What do the insights provided by the author(s) of any chapter in this book reveal about the state of reasoned discourse in our society?

 Tell Me

Share with the class the insights you gained from your chosen Listen to Me, View Me, or Read Me selection.

Imagine that you've started late on preparing a speech on the topic of affirmative action. Because time is of the essence, you ask a friend if you can borrow a research paper that your friend wrote on the same subject. You reason that it probably contains the kind of research you would find if you only had the time to investigate the topic yourself. Explain why you would or would not use the paper your friend provides. Also indicate, if you decide to use it, whether you consider your use of your friend's paper to be plagiarism.

Key Chapter Terminology

Communication
Works

online learning center

www.mhhe.com/gamble8

Use the Communication Works CD-ROM and the Online Learning Center at www.mhhe.com/gamble8 *to further your knowledge of the following terminology.*

bar graph 462
Boolean search 449
definitions 455
examples 456
illustrations 456
line graphs 463

listserv 451
pictographs 464
pie, or circle, graph 462
statistics 455
testimony 457

Test Your Understanding

Go to the *Self Quizzes* on the Communication Works CD-ROM and the book's Online Learning Center at www.mhhe.com/gamble8.

Communication
Works

online learning center

www.mhhe.com/gamble8

Notes

1. See Ted Spencer. "The Internet Comes of Age for 1997." *Spectra,* January, 1997, p. 5.

2. Randy Reddict and Elliot King. *The OnLine Student.* Fort Worth, TX: Harcourt, Brace College, 1996, p. 3. Information on conducting research, pp. 161–179, is particularly valuable.

3. Jeffrey Graham. "Thrill of Hunt Lures Google Competitors." *USA Today,* May 13, 2002, p. 4D.

4. For a more comprehensive treatment of supporting materials, see Teri Gamble and Michael Gamble. *Public Speaking in the Age of Diversity,* 2nd ed. Boston: Allyn & Bacon, 1998, chaps. 7 and 8.

5. Robert L. Dilenschneider. "Spin: Can It Save You or Sink You?" *Vital Speeches of the Day* 66:4, December 1, 1999, p. 123.

6. Manuel Goni. "Hazing: When Rites Become Wrongs," *Winning Orations.* Mankato: MN: Interstate Oratorical Association, 2001, pp. 1–3.

7. Chandra Palubiak. "To Tattoo or Not to Tattoo." *Winning Orations.* Mankato: MN: Interstate Oratorical Association, 2002, pp. 11–13.

8. Jonathan Hakala. "We Must Rebuild the Towers." *Vital Speeches,* February 1, 2003, 66:8, pp. 251–253.

9. For a discussion of the power of examples in public speaking, see Gamble and Gamble; and Scott Consigny. "The Rhetorical Example." *Southern Speech Communication Journal* 41, 1976, pp. 121–134.

10. Solomon D. Trujillo. "Two Lives: The One We Make Defines Our Legacy." *Vital Speeches of the Day* 66:6, January 1, 2000, p. 169. Reprinted with permission.

11. Tony Martinet. "Parents: Poor Losers." *Winning Orations.* Mankato, MN: Interstate Oratorical Association, 2002, pp. 77–79.

12. Rebekah Olson. "Cherish Diversity." *Winning Orations.* Mankato, MN: Interstate Oratorical Association, 1999, p. 142. Reprinted with permission.

13. Sara Gronstal. "A Fungus among Us." *Winning Orations.* Mankato: MN: The Interstate Oratorical Association, 2002, pp. 27–29. Reprinted with permission.

14. Stacy Champagne. "The Patriot Act—Enduring Freedom?" *Winning Orations,* Mankato: MN: Interstate Oratorical Association, 2002, pp. 29–31. Reprinted with permission.

15. Theresa McGuiness. "Greeks in Crisis." *Winning Orations.* Mankato, MN: Interstate Oratorical Association, 2000, p. 75. Reprinted with permission.

16. Kelly Sonderup. "Phthalates: The Insidious Danger of Soft Plastic." *Winning Orations.* Mankato: MN: Interstate Oratorical Association, 2002, pp. 56–58. Reprinted with permission.

17. George W. Bush. "Shuttle Columbia Tragedy." *Vital Speeches of the Day* 69:9, February 15, 2003, p. 258.

18. The power of repetition and restatement is stressed in most books on public speaking, including Gamble and Gamble.

18a. "I Have a Dream" by Martin Luther King, Jr. Reprinted by arrangement with the Estate of Martin Luther King, Jr., c/o Writers House as agent for the proprietor, New York, NY. Copyright © 1963 Dr. Martin Luther King, Jr., copyright renewed 1991 Coretta Scott King.

19. Earnie Deavenport. "Beyond the Moral Equation." *Vital Speeches of the Day* 69:6, June 1, 2003, pp. 501–503.

20. "Hillary Rodham Clinton Honors the First Women's Rights Convention." In S. Michele Nix, ed. *Women at the Podium.* New York: HarperCollins, 2000, pp. 186–198.

21. Barbara Slavin and John Diamond. "Case Is Stronger When 'Biggest Dove' Makes It." *USA Today,* February 6, 2003, p. 10A.

22. V. Johnson. "Picture-Perfect Presentations." *Training and Development Journal* 1989, pp. 43, 45.

23. C. Wilder. *The Presentation Kit.* New York: Wiley, 1990.

24. John M. Broder. "NASA Now Doubts Tank Foam Debris Doomed Columbia." *New York Times,* February 6, 2003, p. A1.

25. "Romance on the Web." *Newsweek,* May 12, 2003, p. E20.

26. Mark Thompson. "Bush's New Nuclear Push." *Time,* May 26, 2003, p. 22.

27. Perry Bacon, Jr., and Eric Roston. "Stop Calling Us." *Time,* April 28, 2003, pp. 56–58.

28. "Tracking the Global Spread." *Newsweek,* May 5, 2003, p. 31.

29. *Discover.* June, 2003, pp. 42–47.

30. W. I. Ringle and W. D. Thompson. *TechEdge: Using Computers to Present and Persuade.* Needham Heights, MA: Allyn & Bacon, 1998.

31. L. Zuckerman. "Words Go Right to the Brain, but Can They Stir the Heart?" *New York Times,* April 17, 1999, pp. A-17–A19.

32. Greg Jaffe. "What's Your Point, Lieutenant? Just Cut to the Pie Charts." *Wall Street Journal,* April 26, 2000, pp. A1, A6.

33. June Kronholz. "PowerPoint Goes to School." *Wall Street Journal,* November 12, 2002, pp. B1, B6.

34. Jan Parker. "Absolute PowerPoint." *New Yorker,* May 28, 2001, pp. 76–87.

35. Parker.

36. See David Shenk. *Data Smog: Surviving the Information Glut.* San Francisco: Harper Edge, 1997.

37. Shenk, p. 93.

38. "College Faked Photo in Pitch for Diversity." *The Record,* September 21, 2000, p. A-13.

Designing Your Speech: Organizing Your Ideas

After finishing this chapter, you should be able to

1. Identify main and subordinate ideas.

2. Create a complete sentence outline.

3. Identify five methods of ordering ideas.

4. Use internal summaries and transitions effectively.

5. Develop an effective introduction and conclusion.

6. Use a tryout to refine a speech.

Every speech ought to be put together like a living creature, with a body of its own, so as to be neither without head nor without feet, but to have both a middle and extremities, described proportionately to each other and to the whole.

—Plato

Tell me to what you pay attention and I will tell you who you are.

—José Ortega y Gasset

Our lives are now so busy and cluttered with details that many of us have become obsessed with the need for order.[1] We hire closet experts to organize our closets. We use hand-held computers, more commonly known as personal digital assistants (PDAs), to organize our day. Disorder has become so discomforting that people make careers out of helping others bring order to their lives. Organization is important to the speaker as well. You can have the best ideas in the world and the most impressive and eye-opening support, but if you are unable to organize your ideas and integrate your support so that the audience can follow what you're trying to communicate, you might as well not speak at all. Organization is one of the main challenges you will have to face as a speech maker. It is the second step in the topic development stage of preparing a speech.

What is your goal when you are organizing ideas? Primarily, you want to order your materials so that communication between you and your audience will be facilitated. How can you accomplish this? You must plan. Just as an architect develops a plan for a building, so you must develop a plan for your speech. Your plan shows the structure you will adhere to—the developmental sequence you think will work best. Of course, just as an architect considers numerous designs before selecting one, you should test potential patterns to determine which one will best clarify and amplify your ideas. Fortunately, you do not have to grope your way through a thicket of possibilities. Communication theorists have developed guidelines to help you with this phase.

Go to the *Online Learning Center* at www.mhhe.com/gamble8 and answer the questions in the *Self Inventory* to evaluate your understanding of speech outlining.

BUILDING THE OUTLINE: A SPEECH FRAMEWORK FOR SUCCESS

An audience has to be able to follow your speech for it to be effective. Without good organization, a speech's message may remain fuzzy and difficult for the audience to follow. Since receivers rarely interrupt speakers during the course of their speeches to seek clarification, and because they do not usually

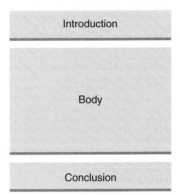

FIGURE 16.1
Framework for a Speech.

have access to transcripts or tapes of presentations, speakers need to organize the ideas of their speeches so that receivers comprehend them the first time they hear them. Receivers have no rewind button to push if they become distracted or confused. Thus, speakers must therefore structure their messages so that confusion is kept to a minimum.[2]

As we saw in Chapter 7, not everyone is a skillful listener. For this reason, you should base your organization on the principle of redundancy. In other words, to ensure comprehension, you will need to build a certain amount of repetition into your speech. Only if this is done will listeners be able to follow your ideas easily. This basic developmental principle is often expressed as follows: Tell them what you are going to tell them, then tell them, and finally tell them what you have told them.

One of the best ways to organize a speech is the introduction-body-conclusion format (see Figure 16.1), called a **speech framework** because it provides a frame, or skeleton, on which any speech or other formal presentation can be built.

Any speech you develop should be organized according to this framework. Your introductory remarks and your concluding statements should each take up approximately 10 to 15 percent of the total presentation. That leaves 70 to 80 percent of your time for developing the ideas contained in the body of your speech. Since the body will be the main portion of your presentation, it is often advisable to begin by preparing this part of the speech; once the body is set, you can move on to develop the introduction and the conclusion. Let's consider the three key parts of a speech in that order: body, introduction, and conclusion.

speech framework
a skeleton for speech development

ORGANIZING THE BODY OF YOUR PRESENTATION

As you begin to outline the body of your speech, you will want to build a suitable structure onto which you can place your ideas. You develop this structure in stages. During the first stage of outline development, you create a *preliminary working outline*. This sparse outline has points containing one or two words that eventually will achieve fuller form in the second stage, the full sentence outline. You develop the *full sentence outline* only after you have researched and fully developed the ideas of your stage. Ultimately, during the third stage of outline preparation, you will transform your full sentence outline into an *extemporaneous outline, or speaker's notes,* that you will then use as your guide when you deliver your speech.

Outlining Principles: Identifying Main and Subordinate Ideas

Let's imagine that you have created the following working plan, or outline, for a speech about affirmative action:

I. Definition
II. Purposes
III. Outcomes
IV. Why under attack

Your next task is to develop those topics. As you begin the development process, you need to keep uppermost in your mind the fact that your audience is unlikely to recall a long, wandering, unstructured collection of data. Thus, after you have conducted your research, you will need to develop a full sentence outline that distinguishes between your **main ideas**—your speech's subtopics that directly support your thesis—and your **subordinate ideas**—those ideas that function as support or amplification for your main ideas or subtopics.

In many ways, subordinate ideas can be viewed as the foundation on which larger ideas are constructed (see Figure 16.2). Consequently, you should begin the organizational process by arranging your materials into clusters of main and subordinate ideas. As you do this, you will be able to determine which evidence supports the main ideas and which supports the subordinate ideas. Your main ideas will be, say, two to five major points that you want the audience to remember.

If you are developing a speech on affirmative action programs, you might begin as follows:

Purpose: To inform the audience about affirmative action

Behavioral objective: After listening to my speech, audience members will be able to define affirmative action, identify its uses and results, and explain why it is a policy under fire.

main ideas

the main points of a speech; the subtopics of a speech

subordinate ideas

ideas that amplify the main ideas or subtopics of a speech

FIGURE 16.2
Construction of an Idea.

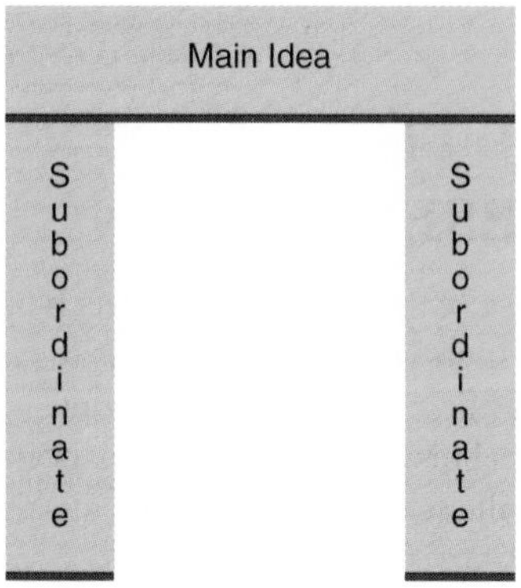

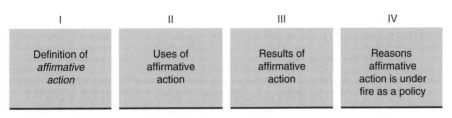

FIGURE 16.3
Dividing a Thesis into Major Points.

Thesis: The definition, uses, and results of affirmative action have contributed to its being a policy under fire. (See Figure 16.3.)

You are now off to a good start. Next, you need to develop these major points into complete sentences using parallel structure—that is, using sentences with similar or matching styles.

   I. Affirmative action can be defined as any action taken to ensure or affirm equal opportunity for oppressed or previously disadvantaged groups.

  II. Affirmative action is used in hiring and college admissions decisions.

III. Affirmative action has benefits and drawbacks.

IV. Affirmative action is under fire for being reverse discrimination.

Many people find it helpful to pull together clusters of information that support their main ideas, as follows:

I. Main idea
  A. Subordinate idea
    1. Sub-subordinate idea
    2. Sub-subordinate idea
  B. Subordinate idea
    1. Sub-subordinate idea
    2. Sub-subordinate idea

When you take the time to prepare an easy-to-follow structure for your speech, in addition to enhancing receiver perceptions of your competence and adding to the personal credibility you have in their eyes, your efforts also help fulfill receiver expectations. That is, the main points of a speech alert receivers to listen for supporting information. Because they are not struggling to give order to a disordered array of information, they can focus instead on the thesis of your speech and the support you offer to build your presentation. Taking time to develop an outline has a third benefit, as well. Because you know what information you are using to support each main point of your speech, your delivery of the speech will be improved. Since your ideas are carefully laid out before you, instead of having to concentrate on what to say next, you free yourself to focus on establishing a good relationship with your receivers.

If you have taken notes on cards, you can lay out or pattern the body of your speech in the following way:

Purpose:

I. Main idea
  A. (Supports I)   B. (Supports I)
    1. (Supports A)   1. (Supports B)
    2. (Supports A)   2. (Supports B)
    3. (Supports A)

II. Main idea

   A. (Supports II)

   B. (Supports II)

Notice that the outline you develop indicates the relative importance of each item included in it. The main points—Roman numerals I, II, III, and so on—are the most important items you want your audience to remember. Your sub-points—capital letters *A, B, C,* and so on—are supportive of but less important than the main points. Likewise, sub-subpoints—Arabic numbers 1, 2, 3, and so on—are supportive of but less important than subpoints. Remember to line up the entries in your outline correctly. Locate the main ideas closest to the left margin. The subpoints underlying the main points should begin directly underneath the first letter of the first word of each main point. Keep in mind that a traditional rule of outlining is that at least two subpoints must support every main point.

Items that support the sub-points begin directly underneath the first letter of the first word of each subpoint. Indicate the supporting materials for the sub-subpoints with lowercase letters (a, b, c, and so on). In this way, the full sentence outline functions as a visual representation of the supportive underpinnings for ideas. In general, there should be at least a 3 to 1 ratio between the total words in your speech and the number of words in your outline.

A final outline, using symbols and indentions might look like the following:

Purpose: To inform audience members about the myths and realities concerning severe acute respiratory syndrome (SARS)

  I. Several myths about SARS are prevalent in society today.

    A. Many people believe that SARS is the next major global epidemic.

      1. Some fear it will rival the 1918 influenza epidemic.

      2. Others fear it will become the plague of our times.

    B. The reality is that SARS is being brought under control.

      1. A significant drop in cases has been seen in China.

      2. Canada has nearly eradicated the disease within its borders.

 II. Many questions remain regarding future efforts to combat SARS.

    A. Developing a vaccine to combat SARS is challenging.

      1. The SARS virus constantly mutates into new forms.

      2. The SARS virus may jump from animals to humans.

    B. It is unclear whether there is a seasonal pattern to SARS.

      1. SARS may arise in the fall and retreat during the summer.

      2. SARS outbreaks may reappear every year or every few years.

    C. Profiteering poses potential problems.

      1. The costs of medical drugs and equipment are increasing in SARS-afflicted areas.

      2. The costs of herbal remedies and basic foods are increasing in SARS-afflicted areas.

Giving Order to Your Ideas Using Traditional and Nontraditional Formats

Speeches have either a linear or a nonlinear format. Western cultures favor a linear organization, while non-Western cultures favor organizational nonlinear formats. As Richard Nisbett notes, there appears to be a geography of thought when it comes to both the development of a worldview and the frameworks of thinking that support it.[3] In his book *The Geography of Thought: How Asians and Westerners Think Differently . . . and Why,* Nisbett notes that human cognition and reasoning preferences differ, depending on whether you were brought up in a Western or an Eastern culture. According to Nisbett, East Asians are more holistic and contextual in their perceptions, while Westerners have more of a tunnel-vision perceptual style that depends more on identifying with what is prominent in a situation and remembering it. Persons from Eastern cultures tend to tolerate subtleties and deal in relationships (the stress is placed on intuitive thinking and informal logic, not the use of categories—for example, the practice of feng shui is not atomistic but extraordinarily complex). On the other hand, persons from Western cultures tend to be analytic, prefer absolutes, and deal in categories (the stress is placed on categorization and rational/logical thinking—for example, delivering a speech entitled Six Ways to Increase Your Self-Esteem). East Asian persons start out by focusing on the context, not zeroing in on an object of interest. Westerners begin by focusing on a central object.

These preferences affect how persons from Eastern and Western cultures prefer to organize their ideas. According to Nisbett, in the West, we start out with a general statement and give suggested solutions. We present the evidence in favor of our position. We argue against the reasons that others might not accept the position we have taken. We summarize and offer a conclusion. In the East, they do not do it this way. Instead, they cycle back into the same topic from different directions.[4] Nisbett suggests that the following example—offered by an English professor, which focuses on writing but could equally focus on public speaking—reveals this difference in methodology:

> I was surprised when one of my students who had been a teacher in China before coming here told me that she didn't understand the requirements of essay structure. I told her to write a thesis statement and then prove its three points in the following paragraphs. She told me if she wrote this way in China she would be considered stupid. "In China," she said, "essays were written in a more circular fashion moving associated ideas closer and closer to the center."[5]

While we need to be cautious about overgeneralizing, especially since persons from one culture who spend time in another culture tend to tune their thinking style into the culture in which they are interacting, we will see these differences surface as we explore both linear and nonlinear organizational formats. You need to order the ideas in your speech in a way that will make sense to your audience.

Traditional Organizational Formats

Traditional organizational formats display a linear logic and are typical of the prototypes many North American speakers use to make sense of information.

A speech has a linear organization if its main points develop and relate directly to the theses or topic sentence that comes early in the presentation. We will look at five traditional approaches to ordering material: (1) chronological, or time, order; (2) spatial order; (3) cause-and-effect order; (4) problem-and-solution order; and (5) topical order. Prior to doing this, let us examine some pointers to keep in mind when drafting an outline for any of these traditional approaches.

Tips for Drafting the Body of the Outline   The body is the part of the speech that develops and explains the key ideas you have gathered in support of your topic or thesis. Your first task in drafting an outline is to identify potential main points for use in your speech. Once you have done this, you need to select the main ideas (usually between two and five) that are most important to the success of your presentation; the ideas you select are the ones you believe will be most useful to you in fulfilling your primary purpose for speaking.

Each main point in the outline you develop should be a sentence that summarizes your supporting material. Main points should be similarly constructed. They should exhibit parallel structure. For example, if your first main point uses a subject and verb construction, so should each of your other main points. Main points should also contain vivid and descriptive language designed to interest receivers. For example, the following set of main ideas does not contain parallel structure or effective use of language:

> Few breeds of dogs are as intelligent as poodles.
> Poodles like to explore their environment.
> Have one, and you'll find that these dogs like human contact.

In contrast, the sentences in the next set have parallel structure and make better use of descriptive language:

> Poodles are one of the most intelligent breeds of dogs.
> Poodles are naturally curious and creative as they explore their environment.
> Poodles make wonderful pets because they thrive on human contact.

chronological, or time, order

an organizational format that develops an idea using a time order

Chronological Order   **Chronological, or time, order** involves developing an idea or a problem in the order in which it occurs or occurred in time.

One student, for example, used chronological order to describe the events that resulted in the elephant's becoming an endangered species:

Purpose: To explain why the elephant is becoming an endangered species

  I. Until the early 1900s, elephants had little reason to fear people.
 II. During the 1920s, elephants were slaughtered as the demand for ivory products increased in the United States and Europe.
III. Within the past 20 years, products made from ivory have also come to be prized in the Far East.

As you can see, this student has considered the steps leading up to the present situation in the order in which they occurred. In addition, each main point the speaker used covers a particular time period. Since the main points describe a sequence of happenings, they help the audience keep track of where the speaker is in time.

Another student used chronological order for a speech on the insanity defense:

Purpose: To examine the history of the insanity defense in criminal jurisprudence

I. In the seventeenth and eighteenth centuries, belief in witchcraft influenced popular legal conceptions of mental disorder.

II. The nineteenth-century showcase for the insanity defense was the trial of Daniel M'Naghten, a political assassin.

III. Not until 1954 did the courts begin to acknowledge that a wide variety of diseases or defects may impair the mind.

IV. As we enter the new millennium, the legacy of the Jeffrey Dahmer case and the public's reactions to it again raise questions regarding our attitude toward crime, punishment, and personal responsibility.

> *Think of three topics you could develop using chronological order. Why do they lend themselves to that arrangement?*

Any event that has occurred in time can be examined chronologically. With a time-ordered presentation, it is up to you to decide where to begin and end your chronology and what events to include. As you might expect, time order is most often used in informative speeches. (See Figure 16.4.)

Spatial Order   Spatial order describes an object, a person, or a phenomenon as it exists in space. An object, for example, might be described from

Top to bottom
Bottom to top
Left to right
Right to left
Inside to outside
Outside to inside

spatial order

an organizational format that describes an object, a person, or a phenomenon as it exists in space

With spatial order, you must select one orientation and carry it through.

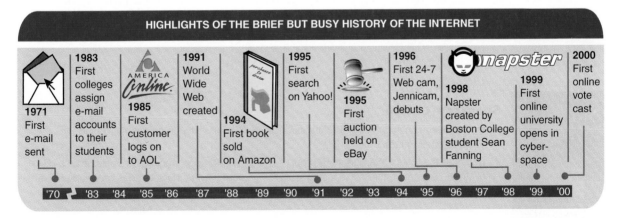

FIGURE 16.4   *Could you develop an informative speech on the history of the Internet using this time line?*

One student used spatial order to explain the appearance and functioning of a beehive:

I. Outside the hive
II. Inside the hive

Another student used a spatial pattern to discuss the different kinds of natural disasters that plague different sections of the United States:

I. States along the East Coast of the United States are hurricane-prone.

II. States in the central region of the United States are tornado-prone.

III. States along the West Coast of the United States are earthquake-prone.

Like chronological order, spatial order is used most frequently in informative speeches.

Visuals, like the one held by this attorney, reinforce presented information—would you find this visual effective were you on the jury?

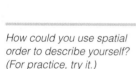

How could you use spatial order to describe yourself? (For practice, try it.)

Visuals can be used effectively to reinforce information contained in a spatially ordered presentation—whether you intend to discuss the components of a computer, the terrain of a national park, the design of a new car, or the floor plan of a house or an apartment. Using spatial order involves organizing your ideas according to an area concept, which should be reflected in the main points of the outline.

cause-and-effect order
an organizational format that categorizes a topic according to its causes and effects

Cause-and-Effect Order **Cause-and-effect order** requires you to categorize your material into things related to the causes of a problem and things related to its effects. It is then up to you to decide which aspect you will explore first. Thus, in a speech on drunk driving, you might begin by

Skill BUILDER

Speaker's Choice

1. Find a rock, a shell, a piece of driftwood, or some other natural object.

2. Describe the object to a partner, a group of students, or the entire class, using spatial order.

3. Explain why your spatial ordering took the form it did.

4. Would approaching the object from a different angle have altered your audience's understanding and appreciation? How?

discussing the percentage of drivers during a certain period who were drunk when involved in car accidents (cause). You might then discuss the number of deaths each year that are attributed directly to drunk driving (effect).

One student used cause-and-effect order in a speech on chemical dependency, first discussing the physiological and psychological causes of chemical

Sound Bites

Ethics &
COMMUNICATION

"Hey, do you want to be on the news tonight or not? This is a sound bite, not the Gettysburg Address. Just say what you have to say, Senator, and get the hell off."

Are sound bites—public presentations of positions that usually last no more than 90 seconds—an effective way of informing the electorate? Why or why not?

How organized must a speaker be to present ideas or urge action in this manner? What organizational format do you believe lends itself best to this type of presentation? Is 90 seconds or less enough time to deliver a message designed not just to inform but also to influence? Explain your position.

How could you use cause-and-effect order to explain a recent disagreement you had with an instructor, an employer, a friend, or a family member?

dependency and then considering the health-related effects of being chemically dependent:

I. Chemical dependency appears to have several causes, some physical and some psychological.

II. Chemical dependency has adverse effects on health.

You can vary this approach by discussing the effect before the cause. In the following example, a student used effect-and-cause order to reveal the causes of excessive stress among students:

I. The number of students suffering from stress-related ailments is increasing at an alarming rate.

II. Experts on such ailments have identified four major explanations for this increase.

Cause-and-effect order and effect-and-cause order are quite versatile. They are used in both informative and persuasive speeches.

problem-and-solution order

an organizational format that identifies the problems inherent in a situation and presents a solution to remedy them

Problem-and-Solution Order **Problem-and-solution order** requires you to (1) determine what problems are inherent in a situation and (2) present a solution to remedy them. Thus, you might discuss the problems that develop when many students entering college are deficient in writing skills. The second portion of your speech can then suggest a number of ways the identified problem might be alleviated (perhaps, for example, by expanding tutoring programs or offering noncredit remedial courses). If you wanted to speak about increased crime in your community using problem-and-solution order, your first task could be to establish in the minds of your listeners that a problem did indeed exist. From there, you could proceed to suggest various solutions.

One student used problem-and-solution order to argue that her state should drop the legal definition of intoxication to a blood alcohol level of 0.08:

I. The problems caused by intoxicated teenagers are increasing.

II. Lowering the legal definition of intoxication to a 0.08 blood alcohol level will do much to alleviate the situation.

Problem-and-solution order is most frequently employed in persuasive speeches.

topical order

an organizational format that clusters material by dividing it into a series of appropriate topics

Topical Order At times, a speech may not fit neatly into any of the patterns previously described. When this happens, you may choose to develop or cluster your material by arranging it into a series of appropriate topics. This is **topical order.** Examples of topical order include the following categorical arrangements: advantages and disadvantages of a proposal; social, political, and economic factors that contribute to a problem; perceptions of upper-class, middle-class, and lower-class people on an issue. When you use topical order, you may find that you can intermingle cause-and-effect, time, problem-and-solution, or spatial order within the topical order.

A student used topical order to argue in favor of active euthanasia (mercy killing):

I. Euthanasia is merciful.

II. Euthanasia is death with dignity.

Because of its wide applicability, topical order is used very frequently.

Support All Main Points   While each example in the previous sections contained only main points, in a developed outline, each of these points should be supported by information, including examples, definitions, and visual aids, that pertain to the subject in the main point they support and enable the audience to understand why the main point is true. Usually, two to four subpoints are offered in support of a main point.

For practice, for each of the main points in the preceding examples, conduct research in an effort to identify two to four subpoints to support each main point.

Nontraditional Formats

In developing an outline, a number of organizational patterns can be used in place of a linear framework. You should use one of the nontraditional patterns discussed in this section if you believe the cultures and dispositions of the persons in your audience warrant it. While a number of us prefer to use **linear logic** to develop our ideas, others of us—including some persons from Native American, Asian-American, or Latino cultures—do not. As we deduce from the preceding prototypes, linear logic develops ideas step-by-step, relying on facts and data to support each main point. In contrast to formats that depend on linear logic are formats that are more indirect and less explicit in offering hard evidence and proof in defense of a point. These patterns are called **configural formats.**

linear logic

the step-by-step development of ideas; the reliance on facts and data to support main points

configural formats

organizational patterns that are indirect and inexplicit

Instead of previewing, spelling out, and discussing each key point, one at a time, persons who prefer configural thinking approach their subject from a variety of perspectives and rely on examples and stories to carry the crux of their message; they also rely on receivers to understand the messages implied by the examples and stories used. Because they believe the explicit stating of a message is unnecessary, speakers who use a configural style do not bluntly tell receivers their conclusion or call on them to make a specific response; instead of ensuring that the conclusion is obvious to receivers, the speakers lead them to their conclusion indirectly and by implication. Thus, configural frameworks require receivers to do more work.

While persons in cultures who favor the use of configural patterns might not categorize them in this way, Westerners do identify three kinds of configural systems of organization. First is the deferred-thesis pattern, in which the main points of a speech gradually build to the speaker's thesis, which he or she does not indicate until the speech is nearly over. Second is the web pattern, in which threads of thought refer back to the speaker's central purpose; while to Western ears the speaker may seem to be "off topic" at points, to receivers in other cultures the tangents the speaker explores are connected to the speaker's topic and make it more meaningful. Third is the narrative pattern, in which the speaker tells a story without stating a thesis or developing it with main points. When using this pattern, the speaker may only "discover" the main point via a series of illustrations and parables.

The following speech outline is organized configurally. As such, it requires the audience to participate more actively in interpreting what the speaker implies.

Purpose: To persuade my audience that *E-coli* presents problems for our food supply

I. A hypothetical food worker, Jake, who is employed in a meat packing plant, inadvertently infects the plant's meat supply with *E-coli*.

II. Jake's carelessness contributes to the infection of a number of persons in an array of cities across the United States.

III. The plant is closed because of *E-coli* contamination.

IV. Today, members of the families of those who were sickened by *E-coli* ask the federal government, "How can our food supply be made safe?"

In your opinion, should speakers match the organizational format they use to the preferred perceptual system of the receivers?

As the speaker embellishes each of the ideas identified in the outline during his or her presentation, it is up to the receivers to interpret the meaning of the speaker's narrative from the stories, examples, and testimony offered. The speaker will not state directly what receivers should think or do but will rely on them to draw their own conclusions and come up with their own solutions.

You'll recall from Chapter 2 that members of low-context cultures, such as the United States, are usually more direct in how they convey information to others than are members of high-context cultures, such as Latin America, Japan, and Saudi Arabia. To low-context receivers, the speaker from a high-context culture may come off as vague or deceptive because of his or her reluctance to be direct, explicit, or obvious. In contrast, high-context receivers prefer to receive information through examples, illustrations, and other indirect means of expression.[6]

Connecting Your Ideas: Internal Summaries and Transitions

To transmit your ideas to an audience with clarity and fluidity using linear logic, you will need to use internal summaries and transitions to move from one idea to the next.

internal summaries

rhetorical devices designed to help listeners remember content

The body of a speech organized according to linear logic contains brief **internal summaries;** these are designed to help listeners remember the content. The following are examples: "Thus far we have examined two key housing problems. Let us now consider a third." "The four characteristics we have discussed thus far are . . . ." Besides helping the audience recall the material,

EXPLORING

Diversity

Is Paying Attention Cultural?

Edward T. Hall suggests that "culture . . . designates what we pay attention to and what we ignore." If this is so, how can speakers ensure that audience members who belong to other cultural groups will pay attention to the right things? In other words, how can speakers target crucial ideas and emphasized points? How can a speaker be sure that listeners are not paying attention to the wrong thing and screening out what they should be concentrating on?

Source: Edward T. Hall. *The Hidden Dimension.* New York: Doubleday, 1966.

transitions—connective words and phrases—facilitate the speaker's movement from one idea to another; in effect, they bridge gaps between ideas so that there are no abrupt switches.[7]

transitions

connective words and phrases

To indicate that additional information is forthcoming, you might use such transitional words and phrases as *equally important, next, second, furthermore, in addition,* and *finally.* To signal that you will be discussing a cause-and-effect relationship, you can use the expressions *as a result* and *consequently.* To indicate that there is a contrasting view to the one being elaborated, you could use phrases such as *after all, and yet, in spite of,* and *on the other hand.* To indicate that you are summing up briefly, you can say *in short.* Expressions such as *likewise* and *similarly* signal that a comparison will be made. The phrases *for example* and *for instance* let the listeners know that a point will be illustrated.

While few in number, transitions help the audience follow a speech. Do you consciously plan good transitions?

BEGINNINGS AND ENDINGS

Once you've outlined the body of your speech and considered the need for transitional devices, you are ready to "tell them what you are going to tell them" and "tell them what you have told them." In other words, it's time to develop your introduction and conclusion.[8]

The Introduction

All too frequently, the introduction is overlooked or neglected because speakers are in too much of a hurry to get to the heart of the matter. However, in public speaking, just as in interpersonal communication, first impressions count. Thus, it is essential that you make the first few minutes of your speech particularly interesting.

Functions of the Introduction

The functions of your introduction is to gain the attention of the audiences members, to make them want to listen to your speech, and to provide them with an overview of the subject you will be discussing. The art of designing introductions is much like any other art; that is, it requires creative thinking. You will need to examine your purpose, the speech itself as you have developed it, your analysis of the audience, and your own abilities.

The opening moments of contact, with one person or with a multitude, can affect the developing relationship either positively or negatively. Unquestionably, the first few moments of your speech—the introduction—will affect your audience's willingness to process the remainder. It is at this point that people will decide whether what you have to say is interesting and important or dull and inconsequential. If your introduction is poorly designed, your audience may tune you out for the remainder of your speech. On the other hand, a well-designed introduction can help you develop a solid rapport with the audience and thus make it easier for you to share your thoughts.

The material you include in your introduction must be selected with care. Since in all likelihood your listeners have not been waiting in line for several days to hear you speak, you will need to work to spark their interest; you will need to motivate them to listen to you. Student speakers sometimes go

In the introduction, one of the speaker's goals is to build rapport with the audience.

Use brainstorming to devise a number of ways you could introduce yourself to a group of people you don't know.

overboard in trying to accomplish this objective. Some have been known to yell or throw books across the room; in one case, a student fired a blank from a starter pistol. Such devices are certainly attention-getters, but startling an audience can turn your listeners against you. (After all, it is difficult to listen to ideas or evaluate content if you fear for your safety.) Other speakers look for a joke—any joke—to use as an attention-getter. Unfortunately, a joke chosen at random is seldom related to the topic and thus can confuse or even alienate listeners rather than interest and involve them. (A well-chosen anecdote, however, can be very effective.) Some speakers insist on beginning with statements like "My purpose here today is . . ." or "Today, I hope to convince you . . . ." Such openings suggest mainly that the speech maker has forgotten to consider motivation and attention.

Years ago, television shows began simply by flashing the title of the program onto the screen. Today, however, it is common to use a teaser to open a show. The teaser usually reveals segments of the show designed to arouse the interest of potential viewers—to encourage them to stay tuned. Without this device, many viewers would probably switch channels. Your listeners, of course, cannot switch speakers, but they can decide not to listen actively to what you have to say. Therefore, you, too, must design a teaser to include in your introduction—material that will interest and appeal to your audience.

Types of Introductions

Effective speech makers begin in a number of different ways. They may relate an unusual fact, make a surprising statement, or cite shocking statistics. Or they might ask a question, compliment the audience, or refer to the occasion. Sometimes they use a humorous story or an illustration as a lead-in. Sometimes they rely on a suspenseful story or a human interest story to capture their listeners' attention. Audiences respond to stories about people. For this reason, the plight of a family left homeless by a fire might be used effectively to open a speech on fire prevention, and a description of people severely injured in an automobile accident might introduce a speech supporting the use of air bags. If you have selected a topic because you have a personal interest in it, you can use a personal anecdote to begin your presentation. Let us examine a few examples of these approaches.

Some of the most effective introductions use humor, as in the following examples—the first from a speech by Tim Norbeck of the Connecticut State Medical Society, speaking to a medical association gathering; the second from a speech by Ted Koppel, host of ABC's *Nightline;* and the third from a speech by a speech professor, Richard L. Weaver, and delivered to a staff professional development workshop. Which do you think is the strongest introduction and why?

> Bethel, Connecticut–born P. T. Barnum, the great showman, used to exhibit what he advertised as a "happy family." This family consisted of a lion, a tiger, a wolf, a bear, and a lamb, all in one cage.
>
> "Remarkable," said a visitor to Mr. Barnum. "How long have these animals lived together this way?" "Eight months," Barnum replied. "But occasionally we have to replace the lamb."
>
> There can be no lambs in this, the belligerent cradle of the insurance industry called Connecticut.
>
> Health care delivery in Connecticut has become a war zone—our state is indeed a true microcosm of America.[9]

> Let me tell you what is passing through some of your minds, as I begin this commencement address. I say "some" because I know there are several of you here this morning nursing such excruciating hangovers, that the only thought making the transition from one synapse of your brain to another is "Let it be over with soon, please."
>
> It will be.
>
> Also floating around out there are the inevitable "He's a lot shorter than I thought he was." And then, of course, a few of the "It's gotta be his real hair. Nobody who makes his kind of money would buy a rug that cheap."
>
> Aren't you embarrassed for being that predictable?
>
> As a veteran of these events, both on the delivery and receiving end, let me tell you what's on the minds of my fellow veterans among the faculty. Actually, it bears a striking resemblance to what those of you with hangovers are thinking: only since they're faculty members it's somewhat more elegantly phrased: "I am prepared," they are saying to themselves, "to indulge your banalities, Koppel, if you will only do so succinctly."[10]

> I teach speech communication. But I want you to know that I do not take personal responsibility for the oral communication of most of our college graduates. For today's college graduates, the words they use to start almost every conversation are "you know . . ." And for some, that is the sum and substance of what they have to say as well.
>
> Some people would claim that I am responsible for what should follow the "you know." I say no. I, like you, am a member of a university, and you know what they say about universities: a university is a disorganized institution composed of individuals linked together by a common concern for coffee and car parking! How can you hold me responsible?

It kind of confirms what I overheard the other day: One fellow said, "What do you do if you find two professors up to their necks in sand?" And the other fellow said, "Send for more sand."

There is a story of a wealthy man who called his servant in and told him that he was leaving the country for a year and that while he was gone, he wanted the servant to build him a new house. The wealthy man told him to build it well, and that when he returned, he would pay all the bills for material and for his labor.

Shortly after the employer left, the servant decided that he was foolish to work so hard, so he started cutting corners and squandering the money he saved. When his master came back, he paid all the bills, and then asked the servant, "Are you satisfied with the house?" When the servant said that he was, the master said, "Good . . . because the house is yours. You can live in it the rest of your life."

. . . Speaking of skills and abilities . . . a young man who had been hired by the personnel department of a large supermarket chain reported to work at one of the stores. The manager greeted him with a warm handshake and a smile, handed him a broom and said, "Your first job will be to sweep out the store."

"But," the young man said, "I'm a college graduate."

"Oh, I'm sorry," the manager said, "I didn't know that. Here, give me the broom, and I'll show you how."

As a supervisor, I ask you, are you motivating the motivators to build the kind of houses that they (or you) would be happy to live in for the rest of their (or your) lives?[11]

Examples also make effective introductions. One student, Ajay Krishnan of Rice University, used the following example to begin his speech on automobile repair fraud:

On September 28 of last year, 34-year-old Mark Hartman took his car to the local Econo Lube 'n Tire in Tucson, Arizona, for its regular oil change. While he was waiting, the manager asked him over to the service bay, and told him the shocking truth about his 1990 Chevy Corsica. Using a large chart, the manager pointed out that new cars should have red transmission fluid, whereas Mr. Hartman's transmission fluid was brown, meaning that the car was on the verge of a $3,500 breakdown. Unsure of what to do, Mr. Hartman desperately turned to his owner's manual to try to learn anything at all about his car's transmission. If nothing else, the manual made one fact abundantly clear: the manager was lying. Nothing was wrong with Mark Hartman's car.[12]

When used in introductions, illustrations can add drama, as is seen in the following introductory remarks of Erin O'Dell of Kansas State University.

When Susan and Gary Wilson bought their new home, they thought their dreams came true. They moved into a wonderful, upper-class neighborhood, with wonderful upper-class neighbors. One such neighbor, Steven Glover, was entrusted to watch over the family's home while the family was away on vacation. Glover had been a longtime friend and a member of the clergy at the Wilsons' church, but when months later Glover started commenting on how Susan was doing her hair in the bathroom, and making comments on other parts of their private lives, the Wilsons became suspicious. What they eventually found shocked them. Glover had secretly placed cameras in the Wilsons' bathroom, and above their bed, and was watching them in their most intimate moments.[13]

Students Erin Gallaher and Adrienne Hallett both used suspense to make their points. Which of the introductions do you think is more effective? Erin's speech began this way:

> Flip through any furniture catalog, and you'll be sure to note descriptions of color, style, fabric, and texture. When deciding to purchase a new sofa or armchair, most likely you'll carefully weigh options like "to recline or not to recline"—that is the question.
>
> But there is something that most people never even consider when they're shopping for upholstered furniture. What is this hidden feature? It's the extremely flammable polyurethane foam found in the cushions of virtually every piece of upholstered furniture in your home.[14]

Adrienne's speech began this way:

> He showed all of the classic symptoms. His response time was slowed, his judgement was impaired, but he thought he could handle it. As he drove home along the Interstate, his car swerved onto the shoulder of the road, running over and killing a man who was trying to change a flat tire. When the police questioned him later, he didn't remember a thing. What caused this Ohio man's actions is something we have all been guilty of, yet we won't readily admit it. Although the U.S. Department of Transportation estimates that it kills 13,000 people annually, no one will be taking the keys, calling a cab or taking a stand on this issue. Whenever we get into the driver's seat, we must be prepared for the risk presented by an impaired driver—surprisingly, not from alcohol but from a lack of sleep.[15]

Another student began a speech by asking a rhetorical question:

> Do you know who you voted for in the last presidential election? I bet you don't. I bet you think you voted for the Democratic, Republican, or Independent candidate. But you didn't. You voted to elect members of the electoral college. In the course of my speech, I will explain why this practice is undemocratic, un-American, and unacceptable.

Another student used frightening facts to jolt her audience:

> In the time it takes me to complete this sentence, a child in America will drop out of school. In the time it takes me to complete this sentence, a child in this country will run away from home. Before I finish this presentation, another teenage girl will have a baby.
>
> We have a country [that] is gripped by a lost generation. This is an invisible group of kids lost and alone on the streets. On their own, they are hungry, sick, and scared. They are victims of our society. They are victims who desperately need help.
>
> In this presentation I will show you how we can all help these kids.

Finally, many speakers use startling statistics to capture the audience's interest. The following example is from a speech entitled "Homeless Gay and Lesbian Youth: Confronting an Unseen Problem," by Daniel Roth:

> Handcuffed to a chair, packed in a room in a family court holding tank with two dozen other children, Max, 15, began to think about his recent past. Max left his mother's New York apartment a month before because he could no longer take the beating from his mother's boyfriend. He had lived in a "squat house" for three weeks, until the cops came down on him and bolted him to the chair. Max had told his mother and her boyfriend he was gay the month before, which was when the beatings began. Even though the United States Declaration of Independence claims all men are created equal, Max was

discovering the United States has declared a state of inequality for hundreds of thousands of American youth like him.

That night, Max was transferred to a group home with eight teenage boys who beat him nearly unconscious. The adults at the small residence failed to respond to his screams. The adults solved the problem by giving Max $2, and at 4 a.m., showing him the door. That night Max became one of the 42 percent of homeless youth who are gay and lesbian, according to the February 10, 1999, *St. Louis Post Dispatch*. In order to stop this injustice, we must first better understand the problems that force gay youth onto the streets so that we know what we can do to help them.[16]

The Preview

If your speech is organized in a linear fashion, after you have used your introduction to spark interest and motivate your audience to continue listening, it is necessary for you to preview your speech. That is, you need to let your audience know what you will be discussing. Consider the following examples of previews by student speakers:

> There are three "weight classes" of people in our society: the overweight, the underweight, and those who are the right weight. Unfortunately, many people fail to understand the role weight plays in their lives. Your weight affects how your body functions. Let's explore how.

> People have traditionally relied on oil or gas to heat their homes. Today, solar energy is gaining favor as an alternative. However, I believe there are four good reasons why it is inappropriate to consider installing a solar energy system in your home at this time.

Your preview should correspond to your purpose statement. It should let your audience know what to listen for. Additionally, by presenting it after you have gotten your listeners' attention and motivated them to continue paying attention, you ensure that your purpose statement will get a fair hearing.

The Conclusion

The conclusion summarizes the presentation and leaves your listeners thinking about what they have just heard. It provides a sense of closure.

Functions of the Conclusion

The conclusion's summary function may be considered a preview in reverse. During your preview, you look ahead, revealing to your listeners the subject of your efforts. During the summary, you review for them the material you have covered. For example, a summary might begin "We have examined three benefits you will derive from a new town library." During the remainder of this summation, the three benefits might be restated, to cement them in the minds of the listeners.

Inexperienced speech makers sometimes say that the summary appears to be superfluous ("After all, I've just said all of that not more than two minutes ago"). However, it is important to remember that you are speaking for your listeners, not for yourself. The summary provides some of the redundancy mentioned earlier; it enables audience members to leave with your ideas freshly impressed on their minds. In addition to refreshing your listeners' memory, the conclusion can help clarify the issues or ideas you have just discussed.

An effective conclusion heightens the impact of a presentation.

Besides serving as a summary, your conclusion should be used to heighten the impact of the presentation. You can do this in a number of ways. One popular technique is to refer to your introductory remarks; this gives your speech a sense of closure. If, for example, you are speaking about child abuse and you begin your presentation by showing pictures of abused children, you might paraphrase your opening remarks and show the pictures again, to arouse sympathy and support. Quotations and illustrations also make effective conclusions. For example, if you are speaking about the problems faced by veterans of the Gulf Wars, you could provide a moving conclusion by quoting some veterans or retelling some of the challenges they face. You are also free to draw on your own experiences when designing a conclusion. Keep in mind that, as they do with introductions, audiences respond to conclusions that include personal references, surprising statements, startling statistics, or relevant humor.

Types of Conclusions

Let's examine how some conclusion techniques work in practice. One student, for example, used an illustration to end a speech called "The Nature of AIDS":

> I take their hand and talk to them. I tell them I was happy I could make things easier. Then I say, "Thank you for letting me work for you." But every night before Jerry Cirasulolo goes to sleep, he also recites a little prayer: "Please God, give me the strength to keep on caring. And please don't let me get AIDS."

In a speech on identity theft, speaker R. J. Holmes concluded with a set of startling statistics:

> Today, we have become more and more careless about how we handle our money and the responsibilities associated with it. After identifying the problem,

realizing the dangers, and looking at ways to take back who we are as consumers, we can understand that identity theft is an issue which cannot be ignored. It may not seem like such a big problem to our generation, but with 74 percent of college students using one or more credit or charge cards, we are all the more vulnerable to becoming future victims of identity theft.[17]

Recognizing the effectiveness of statistics and rhetorical questions, Brian Swenson, a student at Dakota Wesleyan in South Dakota, ended a speech on guns and children with these words:

Today we have looked at a few cases of child shootings, some facts and statistics about child shootings, and what you should do if you own a gun to prevent this from happening to your children or other children. Now, maybe you still think that you don't need to lock up your gun and that this won't happen to you; but I have one more figure for you. One child is killed every day with a handgun, and for every child killed ten others are injured. Now, I have a question for you. Is your child going to be one of the ten that are injured, or is it going to be the one that is killed? The choice is yours.[18]

Quotations can increase the impact of a conclusion. Former attorney general Robert Kennedy often ended his speeches with the following words by the poet Robert Browning:

Some men see things as they are, and ask, "Why?" I dare to dream of things that never were, and ask—"Why not?"

Humor, when used appropriately, can help keep people on your side. One student ended a speech directed at first-year students with the following "letter":

Dear Mom and Dad:

Just thought I'd drop you a note to clue you in on my plans.

I've fallen in love with a guy named Buck. He quit high school between his sophomore and junior years to travel with his motorcycle gang. He was married at 18 and has two sons. About a year ago he got a divorce.

We plan to get married in the fall. He thinks he will be able to get a job by then. I've decided to move into his apartment. At any rate, I dropped out of school last week. Maybe I will finish college sometime in the future.

Mom and Dad, I just want you to know that everything in this letter so far is false. NONE OF IT IS TRUE.

But it is true that I got a C in French and a D in math. And I am in need of money for tuition and miscellaneous.

Love, _____

In a speech on the impact of technology, management consultant Chester Burger concluded his speech with the following observation and quotation:

In 1943, Thomas Watson, the chairman of IBM, said, "I think there is a world market for maybe five computers." Even a great visionary such as Mr. Watson couldn't foresee what would happen.[19]

In a speech on automobile insurance, one speaker included the following quotations from accident reports in his conclusion:

Coming home I drove into the wrong house and collided with a tree I don't have.

The other car collided with mine without giving warning of its intention.

I thought my window was down, but found it was up when I put my head
through it.

I pulled away from the side of the road, glanced at my mother-in-law, and
headed over the embankment.

I had been driving for 40 years when I fell asleep at the wheel and had an
accident.

I had been shopping for plants and was on my way home. As I reached an
intersection, a hedge sprang up, obscuring my vision.

In Summary: Using Introductions and Conclusions

To increase the effectiveness of your introductions and conclusions, use some
of these techniques:

Humor, when appropriate

Interesting illustrations or quotations

Rhetorical questions

Surprising statements or unusual facts

Startling statistics

TECHNOLOGY AND ORGANIZATION: THE HOME PAGE

Just as information is ordered in a speech, so collections of information—
including text, images, audio, video, and other types of data—are stored and
ordered in Web sites. A Web site opens with a **home page,** which details the
information in the site. The home page contains a title indicating what the
site is about, as well as headings that divide or categorize the topics or section to be found on the other Web pages within the site. (In addition, the
sections usually contain several paragraphs that elaborate on a specific topic.)
The home page may also contain links to other documents on the site or elsewhere on the Web. Thus, every home page is a graphical jumping-off point
to informational resources.

Web sites exist on virtually every subject. Public schools may host Web sites
that contain information about projects. Companies such as Apple, Levi Strauss,
and Coca-Cola all sport Web sites. When you visit a Web site, be sure to review
the home page to determine the organization of information in the site.

home page

the opening page of a Web
site, which details the
structure and ordering of
information in the site

ANALYZING YOUR PRESENTATION: THE TRYOUT

In the theater, playwrights, producers, directors, and performers would never
open an important show without first conducting a series of tryouts, or preview performances. These performances, often staged before invited guests or
audiences who pay reduced prices, give the cast and backers an opportunity
to experience audiences' reactions and, if necessary, make needed alterations.
As a speech maker, you would be wise to give yourself the same advantage.

Web Site Evaluation

Using a URL (uniform resource locator) or Web address, locate one of the following Web sites or a Web site of your choice:

Quotations (http://www.columbia.edu/acis/bartleby/bartlett)

Organization and outlining (http://www.inspiration.com/general_biz.html)

Almanacs and encyclopedias (http://www.infoplease.com)

Centers for Disease Control and Prevention (http://www.cdc.gov)

A great weather map (http://mit.edu:8001/usa.html)

Apple Computer (http://www.education.apple.com)

CNN (http://www.cnn.com)

Greenpeace International (http://www.greenpeace.org)

On the basis of your knowledge of effective organization, evaluate the extent to which the site is either well or poorly organized. Pay attention to your first impression of the site, the difficulty or ease you experience in trying to make sense out of it, the last impression you are left with prior to exiting the site, and whether you would choose to visit the site again.

Focus on Service Learning

How can an understanding of worldviews enable you to help a speaker from an Eastern culture deliver a speech to a predominantly Western audience and vice versa?

Once you've researched your topic, identified your supporting materials, and outlined your presentation, it's time to become your own audience—to explore the sound and feel of your speech. Three essential ingredients in your first tryout are your speech notes, a clock or wristwatch, and a tape or video recorder so that you can review the exact words you use to express your ideas. Before starting, check the time and turn on the recorder. You can then begin speaking. In effect, what you are doing is preparing an oral rough draft of your presentation.

What are you trying to determine? First, you want to know if your presentation consumes too much or too little time. If a run-through takes 25 minutes and your time limit is 5 minutes, you have serious revision ahead of you. If, on the other hand, you have designed a "60-second wonder," you may find that you need to go back to the library for more material. Second, as you actually listen to your speech, you should be alert for ideas that are not expressed as clearly as you would like. Third, you may find that the same thoughts are expressed again and again and again—more than is necessary for redundancy. Fourth, you may realize that the structure is confusing because of missing or inappropriate transitions. Fifth, you may have failed to develop an effective attention-getter. Sixth, the information in the body of your presentation may be too detailed or too technical for your audience. Seventh, your conclusion may not satisfy the psychological requirements you've established for it.

You can use the items on the following checklist to analyze the first tryout of your speech:

Topic

Date

Specific purpose

Length of presentation

Introduction

Attention-getter
Preview
    Most effective components
    Changes needed
Body
    Main points
    Support
    Most effective components
    Changes needed
Conclusion
    Summation function
    Psychological appeal
    Most effective components
    Changes needed

A modular approach is useful in making revisions. Electronic equipment is often designed with modules, which you can remove for repairs or replacement; similarly, you can extract selected modules from your outline to revise them, replace them, or delete them. For example, if you find that your main attention-getter is not as effective as it could be—improve it. If the supporting material under, say, the second main point in the body of your speech is confusing, rewrite it. If an illustration is too long and drawn out, shorten it. In other words, your goal during the tryout is to refine your speech until it is as close as possible to the one you will actually present. Once you reach that point, it is time to think about your delivery. Although we will consider delivery in depth in Chapter 17, before we do that, we need to discuss the importance of the preparation of an extemporaneous outline in your effectiveness as a speaker.

WORKING WITH AN EXTEMPORANEOUS OUTLINE

When you deliver an extemporaneous speech, instead of speaking from a script or word-for-word manuscript, you usually speak from brief notes. In order to be able to speak extemporaneously, you need to prepare an extemporaneous outline. Recall that an extemporaneous outline contains brief notes that remind the speaker of the key parts of the speech and make reference to the support the speaker will use to develop each point. The time for speakers to prepare an extemporaneous outline is after they have practiced delivering the speech a few times using a more detailed outline. Once speakers are comfortable and familiar with the speech, they are ready to rely on only the extemporaneous outline during their final practice sessions.

The extemporaneous outline should be prepared using regular 8½- by 11-inch paper, or notes should be entered on 5- by 7-inch note cards. Whatever format you opt to use, be sure to include the following: reminder phrases for the introduction; a statement of the central idea or thesis; brief notes on the main points and subpoints, including the complete names of sources or citations for references; transition reminders; and reminder phrases for the conclusion of your speech.

While the goal is to keep the extemporaneous outline as brief as possible so you won't be tempted to read your notes instead of maintaining eye contact with audience members, you will want to include a number of delivery cues in the card's margins, such as "emphasize" or "hold up the visual aid," much as an actor marks up a script, to help facilitate your speaking smoothness.

Revisiting Chapter Objectives

1. **Identify main and subordinate ideas.**   Organization is one of the main challenges facing the speech maker. Part of the organizational challenge is to distinguish between main and subordinate ideas. Main ideas are the primary points of a speech. Subordinate ideas amplify the main ideas.

2. **Create a complete sentence outline.**   One of the best ways to organize your speech is to build its framework and prepare a complete sentence outline using the introduction-body-conclusion format. Since the body of the speech is the main part of your presentation, it should be prepared first.

3. **Identify five methods of ordering ideas.**   There are five generally accepted ways based on linear logic to order the ideas in a speech: (1) chronological order, (2) spatial order, (3) cause-and-effect order, (4) problem-and-solution order, and (5) topical order. Speakers from a number of cultural groups prefer to use configural logic to structure their ideas.

4. **Use internal summaries and transitions effectively.**   When you use linear logic, the body of your presentation must also have internal summaries and transitions to help listeners recall the content. (Professional speakers today must be prepared to give very short synopses—sound bites—to the media if they want to appear on the air.)

5. **Develop an effective introduction and conclusion.**   After the body of the speech has been completed, you are ready to prepare the introduction and conclusion. The introduction should gain the attention of the audience members, make them want to listen to your speech, and provide them with an overview of the subject to be discussed. Devices used to enhance introductions include humor, illustrations, questions, surprising statements, and statistics.

The purpose of the conclusion is to summarize the material covered, heighten the impact of the presentation, and enable the audience to leave the occasion with your ideas freshly impressed on their minds. Devices used to increase the effectiveness of conclusions include surprising statements, rhetorical questions, quotations, and humor.

6. **Use a tryout to refine a speech.**   When you have completed the outline for the entire speech, you should become your own audience: Try out the speech and analyze the results. Be sure to take into account any cultural barriers that might affect your presentation to be sure that your presentation is clear to all members of your audience.

Resources for Further Inquiry and Reflection

To apply your understanding of how the principles in Chapter 16 are at work in our daily lives, consult the following resources for further inquiry and reflection. Or, if you prefer, choose any other appropriate resource. Then connect the ideas expressed in your chosen selection with the communication concepts and issues you are learning about both in and out of class.

 Listen to Me

"Ode to Billie Joe" (Bobby Gentry)
"Cats in the Cradle" (Harry Chapin)
"Scenes from an Italian Restaurant" (Billy Joel)

What organizational schema does the speaker use to tell the song's story? Why do you think that this story structure was selected? Could the song have been organized using another approach? Why or why not?

 View Me

Mars Attacks!   *Independence Day*

Compare and contrast the main speeches of the chief executive in each film. How does each commander-in-chief structure his address? Which do you evaluate as more effective and why?

 Read Me

Jerome Lawrence. *Inherit the Wind*. New York: Random House, 1955.

How do both sides on the evolution/creationism debate begin, develop, and end their presentations to the court?

 Tell Me

Share with the class the insights you gained from your chosen Listen to Me, View Me, or Read Me selection.

Find examples that enable you to support or negate the following: It is equally effective to develop a speech using formal rules of logic or holistically.

Key Chapter Terminology

Use the Communication Works CD-ROM and the Online Learning Center at www.mhhe.com/gamble8 to further your knowledge of the following terminology.

cause-and-effect order 490

chronological, or time, order 488

configural formats 493

home page 503

internal summaries 494

linear logic 493

main ideas 484

problem-and-solution order 492

spatial order 489

speech framework 483

subordinate ideas 484

topical order 492

transitions 495

Communication Works

online learning center

www.mhhe.com/gamble8

Communication
Works

online learning center

www.mhhe.com/gamble8

Test Your Understanding

Go to the *Self Quizzes* on the Communication Works CD-ROM and the book's Online Learning Center at www.mhhe.com/gamble8.

Notes

1. See, for example, Margaret J. Wheatley. *Leadership and the New Science.* San Francisco: Berrett-Koehler, 1994.

2. Several studies reveal how organization affects reception. For example, see Christopher Spicer and Ronald E. Bassett. "The Effect of Organization on Learning from an Informative Message." *Southern States Communication Journal* 41, 1976, pp. 290–299; and Johen E. Baird, Jr. "The Effects of Speech Summaries upon Audience Comprehension of Expository Speeches of Varying Quality and Complexity." *Central States Speech Journal* 25, 1974, pp. 119–127.

3. Richard Nisbett. *The Geography of Thought: How Asians and Westerners Think Differently . . . and Why.* New York: The Free Press, 2003.

4. National Public Radio. "Analysis: Geography of Thought." *Talk of the Nation* broadcast of interview of Richard Nisbett by Neal Conan, March 3, 2003.

5. National Public Radio.

6. Myron W. Lustig and Jolene Koester. *Intercultural Competence: Interpersonal Communication across Cultures,* 3rd ed. New York: Longman. 1999.

7. D.L. Thislethwaite, H. deHaan, and J. Kamenetsky suggest that a message is more easily understood and accepted if transitions are used; see "The Effect of 'Directive' and 'Non-Directive' Communication Procedures on Attitudes." *Journal of Abnormal and Social Psychology* 51, 1955, pp. 107–118. Also of value on this aspect of speech organization is E. Thompson. "Some Effects of Message Structure on Listeners' Comprehension." *Speech Monographs* 34, 1967, pp. 51–57.

8. For a more comprehensive treatment of introductions and conclusions, see Gamble and Gamble. *Public Speaking in the Age of Diversity,* 2nd ed. Boston: Allyn & Bacon, 1998, Chap. 10.

9. Tim Norbeck. "The Patient Must Get Some Protection." *Vital Speeches of the Day* 66:12, April 1, 2000, p. 372. Reprinted with permission.

10. Ted Koppel. "What Passes and What Lasts." *Vital Speeches of the Day* 60:19, July 15, 1994, p. 583. Reprinted with permission.

11. Richard L. Weaver II. "Motivating the Motivators." *Vital Speeches of the Day* Vol 62 Issue 15 May 15, 1996, p. 466. Reprinted with permission.

12. Ajay Krishnan. "Is Mr. Goodwrench Really Mr. Rip Off?" *Winning Orations.* Mankato, MN: Interstate Oratorical Association, 1998, p. 120. Reprinted with permission.

13. Erin O'Dell. Untitled. *Winning Orations.* Mankato, MN: Interstate Oratorical Association, 2000, p. 43. Reprinted with permission.

14. Erin Gallaher. "Upholstered Furniture: Sitting in the Uneasy Chair." *Winning Orations.* Mankato, MN: Interstate Oratorical Association, 2000, p. 99. Reprinted with permission.

15. Adrienne Hallett. "Dying in Your Sleep." Northfield, MN: Interstate Oratorical Association, 1995, p. 27. Reprinted with permission.

16. Daniel Roth. "Homeless Gay and Lesbian Youth: Confronting an Unseen Problem." *Winning Orations.* Mankato, MN: Interstate Oratorical Association, 2000, p. 108. Reprinted with permission.

17. R. J. Homes. "Other People's Money: The Problem with Identity Theft." *Winning Orations.* Mankato, MN: Interstate Oratorical Association, 1998, p. 39. Reprinted with permission.

18. Brian Swenson. "Gun Safety and Children." *Winning Orations.* Mankato, MN: Interstate Oratorical Association, 1990, p. 101. Reprinted with permission.

19. Chester Burger. "Sooner Than You Think." *Vital Speeches of the Day* 66:23, September 15, 2000, p. 715.

Delivering Your Speech: Presenting Your Ideas

After finishing this chapter, you should be able to

1. Assess your level of speech anxiety.

2. Use deep-muscle relaxation, thought stopping, visualization, and other techniques to reduce speech anxiety.

3. Discuss four types of delivery: manuscript, memorized, impromptu, and extemporaneous.

4. Identify how the speaker can use visual and vocal cues to advantage.

5. Analyze a speech maker's performance (including your own) in terms of content, organization, language, and delivery.

The human brain is a wonderful thing. It operates from the moment you're born until the first time you get up to make a speech.

—Howard Goshom

The greatest mistake you can make in life is to be continually fearing you will make one.

—Elbert Hubbard

Your research is finished. Your speech is prepared. You have been assigned a presentation date. What happens next? If you're like most speakers, you shift your focus to thinking about delivering your presentation. As your focus shifts, you begin to feel more anxious. Maybe you feel tired or suffer from indigestion. Your back may hurt or you may feel a headache coming on. There are a host of ailments correlated with anxiety.[1] You feel so anxious that you wonder if you will really gather the courage to stand and speak before an audience. The answer is "Of course, you will!" You can overcome whatever anxiety you feel by understanding its sources, learning to cope with your fears, using strategies to handle both the physical and mental symptoms of anxiety, and finally methodically rehearsing your presentation, because the greatest fear that many speakers have is forgetting what they are going to say.[2]

DEALING WITH ANXIETY AND SPEECH FRIGHT

One prominent motivational speaker begins his presentations as follows:

Go to the *Online Learning Center* at www.mhhe.com/gamble8 and answer the questions in the *Self Inventory* to evaluate your understanding of speech anxiety.

I couldn't sleep last night. I finally got up at 4 this morning. I got dressed and went through this presentation 37 times. And guess what? You loved it. [Gentle laughter.] And let me tell you one thing I'll never forget about this group. That is, when I got introduced, everyone was standing. [More laughter.] Tell you what I'm going to do. I'm going to reintroduce myself, and what I want you to do is just give me the welcome you gave me this morning. Just pump it up, OK? Are you ready? [Music pulses.] Ladies and gentlemen, all the way from Atlanta, GA. If you forget everything I say, don't forget this. . . . You are the best at what you do because of one main thing: Attitude. [The audience stands and cheers.][3]

Rehearsal is an integral part of speech preparation. It also helps decrease anxiety.

What attitude do you have toward speaking in public? Fear, or anxiety, is something that affects most public speakers.[4] It is so common that, when queried, many persons answer that they would rather be in the casket at a funeral than be delivering the eulogy. Thus, if you experience a certain amount of apprehension before, during, or after presenting a speech, rest assured that you are not alone.[5] Students sometimes allow their fears to get the better of them. Instead of using anxiety as a positive force, they let it overwhelm them. To combat this, in this chapter we'll look at ways to make speech fright, or **speech apprehension** (fear of speaking to an audience), one form of **communication apprehension** (fear of communication, no matter what the context) actually work for you.

Approximately 20 percent of the U.S. population is "trait" communication apprehensive. This means that they exhibit a predisposition to being apprehensive and display escalated nervousness levels in most, if not all, communication situations. On the other hand, nearly all of us experience occasional "state" communication apprehension. This means that, when facing a specific situation, such as public speaking, we display a somewhat elevated nervousness level.[6] To determine your communication apprehension score, you can take the self-analysis quiz included in the section "Self-Analysis: How Anxious Are You?" or access The Perceived Report of Communication Apprehension (PRCA) developed by James McCroskey, cited on his Web page (http://www.as.wvu.edu/~jmccrosk/jcmhp/html) under Publications.

speech apprehension
fear of speaking to an audience

communication apprehension
fear of communication, no matter what the context

Is Compulsory Speech Making Fair?

Studies show that many people fear public speaking more than they fear death. Is it fair to demand that all students face up to their fear and take a course that requires them to deliver at least one speech? Are there other options that could provide the same skills without actually involving standing in front of an audience? Explain your opinion.

Ethics & COMMUNICATION

Understanding Your Fears

Self-Analysis: How Anxious Are You?

How anxious are you about delivering a speech? Use the following inventory to find out. Although this inventory is not a scientific instrument, it should give you some indication of your level of fear. Note that you must display some level of anxiety to be categorized as "normal." If you had no anxiety about speaking in public, you would not be considered normal; what's more, you would probably not be a very effective speech maker.

For each statement, circle the number that best represents your response:

1. I am afraid I will forget what I have to say.
   Not afraid   1   2   3   4   5   Extremely afraid

2. I am afraid my ideas will sound confused and jumbled.
   Not afraid   1   2   3   4   5   Extremely afraid

3. I am afraid my appearance will be inappropriate.
   Not afraid   1   2   3   4   5   Extremely afraid

4. I am afraid the audience will find my speech boring.
   Not afraid   1   2   3   4   5   Extremely afraid

5. I am afraid people in the audience will laugh at me.
   Not afraid   1   2   3   4   5   Extremely afraid

6. I am afraid I will not know what to do with my hands.
   Not afraid   1   2   3   4   5   Extremely afraid

7. I am afraid my instructor will embarrass me.
   Not afraid   1   2   3   4   5   Extremely afraid

8. I am afraid audience members will think my ideas are simplistic.
   Not afraid   1   2   3   4   5   Extremely afraid

9. I am afraid I will make grammatical mistakes.
   Not afraid   1   2   3   4   5   Extremely afraid

10. I am afraid everyone will stare at me.
    Not afraid   1   2   3   4   5   Extremely afraid

Next, add the numbers you chose and rate yourself as follows:

41–50 Very apprehensive	11–20 Overconfident
31–40 Apprehensive	10 Are you alive?
21–30 Normally concerned	

Causes of Speech Apprehension

Before we can cope with our fears, we need to develop a clearer understanding of what causes them. Following are some of the more common causes of speech apprehension.

Fear of Inadequacy   If adequacy is a state of feeling confident and capable, inadequacy is just the opposite—that is, feeling inferior and incapable. Feeling inadequate may cause us to assume that we will be unable to cope with writing or speaking. Do you fear to take risks because you imagine your performance will not be good enough or will be judged inadequate or not up to par? When you disagree with something you have read or heard, do you feel more comfortable swallowing hard and sitting quietly than you do speaking up for or writing about what you think is right? Is it easier for you to go along with a group than to write or speak your objections to other people's actions or words? If you feel inadequate, you probably prefer to play it safe; you do not want to put yourself in a position where you might feel even more inadequate.

Fear of the Unknown A new job may cause us to feel fearful because our co-workers, the situation, and our responsibilities are unfamiliar, unknown, or still unclear. We may fear writing a paper or delivering a speech for the same reasons. Each new event has a threatening, unknown quality—a quality that many people prefer not to deal with. When such an event involves writing or speaking, we may be afraid because we do not know how people will react to what we write or say. We simply are more comfortable with what is familiar— with the tried and true. Although we have a cognitive understanding of what is and is not likely to happen before an audience or in the mind of a reader, we let our feelings take charge, causing us to react emotionally and behave irrationally.

Fear of Being Judged How sensitive are you to the judgment of others? Are you concerned about a friend's opinion of or judgment about you? An instructor's? Do you believe that what an audience, a reader, or an instructor concludes about you is necessarily true? Sometimes we become so sensitive to the judgments of others that we try to avoid judgment altogether. Public speaking is one situation in which such an attitude is common.

Fear of Consequences Basically, one of two things can result from giving a speech: The audience may like it or may dislike it. That is, it will be a success or a failure. This basic result may then have further consequences. In the classroom, for example, an unsatisfactory speech may result in a failing grade. In a business situation, it may result in the loss of an important account. Whatever the consequences, the speaker must be prepared to deal with them.

Learning to Cope with Your Fears: Controlling Anxiety

One of the best ways to cope with the fear of speech making is to design and rehearse your presentation carefully. The systematic approach suggested in this chapter covers both design and rehearsal and should—at least in theory— decrease your anxiety by increasing your self-confidence. However, theory and reality do sometimes diverge and, preparation notwithstanding, you may still find that you experience some anxiety about your speech. Let us now see how such anxiety can be controlled.

Symptoms of Anxiety

The first thing you need to do is recognize the actual bodily sensations and thoughts that accompany and support your feelings of nervousness.

Examine the symptoms that you and others in your class identify. Do your lists include any of these physical symptoms?

Rapid or irregular heartbeat

Stomach knots

Shaking hands, arms, or legs

Dry mouth

Stiff neck

Lump in the throat

Nausea

Diarrhea

Dizziness

When people are asked about fear-related thoughts, they often make statements like the following. Were any of these included on your lists?

"I just can't cope."

"I'm irritable."

"I'm under such pressure."

"This is a nightmare."

"I know something terrible is going to happen."

"Why does the world have to crumble around me?"

Once you have identified the physical and mental sensations that accompany fear, your next step is to learn how to control these reactions.[7] The next sections describe behavior modification techniques that can help you.

Deep-Muscle Relaxation: Overcoming Physical Symptoms

Muscle tension commonly accompanies fear and anxiety. However, a muscle will relax after being tensed. Deep-muscle relaxation is based on this fact.

Try this: Tense one arm. Count to 10. Now relax your arm. What feelings did you experience? Did your arm seem to become heavier? Did it then seem to become warmer? Next, try tensing and relaxing one or both of your legs. When you examine what happens, you'll see why it is reasonable to expect that you can calm yourself by systematically tensing and relaxing various parts of your body in turn.

Skill BUILDER

Tense and Relax

1. Imagine that your body is divided into four basic sections:
   a. Hands and arms
   b. Face and neck
   c. Torso
   d. Legs and feet
2. Sit comfortably. In turn, practice tensing and relaxing each of these four sections of your body.
   a. *Hands and arms.* Clench your fists. Tense each arm from shoulder to fingertips. Notice the warm feeling that develops in your hands, forearms, and upper arms. Count to 10. Relax.
   b. *Face and neck.* Wrinkle your face as tightly as you can. Press your head back as far as it will go. Count to 10. Relax. Roll your head slowly to the front, side, back, and side in a circular movement. Relax.
   c. *Torso.* Shrug your shoulders. Count to 10 in this position. Relax. Tighten your stomach. Hold it. Relax.
   d. *Legs and feet.* Tighten your hips and thighs. Relax. Tense your calves and feet. Relax

"Calm"

1. Work through the procedure described in the text for releasing tension.

2. As soon as you experience the warm feeling throughout your body, say to yourself, "Calm." Try this several times, each time working to associate the "de-tensed" feeling with the word *calm*.

3. The next time you find yourself in a stress-producing situation, say, "Calm," to yourself and attempt to achieve the de-tensed state.

You will want to try using the Skill Builder "Tense and Relax" several times before you actually present a speech. Many students report that butterflies or tensions tend to settle in particular bodily sections. Thus, it can be helpful to check the bodily sensations you feel when anxious, and personalize "Tense and Relax" to deal with your individual symptoms.

Thought Stopping: Overcoming Mental Symptoms

Anxiety is not simply a physical phenomenon; it also manifests itself cognitively—that is, in thoughts. Thus it is important to work to eliminate the thoughts associated with anxiety, as well as the bodily symptoms.

Many people use the word *relax* to calm themselves. Unfortunately, *relax* doesn't sound very relaxing to some people. You can substitute the word *calm*. Try the Skill Builder "Calm."

A variation on the "calm technique" is to precede the word *calm* with the word *stop*. When you begin to think upsetting thoughts, say to yourself, "Stop!" Then follow that command with "Calm"—for example,

> "I just can't get up in front of all those people. Look at their cold stares and mean smirks."
>
> "Stop!"
>
> "Calm."

You may find that you can adapt this thought-stopping technique to help you handle symptoms of anxiety in interpersonal situations.

Visualization: A Positive Approach

Sports psychologists use a technique called visualization to help athletes compete more effectively. The athletes are guided in visualizing the successful completion of a play or a game. They are asked to imagine how they will feel when they win. Eventually, when they go out on the field to compete, it is almost as if they have been there before—and have already won.

You may want to try this technique to boost your confidence as a speaker. Sit in a quiet place. Picture yourself approaching the podium. See yourself delivering your presentation. Then hear your audience applaud appreciatively. After you have actually delivered the speech, answer these questions: Did the experience help you control your anxiety? Did it help you succeed?

Think you can or think you can't; either way you will be right.

—Henry Ford

Other Techniques

Speakers report that other techniques can also help reduce speech apprehension. Some try to include a bit of humor early in the speech to get a favorable response from the audience right away. They say that such a reaction helps them calm their nerves for the remainder of the presentation. Others look for a friendly face and talk to that person for a moment or two early in the speech. Others use charts, graphs, and other visuals to help them organize the material. In this technique, the visual shows the next major point to be covered, eliminating the necessity for the speaker to remember it or refer to notes. Still others report that they rehearse a speech aloud, standing in front of an imaginary audience and "talking through" the material again and again. What other techniques have you and your classmates found helpful?

Remember, no matter how you choose to deal with it, fear is a natural response to public speaking and can probably never be eliminated completely. But you do need to learn to cope with fear; only in this way will you be able to deliver a successful, well-received presentation.

REHEARSING YOUR PRESENTATION

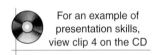

For an example of presentation skills, view clip 4 on the CD

All speakers need to rehearse their presentations. It is common knowledge that presidents practice by videotaping and reviewing their performance before delivering an address. Corporate leaders often spend hours rehearsing and refining the presentations they will deliver at sales meetings, stockholders' meetings, and so on. Actors, obviously, rehearse before a new play or production opens. It stands to reason that only the most foolhardy and unconcerned souls would undertake to deliver a speech that they have not adequately rehearsed.

By now, you have tried out your presentation orally at least once. During the tryout stage, your purpose was to analyze your speech in order to identify any changes that needed to be made. That done, you are now ready to begin rehearsing the speech as you will deliver it.

Options for Delivery

There are four general types of delivery available to you as a speech maker: (1) manuscript, (2) memorized, (3) impromptu, and (4) extemporaneous. We will briefly examine all four options.

Manuscript Speeches

manuscript speech

a speech read from a script

A **manuscript speech** is written out word-for-word and then read aloud by the speech maker. Manuscript speeches are most common when it is imperative that precise language be used. For example, since presidential addresses are likely to be under close scrutiny not only in this country but throughout the world, they often are read from a typed page or a TelePrompTer. When corporate speakers are discussing matters with sensitive legal and commercial aspects, they may choose to deliver a manuscript speech.

Unfortunately, the use of a manuscript tends to reduce eye contact between speaker and audience. Furthermore, speakers reading aloud often sound as if they are reading to, rather than talking to, the audience, and thus it is difficult, if not impossible, to establish the much needed conversational tone.

Memorized Speeches

A **memorized speech** is a manuscript speech that the speaker has committed to memory. This delivery style frequently takes on a canned tone—often glaringly. Also, speakers who have memorized their lines are less able to respond to audience feedback than they would be if they were working from notes. Additionally, of course, there is the problem of retention. Speech makers who insist on memorizing their presentations word-for-word often find themselves plagued by memory lapses, leading to long, awkward silences, during which they valiantly attempt to recall forgotten material. You may want to memorize certain key words, phrases, or segments of your speech, but at this point in your career there is little reason for you to commit the entire presentation to memory.

memorized speech
a manuscript speech committed to memory

Impromptu Speeches

An **impromptu speech** is a speech you deliver spontaneously, or on the spur of the moment without formal preparation. In many ways, it is the antithesis of a memorized speech. Memorization requires extensive preparation, but someone who must deliver an impromptu speech often has no more than a few seconds or minutes to gather his or her thoughts. An impromptu speaking situation may arise, for example, when a boss unexpectedly asks an employee to discuss the status of a project that is still in its developmental stages. If you are faced with such a request, you will need to rely on what you have learned about patterning your ideas; using the introduction-body-conclusion format will facilitate your task.

impromptu speech
a speech delivered spontaneously or on the spur of the moment

Extemporaneous Speeches

An **extemporaneous speech** is researched, outlined, and then delivered after careful rehearsal. Extemporaneous speaking is more audience-centered than any of the preceding options. Since the speech is prepared in advance and rehearsed, the speaker is free to establish eye contact with the members of the audience and to respond to feedback. In addition, because extemporaneous speakers may use notes, they are not constrained by a need to commit the entire presentation to memory. Nor are they handicapped by a manuscript that must be read word-for-word, inhibiting their adaptability.

extemporaneous speech
a speech that is researched, outlined, and delivered after careful rehearsal

Unfortunately, many speakers confuse manuscript, memorized, and impromptu speeches with extemporaneous speeches. Although asked to give an extemporaneous speech, they may insist on writing it out word-for-word and then either memorizing or reading it. Or they may spend too little time preparing the speech and deliver what is essentially a poorly developed impromptu presentation. This sort of misconception defeats their purpose and decreases their effectiveness as speech makers. The extemporaneous speech has been found most effective for most public speakers. Above all, don't turn extemporaneous speaking into what it is not.

Visual Considerations

When we speak in public, we have three basic kinds of tools at our disposal: (1) verbal, (2) visual, and (3) vocal. By this time, you have exerted considerable effort to develop the verbal aspects of your presentation. We now need to devote some time and attention to the visual and vocal dimensions. This section takes up visual considerations.

In addition to your ideas, what aspects of yourself do you want to communicate to an audience? If you're like most speakers, you want your audience to accept you as a credible source. As we will see in Chapter 19, this means that you want your listeners to consider you competent, trustworthy, and dynamic.

How is credibility communicated? Obviously, it is conveyed verbally, through the content and structure of language. However, far too frequently, speakers forget that credibility is also conveyed through visual and vocal cues. As we noted in Chapter 6, the nonverbal components of a message account for at least 65 percent of the total meaning transmitted to listeners. Thus, the visual and vocal dimensions of your speech merit careful attention.

Let's first consider visual cues. How do you think a speech maker should look standing before an audience? Close your eyes and picture his or her clothing, posture, gestures, movements and facial expressions, and use of eye contact.

Clothing

During the 2000 presidential debates, both the Democratic candidate, Al Gore, and the Republican candidate, George W. Bush, arrived at the first debate wearing dark suits, white shirts, and that traditional power symbol, the

The clothing a speaker wears should reinforce, not detract from, the presentation.

solid red tie. One fashion designer noted: "They both looked exactly the same, which I think is a reflection of how the Republican Party is trying to look Democratic and somehow the Democratic Party is becoming more Republican. They're mirroring each other and merging into one thing."[8] Others found differences in the nuances of their apparel. One fashion creative director noted that, while they looked the same, in terms of what their clothing means, they were worlds apart. For example, Vice President Gore wore a three-button suit, and the shoulders were softer, connoting more of a European sensibility than Governor Bush's stiffer, two-button suit. In addition, the points of the vice president's shirt collar were far narrower than the ones on Governor Bush's shirt, whose collar had a more conservative look.[9]

In deciding what to wear when you deliver your speech, you should consider the topic, the audience, and the occasion. Sometimes, in contrast to the candidates previously mentioned, speakers make thoughtless errors in dress. For example, one student delivered a very serious tribute to a well-known leader while wearing a shirt emblazoned with a huge Mickey Mouse emblem. (When asked why, he responded, "I didn't think anyone would notice.") One woman addressing a group of executives on the need for conservatism in office attire chose to wear a bright red suit, polka-dot silver blouse, and floppy, red and silver hat. (Audience members later commented on the dichotomy between her topic and her own clothing.)

Be aware that it's up to you to choose what you will wear. Your clothing does not choose you.

Posture

As a public speaker, you will almost always be expected to stand up when addressing your audience. Thus, unless you are physically challenged—in which case, your audience will, of course, understand—you should expect to be on your feet. Although this may seem obvious, the problem is that standing is something many of us do not do very well. Your posture communicates; it sends potent messages to the audience. Speakers often seem to forget this, assuming a stance that works against them rather than for them. For example, some speakers lean on the lectern or actually drape themselves over it as if unable to stand without its assistance. Some perch on one foot like a crane. Some prop themselves against the wall behind them, giving the impression that they want to disappear into it.

To prepare yourself to stand properly in public, you should assume your natural posture and ask others to evaluate it. Are you too stiff? Do you slouch? Do you appear too relaxed? Feedback can help you put your best posture forward when you rise to speak.

Gestures

As we noted in Chapter 6, gestures are movements of a speaker's hands and arms. The gestures you use when speaking in public may be purposeful, helping reinforce the content of your speech, or purposeless, detracting from your message. A problem most of us encounter is that we have certain favorite gestures that we are unaware of doing—things like scratching our neck, putting our hands into and out of our pockets, jingling our keys or jewelry, or smoothing our hair. Such mannerisms often become intensified when we find ourselves faced with a stressful situation such as speaking in public. In fact, when people are nervous, it is not unusual for them to add new gestures to their repertoire of annoying mannerisms. Speakers will sometimes tap a pencil or ring on the lectern or even crack their knuckles—things they would never do in normal circumstances.

Gestures can, however, serve a number of useful purposes. They can help you emphasize important points, enumerate your ideas, or suggest shapes or sizes. Thus, your job with regard to gestures is really twofold. First, you need to work to eliminate annoying gestures; second, you need to incorporate appropriate gestures that can be used to enhance the ideas contained in your speech.

Movements and Facial Expressions

It's important to understand that your presentation really begins as soon as you are introduced or called on to speak—that is, before you have uttered your first syllable. The way you rise and approach the speaker's stand communicates a first impression to your listeners. Similarly, your facial expressions as you complete your speech and your walk as you return to your seat also send important signals to your audience. Far too many speech makers

Stand up before the class and recite the alphabet. As you do so, make as many annoying gestures as you can. Then recite the alphabet a second time. During this second recitation, make gestures that are as appropriate as possible.

Eye contact draws receivers into a presentation.

approach the lectern in inappropriate ways. For example, they may walk in a way that broadcasts a lack of preparation. Some even verbalize this by mumbling something like "I'm really not ready. This will be terrible." Others apologize for a poor showing all the way back to their seats.

Consider carefully your way of moving to and from the speaker's stand. The way you move communicates whether or not you are in control. You may have noticed that confident people walk with head erect, follow a straight rather than a circuitous path, proceed at an assured rather than a hesitant or frenetic pace, and use open rather than closed arm movements.

Eye Contact

Eye contact also communicates. Unfortunately, some speakers "talk" to walls, chalkboards, windows, trees, or the floor rather than to their listeners. Some speakers seem embarrassed to look at any audience members; others seek the attention of one person and avoid looking at anyone else. Some student speakers avoid meeting the eyes of the instructor during a speech; others focus on him or her exclusively.

Be sure that your gaze includes all the members of the audience. Look at each individual as you deliver your speech. Such contact will draw even the most reluctant listeners into your presentation.

Vocal Considerations

Obviously, the voice is one of our main tools in speech making. Your voice is to your speech as the artist's brush is to a painting. The brush carries colors to the canvas just as your voice transmits ideas to your listeners. In Chapter 6, we considered four basic vocal dimensions: volume, rate, pitch, and quality. You should review this material during your rehearsals, keeping in mind that your goal is to use your voice to reinforce the content of your speech.

To respond to your ideas, your audience must, of course, first hear them. Maintaining your voice at an appropriate volume is your responsibility. If you are to address a group in a large auditorium, a public-address system will probably be provided. The system should be of good quality and have sufficient power for the space. If you are addressing a group in a smaller room, you will probably be expected to speak without amplification. By observing the people in the rear, you should be able to determine if you are speaking loudly enough for them to hear you easily. If you notice that any of the audience members look confused or upset, speak up. On the other hand, if your voice is normally loud and you notice that those seated nearest to you are cringing, turn down your volume a bit.

With regard to pitch, try not to fall into the monotone trap. If you maintain one predominant tone throughout your presentation, you will create a sense of boredom in the audience. Use pitch to reflect the emotional content of your material; use it to create interest.

Like volume and pitch, rate also communicates. Speaking too quickly or too slowly can impede understanding. Thus, respond to feedback from your audience and speed up or slow down your pace as appropriate.

Nonfluencies are a problem every public speaker needs to consider. "Uhs" and "ums" are normal in communication encounters, but they are not expected in speech making. During person-to-person conversations, we realize that people are thinking about or planning what they are going to say next. In contrast, we expect public speakers to have prepared their remarks carefully, and thus we are less tolerant of their nonfluencies. You should attempt to eliminate nonfluencies from your delivery as much as possible.

Rehearsal Procedures: Communicating Confidence

Rehearsal—careful practice of your presentation—can help you acquire the confidence you need to deliver an effective speech. At this point, you have prepared an outline and appropriate visuals. Your task is to synthesize these ingredients into a polished presentation. Although rehearsal is a highly individualized matter, you can use some basic guidelines.

First, begin the rehearsal process by reading through your outline several times, developing a list of key words and main points to be covered. These may become the basis of your delivery notes.

Second, learn your first and last sentences. Many speakers find it helpful to commit the first and last sentences of an address to memory. If you do not memorize your opening and closing sentences, you should at least become very familiar with them. (As one student put it, "That way I know that I'll be able to start and stop the speech.")

Third, conduct a preliminary auditory rehearsal. Stand up and face an imaginary audience. Present the entire speech. Time yourself. This will give you an idea of how the final address will sound.

Keep a log of your progress during rehearsals. Each time you rehearse, note the location of the rehearsal, the problems you encountered, the changes you made, and any progress you observed.

"I'm practicin' my speech."

© Bil Keane. Reprinted with special permission of King Features Syndicate.

Fourth, conduct additional rehearsals. Rehearse for several days, sometimes alone, at other times before a small group of friends or relatives. If you want, use an audio- or videocassette recorder.

When rehearsing, be sure to incorporate all your audio and visual aids into the presentation. Also, practice delivering the speech in several locations; this will help you get used to the foreign feel of the room where the speech will actually be presented. Your goal is to develop a flexible delivery—one that will enable you to meet the unique demands of the live audience.

GIVING THE SPEECH: SOME FINAL TIPS

If you follow the developmental plan outlined in this book, you should find yourself ready and eager to deliver your speech. Not only will you have carefully prepared and rehearsed your address, you will also have at your disposal tested techniques to help you control your nerves. At this juncture, you should need only a few additional pointers:

1. Arrive at your speaking location with ample time to spare. Be sure that you have prepared equipment to hold your notes and presentation aids.

2. If you are going to use a public-address system or other electronic equipment, test it so that you will not have to adjust the volume or replace bulbs or batteries unnecessarily during your presentation.

3. Give ample consideration to your clothing and appearance. Your confidence and believability will increase if you look the part. (But don't distract yourself with worries about your appearance while you are speaking.)

4. Let your audience know you are prepared by the way you rise when introduced and by walking confidently to the podium.

5. While speaking, work to transmit a sense of enthusiasm and commitment to your listeners. Some speech makers find it useful to write the word *enthusiasm, commitment,* or *confidence* on a 3- by 5-inch card that they take with them to the speaker's stand. The card helps them remember to communicate these qualities.

6. Complete your speech before returning to your seat. You've worked hard to communicate your credibility to audience members; don't blow it in the last few seconds. Last impressions, like first impressions, count.

AFTER THE SPEECH: EVALUATING YOUR EFFECTIVENESS

As soon as you have completed your presentation, the first question you will ask yourself is "How did I do?" No doubt you will also want to know what your peers and your instructor thought of your performance.[10] You and your listeners can evaluate your speech by analyzing how effectively you were able to handle each of the following: content, organization, language, and delivery.

Multicultural Communication Classes

EXPLORING
Diversity

Although made over two decades ago, the observations of communication scholar Dean Barnlund ring even more true today: Few communication classes are composed of students who are "cultural replicas" of each other. A number of students in your class may speak in different native tongues (English is their second language); they may also move at different paces, gesture in different ways, and respond to or seek different values.

What kinds of challenges do these differences pose for speakers and for listeners? Explain.

Should we expect that foreign students in the United States be cultural replicas of Americans? Why or why not?

Content

Was the subject of your speech appropriate? Was it worthwhile? Was your purpose communicated clearly? Did you research the topic carefully? Were your audiovisual aids helpful? Did you use a variety of supports? Were your main points adequately developed? Were your main divisions of speech effectively bridged by transitional words and phrases?

Organization

How effective was your organizational approach? Did you begin with material that gained the attention of the audience? Did you preview each main point? Were your main points arranged in a logical sequence? Was the number of main points appropriate for the time allotted? Was your organizational design easily discernible? Did your conclusion provide a sense of closure? Did it motivate listeners to continue thinking about your presentation?

Language

Was the language you used to explain your ideas clear? Was it vivid? Did your speech sound as if it should be listened to rather than read? Could any of the words or phrases you used have been considered offensive to any audience members?

Delivery

Did you maintain effective eye contact with the members of the audience? Did you approach the speaking situation confidently? Were you able to use an extemporaneous style of delivery? Could you be heard easily? Was your speaking rate appropriate? Did you articulate clearly? Were you able to convey a sense of enthusiasm as you spoke? Did your gestures help reinforce your content?

TECHNOLOGY: AN AVENUE FOR REDUCING SPEECH-MAKING ANXIETY

The Internet is not just a resource for researching issues. It can also be used to collect and analyze information from persons representing virtually every imaginable point of view on every imaginable subject, including speaking

Speech Making on the Web

You have just been employed by a company called Speech Masters. During your first week on the job, you are instructed to compare and contrast the public speaking attitudes and speech-making styles of one of the following groups: Asian Americans, Hispanics, African Americans, or Native Americans. You decide to use the Internet as your research tool. Prepare a one-minute presentation detailing your research findings.

Compare your findings with those of others in your class.

Debriefing Yourself

Before joining in a discussion of your effectiveness as a speech maker, make two lists:

1. What I believe I did well
2. What areas I believe need improvement

anxiety. Using the Web, you can find information about relaxation techniques, share personal stories and experiences, or even use Internet or video phone to pretest the delivery of your speech and see how others unknown to you respond to it.

Among the Internet sites devoted specifically to public speaking are

http://www.mwc.edu/~bchirico/psanxinf.html
http://speeches.com/index.shtml
http://www.ukans.edu/cwis/units/coms2/vpa/vap.htm

The first contains clues on how to overcome public speaking anxiety (PSA). The second contains excellent speechwriting resources that you can access for help in speech preparation. The site also offers a speech archive, links to speeches on the Web, and help in writing. The third is an online tutorial you can use to improve your speech-making skills.[11]

A PERFORMANCE INVENTORY

The Skill Builder "Debriefing Yourself" can help you conduct a personal performance inventory.

When it is time for the audience members to comment on your presentation, they, like you, should consider the positive dimensions of your performance before making recommendations for improvement. Speaker and audience alike should remember that analysis is designed to be constructive, not destructive. It should help build confidence. It should not destroy the speaker's desire to try again.

Your instructor will probably provide you with a more formal analysis of your work, using an evaluation form similar to the one shown in Figure 17.1. Whether or not your instructor uses Figure 17.1, you will find it helpful as a personal guide.

Focus on Service Learning
How can you use what you know about speech apprehension, delivery, or credibility to prepare a volunteer for a community group to take his or her message "on the road"?

FIGURE 17.1
Evaluation Form.

Name: _____ Speech: _____

Specific purpose: _____

1. Content
___ Based on accurate analysis of speaking situation.
___ Specific goal of speech was apparent.
___ Subject appropriate, relevant, and interesting to intended audience.
___ All material clearly contributed to purpose.
___ Had specific facts and opinions to support and explain statements.
___ Support was logical.
___ Handled material ethically.
___ Used audiovisual aids when appropriate.
___ Included a variety of data—statistics, quotations, etc.
___ Moved from point to point with smooth transitions.

2. Organization
___ Began with effective attention-getter.
___ Main points were clear statements that proved or explained specific goals.
___ Points were arranged in logical order.
___ Each point was adequately supported.
___ Concluded with memorable statement that tied speech together.

3. Language
___ Ideas were clear.
___ Ideas were presented vividly.
___ Ideas were presented emphatically.
___ Language was appropriate for intended audience.

4. Delivery
___ Prepared oneself to speak.
___ Stepped up to speak with confidence.
___ Maintained contact with audience.
___ Sounded extemporaneous, not read or memorized.
___ Referred to notes only occasionally.
___ Sounded enthusiastic.
___ Maintained good posture.
___ Used vocal variety, pitch, emphasis, and rate effectively.
___ Gestured effectively.
___ Used face to add interest.
___ Articulation was satisfactory.
___ On finishing, moved out with confidence.
___ Fit time allotted.

Additional comments:

Reflect and Respond

According to poet e. e. cummings, "Most people are perfectly afraid of silence." Do you agree with cummings? Provide reasons and examples to explain your position.

Which do you believe most people fear *more* and why—silence or speaking in public?

Finally, what do the quote by e. e. cummings and the following one, by Daniel Webster, have in common?

If all my talents and powers were suddenly taken from me by some inscrutable providence, and I were allowed to keep only one, I would unhesitatingly ask to be allowed to keep my power of speaking for with that one, I would quickly regain all the others.

Thinking
CRITICALLY

Another means of evaluating your own effectiveness as well as the effectiveness of other speakers is to evaluate the credibility of the evidence included in a presentation. Such an evaluation form appears at the end of Chapter 19.

Revisiting Chapter Objectives

1. **Assess your level of speech anxiety.**   Anxiety, or fear, affects all speech makers. One of the best ways to cope with speech fright is to design and rehearse your presentation carefully. In addition, you should learn to recognize the causes of fear, as well as the physical and mental sensations that accompany it, so that you can learn to control your reactions with appropriate behavior modification techniques.

2. **Use deep-muscle relaxation, thought stopping, visualization, and other techniques to reduce speech anxiety.**   Among the techniques you can use to reduce speech anxiety are thought stopping and visualization. Both of these techniques help eliminate the thoughts and symptoms associated with fear—the first by stopping the fear inducing process, the second by boosting confidence.

3. **Discuss four types of delivery: manuscript, memorized, impromptu, and extemporaneous.**   There are four general options for delivery: (1) A manuscript speech is written out word-for-word and then read aloud. (2) A memorized speech is a manuscript speech committed to memory. (3) An impromptu speech is delivered on the spur of the moment. (4) An extemporaneous speech is researched, outlined, and delivered after careful rehearsal.

4. **Identify how the speaker can use visual and vocal cues to advantage.**   In delivering the speech, you have three basic kinds of tools at your disposal: verbal, visual, and vocal. Far too often, the verbal component is overemphasized, while the nonverbal aspects are underemphasized. Effective speech making requires that you pay attention to the visual aspects of your delivery, such as your clothing, posture, gestures, movements, and use of eye contact, and that your vocal cues reinforce—rather than sabotage—the content.

5. **Analyze a speech maker's performance (including your own) in terms of content, organization, language, and delivery.**   Careful rehearsal of your presentation can help you develop the confidence and competence required to deliver an outstanding speech. To ensure continued improvement, you should conduct postpresentation analyses, which will enable you to profit from each speaking experience.

Resources for Further Inquiry and Reflection

To apply your understanding of how the principles in Chapter 17 are at work in our daily lives, consult the following resources for further inquiry and reflection. Or, if you prefer, choose any other appropriate resource. Then connect the ideas expressed in your chosen selection with the communication concepts and issues you are learning about both in and out of class.

 Listen to Me

"Help!" (The Beatles)

How do the pleas of the speakers in the song reflect your own when you are asked to give a speech? How can you use others to help you improve both your speech-making effectiveness and readiness to speak?

 View Me

Dave   *Maid in Manhattan*
Bulworth

What lessons can you derive from the presentations of the title or supporting character? How would you evaluate the public performances of Dave, Bulworth, or the 10-year-old son in *Maid in Manhattan*? Explain.

 Read Me

Philip G. Zimbardo. *Shyness*. New York: Jove, 1987.

How can combating shyness prepare you to be a better speaker?

 Tell Me

Share with the class the insights you gained from your chosen Listen to Me, View Me, or Read Me selection.

Advertisements and public speakers have a number of characteristics in common. Both aim to inform as well as persuade. Their effectiveness depends on whether they are able to attract the interest of receivers, arouse their needs, and motivate them to listen and respond. The delivery of the characters in the ad, the images they project, together with the credibility of the spokespersons also affect an ad's overall impact. The same holds true for a speaker: delivery, image, and credibility interact to enhance or detract from the speaker's effectiveness. Those are the similarities. What differences do you see between public speakers and advertisements?

Key Chapter Terminology

Use the Communication Works CD-ROM and the Online Learning Center at www.mhhe.com/gamble8 *to further your knowledge of the following terminology.*

communication apprehension 511
extemporaneous speech 517
impromptu speech 517

manuscript speech 516
memorized speech 517
speech apprehension 511

 Communication
Works

 online learning center

www.mhhe.com/gamble8

Test Your Understanding

Go to the *Self Quizzes* on the Communication Works CD-ROM and the book's Online Learning Center at www.mhhe.com/gamble8.

Communication
Works

www.mhhe.com/gamble8

Notes

1. See, for example, "Ailments Correlated with Anxiety." *USA Today,* June 3, 2003, p. 1A.

2. J. B. Donovan. "Power to the Podium: The Place to Stand for Those Who Move the World." *Vital Speeches of the Day* 58, 1991, pp. 149–150.

3. Ellen Joan Pollock. "The Selling of a Golden Speech." *Wall Street Journal,* March 2, 1999, p. B1.

4. See, for example, Timothy L. Sellnow. "Controlling Speech Anxiety." Paper presented at the annual meeting of the Speech Communication Association, Chicago, IL, October 29–November 1, 1992; Marianne Martin. "The Communication of Public Speaking Anxiety: Perception of Asian and American Speakers." *Communication Quarterly* 40, summer 1992, pp. 279–288; and James McCroskey, Steven Booth Butterfield, and Steven K. Payne. "The Impact of Communication Apprehension on College Student Retention and Success." *Communication Quarterly* 37, spring 1989, pp. 100–107.

5. Eleanor Blau. "Taking Arms against Stage Fright." *New York Times,* September 20, 1998, p. AR-33.

6. J. D. Mladenka, C. R. Sawyer, and R. R. Behnke. "Anxiety Sensitivity and Speech Trait Anxiety as Predictors of State Anxiety during Public Speaking." *Communication Quarterly* 46, 1998, pp. 417–429.

7. For a more detailed guide to fear-control training, see Joe Ayres and Tim Hopf. "Visualization: Reducing Speech Anxiety and Enhancing Performance." *Communication Reports* 1:1, winter 1992, pp. 1–10.

8. Ginia Bellafante. "Read My Tie: No More Scandals." *New York Times,* October 8, 2000, sec. 9, pp. 1, 9.

9. Bellafante.

10. See the published proceedings of the Speech Communication Association's Summer Conference on Assessment, Washington, DC, August 4–7, 1994. In addition, the 1994 meeting of the Speech Communication Association (New Orleans, November 19–22) featured a short course: "A Workshop on Assessing Interpersonal, Public Speaking, and Listening Competence in the Fundamentals Course."

11. A number of useful Internet sites are contained in Cynthia B. Leshin. *Internet Investigations in Business Communication.* Upper Saddle River, NJ: Prentice Hall, 1997.

Informative
Speaking

After finishing this chapter, you should be able to

1. Define *informative speaking.*

2. Distinguish among three types of informative discourse.

3. Explain how to create information hunger and increase listeners' comprehension.

4. Develop and present an informative speech.

We now face the prospect of information obesity.

—David Shenk

There are things that are known and things that are unknown; in between are doors.

—Anonymous

Go to the *Online Learning Center* at
www.mhhe.com/gamble8
and answer the questions in the *Self Inventory* to evaluate your understanding of speech topics.

We live in the age of information. While information is, of course, valuable, David Shenk, author of *Data Smog: Surviving the Information Glut,* notes: "Just as fat has replaced starvation as this nation's number one dietary concern, information overload has replaced information scarcity as an important new emotional, social, and political problem."[1] The real problem facing the public speaker today is how to make information understandable. With the sum of human knowledge increasing at an unparalleled rate, are you prepared to communicate what you know to others in a way that creates interest so that they will listen, explain it in a way that enhances receiver understanding, and discuss it in a manner that helps audience members remember it?

In Chapter 14, we examined two categories of speech making—informative and persuasive—and you had an opportunity to formulate sample purpose statements for each type. At this point, you can increase your ability to prepare and deliver effective informative speeches by applying your general knowledge and skills to this situation.

SPEAKING INFORMATIVELY

informative speech

a speech that updates and adds to the knowledge of receivers

How many people do you know whose job requires them to deliver speeches? What percentage of their time is devoted to preparing and delivering speeches?

What's happening? How does it work? What's going on? What is it? What does it mean? These are the kinds of questions that an **informative speech** attempts to answer. Whenever you prepare an informative speech, your goal is to offer your audience members more information than they already have about the topic. Your objective is to update and add to their knowledge, refine their understanding, or provide background.[2]

How does the informative speech relate to your life? What informative messages have you received recently? Have you read an online survey? Listened to a televised news report? A radio commentary? Have you received instructions or directions from a friend, an employer, a co-worker, or an instructor? Our world is filled with informative messages, which we depend on. Many of these messages are informal, but others have been carefully planned, structured, and rehearsed to achieve maximum impact. In today's world, it has become increasingly important to develop the ability to share information with other people. Unless you are adept at sending and receiving informative messages, you will be unable to establish common understanding.

The authors of this book once worked with a corporate vice president who—although he had a fine mind and excellent analytical abilities—considered the process of passing information on to people both above and below him in the organizational hierarchy a "deadly bore." He saw little need to inform others of his activities or his accomplishments. Not surprisingly, he no longer holds his former position of power and influence. When his company merged with another organization, he lost his job—primarily because he was unable to explain his responsibilities and achievements to the new administration. Knowing how to design and deliver effective informative messages has important implications for our careers and our lives.[3]

TYPES OF INFORMATIVE PRESENTATIONS

Let's now consider three types of informative speeches: (1) messages of explanation (speeches of demonstration that explain the how or how-to of a subject), (2) messages of description (speeches that describe what a person, an object, or an event is like), and (3) messages of definition (speeches that define what something is).

Explanations

If your purpose is to explain how to do something (for example, how to motivate employees), how something is made (for example, how to make glass), how something works (for example, how a slot machine works), or how something develops or occurs (for example, how tornadoes form, how an atomic reaction occurs), then you are preparing to deliver an explanation of a process.

Detroit Shock coach Nancy Lieberman-Cline, center, gives some instructions to the team as Astou Ndiays, right, looks on. Lieberman-Cline is regarded as one of the most skilled players ever in women's basketball history. That helps make her a demanding taskmaster as she directs the Shock. Here she is most likely explaining to them how to execute a play.

Ethics & COMMUNICATION

Assessing Informative Speaking Skills

People rely on informative speaking almost constantly when on the job; the need to inform others and be informed by others is experienced daily throughout life. Should we, therefore, assess who has and who has not mastered the skills needed to deliver and process informative discourse on the job or in other settings?

If not, why not? If so, how?

Skill BUILDER

A Demonstration

Design and present a three- to five-minute speech in which it is your purpose to demonstrate how to do something or to explain how something works. An outline is required.

Your primary goal is to share your understanding of the process or procedure with your listeners and, in some instances, to give them the skills they need to replicate it.

What processes are you equipped to speak about?

When organizing a message of explanation, you must be especially careful to avoid overcondensing the data. It is not uncommon for an inexperienced speaker to recite a long list of facts that merely enumerate the steps involved in a process. This kind of perfunctory outline is hard for an audience to follow. You would be wise, instead, to use meaningful information groups. For example, grouping information under such headings as "Gathering Ingredients," "Blending Ingredients," and "Adding the Garnish" would be considerably more effective than simply relaying 15 steps involved in preparing a chocolate mousse. Besides facilitating understanding, this grouping system also helps the audience retain the material.

It is also important to consider the length of time it will actually take to accomplish your objectives in a process speech. Take a tip from televised cooking shows. Notice how an on-the-air chef always demonstrates some parts of the process live but has other parts of the dish prepared in advance to save time. This technique can be of great value to you, too.

Descriptions

One of your responsibilities as a speaker is to be able to describe a person, place, or thing for your listeners. For instance, if you were a site-location specialist for a fast-food chain, you would have to describe potential store locations to the management. If you were a spokesperson for a nuclear plant that had experienced a radiation leak, you would have to describe the location and extent of the mishap to the media. If you were a sales manager, you would need to describe the advantages of your organization's new product line to your sales force. Whatever the nature of a descriptive message, your aim is to

A Description

Design and present a three- to five-minute speech in which you describe an object, a place, a structure, or a person. Use spatial order, as discussed in Chapter 16, to organize the speech. An outline is required.

help your listeners form mental closeups of places, people, or things. To do this, you need to find ways to describe condition, size, shape, color, age, and so on to make your subject come alive for your audience.

Of course, visual aids of the type discussed in Chapters 15 and 16 are particularly relevant to a descriptive presentation. For example, photographs, maps, and drawings can make it easier for you to describe a significant archaeological dig, the pathos of a homeless person, the appearance of a high-tech artificial limb, or the blight of an inner-city slum. In a descriptive speech, you paint with words.

Whatever your topic, you will want to ensure that the words and phrases you select will evoke the appropriate sensory responses in your listeners. To do this, you will need to communicate how your subject looks, tastes, smells, feels, and sounds.

Definitions

"What do you mean?" is a common question. In most cases, it is used when the questioner is seeking clarification or elaboration of ideas from a speaker. Sometimes a satisfactory answer can be supplied in a sentence or two. At other times, however, it takes a speech, or even a book, to define a concept adequately. For example, books with titles such as *Data Smog, The Age of Paradox, Emotional Intelligence, Theory Z, Leader Effectiveness Training, The Age of Missing Information,* and *Happiness Is . . .* are actually extended definitions: The authors are discussing their meaning for a particular concept or idea. An informative speech of definition likewise provides an audience with an explanation of a term. "Shyness," "The Grief Cycle," "ESP," and "Muscular Dystrophy" are among the topics for which a definitional presentation would be appropriate.

What Does It Mean?

1. Working individually or in groups, list topics for a speech of definition.
2. Select five of the topics and develop purpose statements for them (see Chapter 16).
3. Design and present a three- to five-minute speech in which you define a concept or an idea. Organize it carefully and submit an outline.

Can you think of others? Many students find that topics such as "Racial Profiling," "The Meaning of Obscenity," "Prejudice," "Friendship," and "Sexual Harassment" give them the freedom they need to develop effective speeches of definition.

Since many of the concepts you may choose to define will have connotative, or subjective, meanings not traditionally found in dictionaries, not all members of your audience will agree with the definition you present. On one television talk show, for example, two experts on shyness were unable to agree on what it means to be shy. It is necessary, therefore, to organize a definitional speech in a way that will be clear and persuasive. For example, how would you define *shyness*? To explain your meaning for the term, you might offer examples of what it feels like to be shy, describe how a shy person behaves, and then go on to discuss the consequences of shyness. Perhaps you would explain shyness by comparing and contrasting a shy person with an extrovert. Or you might choose to discuss the causes of shyness and then focus on different types or categories of shyness. No matter how you choose to order your ideas, your organization should be suggested by the topic and grow out of it.

EFFECTIVE INFORMATIVE SPEECHES: INCREASING YOUR LISTENERS' INTEREST AND COMPREHENSION

To develop an effective informative speech, you need to accomplish several tasks: (1) make your listeners want to learn more about the topic; (2) communicate the information clearly by seeking information balance (3) emphasize key points; (4) find ways to involve audience members in your presentation; and (5) provide the information in ways that will make it memorable, by using novelty, creativity, and audiovisuals. Let's look at these tasks.

Create Information Hunger

Which speakers you have listened to succeeded in increasing your hunger for knowledge about a topic? What did they do to accomplish this?

Your primary goal in an informative speech is to deliver a message of explanation, description, or definition, but it is equally important to make your presentation interesting, intellectually stimulating, and relevant (that is, significant or personally valuable) for your listeners. In other words, you need to work to increase each listener's need to know and hunger to receive your message.

You will be more adept at creating information hunger if you have analyzed your audience carefully (see Chapter 14). Then, by using appropriate vehicles, you will be able to generate the interest that will motivate them to listen to the information you want to share. Remember to use the attention-getting devices discussed in Chapter 16. For example, you can relate your own experiences or the experiences of others; you can ask rhetorical questions; you can draw analogies for your listeners to consider. You can also arouse the audience's curiosity; and you can incorporate humor or use eye-catching visual aids.

Obviously, your effectiveness as a speaker will increase to the extent that you present your information creatively and are successful in arousing the desire and the need to know among audience members.

Seek Information Balance

Listeners will become informed as a result of your speech only if they are capable of processing the information you deliver. A common danger in informative speaking is that your audience will experience information overload. **Information overload** is created in two ways: (1) The speech maker delivers far more data about the topic than the audience needs or wants. This confuses the listeners and causes them to tune out what is being communicated. (2) The speech maker presents ideas in words the listeners do not understand. Instead of using clear language and speaking at a level the audience can comprehend, the speaker creates frustration among audience members by using unfamiliar jargon or words that soar beyond the reach of the listeners' vocabulary. Forgetting that an informative speech will fail if its ideas are superfluous or unclear, some speakers end up talking to themselves rather than to the audience.

Remember, your speech does not have to be encyclopedic in length or sound impressively complicated to merit the audience's attention. But it must by all means be understandable.

A speaker who tries to avoid information overload will often overcompensate and create a situation of information underload. **Information underload** occurs when the speaker underestimates the sophistication or intelligence of the audience members and tells them little that they do not already know.

As a speech maker, you need to strike a balance, providing neither too little information nor too much. As a rule, effective speech makers neither underestimate nor overestimate the capabilities of the audience. Instead, they motivate their listeners to want to fill in any information gaps. To motivate your listeners, do not overkill your subject by saturating the listeners with so much material that they lose interest; instead, choose supporting materials carefully to achieve your objectives, using an appropriate mix of new information and more familiar support. Once one point is made, be ready to move on to the next one.

Emphasize Key Points

As we discussed in Chapter 15, emphasis can be created through repetition (saying the same thing over again) and restatement (saying the same thing in another way). As long as you do not become overly repetitious and redundant, these devices will help your listeners process and retain the main points of your speech.

Focus on Service Learning

How can you help a community group leader cope and deal more effectively with the challenges posed by information overload?

information overload
the situation that occurs when the amount of information provided by a speech maker is too great to be handled effectively by receivers

information underload
the situation that occurs when the information provided by a speech maker is already known to receivers

---

Conveying Information across Cultures

Through informative presentations, speakers attempt to describe something, demonstrate how something works, or explain a concept. Their goal is to convey knowledge and understanding. For this goal to be realized, the information they want to share must be communicated clearly.

However, people who *seem* to speak the same language may in reality come from divergent backgrounds. How can such speakers hope to communicate clearly with each other? How can an appreciation of the communicative behavior of people from cultures different from your own facilitate this effort?

EXPLORING
Diversity

The organization of your speech can also reinforce your main ideas. Remember that you can use your introduction to preview ideas in your conclusion and to help make those ideas memorable. Transitions and internal summaries also help create a sense of cohesiveness.

Involve Your Listeners

The relationship between audiences and speakers is changing. Contemporary audiences are restless. They are used to playing video games and talking back to small screens. Public speakers need to work to channel the nervous energy of their audience members.[4] People learn more if they become involved with the material that is being presented to them. Effective speech makers do not view the audience as a passive receptacle; rather, they work to find ways to let the audience take an active part in the presentation. For example, the audience may be called on to perform an activity during the presentation. If you are giving a speech on how to reduce stress, you might have your listeners actually try one or two stress-reducing exercises. Or if your speech topic is "How to Read an EKG," you might pass out sample EKGs for audience members to decipher.

Provide Information Memorably

Remember that people want to understand and remember information that they perceive as relevant to their own lives. Few of us would have much interest in a speech on the development of bees. If, however, we found that the bees we are hearing about are a new species of killer bee that is extremely resistant to common insecticides, and that droves of these bees are on the way to our community and will arrive within the next two weeks, we would develop an intense interest very quickly.

Receivers learn more when directly involved in a presentation.

Audiences also want to listen to new information. In this case, the term *new* means "new to them." A historical blunder may be new in this sense, and it may be relevant to a college or business audience today. The cable television industry has found that weather is worthy of its own channel; the weather forecast is constantly being updated and is therefore considered new.

Audiences also respond well to information that is emphasized. You can use your organization of main ideas to emphasize material you want people to retain.

Repetition can help as well; audiences respond to information that is repeated. Martin Luther King, Jr., understood the value of repetition in his "I Have a Dream" speech. Jesse Jackson uses repetition to foster his audiences' retention as well as their emotional involvement. As you prepare your informative speech, look for ways to let repetition augment your message.

Novelty and Creativity

An effective speaker looks constantly for ways to approach information from an unusual direction. If you are the fifth speaker that your audience will hear on the homeless, you must find a different slant or approach to the topic, or the audience may be bored from the outset. You might try taking a different point of view—through the eyes of a child, for example. Look for analogies that bring topics home to an audience: "The number of people entering teaching today is diminishing. The teaching profession is like a stream drying up." Try other ways to complete this analogy. As you prepare your presentation, remember that you are looking for creative ways of bringing your topic to life for the audience.

Take your mind out every now and then and dance on it. It is getting all caked up.
—Mark Twain

Audiovisual Aids

You will want to include audiovisual aids in an informative presentation. Remember first, though, that you are your primary visual aid. The way you stand, walk, talk, and gesture is extremely important to the effectiveness of your presentation. Avoid hiding behind the lectern; avoid reading your notes. Move to the side. Use gestures to show the size and shape of objects. If an article of clothing is important to your topic, you may want to wear it. Foreign students, for example, sometimes wear clothing from their homeland when they give informative speeches about their culture.

Take objects, or make simple models if you cannot take the objects themselves. Use charts and graphs when appropriate. If you have access to a computer and can manipulate spreadsheet software, you can create computer-generated bar, line, and pie graphs. You can then have a graph converted to a transparency at a local copy shop so that it can be used with an overhead projector.

You can also consider using video and audio clips to create interest. Camcorders can be used to conduct interviews or show processes at work. One student, for example, interviewed other students about campus parking problems. Another showed a brief tape of a chemical reaction that could not have been demonstrated safely in the classroom.

The Internet is another source of visuals you can use to enhance your speech. As you visit various Web sites, you will find images, charts, and graphs that you can incorporate into your presentation to help communicate your message.

TECHNOLOGY AND THE INFORMATIVE SPEAKER

Our society is facing a knowledge gap. The growth in new technologies is allowing certain groups of people to have access to greater amounts of information. Because newer communication technologies require that users have both the skill to use them and the money to afford them, specialized knowledge and wealth enable some people to acquire more information than those who are not as fortunate. Today, technological access and opportunities to gain knowledge go hand in hand. As researchers Jeanie Taylor and Cheris Kramarae note, "If the future of information is electronic, we need to ensure access for everyone, not just an elite. We imagine computer terminals connected to community systems in laundromats, homeless shelters, daycare centers, etc.—with sufficient support so that most people have access to the Internet." They continue by noting that poor is the "community that knowlingly allows whole segments of our real world to be excluded from the Internet."[5]

Significant efforts are being made to decrease the size of the knowledge gap. Once we are able to gain access to information, it is freely available on the Internet. Electronic mailing lists and discussion groups are key Internet resources for finding and sharing information. There is a wide array of special interest lists where individuals can join a virtual community on a topic of interest and receive electronic mail in the form of a report, an article, an abstract, or a personal reaction. The following are two of the best resources for finding such mailing lists:

> http://www.liszt.com
> http://www.tile.net/tile/listserv/index.html

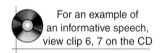

For an example of an informative speech, view clip 6, 7 on the CD

In addition, you can request information on listserv mailing lists for a particular subject by sending an e-mail message to LISTSERV@vm1.nodak.edu.

Usenet groups are similar to listserv groups, only larger. A usenet group is a distributed bulletin board system (BBS) comprising thousands of specialized discussion groups. Once you subscribe to a newsgroup, you can scan the group's messages and send your own comments or questions.

When preparing an informative speech, you use a search directory such as "AltaVista," "Excite," "Infoseek," or "Yahoo!" to search for information on your chosen topic. You would then explore the links that seem to contain the most promising information. If you receive too much information—remember the dangers of information overload—you will want to narrow your search. If you receive too little information—remember the dangers of information underload—you will want to broaden your search.

e-SEARCH

Web Sites

Choose any one of the suggested topics in this chapter for an informative speech. Using a search engine of your choice, develop a list of Web sites you could visit to develop the topic into a speech. Identify the title of the Web page and the URL (uniform resource locator), or address. Which of the Web sites seem most promising? Least promising? Why?

Reflect and Respond

Agree or disagree with the following statement; supply reasons and examples that support your stance:

All information is persuasive. Thus, there is no such thing as an informative speech.

Then examine the sample informative speech outline and speech transcript that follow. Discuss how each sample can be used in defense of the position you have taken.

Thinking
CRITICALLY

SAMPLE INFORMATIVE SPEECH OUTLINE

Sentence Outline

Topic: Mad cow disease

Purpose: To inform the class about the nature, causes, means of transmission, and symptoms of bovine spongiform encephalopathy (mad cow disease)

Central idea: It is important for us to understand the facts about mad cow disease.

Introduction I. On February 7, 2002, the *New York Times* reported that an Italian woman was afflicted with mad cow disease. That brought the number of human cases of the disease to over 100 worldwide. Among those concerned with this seemingly small number of human cases is McDonald's. McDonald's has seen its stock slide 40 percent as a direct result of MCD.

The purpose statement and central idea guide the speaker in developing the outline.

The use of statistics, a rhetorical question, personalization, and a visual aid draw receivers into the speech.

The use of an actual McDonald's box enhanced the speaker's presentation.

continued

The speaker reveals the speech's purpose.

II. (Show McDonald's hamburger box visual.) Mad cow disease also threatens you and me.

III. Today I would like to tell you about the nature, causes, means of transmission, and symptoms of bovine spongiform encephalopathy (mad cow disease).

Transition to main point I: First, let's explore what mad cow disease really is.

The speech's body is organized into four main points, each with a number of subpoints. Note that every entry in the body is a complete sentence and contains only a single idea.

Body

I. Mad cow disease is a fatal disease.

　A. The disease enters and destroys the brains of cattle and other animals, including sheep, deer, and elk.

　B. Since 1986, over 200,000 cows worldwide have been diagnosed with the deadly disease.

　C. Recently the CBS program *60 Minutes II* showed what mad cow looks like in a dying cow. (Show video clip: *60 Minutes*.)

The speaker uses a definition, statistics, and a video to develop the first main point of the speech.

Transition to main point II: Now that we have seen the results of the disease, let's consider its cause.

II. According to Dr. Stanley Prusiner, the cause of mad cow disease is a deformed prion that kills the brain.

　A. The prion is a new infectious particle.

　　1. The prion literally pokes holes in the brains of animals.

　　2. Eventually the brain looks much like this piece of Swiss cheese. (Visual: samples of Swiss cheese)

　B. According to Dr. Robert Gallo, MCD cannot be killed.

　　1. Antibiotics are not effective.

　　2. Cooking does not kill the disease.

The speaker uses a definition, a dramatic visual, and startling facts to develop the second main point of the speech.

Transition to main point III: Next, we need to examine how the disease is spread.

III. Mad cow disease spreads through infected feed.

　A. In the 1980s, cattle feed producers began feeding the ground-up parts of deceased animals to living cows.

　　1. Healthy cows ate the remains of infected cows.

　　　a. This process is called "rendering."

　　　b. In Sheldon Rampton and John Stauberr's *Mad Cow USA,* Van Smith, a news reporter describes rendering: "A load of guts, heads, and legs recently retrieved from a local slaughterhouse sits stewing in one of the raw material bins at the plant's receiving bay. It will be fed into the hogger, a shredder that grinds up the tissue before it is deep fried in cookers charged with spent restaurant grease and blood."

Testimony and imagery enable the speaker to develop the speech's third main point.

　B. The disease spreads to humans when they eat infected cows.

　　1. According to reporter Sandra Blakeslee, the human variant of mad cow disease, new variant Creutzfeld-Jacob disease, (new variant CJD) first appeared in 1995 in young people in England.

The speaker uses a series of dramatic images to develop the last main point of the speech.

2. The brains of new variant CJD victims are filled with holes—similar to the holes found in the brains of diseased cows.

3. CJD kills within 18 months.

C. Dietary supplements and vaccines may also spread CJD to humans.

1. Supplements such as Male Power and Brain Nutrition contain extracts from cattle organs.

2. The *New York Times* lists vaccines such as polio, diptheria, and tetanus as also containing ingredients from cows.

Transition to main point IV: Now that we have discussed how MCD can be transmitted, let's talk about its symptoms.

IV. Mad cow disease has a number of symptoms.

A. Cows lose weight, are skittish, behave belligerently, and appear confused.

B. People experience paranoia, suffer from lack of coordination, and lapse into a coma.

Conclusion

I. Today we have explored the nature, causes, means of transmission, and symptoms of deadly mad cow disease.

II. It is possible that mad cow, a disease with no known cure, could be the plague of our time. In fact, on Christmas Eve, 2003, the press reported that the U.S. may have its first case of mad cow. Hamburger anyone? (Visual: Hold up the McDonald's fast-food container shown in the introduction.)

The speaker summarizes what the speech has accomplished and uses a visual that refers receivers back to the speech's introduction, providing a sense of closure.

SAMPLE INFORMATIVE SPEECH

Topic: Mad cow disease

Purpose: To inform the class about the nature, causes, means of transmission, and symptoms of bovine spongiform encephalopathy (mad cow disease)

Central idea: It is important for us to understand the facts about mad cow disease.

On February 7, 2002, the *New York Times* reported that an Italian woman was afflicted with spongiform encephalopathy, better known as mad cow disease. That means that, to date, over 100 cases of this disease have been reported around the world. Among those especially concerned about this seemingly small number of cases of the disease is McDonald's. Why is McDonald's concerned? On January 25, 2002 [show McDonald's hamburger box visual], *Wall Street Journal* reporter Shirley Leung, in her article "McDonald's Net Sinks 40% on Fears over Slump, Mad-Cow Disease," noted that the net worth of the McDonald's corporation had shrunk 40 percent—in large part because of the threat posed by mad cow disease. Mad cow disease, however, doesn't only

Does the speaker succeed in gaining your attention? Do you feel the topic of the speech has relevance?

Do you find the use of this visual effective? Is there any other visual you might have considered using in the introduction?

continued

How effective do you find the speaker's orientation? Does it prepare you for what is to come?

Does this transition accomplish its purpose? Is it lengthy enough?

What is the speaker aiming to accomplish with the first main point? Even though you are not able to watch it, do you believe that the use of a brief video is appropriate and facilitative of the speaker's purpose?

Is the speaker's choice of expert appropriate? Is the speaker's explication easy to follow?

How do you respond to the speaker's choice of a visual aid? Does it advance the speaker's goal?

Would you change this transition in any way?

How do you respond to the speaker's use of rhetorical questions? Do you think the device is overused?

threaten McDonald's. It also threatens us. Today I would like to explain to you what mad cow disease is, how it is caused, its means of transmission, and what the symptoms of the disease are.

First, let's examine what bovine spongiform encephalopathy is.

Mad cow disease is a fatal disease that attacks the brains of cattle. It is one of a family of brain-destroying diseases that affect many species, including sheep, deer, elk, and humans. Mad cow disease made its first known appearance in cattle in England in 1984. It was diagnosed in 1986. Since then, over 200,000 cows have fallen ill with mad cow disease.

A few years ago, the CBS program *60 Minutes II* showed us what mad cow disease looks like in an afflicted cow. [*Show video: Opening segment of the 60 Minutes II presentation.*]

What causes such a horrible disease? The cause of mad cow disease is a mutant protein, a prion, that kills the brain. CBS news correspondent Wyatt Andrews, in a report that aired January 31, 2001, revealed that, according to Dr. Stanley Prusiner, who won the Nobel Prize in medicine for his work with this prion, "The prion is a completely new infectious particle. It's not a virus, not a bacterium, not a fungus. It's a natural protein in mammals that can mysteriously deform itself, replicate, and concentrate in the brain." Thus, mad cow disease is composed of deformed prions, deadly variants of proteins that occur normally in nerve cells. According to the prion hypothesis, an abnormally shaped prion is eaten and absorbed into the bloodstream. It then crosses into the nervous system. The abnormally shaped prion changes normal prions into abnormal ones. The nerve cells try to get rid of the abnormal prions but can't. Because the nerve cells can't digest the abnormal prions, they accumulate and die. When the deadly prions enter the brains of animals, they literally poke holes in them. Over time, the brains become so filled with holes that they resemble this sample of Swiss cheese [show visual aid]. By this time, due to numerous nerve cell deaths, the brains can no longer function and the cows literally shake to death. Dr. Robert Gallo, a University of Maryland researcher who was also interviewed by Wyatt Andrews for CBS News, tells us that, unfortunately, nothing is as indestructible as a prion. Neither antibiotics nor heat is effective in killing a prion. A prion, it seems, can survive a temperature as high as 600 degrees Centigrade. Thus, cooking meat does not kill the prion.

Now that we know what mad cow disease is, let's consider how the disease is spread.

How did mad cow disease get into cattle in the first place? The theory is that mad cow disease got into cattle as a result of infected sheep that were ground up and added to the cattle feed. In the 1980s, producers of cattle feed (which often included ground meat and bone meal by-products from sheep) changed the way they processed feed. The change somehow enabled the scrapie disease agent to survive the cattle feed production process. As a result, contaminated food was fed to cattle.

Why were parts of dead animals fed to cattle in the first place? The answer is simple. In order to avoid waste, it was common for countries such as Great Britain to dispose of tons of animal waste by grinding the waste into meal and feeding it to cattle, unaware that the waste being used might contain the fatal brain-wasting disease. The process by which this is accomplished is called rendering. Over time, according to Sheldon Rampton and John Stauber, authors of the book *Mad Cow USA,* healthy cattle were fed contaminated feed that came from the waste of cows already infected with mad cow disease. In other words, healthy cows ate the remains of infected cows, caught the disease, and became sick. As reported in Rampton and Stauber's *Mad Cow USA,* Baltimore newspaper reporter Van Smith described the rendering process like this:

> A load of guts, heads, and legs recently retrieved from a local slaughterhouse sits stewing in one of the raw material bins at the plant's receiving bay. It will be fed into the hogger, a shredder that grinds up the tissue before it is deep fried in cookers charged with spent restaurant grease and blood. Suddenly a hot gust of wind blows droplets of it on us. As the bloated stomachs and broken body parts slide from the trailer bed to the bin, the workman shouts out, "Watch out for the splatter."

It is the practice of rendering that researchers believe led to the spread of the disease. In effect, newly infected cows were slaughtered and then their brains and spinal cords were put back into animal feed. The feed was given to more cows, spreading the disease. Ultimately, human beings also ate the beef of cows that ate the feed containing the abnormal prions that cause mad cow disease. It was humans' eating the diseased meat of infected animals that enabled the disease to cross the species barrier.

In 1995, the first case of a new form of Creutzfeld-Jacob disease, called new variant CJD, was diagnosed in Great Britain. Reporter Sandra Blakeslee, author of the article "On Watch for Any Hint of Mad Cow Disease," which appeared in the *New York Times* on January 30, 2001, tells us that, unlike traditional Creutzfeld-Jacob disease, a deadly illness due to genetic causes that affects about one in a million, typically older, people, new variant CJD also occurs in younger people, who, it is believed, get the disease by eating contaminated beef. The brains of new variant CJD human victims have prion-caused holes similar to those found in the brains of mad cow–infected cows. New variant CJD usually kills its human victims within 18 months from the onset of their symptoms.

This is not the whole story, however. The disease may be spread to humans in at least two other ways as well. Since 1991, the United States Department of Agriculture has prohibited the importation of the tissues and organs of cattle from countries that have been shown to have animals afflicted with mad cow disease. Most recently, the Agriculture Department forbid the importation of beef from Canada when a member of a cattle herd there was found to have died from mad cow disease. Unfortunately for us, these government regulations do not specifically apply to cosmetics or products used in dietary supplements. According to *USA Today* reporter Anita Manning, in an article titled "U.S. Supplements May Harbor Mad Cow Disease," issued on January 22, 2001, dietary supplements, including ones labeled "Male Power" and "Brain Nutrition," could contain imported extracts from brains, testicles, and other

What does the speaker do to add credibility to the information being provided to receivers?

Can you imagine yourself reading this description? How could delivery be used to enhance impact?

How would you evaluate the speaker's use of research? In your opinion, does the research add to the speaker's credibility?

continued

cattle organs. In addition, Melody Peterson and Greg Winter reported in their article, "5 Drug Makers Use Material with Possible Mad Cow Link," which appeared in the February 8, 2001, issue of the *New York Times,* that vaccines, including some given to millions of American children, such as polio, diphtheria, and tetanus, as well as the vaccine given to soldiers to protect against anthrax, could also contain ingredients from mad cow–infected animals.

Now that we have discussed how mad cow disease can be transmitted, let's talk about its symptoms.

How can you tell when an animal or a human is infected with mad cow disease? Unfortunately, there is no current way to diagnose the disease before symptoms appear. The symptoms of the disease are horrific in both cows and humans. Cows lose weight, become skittish, act belligerently, appear confused, and suffer paralysis. People experience psychotic problems; become paranoid; suffer from a lack of muscle coordination; experience spasms, terrible tremors, and hearing and vision loss; and eventually suffer from dementia and lapse into a coma. There is no treatment or cure for the disease currently available. No one knows how many animals are harboring mad cow disease or how many people are infected with it.

Today we have explored the nature, causes, means of transmission, and symptoms of mad cow disease. The advent of mad cow disease and its human form, new variant Creutzfeld-Jacob disease, means that we may be living in a mad, mad, mad, mad world. If, like me and Nobel Prize–winning scientist Dr. Prousiner, you're wondering if mad cow disease could turn out to be the plague of the twenty-first century, consider this: 10 to 15 years or more can elapse from the time one eats meat from a mad cow–diseased animal until symptoms occur in a human. In fact, on Christmas Eve, 2003, the press reported that the U.S. may have its first case of mad cow. Thus, only time will tell if we have this disease. McDonald's anyone? [Hold up visual.]

Are the speaker's description of symptoms vivid enough for you? If you were giving the speech, would you have included another visual aid prior to the speech's conclusion?

Does the speaker effectively summarize the speech? What does the speaker do to give the speech a sense of closure? How else might the speaker have concluded the speech?

In your opinion, did the speaker provide you with information that you need and can use?

Works Consulted

Andrews Wyatt. "The Science of Mad Cow Disease." *CBS News,* January 31, 2001.

Blakeslee Sandra. "On Watch for Any Hint of Mad Cow Disease." *New York Times,* January 30, 2001, p. F3.

"Italy: Mad Cow Disease Infects Woman." *New York Times,* February 7, 2002, p. A6.

Leung Shirley. "McDonald's Net Sinks 40% on Fears over Slump, Mad-Cow Disease." *Wall Street Journal,* January 25, 2002, p. A16.

Manning Anita. "U.S. Supplements May Harbor Mad Cow Disease." *USA Today,* January 22, 2001, p. 7D.

Peterson Melody and Winter Greg. "5 Drug Makers Use Materials with Possible Mad Cow Link." *New York Times,* February 8, 2001, pp. C1, C5.

Rampton Sheldon and Stauber John. *Mad Cow, USA.* Monroe, ME: Common Courage Press, 1977.

Ridley Matt. "Mad Cow Disease Is a Little Less Scarier." *New York Times,* May 25, 2003, p. wk3.

Wald Matthew and Lichtblau. "U.S. Is Examining a Mad Cow Case, First in Country." *New York Times,* December 24, 2003, A1, 19.

SAMPLE SPEAKER'S NOTES

Topic:	Mad cow disease
Purpose:	To inform the class about the nature, causes, means of transmission, and symptoms of bovine spongiform encephalopathy (mad cow disease)
Central idea:	It is important for us to understand the facts about mad cow disease.

Introduction

   I. February 7, 2002, the *New York Times* reported the 100th case of MCD.

  II. *Wall Street Journal* reporter Shirley Leung, "McDonald's net sinks 40% on fears over slump, Mad-Cow Disease."

 III. Today I would like to tell you about the nature, causes, means of transmission, and symptoms of MCD.

Body

   I. What MCD is

     Fatal

     200,000 cows diagnosed

     60 Minutes video example

  II. Cause

     Mutant prion kills the brain.

     Nobel Prize winner Dr. Stanley Prusiner: "The prion is a completely new infectious particle. It's not a virus, not a bacterium, not a fungus. It's a natural protein in mammals that can mysteriously deform itself, replicate, and concentrate in the brain." (CBS News, January 31, 2001)

     Brain looks like a piece of Swiss cheese. Visual: Swiss cheese

     Wyatt Andrews (CBS News): There's nothing as indestructible as a prion.

 III. How MCD is spread

     Ground-up sheep and cow parts fed to cattle

     Through the rendering process

     Described by Baltimore newspaper reporter Van Smith in *Mad Cow USA:* "A load of guts, heads, and legs recently retrieved from a local slaughterhouse sits stewing in one of the raw material bins at the plant's receiving bay. It will be fed into the hogger, a shredder that grinds up the tissue before it is deep fried in cookers charged with spent restaurant grease and blood. Suddenly a hot gust of wind blows droplets of it on us. As the bloated stomachs and broken body parts slide from the trailer bed to the bin, the workman shouts out, 'Watch out for the splatter.'"

     Human form of mad cow disease, CJD

        Reporter Sandra Blakeslee *NYT* report, January 30, 2001

        Brains look like Swiss cheese, too.

continued

In cosmetics and dietary supplements, such as Male Power.

> *USA Today* Reporter Anita Manning Report, January 22, 2001
>
> Melody Peterson and Greg Winter Report, February 8, 2001

IV. Symptoms: How do you know if a cow or human is infected?

Cows lose weight, skittish, confused.

People suffer lack of coordination and paranoia. There is no treatment.

Conclusion

I. Today we have explored the nature, causes, means of transmission, and symptoms of MCD.

II. Reference back to Dr. Prousiner

III. It is possible that mad cow could be the plague of our times. Hamburger, anyone?

IV. Visual: Fast-food hamburger

Revisiting Chapter Objectives

1. **Define *informative speaking.*** The goal of the informative speaker is to offer audience members more information than they presently have about a topic. The information speaker aims to update and add knowledge, refine understanding, or provide background.

2. **Distinguish among three types of informative discourse.** There are three kinds of informative speaking with which you need to be familiar: (1) messages of explanation (speeches of demonstration that explain the what or how to of a subject, (2) messages of description (speeches that describe what a person, an object, or an event is like), and (3) messages of definition (speeches that define what something is).

3. **Explain how to create information hunger and increase listeners' comprehension.** A primary goal of the informative speech is to increase each listener's need to know and hunger to receive a message. To do this, speakers need to analyze the audience and use appropriate attention-getting devices to generate receiver interest in their topics. At the same time that speakers work to create interest in receivers, they also need to avoid overloading or underloading receivers with information.

4. **Develop and present an informative speech.** Being able to design and deliver an effective informative speech has important implications for both your career and your life. An effective informative speech makes listeners want to learn more about the topic, communicates information clearly, involves audience members, and delivers information in a way that makes the speech memorable.

THE **Wrap-Up**

Resources for Further Inquiry and Reflection

To apply your understanding of how the principles in Chapter 18 are at work in our daily lives, consult the following resources for further inquiry and reflection. Or, if you prefer, choose any other appropriate resource. Then connect the ideas expressed in your chosen selection with the communication concepts and issues you are learning about both in and out of class.

 Listen to Me

"You Talk Too Much" (Joe Jones)
"The Wreck of the Edmund Fitzgerald" (Gordon Lightfoot)

What lesson(s) can a speaker deduce from the laments of these songs' singers?

 View Me

All the President's Men   *Silkwood*
Erin Brockovich   *My Cousin Vinnie*

To what extent did information hunger drive the investigation featured in each of the preceding films? What did the investigator do to enhance receiver comprehension of his or her discoveries?

 Read Me

David Shenk. *Data Smog: Surviving the Information Glut*. New York: HarperCollins, 1997.

Can we receive too much information? If yes, what are our options? If no, what steps should we take to facilitate our powers of information processing?

 Tell Me

Share with the class the insights you gained from your chosen Listen to Me, View Me, or Read Me selection.

Large quantities of spam, much of it with deceptive titles, are clogging the information arteries of our computers. In your opinion, should spam be regulated or censored to keep it out of our e-mail boxes? Should the sender of spam be assessed a fee?

What should we do to keep the information arteries of our mind clear of information clutter? With the voluminous amounts of information being created daily, what guidelines can we use to filter in, not out, what we need to know?

Key Chapter Terminology

Use the Communication Works CD-ROM and the Online Learning Center at www.mhhe.com/gamble8 to further your knowledge of the following terminology.

information overload 535   informative speech 530
information underload 535

 Communication **Works**

 online learning center

www.mhhe.com/gamble8

Test Your Understanding

Go to the *Self Quizzes* on the Communication Works CD-ROM and the book's Online Learning Center at www.mhhe.com/gamble8.

Communication
Works

www.mhhe.com/gamble8

Notes

1. David Shenk. *Data Smog: Surviving the Information Glut.* New York: HarperCollins, 1997, p. 29.

2. Although compiled years ago, a valuable source to consult is Charles Petrie. "Informative Speaking: A Summary and Bibliography of Related Research." *Speech Monographs* 30, 1963, pp. 79–91.

3. For a discussion on the informative speech, see Douglas Ehninger, Bruce Gronbeck, Ray McKerrow, and Alan Monroe. *Principles and Types of Speech Communication.* New York: HarperCollins, 1992.

4. See for example, Brendan Lemon. "Audiences Today Are Getting In on the Act." *New York Times,* October 8, 2000, pp. AR-5, AR-22.

5. Quoted in Karen A. Foss, Sonja K. Foss, and Cindy L. Griffin. *Feminist Rhetorical Theories.* Thousand Oaks, CA: Sage, 1999, p. 51.

Persuasive Speaking

After finishing this chapter, you should be able to

1. Define *persuasive speaking*.

2. Define and distinguish between *attitudes* and *beliefs*.

3. Distinguish between logical and fallacious reasoning.

4. Explain the concept of credibility.

5. Develop and present a persuasive speech.

Man is the only animal that laughs and weeps; for he is the only animal that is struck with the difference between what things are and what they ought to be.

—**William Hazlitt**

It is not enough to identify the gene that predetermines the prospect of Alzheimer's disease if we go through the prime of life with a closed mind.

—**Tom Brokaw**

Countless times a day, you come into contact with people whose goal is to influence you or whom you attempt to influence. "Vote for me," the candidate advises. "Buy me," reads the ad. "Attend my rally," cries the advocate. "Support my cause," demands the lobbyist. "Give money to our movement," pleads the fund-raiser. Persuasion, the process of changing or reinforcing attitudes, beliefs, values, or behavior, is an integral part of our everyday activities. Advertisers, public relations professionals, politicians, religious leaders, and numerous others have the same primary goal—persuading you.

Our aim in this chapter is to increase your ability to prepare, present, and process persuasive speeches by showing you how to apply your general knowledge and skills to this special type of discourse.

SPEAKING PERSUASIVELY

persuasive speech

a speech whose primary purpose is to change or reinforce the attitudes, beliefs, values, and/or behaviors of receivers

Go to the *Online Learning Center* at www.mhhe.com/gamble8 and answer the questions in the *Self Inventory* to evaluate your understanding of fallacious reasoning.

When you deliver a **persuasive speech,** your goal is to modify the thoughts, feelings, or actions of your audience. You hope that your listeners will change attitudes or behaviors you do not approve of and adopt attitudes and behaviors that are compatible with your interests and the way you see the world. Persuasive discourse is becoming increasingly important; more than ever, we are concerned with being able to influence others.[1]

Today's communication environment demands effective persuasion skills. If you are negotiating for a piece of property for your new corporate headquarters, trying to persuade a town planning board to change zoning laws, speaking to a jury to persuade them to decide in favor of your client, attempting to persuade a company to use your services, running for public office, working on behalf of Amnesty International, or participating in any of thousands of other causes, you will have opportunities to practice and refine the presentation skills you are learning in this class.

"I found the old format much more exciting."

PURPOSES OF PERSUASION: THOUGHT AND ACTION

We can analyze the goals of persuasive speakers by examining what they want their speeches to accomplish. For example, a speaker may believe that flying saucers exist, even though most of the audience may not. A speaker may oppose bilingual education, while others support it. A speaker may want audience members to become organ donors, and the audience members may feel some reluctance about making that commitment. The objective of the speaker, sometimes referred to as the **proposition** of the speech, indicates what type of change the speaker would like to create in audience members. Typically, speakers want one or both of two general outcomes: They want to convince listeners that something is so (that is, to change the way audience members think), or they want to cause audience members to take an action (that is, to change the way they behave). Whatever the general nature of the proposition, it most likely will reflect at least one of the following persuasive goals: adoption, discontinuance, deterrence, or continuance.[2]

Many theorists contend that, to persuade audience members to act differently, you must first persuade them to think differently. Do you agree?

proposition

a statement that summarizes the purpose of a persuasive speech

When your goal is adoption, you hope to persuade the audience to accept a new idea, attitude, or belief (for example, that genetically engineered food is hazardous to health), with the hope that in time that belief will also be supported by action (your listeners will eliminate genetically engineered products from their diet). When your goal is discontinuance, you hope to persuade audience members to stop doing something they are now doing (stop drinking alcohol while pregnant, for example). When your goal is deterrence, you want to persuade the audience to avoid an activity or a way of thinking (for example, "If you don't smoke now, don't begin." "If you believe that every woman has the right to exercise control over her own body, don't vote for candidates who would make abortions illegal."). Finally, if your goal is the continuance of a way of believing or acting, you want to encourage people to continue to think or behave as they now do (for instance, keep purchasing products made in the United States).

To what extent do you think job effectiveness is related to the ability to influence others? Explain your answer.

Adoption and discontinuance goals involve asking listeners to alter their way of thinking or behaving, whereas deterrence and continuance goals involve asking them not to alter the way they think or behave but, rather, to reinforce or sustain it. In general, persuaders find it easier to accomplish deterrence and continuance objectives. That doesn't mean, however, that accomplishing adoption or discontinuance goals is impossible. They may be more difficult to achieve, but if the speaker uses a variety of appeals and a sound organizational scheme and has credibility, these goals can also be realized.

TYPES OF PERSUASIVE SPEECHES

Persuasive speeches may be categorized as focusing on questions of fact, value, or policy. Selecting which kind of speech you will present is among the first tasks you need to complete. By choosing one type over the others, the speaker formally decides to speak on what is or what is not **(proposition of fact)**, how good or bad something is **(proposition of value)**, or what ought to be **(proposition of policy).**

proposition of fact
a persuasive speech with the goal of settling what is or is not so

proposition of value
a persuasive speech that espouses the worth of an idea, a person, or an object

proposition of policy
a persuasive speech on what ought to be

The following are sample propositions of fact:

Date rape is on the rise.
Parental abuse of children participating in sports is increasing.
DNA is the ultimate fingerprint.
High-fiber diets prevent cancer.
The United States is vulnerable to terrorist attacks.
Poor intelligence hastened the start of the war against Iraq.

Good propositions of fact cannot be resolved with just a yes or a no answer. Instead, they are open to debate, and settling them typically requires close examination and careful interpretation of evidence, usually from a number of documents or sources. When speaking on a proposition of fact, the speaker must provide enough evidence to convince receivers of the factual nature of the statement.

The following are examples of propositions of value:

Affirmative action policies are morally justifiable.

Same-sex high schools are better than co-ed high schools.

Sex education belongs in school.

It is wrong for hospitals to continue to employ incompetent physicians.

Using persons in developing nations as guinea pigs for drug testing is unethical.

Attacking the roots of terrorism is a worthwhile endeavor.

Propositions of value explore the worth of an idea, a person, or an object. Like questions of fact, they require more than a simple answer, or in this case, a true or false response. When speaking on a proposition of value, the speaker must convince receivers that the evaluation contained in the proposition is valid. This usually requires that the speaker also explore one or more propositions of fact. For example, you probably won't be effective advocating for the premise that fetal tissue research is morally justifiable until you establish that such research is necessary.

The following are sample propositions of policy:

Trash facilities should not be located in low-income, minority neighborhoods. National health insurance should be provided to all citizens of the United States.

Gay and lesbian partners should be permitted to marry.

Dental units should contain water that conform to at least the minimal standards for drinking water.

We should all be vegetarians.

The quality of education in the United States must be improved.

When speaking on a proposition of policy, the speaker goes beyond questions of fact or value. Instead, the speaker must demonstrate a need for the policy and earn audience approval and/or support for the policy in question.

PERSUADING EFFECTIVELY

Whenever we try to cause others to change their beliefs, attitudes, or behaviors, or whenever others try to influence us, we are participating in the persuasive process.[3] Let's examine some procedures you can use to increase your persuasiveness as a speaker.

Identify Your Goal

To be a successful persuader, you must have a clearly defined purpose. You must, in fact, be able to answer these questions:

What response do I want from audience members?

Would I like them to think differently, act differently, or both?

Which of their attitudes or beliefs am I trying to alter? Why?

Unless you know what you want your listeners to think, feel, or do, you will not be able to realize your objective.

Know the Receivers You Are Trying to Reach

Acting on a good idea is better than just having a good idea.

—Robert Half

The nature of your task is partly related to the extent and type of change you hope to bring about in people. The task will be simplified if you have some idea of how the audience members feel about whatever change you are proposing. For example, to what extent do they favor the change? How important is it to them? What is at stake? The more ego-involved the members of your audience are, the more committed they will be to their current position; hence, the harder it will be for you to affect them.[4]

Understand the Factors Affecting Your Listeners' Attitudes

To be able to influence others, you need to understand the favorable and unfavorable mental sets, or predispositions, that audience members bring to a speech; that is, you need to understand **attitudes**—how they are formed, how they are sustained, and how they may be changed by you. The following forces or factors are among the most important influences on our attitudes.

attitudes

predispositions to respond favorably or unfavorably toward a person or subject

Family

If you say it enough, even if it ain't true, folks will get to believing it.

—Will Rogers

Few of us escape the strong influence exerted by our families. Many of our parents' attitudes are communicated to us and are eventually acquired by us. As communication theorists Scott Cutlip and Alan Center write, "It is the family that bends the tender twig in the direction it is likely to grow."[5]

Religion

Not only believers but also nonbelievers are affected by religion. In fact, the impact of religion is becoming ever more widespread as religious organizations strive to generate and guide attitudes on such social issues as abortion, civil rights, the death penalty, child abuse, and divorce.

Education

More people than ever are attending school; they start young (sometimes before the age of 5), and many attend until they are in or beyond their twenties. Moreover, the traditional role of the school has expanded, since large numbers of adults are now returning to complete their education, some by

Skill

BUILDER

Controversial Issues

Prepare a three- to four-minute presentation explaining your attitude on a controversial issue, such as medical privacy, abortion, human cloning, or gun control. Discuss the forces and factors that led you to form your attitude, and explain what would have to happen for you to change your attitude.

taking online courses. The courses taught, the instructors who teach them, the books assigned, and the films shown all help shape attitudes.

Socioeconomics

Economic status and social status also shape our attitudes. Our economic status helps determine the social arena we frequent. Our view of the world is likewise affected by the company we keep and the amount of money we have.

Culture

As seventeenth-century poet John Donne wrote, "No man is an island, entire of itself." From the crib to the coffin, we are influenced by others—in person and through the media. The groups we belong to, our friends, and the fabric of the society in which we find ourselves all help mold us. Our social environment contains ingredients that help determine our mental sets and in turn our attitudes. We shape our social institutions and are reciprocally shaped by them.

Understand Your Listeners' Beliefs

Your persuasive efforts will be facilitated if you understand not only your listeners' attitudes but also their beliefs—and if you understand how audiences might respond when their important beliefs are challenged.[6]

Attitudes and beliefs are, of course, related—in fact, the two terms are sometimes used interchangeably—but they are not the same thing. We might say that attitudes and beliefs are related to each other as buildings are related to bricks, beams, boards, and so on. That is, in a sense, **beliefs** are the building blocks of attitudes. Whereas attitudes are measured on a favorable–unfavorable scale, beliefs are measured on a probable–improbable scale. Thus, if you say that you think something is true, you are really saying that you believe it. According to psychologist Milton Rokeach, your belief system is made up of everything you agree is true. This includes all the information and biases you have accumulated from birth. Your disbelief system, which is composed of all the things you do not think are true, develops along with your belief system. Together, the two significantly affect the way you process information.[7]

It is necessary to recognize that, to your listener, some beliefs are more important than others. The more central or important a belief is, the harder audience members will work to defend it, the less willing they will be to change it, and the more resistant they will be to your persuasive efforts.

Use Two Principles of Influence: Consistency and Social Proof

When you are speaking persuasively, you should be aware of two significant principles. First, we all have a desire to be consistent with what we have already done. In other words, once we take a stand, consistency theory tells us that our tendency is to behave consistently with that commitment.[8] Therefore, it is important to determine how your speech can engage this tendency toward

How do you react when someone questions your position on what you consider a critical issue? Why?

beliefs
confidence in the truth of something

consistency

the desire to maintain balance in our lives by behaving according to commitments already formed

social proof

the determination of what is right by finding out what other people think is right

consistency. If you can find a way to get audience members to make a commitment (to take a stand or go on record), you will have set the stage for them to behave in ways consistent with that stand.

Second, we all respond to **social proof.** That is, one method we use to determine what is right is to find out what other people think is right.[9] You can use the actions of others to convince your listeners that what you're advocating is right. As motivation consultant Cavett Robert notes: "Since 95 percent of the people are imitators and only 5 percent initiators, people are persuaded more by the action of others than by any proof we can offer."[10]

Reason Logically

You will be more apt to achieve the goal of a successful persuasive speech if you can give your listeners logical reasons that they should support what you advocate. The most common forms of logical reasoning are deduction, induction, causal reasoning, and reasoning from analogy.

Deduction

deduction

reasoning that moves from the general to the specific

When we reason deductively, we move from the general to the specific. In other words, when using **deduction,** we offer general evidence that leads to a specific conclusion. The following example moves from the general to the specific:

> *Major premise:* People who study regularly instead of cramming usually get better grades.
>
> *Minor premise:* You want to get better grades.
>
> *Conclusion:* Therefore, you should study regularly instead of cramming.

You can evaluate deductive reasoning by asking the following two questions:

1. Are the major premise and the minor premise (or minor premises) true?
2. Does the conclusion follow logically from the premises?

Be sure to give the necessary evidence to buttress your major and minor premises.

Induction

induction

reasoning that moves from specific evidence to a general conclusion

When we reason inductively, we move from specific evidence to a general conclusion. The following is an example of **induction;** it moves from the specific to the general—from a series of facts to a conclusion:

> *Fact:* After growing up on a diet of television violence, Ronnie Zamora committed a murder.
>
> *Fact:* After watching the film *The Program,* a group of teenagers imitated a scene in the movie by lying down on the center line of a highway.
>
> *Fact:* After two youths viewed an episode of *Beavis and Butthead,* 2-year-old Jessica Matthews died when her 5-year-old brother set the house on fire by playing with matches, as shown on the show.
>
> *Conclusion:* Violence depicted on television and films is copied in real life.

Whenever speakers use what is true in particular cases to draw a general conclusion, they are reasoning by induction. For instance, we are reasoning inductively if we conclude that sexualized violence against women shown on MTV videos leads to acts of sexualized violence against women in real life because, in a number of cases, men have enacted in real life the situations they have seen on the videos.

You can evaluate inductive reasoning by asking the following two questions:

1. Is the sample of specific instances large enough to justify the conclusion drawn from them?
2. Are the instances cited representative, or typical, ones?

Causal Reasoning

When we reason from causes and effects, we either cite observed causes and hypothesize effects or cite observed effects and hypothesize causes. We use **causal reasoning** every day. Something happens, and we ask ourselves, Why? Similarly, we speculate about the consequences of certain acts; that is, we wonder about what effects they have. The following statements illustrate causal reasoning:

causal reasoning
speculation about the reasons for and effects of occurrences

Smoking cigarettes can cause cancer.
Smoking cigarettes can cause heart disease.
Smoking cigarettes can cause problems during pregnancy.
Cigarette smoking is hazardous to your health and should be eliminated.

To evaluate the soundness of causal reasoning, ask the following questions:

1. Is the presumed cause real or false?
2. Is the presumed cause an oversimplification?

Reasoning from Analogy

When we use **reasoning from analogy,** we compare like things and conclude that, since they are alike in a number of respects, they are also alike in some respect that until this point has not been examined. For example, if you wanted to argue that the methods used to decrease the high school dropout rate in a nearby city would also work in your city, you would first have to establish that your city is similar to the other city in a number of important ways—number of young people, number of schools, skill of personnel, financial resources, and so on. If you said that the two cities were alike except for the fact that your city had not instituted such a program and that its dropout rate was therefore significantly higher, you would be arguing by analogy.

reasoning from analogy
reasoning by comparison

To check the validity of analogical reasoning, ask the following questions:

1. Are the two things being compared alike in essential respects? That is, do the points of similarity outweigh the points of difference?
2. Do the differences that do exist matter?

Reason Ethically

Ethical speakers do not employ logical fallacies. A fallacy is an error in logic; it is flawed reasoning. When a speaker attempts to persuade using flawed

Ethics & COMMUNICATION

Illogical Reasoning

When logic fails, speakers sometimes substitute logical fallacies in its place. Additional reasoning fallacies speakers may flaw their speeches with are the following:

The hasty generalization: being too quick to jump to a conclusion

The slippery slope: asserting that one action will set in motion a chain reaction

The appeal to tradition: telling receivers that things have always been done a certain way

Using the Internet, books of published speeches, or issues of *Vital Speeches of the Day,* locate examples of fallacious reasoning. Explain why you believe the logic is flawed in each example.

---

reasoning, in addition to misusing the reasoning process, he or she is also abusing the persuasion process. The following are among the most common fallacies that speakers should avoid. (Other logical fallacies are noted in Ethics & Communication, "Illogical Reasoning.")

Argumentum ad Hominem

argumentum ad hominem

the use of name-calling in an argument

When you present your audience with an **argumentum ad hominem,** you inject name-calling into your speech. It is literally an "argument against the man" (or woman). You appeal to receivers to reject an idea because of a flaw in a person associated with that idea. You attack a person's character instead of his or her stand on an issue. "She's just a left-wing liberal" and "He's just a member of the radical right" focus attention on the person and not his or her ideas.

Red Herring

red herring

a distraction used to lead the receiver to focus on an irrelevant issue

The term **red herring** derives its meaning from an act performed during English fox hunts, in which hunt masters would drag red herrings across trails in an effort to divert the hunting dogs from chasing the foxes. When you use a red herring in your speech, your goal is to send the audience on a wild goose chase. By causing receivers to focus on one or more irrelevant issues, you prevent them from considering the issue actually under discussion. For example, in an effort to negate the right of women to have abortions, one speaker attempted to deflect the focus of receivers by concentrating instead on the cost of health insurance.

False Division

false division

the polarization of options, when, in fact, many options exist

When you use a **false division** in your speech (a false dichotomy, dilemma, or either-or argument), you require audience members to choose between two options, usually polar opposites, when in reality there are many options in between. The following are examples of the false division at work: "If you believe in flag burning, you don't believe in the country." "If you don't like the policies of the United States, go back to your native country." "If you are not part of the solution, then you are part of the problem." "Either we eliminate gun control, or only outlaws will have guns."

Post Hoc, Ergo Propter Hoc (False Cause)

post hoc, ergo propter hoc

the identification of a false cause

When your argument is based on the assumption of **post hoc, ergo propter hoc,** you identify a false cause; that is, you lead your receivers to assume

The speeches of speakers from groups such as the Ku Klux Klan usually contain an array of logical fallacies.

mistakenly that one event causes another merely because they occur sequentially. For example, one speaker pointed out that a decrease in abortions in the United States began about the same time as increased opportunities in sports for women. While a causal link may exist, the speaker has to supply evidence to establish a definitive link between the two phenomena. Correlation is not causation.

Argumentum ad Populum (Bandwagon Appeal)

An **argumentum ad populum** is a bandwagon appeal—that is, an appeal to popular opinion. The speaker who uses such a fallacy tells receivers that, because "everyone is doing or supporting it," they should too. Widespread acceptance of an idea, however, does not mean the idea is sound. Rather than rush to judgment based on what everyone else is saying or doing, you should consider the facts carefully and decide for yourself.

argumentum ad populum

a bandwagon appeal; an appeal to popular opinion

Argumentum ad Verecudiam (Appeal to Authority)

When you inject an **argumentum ad verecudiam** fallacy into your speech, you use the testimony of someone who is not an expert on your subject and does not possess the credentials that would permit him or her to make a claim or endorsement. Name recognition and expertise are not synonymous. For instance, while the Backstreet Boys may be well-known performers and experts on music or MP3, when it comes to talking about the foreign policy of the United States, their value as a source decreases.

argumentum ad verecudiam

an appeal to authority

Gain Your Listeners' Attention

Before you can persuade or convince other people, you must first get their attention. In his book *The Art of Persuasion*, Wayne Minnick relates how a 9-year-old girl succeeded in getting the undivided attention of a male guest at her party. It seems that all the boys had gathered at one end of the room, talking to each other and ignoring the girls. "But I got one of them to pay attention to me, all right," the little girl assured her mother. "How?" inquired the mother. "I knocked him down!" was the undaunted reply.[11]

You should not knock your listeners down to get their attention, but you will need to find ways to encourage them to listen to you. It is your responsibility to put them into a receptive frame of mind. You can do this in several ways. You can compliment your listeners. You can question them. You

To what extent must friends, co-workers, politicians, and advertisers compete to get your attention? Which strategies are the most effective? Why?

can relate your message directly to their interests, or you can surprise them by relating to them in an unexpected way. Once you have the attention of your listeners, you must continue to work to hold it.

Make Your Listeners Feel As Well As Think

Following is an excerpt from a student's speech on the issue of Palestinians jailed without trial in Israel. In it, the student quotes from a letter written by a Palestinian prisoner to an Israeli officer who was sentenced to jail himself for refusing to serve as a jailer for the political detainees because of his belief that the practice of administrative detentions was wrong. Why do you think that the use of this passage in the student's speech is effective?

> Who are you, officer?
>
> I want to write to you, but first I have to know who you are. I have to know the reasons that moved you to act as you did. I have to know how you arrived at this principled decision of conscience; how you chose such a unique rebellion, so unexpected.
>
> What's your name? Where do you live? What do you do? How old are you? Do you have children? Do you like the sea? What books do you read? And what are you doing now in the cell where you are held? Do you have enough cigarettes? Is there someone who identifies with you over there? Do you ask yourself, "Was it worth paying the price?"
>
> Can you see the moon and stars from the cell window? Have your ears grown accustomed to the jangle of the heavy keys, to the creak of the locks, to the clang of the metal doors? . . . Do you see in your sleep fields of wheat and kernels moving in the wind? Do you see expanses of sunflowers, and are your eyes filled with yellow, green and black hues, and the sun tans you, and you smile in your sleep, and the walls of the cell tumble and fall, and an unknown person waves his hand to you from afar? . . .
>
> Don't you have regrets? Didn't you have doubts when they told you: "They're dangerous; they belong to Hamas, to Islamic Jihad and the Popular Front? Don't you trust our security services? Do you really believe that we are ready to throw innocent people in jail?"
>
> Why do I feel as if I know you? . . .
>
> Anonymous lieutenant, whatever your name is, sleep well; sleep the peaceful slumber of someone whose conscience is clear.

Effective speakers develop emotional appeals designed to make audience members feel.

Many changes in human behavior have resulted from messages that combined emotional appeals with rational reasons. Since few people will change their attitudes or take action if they are unmoved or bored, effective speakers develop emotional appeals that are designed to make listeners feel.[12] Whether the feeling evoked is sadness, anger, fear, sympathy, happiness, greed, nostalgia, jealousy, pride, or guilt depends on the speaker's topic and the response desired.

Ronald Reagan understood the need for emotion. He chose a poem to close his presidential tribute to the astronauts lost in the *Challenger* disaster:

> Let us close with these lines written by a 19-year-old World War II fighter pilot, John Gillespie Magee, Jr., shortly before his own death in the air:

High Flight

Oh, I have slipped the surly bonds of Earth.
And danced the skies on laughter-silvered wings:
Sunward I've climbed and joined the tumbling mirth
Of sun-split cloud—and done a hundred things
You have not dreamed of—wheeled and soared and swung
High in the sunlit silence. Hov'ring there.
I've chased the shouting wind along and flung
My eager craft through footless halls of air.
Up, up, the long delirious burning blue
I've topped the wind-swept heights' easy grace
Where never lark or even eagle flew—
And, while with silent lifting wing I've trod
The high untrespassed sanctity of space.
Put out my hand and touched the face of God.[13]

Your goal should be to compel your listeners to remember your ideas and proposals; to do this, you will need to arouse their feelings. As a speaker, you must appeal not just to your listeners' heads but also to their hearts. Thus, although your speech should be grounded in a firm foundation of logic and fact, it should also be built on feelings.

Evoke Relevant Needs and Issues

Balance is a state of psychological health or comfort in which our actions, feelings, and beliefs are related to each other as we would like them to be. When we are in a balanced state, we are content or satisfied. Thus, we engage in a continual struggle to keep ourselves in balance. What does this imply for you as a persuasive speaker? If you want to convince your listeners to change their attitudes or beliefs, you must first demonstrate to them that a current situation or state of affairs has created an imbalance in their lives and that you can help restore their balance. The simple introduction of imbalance, or dissonance (whether that imbalance, or dissonance, is experienced by receivers for real or created vicariously by the speaker) motivates change in receiver thinking or behaving. Thus, speakers may deliberately create dissonance in receivers and then suggest what receivers need to think or do in order to be able to alleviate their dissonance and restore their sense of balance. It is our inner drive for balance that helps explain our positive responses to an array of persuasive appeals.

Remember that human behavior depends on motivation. If you are to persuade people to believe and do what you would like them to do, you must make your message appeal to their needs and goals.

One popular device used to analyze human motivation is a schematic framework devised by famous psychologist Abraham Maslow.[14] In **Maslow's hierarchy of needs,** motivation is seen as a pyramid, with our most basic needs at its base and our most sophisticated needs at its apex (see Figure 19.1). Maslow defined survival needs as the basic necessities of life: shelter, food, water, and procreation. Safety needs include the need for security and the need to know that our survival requirements will be satisfied. At the third level are love and belonging needs. Once these are met, our esteem needs can be addressed. Esteem needs include self-respect and the respect of others. Our efforts to succeed are often attempts to satisfy our esteem needs, because success tends to

balance

a state of psychological comfort in which one's actions, feelings, and beliefs are related to each other as one would like them to be

In your opinion, is it reasonable for speakers to cause receivers to experience dissonance in order to get them to believe something or do something? Is causing receivers to feel at risk, insecure, or vulnerable by manufacturing dissonance unethical? What if the speaker exaggerates the risk receivers face just to accomplish a goal? What if the risk isn't really there at all?

Maslow's hierarchy of needs

a model that depicts motivation as a pyramid with the most basic needs at the base and the most sophisticated at the apex

FIGURE 19.1
Maslow's Hierarchy of Needs.

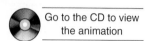

Go to the CD to view
the animation

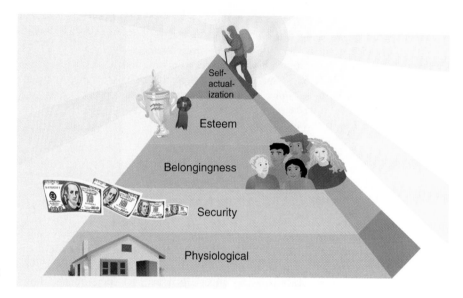

From Abraham Maslow, *Toward a Psychology of Being.* Copyright © 1962. Reprinted by permission of John Wiley & Sons, Inc.

attract respect and attention. At the peak of Maslow's hierarchy is the need for self-actualization. When we satisfy this, we have realized our potential; that is, we have become everything we are capable of becoming.

How does Maslow's hierarchy relate to you as a persuasive speaker? Find out by trying the Skill Builder "Climbing the Motivation Pyramid." Remember that salient needs make salient motives. Your goal is to make your receivers identify your proposal with their needs. Whenever you attempt to do this, you will probably have to involve personal feelings.

Promise a Reward

When you are speaking persuasively, demonstrate how your listeners' personal needs can be satisfied by your proposal. You should stress how your ideas can benefit the people you are trying to persuade. Make them believe that your proposal will supply a reward.

Skill BUILDER

Climbing the Motivation Pyramid

For each of the following situations, identify the types of appeals you could use to persuade listeners to believe or behave as you would like them to. First, imagine a particular type of audience. Second, aim a part of your persuasive effort at each level of Maslow's levels on the hierarchy pyramid. Which level and which appeal do you think would be most effective? Explain your reasons.

1. You want to persuade someone to stop smoking.

2. You want to persuade someone to donate blood.

3. You want to persuade someone to support capital punishment.

4. You want to persuade someone to protest against using domestic animals for experimental research.

Remember, however, that different audiences value different types of rewards. For practice, think of three different types of audiences and identify the most important needs of each. Imagine that you are a salesperson trying to persuade each of those audiences to buy one of the following items: (1) guitar, (2) plant, (3) dog, (4) hat, (5) attaché case. Describe the strategies you would use with each group. What adaptations would you make? To what extent would you display your awareness of individual differences?

It is important to remember that people are usually preoccupied with how something will benefit them personally. Your listeners, whoever they are, will want something in return for behaving as you would like them to behave.

What are your own most important needs? How might someone use this information to persuade you to buy one of the items listed in the text?

MONROE'S MOTIVATED SEQUENCE: A FRAMEWORK FOR PERSUASIVE SPEAKING

One organizational framework that persuasive speakers have found particularly effective in motivating receivers to respond positively to their purpose is **Monroe's motivated sequence.**[15] Based on the psychology of persuasion, Monroe's framework is composed of five phases, which sequentially move receivers toward accepting and acting on a speaker's proposition. Its persuasive structure especially meets the needs of speakers who desire to move audience members to action.

Monroe's motivated sequence

a speech framework composed of five phases— attention, need, satisfaction, visualization, and action

Phase One: Attention. At the outset of a speech, the speaker's primary task is to gain the audience's attention. The speaker entices the collective appetite of receivers in an effort to spark interest in his or her proposal. (In effect, you say, "Pay attention." Perhaps you enhance receivers' interest by asking a question, referring to their experiences, using an illustration or a dramatic story, supplying startling statistics, or providing an eye-catching visual. As a result of what you say or do, your audience members should realize why your message is important to them and why they should listen to what you have to say.)

Phase Two: Need. The speaker demonstrates for receivers that the present situation poses serious problems. He or she explicitly states the need and illustrates it with a variety of supporting materials. By revealing what is wrong to receivers and relating the need to their interests and desires, the speaker prepares them for the problem's solution. (In this stage, you say, "This is wrong, and here is what we need to do about it." In addition to identifying the problem or need, you illustrate it with specific examples. In addition, you support the need's existence with illustrations, statistics, testimony, or other forms of support. Your objective is to show how the identified need has an impact on the lives of audience members and how it affects their personal or professional goals, health, happiness, and/or financial security, for example.)

Phase Three: Satisfaction. Having shown the audience members that a need exists, the speaker's next task is to satisfy their desire for a solution. (Here, you tell receivers, "I have a way to solve the problem." You present your plan, explain it fully to receivers, and help them recognize that solving the problem will satisfy their interests and desires. By using examples and illustrations to flesh out what you want audience members to believe or do, and explaining why you are asking them to believe or do this, you help them understand how they can satisfy the need you described previously.)

Phase Four: Visualization. The speaker visualizes the plan's benefits for receivers, describing how things will improve when the plan is put into action. (In this phase, you say, "This is how my plan will meet your needs, alleviate the problems you face, and help make things better." You demonstrate the benefits audience members will receive once they act upon your ideas; if desired, you also explore the negative effects receivers will suffer if they fail to act on your plan.)

Phase Five: Action. The speaker's next task is to move receivers in a particular direction by telling them what they should do to ensure that the need is satisfied. In effect, the speaker asks receivers to support the policy and act on it. (In this phase, you say, "Here's what I would like you do." You conclude with an appeal that reinforces their commitment to putting your solution to work. You are telling them to act.)

Focus on Service Learning
Use Monroe's motivated sequence to write a speech that supports the fund raising efforts of your college or a local charity.

The following outline illustrates how the motivational sequence can be used to design a presentation advocating that we should not drive when drowsy.

Introduction

(Attention)

I. It was after midnight when six students walking to a fraternity party were killed when Brandon Kallmeyer fell asleep at the wheel of the pick-up truck he was driving, veered off the road, and hit them.

II. Over 100,000 accidents occur every year because drivers fall asleep at the wheel.

III. The problem of people driving while drowsy is increasing.

IV. Today I would like to explore why it is important to us to examine this problem, why it continues to escalate, and what steps we can take to help alleviate it.

Body

(Need)

I. We have put sleep on the back burner.
   A. Everyone needs approximately eight hours of sleep a day to function effectively the next day, but we average only about six hours of sleep a night.
   B. The most important sleep hour is the REM stage, which occurs between the seventh and eighth hour.

II. Sleep-deprived persons pose serious dangers on the road.
   A. Highway patrol officers report stopping motorists who appear drunk, only to discover they are fatigued.
   B. Drowsy driving is approaching a national epidemic.

III. The drowsy driving problem can be alleviated once we fully understand its causes.

(Satisfaction)
   A. We are poor judges of our own sleeplessness.

B. Alcohol consumption contributes to becoming sleepy behind the wheel.

C. Comfortable drive is a contributing factor to becoming tired.

IV. Tragedy can be prevented if we take the proper steps.

(Visualization)

A. Imagine what would happen if the Federal Highway Administration added more rumble strips designed to wake us up when we began to veer off the road.

B. Imagine what would happen if cars were equipped with AutoVue cameras that emit rumble strip–like sounds when a driver drifts out of a lane.

V. There are some steps we can take personally to protect ourselves.

A. We can take naps to fight fatigue.

(Action)

B. We can sleep the recommended seven to eight hours a night.

Conclusion

I. Six innocent students were killed because someone didn't take action to avoid the tragedy.

II. It is time to get the sleep that could save our lives and the lives of others.[16]

BECOMING A MORE CREDIBLE PERSUADER

credibility

the receiver's assessment of the competence, trustworthiness, and dynamism of a speaker

According to attorney Gerry Spence, your success as a persuader will be determined in part by what your "targets" think of you—in other words, by your **credibility.**[17]

For some groups of people, the Dalai Lama is considered a highly credible speaker.

When we use the term *credibility,* we are talking not about what you are really like but about how an audience perceives you. If your listeners accept you as credible, they probably believe that you are a person of good character (trustworthy and fair) and are knowledgeable (trained, competent to discuss your topic, and a reliable source of information) and personable (dynamic, charismatic, active, and energetic). As a result, your ideas are more likely to get a fair hearing. However, if your listeners believe that you are an untrustworthy, incompetent (not sufficiently knowledgeable about your topic), and passive (lacking in dynamism), they are less likely to respond as you desire.

It is entirely possible—even probable—that your listeners may consider you more credible about some topics than others. For example, the following are two pairs of imaginary statements. Which statement in each pair would you be more inclined to accept?

> The United States must never negotiate with terrorists. Strength is the only language they will understand.
>
> —Madeleine Albright

> The United States must never negotiate with terrorists. Strength is the only language they will understand.
>
> —Madonna

> The world of contemporary music has room in it for everyone. The message music sends is tolerance.
>
> —Jewel

> The world of contemporary music has room in it for everyone. The message music sends is tolerance.
>
> —Hillary Rodham Clinton

If you're like most people, you find the first statement in each pair more credible. The source cited for the first statement seems obviously more

---

EXPLORING Diversity

Persuasion and Assumed Similarity

LaRay M. Barna, an intercultural communication theorist, points out that we are all influenced by our cultural upbringing, and, while we tend to assume that other people's needs, desires, and basic assumptions are the same as our own, often they are not. How can assumed similarity—the belief that we all have similar thoughts, feelings, attitudes, and nonverbal codes—cause problems for persuasive speakers? For example, while Americans tend to value materialism, success, and rationality, Arabs are more likely to value self-respect, courage, and honor. Arabs also value storytelling, eloquence, and the ability of words to spark emotional responses in others. To this end, they use emphatic assertions to convey their seriousness. When such assertions are missing, others may assume that an Arab speaker means the opposite of what was said.[18]

Based on this realization, in your opinion, is it more beneficial for a persuasive speaker to assume *differences* rather than similarity? Explain.

What should the speaker do if members of the audience come from a variety of cultures, some who expect a more formal style of delivery than the speaker is used to, some who expect the speaker to begin by humbling himself or herself and making respectful references to the audience, some who expect the speaker to be restrained rather than overly expressive, some who expect the speaker to rely on narratives rather than formal logic or standard inductive or deductive structures, and so on?

knowledgeable about the subject. Another way of saying this is that you may be judged more credible by certain types of audiences than by others.

Regardless of the circumstances, however, it will be up to you to build your credibility by giving your listeners reasons to consider you competent, trustworthy, and dynamic.[19] To help listeners see you as competent, you can describe your own experiences with the subject and suggest why you feel you've earned the right to share your ideas. You can help your listeners see you as trustworthy by demonstrating respect for different points of view and communicating a sense of sincerity. To help listeners see you as dynamic, speak with energy, use assured and forceful gestures, and create vocal variety.[20]

Note that the audience's assessment of your credibility can change during your presentation or as a result of it. Thus, we can identify three types of credibility:

Initial credibility is your credibility before you actually start to speak.

Derived credibility is your credibility during your speech.

Terminal credibility is your credibility at the end of your speech.

initial credibility

a measure of how an audience perceives a speaker prior to the speech-making event

derived credibility

a measure of a speaker's credibility during a speech-making event

terminal credibility

a measure of a speaker's credibility at the end of a speech-making event

Of course, if your initial credibility is high, your task should be easier. But keep in mind that your speech can lower your initial credibility—and that it can also raise your initial credibility. What you say and how you say it are important determiners of credibility.

As Ralph Waldo Emerson wrote,

> The reason why anyone refuses his assent to your opinion, or his aid to your benevolent design, is in you. He refuses to accept you as a bringer of truth, because, though you think you have it, he feels that you have it not. You have not given him the authentic sign.

In brief, persuasive speaking involves more than simply communicating with others in a public setting. It includes your responsibility to familiarize yourself with the beliefs, attitudes, and needs of those you hope to persuade. Only by doing so will you be in a position to influence others—and to understand how they may try to influence you.

Ethics & COMMUNICATION

Big and Little Lies

What kinds of communication choices do you make when attempting to accomplish a goal? What would you do to get others to comply with your wishes? Would you lie? Would you cheat? In your opinion, is it acceptable for a speaker to manipulate receivers?

Do you think Martha Stewart's credibility was damaged by accusations of insider-trading?

Our society has been criticized for being a "culture of cheating."[21] From the schoolyard to the White House, from the boardroom to the war room, from the ball field to the farm field, cheating appears to go on everywhere. We saw it with the presentation of the reasons for going to war against Iraq, and we saw it with the alleged "rescue" of Private Jessica Lynch and the ensuing accusation that "the Pentagon tried to pull a fast one."[22] We saw it with Enron. We saw it with ImClone. Politicians and CEOs fudge statements, exaggerate the value of evidence, and fabricate claims. Some lies are told "to protect national security," some to protect the president's skin; some are just boasting. What is more, it appears that the "cheaters prosper until they get caught."[23]

What damage, if any, do you believe is done to a speaker's credibility when receivers discover that he or she has lied to them? Is a speaker's tendency to exaggerate as harmful as committing a lie of omission or telling an outright lie? Do the ends, in your opinion, ever justify the means? In other words, is it acceptable for a speaker to make up facts if his or her goal is a worthy one?

Would you ever lie to receivers? Would you make up statistics, pass off as true a narrative you knew to be hypothetical, or tamper with visuals if you knew that doing so would help you realize the objective(s) of your speech?

TECHNOLOGY AND THE PERSUADER

We live in an age when image manipulation is a reality. Today, it is becoming increasingly difficult for us to know when something is real and when it is not. Currently, computer simulations are used in both news reports and live presentations. When speakers explained to the public the outcomes of battles fought during the UN–Iraq war, for example, graphic models or simulations that represented the movement of tanks and the results of air strikes were used to enhance those reports.

Let us try to imagine how virtual reality might affect the audiences of public speakers in years to come. Vivid computer simulations will certainly present receivers with a number of processing challenges. For example, is there such a thing as an objective simulation, or are simulations used by speakers to help internalize the reality that speakers would like receivers to support? And even if the image announces on its face that it is a simulation, doesn't it nonetheless by its very presence have persuasive impact? Is it not possible that the speaker who can stage the most convincingly persuasive simulations will succeed in having receivers think or do anything and win their minds and hearts?[24] In the future, when virtual reality is in full bloom, it may enable receivers to not just hear and see the speaker but also live the ideas expressed in the speech. The speaker's audience may be able to share more fully the dramatic moments or illustrations of a speech once they are transformed into multisensory stories. Audience members may be able to feel that they share a cardboard shelter with a homeless person or are in the middle of a rain forest. The sensory richness the speaker is able to provide may reduce the receiver's capacity to reason logically. In short order, the emotional power of virtual reality may become a powerful, though ethically questionable, tool for persuasive speakers. As with any new communication medium, however, it is neither good nor bad in itself. How it will be used by speakers is what matters.

How Real Is Real?

Compare and contrast virtual reality with hypothetical examples. How are they similar? How are they different? Some say they are both ploys manufactured by the speaker to involve receivers in a hallucination that serves the speaker's purpose only. Others say they are nothing more than models that provide information and enable receivers to visualize the speaker's intention more fully.

To what extent do you agree or disagree with each of these perceptions?

e-SEARCH

Reflect and Respond

Agree or disagree with the following statement; give reasons and examples that support your stance.

All persuasive speaking is informative. There is no such thing as a purely persuasive speech.

Then, using both the outline and transcript of the persuasive speeches that follow in the text, provide examples from each that support the position you have taken.

Thinking CRITICALLY

DELIVERING A PERSUASIVE SPEECH

As a persuasive speaker, you must show a great deal of interest in and enthusiasm for your topic. At the moment of presentation, it must become the most important issue in the world for both you and your listeners. The audience must feel that you have a strong conviction about the topic and the solution you suggest.

Be aware that audience members may object to what you say. As a persuader, you need to be able to handle objections in an effective manner. First, be prepared for opposing points of view. Anticipate your audience's concerns and rehearse possible answers. Second, consider the source of objections. For example, audience members may dispute your facts. If you make a statement about the number of millionaires in your state and an audience member has just completed a study on wealth in the United States and has up-to-date statistics, you will need to agree, restate your findings, or suggest that this is a good point, which you both should explore. An effective way to handle opposing views is to agree with them as much as possible. "I agree that life insurance may not be the best investment . . ." is a disarming technique often used by sales representatives to counter objections to purchasing insurance.

Answer any argument in a professional manner. Do not become angry that anyone would dare question your reasoning. Remember that your credibility is at stake while you are speaking in front of others. Respond to the question or objection in an authoritative manner and move on to other questions. Maintain control.

For an example of a persuasive speech, view clip 8, 9 on the CD

SAMPLE PERSUASIVE PRESENTATIONS

Topic:	The Patriot Act[25]
Purpose:	To persuade the audience that we need to work to restore the freedoms we lost due to passage of The Patriot Act
Thesis:	The Patriot Act has trampled the freedoms of Americans.
Introduction	I. "They that would give up liberty just for a little safety deserve neither liberty nor safety." These words, delivered by Benjamin Franklin in 1778, ring as true to our ears today, over 225 years later.
	II. In October 2001, Congress passed the "Provide Appropriate Tools Required to Intercept and Obstruct Terrorism Act"— better known as The Patriot Act.
	A. The focus of the bill is on safety, not liberty.
	B. According to the *Washington Post,* the Justice Department is contemplating expanding the bill.
	III. In order to understand the dangers inherent in The Patriot Act, we must first explore the root of The Patriot Act's flaws; second, examine the problems associated with this act; and third, look into some solutions to see what we can do to help

By starting with a quotation from the Revolutionary War era and tying it to today, the speaker attempts to draw receivers into the speech.

Having aroused the interest of receivers, and indicating that a problem exists, the speaker reveals the subject of the speech and specifically identifies the speech's objective.

restore the freedoms we have lost while continuing to ensure our safety.

Body

I. The roots of The Patriot Act are flawed.

    A. The Patriot Act was passed out of fear.

        1. According to National Public Radio, because of fear, elected officials reached for a blanket of safety.

        2. The means devised to make us safe take away from us what we want to protect.

    B. The Justice Department stifled debate.

        1. Questioning the bill was labeled as "un-American."

        2. The stifling of debate is as heinous in the post–9/11 era as it was in the 1950s.

II. The Patriot Act has a number of problems.

    A. The Patriot Act is ineffective in fighting the war on terrorism.

        1. According to *The London Daily Telegraph,* only 3 of the 700 suspected terrorists detained and the 300 arrested have been found guilty.

        2. Persons convicted under The Patriot Act have been low-level cell members.

        3. Consider the story of Vasilly Rajah, who was deported by the Justice Department, which declared him a risk to national security.

            a. Rajah was here legally.

            b. Rajah's wife died on 9/11 in Tower II.

    B. The Patriot Act infringes on the rights we cherish.

        1. According to the *Washington Post* of November 19, 2002, The Patriot Act enables federal agencies to tap our phone lines and access our e-mail.

        2. The Patriot Act is in conflict with the Fourth Amendment to the Constitution of the United States.

        3. The Patriot Act invades our right to privacy.

            a. Federal agencies can access library records, including Internet usage.

            b. Federal agencies can investigate us because of the research we do.

            c. Persons seen as assisting an organization considered terrorist—even Greenpeace—may have their citizenship revoked.

III. We must stand up for our civil liberties.

    A. Research The Patriot Act.

    B. Know what your civil liberties are.

        1. Contact your local city council office.

        2. ABC News notes that over 35 municipalities have chosen not to abide by The Patriot Act.

    C. Alter your attitudes toward liberty and safety.

    D. Remember the sacrifices of our nation's early patriots.

The speaker identifies the first reason for the position taken in the speech and supports this reason with specific examples.

The speaker uses dramatic statistical evidence and an emotionally charged illustration to support the second main point of the speech.

The speaker also supports the second main point by supplying a litany of reasons with which receivers can identify.

The speaker involves receivers by telling them what they can do to help remedy the situation.

The speaker reminds receivers why they need to be vigilant.

continued

The speaker uses an effective example to strengthen the position espoused by the speech.

Conclusion

I. Khalid Sheik Mohammad was captured on March 1, 2003, without any use of The Patriot Act.

II. Let us not give away our freedoms.

Sources

The "Provide Appropriate Tools Required to Intercept and Obstruct Terrorism Act," also known as The Patriot Act, accessed at www.house.gov

National Public Radio, February 9, 2003.

London Daily Telegraph, February 10, 2003.

Washington Post, November 19, 2002.

Baltimore Sun, March 8, 2003.

ABC News.

A Speech: The Patriot Act and Our Civil Rights[26]

Topic: The Patriot Act

Purpose: To persuade the audience that we need to work to restore the freedoms we lost due to passage of The Patriot Act

Thesis: The Patriot Act has trampled the freedoms of Americans.

Do you think that starting with a 225-year-old quotation is a good idea? Does the speaker's opening succeed in capturing your attention and motivating you to want to hear more? What other means might the speaker use to pull you into the speech? Could the speaker have benefited from the use of a visual aid?

"They that would give up their liberty just for a little safety deserve neither liberty nor safety." These words, spoken by Benjamin Franklin warn of the loss of precious freedom out of fear. While Franklin first delivered his warning in 1778, this patriot's words still ring true over 225 years later.

On October 11, 2001, the United States Congress overwhelmingly approved the "Provide Appropriate Tools Required to Intercept and Obstruct Terrorism Act"—better known as The Patriot Act. At the time of the bill's introduction, the question was raised: "Which is more important: liberty or safety?"

And now more than a year since the bill was enacted, a new question has arisen: Is the sacrifice of liberty in the name of safety ever enough? *The Washington Post,* on February 8, 2003, reported that the Justice Department is currently considering expanding The Patriot Act beyond its already intrusive powers. The Patriot Act has trampled our American freedoms, and before we find these freedoms slipping even further from our grasp, we must address the issue.

How effective do you find the speaker's orientation? Does it help clarify the major parts of the speech?

In order to better understand the dangers that are inherent in The Patriot Act, we must first explore the roots of The Patriot Act's flaws, then examine the problems associated with the act, before finally looking into some solutions to see what we can do to help restore the freedoms we have lost while continuing to ensure our safety.

How would you describe the basic speech-making structure of the speech?

In a situation such as the one we face with The Patriot Act, we can pinpoint The Patriot Act's flaws without political bias. Our elected officials, regardless of political affiliation, did what any of us would have done in a time of such fear. They reached for the closest blanket of safety. However, it is the means by which some sought safety that contradicted the very essence of what we want to protect.

National Public Radio transcripts of February 9, 2003, report that, while the bill was passed in less than a month on the floor of Congress, during that time Justice Department officials effectively had all the debate stifled—not through any direct means but, rather, by implying that any questioning of this bill would be seen as "un-American," a term that was as heinous in the post–9/11 days as it was to be called a Communist during the 1950s. From this lack of discussion, the American system was cheated, diverted away from the intentions this nation was founded upon. But this diversion away from the Constitution would not be the last.

In our search for safety, we have seen several problems inherent with The Patriot Act, including the general ineffectiveness of the bill and the gross infringement of our civil liberties.

Primarily, The Patriot Act has yet to prove its worth in fighting the war on terrorism. *The London Daily Telegraph* of February 10, 2003, reports that in the United States there have been more than 700 detentions and 300 arrests of suspected terrorists. Of these, 3 have been found guilty. While certainly any convictions are helpful, the 3 who were convicted were admittedly lower-level cell members. Furthermore, when federal agencies decide to implement their strictest penalties, the chances of subduing a person who is a real risk are minimal at best. Consider the ironic story of Vasilly Rajah—a Russian immigrant who was recently deported after the Justice Department had him declared a risk to national security. Apparently Rajah's career as a computer software engineer raised a red flag on his record. His lack of a Green Card led to his being sent home. But Rajah wasn't living in America illegally. He was married to Tatiana Rajah, a Russian immigrant who had her nationalization papers. But when Tatiana died, Vasilly was no longer considered a conditional citizen. He was sent back to Russia without his now motherless children, who were born in the United States and therefore allowed to stay. The truly tragic twist in his story lies in the death of Tatiana, who was working in Tower Two of the World Trade Center on September 11th. Because of this legislation, passed as a result of September 11th, Vasilly Rajah, a man widowed by the attacks, was deported without ever being convicted of a crime. But having an ethnic-sounding name is not a prerequisite for being victimized by this bill.

Along with being generally ineffective, The Patriot Act is truly a misnomer. Certainly nothing that works to infringe on the rights of citizens can be considered the act of a patriot. *The Washington Post* of November 19, 2002, explains one of the greatest infringements on our civil liberties. The Fourth Amendment to the Constitution states that "the right of the people to be secure in their persons, houses, papers, and effects against unreasonable searches and seizures shall not be violated." However, using powers granted in The Patriot Act, federal agencies may now tap any individual's phone line and access any individual's e-mail content, using only the pretense of a suspicion of cooperating

Do you find the use of a National Public Radio transcript credibility-enhancing?

Does the speaker's use of another historical example and the indirect reference to the McCarthy era help advance the speech's purpose?

Does this transition facilitate the receivers' job?

Are the problems the speaker cites convincing? Does the speaker supply enough evidence to build a case?

Is the illustration the speaker provides effective? Do you think that the speaker needs to supply others?

In your opinion, does the speaker do a sufficient job of personalizing the problems with The Patriot Act for receivers? What proof does the speaker offer in support of the act's problems? Do you think the speaker ever gets overly dramatic?

continued

with terrorism as a reason. The Patriot Act is in conflict with a cornerstone of American democracy and, as such, works only to infringe on our civil liberties.

The Patriot Act also invades our right to privacy. One of the powers granted in The Patriot Act allows federal agencies to access public library records, as well as the records of Internet searches conducted in public libraries. These libraries include libraries located on campuses of public universities as well. In response, in February 2002, the American Library Association issued a newsletter warning its members to comply with any search request but to immediately seek legal counsel. To put this in another context, my own personal library records, just from researching this speech, could constitute my being seen as a threat to national security. Think about it. How many times have you researched an issue that could be considered questionable in the eyes of a federal agent?

Perhaps most shocking of all is a new provision being sought by the Justice Department. *The Baltimore Sun,* March 8, 2003, reports that, if the new Patriot II bill passes Congress, any individual seen as assisting an organization considered terrorist by nature may have his or her citizenship revoked. According to the article, using the wording of the bill, an action as passive as donating fifty dollars to Greenpeace could leave you without a country to call home. Ironically enough, with these newly proposed provisions you may no longer have to worry about infringements upon your rights as a citizen, because you may not be one.

What do you think of the suggestions the speaker offers for action? Are the speaker's suggestions ones receivers can easily follow?

Before it is too late, we must stand up for our civil liberties. And only through personal resolve may we once again deserve both our liberty and our safety, for, as Thomas Jefferson said, "The people are the only sure reliance for the preservation of liberty."

Initially in this fight to take back what is rightfully ours, we must arm ourselves with the strongest weapon democracy holds—knowledge. Research this issue for yourselves because I could not even read you The Patriot Act in 10 minutes. You can read The Patriot Act as well as the U.S. Constitution online at www.house.gov or in your local library. Don't worry. At least for now, reading the Constitution is still a protected right.

Knowing what your civil liberties are and knowing what rights are afforded you as a citizen is not just in your best interest; it is also your responsibility. But knowing what your civil liberties are is only the first step. Now you have to let your voices be heard. But you do not necessarily have to write to Washington just yet. You can just walk down to your local city council office, for, as ABC News points out, over 35 municipalities across the country—including Ann Arbor, Michigan; Oakland, California; and Madison, Wisconsin—have voted not to abide by the rulings of The Patriot Act. These cities have given their city workers, including their police forces, the option of not assisting any investigation that infringes on civil liberties.

In closing, does the speaker provide a sufficient summary of the speech for receivers?

Most important, we have to alter our attitudes toward liberty and safety. After September 11th, we were all afraid for our national security and for our personal safety. Unfortunately, our officials were not immune from the same concerns. But the path they chose did more harm than good. We must remember the first patriots of this nation, who believed that our liberty and safety were not mutually exclusive ideas. Rather, they believed that we deserve not only to live, but to live free, and in their ultimate sacrifice, they ensured we would never have to endure infringement upon our liberties simply to be temporarily safe.

On March 1st of this year, the United States captured Khalid Sheik Mohammed, one of the top lieutenants in the Al-Qaeda network. Thankfully, this proves to be a great step toward protecting our nation. But it also teaches a very important lesson. Khalid Sheik Mohammed, to date the most noted arrest in the war on terrorism, was captured without any use of The Patriot Act.

Our nation has already seen too much tragedy and felt too much sorrow. Let us not compound our regrets by giving away that one thing that truly makes us all Americans—our freedoms.

Does the introduction of a new example in the conclusion help the speaker's case?

Does the conclusion provide the speech with a sense of closure?

Were you the speaker, what would you do differently?

SAMPLE SPEAKER'S NOTES

Topic: The Patriot Act[27]

Purpose: To persuade the audience that we need to work to restore the freedoms we lost due to passage of The Patriot Act

Thesis: The Patriot Act has trampled the freedoms of Americans.

Introduction   I. "They that would give up liberty just for a little safety deserve neither liberty nor safety. These words, spoken by Benjamin Franklin, warn of the loss of precious freedom out of fear. While Franklin first delivered his warning in 1778, the patriot's words still ring true over 225 years later.

II. In October 2001, Congress passed the "Provide Appropriate Tools Required to Intercept and Obstruct Terrorism Act"—better known as The Patriot Act.

    A. <u>Washington Post</u>, February 8, 2003—considering expansion of act

    B. Act tramples freedom.

III. In order to understand the dangers inherent in The Patriot Act, we must first explore the root of The Patriot Act's flaws, then examine the problems associated with the act before finally looking into some solutions to see what we can do to help restore freedoms we have lost while continuing to ensure our safety.

Body   I. Patriot Act Flawed

    Passed out of Fear

    Debate was stifled—National Public Radio, February 9, 2003

continued

II. Patriot Act Has Problems

Ineffective

London Daily Telegraph, February 10, 2003: Only 3 convictions out of 700 detained and 300 arrested

Low-level cell members

Story of Vasilly Rajah and wife Tatiana

Patriot act infringes on rights: Washington Post, November 19, 2002.

Conflicts with fourth amendment

Phone and e-mail taps

Invades Privacy, American Library Association, February 2002 newsletter

Danger of Revocation of citizenship—Baltimore Sun, March 8, 2003, and Patriot II Bill

III. Stand up for civil Liberties: Jefferson—"The people are the only sure reliance for the preservation of liberty."

Research and www.house.gov

Know civil Liberties

Change attitudes about liberty and safety

Recall early patriot sacrifices

Conclusion   I. Capture of Khalid Sheik Mohammed, March 1, 2003

II. Don't give Freedoms away.

EVALUATING THE PERSUASIVE SPEECH

While the evaluation form featured in Chapter 17 can be used to evaluate persuasive speeches, there are a number of criteria to keep in mind when evaluating persuasive discourse. Use the following checklist as a guide:

Rate the following criteria from 1 to 5; 1 represents "not at all" or "barely accomplished" and 5 represents "fully accomplished."

____ Did the speaker's introduction fulfill its purpose?

____ Was the speaker's proposition clearly understood?

____ Were the reasons the speaker offered in support of the proposition clear?

____ Was the speaker's use of testimony effective?

____ Was the organizational pattern used by the speaker appropriate and easy to follow?

____ Was the speaker's use of language vivid, appropriate, and motivating?

____ Was the speaker effective in establishing his or her own credibility?

____ Did the speaker's conclusion accomplish its purpose?

____ Did the speaker conduct himself or herself ethically?

____ Was the speaker's delivery effective?

Check one and only one of the following:

The speech was ____ superior ____ above average ____ average ____ below average ____ poor

Revisiting Chapter Objectives

1. **Define *persuasive speaking*.** Persuasive speaking is the means a speaker uses to modify the thoughts, feelings, or actions of receivers so that they change the attitudes or behavior that the speaker does not approve and, instead, adopt attitudes and behaviors compatible with the speaker's interests and worldview. The proposition of the speech indicates the kind of change the persuasive speaker would like to create in receivers.

2. **Define and distinguish between *attitudes* and *beliefs*.** In order to influence receivers, speakers need to address their attitudes and beliefs. Attitudes are the mental sets, or predispositions, receivers bring to a speech. Beliefs are the building blocks of attitudes. A receiver's belief system is comprised of everything the receiver believes to be true. Whereas attitudes are measured on a favorable–unfavorable scale, beliefs are measured on a probable–improbable scale. The more central a belief, the harder it is to change.

3. **Distinguish between logical and fallacious reasoning.** Speakers who give their receivers logical reasons to support their propositions improve their chances of realizing their speech-making goals. By using deductive and inductive reasoning, causal reasoning, and reasoning from analogy, speakers can build their case and earn receiver support. Ethical speakers do not rely on fallacious reasoning to win the support of receivers. Among the logical fallacies unethical speakers use are argument ad hominem, red herring, false division, false cause, the bandwagon appeal, and the appeal to authority.

4. **Explain the concept of credibility.** A speaker's success as a persuader is in part determined by his or her credibility—or how an audience perceives him or her. In order to find a speaker credible, receivers need to believe the speaker is a person of good character, is knowledgeable, and is personable. The assessment of a speaker's credibility can change during or as a result of a speech.

5. **Develop and present a persuasive speech.** The job of the persuader is to build an effective case, which includes well-supported reasons and appeals for accepting a speaker's proposition. The audience members must be drawn into the speech, sense the speaker's conviction and belief in the position he or she is advocating, and be reminded at the conclusion of the speech of what they need to believe and/or do.

Resources for Further Inquiry and Reflection

To apply your understanding of how the principles in Chapter 19 are at work in our daily lives, consult the following resources for further inquiry and

THE Wrap-Up

reflection. Or, if you prefer, choose any other appropriate resource. Then connect the ideas expressed in your chosen selection with the communication concepts and issues you are learning about both in and out of class.

Listen to Me

"Let It Be" (The Beatles)
"Truth No. 2" (Dixie Chicks)
"We Didn't Start the Fire" (Billy Joel)
"Let's Roll" (Neil Young)

Compare and contrast the attitudes toward persuasion and change expressed in any of these songs with your own attitudes. What does the song you chose suggest about potential subjects for a persuasive speech?

View Me

Wall Street   *Bowling for Columbine*
Malcolm X

What do we learn about the ethics and persuasive approaches favored by featured characters from their own words and actions?

Read Me

Robert B. Cialdini. *Influence: The Psychology of Persuasion,* rev. ed. New York: Quill, 2000.
Anthony Pratkanis and Elliot Aronson. *Age of Propaganda: The Everyday Use and Abuse of Persuasion,* rev. ed. New York: Friedman, 2000.

In what ways, if any, do tactics of persuasion influence the susceptibility of receivers?

Tell Me

Share with the class the insights you gained from your chosen Listen to Me, View Me, or Read Me selection.

Do you think the President is an effective persuasive speaker? Explain why or why not.

Key Chapter Terminology

Communication
Works

www.mhhe.com/gamble8

Use the Communication Works CD-ROM and the Online Learning Center at www.mhhe.com/gamble8 *to further your knowledge of the following terminology.*

argumentum ad hominem 558
argumentum ad populum 559
argumentum ad verecudiam 559
attitudes 554
balance 561
beliefs 555
causal reasoning 557
consistency 556
credibility 565
deduction 556
derived credibility 567
false division 558
induction 556
initial credibility 567

Maslow's hierarchy of needs 561
Monroe's motivated
  sequence 563
persuasive speech 550
post hoc, ergo propter hoc 558
proposition 551
proposition of fact 552
proposition of policy 552
proposition of value 552
reasoning from analogy 557
red herring 558
social proof 556
terminal credibility 567

Test Your Understanding

Go to the *Self Quizzes* on the Communication Works CD-ROM and the book's Online Learning Center at www.mhhe.com/gamble8.

Notes

1. For an excellent explanation of why we study persuasion, see Deirdre D. Johnston. *The Art and Science of Persuasion*. Dubuque, IA: Brown & Benchmark, 1994. For an analysis of key theories of persuasion, see Dominick A. Infante, Andrew S. Rancer, and Deanna F. Womack. *Building Communication Theory*, 3rd ed. Prospect Heights, IL: Waveland, 1997. An interesting discussion also occurs in Jay A. Conger. "The Necessary Art of Persuasion." *Harvard Business Review* 76:3, May–June 1998, pp. 84–95.

2. See Wallace Folderingham. *Perspectives on Persuasion*. Boston: Allyn & Bacon, 1966, p. 33; and James Price Dillard. "Persuasion Past and Present: Attitudes Aren't What They Used to Be." *Communication Monographs* 60:1, March 1993, pp. 90–97.

3. For an interesting definition and discussion of persuasion, see Anthony Pratkanis and Elliot Aronson. *The Age of Propaganda*, rev. ed. New York: Freeman, 2000; and Robert B. Cialdini. *Influence: Science and Practice*, 4th ed. Boston: Allyn & Bacon, 2000.

4. For a discussion of now-classic studies, see M. Sherif and C. Hovland. *Social Judgment*. New Haven, CT: Yale University Press, 1961; and C. Sherif, M. Sherif, and R. Nebergall. *Attitude and Attitude Change*. Philadelphia: Saunders, 1965. For a very understandable explanation, see also E. Griffin. *A First Look at Communication Theory*, 4th ed. New York: McGraw-Hill, 2000.

5. Scott Cutlip and Alan Center. *Effective Public Relations*. Englewood Cliffs, NJ: Prentice-Hall, 1985, p. 122.

6. A framework for understanding the importance of beliefs is provided by Martin Fishbein and Icek Ajzen. *Belief, Attitude, Intention and Behavior: An Introduction to Theory and Research*. Reading, MA: Addison-Wesley, 1975. See especially Chapters 1 and 8.

7. Milton Rokeach. *The Open and Closed Mind*. New York: Basic Books, 1960.

8. Prominent theorists such as Leon Festinger, Fritz Hieder, and Theodore Newcomb consider the desire for consistency a central motivator of behavior. For a more contemporary discussion of the topic, see Robert B. Cialdini. *Influence*. rev. ed. New York: Quill, 2000.

9. Cialdini, p. 116.

10. Cialdini. See also Mike Allen. "Determining the Persuasiveness of Message Sidedness: A Prudent Note about Utilizing Research Summaries." *Western Journal of Communication* 57:1, winter 1993, pp. 98–103.

11. Wayne Minnick. *The Art of Persuasion*. Boston: Houghton Mifflin, 1968.

12. For a discussion of the role of affect, see, for example, Mary John Smith. *Persuasion and Human Action*. Belmont, CA: Wadsworth, 1982.

13. "High Flight" quoted by President Ronald Reagan in his speech to commemorate the *Challenger* crew, January 28, 1986.

14. Abraham Maslow. *Motivation and Personality*. New York: Harper & Row, 1954, pp. 80–92.

15. Bruce E. Gronbeck, Raymie E. McKerrow, Douglas Ehninger, and Alan H. Monroe. *Principles and Types of Speech Communication*, 15th ed. New York, Allyn and Bacon, Boston, 2002.

16. Based on a speech by Amanda Taylor. "Drowsy Driving: A Deadly Epidemic." *Winning Orations*. Mankato, MN: Interstate Oratorical Association, 2000, pp. 12–15.

17. Credibility has received much attention from researchers. See, for example, James M. Kouzes and Barry Z. Posner. *Credibility*. San Francisco: Jossey-Bass, 1993.

18. J. W. Anderson. *The Howard Journal of Communications* 2:1, winter 1989–1990, "A Comparison of Arab and American Conceptions of 'Effective' Persuasion," pp. 81–114.

19. Speakers can establish credibility early in a speech. For example, see R. Brooks and T. Scheidel. "Speech as Process: A Case Study." *Speech Monographs* 35, 1968, pp. 1–7.

20. Nonverbal aspects of credibility are discussed in more detail in Chapter 17.

21. Bob Ivry. "From White Lies to the White House." *The Record,* June 8, 2003, pp. A-1, A-16.

22. Mark Bowden. "Sometimes Heroism Is a Moving Target." *New York Times,* pp. WK1, WK4.

23. Bowden.

24. For a discussion of this issue, see Frank Biocca and Mark R. Levy, eds. *Communication in the Age of Virtual Reality.* Hillsdale, NJ: Lawrence Erlbaum Associates, 1995.

25. Developed as part of a class exercise by students in public speaking courses at the College of New Rochelle, New Rochelle, New York, and at New York Institute of Technology, New York City, New York, during the academic year 2002–2003.

26. Transcribed from a video-taped speech made by Paul Yeager. "The Patriot Act and Our Civil Rights," *Winning Orations,* Mankato, MN: Interstate Oratorical Association, 2003. Reprinted by permission.

27. Developed as part of a class exercise by students in public speaking courses at the College of New Rochelle, New Rochelle, New York, and at New York Institute of Technology, New York City, New York, during the academic year 2002–2003, using a transcript made of the videotaped speech by Paul Yeager. "The Patriot Act and Our Civil Rights." *Winning Orations.* Mankato, MN: Interstate Oratorical Association, 2003.

Mass Communication and Media Literacy

After finishing this appendix, you should be able to

1. Define *media literacy* and *mass communication.*

2. Describe how our traditional media environment has changed.

3. Explain the functions performed by the media.

4. Identify the roles the media play in your life.

5. Assess how the media affect perception.

6. Take a stand on the following media-related issues: violence, privacy, media-induced passivity or anxiety, and the advertising of unhealthy products.

How did the media influence your perceptions of 9/11 and the War with Iraq? As you read about, viewed, and listened to reports of these events, were you merely a consumer of news reports, or were you a critical consumer of all the media you had access to? To what extent, if any, did you augment your use of traditional media with computer-mediated communication (CMC)?

As extensions of our psychic and sensory powers, the media have a way of shaping us even as we are shaping them. Understanding media has a lot to do with understanding me.

—John Culkin

Which of these media do you spend the most time with? Why?

On September 11, 2001, most of us were glued to our television sets. With our own eyes, we witnessed the destruction caused by terrorists who turned airplanes into bombs. We took in the horrific image of the second plane slamming into the second tower of New York City's World Trade Center. Over and over again, we saw replays of the devastation at Ground Zero and at the Pentagon. The media mesmerized us, as they involved all of us in what was occurring. Because the majority of Americans get their information regarding what policies to support and what to be afraid of from the news media, the media helped frame our perception of the events and the issues they precipitated.[1]

During the 2003 war against Iraq, U.S. forces jammed computer transmissions and bombed the broadcast stations and other mass communication facilities of Iraq. The goal was to eliminate the Iraqi government's ability to communicate with the Iraqi people. The mass media and emerging technologies can be powerful weapons in times of war. When the United States declared victory in Iraq, one of the first things President George W. Bush did was broadcast a message to the Iraqi people. The mass media and emerging technologies can be powerful tools in times of peace. They are also powerful forces in our personal and professional lives.

The Internet. E-mail. Cellular telephones. Our television set. A magazine. This book. A radio. CDs. DVD. MP3. A videocassette recorder. The newspaper. A movie. These are just some of the media and machine-assisted technologies that are influencing how we communicate and what we communicate about. Headlines, Web pages, bulletins, advertisements, publicity and video news releases, DJs, VJs, life glorified, life horrified, the all-too-real, the not-so-real, the possible, and the impossible—all are brought to you by mass media industries, all affecting who you are, how you think, how you form relationships, and how you live, play, and work.

This chapter is about you and your relationship to and interaction with the media-saturated environment and converging technologies that now permeate your world. The topics we explore will help you make sense of the role that mass communication and new communication technologies play in your day-to-day life. They will also help you develop your **media literacy**—the ability to interpret mindfully the positive and negative meanings and effects of the media messages you encounter instead of accepting unquestioningly the images presented in those messages.[2]

DEFINING *MASS COMMUNICATION:* THE WAY IT WAS

Like the other forms of communication we have explored, mass communication is a mix of the following ingredients: people, messages, channels, noise, feedback, fields of experience, context, and one or more effects. But it is also different from other types of communication in a number of significant ways. First, mass communication is capable of reaching tens of thousands—even millions—of people, most of whom the sender does not know personally, and it is capable of reaching these people simultaneously. Second, it relies on technical devices, intermediate transmitters, or machines to disseminate its messages widely and rapidly to scattered, usually heterogeneous, audiences who usually remain unknown to each other. Third, the message is public; it is available to many people who decide whether or not they will attend to it or receive it. Fourth, the source in the mass communication situation is a formal organization; thus, mass communication is the product not of one individual but of a group of persons who do their best to get your attention so that you will consent to become part of their audience. Fifth, mass communications are controlled by many gatekeepers, individuals who can exercise control over the message that will travel through the mass medium to reach the public. Sixth, feedback is typically minimal and more delayed than it is in other types of communication. On the basis of these distinguishing characteristics, we can define mass communication as the process of transmitting messages that may be processed by gatekeepers before being transmitted to large audiences via a channel of broad diffusion, such as a print, an audio, or a visual medium.

The mass media and the emerging technologies are tools—instruments of communication—which, depending on how we use them, can either enable us to overcome barriers caused by time and space and extend our ability to interact with each other or take away from the time we have available for family and friends.[3] They can immerse us in a world community or drown us in a virtual community, which some critics contend is not a community at all.

New technologies are changing our definitions for commonly used words. How for example, are the words community *and* conversation *employed by those who use the Internet?*

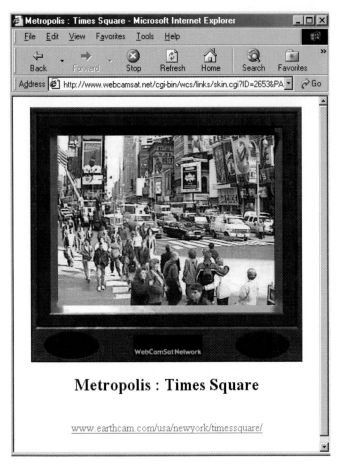

Our daily lives can be broadcast around the world via web cams.

To what extent, if any, does your use of media impede or enhance the time you spend communicating with other persons? Explain.

prosumers

consumers who produce the material of consumption themselves

time shifting

the ability to watch media offerings at a time convenient to you

THE CHANGING MEDIA ENVIRONMENT: THE WAY IT IS

While there are differences between mass communication and the other kinds of communication we have explored in this text, our mediated and technologically enriched communication environment serves as a backdrop for all our other communication experiences, including interpersonal, group, organizational, and public communication.

Rapid changes in technology, however, are also rapidly changing mass communication by enabling us to take a more active role in media processing. In addition to feeding on prepared and programmed media offerings that are presented to us, we now also function as **prosumers**—consumers who produce the material of consumption ourselves. We create Web pages for ourselves. We become Webcasters. We have the capability to function as the creators and editors of a personally tailored communication environment, which we can choose to share with others.

Media are merging and converging. Newspapers, magazines, broadcasting, books, and advertising now also appear in cyberspace. Books are commonly packaged with accompanying computer disks. Today in the United States, more computers are sold than TV sets.[4] The time people spend using personal computers is starting to eat away at the time they spend viewing television or using other media.[5]

Television is also changing; ABC, NBC, CBS, PBS, and Fox no longer have a monopoly on viewership. The popularity of cable continues to grow. Many cable systems now offer from 50 to over 500 channels. Media scarcity is disappearing as an issue. Content once directed at mass audiences is suddenly being tailored to reflect the interests of smaller groups. In addition, the **time shifting** that videocassette recorders and pay-per-view TV precipitated means we no longer have to watch the programs at the same time as everyone else.

We are becoming more user-active. We are changing from couch potatoes to insatiable chatterers and Web surfers who think nothing of spending hours visiting with others in computer chat rooms, playing virtual reality games into the wee hours of the morning, or downloading CDs, music videos, and movie previews. Each of us has the ability to set up an Internet site, provide a service, and make money doing so. The lines between consumer and provider are blurring.

Also blurring are the lines among interpersonal communication, mass communication, and mediated interpersonal communication. With the exception of pure face-to-face contact, e-mailing, diary-like Web logs **(blogs)**, audio- and video-conferencing, instant messaging and Internet relay chat rooms, and multiuser environments **(MUDs)** preserve many of the qualities of personal interaction we discussed in earlier chapters, including the significant promotion of interaction and opportunities for feedback.

We use and adapt many of the same means we rely on to get to know someone when interacting face-to-face to get to know someone we are interacting with via computer. We make inferences about the person's values, personality, and appearance and seek to reduce our uncertainty by asking questions, particularly questions that will allow us to come to know and understand the inner self of our online partner.[6]

New technologies are promoting other changes as well. First, the pace of technological change is increasing. We now need to learn new technologies every three or four months; computers evolve so quickly that they become obsolete almost as soon as we purchase them.[7] Whereas it used to take significant periods of time for innovations such as the telephone and television to be diffused throughout society, the use of mobile phones and the Internet spread much more rapidly. Second, communication technologies are being melded together. Computers have merged with media. We now have interactive television; the merging of cable, television, telephone, and computer technology; and the Internet, a medium of print, graphics, photography, video, and/or sound, which merges computer and phone technology. We are witness to mediamorphosis—the metamorphosis of old media into new media.[8] Third, we are experiencing media demassification. We have many more media choices. Media are being aimed at smaller and smaller segments, narrower audiences, of the overall media marketplace. In your opinion, what would be the ultimate new communication/media technology that could target and speak directly to you?

blog
a web log

MUD
multi-user environment

According to author and cultural critic Neil Postman, new technologies always produce winners and losers. Who are the current winners? Losers? Why?

My Broadcast Life

Using Webcams hooked to their computers, an increasing number of people are transforming themselves into Internet stars by broadcasting their daily lives around the world. An explosion of Webcam-based sites, such as earthcam.com and cutecouple.com, allows Internet users to eavesdrop on, observe the most intimate moments of, and establish instant virtual friendships with the Webcam's operators as they go about their business of living and loving at home while online.[9]

Would you ever use a Webcam to broadcast your personal life over the Internet? If so, why? If not, why not? Would you or have you frequented any sites such as those mentioned previously? If you have, what site or sites did you view? To what extent, if any, did you feel like a voyeur as you observed the site and its interactants? Did you ever feel compelled to turn away or disconnect? Did you chat with the "actors" online? Why, in your opinion, do Webcam operators choose to allow others to invade their privacy? Do you see any dangers in their actions? To what degree, if any, do you believe that such sites threaten your privacy as well?

Media
WISE

THE FUNCTIONS OF THE MASS MEDIA AND MACHINE-ASSISTED COMMUNICATION

There are a number of ways the mass media and the new technologies are making daily life easier for us. Among the functions they serve are the following.

Information and Surveillance

What recent examples can you offer of media providing the functions identified in the text? Be specific.

Both traditional mass media and the Internet inform us and help us keep a watch on our world; they serve a surveillance function. They provide us with the news, information, and warnings we need to make informed decisions. For instance, they let us know when we are threatened by an impending hurricane, fire, or volcano; an economic crisis; or war. They also give us helpful and useful information that we can use not just in times of crisis but also in daily life. How, for example, do we find out what's playing at the local theater? How do we learn what new products are out there for us to try? How do we identify the latest fads and fashions? We consult the media.

Agenda Setting and Interpretation

The media set our agendas and help structure and interpret our lives. Professional communicators who work in media choose what topics we will read about, hear about, and view.[10] Stories that are given prominence in the media are believed to be more important than those that are glossed over or ignored. Issues that the media cover and/or discuss in editorials tend to consume our interest as well.

The range of analyses and evaluations we open ourselves to can affect whether or not we will be exposed to differing points of view and whether or not we will be in a position to evaluate all sides of an issue before we take a position.

The extensive access we now have to information means we need to take extra special care in assessing its value and accuracy. For example, messages posted by individuals on the Internet may be reliable or suspect; they may contain sound information or be based entirely on rumor; they may be extremely important or trivial.

Connective Links

The media help us connect with diverse groups in society. Although we may not get the same pleasure from them as we might get from interacting face-to-face with other human beings, the media and new technologies do enable us to keep in contact with our politicians, keep a finger on the pulse of public opinion, and align ourselves with others who have the same concerns. In fact, the media and new technologies have a "public-making" ability. They help create totally new social alignments by connecting persons who are unaware that others share their interests.

Socialization and Value Transmission

The media help socialize us. Through old and new media, we supplement what we have already internalized about behavior and values in direct encounters with other people. The media show us people in action; their portrayals help us assess the preferred patterns of behavior and appearance. By so doing, they teach us social norms and values and help us learn what is expected of us, including how we are supposed to think, act, and look. Thus, they participate in our socialization.

Persuasion

The media are used to persuade us and to benefit the originators of messages. For example, advertising and public relations are filled with people whose task is to use the media to further their persuasive goals. Thus, the media provide platforms for idea and product advocates. It is their ability to persuade and sell so effectively that sustains and nourishes most of our media. Let us not forget that the media are predominantly industries that must turn a profit to stay in business.

Currently, advertising is undergoing a change from mass media advertising to database marketing. No longer are campaigns aimed solely at large audiences of anonymous receivers.

Entertainment

The media entertain. All the media expend a portion of their energies trying to entertain their audiences. For instance, even though the newspaper is a prime medium of information, it also contains entertainment features, such as comics, crossword puzzles, games, and horoscopes. Television, motion pictures, recordings, fiction books, and some World Wide Web sites, radio stations, and magazines are devoted primarily (although not exclusively) to entertainment. Even most news today is a mix of information and entertainment.[11] Neil Postman, in the book *Amusing Ourselves to Death,* suggests that the entertainment functions of the media might be distracting us from taking social issues seriously. He fears that we might, as the title warns, amuse ourselves to death.[12] Do you agree?

THE ROLE OF THE MASS MEDIA IN YOUR LIFE

For a moment, try to conceive of our society without any one of the media. Imagine what it would be like to have no radio, CDs, television, movies, or access to the Internet. Every now and then, just to assure ourselves that it is we who control the media and not the media that control us, we tell ourselves that we could get along just fine without them. But could we really do so?

Have you ever tried to give up using a particular medium? Were you successful? Why or why not?

Large numbers of us today spend more time with the media than we do with close relatives or friends. For instance, it is estimated that 51 percent of U.S. households now own three or more TV sets, 92 percent own a VCR, and 76 percent are wired for cable.[13]

Skill
BUILDER

Self-Survey

For the next week, survey your personal media habits. To do this, simply log the amount of time, in 15-minute units, you spend consuming each medium identified below. When the week is over, total your consumption units for each medium. Then divide each total by 4 to determine the number of hours you spent with each medium. To which medium or media did you devote the most time? The least time? Why do you think that was so? Finally, total the hours for all the media. That figure represents the number of hours you spend with media during a typical week. Do the number of hours surprise you?

Example

	Mon	Tue	Wed	Thu	Fri	Sat	Sun	Total Units	Total Hours
Newspapers	//		/		/		////✝	9	2¼

Daily Log

	Mon	Tue	Wed	Thu	Fri	Sat	Sun	Total Units	Total Hours
Newspapers									
Magazines									
Books									
Radio									
CD player									
Film									
Television									
VCR									
Internet									

Total hours for all media: _____

The total media use figures are also impressive. The typical American spends 3,400 hours a year consuming the output of the media—whether that be print materials, broadcasting, films, recorded music, or the Internet. That's almost 40 percent of the hours in a year, 40 percent of the hours in our lives. It is more time than we spend sleeping (2,900 hours).[14] Recent Department of Education figures suggest that the typical American child between the ages of 2 and 18 spends 1,500 hours a year watching television. The same child spends only 75 hours a year speaking with his or her parents.[15]

In terms of time allocation, 80 percent of our media hours are invested in television and radio. In fact, the average American spends 15 hours of "free time" each week watching television, while spending only 6.7 hours socializing.[16] Other studies reveal that the television is turned on an average of 6 hours and 47 minutes a day in U.S. households.[17] Our reading averages about an hour a day, split among newspapers, books, and magazines. Estimates are that, as we make our way through the first decade of the twenty-first century, we will spend even more time with the media—perhaps an additional 119 hours yearly of our time—with an increasing percentage of it devoted to the Internet.[18] In addition, for the first time in the United States, more women than men are logging on to the Internet.[19]

How We Use the Media

We use the media to learn about things in general and to satisfy our curiosity. We use the media to seek relief from boredom, to vent our emotions, to relax, and merely to pass the time. We may even program our day by them. For example, we may rise to the sounds of music or news on the radio; dress while watching *Today, Good Morning America,* or *Imus;* eat breakfast while perusing the morning paper or checking CNN online; travel to work while listening to favorite radio stations or CDs; eat lunch while checking our hand-held computer or reading a book or magazine; travel home again accompanied by the radio or CDs; eat dinner while listening to or watching the evening news; fill the evening hours and unwind by watching TV or a video, surfing the Internet, or going to a movie; and, finally, fall asleep with the TV, CD player, or radio on. All this media contact helps fulfill a kaleidoscope of personal needs.

We sometimes use the media to fulfill our affiliation needs. The media provide us with fuel for real-life conversations, they help us escape from feelings of loneliness, and they may even substitute for relationships missing in our own lives by providing us mediated or parasocial relationships in their place. When this happens, we come to believe that the media's personalities are also our friends. For some of us, immersion in the mass media has succeeded in making the mediated world our real world.

We also use the media to withdraw from or postpone human contact. By focusing on the media's content, we free ourselves from having to focus, at least for the moment, on the things we need to do or the people we need to see. The media can also help isolate us from others. For example, a person reading a newspaper or wearing earphones appears to be less approachable. In addition, the prevalence of multi-TV-set households enables family

Provide examples of how people you know use the media to help meet both their personal and their professional needs.

As long as there have been cars, there have been drivers who pay more attention to their cell phones, radios, friends, grooming or eating than to steering. What effect do the increasing number of digital connections have on your life?

members to retreat into self-created cocoons and watch different shows in different rooms.[20]

The increasing number of digital connections we have access to places us in multiple transits. We're in a car, but also conversing with our boss or perhaps a counselor. We're in a park with a friend but also hooked up to a device that can organize the next day's schedule, access e-mail, or surf the Internet. Today, instead of "being in the here and now," we imagine we have the ability to be everywhere as well as "here."[21]

How the Media Affect Us

Our intensive media culture affects all of us. The media occupy central places in our lives. Depending on how we use them, the media can help us share experiences, or they can fragment our society and divide us into subcultures. They can encourage diversity or sameness. They can help us connect or keep us from connecting with each other.

The Media Provide Models

The media affect our awareness, knowledge, attitudes, and behavior. Between 20 and 25 percent of teenagers, for example, say they learn about moral values and interpersonal relationships from the media. The media are influential in shaping what we know, whom we want to be like, and what we think.

To be sure, the media have a huge role in defining our culture. In your opinion, do U.S. media promote a "have whatever you want whenever you want it" culture? Do you think they are coarsening our culture? Why or why not? What, if any, elements in our media culture do you find personally offensive or harmful?

The Media Create and Perpetuate Stereotypes

How have media portrayals influenced the way you perceive the following groups: Arabs, Asians, Native Americans, Latinos, African Americans, Caucasians? How have they affected your expectations for men and women? For members of the medical profession? The legal profession? Law enforcement? Yourself? Be specific.

Media content presents various careers, subjects, and ethnic groups in stereotyped ways. For example, between one-fourth and one-third of all TV time consists of shows highlighting cops and robbers. And almost 90 percent of the crimes depicted in these shows are solved. Real life cannot produce such figures.

The media overrepresent violent crimes. While only 10 percent of the crimes committed in real life are violent, on television approximately 60 percent of the crimes depicted are violent.

The media are affecting our perception of various groups. Media images of Latinos, African Americans, Native Americans, strong women, and Arabs are apt to be negative. For years, for example, when portrayed in the popular media, Native Americans were apt to come across as vicious, cruel, lazy, and drunk.[22] In similar fashion, when portrayed in media offerings, Arab men are frequently portrayed as terrorists, oil-rich sheiks, or desert nomads, while Arab women are rarely seen or are presented as members of harems or as belly dancers. According to columnist Russell Baker, "Arabs are the last people . . . whom Hollywood feels free to offend en masse."[23] Similarly, only about 10 percent of television characters are African American.[24] In general, African-American males are frequently depicted as athletes or entertainers and as lazy or unlawful. Latinos are also underrepresented in the media, constituting a scant 1.5 percent of the total television character population.[25] A one-week boycott of network television by a coalition of Hispanic organizations was called for in an effort to focus attention on the dearth of prime-time acting

Whom Do You See?

Spend some time watching films and videos, viewing prime-time programs, and looking at advertisements that appear in these offerings as well as in various popular magazines.

As you do so, keep a record of the stimulus item attended to and the number of men, women, and minorities, including Asians, Latinos, African Americans, and Arabs, that appear in each. Also note the number of main and background roles performed by the males, females, and minorities and the nature of each role—that is, if the presented character or model was young or old, was attractive or unattractive, was likable or unlikable, and was serving as a positive or a negative role model. Also provide a list of attributes and traits for each role.

Compare and contrast your findings with those of your peers, and discuss their implications. To what extent, if any, do you believe the media help bias our attitudes toward any of the aforementioned groups?

EXPLORING

Diversity

roles for Latinos.[26] In addition, when Latinos are featured, they are infrequently cast in a positive light, being shown instead as violent or lazy, uneducated, and unconcerned with their future.[27] The majority—80 percent—of all television characters are White Americans. In general, women are shown as concerned with their looks, their relationships, and their family, while men are shown as concerned with their careers. The marital status is apparent for about 80 percent of the women but only 45 percent of the men. As for socio-economic status, approximately 50 percent of the characters on television are wealthy, and a large percentage are professionals or occupy managerial positions. What is noteworthy is that media portrayals of a group can influence the extent to which the group perceives itself similarly and as a result begins to question its ability to fit into society.[28]

Thus, the media present us with myriad stereotypical images that real life often contradicts. Vicarious contact, however, takes a toll. Over time, heavy usage may result in the cultivation of perceptions of reality that are consistent with the view of the distorted world depicted in the media. Heavy television viewers, for example, consistently overestimate the number of persons who commit serious crimes, the number of married persons who have affairs, and the number of couples who divorce, while underestimating the number of elderly persons in our society. Even though media watching appears to cause viewers to exaggerate the seriousness of society's problems, when questioned, many people underestimate the influence that the media have on them.[29]

Critic Walter Lippman, in his now-classic work *Public Opinion,* defined stereotypes as "pictures in our heads." What pictures do you see when you come across the following terms: *feminist, Italian, sports icon, military general, SARS-infected person?* How much influence, if any, do you believe the media have had in helping you construct that picture?

If some of the basic lessons we learn about life are learned from the media, what exactly are we currently being taught?

The Media Influence Our Real-Life Experiences

There is a link between media images and people's views of reality. We tend to prefer mediated reality and sometimes try to apply it to our own lives. Media images help shape our opinions about how our bodies should look and how the sexes should interact. For example, women are approving of Hollywood's strong but selfless male characters, such as one fisherman in the movie

Where Do You Draw the Line?

When the shooting began at Columbine High School several years ago, the speed with which survivors turned up on camera was astounding. What led to such behavior on the part of the media? What is the impact of such media attention and intrusiveness?

Before you answer those questions, consider the insights of a photographer who described an incident that occurred over two decades ago. As you read his story, ask yourself if you believe that a photographer working today would act similarly.

It was early in the spring—a day of pale sunlight and trees just beginning to bud. I was a young police reporter, driving to a scene I didn't want to see. A man, the police-dispatcher's broadcast said, had accidentally backed his pickup truck over his baby granddaughter in the driveway of the family home. It was a fatality.

As I parked among police cars and TV-news cruisers, I saw a stocky, white-haired man in cotton work clothes standing near a pickup. Cameras were trained on him, and reporters were sticking microphones in his face. Looking totally bewil-

dered, he was trying to answer their questions. Mostly he was only moving his lips, blinking and choking up.

After a while the reporters gave up on him and followed the police into the small white house. I can still see in my mind's eye that devastated old man looking down at the place in the driveway where the child had been. Beside the house was a freshly spaded flower bed, and nearby a pile of dark, rich earth.

"I was just backing up there to spread that good dirt," he said to me, though I had not asked him anything. "I didn't even know she was outdoors." He stretched his hand toward the flower bed, then let it flop to his side. He lapsed back into his thoughts, and I, like a good reporter, went into the house to find someone who could provide a recent photo of the toddler.

A few minutes later, with all the details in my notebook and a three-by-five studio portrait of the cherubic child tucked in my jacket pocket, I went toward the kitchen, where the police had said the body was.

I had brought a camera with me. . . . Everybody had drifted back out of the

The Perfect Storm, who, as the water rises above him, utters his last words: "This is going to be hard on my little boy." The tough guy and nurturing male rolled into one is a departure from the self-absorbed male or the male portrayed as wimp or beast. Women report that they want to be married to men who are humble yet determined to persevere, men who are sensitive but make them feel safe.[30] Mediated reality, for the most part, however, frequently is a lot sexier, more intense, and more humorous than real life. Thus, we often end up disappointed or disillusioned. Our relationships are rarely as exciting as those presented to us by the media. Our bosses and co-workers are rarely as attractive as those we meet in media offerings. Physicians and lawyers are rarely as successful treating us or winning our cases in real life as they are on the screen. Real life falls short when measured against a mediated ideal standard.

MEDIA ISSUES

Controversial issues abound in the volatile world of mass and machine-assisted communication. Among the many issues hotly debated today are privacy and media responsibility, the effects of violence, media-induced passivity and anxiety, and the advertising of unhealthy products.

house together—family, police, reporters, and photographers. Entering the kitchen, I came upon this scene:

On a Formica-topped table, back-lighted by a frilly curtained window, lay the tiny body, wrapped in a clean white sheet. Somehow the grandfather had managed to stay away from the crowd. He was sitting on a chair beside the table, in profile to me and unaware of my presence, looking un-comprehendingly at the swaddled corpse.

The house was very quiet. A clock ticked. As I watched, the grandfather slowly leaned forward, curved his arms like parentheses around the head and feet of the little form, then pressed his face to the shroud and remained motionless.

In that hushed moment I recognized the makings of a prize-winning news photo-graph. I appraised the light, adjusted the lens setting and distance, locked a bulb in the flashgun, raised the camera and com-posed the scene in the viewfinder.

Every element of the picture was per-fect: the grandfather in his plain work

clothes, his white hair backlighted by sun-shine, the child's form wrapped in the sheet, the atmosphere of the simple home suggested by black iron trivets and World's Fair souvenir plates on the walls flanking the window. Outside, the police could be seen inspecting the fatal rear wheel of the pickup while the child's mother and father leaned in each other's arms.

I don't know how many seconds I stood there, unable to snap that shutter. I was keenly aware of the powerful story-telling value that photo would have, and my pro-fessional conscience told me to take it. Yet I couldn't make my hand fire that flashbulb and intrude on the poor man's island of grief.

At length I lowered the camera and crept away, shaken with doubt about my suitability for the journalistic profession. . . . Every day, on the newscasts and in the papers, we see pictures of people in ex-treme conditions of grief and despair. Hu-man suffering has become a spectator sport. And sometimes as I'm watching news film, I remember that day.

I still feel right about what I did.[31]

Personal Privacy and Media/Technological Responsibility

There is a difference between what the media and technology can and cannot do according to law (the legal constraints placed on the media) and what they should and should not do (the ethical constraints that govern the decision-making processes of today's media/technology practitioners). In the business world, for example, managers are increasingly monitoring the computer activities of employees. Monitoring software programs afford them access to every online or offline message an employee sends, every Web site he or she visits, everything written in a chat room—every key he or she strokes. Some com-panies do not even notify their employees of their monitoring capabilities or activities. A surveillance society in the workplace is becoming a reality. And it is legal as long as employers do not violate labor and antidiscrimination laws, by targeting union organizers or minorities, for example.[32]

Another of the more controversial media trends is tabloid journalism offerings. Vehicles that use a tabloid format focus on sex, crime, and the sen-sational; tend to be overzealous; and typically exploit their subjects, even pay-ing for information and photographs. In the tabloid press, there's plenty of excess—lurid photos and descriptions of extreme emotional distress. If tabloid journalism is televised, there's plenty of screaming, cursing, and confronting.[33] Shock and surprise rule. Insensitivity and voyeurism reign supreme.

Which, if any, tabloid vehicles do you read or view? What attracts you to them?

To what extent, if any, do you believe that the media and new technologies have invaded or are presently invading your privacy? Provide examples.

Have the media become overzealous in their coverage of disasters, controversial issues, and, especially, celebrities and other well-known personalities? By using questionable reporting techniques, besieging people as they do, and telling us things about them that may be untrue and that we probably do not have a need to know, are reporters, news photographers, and the paparazzi ("buzzing insects" in Italian) invading the privacy of others or merely exercising their First Amendment rights by giving the public what it wants?

From the media's point of view, privacy is a nonissue. The media, after all, are in the business of not leaving well-known people alone. But how much coverage is too much coverage? Where should the line be drawn between reasonable and unreasonable media conduct?

The privacy issue affects us personally as well. With the prevalence of information about us that others are privy to, we also fear identity theft. Once someone gains access to our Social Security number or credit card information, they can become us electronically. As a result, privacy advocates are beginning to ask, Does the Internet know too much? Web site after Web site provides us access to online information only after soliciting our answers to personal questions. Once such information is obtained, some sites track our movements online. Thus, they know the topics we research online and can design online ads to appeal to our interests. The open, free-for-all atmosphere of the Net has contributed to such tracking efforts. The question is, Does the Internet make getting public information about each other too easy? Critics note that, while most of us would never think of spending hour after hour pouring through public records to find out information about another person, when we can gain access to that information with only a few clicks, we might all seek it out.[34] Such fears about one's privacy, the confidentiality of e-mail, or the possibility of having someone impersonate them have even kept some people from using the Internet.[35]

Lack of privacy on the Internet is not our only fear, however. If you use company health insurance, your employer probably has access to the details of your medical history. If you use a cell phone, your calls may be able to be intercepted by eavesdroppers. Everything you charge on a credit card is in a database. Surveillance cameras are in banks, hotels, even houses of worship. With The Patriot Act I and II, so is the government. Some call our loss of privacy "Orwellian." Remember *1984*, Orwell's classic work on the erosion of privacy. Orwell envisioned a future in which the state uses video surveillance, media control, and the rewriting of history to exert its authority over citizens. Although Orwell's work was fiction, technology has made it possible for our every move to be watched and words we think we are speaking in private to be listened to. Technology has the potential to turn the surveillance function of the media upside down. Privacy is in danger of shriveling away. And remember, your employer is allowed to read e-mail and more.

Lessons about Media Violence

Do depictions of violence in the media increase the amount of aggressiveness in society, or do they lead us to want to take positive social action in an effort to ward off such violence? Do dramatized acts of violence cause people to engage in similar acts, or do they reduce acts of aggression instead? Are violent cartoons a danger to children? Are CDs with violent lyrics, such as those by Eminem, harming teenagers? While experts disagree as to how to answer these questions, research does reveal that depictions of violence may be emotionally arousing for some people and under some conditions may lead to aggressive behavior in children.

Research demonstrates that observational learning can work for good and bad. While the media are capable of providing us with numerous prosocial examples of how we should behave, they are also adept at providing us with a host of deviant behaviors. Sometimes, unfortunately, individuals imitate the violent behavior portrayed in media offerings. For this reason, some contend that violence on television or in film should never go unpunished.

Others, however, downplay the effect of media violence by suggesting that, instead of encouraging us to emulate such acts, violent portrayals actually have a cathartic effect. Supporters of **catharsis theory,** which can be traced back to Aristotle, contend that watching violence enables individuals to let off steam vicariously by fantasizing the release of pent-up frustrations that might otherwise fester dangerously or explode. By fantasizing and viewing episodes of violence, theorists note, we become less apt to exhibit such violence in real life.

Much evidence, on the other hand, tends to lie with supporters of Albert Bandura's **aggressive stimulation theory.**[36] In his research, Bandura found that children who were shown films of people aggressively punching and beating a large inflated doll demonstrated an increase in such behavior in their own lives. The implication was that children exposed to violence in the media used the examples shown them as models to emulate during their own person-to-person interactions.

In 2001, the surgeon general of the United States released a report discussing the link between mediated violence and violence in society. The report's conclusion was that a statistically significant relationship between exposure to mediated violence and violent behavior exists.[37] The American Academy of Pediatrics echoes the concerns expressed by the surgeon general, noting that as much as 10 to 20 percent of real-life violence may be attributable to mediated violence.[38]

In contrast to these two polar theories is Wilbur Schramm, Jack Lyle, and Edwin Parker's **catalytic theory,**[39] which proposes that, while the media may play a role in real-life violence, they are not apt to trigger it. But in those infrequent times when the media do serve as a catalyst for more vulnerable

Which of these theories do your personal experiences affirm as the most valid? Explain.

catharsis theory
the contention that the viewing of violence makes one less apt to exhibit violence

aggressive stimulation theory
the contention that the watching of violence stimulates aggression in the viewer

catalytic theory
the contention that, while the media may play a role in real-life violence, they will trigger it only if a viewer is predisposed to violence or is particularly vulnerable

Viewing Violence

For each of the following instances, imagine that you are the parent of a young child:

Instance 1: Your child asks if he or she can watch a program that you know will contain violence and at least one assault. Would you allow your child to watch the show? Why or why not?

Instance 2: Your child tells you that two people are fighting outside your home. He or she asks your permission to watch that fight. Do you consent to this request? Why or why not?

Compare and contrast the two questions asked by your child and the outcomes of the experience he or she would have if you answered (1) both questions affirmatively, (2) the first question affirmatively and the second negatively, or (3) both questions negatively.

Skill
BUILDER

What effects, if any, do you believe that depictions such as this scene from one of The Terminator *films have on you and other viewers?*

targets, such as the hyperactive or the unstable, they will do so only if those affected experience a heavy diet of media violence, the violence portrayed is terribly realistic, and/or the violent person depicted in the media offering is shown as being rewarded for his or her violent acts.

Thus, we are left to conclude that for *some* children under *some* conditions, *some* television is harmful. For *other* children under the same conditions, or for the same children under *other* conditions, it may be beneficial. For *most* children, under *most* conditions, *most* television is probably neither particularly harmful nor particularly beneficial.

Increasing amounts of verbal violence also abound on television talk shows. Have we learned to prefer what one journalist refers to as "acrimony over civility and conflict over resolution"?[40] Why do ratings suggest that we are aroused when we see a host decimate a guest by repeatedly interrupting and/or cutting away to a commercial? Some hosts have become like attack dogs, transforming what could be a forum into a mélée. Do we now thrive on seeing others embarrassed or shamed by a verbally violent host? What do you think?

Media-Induced Passivity or Anxiety

Do you find that traditional and new media have contributed to your becoming more or less passive? More or less anxious? More or less violent? More or less intelligent? Why do you think this is so?

Television, in particular, has been singled out as a passive entertainment medium. Adolescents and adults alike report feeling more passive, uninvolved, relaxed, and unchallenged when watching TV than when engaged in other activities.[41] Heavy viewers of television are also more apt to describe themselves as less happy, friendly, and positive than are light viewers.[42] We bring low expectations to the event when we watch TV. Watching television is perceived to be easy, to demand little of us: thus, we invest little mental effort in it. We tend not to take television viewing seriously.

Informanxiety

To what extent, if any, has the Internet contributed to your wishing that humans could absorb information at a faster rate—that is, to your experiencing "informanxiety"? What did you do about this "technostress" wish? In what ways, if any, has the Internet enhanced self-induced feelings of confusion rather than self-induced feelings of enlightenment? How did you respond to those feelings? To what extent are you or is someone you know dependent on the computer? How has this attachment affected you and others? Be specific.

If, as media theorist Marshall McLuhan says, "The media is the message," and if, as media ecologist Neil Postman suggests, "Once a technology is admitted into society, it plays out its own hand; it does what it is designed to," then, in your opinion, what is the Internet's message, what was it designed to do, and what changes is it precipitating in us and our world?

On the other hand, information overload caused by a plethora of information media and the sheer quantity of information is causing some of us to feel helpless or overwhelmed, contributing to our becoming overly anxious and fearful.[43] Similarly, the sheer magnitude of information available on the Internet is leaving some of us with a drowning feeling: We are awash in information; we have greater access to information than any normal person can handle; and we don't know how to cope with this flood of information. We are fearful that we do not understand what we need to understand, have not learned what we need to know, and have not captured the information we should possess. Feeling we can never catch up with the information glut, we tend to fall prey to information-induced anxiety created by our message-dense society. The media follow and pursue us. They burden us with the conception that we can do everything and be everywhere. Our beepers, our cell phones, and our hand-held computers come along for the ride—from school to the office, from the office to the home, from the home to the store, from the store to vacation.

The Advertising of Inaccurate Images and Unhealthy Products

What do today's advertisements reveal about the roles of men, women, and minority groups in our society? Which persons are shown as homemakers? Which persons are depicted in professional roles? When advertisers put people from different groups in their place, into what type of place are they put? Who is shown serving? Who is shown receiving service?

Women and minority groups are unhappy with the ways they are depicted in ads. Women, for example, believe that advertising often treats them as sex objects and fails to realistically portray their changing roles.[44] According to research, advertisements tend to locate the source of women's power in their beauty, causing women to fear growing old or being unattractive. In addition, advertisers tend to portray women in terms of reproductive and family relationships. Sexual images and sexual references in advertising do not seem to be abating.

Provide examples of ads that you believe contribute to inaccurate depictions of men, women, and members of minority groups.

Thinking CRITICALLY

Reflect and Respond

Agree or disagree with the following Leo Bogart quotation; supply reasons and examples that support your position.

In its brief history television has become the American people's most important source of ideas, apart from interpersonal contact.

Latinos and African Americans object to their portrayals and their under-representation in ads, especially in ads with business settings. When they are included in ads, it's often in a background or secondary role.

Some critics of advertising also contend that it contributes to both excessive alcohol consumption and cigarette addiction. Until recently, the distilled spirits industry voluntarily refrained from airing broadcast commercials. Now, after almost a half century of broadcast and cable abstinence, the hard liquor world wants its share of the audience.

Should ads that threaten our health be allowed? Should advertisers be permitted to use any mass medium to present images of youth, vitality, and fun to sell products that are harmful and can kill us? If, however, we advocate banning ads for potentially dangerous products such as cigarettes and liquor, shouldn't we then also ban advertising for explicit books and movies or suggestive clothes as well? After all, some say, sex through AIDS kills too. Therefore, shouldn't products that promote unhealthful activities and that lure or entice consumers with trendy images also be eliminated? These are some of the controversial questions facing us today. How do you respond to them?

Focus on Service Learning

Choose a local elementary/junior or senior high school. Identify a media issue of interest to you, and prepare a brochure about that issue for distribution in the school.

Revisiting Appendix Objectives

1. **Define *media literacy* and *mass communication*.** Media literacy is the ability to interpret mindfully the positive and negative meanings and effects of the media messages we encounter instead of accepting unquestioningly the images presented in those messages. Mass communication is the process of transmitting messages that may be processed by gatekeepers prior to being transmitted to large audiences via a channel of broad diffusion such as a print, an audio, or a visual medium.

2. **Describe how our traditional media environment has changed.** Rapid changes in technology are changing the media environment and the relationship we have with various media. Our newly technologically enriched communication environment shadows our communication experiences, including interpersonal, group, organizational, and public communication. In addition to being media consumers, we now also can be prosumers—consumers who produce the material of consumption themselves. We can personally tailor a communication environment to reflect our unique needs and interests. In addition, the media continue to merge and converge. Newspapers, magazines, broadcast information, books, and advertisments also appear in cyberspace.

THE Wrap-Up

3. **Explain the functions performed by the media.**   Among the functions old and new media serve are information and surveillance, agenda setting and interpretative, connection, socialization and value transmission, persuasive, and entertainment.

4. **Identify the roles the media play in your life.**   Each of the media, old, new, and emerging, affect how we live our lives. Many of us spend more time with the media than we do sleeping or spending time with close relatives or friends. We use the media to learn about things, to fulfill affiliating needs, and/or to withdraw from human contact.

5. **Assess how the media affect perception.**   The media affect our awareness, knowledge, and attitude and behavior. They provide us with models, create and perpetuate stereotypes, and influence our real life experiences by cultivating in some of us distorted perceptions of reality.

6. **Take a stand on the following media-related issues: privacy, violence, media-induced passivity or anxiety, and the advertising of unhealthy products.**   Developing an understanding of the interplay between individuals and the media is critical. Even more critical is developing an understanding of an array of issues precipitated by media practices in an effort to discover ways to control, rather than be controlled by, media influences. Debating and drawing our own conclusions regarding issues such as privacy, mediated violence, media-induced passivity or anxiety, and the advertising of unhealthy products are becoming increasingly important as we attempt to make sense of media changes and cope with the omnipresence of media in our lives.

Resources for Further Inquiry and Reflection

To apply your understanding of how the principles in the Appendix are at work in our daily lives, consult the following resources for further inquiry and reflection. Or, if you prefer, choose any other appropriate resource. Then connect the ideas expressed in your chosen selection with the communication concepts and issues you are learning about both in and out of class.

 Listen to Me

"American Pie" (Don McLean)
"Candle in the Wind" (Elton John)

Both songs speak of the lasting effects media figures have on our lives. Use your selected song as a stimulus to discuss the media figures whose influence you believe will be as long-lasting as those in McLean's or John's now-classic works.

 View Me

Broadcast News	*The Truman Show*
Network	*You've Got Mail*
Pleasantville	

Each of these films explores how a particular medium of communication affects our lives. In the process, the excesses of the medium itself are exposed. Choose one film and use it to discuss the roles you believe the highlighted medium plays in your own life and whether its influence is primarily positive or negative, and why.

Read Me

Al Franken, Lies and the Lying Liars Who Tell Them: A Fair and Balanced Look at the Right. New York: E. P. Dutton, 2003.

Bernard Goldberg. *Bias.* Washington, DC: Regnery, 2002.

Jerzy Kosinski. *Being There.* New York: Bentam Books, 1970.

These works explore the influence of media in our lives. Use one to discuss the extent to which you believe the media participate in the social construction of reality.

 Tell Me

Share with the class the insights you gained from your chosen Listen to Me, View Me, or Read Me selection.

In a brief presentation, agree or disagree with the following statement by famed television and film director Alfred Hitchcock, with reasons for your stance:

One of television's great contributions is that it brought murder back into the home where it belongs. Seeing a murder on television can be good therapy. It can help work off one's antagonisms.

Key Appendix Terminology

Communication **Works**

www.mhhe.com/gamble8

Use the Communication Works CD-ROM and the Online Learning Center at www.mhhe.com/gamble8 *to further your knowledge of the following terminology.*

aggressive stimulation theory A-15	media literacy A-3
blogs A-5	MUDs A-5
catalytic theory A-15	prosumers A-4
catharsis theory A-15	time shifting A-4

Test Your Understanding

Communication **Works**

online learning center

www.mhhe.com/gamble8

Go to the *Self Quizzes* on the Communication Works CD-ROM and the book's Online Learning Center at www.mhhe.com/gamble8.

Notes

1. See, for example, E. Texeira. "Coverage of Youth Crime Promotes Fear, Study Says." *Los Angeles Times,* p. B3.

2. See W. James Potter. *Media Literacy.* Thousand Oaks, CA: Sage, 1998.

3. B. Haring. "Internet Vet Wary of Superhighway's Direction." *USA Today,* April 6, 1995, p. 7D.

4. A. C. Powell. "Diversity in Cyberspace." Address presented to the Association for Education in Journalism and Mass Communication, Washington, DC, 1995.

5. D. Lieberman. "Home PCs Draw Viewers Away from TVs." *USA Today,* November 16, 1995, p. 1B.

6. J. Hancock and P. Dunham. "Impression Formation in Computer-Mediated Communication Revisited: An Analysis of the Breadth and Intensity of Impressions." *Communication Research* 28, 2001, pp. 325–332; and L. Pratt, R. Weisman, M Cody, and P. Wendt. "Interrogative Strategies and Information Exchange in Computer-Mediated Communication." *Communication Quarterly* 47, 1999, pp. 46–66.

7. D. Shenk. *Data Smog: Surviving the Data Glut.* New York: HarperCollins, 1997.

8. Roger Fidler. "New Media Theory." In Eric P. Bucy, ed. *Living in the Information Age.* Belmont, CA: Wadsworth, 2002, pp. 21–29.

9. See, for example, "The Webcam Explosion." MSNBC, August 13, 2000.

10. J. Wilson and S. L. Wilson. *Mass Media/Mass Culture,* 4th ed. New York: McGraw-Hill, 1998.

11. J. Katz. "Rock, Rap and Movies Bring You the News." *Rolling Stone,* March 5, 1992, pp. 33–40, 78.

12. Neil Postman. *Amusing Ourselves to Death.* New York: Viking, 1985.

13. Ellen Graham. "Where Have All the Viewers Gone?" *Wall Street Journal,* June 27, 1997, pp. R1, R4.

14. Richard Harwood. "The Media Get 40 Percent of Our Time." *The Record,* December 3, 1996, p. L-13.

15. Michael Medved. "Peeping Tom TV Exploits Loneliness, Not Urge to Snoop." *USA Today,* July 10, 2000, p. 17A.

16. Michael Raphael. "Study Finds Leisure Time Increasing." *The Record,* June 5, 1997, p. A-15.

17. "A Quick Look." *The Record,* April 22, 1996.

18. Harwood.

19. Anita Hamilton. "Meet the New Surfer Girls." *Time,* August 21, 2000, p. 67.

20. Ellen Graham. "The New Living-Room Detente." *Wall Street Journal,* June 27, 1997, p. R4.

21. Douglas Foster. "Burdened with Being Everywhere." *New York Times,* August 19, 2000, p. A-15.

22. See Alexis Tan, Yuki Fujioka, and Nacy Lucht. "Native American Stereotypes, TV Portrayals, and Personal Contact." *Journalism and Mass Communication Quarterly* 74:2, summer 1997, pp. 265–284.

23. Jack G. Shaheen. "Arabs: Hollywood's Favorite Bad Guys." *The Record,* August 28, 1997, p. L-11.

24. Potter, p. 163.

25. Potter.

26. Joseph Hanania. "White Out: Latinos on TV." *TV Guide,* August 28, 1999, pp. 26–28, 67.

27. See, for example, National Council of La Raza. *Don't Blink: Hispanics in Television Entertainment.* Washington, DC: Center for Media and Public Affairs, 1996.

28. Charles R. Taylor and Hae-Kyong Bang. "Portrayals of Latinos in Magazine Advertising." *Journalism and Mass Communication Quarterly* 74:2, summer 1997, pp. 285–303.

29. Potter, p. 29.

30. Greg Zoroya. "The Men of Our Dreams." *USA Today,* July 11, 2000, p. 1D.

31. James Alexander Thom. "The Perfect Picture." *Reader's Digest,* August 1976, p. 113. Reprinted with permission.

32. Charlotte Faltermayer. "Cyberveillance." *Time,* August 14, 2000, pp. B22, B25.

33. Janice Kaplan. "Are Talk Shows Out of Control?" *TV Guide,* April 1, 1995, pp. 10–15.

34. Thomas E. Weber. "Privacy Concerns Force Public to Confront Thorny Issues." *Wall Street Journal,* June 19, 1997, p. B6.

35. Joshua Quittner. "Invasion of Privacy." *Time,* August 25, 1997, pp. 28–35.

36. Albert Bandura. *Social Learning Theory.* Englewood Cliffs, NJ: Prentice Hall, 1977.

37. *Youth Violence: A Report of the Surgeon General,* 2001. http://www.surgeongeneral.gov.

38. American Academy of Pediatrics. "Children, Adolescents, and Television." *Pediatrics* 107, 2001, pp. 423–426.

39. Wilbur Schramm, Jack Lyle, and Ed. Parker. *Television in the Lives of Our Children.* Stanford, CT: Stanford University Press, 1961.

40. Bruce Kluger. "Why Do Mean-Spirited TV Shows Lure Americans?" *USA Today,* January 20, 2003 p. 13A.

41. Aletha C. Huston, N. Feshbach, P. Katz, H. Fairchild and E. Donnerstein. *Big World, Small Screen.* Lincoln: University of Nebraska Press, 1992, p. 93.

42. Huston. et al.

43. See, for instance, Richard Saul Wurman. *Information Anxiety.* New York: Doubleday, 1989; and David Shenk. *Data Smog: Surviving the Information Glut.* New York: HarperCollins, 1997.

44. Jane L. Levere. "The Media Business: Advertising." *New York Times,* July 12, 1996, p. D-5.

acceptance the expression of a willingness to receive and respond to a message.

accommodation the means by which co-culture members attempt to maintain their identity even while striving to establish relationships with members of the dominant culture.

accommodator in a conflict, the person who gives in to the demands of another so that they are able to coexist in peace.

achieved leader a person who displays effective leadership behavior without being appointed or directed to do so.

acquaintanceships relationships with persons known by name but with whom interaction is usually limited in scope and quality.

affect blends the facial movements that accompany the communicating of multiple emotions.

affection the need to express and receive love; the need to experience emotionally close relationships.

aggressiveness the expression of one's own thoughts and feelings at another's expense.

aggressive stimulation theory the contention that the watching of violence stimulates aggression in the viewer.

allness the erroneous assumption that a person can know all there is to know about a particular person, object, or event.

allocentric exhibiting a collectivistic orientation.

analogic the continuous stream of nonverbal cues.

appraisal interview an interview with the goal of performance evaluation.

argumentum ad hominem the use of name-calling in an argument.

argumentum ad populum a bandwagon appeal; an appeal to popular opinion.

argumentum ad verecudiam an appeal to authority.

artifactual communication the use of personal adornments such as clothing, jewelry, makeup, hairstyles, and beards.

assertiveness the honest, clear, and direct communication of one's thoughts and feelings while displaying respect for the thoughts and feelings of others.

assimilation the means by which co-culture members attempt to fit in with members of the dominant culture.

attitudes predispositions to respond favorably or unfavorably toward a person or subject.

attribution theory a theory analyzing how we explain events and people.

audience adaptation the process of adjusting one's speech to a particular audience.

audience analysis the gathering of information about an audience that is relevant to the speech topic.

autistic society a society whose members are at home with computers but disadvantaged when it comes to establishing human intimacy; the opposite of a high-tech–high-touch society.

autocratic, or authoritian, leaders directive leaders; leaders who dominate group decision making.

avoider in a conflict, one who uses the unproductive conflict strategy of mentally or physically fleeing the conflict situation.

avoiding the relationship stage that finds interactants seeking not to have contact with each other.

balance a state of psychological comfort in which one's actions, feelings, and beliefs are related to each other as one would like them to be.

bar graph a graph used to show the performance of one variable over time or to contrast various measures at a point in time.

behavioral interview a hiring interview in which an employer seeks specific examples from prospects of times when specifically desired skills were exhibited.

beliefs confidence in the truth of something.

blind area the pane of the Johari window representing the part of the self known to others but not known to oneself.

blindering the process by which one unconsciously adds restrictions that limit one's perceptual capabilities.

blogs Web logs.

body the main segment of a speech.

bonding the commitment stage of a relationship, which involves the formal recognition of the relationship.

Boolean search a key word search.

brainstorming a technique designed to generate ideas.

breadth the number of topics you discuss with another person.

bridges persons in groups who have intragroup contacts and who communicate with one or more persons in another group or clique.

bypassing the pattern of miscommunication that occurs when individuals think they understand each other but actually miss each other's meaning.

case interview a hiring interview in which the employer presents the interviewee with a business case to solve.

catalytic theory the contention that, while the media may play a role in real-life violence, they will trigger it only if a viewer is predisposed to violence or particularly vulnerable.

catharsis theory the contention that the viewing of violence makes one less apt to exhibit violence.

causal reasoning speculation about the reasons for and effects of occurrences.

cause-and-effect order an organizational format that categorizes a topic according to its causes and effects.

channels media through which messages are sent.

chronemics the study of time use.

chronological or time, order an organizational format that develops an idea using a time order.

circumscribing the relationship stage that finds both the quality and quantity of communication between the parties decreasing.

civil inattention the avoidance of sustained eye contact with strangers; the polite ignoring of others so as not to infringe on their privacy.

clique a group of individuals who have a majority of their contacts with each other.

closed questions highly structured questions that can be answered with a simple yes or no or in a few words.

closure the means we use to perceive a complete world.

co-cultures, or subcultures members of the same general culture who differ in some ethnic or sociological way from the parent culture; groups of people who have a culture of their own outside the dominant culture.

code words words that are discriminatory.

cohesiveness the property of togetherness; a measure of the extent to which group members stick and work together.

collectivistic cultures cultures in which group goals are stressed.

communication the deliberate or accidental transfer of meaning; that which occurs when someone observes or experiences behavior and attributes meaning to it.

communication apprehension the fear of communicating.

communication network the pathway for messages; an organizational structure through which messages are sent and received.

comparison level a measure of the rewards and profits individuals expect to gain from a relationship.

comparison level for alternatives a comparison of the rewards attained from a present relationship with those expected to be derived from an alternative relationship.

competitive forcer in a conflict, a participant who exhibits a win-lose attitude.

competitive goal structure a goal structure in which members work to hinder one another's efforts to obtain a goal.

competitive listening the practice of manufacturing information to fill listening gaps.

competitive set a readiness to perceive a conflict in all-or-nothing terms; the belief that, to win, one must defeat others.

complementarity the attraction principle stating that opposites attract.

complementary interaction communication in which interactants engage in opposite behavior.

complementary relationship a relationship based on differences.

compromiser in a conflict, a participant who seeks a middle ground.

computer graphics computer-generated visual aids.

conclusion the final segment of a speech.

configural formats organizational patterns that are indirect and inexplicit.

confirmation communication in which one acknowledges the presence of another and indicates acceptance of the other's self-concept.

conflict perceived disagreement about views, interests, and goals.

conflict grid a model portraying the styles individuals use to resolve conflicts.

connotative meaning subjective meaning; one's personal meaning for a word.

consistency the desire to maintain balance in our lives by behaving according to commitments already formed.

contact cultures cultures whose members relish the intimacy of contact when interacting.

content conflict the type of conflict that arises when people disagree over matters of fact.

content level the information or data level of communication.

context the setting of communication.

control the need to feel we are capable and responsible and are able to exert power and influence over our relationships.

cooperative goal structure a goal structure in which the members of a group work together to achieve their objectives.

cooperative set the readiness to perceive a conflict situation in such a way that a means to share the rewards can be discovered.

cost-benefit/social exchange theory the theory stating that we work to maintain a relationship only as long as the benefits we perceive for ourselves outweigh the costs.

counseling interview an interview designed to provide guidance and support for the interviewee.

credibility the receiver's assessment of the competence, trustworthiness, and dynamism of a speaker.

critical thinking the careful and deliberate process of message evaluation.

cultural imperialism the expansion of dominion of one culture over another culture.

culturally confused lacking an understanding of cultural difference.

cultural nearsightedness the failure to understand that we do not all attribute the same meanings to similar behavioral cues.

cultural pluralism the adherence to the principle of cultural relativity.

cultural relativism the acceptance of other cultural groups as equal in value to one's own.

culture a system of knowledge, beliefs, values, customs, behaviors, and artifacts that are acquired, shared, and used by members during daily living.

cyberbole exaggerated claims about the effects that new technologies have on society.

cyberspace the digital world of computers and online communication.

decision by consensus a group decision reached and supported by all members of the group.

deduction reasoning that moves from the general to the specific.

deep-muscle relaxation a means of overcoming the physical symptoms of speech anxiety.

defensive behavior behavior that occurs when one perceives a threat.

defensive listening the practice of perceiving remarks made by another as a personal attack.

definitions explanations of what stimuli are or what words or concepts mean.

democratic leaders leaders whose leadership style represents a reasonable compromise between the authoritarian and laissez-faire styles.

demographics the social categories into which people can be grouped, including age, gender, family orientation, religion, cultural background, occupation, socioeconomic status, educational level, and membership in organizations.

denotative meaning dictionary meaning; the objective or descriptive meaning of a word.

depth a measure of how central the topics you discuss with another person are to your self-concept.

derived credibility a measure of a speaker's credibility during a speech-making event.

DESC script a system for expressing one's feelings and for understanding the feelings of another (*DESC* stands for *d*escribe, *e*xpress, *s*pecify, and *c*onsequences).

designated leader a person given the authority by an outside force to act as leader.

dialectical tensions tensions that occur when relationship goals conflict; relationship differences that usually revolve around differences in the desires for connection and autonomy, predictability and novelty, and openness and privacy.

dialogic listening listening that focuses on what happens between people as they respond to each other, work toward shared understanding, and build a relationship.

differentiating the relationship stage in which two people reestablish their individuality.

digital the word level of communication.

disclaimer remarks which diminish a statement's importance.

disconfirmation communication that indicates one's lack of interest in another person; a failure to acknowledge the contributions of another person.

disqualification communication that invalidates a message sent.

distance relating the use of e-mail, chat rooms, instant messages, and the Internet to facilitate relationships.

dominant culture the culture in power; the mainstream culture.

effect the emotional, physical, and/or cognitive outcome of communication.

ego conflict the type of conflict that arises when individuals connect winning or losing and self-worth.

emblems nonverbal cues that directly translate words or phrases.

emoticons symbols that replace nonverbal cues during machine-assisted communication.

emotion the feeling one experiences in reaction to a person or situation.

emotion state a particular emotional process of limited duration and varying intensity.

emotion traits a tendency to experience a specific emotion when interacting.

emotional appeals appeals designed to evoke various feelings in receivers.

emotional contagion the catching of a mood from another person.

emotional intelligence the ability to motivate oneself, to control impulses, to recognize and regulate one's moods, to empathize, and to hope.

emotional isolationists persons who seek to avoid situations that may require the exchange of feelings.

emotive language words that reveal feelings.

empathic listening listening to help others.

empathy the ability to feel another's feelings.

essentials of communication those components present during every interpersonal, small-group, public, and mass communication event.

ethnocentrism the tendency to see one's own culture as superior to all others.

euphemism the substitution of a pleasant term for a less pleasant one.

evaluative feedback a response that is judgmental—that is, positive or negative.

evasive language words that disguise feelings.

examples representative cases.

exit interview an interview conducted when a person leaves an organization.

experimenting the relationship stage that involves the exchange of small talk.

expert power power dependent on a person's knowledge.

extemporaneous outline, or speaker's notes an outline developed from a full sentence outline.

extemporaneous speech a speech that is researched, outlined, and delivered after a rehearsal period.

extensional orientation focusing on the world of experience; the refusal to be blinded by a label.

external feedback a communicative response from another.

facework the means used to present a public image.

facial management techniques the techniques used to attempt to conceal facial behavior, including emotion intensification, deintensification, neutralization, and/or masking.

fact that which is known to be true on the basis of observation.

false division the polarization of options, when, in fact, many options exist.

feedback verbal and nonverbal cues sent out in response to another person's communication; information returned to a message source.

figure-ground principle a strategy that facilitates the organization of stimuli by enabling us to focus on different stimuli alternately.

first impressions initial judgments about people.

fixed-feature space space that contains relatively permanent objects.

flame war a conflict that occurs in cyberspace.

flames insults delivered online.

formative feedback a timed negative response, usually provided right before an activity is to be performed again.

fraudulent listening pseudolistening.

friendly relations the friendship stage involving small talk.

friendships relationships that exist when persons seek each other out and exhibit a strong mutual regard for each other.

full sentence outline an outline developed after researching a topic.

functional theory the leadership theory suggesting that several members of a group should be ready to lead because various actions are needed to achieve group goals.

Galatea effect the principle that we fulfill our own expectations.

gatekeeping the filtering of messages from source to receiver.

geekspeak online talk that disparages human beings and treats them like machines.

gender-lects Deborah Tannen's term for language differences attributed to gender.

graph a pictorial device used to present quantitative relationships.

grief process a mourning process composed of five stages: denial, anger, guilt, depression, and acceptance.

group a collection of individuals who interact verbally and nonverbally, occupy certain roles with respect to one another, and cooperate to accomplish a goal.

group climate the emotional atmosphere of a group.

group communication communication with a limited number of other persons during which information is shared, ideas developed, decisions made, and/or problems solved.

group conflict conflict that occurs when a group member's thoughts or acts limit, prevent, or interfere with another group member's thoughts or acts.

group goals a group's motivation for existing.

group norms informal rules for interaction in a group.

group patterns of communication the patterns of message flow in a group.

group role-classification model the model proposed by Benne and Sheats describing functions participants should and should not seek to perform in groups.

group structure member positions and roles performed.

groupthink an extreme means of avoiding conflict that occurs when groups let the desire for consensus override careful analysis and reasoned decision making.

habitual pitch the pitch (of the voice) one uses most often.

halo effect the perceiving of qualities that are primarily positive.

haptics the study of the use of touch.

hearing the involuntary, physiological process by which we process sound.

hidden area the pane of the Johari window representing the part of the self that contains information about the self known to oneself but hidden from or unknown to others.

high-context communication a tradition-bound communication system that depends on indirectness; a culture whose members place less reliance on explicit verbal messages and more emphasis on the preservation of harmony.

high-intensity conflict a conflict in which one party seeks to destroy or hurt the other party.

high power distance cultures cultures based on power differences in which subordinates are quick to defer to superiors.

high-tech–high-touch society a technologically oriented society whose members value personal contact; the opposite of an autistic society.

hiring interview an interview conducted for the purpose of filling an employment position.

home page the opening page of a Web site, which details the structure and ordering of information in the site.

hyper-competitiveness the contention that one needs to defeat another to achieve one's goals.

horn effect the perceiving of qualities that are primarily negative.

idiocentric exhibiting an individualistic orientation.

illustrations stories, narrative pictures.

"I" messages messages that convey feelings about the nature of a situation without passing judgment on the actions of another.

impression management the creation of a positive image designed to influence others.

impromptu speech a speech delivered on the spur of the moment, with little or no preparation.

inclusion the need for social contact.

individualistic cultures cultures in which individual goals are stressed.

induction reasoning that moves from specific evidence to a general conclusion.

inference a conclusion that cannot be verified by observation; an assumption with varying degrees of accuracy.

informal space space that is highly mobile and may be quickly changed.

information-gathering interview an interview with the goal of collecting information, opinions, or data about a topic or person.

information overload the situation that occurs when the amount of information provided by a speech maker is too great to be handled effectively by the listeners; the speech maker may provide more data than is necessary or use unclear language or jargon.

information underload the situation that occurs when the information provided by a speech maker is already known by the listeners.

informative speech a speech whose primary purpose is to impart knowledge or to teach.

initial credibility a measure of how an audience perceives a speaker prior to the speech-making event.

initiating the first stage in a relationship; the point at which persons first make contact.

integrating the relationship stage when two persons are identified as a pair.

intensifying the relationship stage during which persons become good friends.

intensional orientation the preoccupation with labels.

intercultural communication the process of interpreting and sharing meanings with individuals from different cultures.

interethnic communication the process of interpreting and sharing meanings with individuals of different ethnic origins.

internal feedback a response you give yourself as you monitor your own behavior.

internal summaries rhetorical devices designed to help listeners remember content.

international communication communication between persons representing different nations.

interpersonal communication communication with another; the relationship level of communication.

interpersonal conflict a struggle between two or more people.

interpersonal relationship a meaningful connection between two persons.

interracial communication the process of interpreting and sharing meanings with individuals from different races.

interview the most common type of purposeful, planned, decision-making, person-to-person communication; a form of communication involving two parties, at least one of whom has a preconceived and serious purpose and both of whom speak and listen from time to time.

intimate distance a distance ranging from the point of touch to 18 inches from a person.

intracultural communication the process of sharing meaning with members of one's own racial or ethnic group or subculture.

intrapersonal communication communication with the self; communication that involves one person.

intrapersonal conflict an internal struggle.

introduction the initial segment of a speech.

isolates persons who do not feel well integrated into a group and have few, if any, contacts with others.

Johari window a model containing four panes (the open, blind, hidden, and unknown areas) used to explain the roles that self-awareness and self-disclosure play in relationships.

kaleidoscope thinking the taking of existing data and twisting it or looking at it from another angle.

killer looks looks that discourage or inhibit the generation of ideas.

killer phrases comments that stop the flow of ideas.

kinesics the study of human body motion, or body language.

language a unified system of symbols that permits the sharing of meaning.

laissez-faire leaders nondirective leaders.

leadership the ability to influence others.

legitimate power power by virtue of position.

liaisons persons who do not belong to any one group or clique but who link persons of one group with persons in another.

linear logic a step-by-step approach to developing ideas that relies on facts and data to support main points.

line graphs graphs used to illustrate trends, relationships, or comparisons over time.

linguistic determinism the belief that language influences one's interpretation of the world.

linguistic prejudice the use of prejudiced language.

linguistic relativity the belief that persons who speak different languages perceive the world differently.

listening the deliberate, psychological process by which we receive, understand, and retain aural (heard) stimuli.

listening level–energy involvement scale a scale that describes energy expenditure during listening.

listserv an e-mail list of people who share interests in and knowledge of a topic.

loneliness a perceived discrepancy between desired and achieved social relationships.

low-contact cultures cultures whose members value privacy and maintain distance when interacting.

low-context communication a system that encourages directness in communication; a culture in which self-expression is valued.

low-intensity conflict a conflict in which the parties seek solutions beneficial to all parties involved.

low power distance cultures cultures that believe that power should be used only when legitimate.

main ideas the main points of a speech; the subtopics of a speech.

maintenance roles group roles designed to ensure the smooth running of a group.

manuscript speech a speech read from a script.

marginalized group a group whose members feel like outsiders.

markers items that reserve or set the boundaries of our space.

Maslow's hierarchy of needs a model that depicts motivation as a pyramid, with the most basic needs at the base and the most sophisticated needs at the apex.

mass communication the process of transmitting messages that may be processed by gatekeepers before being transmitted to large audiences via a channel of broad diffusion, such as a print, an audio, or a visual medium.

media literacy the ability to interpret mindfully the positive and negative meanings and effects one encounters in the media.

medium-intensity conflict a conflict in which the parties are committed to winning but believe that winning is sufficient.

melting pot philosophy the philosophy advocating the assimilation of different cultures into the dominant culture.

memorized speech a manuscript speech that the speaker commits to memory.

message the content of a communicative act.

microfacial, or micromomentary, expression an expression, lasting no more than one-eighth to one-fifth of a second, that usually occurs when an individual consciously or unconsciously attempts to disguise or conceal an emotion and that reveals an actual emotional state.

mixed message an incongruent message that occurs when words and actions contradict each other.

monopolistic listening the practice of defending one's right to speak while denying others the right to be listened to.

Monroe's motivated sequence a speech framework composed of five phases—attention, need, satisfaction, visualization, and action—that sequentially moves receivers toward accepting and acting on a speaker's proposition.

moving toward friendship the friendship stage involving personal disclosures; the stage during which individuals move beyond serendipitous encounters.

MUDS an online multi user environment.

multitasking clothing clothing with built-in electronic gadgetry.

MYGLO acronym for "my eyes glaze over."

nascent friendship the friendship stage during which individuals increase the regularity of their interactions and consider each other friends.

need for affection the need to express and receive love; the need to experience emotionally close relationships.

need for control the need to feel we are capable and responsible and are able to exert power and influence over our relationships.

need for inclusion the need for social contact.

negative feedback a communicative response that extinguishes behavior in progress.

netiquette the rules of the Internet.

noise anything that interferes with or distorts the ability to send and receive messages.

nonassertion that which occurs when one hesitates to display one's feelings and thoughts.

nonassertiveness a failure to stand up for one's rights; the suppression of one's thoughts or feelings as a result of fear or shyness.

nonevaluative feedback a nondirective response.

nonfluencies meaningless sounds or phrases that disrupt the natural flow of speech; hesitation phenomena.

nonverbal communication the kinds of human responses not expressed in words.

online, or machine-assisted, communication communication via computers and the Internet.

onlinespeak the informal communication style that marks electronic communication.

open area the pane of the Johari window representing the part of the self containing information known both to the self and to others.

open questions questions that offer the interviewee freedom with regard to the choice and scope of an answer.

paralanguage the study of the voice as a nonverbal cue; the vocal cues that accompany spoken language.

paraphrasing restating in your own words what another has said.

perception the process by which we make sense out of experience; the means by which we make experience our own.

perceptual constancy the desire to perceive experience exactly as we have perceived it in the past.

perceptual sets expectations that produce a readiness to process experience in a predetermined way.

personal distance a distance ranging from 18 inches to 4 feet from a person.

persuasion interview an interview with the goal of attitude and behavior influence.

persuasive speech a speech whose primary purpose is to change or reinforce the attitudes, beliefs, values, and/or behaviors of receivers.

phatic communication communication designed to open the channels of communication.

pictographs graphs that use sketches to represent concepts.

pie, or circle, graph a circle with the various percentages of the whole indicated by wedges; a means of showing percentage relationships.

pitch the highness or lowness of the voice.

positive feedback a communicative response that enhances behavior in progress.

post hoc, ergo propter hoc the identification of a false cause.

prejudice a biased, negative attitude toward a particular group of people; a negative prejudgment based on membership in a social category.

prejudiced language sexist, ageist, or racist language; language disparaging to the members of a co-culture.

preliminary working outline a sparse outline containing only key words.

preview the section of the speech that lets the audience know what the speaker will be discussing.

primacy effect the tendency for a first impression to exert more influence than what comes later; the ability of one's first impression to color subsequent impressions.

primary questions questions used to introduce the exploration of a topic.

probing a nonevaluative response that asks for more information.

problem-and-solution order an organizational format that identifies the problems inherent in a situation and presents a solution to remedy them.

problem-solving collaborator in a conflict, a participant who exhibits a win-win attitude.

proposition a statement that summarizes the purpose of a persuasive speech.

proposition of fact a persuasive speech with the goal of settling what is or is not so.

proposition of policy a persuasive speech on what ought to be.

proposition of value a persuasive speech that espouses the worth of an idea, a person, or an object.

prosumers consumers who produce the material of consumption themselves.

proxemics the study of space.

pseudoconflict a situation with only the appearance of a conflict.

psychographics categories into which persons may be grouped based on their attitudes, motivations, values, and level of information and commitment with respect to a topic.

public communication communication designed to inform, persuade, or entertain the members of an audience.

public distance a distance that is beyond 12 feet from a person.

public speaking the act of preparing, staging, and delivering a presentation to an audience.

purpose statement an infinitive phrase describing the goal of a speech.

purr words words with highly positive connotations.

Pygmalion effect the principle that we fulfill the expectations of others.

qualifiers words that lack certainty and make phrases tentative.

quality circles small groups of employees who meet regularly to discuss organizational life and the quality of their work environment; recommendations for improving products and work procedures are made during these meetings.

questions of fact questions concerned with the truth or falsity of a statement.

questions of policy questions that help determine what future actions, if any, should be taken.

questions of value questions that involve subjective judgments of worth.

racist language language that denigrates a person because of race.

rate the speed at which one speaks.

reasoning from analogy reasoning by comparison.

receivers persons who receive, decode, and interpret messages.

reciprocal turn taking the changing of the speaking and listening roles during conversation.

red-flag words words that evoke an emotional response and drop listening efficiency to zero.

red herring a distraction used to lead the receiver to focus on an irrelevant issue.

referent power power dependent on one's desire to identify or be like another person.

reflective-thinking framework a system for decision making and problem solving that is designed to encourage critical inquiry.

rejection the expression of disinterest in communication; communication that indicates one's rejection of another's self-concept.

relational dialectics theory the contention that relationships oscillate between contradictory goals or desires.

relationship a meaningful connection with another person.

relationship level the interpretation level of communication.

rhetorical question a question asked for effect and without the expectation of an answer.

rigid complementarity a relationship characterized by fixed, unchanging roles.

role-limited interaction the beginning of friendship; the stage during which two individuals make initial contact.

role reversal a conflict-resolution technique in which one acts as the person with whom one is in conflict.

romantic relationship a relationship characterized by commitment, passion, intimacy, and the expectation of permanence.

Sapir-Whorf hypothesis the belief that the labels we use help shape the way we think, our worldview, and our behavior.

search engine a computer program that allows one to look through an entire database of information quickly.

secondary questions probing questions; questions used to follow up primary questions.

selective attention the tendency to focus on certain cues and ignore others.

selective exposure the selection of stimuli that reaffirm existing attitudes, beliefs, and values; the tendency to close oneself to new experiences.

selective listening the practice of zeroing in on only the parts of a message of particular interest to the receiver.

selective perception the means by which one interprets experience in a way that conforms to one's beliefs, expectations, and convictions; the inclination to distort one's perceptions of stimuli to make them conform to the need for internal consistency or closure.

selective retention the tendency to remember that which reinforces one's way of thinking and forget that which opposes one's way of thinking.

self-concept everything one thinks and feels about oneself; one's self-evaluation.

self-conflict the type of conflict that occurs when one person has to choose between two or more mutually exclusive options.

self-directed teams autonomous work groups in which employees are empowered to make decisions and supervise themselves.

self-disclosure the process of revealing to another person information about the self that he or she would not otherwise know.

self-efficacy an optimistic belief in our own competence.

self-enhancement the bolstering of one's self image.

self-esteem how well one likes and values oneself.

self-fulfilling prophecy a prediction or expectation that comes true simply because one acts as if it were true.

self-image the sort of person one perceives oneself to be.

self-serving bias the overemphasis of external factors to explain our own behavior.

self-serving roles group roles that impede the functioning of a group by preventing members from working together effectively.

semifixed-feature space the space in which objects are used to create distance.

senders persons who formulate, encode, and transmit messages.

separation the strategy co-culture members use to resist interacting with members of the dominant culture.

serial communication a chain-of-command transmission.

sexist language language derogatory to one sex.

silence the absence of both paralinguistic and verbal cues.

situational theory the theory of leadership asserting that leadership is situation dependent.

snarl words words with highly negative connotations.

social distance a distance ranging from 4 feet to 12 feet from a person.

social penetration theory the theory stating that our relationships begin with relatively narrow breadth and shallow depth and develop over time.

social proof the determination of what is right by finding out what other people think is right.

spatial order an organizational format that describes an object, a person, or a phenomenon as it exists in space.

speech apprehension fear associated with speaking in public.

speech framework a frame, or skeleton, on which a speech is developed.

speech-thought differential the difference between thinking rate and speaking rate.

stabilized friendship the friendship stage that finds interactants sharing more intimate information because of the belief that the relationship is secure and will continue.

stagnating the stage in a relationship that finds communication between the parties at a standstill.

statistics facts expressed in numerical form.

stereotype a generalization about people, places, or events that is held by many members of a society.

stress interview a hiring interview that includes more than one interviewer firing questions at a single interviewee.

subordinate ideas ideas that amplify the main ideas of a speech.

supportive feedback a nonevaluative response that confirms the significance of a problem or situation.

symbol that which represents something else.

symmetrical escalation a relationship in which individuals compete for control.

symmetrical interaction a relationship in which the behavior of one person mirrors the behavior of another person.

symmetrical relationship a relationship based on similarity.

symptom as communication, the the use of an excuse as a reason for not wanting to communicate.

systematic speaking system a public speaking system composed of four stages: topic selection, topic development, presentation, and postpresentation analysis.

tag questions words that seek verbal confirmation; a tag lies midway between an outright statement and a yes-no question.

task roles group roles designed to help the group realize its objective.

technopoly a culture in which technology monopolizes the thought world.

terminal credibility a measure of a speaker's credibility at the end of a speech-making event.

termination the end stage of a relationship.

territoriality the need to demonstrate a possessive or ownership relationship to space.

testimony someone else's opinions or conclusions.

thought stopping a means of overcoming the mental symptoms of speech anxiety.

time shifting the ability to watch media offerings at a time convenient to you.

tolerance of vulnerability a measure of the degree of trust you place in another person.

topical order an organizational format that clusters material by dividing it into a series of appropriate topics.

toxic communication the consistent use of verbal abuse and/or physical or sexual aggression or violence.

trait theory the theory of leadership asserting that certain people are born to lead.

transformational leader a leader who gives a group a new vision or culture.

transitions rhetorical devices used to bridge ideas.

triangle of meaning a model that explains the relationship that exists among words, things, and thoughts.

twenty-four seven a reference to the ability to maintain contact 24 hours a day, 7 days a week.

type X leader a leader who does not delegate responsibility because he or she does not believe in the abilities of group members.

type Y leader a leader who lets group members grow and develop; a leader concerned with the personal sense of achievement realized by group members.

understanding a nonevaluative response that relies on the use of paraphrasing.

uniform resource locator (URL) a Web page address.

unknown area the pane of the Johari window representing the part of the self that is unknown to oneself and others.

usenet newsgroup a conference system of computer bulletin boards and discussion forums.

value conflict the type of conflict that arises when people hold different views on an issue.

virtual neighborhoods and communities online, surrogate communities.

virtual reality an environment that exists as data in a computer system.

visual dominance a measure calculated by comparing the percentage of looking while speaking with the percentage of looking while listening.

visualization the picturing of experience in the mind; a technique used to help speakers imagine their own speech-making success.

volume the degree of loudness of the voice.

waning friendship the friendship stage during which friends drift apart.

"you" messages messages in which a speaker denies responsibility for a situation by placing blame on another person; the opposite of "I" messages.

Blindering Problem

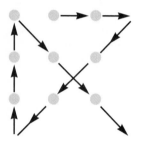

The Detective

1. ?
2. ?
3. F
4. ?
5. ?
6. T

7. ?
8. ?
9. ?
10. ?
11. ?

CREDITS AND ACKNOWLEDGMENTS

Photo Credits